LOGAN TURNER'S

Diseases of the
Nose, Throat and Ear

LOGAN TURNER'S

Diseases of the Nose, Throat and Ear

Edited by

A. G. D. Maran, MD, FRCS (ED), FACS

Head, Department of Otolaryngology,
University of Edinburgh

Tenth Edition

K. M. VARGHESE COMPANY

104–105 Hind Rajasthan Building
Dadasaheb Phalke Road
Dadar
Bombay 400 014, India
1988

First Edition (based on the Third Edition of Porter's 'Throat, Nose, and Ear'), 1924
Second Impression, 1925
Second Edition, 1927
Reprinted, 1928
Reprinted, 1930
Third Edition, 1932
Reprinted, 1934
Fourth Edition, 1936
Reprinted, 1937
Reprinted, 1938
Reprinted, 1940
Fifth Edition, 1952
Sixth Edition, 1961
Reprinted, 1964
Seventh Edition, 1968
Eighth Edition, 1977
Ninth Edition, 1982
Tenth Edition, 1988

British Library Cataloguing in Publication Data

Turner, Arthur Logan
   Logan Turner's diseases of the nose, throat
   and ear.—10th ed.
   1. Otolaryngology
   I. Title   II. Maran, A. G. D.
   617'.51   RF46

ISBN 0 7236 0945 4

John Wright
is an imprint of Butterworth Scientific
Borough Green, Sevenoaks, Kent TN15 8PH England

Typeset by
Bath Typesetting Ltd, 3a Longacre, London Road, Bath

Printed in Great Britain by
Butler & Tanner Ltd., Frome and London

This work is dedicated to the memory of

Arthur Logan Turner MD, LLD, FRCSE

*and to those contributors to the previous editions
who have since died*

Preface to the Tenth Edition

It is now 75 years since Dr W. G. Porter published a short textbook entitled *Diseases of the Throat, Nose and Ear*. Dr Porter was killed on active service in World War I and Dr A. Logan Turner, a past president of the Royal College of Surgeons of Edinburgh, revised the book for its third edition in 1919. Since then a further seven editions have been produced by the Edinburgh consultant otolaryngologists.

At one time it was possible to include enough otolaryngology in a book of this size to make it an acceptable pre-Fellowship study vehicle. Otolaryngology has, however, expanded to such a size that it can only be encompassed in a multi-volume book. The authors see this volume as being directed towards senior students, general practitioners and trainees in otolaryngology who may use it as a preparatory volume in working towards the Fellowship examination in otolaryngology.

This book has been consistently popular in the Middle East, the Indian Subcontinent and South East Asia. The presentation of pathology is widely divergent between the developed and the developing countries. With this in mind the authors have tried not to confine their presentations to pathology as seen in Northern Europe.

The main change in this volume is that the traditional three sections have been split into four. Dr Bryan Dale and Dr Alastair Kerr have completed the difficult task of presenting otology, audiology and otoneurology as an integrated whole. Dr John Murray has rewritten the section on rhinology and Dr David Cowan has presented a completely new section on the enlarging field of paediatric otolaryngology. The editor has slightly modified and enlarged the section on head and neck surgery and Dr Bob Yorston has added some new line drawings.

We are also indebted to Blackwell's Scientific Publications for allowing us to print extracts from *Clinical Otolaryngology*, edited by A. G. D. Maran and P. M. Stell and to the *Journal of Laryngology and Otology* for allowing us to use material from that journal.

The authors would like to thank the publishers for their excellent cooperation in the preparation of this volume and also Mrs Ann White, secretary of the Department of Otolaryngology, for her patience and diligence in preparing the manuscripts.

A. G. D. Maran

Contributors

B. A. B. Dale FRCS (ED)
Consultant Otolaryngologist,
Royal Infirmary and
City Hospital, Edinburgh

D. L. Cowan FRCS (ED)
Consultant Otolaryngologist,
Royal Hospital for Sick Children,
City Hospital and
Western General Hospital, Edinburgh

A. I. G. Kerr FRCS (ED), FRCS (GLAS)
Consultant Otolaryngologist,
Royal Infirmary,
Royal Hospital for Sick Children
and City Hospital, Edinburgh

J. A. M. Murray MD, FRCS (ED), FRACS
Consultant Otolaryngologist,
Royal Infirmary and
City Hospital, Edinburgh

Contents

SECTION 1—THE NOSE (J. A. M. Murray)

1.1	Anatomy and Physiology	3
1.2	Investigation of Nasal Disease	13
1.3	Nasal and Facial Trauma	21
1.4	Epistaxis	30
1.5	Acute Rhinosinusitis	34
1.6	Chronic Rhinitis	38
1.7	Chronic Sinusitis	42
1.8	Allergic Rhinitis and Nasal Polyps	51
1.9	Benign Tumours and Granulomas	56
1.10	Facial Pain	64
1.11	Cosmetic Facial Surgery	67
1.12	Trans-sphenoidal Hypophysectomy	71

SECTION 2—THE HEAD AND NECK (A. G. D. Maran)

2.1	Anatomy of the Pharynx	77
2.2	Investigation of Pharyngeal Disease	80
2.3	Infections of the Pharynx	84
2.4	Benign Disease of the Pharynx	94
2.5	Neck Space Infections	104
2.6	Tumours of the Nasopharynx	109
2.7	Tumours of the Oropharynx	113
2.8	Tumours of the Hypopharynx	116
2.9	Tumours of the Oral Cavity	121
2.10	Benign Diseases of the Oral Cavity	125
2.11	Salivary Gland Disease	129
2.12	Anatomy of the Larynx	142
2.13	Investigation of Laryngeal Disease	150
2.14	Voice Problems	155
2.15	Laryngeal Infections	160
2.16	Rare Laryngeal Tumours	166

2.17	Cancer of the Larynx	171
2.18	Vocal Cord Paralysis	180
2.19	Laryngotracheal Trauma	185
2.20	Tracheostomy	191
2.21	Neck Masses	198
2.22	Cancer of the Nose and Sinuses	209
2.23	Tumours of the Ear	212

SECTION 3—THE EAR (B. A. B. Dale and A. I. G. Kerr)

3.1	Anatomy and Physiology	219
3.2	Investigation of Ear Disease	237
3.3	Audiology and Vestibulometry	246
3.4	Diseases of the External Ear	263
3.5	Acute Otitis Media in Adults	278
3.6	Chronic Otitis Media	282
3.7	Extracranial Complications of Otitis Media	294
3.8	Intracranial Complications of Otitis Media	304
3.9	Otosclerosis	317
3.10	Sensorineural Deafness	322
3.11	Tinnitus	329
3.12	Vertigo	331
3.13	Cerebellopontine Angle Tumours	339
3.14	Otological Trauma	345
3.15	The Facial Nerve	353

SECTION 4—PAEDIATRICS (D. L. Cowan)

4.1	Tonsils and Adenoids	363
4.2	The Catarrhal Child	372
4.3	Laryngeal Stridor	381
4.4	Endoscopy	392
4.5	Intubation and Tracheostomy	396
4.6	Subglottic Stenosis	400
4.7	Tumours of the Head and Neck	402
4.8	Deafness in Children	409
4.9	Acute Otitis Media and Mastoiditis	422
4.10	Secretory Otitis Media	432
Index		443

Section 1

THE NOSE

(J. A. M. Murray)

Chapter 1.1

ANATOMY AND PHYSIOLOGY

THE EXTERNAL NOSE

The external nose is a projecting triangular pyramid directed downwards. Its inferior base is perforated by two nostrils separated by a median septum and its superior root connects directly with the forehead (nasion). The tip or apex of the nose continues cephalically as the dorsum, initially cartilaginous, it then changes to the bony dorsum or bridge. The skin over the bridge of the nose is relatively thin compared with the thick adherent skin of the tip which contains sebaceous glands. The external framework is osseous and cartilaginous (*Fig.* 1.1.1). The nasal bones form the cephalic aspect of the dorsum; each is joined to the frontal bone above the nasal process of the maxilla laterally and to each other medially. Inferiorly they join the upper lateral cartilage which is attached to the underside of the bone for several millimetres. The dorsal aspect of the cartilaginous septum completes the external nose. The lower lateral cartilage completes the external framework. The upper lateral cartilage is continuous in its median upper half with the dorsal septum. A number of small sesamoid cartilages make up the postero-lateral aspect of the external framework.

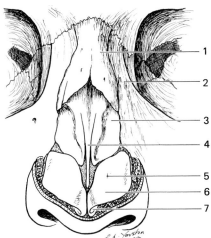

Fig. 1.1.1. The external nose.
1, Nasal bone.
2, Frontal process of maxilla.
3, Upper lateral cartilage.
4, Cartilage of septum.
5, Lower lateral cartilage.
6, Lateral crus.
7, Medial crus.

3

The main muscles acting on the external nose are the three compressors and the four dilators of the nostrils (alae). They are all supplied by the facial nerve. The arterial supply is from the maxillary and ophthalmic arteries and the venous drainage through the anterior facial and ophthalmic veins. The latter drain eventually into the cavernous sinus, hence superficial infection over the nose has the potential to cause the dangerous condition of septic cavernous thrombosis. Lymphatic drainage either follows the anterior facial vein and opens into the submandibular nodes or drains to the preauricular nodes.

THE NASAL VESTIBULE

The entrance to the nasal cavity is lined by hair-bearing squamous epithelium which ends at the mucocutaneous junction; the point at which the nasal cavity proper begins. The columella is the strip of skin, connective tissue and medial crura of the lower lateral cartilage which separates the nostrils.

THE NASAL CAVITY

The nasal fossae are two irregular cavities extending from the mucocutaneous junction with the nasal vestibule in front (the anterior nares) to the junction with the nasopharynx behind (posterior nares or choanae). The lining of the cavity is mainly ciliated columnar epithelium (respiratory type) or olfactory epithelium. Occasionally squamous epithelium encroaches from the vestibule onto the anterior ends of the middle and inferior turbinates.

The bony lateral wall of the cavity is convoluted by three turbinates. The superior and middle are the medial aspect of the lateral mass of the ethmoid bone, and the inferior is a separate bone attached to the maxilla. In cross-section these bones resemble a scroll (concha) or whorl (turbinate). Each turbinate overhangs a channel or meatus. The inferior turbinate covers the inferior meatus and so on. Superior to the superior turbinate is the sphenoethmoidal recess. The superior meatus occupies the posterior third of the lateral wall, the middle meatus the posterior two-thirds and the inferior meatus runs the length of the lateral wall. The olfactory cleft occupies the area between the superior turbinate, cribriform plate and corresponding area of the septum and is lined by specialized olfactory epithelium. Several ducts drain into the nose through the meatuses. The inferior meatus in its anterior aspect receives the nasolacrimal duct. The anterior group of sinuses (frontal, anterior ethmoidal and maxillary) drain into the middle meatus via their ostia (openings). The posterior ethmoidal sinuses drain into the superior meatus and the sphenoid sinus into the sphenoethmoidal recess. At the anterior end of the middle meatus is a ridge—the agger nasi. This represents the nasoturbinal found in many mammals or the 'fourth turbinate'. Posterior to this in the middle meatus runs the hiatus semilunaris which receives the maxillary ostium posteriorly. Posterosuperiorly lies the bulla ethmoidalis which is formed by the anterior ethmoidal cells draining onto or above the bulla. Below the hiatus semilunaris is the uncinate process of the ethmoid which articulates with the inferior turbinate bone (*Fig.* 1.1.2).

The nasal septum separates the two nasal cavities. Posteriorly it is bony and anteriorly it is cartilaginous. The cartilaginous septum is an elastic structure which bends back to shape when deformed. This is achieved by the interlocked stress

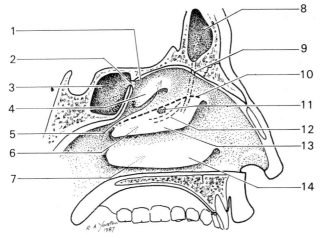

Fig. 1.1.2. Lateral wall of nose.
1, Sphenoethmoidal recess.
2, Ostium of sphenoid sinus.
3, Sphenoid sinus.
4, Superior turbinate.
5, Superior meatus.
6, Middle meatus.
7, Inferior meatus.

8, Frontal sinus.
9, Line of nasofrontal duct.
10, Line of bony attachment of middle turbinate.
11, Position of maxillary sinus ostium in middle meatus.
12, Line of semilunar groove.
13, Middle turbinate.
14, Inferior turbinate.

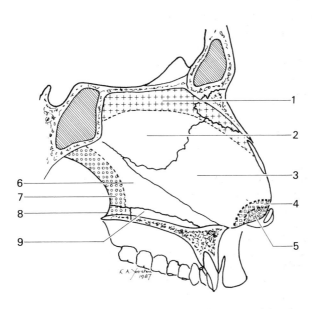

Fig. 1.1.3. The nasal septum showing Cottle's area. The turbinate area of the septum is unshaded in this diagram, and lies opposite the turbinates.
1, Attic area (crosses).
2, Perpendicular plate of ethmoid.
3, Septal cartilage.
4, Valve area (open squares).
5, Vestibular area (cross-hatched).

6, Vomer.
7, Posterior choanal area (open circles).
8, Nasal crest of palatine bone.
9, Nasal crest of maxilla.

system. The outer layers of the septum hold in the inner layers under tension. This arrangement ensures a constantly traumatized area is not deformed by minimal force. It is the only midline structure of the face and theoretically it should be straight.

The septum has been divided into five areas by Cottle (*Fig.* 1.1.3): the vestibule, valve, attic, turbinate and posterior choanal areas. These allow an accurate description of abnormalities.

The attachments of the cartilaginous part of the septum (quadrilateral cartilage) are inferiorly the maxillary crest, posteriorly the vomer and posterosuperiorly the perpendicular plate of the ethmoid. The upper lateral cartilages are attached at the dorsum but otherwise the cartilaginous septum is covered by skin or connective tissue.

The arterial supply to the septum is derived from two sources. The main source is from the external carotid system via the maxillary artery and the sphenopalatine artery. This latter divides into three branches in the nasal cavity, i.e. the inferior turbinate, the middle turbinate and the nasopalatine arteries. They run in the periosteum of the nasal mucoperiosteum. The nasopalatine artery leaves the sphenopalatine foramen and passes along the anteroinferior border of the sphenoid to the septum, where it divides into two. The superior branch lies in the perpendicular plate, the lower just above the maxillary crest. The latter divides again and one of these branches passes through the incisive foramen. The other lesser source from the internal carotid system comes from the anterior ethmoidal artery. This is a terminal branch of the ophthalmic artery and enters the nose through the anterior ethmoidal foramen to supply a variable portion of the superior septum. The other vessels (greater palatine from the maxillary artery, superior labial artery from the facial, infraorbital and superior dental artery from the maxillary and the pharyngeal branch of the maxillary artery) and the posterior ethmoidal from the ophthalmic artery contribute with the main vessels to the highly vascularized area at the anteroinferior aspect of the septum, eponymously termed Little's area or Kiesselbach's plexus (*Fig.* 1.1.4).

The lateral wall of the nose has a similar supply. The inferior turbinate artery supplies the inferior turbinate by three branches, the antral artery and the medial and lateral terminal branches. The middle turbinate artery runs along the lateral surface of the turbinate to the lower border of the bone where it enters a bony canal at the junction of the middle and posterior thirds of the turbinate and breaks into three terminal branches.

The veins form a cavernous plexus beneath the mucous membrane and drain through the sphenopalatine and facial veins. Lesser veins include the superior ophthalmic via the ethmoidal veins to reach the veins of the dura mater.

Lymphatic drainage from the anterior part of the nose is to the submandibular nodes and superior nodes of the deep cervical chain. Drainage from the posterior part is to the middle, deep cervical chain.

The mucous membrane of the nose is intimately adherent to the periosteum or the perichondrium. With the exception of the olfactory area, it is ciliated columnar epithelium interspersed by goblet cells and serous glands. It is thickest and most vascular over the lower aspect of the septum and the turbinate, which permits vascular engorgement to regulate the temperature and humidity of inspired air. The subepithelial thin-walled vessels, serous glands and goblet cells all contribute to the formation of mucus. Mucus has two phases, the gel phase and the sol phase.

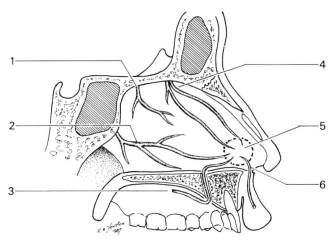

Fig. 1.1.4. Blood supply to the nasal septum.
1, Posterior ethmoidal artery.
2, Nasal branch of sphenopalatine artery.
3, Greater palatine artery.
4, Anterior ethmoidal arteries.
5, Little's area.
6, Septal branch of superior labial artery.

The sol phase is less viscous and is closely applied to the columnar cells. The gel phase overlies this and is moved backwards by hooks on the ends of the beating cilia. Mucus humidifies inspired air and with nasal vibrissae helps trap inspired contaminants.

The nerve supply to the nose is extremely rich. The main sensory supply comes from the maxillary division of the trigeminal nerve from its pterygopalatine branches (nasopalatine, greater palatine and short sphenopalatine nerves). The lateral and medial internal nasal branches of the anteroethmoidal nerve supply the anterior part of the nasal cavity, the floor and anterior end of the inferior turbinate are supplied by the anterior dental branch of the infraorbital nerve (*Figs.* 1.1.5, 1.1.6).

The secretory nerve supply fibres are mainly contained in the Vidian nerve (nerve of the pterygoid canal). The parasympathetic supply is derived from the superior salivatory nucleus in the medulla via the nervus intermedius and facial nerve which it leaves at the geniculate ganglion to form the Vidian nerve. The sympathetic fibres are derived from the superior cervical chain via the sympathetic plexus of the internal carotid artery and join with the parasympathetic fibres in the pterygoid canal. These supply the nasal vasculature; sympathetic stimulation constricts and parasympathetic dilates blood vessels. The glands themselves are under parasympathetic control alone.

PARANASAL SINUSES

These are air-filled cavities lined by an evagination of the mucous membrane of the nose from the nasal cavity into the substance of adjacent skull bones. They are arranged in pairs and are conveniently divided into an anterior and a posterior group. All the anterior group—frontal, ethmoidal and maxillary—drain into the middle meatus of the nose. The posterior ethmoidal cells drain into the superior meatus and the sphenoid into the sphenoethmoidal recess.

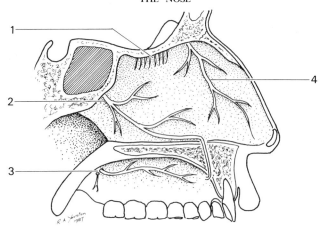

Fig. 1.1.5.   Nerve supply to the septum.
1, Branches of olfactory nerve.   3, Greater palatine nerve.
2, Long sphenopalatine nerve.   4, Medial internal nasal nerve.

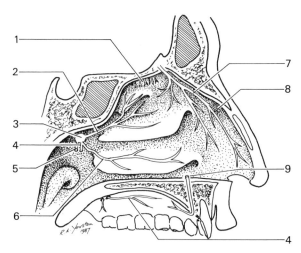

Fig. 1.1.6.   Nerve supply to the lateral nasal wall.
1, Branches of olfactory nerve.   6, Nasal branch of greater palatine nerve.
2, Short sphenopalatine nerve.   7, Lateral internal nasal nerve.
3, Sphenopalatine ganglion.   8, External branch of lateral nasal nerve.
4, Greater palatine nerve.   9, Long sphenopalatine nerve.
5, Lesser palatine nerve.

The Maxillary Sinuses

The maxillary sinus (antrum) is hollowed out of the maxilla. Its apex is formed by the malar process, its base is the lower part of the lateral wall of the nose. Its roof is the floor of the orbit and its narrow floor lies over the alveolar process of the maxilla and the roots of the molar and premolar teeth with its deepest part overlying the second premolar and first molar teeth. The canine and all molar teeth may occasionally be included in the floor. The roots of these teeth may produce eminences into the maxilla or occasionally perforate the bone. The medial wall is the lateral wall of the nasal cavity. The ostium is sited high on the wall, hence drainage is dependent on ciliary action and not gravity. One or more accessory ostia may lie posteriorly to the main one. The posterior wall is the anterior wall of the pterygopalatine and infratemporal fossae. At birth the sinus is rudimentary and growth is slow until the secondary dentition quickly expands it to its average adult size of 35 mm high, 30 mm anteroposteriorly and 25 mm wide with eruption of the third molar tooth (*Fig.* 1.1.7).

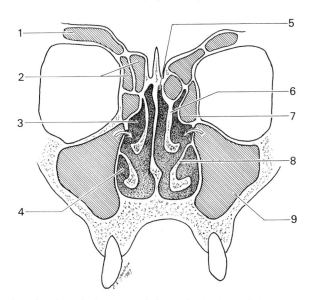

Fig. 1.1.7. Coronal section through the nose and sinuses in the plane of the maxillary ostia. The arrows lie in the maxillary sinus ostia.
1, Frontal sinus.   6, Middle turbinate.
2, Ethmoidal cells. 7, Ethmoidal bulla.
3, Middle meatus.   8, Inferior turbinate.
4, Inferior meatus. 9, Maxillary sinus.
5, Olfactory cleft.

The Frontal Sinuses

These are situated in the frontal bone above the supraorbital margin and root of the nose. They are unevenly divided by a vertical bony septum and vary considerably in size. They probably arise from the anterior ethmoidal cells and are closely related. The frontonasal duct passes through the ethmoidal labyrinth to the middle meatus. The anterior wall is the anterior table of the skull, the posterior wall is related to the frontal lobes. Inferiorly lies the frontonasal duct, medially the orbital roof and posteriorly the extremely variable supraorbital extension.

The Ethmoidal Sinuses

These labyrinths of thin-walled cavities are variable in number and size. They are relatively large at birth. They grow extremely slowly compared with the other sinuses. Laterally lies the medial wall of the orbit (lamina papyraceae) and medially is the nasal cavity. They lie inferior to the anterior cranial fossa, near the midline, at each side of the cribriform plate (fovea ethmoidalis). Some of the cells may invade the surrounding frontal sphenoid and maxillary bones. The anterior groups are small and numerous and drain into the middle meatus. The posterior group drain into the superior meatus.

The Sphenoid Sinuses

These occupy the body of the sphenoid bone. It is unevenly divided by a vertical septum and varies considerably in size. True growth of the sphenoid sinus only occurs at puberty, prior to that there may only be a small indentation with the nasal growth. In about 1 per cent of the population minimal pneumatization is present, in 40 per cent the sinus is pneumatized back to the anterior bony wall of the pituitary fossa (presellar) and in 60 per cent it extends to and under the pituitary fossa (sellar). The ostium is situated anteriorly and drains into the sphenoethmoidal recess.

Laterally the wall is contiguous with the internal carotid artery, the optic nerve and the venous cavernous and intercavernous sinuses. These contain the IIIrd, IVth, ophthalmic and maxillary divisions of Vth and VIth cranial nerves. Superiorly lie the frontal lobes and the olfactory apparatus and posteriorly lies the pituitary fossa. Sphenopalatine nerves and vessels lie in front of the sphenoid and the Vidian nerve lies inferiorly.

PHYSIOLOGY OF THE NOSE

The nose has several functions. It provides an airway for respiration, air-conditions the inspired air, collects the moisture from expired air to prevent excessive loss, provides the voice with a pleasing resonant quality, kills inspired bacteria and viruses, transports mucus posteriorly to lubricate the pharynx, filters suspended particulate matter from inspired air and is an integral part of the olfactory system. This latter function is fully explained later.

Inspired air passes in a wide curve beginning at the nostril, through the upper part of the nose to the posterior choanae. Expired air, however, does not move in a laminar flow of inspired air but is broken up by the turbinates into turbulent flow and the eddies flow through the meatuses. It has been postulated this is because the posterior choana is much larger than the nostril and because the outflow is smaller than the inflow, inevitably there is a degree of recirculation of air.

The subepithelial capillaries, which are fenestrated, humidify inspired air to achieve the optimum conditions for inspired air at the alveolar level. The moisture is evaporated from the mucous blanket overlying the epithelium which is maintained by secretions from the nasal gland. The water concentration of the mucus is maintained by fluid released through the fenestrated capillaries as they pass through the respiratory epithelium. The mucous blanket is formed by two layers, the gel phase and the sol phase. The overlying gel phase has a higher viscosity but in places is patchy. This is the phase which is moved posteriorly by ciliary action. Each cilium is composed of a shaft, basal body, a basal foot and a rootlet. They are 5 mm long and 2–3 mm thick (*Figs.* 1.1.8, 1.1.9).

In the shaft the cytoplasm is occupied by the microtubules, nexin buds, spokes and dynein arms. Microtubules are arranged in the 9 + 2 pattern, i.e. nine

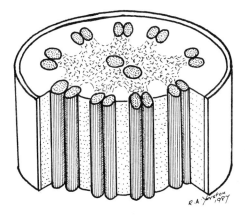

Fig. 1.1.8.   The structure of a nasal cilium near the middle of the shaft.

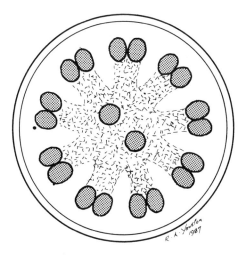

Fig. 1.1.9.   Transverse section of a nasal cilium.

peripheral doublets and two central simple microtubules. They beat forward in an effective stroke pulling the gel phase by the action of hooks on the end of the cilia and beat backward in a recovery stroke. Their action is reminiscent of a field of corn being blown by the wind. This movement is called metachrony as opposed to synchrony where all the cilia beat together. The whole blanket moves in a posterior direction through the posterior choana at an average rate of 6 mm/ minute. Congenital absence of the dynein arms, which normally contain ATP and power the cilia, occurs in Kartagener's syndrome (immotile cilia). These patients have a constantly runny nose, secretory otitis media, chronic sinusitis, bronchiectasis and often situs inversus. Normally the mucous blanket traps particulate matter and delivers it eventually to the acid secretions of the stomach which render it harmless. It also contains antibacterial lysozymes. Drying out of the mucous blanket stops ciliary activity. Thus excessive dry air, a deviated septum or excessive crusting decreases ciliary motion. Warming of inspired air is achieved by dilatation of the large vascular beds of the turbinates. These normally change in volume every 4 hours (the nasal cycle), each side alternating. Thus when one nostril allows a good respiratory airflow the other is effectively warming and humidifying the air.

The sinuses do not appear to have a function. Several unproven hypotheses have been suggested. They may give resonance to the voice or sound protection from transmission of the sound of one's own speech to the ears. They may air-condition inspired air by supplying warm and humid air or may equalize pressures during respiration, alternating between high internal and external pressures. They may have some influence on olfaction as they do in lower animals. They may reduce the weight of the skull or simply act as a protector to the eyes in trauma. They may thermally insulate the skull base and orbit. The most likely explanation is that they are vestigial, having no function, but are the result of development of the middle third of the face, nasal septum and teeth growing out and down and taking with them the outer bony layer.

BACTERIOLOGY

The commensal flora of the nose includes *Haemophilus influenzae*, *Staphylococcus albus* and a large variety of other organisms, including anaerobes. The finding of an organism on a nasal or sinus swab does not necessarily indicate that this is a pathogen or indeed causing symptoms. Up to 50 per cent of hospital personnel are found to be *S. aureus* carriers. The vast majority are asymptomatic but are an important source of infection to patients.

Chapter 1.2

INVESTIGATION OF NASAL DISEASE

HISTORY. The importance of taking an accurate history of nasal symptoms cannot be over-emphasized. The cardinal symptoms are nasal blockage, sneezing, rhinorrhoea, postnasal drip, facial pain, halitosis, snoring, unhappiness from cosmetic deformity and epistaxis and the many disorders of smell. The term 'catarrh' should be used cautiously as it has many different meanings, ranging from nasal obstruction to blobs of thick mucus lying in the larynx. Sinusitis and 'sinus' should not be accepted as a diagnosis until this has been proved. The time of onset of symptoms, periodicity (variable during the day or seasonal), severity, exacerbating or relieving factors and other associated symptoms should be asked for. Each condition will be discussed with its symptoms in subsequent chapters. Other systemic problems should also be discussed whether or not they are apparently related. A full medication history as well as all the medicines used in the past is important. Any family history including atopy, past medical and surgical history, and environmental conditions should be sought.

EXAMINATION. The nose is examined in a good light and any scars are noted. Beware the lateral rhinotomy scar that fades to an invisible line or 'hidden' scars (e.g. the bicoronal incision for a frontal osteoplastic flap operation is behind the hairline). Any deviation of the nasal bones or dorsal cartilaginous septum is noted, as are any deviations of the tip of the nose. A caudal dislocation of the cartilaginous septum is looked for and the intercanthal distance and interpupillary distance may be clinically judged. The cosmetic 'appropriateness' of the nose to the face is noted. Without altering the shape of the nostril the patency of each nostril is estimated by blocking the other one and the clouding of expired air on a shiny surface will confirm this. Sniffing may collapse the alae nasi and listening to the voice may suggest rhinolalia aperta or clausa.

The ears, the mouth and throat must also be examined for evidence of involvement in any nasal condition. Good illumination is necessary to inspect the nasal cavities, i.e. anterior rhinoscopy. Traditionally a bull's eye lamp is shone over the patient's left shoulder and reflected off a concave mirror on the examiner's forehead. The examiner looks through a hole in the middle of this mirror and dilates the nostrils with a speculum (*Fig.* 1.2.1). Modifications of this technique are many but the principle of good illumination of the nasal cavity is essential. Usually only the anterior part of the nostril may be seen in this manner because of the anterior part of the inferior turbinate, but if a better view is needed, the nasal mucosa should be shrunk. Cotton wool soaked in 5 or 10 per cent

13

cocaine hydrochloride, mixed in equal proportions with adrenaline tartrate, is placed in the nasal cavity for 10 minutes. This may be repeated more posteriorly in the nose if necessary.   If a patient faints when this is done, the patient is either allergic to cocaine or has swallowed some and absorbed it very quickly through the gastric mucosa. Normal resuscitative procedures should be instituted in this case but prevention is preferable by spitting out any solution that trickles into the pharynx.

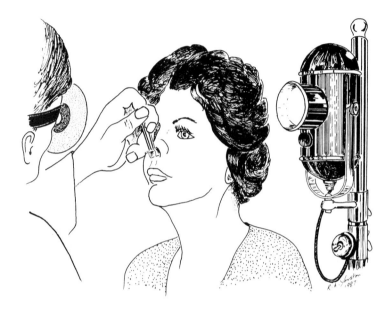

Fig. 1.2.1.   Anterior rhinoscopy.

Deviations of the nasal septum are looked for; bleeding vessels, nasal polyps, abnormalities of the mucosa and secretions should all be described appropriately. Examination of the upper teeth, with percussion if necessary, to exclude local infection, soft palate movement, palpation for a submucous cleft and the noting of a bifid uvula are all essential. The nasopharynx is viewed with a small angled mirror held in the oropharynx, directed cephalically, and a strong light shone onto it. The tongue is held down with a depressor. The mirror should be preheated gently to avoid condensation. This is a difficult examination to perform and many patients cannot relax their soft palate with their mouth open. Encouragement to breathe through the nose may help, but the ability to perform this examination requires considerable practice. The posterior end of the septum is a pale, vertical ridge which gives an anatomical landmark. Laterally lie the posterior choanae with often the posterior ends of the inferior turbinates evident. Further laterally the tubal ridges of the pharyngeal ends of the Eustachian tubes are seen. In the roof posteriorly lie the adenoids and any mucosal abnormality, particularly immediately above the Eustachian tubes (the fossae of Rosenmüller), should alert one to the possibility of a nasopharyngeal carcinoma.

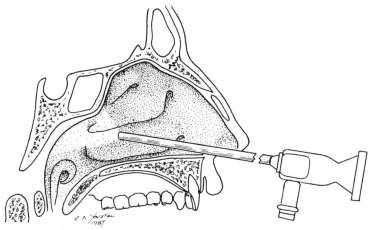

Fig. 1.2.2. Rhinoscopy using an endoscope (antroscope).

ENDOSCOPY. Further advances with fibreoptic endoscopy have facilitated this examination. Cocainization of the nose is almost mandatory and a rigid endoscope is advanced through the anterior nares. A good view of the nasal cavity, including the olfactory groove and various meatuses, is possible before advancing through the posterior nares to view the nasopharynx (*Fig.* 1.2.2). This technique requires considerable practice before proficiency is obtained. A simpler method of viewing the nasopharynx is by using a rigid fibreoptic rod passed through the mouth and directed at right angles to view the nasopharynx. This has the added benefit of closing the mouth around it and allowing nasal breathing which relaxes the soft palate (*Fig.* 1.2.3). In children instrumentation is frightening and should,

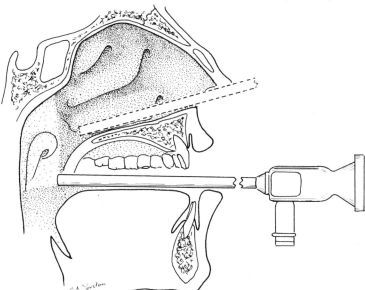

Fig. 1.2.3. The nasopharyngoscope may be passed through the mouth or through the nose (dotted outline).

if possible, be avoided. Often an adequate examination is performed by tilting the tip of the nose up and shining a light up. Digital examination of the child's nasopharynx is not indicated unless under a general anaesthetic. A full examination of the nose and nasopharynx may require a general anaesthetic with direct inspection, palpation, fibreoptic inspection and biopsy.

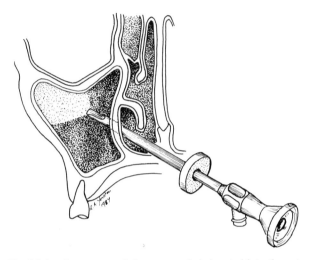

Fig. 1.2.4. Antroscopy. A 6-mm cannula is inserted into the antrum through the inferior meatus, and the antroscope is passed through the cannula.

Fibreoptic examination of the sinuses may be indicated. The nasal cavity is cocainized including the middle meatus. The maxillary ostium is inspected. Using a trocar and cannula, the wall of the antrum is pierced in the inferior meatus and a fibreoptic rod is passed through the cannula (*Fig.* 1.2.4). With practice a good view of the maxillary sinus mucosa is obtained. Biopsy forceps may also be used through the cannula. An alternative route is via the buccolabial sulcus in the canine fossa through the anterior wall of the maxillary sinus (*Fig.* 1.2.5). Direct sight of the sphenoid and ethmoid sinuses is similarly possible. Through a trephine (*see below*) incision, the trocar and cannula may be introduced into the frontal sinuses for visual inspection.

DIAGNOSTIC PROOF PUNCTURE. A trocar and cannula may be introduced through the inferior meatus into the maxillary antrum. A syringe is placed on the end of the cannula after withdrawal of the trocar and sucked back to see if pus is present. A small amount of saline at body temperature is syringed into the sinus and sucked back. By this method any pus in the sinus is collected and sent for culture and the patency of the ostium may be assessed. This diagnostic proof puncture is also used to treat maxillary sinus disease. Caution is necessary in interpretation of the results of nasal swabs. Antibiotic treatment alters the flora considerably, thus the growth of an organism on a swab does not necessarily mean it is a pathogen.

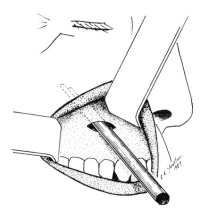

Fig. 1.2.5. Antroscopy. A 6-mm cannula is inserted into the antrum through the canine fossa, and the antroscope is passed through the cannula.

ALLERGY TESTING. The basis of objective testing lies in skin tests. Both the prick test and the intradermal test use an allergen placed on the skin. If the patient has an allergy to this, a wheal and flare will come up within 20 minutes. These are usually performed on the volar aspect of the forearm because, if the patient is highly sensitive, an anaphylactic reaction may result. Containment of the reaction is helped by a tourniquet placed proximally to the reaction and, if necessary, administration of subcutaneous adrenaline. This site has the disadvantage of a small area and the upper back is sometimes used. Normally a control and a histamine-containing solution are used to ensure the patient is not allergic to the carrier substance and does react in the normal fashion to histamine. Depending on the patient's history, a variety of allergens are tested. These may be conveniently grouped under the headings of moulds, pollens, animal dander, the house dust mite and house dust. Usually a mixture of various pollens or moulds is used and, if positive, further testing is indicated to find the particular allergen or allergens. The fact that the test shows a patient to have a specific allergy does not necessarily mean that this allergy is the one causing the symptoms.

The allergic reaction causing rhinitis is classified as a type I reaction involving immunoglobulin E. Plasma levels of IgE may be measured in total in the plasma radioimmunosorbent test (PRIST) and IgE to specific allergens in the radioallergosorbent test (RAST). These do not have any diagnostic superiority over the skin tests and are considerably more expensive, but are of use in the confirmation of the diagnosis or as a 'safety net' in case other methods do not demonstrate the allergen.

SMEARS. An increase in the number of eosinophils in a nasal smear has been shown to be indicative of an allergic rhinitis, but this test is merely supportive and not diagnostic. Blood eosinophilia may also indicate the diagnosis of allergic rhinitis, but it is uncommon for the small shock organ (the nose) to create a systemic imbalance and an eosinophilia is more likely to indicate a larger shock organ, e.g. the lungs.

PROVOCATION TESTS. Nasal provocation tests are occasionally of use. The suspected allergen is squeezed into the nose and the number of sneezes counted. Alternatively a positive result is shown by the change in the number of eosinophils counted from a nasal smear or if rhinomanometry shows a sudden change in nasal resistance. The disadvantage of this test is that it cannot be repeated for half an hour.

RHINOMANOMETRY. Rhinomanometry is the measurement of nasal airflow and nasal airway resistance. It has not yet been standardized or accepted into standard clinical practice and remains a research tool at present. Either the pressure or flow is measured through the nose. The pressure may be standardized and the flow through each nostril measured, or the flow is standardized and the pressure gradient measured. In posterior rhinomanometry the pressure differences between the ambient air and the mouth (nasopharynx) are measured and in anterior rhinomanometry the technique is based on pressure registration from one nostril and flow from the other nostril. Other variations include active and passive respiration using different recording methods. Although it is quite an objective measurement, a significant percentage of patients cannot perform these tests and the equipment is expensive and requires expertise and practice to work.

MUCOCILIARY CLEARANCE TEST. Ciliary motility is relatively easily measured by the saccharine-clearance test. A small piece of saccharine is placed on the anterior end of the inferior turbinate, behind the squamous epithelium mucosa junction. The ciliated epithelium wafts the saccharine molecules backwards until they reach the pharynx, and the patient indicates when he tastes the substance. The normal time for this is up to 20 minutes but the patient must not sniff or hawk in this time. About 20 per cent of normal people have a prolonged time. A positive test may indicate primary immotile cilia, as in Kartagener's syndrome, or secondary as in chronic infection. Modifications of the test include the use of dyes, e.g. sky-blue or orange, or radioactive particles plotted by gamma camera.

RADIOLOGY. The nasal bones may be demonstrated by a plain lateral radiograph, an anteroposterior view, an occipitomental view or from above with a film held in the teeth—an occlusal view (*Fig.* 1.2.6).

The anteroposterior view also demonstrates the bony septum and the turbinates, although these should be adequately seen clinically.

There are several standard views of the sinuses:

1. *Occipitomental.* The head is thrown back to take the petrous bone below the floor of the antrum, thus demonstrating the maxillary antrum best. Occasionally the sphenoid may be seen below the upper incisors if the tilt is enough.

2. *Occipitofrontal.* This 'straight-on' view demonstrates the ethmoidal sinuses and the frontals.

3. *Lateral.* This is the best view for the sphenoid sinus. It also demonstrates the frontal and maxillary sinuses but there is much superimposition and less value is attached to these sinuses on this view. The nasopharynx is also demonstrated. This has been used to demonstrate adenoidal size but cephalometric techniques to avoid skull rotation are necessary to render the findings meaningful.

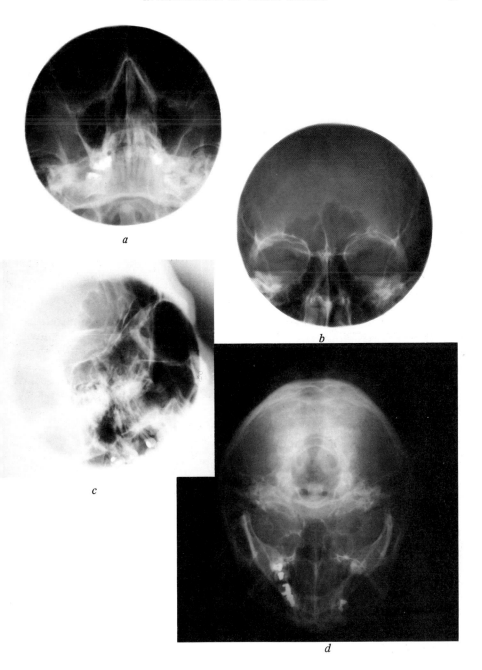

Fig. 1.2.6. Radiography of sinuses.
a, Normal occipitomental view.
b, Normal occipitofrontal (posteroanterior) view.
c, Normal oblique view of ethmoids.
d, Normal submentovertical view.

4. *Submentovertical view*. This shows the ethmoids and sphenoid sinuses.

5. *Oblique views*. These are occasionally helpful to demonstrate the ethmoids.

The relative translucency of the paired sinuses should be studied in comparison with the radiolucent orbit. If the sinuses are clear it is unlikely that sinus disease is present. Mucosal thickening is often seen, particularly in the alveolar recess. This may be indicative of infection but antroscopy will help elucidate the diagnosis.

Tomograms of the sinuses are necessary for assessment of tumours and bone destruction. The method is now being applied to the assessment of sinusitis.

A fluid level is diagnostic of infections but total opacification of the sinus may indicate either a gross infection or a huge polyp. Small polyps seen inside the sinus on radiographs should be inspected by antroscopy to exclude neoplasia, but active treatment of an infective polyp should only be instituted if the patient has associated symptoms. Erosion or thinning of bone indicates an expansive or neoplastic condition requiring further investigation.

Radiology is only a guide to the diagnosis and must always be taken into consideration with all the other information available before a diagnosis is reached. The orthopantomogram is essentially a dental examination. The full dentition may be seen on an elongated radiograph. It shows the teeth and in particular their roots well. Any erosion or bony swellings are readily identifiable.

SCANNING TECHNIQUES. The use of computerized axial tomography has revolutionized the management of several nose conditions, particularly neoplasia. This uses the principle of multiple tomograms of the skull and face taken from different angles, which are processed by a computer, producing various 'slices' through the head. A composite picture is obtained which otherwise is not possible. This is excellent for seeing the orbits and bony erosions around the base of the skull, the anterior cranial fossa and the pterygopalatine fossa. It may be used either horizontally or vertically. However, it is extremely expensive, but with the advent of more sophisticated scanners with higher definition, diagnostic accuracy is high.

The nuclear magnetic resonance imager is another recent development. This works on the principle of identification of hydrogen ion spin, thereby creating a magnetic field. It is at present in its infancy and shows soft-tissue densities better than the CT scanner but does not demonstrate bone well. In effect, it 'strips away' bone from the picture. A full evaluation of its uses for nasal diagnostic purposes is awaited.

Chapter 1.3

NASAL AND FACIAL TRAUMA

Nasal trauma is extremely common. From birth onwards the nose is 'assaulted', but relatively speaking receives little medical attention. Although most incidents of nasal trauma are minor, evidence is rapidly accumulating that the long-term effects are more far reaching than previously understood.

During normal parturition the fetal head is directed caudally and passes through the pelvic brim. The Caucasian head is widest at the occipitonasal diameter. Up to 20 per cent of babies born in this manner are found to have 'squashed' noses. The majority spring back into place but about 1–2 per cent are left with a permanently deviated septum. This may not be apparent initially but subsequently gives rise to nasal obstruction and snuffles. Excessive moulding of the head distorts the posterior aspect of the septum which at this stage of development is cartilaginous and, if not immediately corrected, this eventually develops into a deviated bony septum with consequent problems. Early recognition of septal abnormalities in neonates permits straightening of the septum at this stage and prevention of an 'idiopathic' deviated septum. The technique of depressing the hard palate with a two-pronged instrument, one going in either nostril, and rapid maxillary expansion has its advocates but has not achieved total acceptance in the profession.

Subsequent minor injuries not requiring medical attention may interfere with growth centres by haematoma formation and thereby further deviate the nasal septum. The Fry principle also provides at least a theoretical cause of a deviated cartilaginous septum. The cartilaginous septum is composed of a sandwich of layers, the innermost is held under tension by the outer layers. If one outermost layer is breached as in a traumatic bend of the septum, the innermost tension is lost and the septum remains deviated. Subsequent scarring and fibrosis ensure this deviation remains.

A true fracture through the cartilage will also deviate the septum. Interference with the formation of the maxillary crest allows a true dislocation of the septum laterally into either nasal cavity. This is apparent clinically by protrusion of the caudal end into the medial aspect of the vestibule.

Fractures of the cartilaginous septum may conveniently be divided into two eponymously named fractures (*Fig.* 1.3.1), and a large variety of miscellaneous fractures. The fracture of Jarjavay runs in a horizontal direction parallel with the maxillary crest from the maxillary spine to the vomer and results from trauma directed onto the dorsum of the nose. The fracture of Chevallet runs from the maxillary spine to the nasal bones and results from lateral trauma. Other less specific trauma produces a variety of deviations of the septum which are not

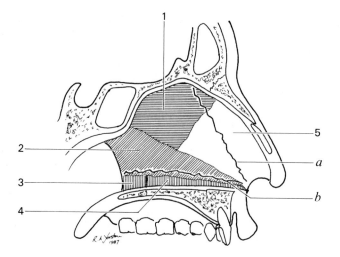

Fig. 1.3.1.   Nasal septum showing fracture of Chevallet (*a*) and fracture of Jarjavay (*b*).
1, Perpendicular plate of ethmoid (horizontal shading).   4, Nasal crest of maxilla (vertical shading).
2, Vomer (diagonal shading).   5, Cartilaginous septum (unshaded).
3, Nasal crest of palatine bone.

constant and may produce either a 'C'- or 'S'-shaped deviation (*Fig.* 1.3.2). The actual shape is not particularly important in relation to symptoms but operatively it must be recognized to allow adequate correction.

The incidence of a deviated septum rises with age. The aetiology of the deviated septum is most probably trauma, although other possible causes include thumb sucking, nose picking and inheritance. The requirement for operation depends solely on the presence of symptoms. Commonly nasal blockage is the predominant symptom, but others include postnasal discharge, cosmetic deformity and epistaxis due to crusting of an exposed part of the septum.

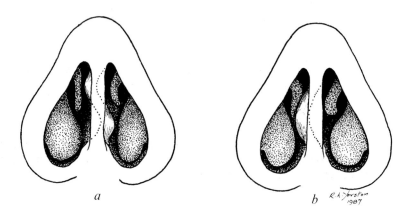

Fig. 1.3.2.   Deformities of the nasal septum.
a, S-shaped.   *b*, C-shaped.

Fractures of the nasal bones themselves can be similarly classified. The unilateral nasal bone fracture is usually depressed and gives the appearance of deviation but in fact there is none. This fracture results from mild lateral violence and can be easily elevated back into position and held there by intranasal packing until healed.

Greater violence fractures the nasal bones across the midline and tends to deviate the nasal bones. Correction of this fracture may require septal surgery as well as manipulation of the bones by Walsham's forceps. These forceps consist of one prong, which is inserted into the nostril and the other, which is rubber-covered and placed on the external aspect of the skin overlying the nasal bone. The bones are then mobilized and reset. The septum can be manipulated using Asche's forceps. These are forceps with parallel prongs placed either side of the septum which is grasped between and the cartilage manipulated back into shape.

A greater degree of trauma may shatter the nasal bones into a comminuted fracture. This is usually associated with a greater septal fracture which runs in a C-shape from immediately under the nasal bones, through the perpendicular plate of the ethmoid and vomer, to end anteriorly in the posteroinferior aspect of the cartilaginous septum (*Fig.* 1.3.3). If the bones are not shattered they are widely deviated in this fracture and the probability of the septal fracture may be surmised by the degree of deviation of the nasal bones. This septal fracture must be reduced or resected at the time of repair, otherwise the deviated septal fragments pull the nasal bones laterally.

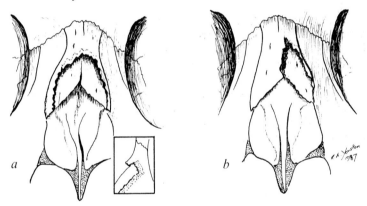

Fig. 1.3.3. Fractures of nasal bones.
a, Central segment fracture. The segment is displaced posteriorly (inset), with splaying of the other nasal bones and fracture of the underlying bony septum. The septal fracture must be reduced or resected at the time of repair, otherwise the deviated septum pulls the nasal bones laterally.
b, Unilateral fracture.

Occasionally greater anterior violence delivered straight on may produce a central segment pushed into the face with comminution of the ethmoid labyrinth, and again septal involvement is common.

COMPLICATIONS

A septal haematoma may result after trauma to the septum. It is common in children because the mucoperichondrium is not closely bound down to the cartilage in this age-group compared with adults. If left it necroses cartilage to produce either an abscess or perforation and thus must be drained under general anaesthesia. Soft rubber drains with packing to prevent recurrence are necessary.

If **infection** does ensue, abscess formation quickly necroses cartilage with the end-result of a deficient cartilaginous dorsum and usually a widened septum which reduces the airway. Venous drainage of this area (*see above*) may lead to the cavernous sinus. If this thromboses as a result, the IIIrd, IVth and VIth cranial nerves and the two upper divisions of the Vth are affected. This condition of **cavernous sinus thrombosis** carries a very high mortality rate and is characterized by exophthalmos and ophthalmoplegia.

A **perforation** may also result from trauma as from many other causes. If small the perforation may produce an irritating whistling noise with respiration and if larger, considerable crusting. If asymptomatic no treatment is necessary. The treatment of a perforation is discussed below.

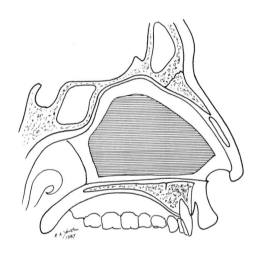

Fig. 1.3.4.   Classical submucous resection of the nasal septum. The area resected is shaded.

SEPTAL SURGERY

The classic septal operation is the submucous resection. This involves incising the mucoperichondrium parallel but 0·5 in (1·25 cm) behind the columella and elevating the mucoperichondrium flap of the septal cartilage. The cartilage is incised in the same parallel line as the mucoperichondrium and the opposite flap is raised. Forceps are inserted either side of the cartilage and it is removed. The original described area of resection is shown in *Fig*. 1.3.4.

This operation, although a great step forward in its time, has several complications. Too much cartilage may be removed, producing a dip immediately distal to the nasal bones on the dorsum or retraction at the nasolabial angle; the typical pugilist's nose. Tears and infection of the mucoperichondrium flaps often produce a permanent perforation, and if too much cartilage is removed the septum can move from side to side with respiration—the 'flapping' septum. It is not uncommon also for some of the offending deviations or spurs to be left even after this extensive removal, particularly a dislocated caudal end of the septum. A variety of other operations have been devised to obviate most of these complications. These retain as much cartilage as possible.

The swing-door technique involves a through-and-through incision through the cartilage at the site of fracture with the free end swung back into line.

The Cottle septoplasty uses inferior tunnels with removal of cartilage along the maxillary crest and elevation of mucoperichondrium only on one side of the septum.

The technique of scarring the cartilage on one side to make the cartilage bend to the other side is used for the majority of gross septal deviations. This incomplete scarring and cross-hatching is dependent on the Fry theory with unilateral release of interlock stresses to cause the septum to bend. Despite the earlier claims of success, this technique has not been found useful as following trauma the rearrangement of collagen fibres in the deviated septum prevents normal behaviour of the cartilage.

The more radical technique of removing the whole cartilaginous septum, destroying any deviations and interlock stresses by morselization and replacement appears to be more successful. Resiting of a dislocated caudal end of the septum is usually part of a septoplasty.

The difference between a submucous resection and septoplasty is more apparent than real. A septoplasty operation is only mandatory in the presence of either a caudally dislocated septum or externally deviated cartilaginous septum which needs correction. To produce a good airway a septum operation tailored to the requests of the case should be done. An experienced rhinologist uses all of the above techniques to a greater or lesser extent, and a standard operation whatever its name will not suit all cases.

In the acutely traumatized nose with gross deviation, replacement of the nasal bones is usually inadequate to reduce the fractures and removal of the bony-cartilaginous septum at their interface is necessary to allow the nose to stay in the middle of the face (*Fig.* 1.3.5).

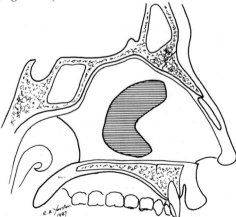

Fig. 1.3.5. Area of resection of a C-shaped fracture in a widely deviated nose.

FRONTAL SINUS FRACTURE

Fractures of the frontal sinus are relatively uncommon. Direct frontal trauma of adequate force may depress the outer table. If this is an isolated fracture with no other involvement and no consequent frontal sinusitis, the fragments may be left alone. Commonly, however, it is not possible to assess adequately the posterior wall or inner table of the sinus. Anteroposterior tomograms and laminograms have been used but direct inspection is usually necessary. Using an osteoplastic flap technique (*see below*), the sinus is opened and the back wall viewed. The importance of adequate reduction of the broken fragments in this area is prevention of cerebrospinal fluid leakage and subsequent meningitis. As cosmesis is important in the forehead, exploration and reduction may be necessary to prevent deformity.

FRONTOETHMOID FRACTURE

Direct trauma aimed around the nasion area may not only fracture the nasal bones (*see above*) but, if severe enough, disrupt the medial canthal ligaments. If these alone are disrupted, the interpupillary distance is not increased but is apparently increased. No change in vision is noted but the distance between the canthi is widened. This is termed pseudohyperteleorism. In contrast, true hyper-teleorism results from an ethmoidal fracture with splaying of the nasal bones and ethmoids and lateral displacement of the lamina papyracea. The interpupillary distance is increased with consequent visual disturbances. Adequate reduction of this fracture is mandatory and may involve wiring of the fragments back into position and holding them across the midline. Occasionally lead plates are placed on the external aspects of the nasal bones and wired in place to hold the bones 'up and out' of such a depressed fracture, but usually intranasal packing with an external splint should be adequate to stabilize the fracture with normal healing.

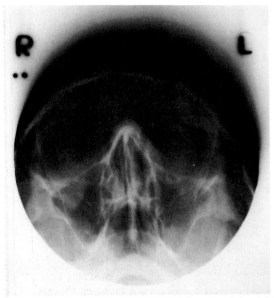

Fig. 1.3.6.   Radiograph showing a 'blow-out' fracture of the right orbit.

BLOW-OUT FRACTURE

The 'blow-out' fracture of the eye is usually the result of direct frontal trauma. The size of a squash ball is ideal to produce this injury, a cricket ball is slightly too large.

Apart from the obvious disruption of the eye itself, increased pressure may rupture the floor of the orbit and extrude the fat content of the orbit. This produces enophthalmos and the appearance of a herniated piece of fat into the roof of the maxillary antrum is the 'tear-drop' sign (*Fig.* 1.3.6).

Correction of this requires exploration of the orbit and reconstitution of the floor, usually with sialastic to prevent a recurrence of the herniation. If this is not achieved, early necrosis of the fat occurs with permanent enophthalmos. Entrapment of the intraorbital muscles is evident with clinical testing but the forced duction test may be required to distinguish globe displacement from actual entrapment. After anaesthetizing the eye the inferior rectus muscle is physically grasped and rotated.

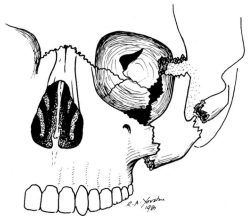

Fig. 1.3.7. Fracture of the lateral third of the maxilla.

ZYGOMATIC FRACTURE

A fracture of the zygomatic arch alone is common. It is treated by elevation with access from the temporal region.

In the malar or tripod fracture all three arms are fractured and the areas depressed. Recognition of this fracture depends on the awareness of the possibility as often soft-tissue swelling obscures the bony outline. Palpation of the infraorbital rim may reveal a step. If the fracture is undisplaced there is no cosmetic problem and if the infraorbital nerve is undamaged, no further active treatment is required. If, however, either of these factors is present, operative reduction is necessary. This can either be open or closed. The closed technique involves making an incision in the temporal area and dissection inferiorly to the zygoma. Elevation of the depressed area often clicks the displaced bone into position (*Fig.* 1.3.7). If this is unstable either the fragments are openly reduced and directly wired or the fragments are reduced by manipulation through the antrum which is packed to avoid redisplacement.

There are three classic Le Fort fractures. Type 1 is the Guérin fracture which involves the lower part of the maxilla. It is quite uncommon to sustain this fracture alone (*Fig.* 1.3.8). The common Type 2 or pyramidal fracture runs more superiorly. It is the result of more severe trauma and usually needs to be reduced under general anaesthesia and held in place by wires. The Type 3 or craniofacial dysjunction is the result of severe frontal violence and is often fatal. All of these fractures are associated with copious bleeding and first aid techniques to avoid death include holding the fracture segment forward to allow a reasonable airway. An even more severe Type 4 injury involving a coronal fracture of the skull has also been described. These fractures are rarely present as classically described above but more often a combination of the various types is usual.

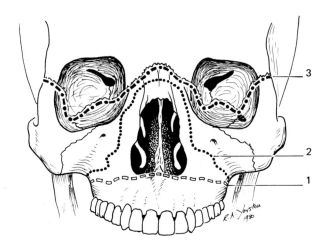

Fig. 1.3.8.   Fractures of the middle third of the face. The numbers correspond to the Le Fort classification.

CEREBROSPINAL FLUID LEAKS

The presence of clear rhinorrhoea following nasal trauma at any stage raises the possibility of a cerebrospinal fluid leak. The commonest area of fracture is the cribriform plate as this is extremely thin. Other possible areas include the posterior wall of the frontal sinus and the floor of the anterior cranial fossa. Postoperatively a trans-sphenoidal hypophysectomy may leak cerebrospinal fluid. The muscle graft used to plug the sphenoid may be deficient, allowing cerebrospinal fluid to leak past.

Confirmation of the diagnosis is obtained by collecting some of the fluid. Cerebrospinal fluid has a high glucose content (approaching serum levels), will make a dry handkerchief stiff and if mixed with blood in the secretions classically produces a 'halo' effect when it stains white bedclothes. In contrast, rhinorrhoea from the turbinates, which is common after nasal trauma, has none of these properties. Further confirmation is obtained by injection of either fluorescein or a radioactive isotope into the CSF via a lumbar puncture. Pledgets placed appropriately in the nose collect the substance. The areas where these are placed are superiorly along the cribriform plate in the sphenoethmoidal recess, in the middle meatus and at the opening of the Eustachian tube in case the leak comes from the middle ear. In practice a CSF leak will undoubtedly contaminate all these, rendering the exact site of leak impossible to locate. Further CT scanning with high resolution localizes the fracture better. The treatment may well involve a craniotomy with a formal repair of dura with fascia lata in reduction of the bony fragments. Lesser leaks are occasionally managed without resort to such extreme surgery and close spontaneously.

Avoidance of meningitis is mandatory in these patients and recurrent bouts of meningitis after nasal or facial trauma should alert the clinician to the probability of a dura leak, even if there is no clinical CSF rhinorrhoea.

SEPTAL PERFORATION

The causes of septal perforation include local trauma (nose picking or iatrogenic), nasal trauma with septal haematoma or abscess formation, and granulomatous conditions, e.g. Wegener's granulomatosis or syphilis. However, many perforations are idiopathic. The symptoms caused vary with size. If the perforation is very small a whistling noise may be heard on respiration. This may be quite distressing and is treated by enlarging the perforation. Crusting with subsequent bleeding may occur with a large perforation. Any underlying causative condition should be treated before specific treatment of the perforation. Medical treatment of the crusting is possible with 25 per cent glucose in glycerol drops or petroleum ointment liberally applied to the nose. Surgical treatment may be ultimately necessary but is in the main unsatisfactory. A variety of operations, including closing the operation with a split-skin graft or the use of septal mucoperichondrial flaps or buccal flaps, have been described. Other possibilities include composite grafts from the pinna or moving septal cartilage to fill the hole. As with other operations, the description of so many differing techniques indicates that none is particularly successful. An alternative treatment, if the condition troubles the patient, is to use a silastic prosthesis.

Chapter 1.4

EPISTAXIS

Epistaxis is common. Seventy per cent of adult males over the age of 60 years have had an epistaxis. The commonest cause is either external trauma or from picking the nose, although this latter aetiology is often classified as idiopathic. Most epistaxes originate from Little's area, not only because of the highly vascular nature of this region but also inspired air tends to be directed onto it causing undue drying and crusting. When this is removed some of the mucosa is often also removed to produce bleeding. Relatively few nosebleeds are seen by a doctor because they are self-limiting.

ASSESSMENT. The aetiological factors for epistaxis include trauma (*see above*), upper respiratory tract infections, foreign bodies, postoperative nose or sinus infections, tumours, elevated blood pressure and disorders of blood vessels and clotting mechanisms. A history will exclude many of the above causes. The blood pressure is often temporarily elevated on admission to hospital but settles with bed rest and sedation. If necessary a full clotting and bleeding screen should be done to exclude haematological problems. A drug-induced nosebleed is not uncommon, particularly in the elderly when taking antiarthritic drugs. Other acquired blood disorders may cause nose bleeding, e.g. idiopathic thrombocytopenic purpura, leukaemia, scurvy, etc. All treatable disorders are naturally corrected as quickly as possible.

TREATMENT. First aid measures include sitting the patient forwards and pinching the nostrils tight. Ice is sucked and put over the forehead until the bleeding stops. If this fails a medical referral is necessary. The simplest method to stop the bleeding is to insert a pledget of cotton wool soaked in an adrenaline solution to the nostril. This is only short acting and when the adrenaline effect wears off in about 20 minutes, the bleeding may return in a greater quantity. If a small bleeding vessel or point can be seen it should be cauterized. Similarly, if the patient presents with a non-acute recurrent epistaxis and the blood vessel can be seen, it should be cauterized. This is done as follows. A pledget of cotton wool soaked in a 1 : 1 solution of adrenaline tartrate and 10 per cent cocaine hydrochloride is inserted into either nostril for 20 minutes. If the vessel is further posterior than this first pack reaches, a further pack should be inserted. Once the mucosa is anaesthetized the offending vessel is cauterized. Other solutions, e.g. lignocaine, may be used to anaesthetize the nose. The substances used for the cautery include silver nitrate, often on the end of an orange stick, trichloracetic acid, chromic acid, bead or electric cautery. Care should be taken to avoid an overdose of 10 per cent cocaine. The safe body dose is 200 mg, thus less than 2 ml should be used and none should be swallowed as it is easily absorbed from the gastric mucosa. If the patient feels faint, either he has had a vasovagal attack, in which case the pulse is slow and regular and recovery is rapid if he is laid flat, or he has been affected by the cocaine, in which case the pulse is rapid. Supportive measures of resuscitation are used when indicated.

In young children and apprehensive adults, electrocautery may be difficult in the clinic situation and they may require a general anaesthetic.

In some patients, despite good illumination and suction, the blood vessel either cannot be seen or cauterized, and physical pressure on the blood vessel is necessary to occlude it. This is achieved by packing and clotting mechanisms will occlude the vessel while the pack is in place.

The pack requires to remain *in situ* for at least 48 hours to allow reasonable clotting. A 0·5 in (1·25 cm) ribbon gauze is soaked in a mixture of bismuth iodoform paraffin paste (BIPP). This substance is antiseptic and can be left in the nose for a considerable time. If this is not used the pack quickly becomes foul and a source of infection. The leading edge of the pack is inserted along the floor of the nostril as far posteriorly as possible and another layer placed on top sequentially and so on. This will eventually totally pack the nostril (*Fig.* 1.4.1).

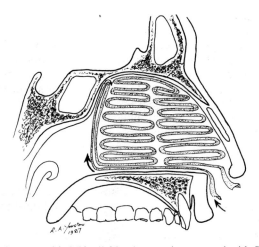

Fig. 1.4.1. Packing the nose with 0·5 in (1·25 cm) gauze impregnated with BIPP. The first fold is directed along the floor of the nose, and the second fold to the roof of the nose (arrows). The packing is then continued in smaller more easily managed loops from floor to roof. The first vertical fold prevents the pack unfolding and escaping into the nasopharynx.

A good pack placed in this manner will control almost all epistaxes. None of the pack should go down into the nasopharynx if it is properly packed. The pack may be left for a prolonged time. If the bleeding continues despite an adequate anterior pack, the patient should be taken to theatre and given a general anaesthetic. Direct inspection of the nose may reveal a specific bleeding point which should be cauterized. More commonly after 48 hours of BIPP packing, the nasal mucosa is raw and bleeding in many places. A posterior pack may be used if the bleeding is predominantly in this area. A small swab or ready-made pledget is inserted into the postnasal space. Ties are taken anteriorly through both nostrils and tied around a bolster covering the columella. These hold the pack in place against the posterior choanae and prevent posterior epistaxis. A further anterior pack is then placed, packing against the posterior pack. The posterior pack stays in place for 48 hours or longer.

Variations on these packs are many. The most popular include some form of balloon. The simplest is designed to fill the nasal cavity and is blown up *in situ* either by air or water. A urinary catheter is the simplest method of inserting a postnasal pack. It is inserted along the floor of the nostril and when in the nasopharynx the balloon is filled. The free edge of the catheter is pulled back away from the patient and the balloon is pulled into and blocks the posterior choanae. As the catheter is elastic the free end is taped under a degree of tension to the nostril to prevent the balloon falling into the oropharynx. Other specifically made balloon catheters have anterior and posterior balloons to fill the nasal cavity and nasopharynx respectively. An adequate time should be allowed for clotting before removal of these balloons.

The patient should be given antibiotics when the posterior packs are *in situ* to prevent otitis media from Eustachian tube blockage.

Sedation is necessary whenever a nasal pack is *in situ*. Not only is the pack uncomfortable but the added anxiety of a nosebleed and a blocked nose may elevate the blood pressure. Care must be taken, however, as packing the nose embarrasses respiration and the arterial Po_2 drops and the arterial Pco_2 rises. This may lead to respiratory failure in the patient with chest problems. Other supportive measures are instituted at an early stage. The pulse and blood pressure are checked and if the patient is shocked an intravenous drip is commenced. A baseline haemoglobin is withdrawn and resuscitation begun with crystalloid fluids. If necessary plasma and blood should be given to restore an adequate circulating volume. If there is any question of an underlying anaemia, e.g. iron deficiency or megaloblastic anaemia, venous blood is withdrawn for estimation before intravenous blood is administered.

If the epistaxis continues, and usually at this stage it has gone on for several days, it may be necessary to clip the feeding arteries to the nose. The maxillary artery from the external carotid artery system feeds the lower part of the nose and the ethmoidal artery from the internal carotid artery system feeds the upper part of the nose. Depending on the area of bleeding, the appropriate vessel is clipped under general anaesthesia. The approach to the anterior ethmoidal artery is via a medial orbital incision with lateral displacement of the orbital contents and lacrimal sac. The artery runs across the operative field and is readily controlled with a stainless-steel clip.

The maxillary artery is encountered in a bed of glistening fat in the pterygopalatine fossa. A Caldwell–Luc incision is made, the antrum entered and a window made in the posterior wall of the sinus. The artery is encountered in the pterygopalatine fossa and teased away from the fat pad. Each tortuous branch is clipped in turn. If these procedures are still unsuccessful at stopping the bleeding, the external carotid artery may need to to be tied off in the neck.

Specific problems in the management of epistaxis include hereditary haemorrhagic telangiectasia or Rendu–Osler–Weber disease. This condition is recurrent and often leads to intractable epistaxis. Apart from repeated local treatment, other therapies include oestrogens, radiotherapy, sclerosants, lining mucosa with placenta, split skin or other similar substances and even, in extreme circumstances, removal of the external nose.

Recent advances in the treatment of epistaxis include the use of embolization of the offending vessel under radiographic control with gel sponge or beads. These are designed to block the bleeding vessel but due to the relatively high risk involved this procedure has not been fully accepted.

ACUTE RHINOSINUSITIS

THE COMMON COLD AND INFLUENZA

The symptoms of the common cold are well-known. Sneezing, nasal blockage and copious rhinorrhoea are usual, with mild pyrexia and headache. These symptoms are common in children, presumably because they have not fully matured their defence mechanisms and also because they cough into each other's faces. Incidences rise transiently when they change schools, e.g. from nursery to primary, presumably as they are exposed to a host of new viruses. Aetiology is related to poor resistance, e.g. extreme fatigue, exposure to cold, poor nutrition, chronic nasal sepsis and obstruction. Five different groups of viruses have been implicated, the influenzae viruses, picorna viruses (Coxsackie, Reo, Echo and rhinovirus), respiratory syncytial virus, parainfluenza virus and adenovirus. Spread is by droplets and dust and incubation time varies from 1 to 3 days. Although clinically there is a wide range of severity of a cold, most are associated with transient mucosal ischaemia followed by swelling, hyperaemia and profuse rhinorrhoea which changes from clear to mucopurulent. At this stage secondary bacterial infection ensues with beta-haemolytic streptococci, pneumococcus and *Haemophilus influenzae*.

If uncomplicated the disease is self-limiting in about 14 days and only supportive measures, e.g. salicylates, etc. are required to control pyrexia and muscular pains, etc. The difference between the common cold and influenza in lay-terms depends on the severity of the illness, although real influenza is caused by the influenza virus. Normally the goblet-cell population, particularly of the inferior turbinate, dramatically increases during this infective process and eventually returns to normal afterwards. This return is often incomplete and with repeated infections the goblet cell population remains high, thereby clinically producing postnasal catarrh or postinfective rhinitis.

Extranasal complications include nasopharyngitis and pharyngitis, sinusitis, pharyngotympanic salpingitis, otitis media, mastoiditis, lymphadenitis, tonsillitis and chest infections.

ACUTE SINUSITIS

This commonly follows a cold but may also follow dental infection, dental extraction, swimming and diving, trauma, or after a nose operation. Predisposing factors include any anatomical abnormalities, e.g. septal deviation, polyps, enlarged adenoids, allergic rhinitis or foreign bodies. Bacterial infection quickly follows any viral insult and the bacteria responsible for acute sinusitis include pneumococci, streptococci, staphylococci, *H. influenzae* and *E. coli*.

The symptoms are acute severe pain across the infected sinuses associated with pyrexia and a general feeling of malaise. The pain may increase in bending forwards. Often the pain is non-specific and the whole face aches. Localized tenderness may indicate the group of sinuses involved, although in the acute situation following a cold a pansinusitis is common.

The pain of sphenoiditis, which is relatively uncommon, is localized to the top of the head and is less specific than the other sinuses. It may produce pain over the trigeminal distribution because of the close proximity of these nerves.

Although the sinus ostium blocks in this condition, it is likely that this is secondary to the acute insult which produces oedema of the sinus mucosa and is not causative. The ostium of the maxillary antrum is high and not gravity-dependent, hence more commonly affected than the other groups of sinuses. Copious nasal catarrh is produced, the sense of smell goes and a general feeling of fullness in the face results.

TREATMENT. Radiology is rarely indicated for diagnosis of the acute phase, as clinically it is so obvious. A raised white-cell count, ESR and positive blood cultures confirm the diagnosis but a small amount of pus identifies the causative organism. The appropriate antibiotic is given over 7 days, either orally or systemically, and decongestants (xylometazoline or pseudoephidrine) used also, either locally or systemically, to open the natural ostia of the sinuses to allow free drainage. If the condition does not resolve with these simple measures, a surgical drainage procedure is necessary. It is essential that adequate antibiotic therapy is given prior to surgery. The most important sinus to drain is the maxillary antrum as this is the 'conductor of the orchestra'. If the sinus settles, oedema in the middle meatus will disappear and permits adequate drainage of the frontal and anterior ethmoidal sinuses. The procedure of puncturing the medial wall of the antrum (*see Fig.* 1.2.4) occasionally transgresses diploic bone which can produce a retrograde septic venous thrombosis with consequent corticothrombophlebitis and cavernous sinus thrombosis, hence the necessity for adequate antibiotic cover.

The actual procedure performed is subject to debate. The author prefers to perform an intranasal antrostomy as, although it represents bigger surgery, it fulfils the surgical aphorism that pus must be adequately drained. The antral wash-out or simple suction of the antral contents only works transiently and requires antibiotics to sterilize the antral contents.

Drainage of the frontal sinus is by trephine, i.e. external drainage through a roof or orbit incision. Cannulation of the nasofrontal duct is not advised as it commonly leads to further problems, e.g. stenosis of the duct.

The ethmoid sinuses usually drain spontaneously and do not require surgery but uncapping of the cells may encourage free drainage. An anterior sphenoidotomy may be necessary to drain sphenoiditis adequately.

Obviously correction of any precipitating factor, e.g. dental infection, etc. should also be instituted. Correction of a septal deviation should probably be deferred until the acute phase is over because of the risk of septal abscess and complications resulting from this.

RECURRENT ACUTE SINUSITIS

This is quite common. Each attack clears up totally before the next commences. The mucosa of the sinus returns to normal between attacks. The aetiological factors include poor resistance, anatomical abnormalities and recurrent viral upper respiratory tract infections. Adequate drainage of this condition which is commonest in the antrum is obtained by an intranasal antrostomy. Although this does not in effect prevent the infection, the severity of symptoms is much lessened. Correction of the underlying aetiological factor should also be undertaken.

COMPLICATIONS. Orbital complications are the commonest. The ethmoid sinuses are separated from the orbit by only a very thin plate of bone, the lamina papyracea. Orbital complications are, thus, commoner in children because of the relatively high number of upper respiratory tract infections associated with large ethmoids in this age-group.

Orbital cellulitis results from thrombophlebitis of the vessels of the mucosa and bone of the inflamed ethmoids and rapidly spreads through the orbit. An abscess results from direct spread from the ethmoids and collects between the lamina papyracea and the orbital periosteum. Clinically the eye is painful and there is considerable swelling of the eyelid. The differentiation of cellulitis or abscess is necessary to make the decision whether to drain the infection surgically or not. A collection of pus in reasonable quantity displaces the globe, producing proptosis and diplopia. Eye movements may be restricted. In this case early drainage is necessary to prevent pressure and septic necrosis of the orbital nerve and blindness. Thrombophlebitis of the vessels may also produce ischaemic necrosis. Infection of the posterior ethmoidal cells is more likely to damage the optic nerve, and visual fields, acuity and the state of the optic disc should be monitored. There are often associated intranasal signs of an ethmoiditis, e.g. pus, and radiographs will confirm ethmoiditis, although the soft-tissue swelling overlying the ethmoids may produce a generally hazy picture.

TREATMENT. A broad-spectrum systemic antibiotic is necessary with intranasal decongestants to allow easy drainage of the pus. If necessary, surgical drainage of the abscess is achieved via an incision in the superomedial aspect of the orbit. The pus often points in this area and a tube should be inserted to allow free drainage for several days.

OSTEOMYELITIS

This only occurs in diploic bone and thus only in the maxilla of children and the frontal sinus in adults. Untreated sinusitis may produce a thrombophlebitis and consequent osteomyelitis. This is less common now in the 'antibiotic age' with adequate treatment of common organisms such as streptococci and staphylococci. Surgical drainage should be through non-diploic bone, e.g. the medial wall of the antrum and the floor of the frontal sinus. Abscesses may form subperiostially and intracranially and require drainage. Clinically there is a build up of dull local pain and oedema of the forehead. This latter sign is situated slightly above the upper limit of the frontal sinus and is called **Pott's puffy tumour.**

INTRACRANIAL COMPLICATIONS

These result from either direct spread or are blood-borne. Direct spread is via the olfactory nerve through the cribriform plate, fracture sites and congenital dehiscences of bone.

Meningitis is the commonest complication. A lumbar puncture is performed to identify the causative organism and high doses of an appropriate systemic antibiotic administered. Before the lumbar puncture it is essential to exclude increased intracranial pressure by looking for papilloedema. A CT scan is necessary to demonstrate hydrocephalus.

A more severe complication is **cortical venous thrombosis**, which is characterized by severe headaches, neck stiffness, altered conscious levels and epileptic fits. **Cavernous sinus thrombosis** results from thrombophlebitis of the frontal, ethmoidal and sphenoid sinuses and ascending infection from the nose and face. Venous stasis causes swelling of the orbital vessels. Clinically there is a high fever, rigors, headaches, a reduced conscious level and cerebral irritation. An ophthalmoplegia results from paralysis of the cranial nerves which travel within the cavernous sinuses, viz. III, IV and VI, and ophthalmic and maxillary nerves. The eyes are proptosed and there is considerable swelling of the area. This condition, although much less common, has a high mortality rate. High levels of broad-spectrum antibiotics are given systemically.

A **brain abscess** may occur in the frontal lobes secondary to frontal sinusitis. Clinically a high index of suspicion is necessary to make the diagnosis as localizing signs are few. A CT scan with enhancement if necessary helps to make the diagnosis. Extradural abscesses may also occur secondary to a frontal sinusitis. Antibiotics are required and a surgical drainage procedure through the frontal sinus is necessary. A subdural abscess is extremely difficult to diagnose. The symptoms are very general until a sudden increase in size may produce a life-threatening situation. A CT scan with contrast enhancement makes the diagnosis, and treatment is a neurosurgical procedure with drainage through multiple burr holes.

Chapter 1.6

CHRONIC RHINITIS

The term chronic rhinitis embraces several different conditions and implies a long-standing inflammation of the nasal mucosa, often producing excessive mucous secretions. Simple chronic infective rhinitis may develop from recurrent acute infective rhinitis. In this situation the goblet-cell population of the nasal mucosa does not revert to normal between attacks (*see* Chapter 1.5) and there is a general increase in mucous secretion. Chronic vascular engorgement of the inferior turbinates also causes nasal blockage. If the cause of these symptoms cannot be identified, the condition is often termed vasomotor rhinitis. This diagnosis is not a specific entity and results from changes in the submucosal vasculature to cause swelling of the inferior turbinates with nasal blockage and rhinorrhoea production. This is a diagnosis of exclusion but should not be used for the postinfective chronic rhinitis state described above.

The predisposing factors for chronic infective rhinitis include a concomitant sinusitis, a depressed immunity and recurrent exposure to viruses, e.g. in association with small children and dry central heating which diminishes the effectiveness of the mucosal defences. Other causes include any local nasal abnormality (e.g. a deviated nasal septum, nasal polyps, etc) and atmospheric pollution (e.g. car exhaust gases, chemical vapours and irritation from chronic local trauma such as nose picking). Clinically the inferior turbinates are large and may obstruct the nostril. The posterior ends are often mulberry like in appearance (purple and engorged). The diagnosis is obvious from the history. A course of antibiotics and decongestants may be curative in the early cases but, for the long-standing case, surgery is usually necessary. Correction of any local nasal abnormality, e.g. a deviated nasal septum, is necessary. When the turbinates have lost their ability to shrink in appropriate circumstances, i.e. when it is hot and humid, a degree of fibrosis and scarring is present in the submucosal areas. Verification of this is obtained by placing a pledget of cotton wool soaked in cocaine and adrenaline in the nostril for 5 minutes. Failure of the turbinate to shrink indicates an irreversible hypertrophy of the turbinate requiring surgery.

TREATMENT. The least invasive treatment is **cautery.** A red hot wire is drawn along the surface of the inferior turbinate from posterior to anterior. Three such parallel lines are drawn. The principle is that the consequent scarring and fibrosis interferes with the vascular bed of the inferior turbinate to decrease its size. In practice considerable surface scarring occurs with crusting. This eventually settles but the submucosal area does not scar. Therefore, the effects of this operation are not long-lasting.

Submucosal diathermy of the inferior turbinates is designed to fibrose the vascular spaces of the inferior turbinates. A needle or Simpson's gun (an insulated nasal needle bare at its end for 1 cm) is pushed through the anterior end of the inferior turbinate to the posterior end. The end of the needle may be palpated by finger in the postnasal space. The patient is earthed and unipolar diathermy is applied to this needle which is slowly withdrawn over 30 seconds and the entry hole diathermized to prevent undue bleeding. This procedure is repeated in a parallel fashion at two levels in the inferior turbinate. This procedure, although superior to cautery of the turbinates, does not have a permanent shrinkage effect and thus does not represent a 'cure'.

Many similar methods of treatment have been described, including cryotherapy and sclerosant injections.

Mechanical reduction in the size of the inferior turbinate is required to remove enormous turbinates. Many different types of **turbinoplasty** have been described. Most involve removal of part or all of the turbinate bone or the overlying vascular area. Attempts are made to maintain the integrity of the nasal mucosa to avoid undue crusting. Although theoretically some of these operations are attractive, in practice they have not achieved widespread acceptance.

Increasingly, the total or near **total inferior turbinectomy** is used. This simple operation removes the offending blockage. The inferior turbinates are fractured medially and the turbinate is removed with scissors. The degree of resection varies from surgeon to surgeon. Some remove only part of the mucosa whereas others remove mucosa and turbinate bone. The main complication of this operation is bleeding. Adequate nasal packing after removal prevents most bleeding but occasionally blood replacement is necessary. The main criticism of this operation is the possibility of postoperative atrophic rhinitis (*see below*). This condition was common 50 years ago but is extremely uncommon in Western society today due to improvements in nutrition, general health and housing. The results of inferior turbinectomy are more long-lasting than the other forms of turbinate surgery, assuming the stimulating factors producing turbinate hypertrophy are dealt with at the same time.

RHINITIS MEDICAMENTOSA

This condition is the result of over-medication with local nasal decongestants. The liberal use of sprays initially brings relief to the patient with enlarged inferior turbinates. Unfortunately, when the effects wear off a rebound phenomenon occurs. Not only is there a reflex vasodilatation from ischaemia, but a build up of metabolites in the turbinate greatly increases the blood supply to this area causing turbinate hypertrophy. If the decongestant treatment is repeated the condition becomes rapidly self-perpetuating and a chronic nasal obstruction unresponsive to decongestant results. The treatment is immediate cessation of the decongestant with replacement by nasal or systemic steroids. If this is not successful then inferior turbinectomy may be required.

VASOMOTOR RHINITIS

This term is used to describe episodic nasal obstruction and watery rhinorrhoea for which no specific cause is identified. Swelling of the inferior turbinate is frequently seen and may appear as the most obvious cause of the obstruction.

Vasomotor rhinitis is an extremely common condition in the Western world and in many instances represents a variation of normal physiology. Autonomic stimulation from a full stomach or bladder, and sexual activity may cause inferior turbinate hypertrophy, as do local pollutants such as tobacco smoke.

Psychological stress, a change in the climate, pregnancy or the contraceptive pill and some of the beta-blocker drugs may cause nasal obstruction by inferior turbinate hypertrophy. Nasal blockage and clear rhinorrhoea are the main symptoms but very often facial aches result from a high-pressure sinus headache due to sinus ostia blockage.

Vasomotor rhinitis is rarely a clear-cut diagnosis as there are many other influencing factors which cause inferior turbinate hypertrophy. Individual toleration of these symptoms varies widely and an accurate assessement of the degree of morbidity is necessary before instituting treatment.

TREATMENT. Medical treatment is by either local or systemic decongestants. Local sprays or drops include xylometazoline, oxymetazoline and ephedrine, but each may lead to rhinitis medicamentosa (*see above*). Systemic decongestants, e.g. pseudoephedrine, may produce systemic side-effects such as dry mouth, constipation and excitability but are useful in some patients with vasomotor rhinitis. They are contraindicated in patients with glaucoma, hypertension, cardiovascular disease and those taking monoamine oxidase inhibitors. Amitryptiline has a side-effect of anticholinergic reaction and dries up the mouth and nose.

Turbinate surgery may be necessary at some stage (*see above*). For the few people with no nasal blockage but profuse rhinorrhoea, section of the autonomic nerve supply to the nose may be useful. This operation divides the parasympathetic and sympathetic supply to the nose as the nerve of the pterygoid canal (Vidian nerve) enters the pterygopalatine fossa. The effect of this operation, however, is not often long-lasting.

VESTIBULITIS

This infection of the anterior nares commonly results from nose picking. In its most severe form, reddening on the outside of the nose tip is accompanied by exquisite tenderness and occasionally boil formation. The treatment is to stop touching the area particularly with dirty fingernails, and use topical antibiotics. These need to be continued for a protracted length of time even after the symptoms have subsided, otherwise the condition recurs. *Staphylococcus aureus* is the most commonly implicated organism and is often present in the anterior nares causing no symptoms. Spread of infection to patients from this source is well-recognized in hospital personnel.

ATROPHIC RHINITIS

In this condition there is excessive crusting in the nose and an associated abnormal patency of the nostril. The idiopathic form usually begins at puberty and is common in females. It may be associated with poor hygiene or living conditions and there appears to be an increased incidence in some races. Many organisms have been implicated in the past but none has been identified as the causal organism.

In the Western world the more common cause is extensive nasal surgery—e.g. when enormous polyps are removed the resultant enormous nostrils may crust unduly causing atrophic rhinitis. Immunosuppression from disease or drugs also causes this condition.

The submucosal vessels undergo an endarteritis and periarteritis, decreasing the blood supply to the mucous membrane. The ciliated columnar epithelium either metaplases to a cuboidal or stratified squamous epithelium or atrophies.

The underlying turbinate bone may also atrophy. The resultant thick viscid secretions rapidly dry to form crusts and produce the characteristic fetor. The condition is then termed ozaena. This fetor is not appreciated by the patient who is anosmic. Crusting in the nose and pharynx causes blockage, pain and bleeding. Crusting in the larynx may cause hoarseness.

Treatment of the underlying condition is necessary. This may take the form of an airway-narrowing operation, e.g. Teflon injection into the inferior turbinate or medializing the lateral wall of the nostril. These types of operations have mixed results and have not gained widespread acceptance. Medical management of the crusts include recurrent steam inhalations, petroleum jelly instilled into the nose and 25 per cent glucose in glycerol drops.

The complete closure of the nostrils, either by an obturator or oversewing them, does relieve the crusting and eventually the epithelium reverts to normal, but patient compliance with either procedure is not high. These operations are most uncomfortable but may well represent the last option in an otherwise intractable condition.

RHINITIS SICCA

This condition is characterized by a dry nose. It may be caused by environmental factors such as exposure to hot, dry desert-like conditions (e.g. men working in furnaces) or exposure to irritant gases (e.g. dry cleaning fluids or other chemical gases). It may also represent part of the sicca syndrome which includes dry eyes and a dry mouth. The excessive crusting which is usually present can be very painful and epistaxis ensues when the crusts come off. The treatment is aimed at softening these crusts with petroleum jelly, repeated steam inhalations or 25 per cent glucose in glycerol nasal drops. Removal from environmental irritant causes will obviously be beneficial.

RHINITIS CASEOSA

This uncommon condition results from a change of the pseudostratified columnar epithelium of the nasal mucosa to a squamous type. This forms a cholesteatomatous mass in the sinuses which erodes through the bony wall. It may be the result of chronic infection or foreign body retention and rhinolith formation. Unilateral nasal obstruction with purulent secretions and epistaxis may be the result. There is an unpleasant smell.

Chapter 1.7

CHRONIC SINUSITIS

Chronic sinusitis implies a long-standing infection of the sinus. The changes in the mucosa over this time may be irreversible and when the original cause of infection is removed the lining will not revert to normal.

Its onset may apparently be insidious but usually there is some acute episode which initiates the infection. Continuation of the infection is enhanced if there is obstruction to the normal sinus ostia. Adequate aeration of the sinus may be all that is required to restore normal ciliary motility and decrease the goblet-cell hyperplasia present in these sinuses. This simple measure may promote restitution of the mucosa to normal. Early cases of chronic sinusitis may be cured in this manner but if the mucosa has become irreversibly changed, removal of it may be necessary before a cure is possible.

MAXILLARY SINUSITIS

PREDISPOSING FACTORS. The commonest causes of chronic maxillary sinusitis are nasal. Long-standing blockage with, for example, adenoidal hypertrophy, deviated nasal septum, nasal polyposis and enlarged inferior turbinates predisposes to sinusitis. Recurrent acute infections leading to blockage of the drainage ostia and chronic irritation from environmental gases may also produce chronic sinusitis.

Teeth may also be the focus of maxillary sinus infection. The 5th, 6th and 7th upper teeth impinge closely on the floor of the maxillary antrum and may indeed penetrate it. Root infections or dental abscesses are commonly the cause of unresolved maxillary sinus infections.

PATHOLOGY. The most common pathological changes are the result of increased vascular permeability causing hypertrophy of the mucosa which may eventually become polypoidal. There is a chronic inflammatory cellular infiltration, particularly around the vessels, and the number of seromucinous glands and goblet cells is increased. Fibrosis of the lamina propria will result and often small multiple abscesses occur in the thickened mucosa.

The other main type is considerably less common. Endarteritis obliterans of the arterioles occurs with loss of the typical respiratory epithelium and general flattening of the epithelium. There is also a dense chronic inflammatory cell infiltrate in the deeper layers.

42

SYMPTOMS. There is usually a copious postnasal discharge which may be greenish-yellow when acutely infected but is often clear. Clinical examination may not demonstrate this but the history will be quite emphatic. Nasal obstruction is usually the result of swelling of the inferior turbinate mucosa consequent on the presence of sepsis.

The severe pain of acute sinusitis is absent, but a deep chronic headache over the forehead, the bridge of the nose and the face is common. This is due to increased pressure in the sinuses (not, as previously reported, a vacuum headache) from a build up of secretions or more commonly, if the maxillary sinuses are the only ones affected, by blockage of the drainage ostia. The timing of the headaches is said to be diagnostic but this is so variable as not to be useful.

The presence of chronic sepsis in the upper respiratory tract may lead to anosmia or cacosmia. There are several causes of total or partial loss of smell but sinusitis, albeit otherwise asymptomatic, should be excluded. Anosmia results from the prevention of inspired and expired air reaching the olfactory groove. Cacosmia (unpleasant smell) is the result of chronic odiferous sepsis.

Chronic irritation inside the nose may produce a vestibulitis or excoriation due to excessive use of the handkerchief. Nosebleeds are also a common accompanying factor. The purulent secretions may also produce oedema of the Eustachian tube orifice with consequent otitis media, granular pharyngitis and chronic laryngitis.

EXAMINATION. Clinical examination is often unhelpful other than indicating a general inflammation of the nasal mucosa but may show purulent secretions or crusts. If the nasal mucosa is shrunk with a lignocaine or cocaine and adrenaline mixture, pus may be seen emanating from the middle meatus. Circumstantial evidence indicating chronic sinusitis includes otitis media and granular pharyngitis in the absence of any specific nasal symptoms.

The diagnosis is usually confirmed on radiography. Several views of the sinuses are recommended (see above). If the radiograph is clear it effectively excludes chronic hypertrophic sinusitis but not the atrophic variety. Thickening of the mucosa is shown on the radiograph; this may be uniform or polypoidal and in extreme circumstances a frank polyp or polyps may be seen. Gross polypoidal formation may produce a totally opacified sinus. Any of the causes of nasal mucosal swelling may produce swelling of the sinus mucosa and other causes of this must be excluded. A fluid level obviously signifies infection. Occasionally rhinitis caseosa may produce erosion of the sinus wall. In this condition a cholesteatoma-like mass forms in the maxillary sinus and behaves like cholesteatoma in the middle ear.

Antroscopy (see above) allows direct vision of the maxillary sinus mucosa and, if necessary, biopsy of it to confirm the diagnosis. This may require a general anaesthetic which in turn allows adequate operative treatment to be carried out at the same time.

Previously the direct proof puncture (see above) was widely used for diagnostic purposes. This procedure used to be performed under local anaesthetic but consumer resistance due to discomfort has led this author to abandon it. It was said that the patency of the ostia and the presence of chronic sinusitis could be demonstrated by this. The former conclusion depends on the force used to wash out the sinus and the latter on the presence of pus in the sinus, which is not a constant finding.

TREATMENT. The principle of treatment is to restore normal mucosa to the sinus lining. This allows the cilia to waft out through the ostium any residual infection. If this is not possible, i.e. when the mucosa has become irreversibly changed, then the mucosa may need to be removed.

The importance of aeration of the sinuses to promote restoration of ciliary motility cannot be over-emphasized. This is achieved with decongestants which decrease swelling around the ostia to allow air exchange. At the stage of chronic changes medical treatment has usually been tried and is of limited value.

Antibiotic treatment should be tried as the condition may not be chronic and irreversible, but if it is then antibiotics will have little value. Correction of predisposing factors to chronic sinusitis is necessary. A deviated septum, nasal polyps and large adenoids, carious teeth and enlarged turbinates require to be treated.

The maxillary sinus is the most commonly affected. If all the sinuses are infected, treatment of the maxillary sinus may often allow spontaneous resolution of the other sinuses.

SURGICAL TREATMENT OF THE MAXILLARY SINUS

Antral lavage. This has been described above. It may open the sinus ostium at least temporarily and clears away mucopurulent material. Concomitant antibiotic treatment is necessary or otherwise the saline left in the sinus will merely reinfect and the condition will not be relieved. An indwelling polythene tube fed through the cannula into the sinus allows repeated 'washouts' of three or more times per day.

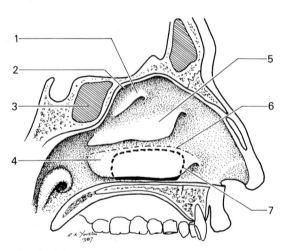

Fig. 1.7.1. The lateral wall of the nose.
1, Superior turbinate.
2, Sphenoethmoid recess.
3, Sphenoid sinus.
4, Inferior turbinate.
5, Middle turbinate.
6, Line of bony attachment of inferior turbinate.
7, Heavy outline marks antrostomy which is made in the inferior meatus lateral to the inferior turbinate.

Intranasal antrostomy. This procedure allows good aeration of the maxillary sinus. It allows ciliary motion to be restored but adequate removal of all irreversibly changed antral lining is not possible through the opening. A large dependent opening in the medial wall of the antrum is made in the inferior meatus. There is a tendency for this to close spontaneously but creation of a large stoma may avoid this (*Fig.* 1.7.1).

Caldwell–Luc or radical antrostomy operation. This procedure is designed to remove the lining of the maxillary sinus which has become irreversibly damaged. An incision is made above the appropriate canine tooth in the buccogingival sulcus (*Fig.* 1.7.2). This should be 3–5 cm long and placed high enough to avoid damaging the dental roots. A hammer and chisel is used to remove part of the anterior wall of the antrum to allow access. All the diseased mucosa is then removed and a large intranasal antrostomy is fashioned. The wound is sutured with absorbable cat-gut sutures. The infraorbital nerve may be damaged if retraction of the cheek is too vigorous. Occasionally a fistula is left after this operation or after dental extraction. Formal repair of this may subsequently be necessary.

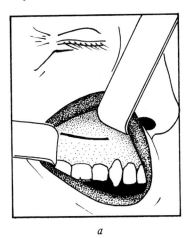 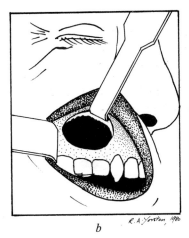

a   b

Fig. 1.7.2.   Caldwell–Luc operation.
a, Incision in canine fossa.
b, Opening through anterior bony wall of antrum.

THE FRONTAL SINUS

The frontal sinus is considerably less often affected and operative treatment should be kept to a minimum. If exploration is necessary the osteoplastic frontal flap operation is used. The frontoethmoidectomy operation is also described.

Mucocoeles

A mucocoele arises in order of frequency in the frontal, ethmoidal, maxillary and sphenoidal sinuses. It can be either a retention cyst of a mucous gland when it is surrounded by thin but normal sinus mucosa, or it can be due to blockage of the sinus ostium and is, therefore, due to retained secretions.

In the early stages the patient is asymptomatic but, particularly in the frontal type, a dull ache develops and a swelling appears at the supramedial aspect of the orbit. The swelling is tender and feels rubbery, not as firm a consistency as bone. Increase in size thins the bone more and pressure may damage the optic nerve or vasculature causing blindness. If infection supervenes it is called a pyocoele and has more sinister consequences. With increasing enlargement the eye may proptose. Radiographs of the sinus will show thinning of the bone and in the case of a frontomucocoele there is displacement of the medial frontal sinus floor downwards. There is also loss of scalloping of the superior border of the sinus and the intersinus septum may be displaced or eroded.

The treatment is evacuation of the contents of the sinus by one of the operations described. Intranasal approaches to the frontal sinus are to be deprecated as they lead to fibrosis and scarring of the frontonasal duct. The subsequent stenosis leads to irreversible frontal sinus changes requiring further surgery. The operation of trephine is to relieve acute infections and is described above.

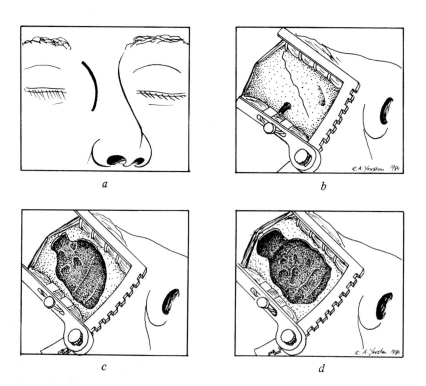

a

b

c

d

Fig. 1.7.3.   Radical frontal sinus operation.
a, Incision.
b, Exposure of ethmoidal vessels.
c, Exenteration of ethmoidal cells.
d, Opening into frontal sinus.

The frontal sinus may be approached from the floor or from above. The frontal ethmoidectomy operation uses a curvilinear incision beginning at the medial end of the eyebrows onto the nasal bone almost to the dorsum and curves back to the maxilla (*Fig.* 1.7.3). The periosteum is incised and elevated. The lacrimal sac is elevated laterally and the orbital periosteum kept intact. Elevation continues posteriorly until the anterior ethmoidal artery is seen and clipped. This represents the level of the cribriform plate and fovea. Dissection must not take place cephalically to this in case the fovea is damaged. An anterior ethmoidectomy is performed. The frontal sinus is entered and a small amount of mucosa may be removed. A large-bore polythene tube is inserted from the frontal sinus into the nose and sutured to the columella. This remains in place for 6 weeks to allow epithelialization of the duct, and it prevents stenosis. The operation is designed to allow adequate drainage of the frontal sinus contents.

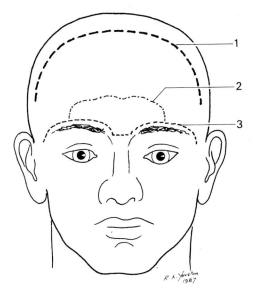

Fig. 1.7.4.   Osteoplastic flap operation.
1, Coronal incision.
2, Periosteal incision, which corresponds to the outline of the frontal sinuses.
3, Eyebrow incision.

To permit an adequate examination or removal of the mucosa of the frontal sinus an osteoplastic flap operation is necessary. The scalp is either lifted superiorly from an eyebrow incision or inferiorly from a behind-the-hairline coronal incision to expose the frontal sinus (*Fig.* 1.7.4). The periosteum is incised around the outline of the sinus except where it attaches at the supraorbital margin. This ensures an adequate blood supply to the flap. The bone is drilled in the same place and the flap elevated down to show the frontal sinus. All diseased mucosa is removed, including any supraorbital extensions. Occasionally fat is used to obliterate the sinus. In this case every shred of mucosa needs to be removed to prevent an infective necrosis of the fat. The frontonasal duct is also obliterated from above to avoid ingrowth of diseased mucosa from here. The bony flap is replaced and the cosmetic result after suturing is good.

If the frontal bone is chronically infected it may very occasionally need to be sacrificed. This ablative procedure is cosmetically very disfiguring but may be corrected with an acrylic plate when the active disease has settled.

ETHMOIDAL SINUS SURGERY

This is usually necessitated by recurrent growth of nasal polyps. There are basically three approaches, the external approach, the intranasal approach and the transantral approach.

The external approach involves an incision longitudinally down the bridge of the nose medial to the eye. The entry to the ethmoids is as described in the previous section. Complete exenteration of all ethmoidal cells may be difficult. It is essential to note the position of the posterior ethmoidal artery. This is usually 4 mm anterior to the optic nerve but is separated by a thick bar of bone. Dissection posterior or superior to the posterior ethmoidal artery must not be done.

The intranasal approach involves dissection lateral to the middle turbinate. This ensures that the cribriform plate is not transgressed. Good vision with minimal bleeding is essential in this procedure to avoid intracranial or optic nerve trauma. Some authorities do this operation using a cocaine paste to shrink the mucosa and avoid excessive bleeding. Endoscopic surgery of the ethmoids is increasingly used.

The transantral approach via the Caldwell–Luc incision approaches the ethmoids from below. This approach is less commonly used now as the other two give adequate control of ethmoid disease.

SPHENOID SINUS SURGERY

The sphenoid sinus is rarely affected on its own. Chronic infection may produce any of the complications of the acute variety. A mucocoele of the sinus may also have a pressure effect on surrounding structures. There are essentially three approaches.

The **external ethmoidectomy** approach is described in relation to hypophysectomy.

In the **intranasal approach** the sphenoid is identified as a midline structure in the posterosuperior wall of the nose and the anterior wall is removed and the lining removed.

A **submucous resection** to the posterior aspect of the nose ensures the dissection remains in the midline. The septal approach is also used via a sublabial incision.

CYSTS OF THE MAXILLARY SINUS

These may masquerade as maxillary sinusitis.

Embryological Cysts

These are a group of less common cysts which arise due to faulty fusion of embryological elements forming the maxilla. They arise in the hard palate and conveniently may be divided into the medial and lateral group.

The medial group:

1. Alveolar cysts separate the upper central incisors.

2. Median palatal cysts lie between the palatine process of the developing maxilla posteriorly.

3. Nasopalatine cysts arise from tissue in the incisive canal or rest in the papilla palatina and present either on the palate or on the nasal floor.

The lateral group:

1. Lateral alveolar cysts—these separate the canine and lateral incisor teeth and represent the line of fusion of the maxillary and premaxillary elements of the palate.

2. Nasoalveolar cysts lie in the lateral half of the nasal floor.

Dental Cysts

These are derived from the epithelium that has been connected with the development of the teeth concerned.

1. Follicular

These result from cystic degeneration within the epithelial layers of the tooth-forming tissues. This prevents further development of the tooth. If it occurs at an early stage it is termed primordial and is commonest in the third molar region of the mandible. The commonest type is the dentigerous cyst which is always anatomically related to the crown of an unerupted tooth, most frequently a maxillary premolar or mandibular third molar.

2. Radicular

These arise from the epithelial remains in the periodontal membrane and are the most common cysts of the jaw. Clinically infected dead tooth roots produce a granulomatous reaction which contains epithelium which produces the cyst. They are thin-walled and tend to recur. Clinically the cyst may produce pain, inflammation, swelling or remain asymptomatic. Enlargement of the cyst produces pressure symptoms and thinning of the bony walls giving a characteristic 'egg shell crackling'. A radiograph of the maxillary sinus may show opacification but an orthopantomogram may be necessary to show a small localized dental cyst.

TREATMENT. If these cysts are symptomatic they should be exenterated. The defect may require to be packed with bone chips.

OROANTRAL FISTULA

An oroantral fistula occurs most frequently through the alveolar border following dental extraction, particularly of the first upper molar teeth, the roots of which may penetrate the bony floor of the antrum. It can also follow attempted removal of a broken tooth root which may have been forced into the maxillary sinus. An oroantral fistula may also result from a radical antrostomy operation when the incision line breaks down. It is also found in association with lower lateral malignant tumours of the antrum.

The most satisfactory treatment is immediate suture at the time of dental treatment, in the absence of a retained root, which will first have to be removed. If this is not carried out, or should it be unsuccessful, food particles will enter the sinus and infection soon becomes established. Pus should be bacteriologically cultured and a radical antrostomy carried out under antibiotic cover. Any foreign bodies must be removed and the bony edges of the fistula trimmed. The fistula itself is best repaired using a mucoperiosteal flap. A palatal flap based on the greater palatine artery is the most satisfactory, unless the fistula is closely surrounded by standing teeth when some difficulty can be experienced in turning and placing this flap in the desired position. In this situation a thinner buccal flap is easier to use. In persistent fistulae of dental origin there is usually a retained root which prevents adequate healing.

Chapter 1.8

ALLERGIC RHINITIS AND NASAL POLYPS

PATHOGENESIS. Allergic rhinitis is very common. Ten per cent of the Western population have hay fever and about 20 per cent a positive skin test. Allergic rhinitis is usually mediated by immunoglobulin E and is classified as a type I pathological reaction. It is an identical pathological process to allergic asthma but the size of the offending allergens is different because the larger particles filter off in the nose while the smaller ones reach the bronchiolar epithelium. Immunoglobulin E is produced from plasma cells which may be regulated by T suppressor lymphocytes or T helper cells. Immunoglobulin E is different from the other immunoglobulins in that its Fc portion has affinity for mast cells and basophils. Thus the Fab portion of the molecule is free and two such molecules combine with the allergen to activate the mast cells. Immunoglobulins G and A have a blocking antibody effect. The disruption of the mast cell leads to the release of many substances including histamine, SRS, leukotrienes and prostaglandin. This is an area of active research in which the full picture is not yet understood. Some of these substances are mediators but histamine and leukotrienes have been shown to cause erythema and bronchoconstriction.

The typical allergens are pollens, moulds, house dust mite and house dust and animal epithelia. Of the pollens, the grasses cause trouble between early June to September, cereals from June to September, weeds throughout the summer, trees from February to early June and flowers from June to October. These timings refer to the UK. Moulds and fungi which have been implicated in allergic rhinitis include aspergillus, candida, cladosporium, *Carvulorium fusarium*, mucor, penicillium, *Alternia alternata* and *Merulia lacrimans* (dry rot). The house dust mite feeds off dead human skin and is, therefore, present in mattresses, soft furnishings and bedroom carpets. The optimum breeding conditions are 25°C and 80 per cent humidity. They reach their peak population in mid to late summer. Many animals produce an allergic reaction in their owner. They include budgerigars, cats, cows, dogs, hamsters, guinea-pigs, horses, rabbits and sheep. Feathers are also implicated, particularly duck, goose and chicken. Salicylic acid has also been implicated as a cause of allergic rhinitis. This substance is contained in most foodstuffs and is extremely difficult to avoid.

Histamine released stimulates the H_1 receptors in the nasal mucosa, thereby producing oedema and rhinorrhoea.

51

ASSESSMENT. Clinically the patient sneezes in response to exposure to the allergen. The associated symptoms include nasal blockage and profuse watery rhinorrhoea and increased lacrimation. The nose may also be itchy. A well-taken history may pinpoint the allergen. The turbinates are classically very pale and swollen but not necessarily. The diagnosis is confirmed by skin tests. The prick test is commonly used whereby the skin is partially broken by a needle and the allergen introduced interdermally. Within 20–30 minutes the classic wheal and flare are seen if the allergen is positive. The reactions are commonly graded from 0 to 4 depending on the size of the wheal. Histamine should also be used to ensure the test has been properly performed. Similarly, the carrier substance is tested to exclude hypersensitivity to this.

Nasal smears may show an increased eosinophil level but the significance of this is poorly understood. There is usually no systemic eosinophilia. The plasma levels of the total immunoglobulin E may be measured. This is the plasma-reactive immunosorbent test (PRIST) and for specific immunoglobulin E the radioallergosorbent test (RAST) is done. Neither of these has any advantage over skin tests in the diagnosis but are more expensive and are only useful if the skin tests are negative as the allergen may not have been tested for.

In **nasal provocation tests** the potential allergen is sprayed into the nose and the number of sneezes counted or any change in rhinomanometry noted. Unfortunately this is extremely time-consuming as each allergen takes 20 minutes to test in order to allow the nose to return to normal after the challenge. It is not, therefore, a standard diagnostic test.

Patch tests are used to determine delayed-type hypersensitivity and the allergen is placed in the skin for 48 hours. The area of the reaction is noted and any allergens identified. This is used more in skin problems and food allergy, the latter being a difficult concept to pinpoint. There is no doubt that some patients are allergic to specific foodstuffs (classically, gluten enteropathy, cows milk and some additives), but the effect on the nose may be minimal compared with the situation discussed above. Similarly, identification of the allergen is tricky and a rotational diet with the exclusion of the suspected foodstuffs on a variable basis is undertaken. The food allergy may also be cyclical—the response is variable and the allergy may not manifest itself on each challenge.

TREATMENT. Avoidance of the allergen is the optimum treatment. Unfortunately, this is rarely possible totally, and in particular with some animals and foodstuffs. Gentle reassuring advice may allow the patient to change his lifestyle minimally with great benefit.

Decongestants. There is a very limited place for local decongestant sprays and drops because of the well-described rebound phenomenon. For a short exposure time requiring a short course of treatment, xylometazoline may be used. This is extremely effective in this situation. Systemic decongestants are more suitable for long-term use but occasionally make the patient feel unwell. This may particularly be so if the decongestant is mixed with an antihistamine which often causes drowsiness.

Oral antihistamines. These have been the mainstay of treatment for many years. Unfortunately their main side-effect is drowsiness. More recent products have claimed not to cross the blood–brain barrier and are not soporific. They are very effective at blocking the H_1 receptors in the nasal mucosa and if tolerated are an excellent way of treating a short-time recurrent allergic rhinitis.

Hyposensitization. This treatment involves the injection of small amounts of antigen to 'mop up' the allergen-specific immunoglobulins in the patient. Theoretically this form of treatment should convey immunity for life but unfortunately in practice this is not always the case. There are many different courses of desensitization. The normal course consists of 18 weekly injections of aqueous extract of the allergen or allergens. Standard alum-precipitated extracts and tyrosine-absorbed glycerinated extracts are available in the shorter courses, e.g. 3 weeks for the common allergens. In principle it is preferable to desensitize only one or two allergens at a time rather than many. The results of pollen and dander desensitization are encouraging but that to the house dust mite and house dust disappointing. If an initial desensitization course is unsuccessful it is doubtful if subsequent courses will be. A further booster course of desensitization from time to time (biannually) may be helpful if the initial course was successful. The main problem with this treatment is the possibility of anaphylaxis, and because of this its use in the UK has been discouraged. Several deaths have been reported and for this reason it is suggested that skin tests are conducted on the volar part of the forearm to allow application of a tourniquet if there is a systemic reaction. Also adrenaline, aminophylline and injectable steroids and antihistamines must be available for such a situation.

Sodium chromoglycate. This substance is said to stabilize the mast cell to prevent the release of granules and their contents. It is a successful means of controlling asthma and in a number of patients is very useful for allergic rhinitis. It has extremely few side-effects and can be used as one of the safest forms of therapy. The patient requires this treatment on a long-term basis.

Steroids. One of the cornerstones in the treatment of allergic rhinitis is the use of steroids as nasal sprays. These are easily used, do not cause atrophy of the nasal mucosa and are not systemically absorbed to any significant amount. The disadvantage is the unlikely possibility of encouraging candidal infections in the nose. For the short-lasting allergy which always comes at a critical time, e.g. examinations, a depot solution of slow-release intermuscular steroid is useful. This may be repeated annually and, provided it is not used more often than this, is now a reasonable alternative. Long-term systemic steroids are to be avoided. This may be necessary in some extremely severe cases of nasal polyps but the side-effects are well documented. The clinician must balance the inconvenience of the polyps against the potential fatal complications of steroid therapy.

SURGICAL TREATMENT. Occasionally turbinate surgery (*see above*) is required to mechanically unblock the nasal airways which have become chronically affected by the allergy. Very occasionally a Vidian neurectomy (*see above*) may be performed to unblock the nose, but only if all other forms of treatment have failed.

NASAL POLYPS

Nasal polyps are round, smooth, soft, translucent, yellow or pale glistening structures attached to the nasal or sinus mucosa by a relatively narrow stalk or pedicle. They are non-tender and move backwards when probed. These features clinically separate them from turbinates. They commonly arise from the ethmoidal sinuses and project into the nasal cavity. They tend to be bilateral and multiple. Unilateral polyps may often not be allergic and other conditions, e.g. antro-choanal polyps, neoplasia and meningocoeles, should be excluded. Clinically polyps cause nasal blockage and a copious postnasal drip. Other symptoms include headaches and anosmia.

Light microscopy shows no remarkable features in polyps but electromicro-scopic studies show many degranulated mast cells. The local IgE is low, however, and so the mechanism of mast-cell rupture is different from a type I allergy.

The aetiology of nasal polyps is poorly understood. Classically they are caused by a combination of allergy and infection. Other known causes include cystic fibrosis and salicylic acid hypersensitivity. It is thought that repeated insults to the mucous lining of the ethmoidal sinuses cause increased blood vessel permeability which in turn causes oedema of the mucosa. Eventually this mucosa, which in effect is the lining of the ethmoids, prolapses out of the sinus. Repeated blowing of the nose encourages growth of the polyp. The increased speed of the air flowing through the nose decreases the pressure in the nasal cavity (Bernoulli's theorem) which pulls down the polyp. The increasing size of the polyp predisposes to infection and the vicious cycle encourages more growth. When extremely large the polyp may actually be seen outside the nostril. The usual investigations are radiography of the sinuses and allergy skin tests.

TREATMENT. Medical treatment is usually incomplete and aimed at relieving symptoms until surgery can be arranged. The medical treatment of polyps is the same as that for allergic rhinitis. Even if the polyps are discovered routinely on anterior rhinoscopy and are asymptomatic, they should be removed and sent for histology. Occasionally what clinically appears to be a polyp turns out to be something quite different.

Surgical treatment is performed under either local or general anaesthesia. If the operation is performed under local anaesthesia the polyps themselves often shrink, which makes removal difficult. However, recurrence is common as there are large parts of the polyps which shrink into the ethmoidal cells. The advantages are that bleeding is less and hospitalization shorter. General anaesthesia on the other hand allows the surgeon excellent access to the ethmoidal polyps.

Recurrence of polyps is common. The patient should use a steroid spray indefinitely to discourage recurrences. Also any obvious aetiological factors should be treated. Despite these measures a number of patients have multiple nasal polyp recurrences which necessitate further surgery. Repeat nasal polypecto-mies are the accepted method of treatment until this necessitates an unreasonable amount of hospitalization and morbidity. At this stage some form of ethmoidec-tomy is indicated. These operations are fully described in the section on ethmoidal surgery.

Polyps which onset in childhood may be very aggressive and lead to misshapen nasal bones. They can splay the bones producing a widened nasal bridge. These, however, are nearly always due to cystic fibrosis, aspirin hypersensitivity or coeliac disease.

CHOANAL POLYP

This uncommon polyp (1 per cent of polyps) arises from the lining of the maxillary sinus. The lining becomes oedematous, exists from the ostium and a polyp forms which enlarges and lies posteriorly in the nose and nasopharynx. The classical presentation is a good inspiratory airway with blockage on expiration. This is the result of the ball-valve effect of the polyp blocking the posterior choana. It is common in adolescence and as the polyp grows produces bilateral symptoms. Anterior rhinoscopy may look normal as only the thin stalk may be present in the nose. The enlarged posterior end may only be seen on posterior rhinoscopy. Radiography of the maxillary sinus will show complete opacification of the affected antrum.

The treatment of this condition is complete removal. Removal of the lining of the sinus is necessary to avoid a recurrence. It is possible to grasp the stalk and move it gently around to tease out the antral lining. More commonly this is not possible and an intranasal antrostomy may be necessary to remove the antral lining. With recurrence a formal Caldwell–Luc procedure should be performed to clear the sinus.

Chapter 1.9

BENIGN TUMOURS AND GRANULOMAS

PAPILLOMA

Papillomas of the nose can arise in two quite unrelated forms—the squamous papilloma of the skin of the nasal vestibule and the inverted papilloma of the respiratory mucosa.

Squamous Papilloma

This appears as a wart-like growth arising from the skin of the nasal vestibule where it causes irritation. It can enlarge to become unsightly or may cause mild epistaxis when traumatized. It is removed by an elliptical incision around its base under local anaesthetic. The incision is closed by sutures.

Inverted Papilloma

This tumour has many names, the most popular is the Schneiderian papilloma. This is the most common benign neoplasm of the nose and sinuses. The aetiology is unknown. It arises almost exclusively from the lateral wall of the nose and only occasionally from the septum. Extension into the ethmoid and maxillary sinuses is very common. It causes symptoms by obstruction to nasal airflow and drainage, thereby precipitating sinus infection. Coincident sinusitis of all groups may produce more symptoms than the papilloma itself. The tumour is soft and friable and may become detached or bleed with hard nose blowing. The surface of the neoplasm is covered with alternating layers of squamous and columnar epithelium, i.e. transitional type of epithelium. Radiography of the sinuses may show thinning of the bony walls as a pressure effect but no frank erosion.

The treatment of inverted papilloma is adequate local excision. If it arises in the maxillary sinus, a radical antrostomy is carried out. If it arises in the ethmoidal sinuses, an external ethmoidectomy is done. For tumours arising from the nasal lining, adequate exposure is obtained through a lateral rhinotomy. Following surgery, adequate follow-up is essential to ensure that any recurrence is dealt with swiftly and it is imperative that any recurrent tumour is examined histologically for evidence of malignant change.

There is coincidental malignancy elsewhere in the upper respiratory tract in about 4 per cent of cases and malignant transformation of the tumour itself occurs in about 8 per cent. Through an intranasal approach and limited excision, almost 60 per cent recur, but using the lateral rhinotomy approach and wide excision, the recurrence rate is 17 per cent.

ANGIOMA

This can arise in two forms: a localized angiomatous mass on the nasal septum, often called a bleeding polypus of the septum, which arises in adults; or an angiomatous malformation of the ethmoidal and maxillary sinuses which presents with very profuse epistaxis in early childhood.

Fibroangioma of the Septum

This presents with epistaxis in adults, and examination of Little's area shows a pedunculated friable red lesion which bleeds easily to the touch. It is completely benign and is removed by a circular incision with an adequate margin of normal mucosa. It is dissected free from the cartilage so that the perichondrium forms the deep layer of the specimen. The bare cartilage soon re-epithelializes.

Angiomas of the Sinuses

These tumours arise from the maxillary and ethmoidal sinuses, manifest themselves in early childhood and present with frightening epistaxis. Cavernous haemangiomas may also arise from the lateral wall of the nose overlying the turbinate. Some idea of their extent is gauged from plain radiography but it is essential to carry out common carotid angiography to obtain an adequate picture of the blood supply. An angioma of the maxillary sinus has a supply from the external carotid system only, but ethmoidal angiomas may well have some supply from the internal carotid as well. Treatment is surgical. The blood supply can be greatly reduced prior to surgery by carrying out embolization through the major feeding artery, but this procedure is most effective when arterial flow is unimpeded. Therefore tying major feeding arteries such as the maxillary or external carotid is to be avoided if embolization is contemplated. Adequate surgical excision is thereafter carried out.

FIBROMAS AND OSTEOMAS

There is a series of tumours of the sinuses which varies from a fibroma, through an intermediate ossifying fibroma to a mature ivory osteoma.

One school of thought believes that these are encompassed along with fibro-osseous dysplasia; the fibromas and osteomas represent one end of the spectrum whereas the fibrous dysplasias represent the other.

Fibromas

These are rare and appear as soft pedunculated lesions. They are treated by adequate local excision.

Ossifying Fibromas

These can occur at any age but are more frequent in the seond and third decades. They arise in the maxillary and ethmoidal sinuses and cause local discomfort and expansion. The normal bony wall of the maxilla may be resorbed and the tumour can manifest itself as a firm swelling of the cheek or as unilateral nasal obstruction due to medial displacement of the antronasal wall. Radiography shows complete opacity of the affected sinus with a 'ground-glass' appearance due to ossification centres within the tumour. Treatment is surgical. Maxillary ossifying fibromas are removed by radical antrostomy and ethmoidal ones by external ethmoidectomy.

Osteomas

Osteomas are most common between the ages of 15 and 35 and are found incidentally on routine radiographs in 1 per cent of the population. Seventy per cent of them are in the frontal sinuses, 25 per cent in the ethmoidal sinuses and 5 per cent in the maxillary and sphenoid sinuses.

The growth is slow and usually eventually produces a secondary mucocoele. If they are asymptomatic then no treatment is required. The symptoms depend on the site and if they obstruct the frontonasal duct, a secondary infection may result. In such cases removal of the osteoma by an osteoplastic flap approach should be undertaken. A Howarth operation gives insufficient access for adequate removal. Occasionally an osteoma can arise in the ethmoidal sinus, giving rise to broadening of the nasal bridge due to its size, in which case it should be removed by an external ethmoidectomy.

FACIAL FIBROUS DYSPLASIA

This denotes a fibro-osseous thickening of the bones of the face. It is unilateral and can affect several facial bones but it must be differentiated from polyosteotic fibrous dysplasia which is a systemic disorder affecting many bones throughout the body. It represents an arrest of the maturation of bone formation at the stage of woven bone. There are varying degrees of fibrosis and in all cases the lesion is diffuse. Teeth are often present in the lesion.

Facial fibrous dysplasia can present as a swelling around the orbit, over the cheek or on the maxillary alveolus. It becomes apparent during childhood and increases in size with growth but it often ceases to expand after the age of 20.

Radiography of the sinuses may show that the extent of the disease can be much greater than is apparent on the surface and a series of sinuses may be obliterated by the abnormal vascular spongy bone.

The diagnosis is made on the history of a slowly developing painless swelling. Cosmetic trimming of the excess bone is necessary in some cases.

NASAL GRANULOMAS

A granuloma is a tumour-like mass of nodular granulation tissue with actively growing fibroblasts and capillary buds due to a chronic inflammatory process. It may occur locally as an isolated event and run a benign course, or it may be a local manifestation of a more generalized disease with a potentially fatal outcome.

Syphilis

Congenital

The inherited form may manifest itself in the first 3 months of life. Constant snuffles with an obstinate nasal discharge which dries to form crusts are often present. The chronic irritation produces fissures of the anterior nares. In a more advanced form, usually at puberty or later, gummatous ulceration may destroy the nasal tissues so that the bridge of the nose is depressed with fetid crusting within the nose. Other stigmata of congenital syphilis include corneal opacities and the pegshaped secondary dentition (Hutchison's teeth).

Acquired

Primary infections of the nose are uncommon. Secondary infections are less common and less troublesome in the nose than elsewhere but appear as mucous patches. The nose is often involved in the tertiary stage. The septum is most commonly involved, but the lateral wall of the nose may also be affected. The stage of gummatous infiltration is rarely seen because, as a rule, ulceration and destruction of tissue have taken place before the patient is examined. The gumma takes the form of an irregular mamillated infiltration, dark red in colour, involving one or both sides of the septum. Usually at this stage the only symptom is nasal obstruction, but there may be headache and severe pain in the nose, which may be swollen and tender. When ulceration occurs it is accompanied by a purulent discharge which tends to dry and form crusts which emit a horrible stench. After removal of the crusts by douching, the nose may be more fully inspected. If the septum is affected it will be found to be perforated, and the perforation usually involves the bony structures as well as the cartilaginous portion. If the process is still active the edges of the perforation will be covered with granulations. The loss of tissue may be so extensive that there may be sinking of the bridge of the nose and even ulceration and destruction of the external nose. The structures of the lateral wall of the nasal cavity may also be extensively ulcerated and in part destroyed.

DIAGNOSIS. When a granular lesion, especially one associated with fetid crusts, is found on the nasal septum syphilis should be suspected. The diagnosis is made on serological testing, the VDRL and TPHA tests being most suitable for acquired syphilis, and the FTA test for late congenital syphilis.

TREATMENT. Penicillin is the treatment of choice. The nose should be kept clean by frequent douching, and all loose sequestra should be removed.

Lupus Vulgaris and Tuberculosis

Lupus vulgaris is the name given to a slowly growing, indolent deep-skin ulcerative condition caused by *Mycobacterium tuberculosis* which affects the nasal vestibule, the septum and the ala. It is more common in females than males, and is more often encountered than frank tuberculosis of the nasal mucosa. If untreated it is slowly destructive and can lead to gross and embarrassing deformity. Tuberculosis of the respiratory part of the nose gives rise to granulation tissue and ulceration with sanguineous mucopurulent discharge.

DIAGNOSIS. All granulomatous lesions of the nose, whether of the skin or the mucosa, must be submitted for pathological examination. Sometimes the histological picture is so characteristic that a firm diagnosis can be made, but in cases of doubt material should be submitted for bacteriological culture for *M. tuberculosis*. A Ziehl–Neelsen stain may show the tubercle bacillus. A Heaf test or Tine test should be diagnostic if performed in increasing concentrations. There is frequently evidence of tuberculosis elsewhere in the body.

TREATMENT. Treatment depends on the sensitivities of the organism, and usually takes the form of a combination of two or more of the following drugs—streptomycin, PAS, isoniazid, rifampicin and ethambutol.

Sarcoidosis

This is a systemic disease. The nasal lesions are distributed on the septum and lateral nasal walls and frequently become secondarily infected, so that the patients complain of general ill-health associated with purulent serosanguineous discharge. There may be associated disfigurement of the skin of the face due to lupus pernio, or there may be erythema nodosum elsewhere on the body. There can be enlargement of the lymph glands in the neck and also increases in size of the major salivary glands which can be associated with a lower motor neurone facial palsy. Cranial nerve palsies are common in this condition. Eye changes due to kerato-conjunctivitis sicca or uveitis may be present.

Radiography of the chest will show enlargement of the hilar glands and, less commonly, infiltration of the lung fields. A presumptive diagnosis can often be made from pathological examination of a biopsy from the nose, but as the histological features are sometimes not truly specific, further confirmation may be required and this is obtained by carrying out a Kveim test. A small piece of active sarcoid tissue is implanted subcutaneously, usually in the leg, and biopsied 6 weeks later. Increased activity on the biopsy is diagnostic. A depressed tuberculin test is also common.

Treatment is either conservative or with systemic corticosteroids. The decision as to whether or not treatment should be started is probably best left to a physician with a special interest in this disease. Acute sarcoidosis often clears spontaneously or it can be treated by anti-inflammatory drugs such as aspirin or phenylbutazone. It has a good prognosis. Chronic sarcoidosis has a less favourable long-term outlook, and steroids should be used to suppress specific symptoms, as there is little evidence that they alter the ultimate outcome in the long term.

Wegener's Granuloma

This is a systemic condition almost always affecting the lungs but also, in the majority, the upper respiratory tract, and the kidneys. It is a necrotizing giant-cell granuloma characterized by the pathological changes of vasculitis from multinucleated giant cells. Any unusual appearance in the nose, particularly an unexplained septal perforation, should stimulate further investigation. The sex incidence is equal and the peak age of onset is the fourth and fifth decades. The ESR is usually raised, there may be microscopic haematuria or chest changes on radiography. These latter may be multinodular or cavitating lesions. If untreated, renal failure will ensue within a few months and death occurs within 1 year of diagnosis. The mainstay of treatment lies with corticosteroids in high doses initially, thereafter tailing the dose to maintenance levels. The immunosuppressive agents cyclophosphamide and azathioprine have been extremely useful in addition to steroids in the treatment of Wegener's granuloma, but the side-effects of these drugs may be serious and thus the dosage must be well-controlled. The prognosis has improved considerably in recent years. The condition must obviously be differentiated from the other granulomas.

Stewart's Granuloma

This extremely uncommon condition consists of an indurated swelling of the nose, nasal vestibule and septum leading to a progressive ulceration of cartilage and bone. Microscopy shows a dense accumulation of cells that are mainly lymphocytes, and some authorities believe this is a variant of a lymphoma. It is initially localized to the nose but later spreads to local lymph nodes and becomes systemic. Local radiotherapy improves the prognosis.

FUNGI

Fungal infections of the nose are usually the result of upset of the body's host defence mechanism or prolonged antibiotic therapy.

Aspergillosis

The acute form, particularly in debilitated patients, may be very aggressive and potentially fatal owing to extension from the nose and sinuses posteriorly into the cranial cavity. There are new antifungal agents (ketoconazole) now available to replace the standard treatment of amphotericin B, but they still have potentially serious side-effects and should be used with extreme care. Chronic aspergillosis of the sinus is not life-threatening and may be asymptomatic, although it is also an important cause of chronic sinusitis.

Mucormycosis

This is a fulminant opportunistic infection which may be rapidly fatal. Rapidly increasing symptoms of nasal blockage and discharge and the presence of a black turbinate are typical of the condition. Systemic antifungal agents are used to treat this infection.

Monilia

The presence of *Candida albicans* in the nose is characterized by white mucosal patches. The whole area is inflamed. Although common in the mouth and larynx, it is less common in the nose. Local nystatin treatment should clear up this non-fatal condition.

Rhinosporidiosis

This usually occurs in young males from India and presents as bleeding polypus of the septum. Other symptoms are obstruction, epistaxis, discharge. Wide excision of the area is necessary. It is transmitted from cow-pats.

SCLEROMA

This condition found mainly in Eastern Europe, the Middle East, Africa, Central and Southern America and Indonesia is due to *Klebsiella rhinoscleromatis*. It is probably linked with poor nutrition and hygiene. Initially the lesion is atrophic and the differential diagnosis is from atrophic rhinitis. The second stage is proliferative with submucous nodule formation and the third stage is fibrotic and cicatricial. Systemic treatment with ampicillin combined with sulphadiazine and trimethoprin in high doses for a prolonged time is suggested. Surgical treatment of the fibrosed area may be necessary when the condition has become quiescent.

LEISHMANIASIS

This condition is rare in the UK, but is met with in Eastern Mediterranean countries and South America. It begins with an induration of the skin of the upper lip, spreading to the cheek and the nasal vestibule. Later there is an ulcerated bleeding granulating area in the anterior part of the lateral wall and floor of the nasal cavity, giving rise to considerable narrowing of the nose.

Similar granulations may appear on the gums. Histological examination of a piece of excised tissue will show the Leishman–Donovan bodies. Treatment is by injections, either intramuscular or intravenous, or organic pentavalent antimony compounds, or, in resistant cases, pentamidine.

LEPROSY

There are two types of leprosy. The tuberculoid type is localized and is well contained. A marked reaction to an intradermal injection of killed *Mycobacterium leprae* is diagnostic compared with the absent reaction of the systemic lepromatous leprosy. This latter type, which more commonly affects the nose, involves initially the subcutaneous nerves and secondarily infects the skin and nasal mucosa. Clinically there are multiple smooth-surfaced macules or papules which coalesce to form nodules. Red granulations are common and enlarge to erode through the septum making a perforation. Eventually total destruction of the cartilaginous and bony framework of the nose results. The diagnosis depends on a biopsy and identification from a Ziehl–Neelsen stain. Long term treatment with dapsone is indicated.

FOREIGN BODIES

Children, especially young children aged 2 or 3 years, frequently push foreign bodies into the nose. Such objects may be classified as organic and inorganic. Inorganic foreign bodies include metal objects, buttons, beads, plastic objects, etc. These may lie undetected for many weeks, giving rise to no symptoms, and occasionally are found accidentally during routine examination. Organic foreign bodies, such as wood, paper, cotton wool or foam rubber, produce a local inflammatory reaction which may proceed to the formation of granulation tissue. There is a nasal discharge from the affected side, and this quickly becomes purulent and foul-smelling and may be blood-stained. The object may swell with the absorption of moisture from the mucus but there is seldom pain. A unilateral nasal discharge is nearly always due to a foreign body and if the discharge has an unpleasant smell this is pathognomonic.

In the early stage the object is situated just within the nostril and is easily seen. In time it moves further into the nasal cavity—possibly due to the child's habit of sniffing or possibly because it is pushed further in—and if the object is organic in origin it becomes encased with mucus, or mucopus. In this event it may not be seen because of the mucopus or the inflammatory swelling of the mucous membrane.

Removal of the foreign body may be easy if it lies in the nostril. It may be flicked out with a probe, or by getting the child to smell pepper and on closing the opposite nostril it may be sneezed out. When the object reaches the nasal cavity and becomes covered with secretions it becomes slippery and not easy to grasp. A child may sit through one attempt at removal but if this fails, and especially if the attempt produces bleeding, he is not likely to endure a second. Accordingly, it is wiser to give the child an anaesthetic for the removal if one attempt has been made or if the object is situated far back at the initial inspection. Removal is accomplished either with cupped forceps or with a metal probe, the distal 5 mm of which have been bent to a right angle. The probe is passed, point downwards, above the object which is pressed to the floor of the nose and then raked out. The probe may fail with such a narrow object as a shirt button because it slips, or with foam rubber which has become adherent to the mucosa. In these cases the use of cup-shaped forceps is preferable. Very occasionally the foreign body may be of such an irregular shape that it cannot be brought out through the anterior naris, and it may have to be pushed gently into the nasopharynx and recovered from there. The surgeon must be aware of the possibility that there may be a second foreign body present, either in the same side or in the opposite one, and after removal of the first object the nose must be examined for this.

RHINOLITHS

Rhinoliths are calcareous masses which are occasionally found in the nose. They may be unilateral or bilateral. The deposit of salts, chiefly calcium and magnesium carbonates and phosphates, takes place around a nucleus which may be organic or inorganic; the nucleus may be a foreign body or merely dried secretions of blood and mucus. Their presence must be considered in any long-standing cases of nasal discharge.

The patient complains of nasal obstruction and discharge. If the rhinoliths have been present for some time they may give rise to considerable destruction of the nasal mucosa with the formation of sequestra of cartilage or bone and the development of an extremely unpleasant odour. Rhinoliths may attain a considerable size and are often irregular in shape. The diagnosis is made by inspection, but if there is any doubt palpation with a probe will disclose the rough hard object.

Treatment is removal under general anaesthesia. The rhinolith may be too large to remove in a single piece and it may need to be broken with a strong pair of forceps before removal in fragments. A brisk haemorrhage during the removal may require packing with ribbon gauze for 2–4 hours.

Chapter 1.10

FACIAL PAIN

Facial pain is not only uncomfortable but has specific emotive connotations. The face is the most easily visible expressive feature and the head has proportionately an extremely large representation on the sensory homunculus of the posterior central gyrus. Most fibres are distributed from the thalamic nuclei to the sensory cortex, emotional centres, visceral reflex areas in the hypothalamus and the temporal lobes where memory of pain is stored. A large variety of extraneous factors—i.e. mood, concentration and drugs—play on the appreciation of pain. Classification of facial pain is helpful to the clinician.

NEURAL PAIN

Primary Neuralgias
Trigeminal neuralgia is the commonest of these. This is a specific clinical syndrome in which there is a chronic recurring paroxysmal pain of brief duration. It is probably caused by an aberrant blood vessel lying on the trigeminal ganglion. The lower divisions of the nerve are most commonly affected. Each attack is a severe jabbing- or stabbing-like sensation beginning near the nostrils and spreading to a wider area. Undoubtedly the pain is triggered by stimulating certain areas. The following actions may begin an attack: chewing, talking, waking, shaving or cold wind exposure. Ipsilateral lacrimation, rhinorrhoea and facial redness are common during the attack. The pain is always unilateral.

Treatment has traditionally been avoidance of the triggering factors and carbamazepine. Many other treatments have been suggested, but the most recent convincing work suggests that separation of the aberrant blood vessel from the trigeminal ganglion is curative. Whether this treatment stands the test of time remains to be seen.

The pain of **glossopharyngeal neuralgia** has similar qualities to trigeminal neuralgia but occurs around the tonsillar area and ear. It is provoked by swallowing, talking or eating and may continue intermittently for hours or days. The only effective long-term treatment is section of the nerve. The site of section of the nerve depends on the site of pain. Identification and sectioning of the nerve through the tonsillar fossa is the most straightforward operation. Intratympanic resection of the nerve is considerably more difficult and although section of the nerve through a posterior fossa craniotomy ensures permanent relief, this latter procedure obviously carries more risk. This uncommon condition may be associated with an elongated styloid process.

Secondary Neuralgias

These are the result of pathology elsewhere in the head and neck which result in facial pain.

Postherpetic Neuralgia

This condition normally occurs after a severe attack of shingles (herpes zoster). It represents a second infection after childhood chicken pox and most commonly in the head and neck affects the first division of the trigeminal nerve. Zoster virus affects the peripheral nerve, the posterior root ganglion and central sensory pathways up to and including the thalamus. The diagnosis is usually obvious from the vesicular rash over the typical distribution of the trigeminal nerve. The pain may alleviate as the rash goes but may remain for 3 months or more after disappearance of the rash. The best treatment is adequate analgesia at the time of the rash as this prevents the neuralgia being prolonged, although once established analgesia may be difficult to obtain.

Central Lesions

Any lesion of the brainstem, e.g. tumours, demyelination, thrombosis or syringomyelia, may all cause ill-defined facial pain. In most of these there is diminished facial sensation or other nervous system involvement. Base-of-skull tumours, including deep lobe tumours of parotid, nasopharyngeal carcinomas or thalamic lesions, may also cause facial pain, although the facial sensation is also affected.

OTHER CAUSES

Pressure on the trigeminal or glossopharyngeal nerves may produce pain. Very rarely an acoustic neuroma involving the trigeminal ganglion or a glomus tumour involving the glossopharyngeal nerve may cause pain. Antral neoplasms invading the pterygopalatine fossae may involve the trigeminal nerve. An intracranial aneurysm of the carotid artery in the cavernous sinus may press on the trigeminal ganglion to produce pain. An elongated styloid process, which is demonstrable on radiographs, occasionally reproduces glossopharyngeal pain.

The teeth most commonly cause facial pain. The pain usually arises from the pulp space or periodontal membrane. Chewing or thermal irritation may be the only apparent stimulants but percussion of the tooth and, if necessary, radiography should confirm the diagnosis. The third molars are commonly found to be incompletely erupted and cause recurrent gingival infection (pericoronitis). Post-dental extraction neuralgia is the result of damage to the dental nerves but usually settles.

Acute infection of the sinuses commonly produces headaches. The frontal sinuses refer pain to the forehead, the ethmoids and maxillary sinuses to the overlying areas, and the sphenoid to the top of the head. Sinus headache may occur at any time of the day. The so-called vacuum sinus headaches due to blockage of the ostia have been shown to be high-pressure headaches resulting from generalized oedema of the ostial mucosa and blockage.

Sluder's neuralgia or the anterior ethmoidal syndrome is pain around the bridge of the nose radiating into the forehead. It is said to originate from the middle turbinate pressing on the septum. Anatomical correction relieves the pain.

Cervical neuralgia may result from neck injuries, specifically a whiplash injury. The intervertebral joints and ligaments when strained refer pain through the posterior primary divisions of the upper cervical nerve.

Vascular pain is a deep throbbing pain which is quite different in character to that of neuralgia.

Periodic migrainous neuralgia: The typical patient who suffers this is male, middle-aged and has an obsessional personality. The pain is intense, paroxysmal and often occurs at 2 a.m. The pain is unilateral and is associated with flushing of the face, lacrimation, nasal blockage and rhinorrhoea. It lasts 2 hours or so then passes off. The treatment for this condition is prophylactic ergotamine, clonidine or other antimigrainous therapy.

Temporal arteritis: This widespread disease may be only manifest locally, producing temporal pain. It usually occurs in the elderly and is a granulomatous arteritis. If untreated it often leads to blindness. The pain is constant and interferes with sleep. The superficial temporal arteries are swollen. The diagnosis depends on a high index of suspicion, a high ESR and a biopsy of the temporal artery. High doses of steroids should be instituted as early as possible until the condition is brought under control.

The **temporomandibular joint** is a potent cause of facial pain. This has been more recently termed the 'myofacial pain dysfunction syndrome'. The pain arises from the receptors within the temporomandibular joint which are stressed. The stress results from uneven strains on the joint from the mandible. The causes of this include dental malocclusion, emotional stress producing masseter spasm and overenthusiastic kissing. The diagnosis may not be obvious immediately and the help of an oral surgeon may be invaluable. Movement of the joint may produce clicking although this is by no means diagnostic. Radiography of the joint may be useful to demonstrate degeneration of the joint.

Correction of the bite, relaxation from stress, or instruction in the art of osculation are the treatments of choice. In the short term a very soft diet with simple analgesia cures a large number of patients who are not seriously afflicted.

Cervical myalgia is a non-specific condition which results from headaches and generalized stress. In turn, spasm of the cervical muscles occurs which produces occipital headaches and the cycle is repeated.

Atypical facial neuralgia: This condition represents those patients who elude a definitive diagnosis. It is possible that the wide variety of symptoms could be attributed to vascular causes. The typical patient is female, middle-aged and edentulous. The pain is aching, shooting or burning, outwith any specific nerve distribution, and is present for prolonged periods of time. Psychological support and reassurance other than analgesia are the only forms of treatment, but thankfully a number of these patients spontaneously improve.

Chapter 1.11

COSMETIC FACIAL SURGERY

Patients may wish to have cosmetic facial surgery, either because they feel they are ugly or deformed or to reverse the effects of ageing. Correction of an ugly face may require a rhinoplasty, otoplasty, mentoplasty or soft-tissue correction and treatment of an ageing face may include a face-lift, blepharoplasty, hair transplant or dermabrasion. Patient selection for these procedures must be undertaken with extreme care as a percentage will have unstable personalities or be frankly psychotic. The results of surgery should be explained frankly and truthfully to avoid disappointment and patient expectation must be realistic.

RHINOPLASTY

This operation may correct cosmetic deformities as well as improve the nasal airway. It is essential to glean from the patient which he wants to ensure he is satisfied. If he merely wishes a good nasal airway, consideration should be given to a purely septal operation. Cosmetic rhinoplasty should be avoided in ethnic or typically racial noses, the over forties and the nose with thick greasy skin. The results of rhinoplasty in these patients are often disappointing, and in those patients who have had previous rhinoplasty.

Nasal Deformity

This may be broken down into the following types:

Deviation—The commonest cause of externally deviated nasal bones or septum is trauma. If sustained at birth the deviation increases with growth and commonly hemiatrophy of the face may also be a cause.

Widening—This may result from juvenile nasal polyposis or congenital abnormality. The dorsum may be too high (a hump)—it projects above a line from the nasofrontal angle to the tip—or too low (a saddle).

Both of these conditions usually result from trauma. A large subperiosteal haematoma produces a hump. A fractured dislocated septum or deficient septum after absorption following a haematoma or abscess will produce a saddle. The dorsum may be too short (the 'Miss Piggy' look) or too long (the 'witch' look). Similarly, the tip may be too long, too short, too high, too low, too broad or too narrow.

The perfect nose is straight and is a uniform width from rhinion to tip. This is the intercanthal distance or the same distance as between the medial and lateral canthus. It occupies no more than the middle third of the face. From the lateral aspect, the nasofrontal angle is 135°. The combined bony cartilaginous dorsum in the male should be slightly humped and in the female slightly low. The nasolabial angle in a female should be 110° and in males 90°. If the external auditory meatus is the centre of a circle, the circumference should touch the tip of the forehead, tip of the nose and tip of the chin. The nose must be fashioned, however, to fit the face.

PREOPERATIVE ASSESSMENT. All deformities should be noted. At present there is no accepted standard grading of external nasal deformities, unlike the Cottle areas of the internal septum. Standardized photographs of the face are taken. They usually include a full frontal, both lateral views and frontal oblique views.

THE OPERATION. A rhinoplasty is made up of:

1. A septoplasty or a submucous resection operation which corrects the septal deformity either by repositioning or by excision.
2. Osteotomies of the nasal bones which completely mobilize them allowing them to be repositioned or narrowed.
3. A tip rhinoplasty by which tip deformities are corrected by remodelling the lower lateral cartilages and the caudal end of the septum.

Correction of the deviated nose. If the bony vault is deviated, medial and lateral osteotomies are done to mobilize the nasal bones so that they can be repositioned. This may be all that is required in a bony deviation, but if cartilage is also deviated this will have to be dealt with. External deviations of the nasal cartilaginous vault can only be dealt with by septoplasty. Internal deviations can be dealt with by either septoplasty or submucous resection. The latter operation gives better functional results but poorer cosmetic results. Which operation is done for an internal deviation depends on whether the patient is more interested in having a good-looking straight nose or a wide nasal airway to relieve obstruction.

Reduction rhinoplasty. This is performed for a nasal hump. If it is bony, cutting off the hump with an osteotome will broaden the nose and so it will have to be narrowed by osteotomies. Cartilaginous humps are removed by separating the upper lateral cartilages from the septum and trimming both of these structures to the required height. Details of operations to reduce the height, length or breadth of the nasal tip are outwith the scope of this book.

Augmentation rhinoplasty. A saddle nose is seldom bony. It is either cartilaginous only, in which case it can be corrected by a free cartilage graft inserted in the dorsum, or both bony and cartilaginous, in which case a bone graft from the iliac crest is required. Operations to heighten or lengthen the nasal tip are often required to correct the deformities left by a cleft lip and palate. It is seldom necessary, however, to broaden a nasal tip.

OTOPLASTY

Protruding or bat ears are always developmental and usually familial. The cause of the deformity is failure of development of the antihelical crease; this failure opens up the scaphoconchal angle and makes the helix very prominent. The deformity appears most marked around the age of 5, but thereafter it recedes a bit due to growth of the head which tends to make prominent ears less noticeable. The other common ear deformity is the cupped ear which is caused by the upper part of the helix being folded downwards over to the antihelix.

TREATMENT. This is best done around the age of 5, either just before or after the child's commencement at school. Numerous operations exist to create the missing antihelix but basically they are of two types. The Mustarde type consists of merely stitching the antihelix into a fold and holding it there with mattress sutures. The Becker, Rosen and Converse operations involve cutting the cartilage to form a better-defined antihelix.

Cupped ears are corrected by a V–Y-plasty on the helix to lengthen it, allowing the pinna to unfurl.

MENTOPLASTY

A chin may be too prominent (prognathic) or too small (micrognathic). Mentoplasty may be performed to correct either of these deformities. The operations may be minor or major. The minor mentoplasties involve adding prostheses or onlays of silastic to increase the projection of the chin or removing a wedge of bone to decrease the size. The major mentoplasties, which are usually performed by oral surgeons, involve moving the whole ramus of the mandible either backwards or forwards in order to correct dental malocclusion as well as cosmetic deformity.

BLEPHAROPLASTY

The earliest noticeable features of ageing appear in the periorbital region. There are two abnormalities:

1. *Blepharochalasis:* wrinkling and redundancy of periorbital skin on both the upper and lower lids.
2. *Periorbital fat pads:* due to a herniation of the periorbital fat through the orbital fascia. These present as puffy eyes affecting both the upper and lower lids.

The treatment of blepharochalasis involves excision of skin from the upper and lower lids and this operation is called blepharoplasty. In the upper lid the skin is excised in an ellipse about 7 mm above the lash margin, and after excision the edges are closed with a subcuticular suture. If fat pads are also present, these are found, excised with great care being taken to achieve haemostasis, and the skin excised and closed as above. Redundant skin from the lower lids is removed by incising just below the lash margin and undercutting the skin and orbicularis oculi muscle to the inferior bony rim of the orbit. The skin is then pulled up and the excess is removed in a strip. If fat pads exist, they are usually found in well-defined pockets. Removal is as described for the upper lids. Occasionally ectropion can result from a lower-lid blepharoplasty but it is usually self-correcting as the orbicularis oculi muscle recovers its tone.

FACE-LIFT

This operation is performed for the removal of facial wrinkles. Facial skin owes its tensile property to its dermal collagen fibres which lie at right angles to the direction of the underlying muscle fibres, and thus to the stretch force. As the skin gets older, the collagen fibres degenerate and their capacity to stretch decreases. The process is accelerated by frequent exposure to sunburn and also in fair-skinned blondes and red-haired people. After weight reduction in the older person the skin becomes loose and redundant.

The operation is done via a very long bilateral incision which stretches from the temporal region within the hair-line, down in front of the ear, behind the ear in the postaural crease and across the nuchal hair-bearing area. The skin is undercut above the parotid fascia and pulled backwards and upwards. The excess is trimmed off. Since nearly all the stitches are in the hair-bearing areas, no scars are usually visible.

DERMABRASION

A face-lift cannot remove wrinkles around the mouth and eyes. These are best dealt with by creating a chemical burn of the surface with a phenol and croton oil solution. Dermabrasion with a wire brush or diamond stone may also be used.

HAIR TRANSPLANTS

The reason for wanting this procedure is loss of the hormonally dependent hair-bearing areas of the male scalp. Hair loss is under genetic, endocrine and ageing control. The technique involves essentially two methods. Either large flaps of non-hormonally dependent hair (the temporal and occipital regions of the scalp) may be swung into the bald area or multiple punch grafts may be taken from a good hair-bearing source and transplanted into the deficient area. The actual technique is outside the scope of this book.

COMPLICATIONS. With any operation there are complications. Unfortunately with no standardization of assessment it is not possible to resort to an arbitrator and the patient's unrealistic expectations may not be fulfilled. Good preoperative counselling should exclude many of these patients from surgery. Many of these patients wish reassurance with the results of surgery, and support from the patient's family and friends, with a positive attitude from the surgeon, is invaluable.

Chapter 1.12

TRANS-SPHENOIDAL
HYPOPHYSECTOMY

Trans-sphenoidal hypophysectomy is carried out on a normal pituitary gland for the treatment of endocrine-dependent tumours (e.g. carcinoma of the breast), and for the alleviation of gross proliferative new vessel formation in diabetic retinopathy, which is too severe for treatment by laser therapy. It is also carried out for the removal of adenomas of the pituitary gland which present with endocrine disease—acromegaly and gigantism; pituitary Cushing's disease and Nelson's syndrome; and hyperprolactinaemic hypogonadism which gives rise to oligo-menorrhoea, infertility or galactorrhoea in women, and to panhypopituitarism in men.

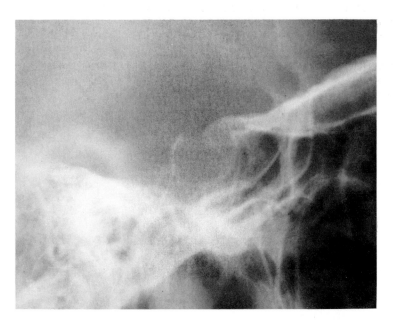

Fig. 1.12.1.   Enlarged lateral radiograph showing an expanded sella turcica with 'double floor'.

71

Requests for trans-sphenoidal hypophysectomy for alleviation of breast carcinoma are decreasing due to improvements in cytotoxic therapy, but it still has a valuable part to play in patients with disseminated disease, and in whom the tumour has been proved to be endocrine-dependent. The only contraindications are infection of the nose and sinuses, superior vena cava block and hepatic failure.

Requests for treatment of pituitary endocrine disease by the trans-sphenoidal route are increasing. The broad indications are the presence of a subdiaphragmatic tumour giving rise to endocrine symptoms. In acromegaly and gigantism, growth hormone levels are raised, and if there is no radiological evidence of enlargement of the sella turcica, treatment is medical with bromocriptine mesylate (Parlodel). When radiological enlargement (*Figs.* 1.12.1, 1.12.2) is evident, but suprasellar extension is not visible on a computerized axial tomography (CT) scan (*Fig.* 1.12.3), a complete trans-sphenoidal hypophysectomy is indicated. If, on the other hand, there is suprasellar extension on the scan, visual field defects are often also present, and removal by a transfrontal approach should be carried out.

In pituitary Cushing's disease and in Nelson's syndrome, ACTH levels are raised and the adenoma is usually small. In the former, removal of the anterior lobe of the pituitary gland by the trans-sphenoidal route is indicated. In Nelson's syndrome the tumour is frequently invasive in character, and a particular effort should be made to remove all hypophyseal tissue from the sella, but even with this meticulous surgery the endocrine results can be disappointing because adenomatous tissue may have invaded the cavernous sinuses.

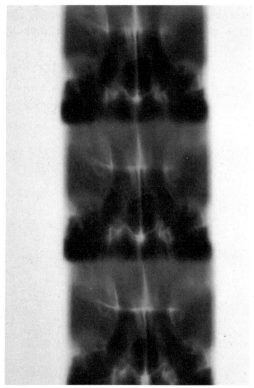

Fig. 1.12.2.   Anteroposterior tomogram showing a depression of the floor of the sella turcica.

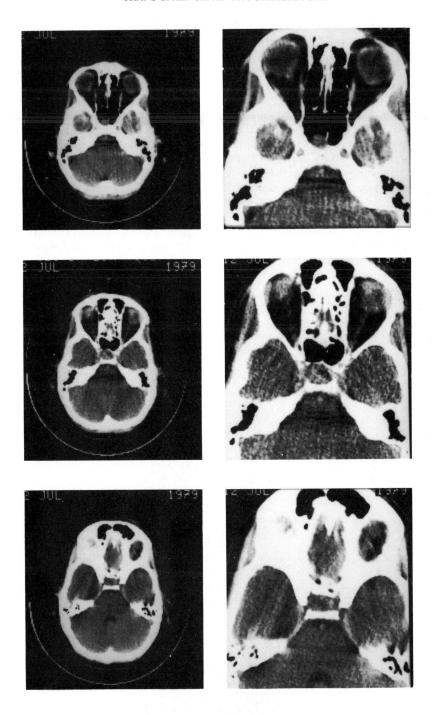

Fig. 1.12.3. CT scan showing enhancement of pituitary tumour with no suprasellar extension.

In hyperprolactinaemic hypogonadism the blood levels of prolactin are increased. This disease has only been recognized for a few years, and optimum treatment is, as yet, not clearly formulated. Women desiring pregnancy, and in whom there is little or no radiological evidence of pituitary enlargement, are probably best treated medically with bromocriptine. A small proportion of these women will not restart spontaneous ovulation because they cannot tolerate sufficient levels of bromocriptine. This group, plus those women complaining of infertility and with moderate sellar enlargement, should be offered trans-sphenoidal hypophysectomy. Prolactin-secreting tumours are usually situated laterally in the gland, and if up to 70 per cent of the anterior lobe, including the whole of the tumour, is removed, prolactin levels should return to normal and ovulation should restart without replacement therapy being required. As there is evidence that prolactin-secreting adenomas can stop growing, it is doubtful if women who have completed their family should be given any treatment at all, but they should be carefully followed up for evidence of continuing growth. Should this arise, and also in the case of those men and women with gross sellar enlargement but no visual defect, the treatment of choice is trans-sphenoidal hypophysectomy.

Section 2

THE HEAD AND NECK

(A. G. D. Maran)

Chapter 2.1

ANATOMY OF THE PHARYNX

The **pharynx** is a fibromuscular tube lined with epithelium. It extends from the base of the skull superiorly to the level of the sixth cervical vertebra where it becomes continuous with the oesophagus (*Fig.* 2.1.1). Anteriorly it communicates with the nasal cavities, the mouth and the larynx, and is thus divided anatomically into the nasopharynx, oropharynx and laryngopharynx (hypopharynx). The lining epithelium is of the stratified squamous type, except in the nasopharynx where columnar ciliated epithelium is found. There are numerous mucous glands. The middle fibrous tissue layer consists of the pharyngobasilar fascia. The outer muscular layer comprises chiefly the three constrictor muscles—superior, middle and inferior—which overlap from below upwards.

The Nasopharynx

This extends from the base of the skull to the level of the hard palate. At the junction of the roof and the posterior wall lies a small mass of lymphoid tissue called the pharyngeal tonsil or adenoids. There is a central mass of the tissue, and there are smaller accumulations of lymphoid tissue laterally around the pharyngeal openings of the auditory (Eustachian) tubes. These tubes connect the nasopharynx with the middle ear cavities, and are lined by columnar ciliated epithelium in continuity with that of the nasopharynx. Anteriorly the nasopharynx communicates with the nasal cavities through the posterior nares. The sensory nerve supply is from the trigeminal nerve.

The Oropharynx

This extends from the level of the hard palate to the level of the hyoid bone. The free edge of the soft palate forms the palatine arch which separates the oral cavity from the pharynx. From its centre the uvula hangs downwards, and from the arch, on either side, run two folds of mucous membrane, raised up by bands of muscle fibres of the palatoglossus and palatopharyngeus muscles, to form the palatoglossal and palatopharyngeal arches, or anterior and posterior pillars of the fauces. The palatine tonsil lies between these folds. The glossopharyngeal nerve, as well as the trigeminal, supplies sensation.

The Hypopharynx

The hypopharynx is that part of the pharynx which extends from the level of the hyoid to the upper end of the oesophagus. It is lined by mucosa, and is enclosed

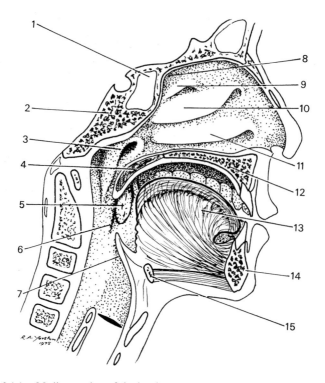

Fig. 2.1.1.   Median section of the head.

1, Sphenoid sinus.	6, Palatopharyngeal fold.	11, Inferior turbinate.
2, Basisphenoid.	7, Epiglottis.	12, Hard palate.
3, Orifice of Eustachian tube.	8, Sphenoethmoidal recess.	13, Tongue.
4, Soft palate.	9, Superior turbinate.	14, Mandible.
5, Palatine tonsil.	10, Middle turbinate.	15, Hyoid bone.

within the three constrictor muscles of the pharynx—superior, middle and inferior. The middle constrictor is attached to the hyoid bone which gives stability to the hypopharynx. Lymphoid tissue is present in the base of the tongue, and is called the lingual tonsil. The vallecula is a recess between the tongue and the anterior surface of the epiglottis. The aryepiglottic folds run from the epiglottis to the arytenoid cartilages and form the walls of the entrance to the larynx. On either lateral side of the aryepiglottic folds is a recess, the pyriform fossa, which forms a channel for food during deglutition. The two pyriform fossae lead to the opening of the upper end of the oesophagus which is situated behind the cricoid cartilage— the postcricoid region. The sensory supply is from the IXth and Xth cranial nerves and this is why pain from a tumour in the area is referred to the region of the ear.

The Palatine Tonsils

The palatine tonsils, more commonly called the tonsils, are masses of lymphoid tissue lying between the faucial pillars. At birth they are of insignificant size, but they enlarge during early childhood, especially between the third and sixth years of age, probably in response to upper respiratory tract infections. Thereafter some regression in size is to be expected, and in old age they atrophy. Each tonsil is described as having an upper pole, a body and a lower pole. About a dozen pitted depressions may be seen on the surface of the body of the tonsil. These are the openings of the tonsillar crypts which extend into the substance of the tonsillar lymphoid tissue. The lateral surface of the tonsil is covered by a fibrous capsule, separating it from the pharyngeal aponeurosis, and providing a convenient plane of separation during the removal of the tonsil. The lower pole of the tonsil is extended on to the dorsum of the tongue, where it is called the lingual tonsil.

The arterial supply to the tonsil derives mainly from the tonsillar branch of the facial artery and the descending palatine artery. The veins drain into the pharyngeal plexus. Lymphatic drainage from the tonsil is into the upper deep cervical nodes, which may enlarge during tonsillar infection. There is an intercommunicating ring of lymphoid tissue in the pharynx, including the pharyngeal tonsils, the palatine tonsils, and the cervical and retropharyngeal nodes; this is called Waldeyer's ring.

Chapter 2.2

INVESTIGATION
OF PHARYNGEAL DISEASE

HISTORY. The commonest complaint in a patient with a disease of the pharynx is probably pain. This can be due to the many lesions of the tonsil described in Chapter 2.3 on infection, but it is also seen in tumours. Tonsil pain is made worse by swallowing and it is typically referred to the ear since the Vth nerve supplies both sites. Pain that is present all the time and causes trismus suggests either a quinsy or a spread of an oropharyngeal tumour to the pterygoid muscles.

The second most common symptom is probably dysphagia. It is essential to get a correct description of this from the patient. Three types exist: (1) True dysphagia is a real difficulty in swallowing food, resulting in food coming back into the mouth, slow eating and loss of weight. It means the presence of a cancer of the hypopharynx or oesophagus until proved otherwise, and is usually progressive. (2) A feeling of a lump in the throat may be the early symptom of a cancer but is usually due to a spasm of the cricopharyngeus secondary to stress, reflux oesophagitis, pharyngeal pouch or pressure from a big thyroid or cervical osteophytes. (3) Difficulty in swallowing due to pain (odondophagia) is seen in pyriform sinus tumours but is most commonly a symptom of tonsillar infection. The patient may also complain of speech problems. Muffled speech can occur in hypopharyngeal and oropharyngeal tumours of some size, and hyponasality is heard if a big nasopharyngeal mass blocks the choanae and pushes the palate down.

Other symptoms include regurgitation of recently eaten food signifying a pharyngeal pouch, and nasal symptoms such as epistaxis and nasal obstruction from nasopharyngeal lesions. Nasopharyngeal tumours can involve the cranial nerves producing symptoms of diplopia, facial pain, incoordinate swallowing, hypernasality from a paralysed palate and dysphonia from a paralysed cord. It may also cause deafness.

Finally one must ask about the appearance of lumps in the neck. Enlarged neck nodes are common in both infections and tumours. The whole larynx may enlarge in pyriform sinus tumours also.

EXAMINATION

1. *Nasopharynx.* This was formerly examined with a tongue depressor and small mirror. It used to take several attempts to view the whole nasopharynx and it was often necessary to spray the soft palate and base of tongue with lignocaine to stop gagging. It is necessary to see both Eustachian tubes, the adjacent fossae of

Rosenmüller, the roof of the nasopharynx and the choanae (*see Fig.* 2.1.1), and this is best done with a straight nasal endoscope.

2. *Oropharynx.* This can easily be seen by depressing the tongue with a spatula (*Fig.* 2.2.1). The examination should be orderly, looking at each of the areas in turn—the tonsils and fauces, the soft palate and the posterior pharyngeal wall. To see the floor of the oropharynx, i.e. the base of tongue and vallecula, the tongue should be pulled forwards and a laryngeal mirror used. The lateral walls and base of tongue should always be palpated if tumour is suspected; the lateral walls to examine for fixation and the tongue base because tumours in this region start deep and come to the surface late.

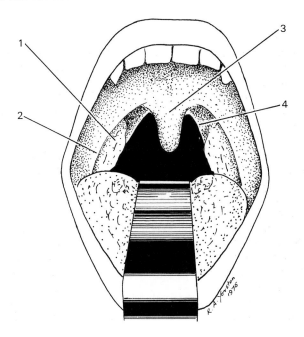

Fig. 2.2.1.   Examination of the oropharynx.
1, Palatine tonsil.   3, Uvula.
2, Palatoglossal fold.   4, Palatopharyngeal fold.

3. *Hypopharynx.* This is examined with a laryngeal mirror and it may be necessary to anaesthetize the area with local anaesthetic to stop gagging. Again the examination should be orderly and both pyriform sinuses should be clearly seen, in addition to the arytenoids and the posterior wall (*see Fig.* 2.13.2). The use of the flexible endoscope helps in the patient who cannot tolerate a mirror.

4. *Neck.* This should be palpated in the routine described in Chapter 2.21. It is important to record exactly the position, number, size and fixation of any nodes. The distribution is helpful. Posterior triangle nodes are often found in viral infections such as mononucleosis and toxoplasmosis, and supraclavicular nodes

are seen in gastro-oesophageal and lung lesions. It is important to palpate the thyroid and to assess the mobility of the larynx. If glands are fixed one should record to what they appear to be fixed, because fixation does not always indicate inoperability.

5. *Other areas*. The eardrums should be examined for evidence of serous otitis media and other causes of pain if the patient complains of referred pain. Tuning-fork tests are necessary. The larynx must be examined for evidence of vocal cord paralysis in nasopharyngeal tumours. Finally, a search is made for a Horner's syndrome and trismus which denote extrapharyngeal spread of tumour.

RADIOGRAPHY

Plain films. In nasopharyngeal disease a simple lateral view gives an indication of the size of the mass. Base of skull views show evidence of erosion of the skull base. Radiography is of little value in oropharyngeal disease, but in hypopharyngeal lesions a simple lateral film of the neck may show an increase in the soft-tissue shadow in the postcricoid region. If this is greater than the diameter of one vertebral body it is abnormal. Plain films of the mandible may show erosion by a tonsillar tumour but this is rare. Chest films may show the presence of a metastasis or of tuberculosis if these are relevant.

Contrast films. The most useful film is a barium swallow which will demonstrate a pharyngeal pouch, an oesophageal web, a hypopharyngeal tumour or pressure from without by a thyroid swelling or cervical osteophytes. A negative barium swallow should not be the final chapter in the investigation; if suspicion of a lesion is high one should proceed to oesophagoscopy. A barium meal is also important if the patient complains of either dysphagia or a feeling of a lump in the throat. Carcinoma or a reflux oesophagitis may be shown. If an angiofibroma of the nasopharynx is suspected a carotid angiogram is performed both to diagnose and to assess the treatability of the lesion.

Scans. CT scans are essential in the evaluation of all nasopharyngeal lesions to assess whether or not there is intracranial spread. In oropharyngeal lesions a CT scan will demonstrate spread to the parapharyngeal space. In hypopharyngeal lesions scans are especially helpful if extraoesophageal spread is suspected at the thoracic inlet (e.g. in a patient with recurrent laryngeal nerve paralysis).

LABORATORY INVESTIGATIONS. In all cases a full blood count and an ESR should be performed. This is especially helpful in infective lesions. Together with this, the monospot test should be asked for if a young adult complains of sore throat and malaise. If the patient has symptoms like glandular fever but with a negative monospot test, blood should be sent for titres against toxoplasma, cytomegalovirus, brucella and HIV.

Any patient with weight loss will need a measure of the serum proteins and electrolytes since hypokalaemia and low serum albumin are common findings. If the Paterson–Brown Kelly syndrome is suspected it is insufficient to test the haemoglobin level only; a serum iron and iron-binding capacity test should be done. Finally, if it is indicated, thyroid function tests and a VDRL and TPHA should be sent.

BIOPSY

1. *Nasopharynx*. This is best done under general anaesthetic with the palate pulled forwards by catheters passed through the nose. A heated laryngeal mirror is used to examine the roof and lateral walls, and examination is helped by the use of the operating microscope. If a lesion is seen then representative pieces are biopsied but care should be taken if an angiofibroma is suspected. In this case prior embolization is suggested. If no lesion is seen biopsies are taken of the fossae of Rosenmüller and the roof, either with multiple bites or with an adenoid curette.

2. *Oropharynx*. Again general anaesthesia is preferred. The biopsy should be of a representative piece of the tumour, not the very edge where dysplastic changes may confuse the report and not the centre of an ulcer which will merely be necrotic. If a lymphoma is suspected the whole tonsil should be removed and not placed in formalin but taken straight to the laboratory so that immunofluorescent antibodies can be studied and the correct classification applied.

3. *Hypopharynx*. Direct laryngoscopy and pharyngoscopy should be performed under general anaesthesia. The main purpose of this is not only to obtain a biopsy but to assess and stage the tumour. Particular note should be taken of the upper and lower limits of any tumour and also any fixation.

Chapter 2.3

INFECTIONS OF THE PHARYNX

In the pharynx the only site to be involved in an infection with any frequency, at least in adults, is the oropharynx. Nasopharyngitis occurs in the early stage of coryza, but is of no significance, and infection of the hypopharynx is virtually unknown. In the oropharynx the lateral wall, the posterior wall and the floor are most often involved causing, respectively, tonsillitis, pharyngitis and lingual tonsillitis. The roof (the soft palate) is rarely infected.

Bacterial infections are now seldom thought to be primary invaders. It is considered that they are often secondary opportunistic invaders following a virus infection. The tonsils, for example, have been shown to harbour a resident Epstein–Barr virus, especially after an attack of mononucleosis. This virus is activated by the same physical factors of chilling and soaking, etc. that stimulate the herpes group of viruses, and so a viral tonsillitis is set up. The tonsil no longer secretes IgA and it is then prime soil for secondary bacteria to invade and cause a bacterial tonsillitis. There are, however, still many primary bacterial infections, such as diphtheria, ulcerative gingivitis etc. which are more common in the developing countries.

ACUTE TONSILLITIS

Acute tonsillitis may affect any age-group but it is most frequently found in children. Streptococci, staphylococci and *Haemophilus influenzae* are the most common organisms, either in pure growth or in combination, but pneumococci may also be cultured.

SYMPTOMS. The symptoms are those of acute pharyngitis but there is usually more constitutional disturbance, especially in the case of children. The onset is often sudden with the temperature rising to 40 °C. The tongue is furred and the breath is offensive. There is some trismus and a constant yet dreaded desire to swallow; dysphagia is considerable and pain radiates up to the ears. There are often abdominal pains due to a mesenteric adenitis.

CLINICAL FEATURES. In the early stages the tonsil is enlarged, red and swollen, while later the infection involves the crypts which fill with fibrin. This turns purulent within the follicles and necrotic areas appear. In this stage the tonsils are congested, swollen and studded with yellow beads of pus which at first appear in the mouths of the crypts but later coalesce. The cervical nodes are enlarged and tender.

DIAGNOSIS. This is usually easy. A throat swab may be taken to isolate the organisms. If there is confluence of the infected material the condition may be mistaken for glandular fever, and a blood film and a monospot test may be necessary. Scarlet fever presents with a similar throat appearance but there is a strawberry tongue in most cases. At times scarlet fever may not be diagnosed until the typical rash appears, but even then the rash may be a streptococcal one which does not desquamate. Skin eruptions due to sensitivity to antibiotics may confuse the picture.

TREATMENT. The patient should be sent to bed, and aspirin in a dose appropriate to the age of the patient may be given every 4 hours until the temperature falls. Antibiotics are usually prescribed, but they must be given for a sufficient period of time, because if they are discontinued too early a relapse may occur. The disadvantage of giving ampicillin in glandular fever is the eruption of a skin rash, but it is most useful in a tonsillitis due to *H. influenzae*. Penicillin, tetracycline or erythromycin may be used. In mild attacks one may be justified in withholding antibiotics to allow the patient to develop his own resistance to the infecting organisms. The administration of fluids is important to prevent dehydration, and they are more acceptable than solid or semisolid food.

ABSCESSES OF THE TONSILS

Peritonsillar abscess (Quinsy)

This consists of suppuration outside the tonsillar capsule, and the swelling can extend to the soft palate and the tonsil may also be pushed medially. The route of infection is probably via a crypt that penetrates or almost penetrates the capsule. The comparison to the internal branchial sinus has been made. A quinsy is usually unilateral and most frequently affects adult males. It may occur at any age, and is much more common in children than is thought. Many extremely fibrous and adherent tonsils are removed from quite young children who have never been suspected of having had a quinsy.

SYMPTOMS. A peritonsillar abscess follows a tonsillitis which appears to settle and then recurs severely on one side. The patient looks ill and his temperature rises to about 40 °C with a rigor. There is acute pain in the throat radiating to the ear, and this makes swallowing so difficult that saliva dribbles from the mouth. The swelling in the throat imparts a thick, muffled tone to the voice.

CLINICAL FEATURES. Examination may be difficult because the patient can only open his jaws slightly, but with good illumination the affected side of the palate is seen to be congested and bulging; the uvula is oedematous, pushed towards the opposite side, and the affected tonsil is usually hidden by the swelling but may have some mucopus on its surface. The cervical nodes are enlarged and tender. If not relieved either by antibiotics or by surgery the abscess may burst or resolve in about 1 week.

TREATMENT. Systemic penicillin should be given in large doses whenever the diagnosis is made, but if it fails to relieve the condition in 24–48 hours the abscess must be opened. A long pair of sinus forceps is plunged into the most prominent part of the swelling and the abscess drained by opening the blades of the forceps (*Fig.* 2.3.1). The throat may first be sprayed with 10 per cent cocaine hydrochloride solution in the adult. This reduces the trismus which makes the operation easier, but it does not relieve the pain of incision, and the patient should be so warned. The immediate relief compensates for the agony. Rapid improvement follows but penicillin should be continued until resolution is complete. The tonsils should be removed 6–8 weeks following a quinsy.

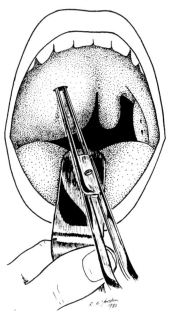

Fig. 2.3.1   Drainage of peritonsillar abscess.

Intratonsillar Abscess

This is uncommon and implies an abscess within the tonsil following retention of pus within a crypt to give pain and dysphagia. The tonsil is swollen and inflamed, but the soft palate does not bulge. It is treated on the same lines as a quinsy.

Chronic Tonsillitis

This may not exist as a separate pathological entity but many patients complain of recurrent short-lived bouts of febrile malaise accompanied by sore throat. A redness of the tonsils and pillars is seen on examination and antibiotics do not seem to eradicate the problem. If the condition is recurrent enough to trouble the patient and if pharyngitis can be excluded then tonsillectomy is advised.

HYPERTROPHY OF THE LINGUAL TONSIL

The lingual tonsil is a mass of lymphoid tissue normally found on the dorsum of the tongue between the vallate papillae in front and the epiglottis behind. Hypertrophy may occur after tonsillectomy, in heavy smokers or in women at the menopause. If the swelling is large it causes the feeling of a lump in the throat. Acute inflammation, or even abscess formation, may occur in the lingual tonsil, and is seen with the help of a laryngeal mirror. Acute infections are treated in the usual manner with antibiotics. Chronic enlargement may be dealt with by cryosurgery.

TUBERCULOSIS OF THE TONSIL

Tuberculosis of the tonsil is now extremely rare in countries where the milk supply is controlled, and it presents no characteristic features. Attention is drawn to the tonsils by the diagnosis of tuberculous cervical nodes. The tubercle bacilli in infected milk are presumed to reach the nodes via the tonsils, which may or may not remain infected. There is no means of diagnosing this by clinical inspection, and the condition is discovered by histological examination after tonsillectomy. This is the more unfortunate because half of the tonsils so sectioned do not show evidence of tuberculosis. It is, however, sound surgical practice to remove the tonsils from children who have a tuberculous cervical adenitis rather than to leave potentially infected tonsils *in situ*. Antituberculous therapy should be started when the diagnosis is made in the nodes.

CALCULUS OF THE TONSIL

A calculus, or tonsillolith, may originate in the upper pole of the tonsil from calcification of cheesy food debris, and it may attain considerable size. It may be seen on the surface or detected with a probe. Sometimes the calculus is extruded spontaneously, or it may be removed with a probe. In many instances the tonsil must be removed, and this is recommended if recurrent infections occur.

RETENTION CYST OF THE TONSIL

White-topped cysts, either single or multiple, are sometimes a source of alarm to patients who notice them. They represent retention cysts in the epithelial lining of the tonsil and if merely punctured tend to recur. Usually reassurance is all that is required but some patients may press for tonsillectomy.

ULCERATIVE GINGIVITIS

Ulcerative gingivitis is a highly infectious and ulcerative lesion of the tonsils. It was common during the First World War, being called trench mouth or Vincent's angina, and the frequency with which it occurred was probably due to lack of hygiene in the cleaning of eating and drinking utensils. It is now much less common. The infection is caused by two Gram-negative organisms, a fusiform bacillus and a spirochaete, which can be isolated together from the ulcers. Ulcerative gingivitis infection may contaminate malignant lesions of the mouth and pharynx.

SYMPTOMS. The patient has a low pyrexia and complains of a sore throat. The cervical nodes may be enlarged. Constitutional symptoms are slight.

CLINICAL FEATURES. Usually only one tonsil is involved, but the membrane may often spread onto the gums and the soft and hard palate. The typical lesion presents as a greyish slough which bleeds easily when it is removed to reveal a deep ulceration of the tonsil. The membrane reforms after removal. There is a characteristic smell from the breath. The infection may persist for several weeks if untreated, but should clear up in a week with appropriate therapy.

DIAGNOSIS. A swab from the affected area will show the causative organisms. Differentiation is from other diseases which produce a membrane—diphtheria and especially nowadays glandular fever. Tertiary syphilis may closely simulate the ulceration of ulcerative gingivitis, and the fact that the two conditions may coexist means that serological tests may be inconclusive.

TREATMENT. The condition responds readily to systemic antibiotics such as penicillin and erythromycin, and to metronidazole (Flagyl) tablets, 200 mg given thrice daily. Apart from this, warm gargles of sodium bicarbonate solution will help to remove the membrane. The patient and his relatives must be warned about the infectious nature of the disease. The patient should be barrier nursed.

DIPHTHERIA

Because of the success of inoculation there is now almost no part of the Western world where the diphtheria bacillus exists as a virulent strain. If it is isolated on a throat swab it will be so avirulent that it will respond to penicillin therapy. The attenuated strain will not cause membrane formation which characterizes the typical infection.

Unfortunately some of the developing countries do not have a successful programme of inoculation, and in these the disease is still found. It affects those in the first 10 years of life, particularly in the 2–3 years age-group. Incubation takes 2–7 days and the onset is insidious with a temperature of some 39·5 °C. The disease is characterized by the appearance of a false membrane on the tonsils, soft palate and posterior pharyngeal wall. The colour of the membrane is usually grey, but it may be white, yellow or dark brown. It is firmly attached to the mucosa, and leaves a bleeding surface when it is removed, after which it quickly reforms. The cervical nodes are enlarged, often markedly so, and tender. The disease may affect the nasal cavities and nasopharynx to produce a fetid and blood-stained discharge. Diphtheria may spread to involve the larynx and trachea where membrane formation imperils the airway.

When the disease is suspected a throat swab is taken and treatment is started without delay. A dose of antitoxin, 10 000 units in a mild case and up to 80 000 units in a severe one, is given. *Corynebacterium diphtheriae* is sensitive to antibiotics, particularly penicillin and erythromycin, and one of these should be prescribed together with the antitoxin to prevent complications.

ACUTE PHARYNGITIS

This is the more frequent variety, occurring primarily during the winter months and less often in autumn or spring. It precedes the common cold, and may accompany influenza, measles, scarlet fever, typhoid fever or smallpox.

SYMPTOMS. The sore throat which ushers in the coryza is accompanied by a feeling of coldness, a slight pyrexia, headache, backache and joint pains. The throat feels dry, raw, uncomfortable or painful, especially on swallowing. There may also be some hoarseness. These symptoms last for a day or two until the coryza, influenza or infectious fever becomes apparent.

CLINICAL FEATURES. On examining the throat there is an obvious redness, and sometimes swelling, of the mucosa of the soft palate, tonsils and posterior pharyngeal wall. The uvula shares in this and occasionally there is some haemorrhage into it. The cervical nodes are palpable and tender. In children the mouth should be examined for Koplik's spots in case the pharyngitis is the precursor of measles.

TREATMENT. As a rule no treatment is required, but if advice is sought the patient should remain indoors and take aspirin 0·3–0·6 g every 4 hours. There is no indication for prescribing antibiotics unless the pharyngitis proceeds to one of the fevers.

CHRONIC PHARYNGITIS

This is a common condition and is due to chronic infection of the aggregates of submucosal lymphatics in the posterior pharyngeal wall. It is seen in heavy smokers and drinkers, and in those who are exposed to industrial or atmospheric pollution. It is also common as a secondary effect of a postnasal drip.

CLINICAL FEATURES. These can vary from a normal-looking pharynx which feels raw, to a posterior wall thick with islands of hypertrophied lymphoid follicles. A frequent finding is a thick vertical band of lymphoid tissue on the posterolateral wall of the pharynx behind the posterior pillar of the fauces—the so-called lateral pharyngeal band. The patient complains of a raw and painful throat without an accompanying elevation of temperature. There is none of the malaise of tonsillitis, and the condition persists for weeks or months. On occasion the pain becomes extreme and is located to a pin-point site, made very much worse by the movement of the pharynx during swallowing. This lasts only for a day or two, and probably represents abscess formation in one of the follicles. The patient may also be tempted to try self-medication on a long-term basis with many of the proprietary brand medicines available, and this in turn may cause a mucositis which is also painful. Secondary infection of the pharynx from a postnasal drip constantly bathing the posterior pharyngeal wall is not uncommon, and is usually seen in patients with chronic rhinitis and sinusitis.

TREATMENT. Avoidance of tobacco is of prime importance to stop the constant irritation. Wearing a mask in industrial pollution might help, but it is difficult to do anything about atmospheric pollution. Titres should be done for mycoplasma because if this is present it will resolve with tetracycline given for at least 1 week. Rhinitis and sinusitis should be dealt with according to the local cause, and treatment with oral and local decongestants may help the pharyngitis if it is due to a postnasal discharge. Persistent hypertrophy of lymphoid tissue on the posterior pharyngeal wall may be treated with the application of cryosurgery.

ATROPHIC PHARYNGITIS

Normally the pharynx is kept moist by minor salivary glands in the submucosa. If these degenerate the submucosa will become thin, the mucosa will be dry and smooth and the patient will have discomfort. It is seen after irradiation of the head and neck, in the elderly, in the Paterson–Brown Kelly syndrome and in Sjögren's disease.

The patient must keep the pharynx moist aided by the use of artificial saliva.

PHARYNGITIS IN BLOOD DISORDERS

Infectious Mononucleosis

Infectious mononucleosis (glandular fever) is a systemic infection thought to be due to the Epstein–Barr virus, and is spread by direct contact with the mouth, such as kissing. It is a disease of young adults and is characterized by an increase in abnormal mononuclear cells in the blood.

CLINICAL FEATURES. In the prodromal period which lasts for 4–14 days there is anorexia, malaise, a low-grade fever and a sore throat of varying severity. The pharynx is very congested and there may be superficial ulcers, especially on the tonsils. Crops of red spots may appear on the palate and last for several days. A transient maculopapular rash is often found. There is enlargement of the cervical nodes, and the postauricular, suboccipital, axillary and inguinal lymph nodes may also be affected. This adenopathy may persist for several months. In about half of the cases there is a moderate enlargement of the spleen. The acute febrile symptoms may continue for several weeks, and relapses are common.

DIAGNOSIS. The diagnosis is confirmed by finding atypical large mononuclear cells in a blood film. A blood count will usually show a leucocytosis of 10.0–$20.0 \times 10^9/l$. Diagnosis is confirmed by a positive monospot test. In over half of the cases the liver enzymes will rise and the ECG may show evidence of myocarditis.

TREATMENT. There is no specific treatment apart from the usual remedies such as soluble aspirin to lower the pyrexia. Antibiotics play no part in the treatment, and ampicillin should never be used as it will cause a skin reaction if given during any phase of infectious mononucleosis. Corticosteroids should be reserved for severe cases, in which they give good results. Tracheostomy may be required rarely.

COMPLICATIONS. These are few but occasionally a peripheral neuropathy may occur involving not only the limbs but also the laryngeal and eye muscles. Some patients become very ill with hepatitis and myocarditis. The airway may be compromised if the tonsils become massive. Many patients remain depressed and devitalized for several months, and during this time the adenopathy, the abnormal blood picture and a positive serological reaction may be found.

Agranulocytosis

This is characterized by a reduction of the neutrophil polymorphs in the blood, and may be associated with pharyngeal ulceration. The cause is a depression of white-cell formation in the bone marrow, and is often drug-induced. The treatment is that of the blood dyscrasia.

Acute Leukaemia

This may also be associated with a necrotic ulceration in the pharynx. Purpuric haemorrhages and a typical leucocytosis of $20·0–100·0 \times 10^9/l$ will confirm the diagnosis.

Lymphoma

Lymphoma may occur in the lymphoid tissue of the pharynx and nasopharynx. There may be unilateral enlargement and ulceration of a tonsil which becomes a dark-purplish colour. The cervical nodes show a characteristic enlargement.

AIDS

This must now be suspected in any 'at risk' patient presenting with pharyngitis/tonsillitis and cervical lymphadenopathy.

FUNGAL INFECTIONS

Moniliasis (thrush) is found with increasing frequency as the result of prolonged antibiotic therapy. It is found also in marasmic infants or poorly nourished children, but it may occur in older patients suffering from a debilitating illness. Creamy-white plaques are found on the tongue and on the buccal and pharyngeal mucosa. These are easily removed with slight bleeding. The condition can also exist in the absence of white plaques. If the condition is suspected in a patient with a diffusely red mouth, salivary washings should be sent to the mycology laboratory. The treatment is by painting the lesions with 1 per cent aqueous solution of gentian violet after each feed. The condition may be treated by systemic nystatin given orally in doses of 100 000 units 4 times daily for 1 week, or amphotericin (Fungilin) lozenges 10 mg 4 times daily.

Candida albicans may be caused by the long-term use of antibiotics, and produces white spots on the tonsils or the posterior pharyngeal wall. The treatment is that for thrush.

Blastomycosis produces shallow granulating ulcers and it responds to a slow intravenous infusion of amphotericin (Fungizone). There is a danger of renal damage if the infusion is not slow. Local lozenges of the same drug (Fungilin) may be allowed to dissolve slowly in the mouth, and have a local effect on the lesion.

SYPHILIS OF THE PHARYNX

Primary syphilis is uncommon, but the tonsil is second to the lip as the most frequent extragenital site. The chancre is unilateral, persists for several weeks and is accompanied by enlarged cervical nodes. Palpation by a gloved finger will disclose that the lesion is of cartilaginous hardness. The discovery of *Treponema pallidum* may confirm the diagnosis.

Secondary syphilis in the pharynx is much more common and much more important in that it is most contagious because the lesion teems with spirochaetes. Initially there is congestion of the palate and fauces, and some tonsillar enlargement, but soon the mucous patch develops. This may be found on any part of the mucosa of the mouth or pharynx, the principal sites being, in order of frequency, the tonsil, the palatine arches, the tongue and the inner aspect of the lips. The patch is round or oval, bluish-grey in colour with a surrounding zone of congestion. The patches may be multiple and symmetrical, and may become confluent. Ulceration takes place, leaving a snail-track ulcer of a dirty grey colour. The cervical nodes are enlarged, and there may be a skin eruption.

Tertiary syphilis does not appear as a gumma for some years after the initial infection. A hard purplish swelling appears on the palate, posterior pharyngeal wall, or, less often, on the tonsil. It may appear in the vallecula between the epiglottis and the tongue, and so be overlooked unless a laryngeal mirror has been employed in routine examination. The gumma breaks down at its centre to form a punched-out ulcer with a greenish-yellow base and red, indurated edges.

Postsyphilitic complications are seen much less frequently now. They were prone to follow hereditary syphilis when they appeared around the age of puberty. The palate may perforate with destruction of tissue or there may be considerable cicatricial stenosis of the pharynx.

SYMPTOMS. The chancre may not cause any symptoms. Secondary lesions cause only slight pain in the throat, although some dysphagia may be felt when ulceration takes place. Pain is rare in the tertiary lesions, and the patient may only complain of a nasal speech or of food entering the nose while eating.

DIAGNOSIS. This must be made from other lesions causing ulceration or membrane formation. The primary and secondary stages are usually recognized, but the gumma may be confused with ulcerative gingivitis or with carcinoma. Serological tests and a biopsy will generally decide the question. Lupus also causes destruction of the pharyngeal mucosa, but is slower and is associated with skin nodules.

TREATMENT. Treatment is that of syphilis, and should be undertaken by a venereologist. Local hygiene is necessary and the highly contagious nature of the mucous patches must be explained to the patient.

TUBERCULOSIS OF THE PHARYNX

Acute miliary tuberculosis is the most common variety found in the pharynx, but is a rare complication of the pulmonary lesion. It is characterized by minute grey or yellow tubercles on the fauces or palate. These rapidly break down into shallow ulcers which spread widely in the mouth and pharynx to cause pain on swallowing, excess salivation, a throaty voice and rapid emaciation. The diagnosis must be made from syphilis, in which pain is absent, and from diphtheria, which is excluded by a throat swab and by a biopsy from the edge of the ulcer. Treatment is by antituberculous therapy with streptomycin, PAS and isoniazid. The prognosis is improving, but the miliary nature of the condition calls for a guarded outlook.

LUPUS OF THE PHARYNX

Lupus rarely attacks the pharynx, but when it does it produces minute pinkish-yellow nodules which resemble the apple-jelly nodes on the skin, which is also affected. The nodules cause some discomfort, but even when they break down, ulcerate and then heal with radiating scars there is little pain. Treatment is largely that for tuberculosis, but calciferol may be prescribed with due care to guard against renal damage.

SCLEROMA

Scleroma is rarely seen in the pharynx. It is most common in Eastern Europe and in Asia. The nose is more often affected than the pharynx. It forms painless, hard infiltrations which on section show hyaline bodies and Mikulicz cells. The diplobacillus may be obtained from the lesions. There is no specific treatment, but tetracycline is the most commonly used drug.

LEPROSY

Leprosy is almost unknown in the UK. Leprosy of the pharynx is secondary to cutaneous leprosy, and gives rise to painless nodules which contract to leave pale cicatrices involving the palate, uvula and faucial pillars. It is caused by the *Mycobacterium leprae* bacillus and is sometimes known as Hansen's disease after the discoverer of the bacillus. The condition is diagnosed by recovering the bacilli from the nasal discharge, and by biopsy of the nodules. Treatment is by dapsone and rifampicin which must be continued for years.

Chapter 2.4

BENIGN DISEASE OF THE PHARYNX

PATERSON–BROWN KELLY SYNDROME

AETIOLOGY. In the USA this is known as the Plummer–Vinson syndrome and it consists of dysphagia, hypochromic microcytic anaemia, angular stomatitis, glossitis and koilonychia. It is more common in females than in males, and also more common on the west coast of Britain than the east coast. The cause of the syndrome is unknown, but since there is an atrophy of all the mucous membranes of the alimentary tract an autoimmune basis may be presumed.

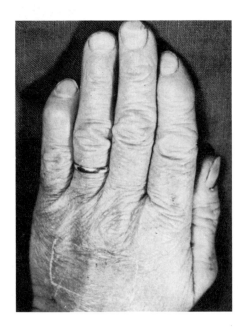

Fig. 2.4.1. Spoon-shaped brittle nails in the Paterson–Brown Kelly syndrome.

CLINICAL FEATURES. While the dysphagia may be very marked, it is not usually severe. The angular stomatitis, glossitis and koilonychia (*Fig.* 2.4.1) may be slight. The characteristic blood picture is a low haemoglobin and a hypochromic microcytic anaemia. All cases will have a low serum iron and consequently a high iron-binding capacity. A small, but significant, proportion of patients with this condition progress to the stage of postcricoid carcinoma. The relationship is not close enough to label the Paterson–Brown Kelly syndrome as a premalignant condition. A curious radiographic finding of unknown cause is a web at the postcricoid region (*Fig.* 2.4.2). This can often be seen at oesophagoscopy and may indeed be a firm diaphragm requiring dilatation, but sometimes a well-marked radiological web may not be seen at oesophagoscopy.

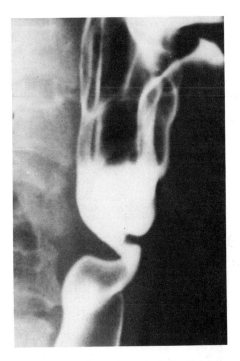

Fig. 2.4.2. Radiograph to show the Paterson–Brown Kelly syndrome with web.

TREATMENT. Iron should be given orally at first until the haemoglobin is within normal limits. From then on, a check should be kept on the serum iron and the iron-binding capacity. When the haemoglobin has been restored to normal the serum iron will still be low and, due to absorption problems, may stay low in spite of oral iron administration. While the serum iron is low, dysphagia will continue, and so if oral iron fails to raise it to the normal level then the patient will require to be given parenteral iron. A check on the course of the disease during the follow-up should always be by means of the serum iron rather than the haemoglobin.

PHARYNGEAL POUCH

AETIOLOGY. The upper end of the oesophagus is guarded by a muscle sphincter called the cricopharyngeus which is normally closed. The lower part of the pharynx has a weak area at the lower part of the inferior constrictor muscle—the so-called dehiscence of Killian (*Fig.* 2.4.3). At this point there is only a mucosal layer, a submucosa and one layer of muscle fibres. If the patient has the habit of a 'double swallow' and develops an abnormally high intrapharyngeal pressure during swallowing, then this weak area will be subjected to pressure. This is reinforced if the cricopharyngeus stays closed longer than usual, or if it has a high state of tonus. Gradually the area expands and soon forms a pouch. Food collects in this small pouch, thus stretching it more and enlarging it. When the pouch gets to a certain size it lies in line with the oesophagus and becomes the natural opening for food (and oesophagoscopes!) to enter. This further increases its size and causes it to expand and to press on the oesophagus when full of food, causing dysphagia.

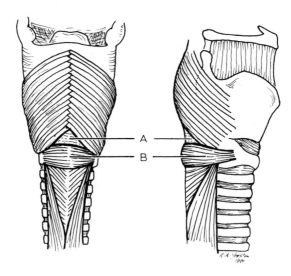

Fig. 2.4.3. A, Site of origin of pharyngeal pouch between oblique and transverse cricopharyngeus (Killian's dehiscence). B, Cricopharyngeal sphincter.

CLINICAL FEATURES. Even when the pouch is small there will be a feeling of a lump in the throat. As the pouch enlarges true dysphagia will follow. When the pouch fills with food during a meal there will come a point when it overflows into the pharynx causing regurgitation of undigested food. Some may overflow into the larynx resulting in coughing fits. A barium swallow will confirm the diagnosis (*Fig.* 2.4.4).

TREATMENT. The most satisfactory treatment of a pouch is to remove it. This is done by making a collar incision on the left side of the neck, retracting the carotid sheath laterally and the laryngopharynx medially, identifying the pouch (which can be made easier by packing it with acriflavine prior to surgery), dividing the neck of the pouch and suturing the opening in layers. If too much is removed there is a danger of stenosis, but if not enough is removed the pouch will recur. A cricopharyngeal myotomy should always be performed, taking care to avoid damaging the recurrent laryngeal nerve.

An alternative method exists of using diathermy coagulation of the common wall between the pouch and oesophagus (Dohlman's operation). This is a simpler and quicker method than excision, but in inexpert hands it can lead to mediastinitis from perforation and damage to the recurrent laryngeal nerves by diathermy. The procedure is done endoscopically using a specially designed oesophagoscope with two beaks—one for the oesophagus and one for the pouch. The stretched wall between the two is clamped and diathermied, again using specially designed instruments.

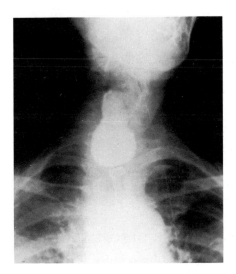

Fig. 2.4.4.   Radiograph showing a pharyngeal pouch.

GLOBUS SYNDROME

Patients with the globus syndrome complain of a feeling of a lump in the throat which is brought on or made worse by anxiety and in which no other organic cause can be found.

Some cases are easy and safe to diagnose as globus—if there is an obvious emotional precipitating cause. The difficult cases are those in which there is no obvious psychological cause. Great care must be taken not to miss an early carcinoma. In this latter group oesophagoscopy must be done in spite of a negative barium examination.

Globus is diagnosed much less now than formerly, because it has been realized that oesophagitis and reflex spasm of cricopharyngeus can mimic the symptoms. In these cases antacids will help the 'globus' symptoms. In the true globus cases, reassurance that no organic disease or cancer is present helps the patient to accommodate to the symptoms which will usually be self-limiting.

It is, however, important to make this a diagnosis of exclusion, at least primarily. The symptoms may be due to extrinsic pressure from a thyroid nodule or cervical osteophytes, or intrinsic problems such as an early carcinoma or a web or a pharyngeal pouch. Indeed, a pharyngeal pouch may be preceded by a globus syndrome due to a hypertonic cricopharyngeus.

Every case should have a barium swallow, and if symptoms persist, an oesophagoscopy. Advances in oesophageal manometry equipment have allowed studies to be performed relating acid reflux to cricopharyngeal hypertonicity. It does not appear that there is a significant relationship, thus casting doubt on the view that the globus syndrome was due to reflex oesophagitis. It now appears that the old name of globus hystericus, while semantically wrong, was nearer the truth.

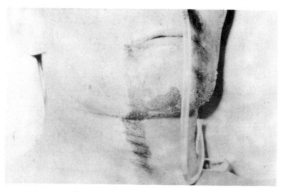

Fig. 2.4.5. Lysol burn. The caustic stain is seen on the mouth and neck. A nasogastric tube has been inserted for feeding.

CORROSIVE BURNS OF THE OESOPHAGUS

This injury is not as common in this country as in the USA, Asia and Africa. It usually occurs in children or potential suicides and the substances swallowed are strong acids or alkalis. High concentrations or large volumes of the substance are the most damaging.

The area first affected is the mouth (*Fig.* 2.4.5) and pharynx, and if the substance is swallowed the middle third of the oesophagus is the site most frequently involved, although the strictures may be multiple. Spillage of the caustic substance onto the larynx may cause oedema.

PATHOLOGY. As with burns elsewhere, the caustic burn of the oesophagus varies in degree. It may involve only the mucous and submucous layers which heal without stricture formation. In more severe burns, necrosis may occur in the oesophageal wall involving all coats. This may heal with fibrosis and stricture formation, or perforation of the oesophageal wall may occur.

TREATMENT. If the substance can be identified attempts should be made to neutralize it. Most patients will have visible burns on the lips, mouth and pharynx. The problem is to decide whether the substance has been swallowed or if it has all been spat out. If doubt exists then it is probably safer to perform oesophagoscopy to see the extent of the burn if it is present. A flexible oesophagoscope should be used in preference to the rigid one. If no burn is visible it may be assumed that no caustic was swallowed, and the oral burns will heal in time.

In cases where there is no doubt that the substance was swallowed there is little to gain by passing an oesophagoscope merely to assess the extent of the burn since the treatment will be unaltered and because there is a real risk of perforating the oesophagus with the instrument. These cases should have a nasogastric feeding tube passed. They should immediately be started on 60 mg prednisolone per day for a week, the dose tapering off thereafter over a further 3–4 weeks. This is given to prevent fibrosis and subsequent stricture formation. Antibiotics should also be given systemically during this period.

After 3 or 4 weeks an oesophagoscopy should be done to assess the presence or absence of stricture formation. At this stage there is less danger of causing a perforation. If a stricture has formed a programme of dilatation should be started.

OESOPHAGEAL STRICTURE

AETIOLOGY. The commonest causes of this are (1) long-standing oesophagitis; (2) surgical correction of hiatus hernia or of a previous stricture; (3) corrosive oesophagitis; (4) cancer of the oesophagus.

Any site may be affected, but due to the nature of the above conditions it is usually found in the middle or lower third of the oesophagus.

CLINICAL FEATURES. The symptoms are a gradually increasing dysphagia with some discomfort at the site of the stricture. On occasion the patient may present as an acute emergency with total dysphagia due to a bolus of meat becoming stuck in the stricture. If the condition is of long duration there will be weight loss.

TREATMENT. In the non-malignant conditions attempts should be made to alleviate the condition by dilatation. The initial dilatations are done at oesophagoscopy using Jackson bougies. Dilatations should be done until the stricture becomes tight. On no account should the stricture be dilated until it bleeds because this leads to more fibrous tissue formation. The dilatations are done at weekly or fortnightly intervals until the maximum lumen is achieved. At this point the patient should be taught to swallow a Hurst mercury bougie before meals to maintain the dilatation. If this regimen is unsuccessful the stricture should be excised surgically and an end-to-end anastomosis performed. This is easier if the stricture is in the lower third than in the middle third where the results are unrewarding.

OESOPHAGEAL PERFORATION

AETIOLOGY. The oesophagus may be perforated in either the neck or the chest. The clinical features and management differ depending on the site.

The commonest cause is perforation by a rigid oesophagoscope, although it is not uncommon with the flexible oesophagoscope. Factors making perforation more likely are a light anaesthetic and a tight cricopharyngeus, biopsy of a malignant growth or an area of severe oesophagitis, a difficult dilatation or a pharyngeal pouch. The oesophagus may also be perforated by chest or neck surgery, by a penetrating wound or spontaneously from a malignant growth, ruptured anastomosis or the Mallory–Weiss syndrome.

CLINICAL FEATURES. Every patient with a perforation of the oesophagus will shortly after the event complain of pain and dysphagia and will have a rising temperature and pulse rate. The pain may be localized to the neck, but since fluids tend to leak down the posterior mediastinum most patients complain of pain between the shoulder blades. If mediastinitis occurs the patient will become very ill. In cervical tears a fullness may develop quite quickly on one side of the neck.

Surgical emphysema will be felt in the neck and over the upper chest. There will be neck tenderness over the site of the leak if it is above the clavicles.

MANAGEMENT. Awareness of the risk of a perforation is important after a difficult oesophagoscopy or any bouginage. Patients at risk should not be given anything other than sterile water for 12 hours after the procedure. If there is pain or elevation of temperature a gastrografin screening should be done.

If there is a perforation then most are managed conservatively because of the difficulty in adequately closing traumatically lacerated tissue. Occasionally, however, thoracotomy is indicated for large intrathoracic perforations.

Each patient should have a nasogastric tube passed and its position checked radiographically. Antibodies should be started and vital signs checked 2–4-hourly.

Collections of fluid outside the oesophagus in the neck or chest should be drained.

ACHALASIA

AETIOLOGY. This is called 'cardiospasm', and is due to a defect in the intramural vagal supply (Auerbach's myenteric plexus). During swallowing there is loss of tone due to a lack of integrated parasympathetic stimulation and non-propulsive motility in the body of the oesophagus. There is also a failure of relaxation at the cardia.

The lower area acts as a stricture and the oesophagus above this becomes very dilated and usually full of food debris.

SYMPTOMS. There are few symptoms until the condition is advanced. The main symptoms are then intermittent difficulty in swallowing associated with discomfort and attacks of regurgitation. As the condition progresses and dilatation occurs, food entering the stomach does not initiate peristalsis, and so large quantities of food collect in the oesophagus. This causes an upset in the swallowing mechanism and the condition becomes progressively worse.

On barium swallow the oesophagus is very dilated, lengthened and occasionally sigmoid in shape (Fig. 2.4.6). When the patient is screened the barium will be seen to be held up for a considerable time and to pass into the stomach only when the pressure reaches a certain level. At the point of delay there is no irregularity and the barium emerges centrally as distinct from neoplasm.

TREATMENT. In mild cases treatment with anticholinergic drugs is successful, but most cases will come to surgery, when a Heller's operation is done.

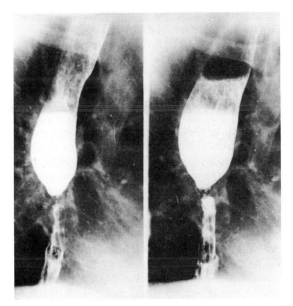

Fig. 2.4.6. Achalasia of the oesophagus, showing greatly dilated oesophagus.

MANAGEMENT OF A PATIENT PRESENTING WITH DYSPHAGIA

About half of the patients with dysphagia present first to an otolaryngologist. He should therefore know how to manage the condition and how to decide which cases should be referred to a thoracic surgeon or to a gastroenterologist, and which cases are best dealt with by his own discipline.

HISTORY. Dysphagia is an all-embracing term meaning difficulty in swallowing, but there are all shades of difficulty ranging from a mere local discomfort to a total hold-up to the passage of food.

The first thing to establish is the nature of the symptoms which are presented by the patient with phrases such as 'Food won't go down', 'Food sticks', 'Food comes back up', 'I've got a feeling of a lump in my throat', etc. It will be appreciated that there is a very distinct difference between food not passing and a mere feeling of discomfort in the throat.

The site of the problem is important. The oesophagus is shorter than one thinks—it begins just above the suprasternal notch—and symptoms from the oesophagogastric junction are often located at the xiphisternal notch. Patients are remarkably accurate in siting oesophageal problems. An example of this accuracy at the upper end is illustrated by the fact that if a foreign body is arrested just above the cricoid level the patient will point above the cricoid, and the foreign body should be seen on mirror examination, but if he points below the cricoid then he will need an oesophagoscopy for visualization of the foreign body.

The severity of the symptoms may be gauged by the amount of food and fluid the patient can swallow. Generally, when the patient is only able to take fluids or very soft foods there will be weight loss to confirm the desperate state of affairs.

An exception to this pattern of events is in achalasia where there is often more difficulty in swallowing fluids than solids.

Pain is not often a feature of dysphagia unless there is some degree of oesophagitis, most commonly due to acid reflux, but is occasionally seen in monilial oesophagitis. A very characteristic pattern of presentation of oesophageal disease is pain and discomfort at the lower end with a feeling of tightness at the cricoid level. This is due to the fact that lower-end oesophagitis causes reflex spasm of the cricopharyngeus muscle.

If there is a total block in the oesophagus the patient will immediately vomit everything he eats or drinks. This type of picture must be differentiated from a later regurgitation of undigested food seen with a pharyngeal pouch. If food builds up and collects in the oesophagus, such as occurs above a stricture, a tumour or an achalasia, then it will eventually overflow, enter the larynx, and cause at first coughing fits, and later aspiration pneumonia.

The age of the patient at presentation gives some idea of the pathology. Children may have congenital problems such as tracheo-oesophageal fistula, web, congenital vascular anomalies or hiatus hernia and they are prone to foreign bodies and corrosive burns. In middle age, while cancer must always be considered, the most likely causes are achalasia, oesophagitis from reflux and hiatus hernia, globus syndrome, Paterson–Brown Kelly syndrome and pharyngeal pouch. In the elderly the cause of dysphagia is cancer of the oesophagus until proved otherwise, although it may be due to osteophytes impinging on the oesophagus, diverticula or strictures from long-standing oesophagitis.

Enquiry must be made into precipitating factors such as the effect of position, various types of food, worry, etc. and alleviating factors such as antacids or tranquillizers.

Associated symptoms such as voice change may signify recurrent laryngeal nerve involvement or pachydermia due to reflux of acid burning the interarytenoid area. A large thyroid or retrosternal thyroid, an aortic aneurysm or a bronchial carcinoma can cause extrinsic pressure, as can osteophytes.

In the past history one must find out about any accidental ingestion of corrosives in childhood, treatment for indigestion or peptic ulcer and irradiation for thyroid or chest conditions.

EXAMINATION

1. *General.* There are few external signs of oesophageal disease. The patient must be weighed and assessed for weight loss. The neck should be carefully palpated for supraclavicular nodes on the left side and also for thyroid nodules or enlargement. The patient should be asked to swallow some water, and the swallowing efforts should be observed, and the neck palpated at the same time. The larynx should be examined for evidence of vocal cord paralysis or pooling of saliva in the pyriform fossa signifying hold-up. Note is taken of the state of the tongue, the corners of the mouth and nails as these are changed in the Paterson–Brown Kelly syndrome. The abdomen should be palpated for any epigastric tenderness.

2. *Laboratory investigations.* All patients should have a full haematological examination and where the haemoglobin is low or the film confirms a microcytic anaemia, a serum iron and iron-binding capacity test should be done. If they are

indicated, the thyroid function tests should be performed and if there has been vomiting or loss of weight the urea and electrolytes ought to be estimated.

3. *Radiography*. This forms the keystone to the examination of oesophageal disease. A barium swallow with or without a barium meal must be done in every case of dysphagia. If any abnormality is seen then it is usually followed up by oesophagoscopy. This is best performed by the person who is going to carry out the future definitive treatment. If no radiographic abnormality is seen then no immediate action need be taken, except in one circumstance. If the patient has ever complained of food sticking during swallowing he should have an oesophagoscopy because this is one of the earliest signs of cancer.

A chest radiograph should also be done in every case to rule out abnormalities that could cause extrinsic pressure, such as aneurysms. When the patient has aspiration problems signs are seen on the chest radiograph that may resemble cannonball secondaries. While these may well represent metastases, they may also denote patches of consolidation due to food debris and infection.

4. *Oesophagoscopy*. This is done with either a rigid or a flexible oesophagoscope.

SNORING

Snoring was until recently a symptom that was ill-understood and thus treated badly. It is a distressing symptom, not only to the performer but also to people in his room, in his building and even adjacent buildings. It is more common in the obese, the male, the over 40-year-old and drinkers. The cause is partial airway obstruction during inspiration which causes vibration of soft tissues in the oropharynx. Some snorers develop hypertension and even the sleep apnoea syndrome. Where simple snoring becomes the sleep apnoea syndrome is arbitrary, but sleep apnoea is usually defined as 30 apnoeic episodes lasting 10 seconds or more in a 6-hour sleeping interval.

Nasal surgery is appropriate where there is an obvious cause such as a polyp or alar collapse. The obese should lose weight and excessive drinkers may modify their habits. The application of continuous positive airway pressure through the nose has been suggested but is cumbersome.

In 1981 the uvulopalatopharyngoplasty (U3P) operation was first described and in most hands gives 90–100 per cent relief of snoring, but it only helps half the cases of sleep apnoea. In this operation the tonsils, the pillars, the uvula and a rim of soft palate are removed. The patients will have a great deal of pain for a week, and regurgitation of fluids and hypernasal speech for 2 weeks.

Chapter 2.5

NECK SPACE INFECTIONS

A fascial space is an area bounded by connective tissue. Deciding whether or not connective tissue is thick enough to be called fascia is rather like deciding the length of a piece of string. This is why there is no general agreement on the numbers of fascial spaces in the neck. Some anatomical texts list up to 20 such spaces, but in clinical practice only three are important, namely the retropharyngeal space, the parapharyngeal space and the submandibular space.

RETROPHARYNGEAL SPACE

ANATOMY. This space lies between the pharynx and the posterior layer of the deep fascia which bounds the prevertebral space (*Fig.* 2.5.1). It extends from the base of the skull to the posterior mediastinum as far as the level of the bifurcation of the trachea. Due to its anterior connection to the pretracheal space, infections can spread to the anterior mediastinum. Mediastinitis due to retropharyngeal infection is, however, rare. What is more common is enlargement of the lymph nodes in this space.

CLINICAL FEATURES IN INFANTS. Retropharyngeal space infection in infants is due to a lymphadenitis secondary to an upper respiratory tract infection. The child will be ill with a high temperature and a sore throat. There will be a smooth swelling on one side of the posterior pharyngeal wall with airway impairment. It may obstruct the posterior nares and push the palate down causing respiratory obstruction. This is made more dangerous by the fact that the infant's spine is short and the larynx is high.

TREATMENT. The abscess is not usually seen until it has fully developed and at this stage the only treatment is incision and drainage. General anaesthetic is dangerous because of the impaired airway. The infant is wrapped in a binder and held upright by a nurse. The abscess is opened with sinus forceps which are plunged into the swelling closed and then opened to release a copious flow of pus which is under considerable tension. The baby is turned face down to allow the pus to escape. This results in an immediate cure. Feeding becomes easy, the temperature drops and movement of the head is once again possible. Antibiotics are not usually necessary.

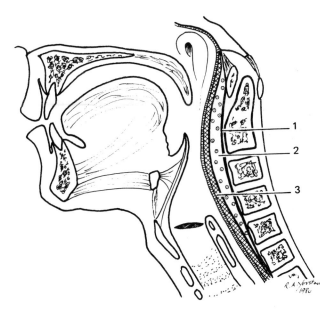

Fig. 2.5.1. Retropharyngeal abscess.
1, Anterior longitudinal ligament.   3, Superior constrictor muscle.
2, Abscess.

CLINICAL FEATURES IN ADULTS. If an adult or an older child has a retropharyngeal infection it is likely to be due to a tuberculous infection of the cervical spine. It is of slow onset and gives rise to pharyngeal discomfort, rather than pain, and to some degree of dysphagia. The lesion of the cervical spine is seen on radiography. The neck nodes and the ears should be examined for associated infection.

TREATMENT. The abscess is opened through an incision over the posterior border of the sternomastoid muscle and the abscess is sought for by dissection between the carotid sheath and the prevertebral muscles and is drained from the neck. Full antituberculous therapy must be ordered.

PARAPHARYNGEAL SPACE

ANATOMY. The parapharyngeal space lies lateral to the pharynx and connects posteriorly with the retropharyngeal space (*Figs.* 2.5.2, 2.5.3). Laterally it is bounded by the lateral pterygoid muscles, the mandible and the retromandibular parotid gland. Medially lies the superior constrictor muscle of the pharynx. It extends from the base of the skull to the level of the clavicle. It does not extend more medial than the larynx. The space contains the carotid artery, the vagus nerve and internal jugular vein, the deep lobe of the parotid gland, the sympathetic trunk and the upper deep jugular lymph nodes.

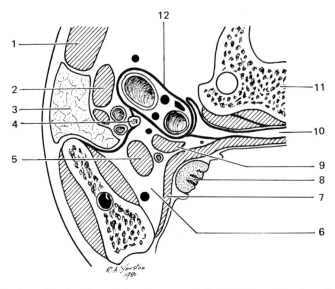

Fig. 2.5.2.   Horizontal section through the pharynx at the level of the tonsil to show the parapharyngeal space.

1, Sternomastoid muscle.	7, Superior constrictor muscle.
2, Digastric muscle.	8, Tonsil.
3, Parotid gland.	9, Stylopharyngeus muscle.
4, Styloid process.	10, Retropharyngeal space.
5, Styloglossus muscle.	11, Axis vertebra.
6, Lateral pharyngeal space.	12, Carotid sheath.

CLINICAL FEATURES. This is a rare site in which to get an infection. Sixty per cent of patients develop it as a complication of tonsillitis or tonsillectomy and 40 per cent as a result of either infection or extraction of the lower third molar tooth. Usually the root of this tooth is outside the space, but if it is slightly lower than normal and near the surface of the mandible it can penetrate the mandible and drain into the space with very little pain locally. Mastoid infection can extend into the space on rare occasions from two routes: first, via the petrous apex and, secondly, via the sheath of the digastric muscles.

There is fever and marked trismus because of spasm in the medial pterygoid muscle. The tonsil, if it is normal, is pushed medially. The most marked swelling is in the neck at the posterior part of the middle third of the sternomastoid. There may also be swelling in the retromolar region.

TREATMENT. Treatment is by incision and drainage. The incision should be vertical at the anterior border of the sternomastoid. This muscle must then be dissected up from the carotid sheath and no pus is usually obtained until dissection reaches medial to the sheath. The space should be opened from the base of the skull to the clavicle and a drain inserted into the lowest part. Antibiotics are given in the postoperative period.

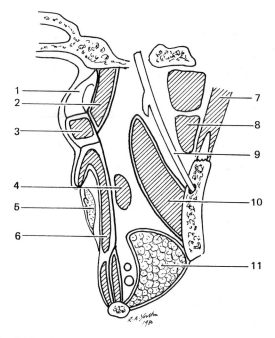

Fig. 2.5.3. Coronal section through prestyloid compartment of lateral pharyngeal space, showing relationship to base of skull, submandibular gland and oropharynx. (After Rouvière and Lederman.)

1, Eustachian tube.
2, Tensor palati muscle.
3, Levator palati muscle.
4, Digastric muscle.
5, Tonsil.
6, Superior constrictor muscle.

7, Temporalis muscle.
8, Lateral pterygoid muscle.
9, Inferior dental nerve.
10, Medial pterygoid muscle.
11, Submandibular salivary gland.

SUBMANDIBULAR SPACE

ANATOMY. The submandibular space is bounded above by the mucous membrane of the floor of the mouth and tongue and below by the deep fascia that extends from the hyoid to the mandible. It is divided into two by the mylohyoid muscle so that the submandibular gland, which is wrapped around the mylohyoid muscle, extends into both parts of the space. The space superior to the mylohyoid muscle is called the sublingual space and contains the sublingual gland. The space inferior to the muscle is the submaxillary space which contains this gland (*see Fig.* 2.11.1). Anteriorly lies the submental space between the two anterior bellies of the digastric muscle.

Infection of the space is known as 'Ludwig's angina'.

CLINICAL FEATURES. This is a rapidly swelling cellulitis of the floor of the mouth and submandibular space secondary to soft-tissue infection, tonsillar infection or infection of the lower premolar and molar teeth. Over 80 per cent of patients have dental disease, and in these patients the lower molars are set eccentrically with the roots closer to the inner than the outer side of the jaw, or the roots of the second and third molars may lie inferior to the mylohyoid line. Root abscesses of these teeth therefore drain into the submaxillary rather than sublingual space. This space may be affected with minimal discomfort from the tooth; pain comes from tension within the bone but if this gives way and drains there is no dental pain. In cases of dental origin the most usual organisms are *Streptococcus viridans* and *Escherichia coli*.

When the infection spreads to the sublingual space the floor of the mouth becomes very swollen and appears as a roll of oedematous tissue rising to the level of the biting edge of the teeth. The tongue is elevated posterosuperiorly and respiratory obstruction is a danger. The patient is very ill with a temperature of over 38°C, with pain, trismus and salivation.

TREATMENT. Treatment is by antibiotics; incision and drainage should be postponed as long as possible because pus is seldom found.

Chapter 2.6

TUMOURS OF THE NASOPHARYNX

CARCINOMA

PATHOLOGY. Nasopharyngeal carcinoma (NPC) is more common in South-east Asia than in Europe. It accounts for 18 per cent of all malignant tumours in China and over 80 per cent of all head and neck cancer (cf. Europe, 6 per cent). In Singapore the normal distribution of the population is 40 per cent Chinese, 30 per cent Malay, 28 per cent Indian and 2 per cent European; the incidence of nasopharyngeal cancer is 87 per cent Chinese, 10 per cent Malay, 3 per cent European and 0 per cent in the Indian population. It is high in the Kenyan, Tunisian and Alaskan Eskimo but low in Japanese, Korean and North Chinese.

Nasopharyngeal carcinoma is multifactorial in origin. The three major risk factors are : (1) A genetically determined susceptibility that allows an EBV (Epstein–Barr Virus) infection in early life of the type that permits (2) the integration of the genomes of the virus into the chromosomes of some naso-pharyngeal epithelial cells, priming them for (3) neoplastic transformation by some environmental nasopharyngotropic carcinogens that have gained entry into the infected cells. However, the only evidence suggesting that EBV may be a cofactor in the genesis of NPC is the regular finding of the DNA of the virus in undifferentiated and poorly differentiated NPC cells. In the southern Chinese there is strong evidence to show that the environmental factor is the ingestion of salted fish (prepared by salting and drying). This is of course not so in the Caucasians, in whom the maximum age incidence is a decade higher than in the Chinese.

The maximum age incidence is in the fifth decade and the male : female ratio is 2 : 1.

Sixty per cent of tumours are squamous carcinoma or lymphoepithelioma, 10 per cent are non-Hodgkin's lymphoma and the remainder may be adenocarci-noma, rhabdomyosarcoma, fibrosarcoma or plasmacytoma.

Most tumours arise from the posterosuperior wall or from the fossa of Rosenmüller. Origin from the floor or the choana is rare.

Fifty per cent of the patients present with no neck nodes palpable (N_0), 1 in 3 have a node on one side (N_1) and 1 in 6 have bilateral nodes (N_2).

CLINICAL FEATURES. Thirty per cent of patients present with nasal symptoms such as epistaxis or rhinorrhoea, 20 per cent with deafness, 20 per cent with a lymph node, 10 per cent with pain and the remaining 20 per cent with cranial nerve palsies, speech and swallowing problems, hoarseness or eye symptoms. In countries where both pulmonary TB and NPC are prevalent, blood-stained morning sputum due to coughed up postnasal drip is often a cause of delay in diagnosis.

On posterior rhinoscopy one may see a large exophytic tumour, but small tumours in the fossa of Rosenmüller may be missed. The palate may be pushed down or paralysed. There may be evidence of fluid in the middle ear or the eardrum may be indrawn. Tests of mobility of the tongue may display a hypoglossal paralysis. Eye function should be tested by an ophthalmologist and one should examine for a Horner's syndrome which would suggest metastases to the retropharyngeal node. Parapharyngeal spread can cause trismus. Alteration of sensation in the face, palate or pharynx would suggest Vth nerve involvement. Finally the neck must be palpated for metastatic lymph nodes.

INVESTIGATIONS. Radiography is the keystone of the investigation. Destruction of the base of the skull may be seen in about 30 per cent of patients—the sites involved may be the petrous apex, foramen lacerum, carotid canal and sphenoid wing. Patients with cranial nerve involvement will show bony destruction five times more commonly than others. Tomograms will be required to delineate the extent of destruction. If biopsy shows lymphoma, pedal lymphangiography will be required.

A CT scan is essential to show involvement of the soft tissue in the parapharyngeal and retropharyngeal space. It will also show tumour extensions through fissures or foramina at the base of the skull. It is, however, useless in detecting small tumours. For finding soft-tissue involvement magnetic resonance imaging is superior to CT scanning.

Audiometry, including impedance tests, will be required if there is any deafness. Field tests and other specialized ophthalmic tests will also be required. Full blood indices are necessary because repeated epistaxis may cause anaemia. The ESR will be raised in lymphoma or midline granuloma.

Biopsy should be done under general anaesthesia with the palate held forwards with rubber catheters. The nasopharynx is examined with a laryngeal mirror or a Yankauer's speculum, and biopsy forceps are passed through the nose. The operating microscope may also be used if no tumour is obvious. If no tumour is visible biopsies should be taken from both fossae of Rosenmüller and also from the roof of the nasopharynx. An adenoid curette may also be used and the scrapings sent for pathological examination.

EBV serology is used in cancer screening in high-risk persons such as first-degree relatives. An elevated serum titre of IgA to the viral capsid antigen (VCA) of 1 : 10 or greater may be the first indication of subclinical NPC. In such cases multiple nasopharyngeal biopsies are warranted.

TREATMENT. Radiation is the treatment of choice for carcinoma and lymphoma. The neck should be included in the field whether or not neck nodes are palpable. Surgery in the form of a radical neck dissection is reserved for patients where lymph nodes are not controlled by radiation or where enlarged nodes appear after the primary has been controlled. If the primary tumour recurs then a further course of radiation can often be given. The combination of radiation and adjuvant chemotherapy appears to offer no significant benefit.

The overall 5-year survival is about 35 per cent, ranging from 75 per cent for early tumours to 15 per cent for late tumours. The presence of cervical metastases does not markedly affect the cure rate. Women have a higher survival rate than men.

If further radiotherapy is used for recurrent tumour complications such as myelopathy, temporal lobe necrosis and cranial nerve paralysis can occur.

The usual staging procedures should be done for lymphomas. If confined to the head and neck, radiation on its own should be used, but if it is more widespread either chemotherapy alone or adjuvant chemotherapy should be used.

ANGIOFIBROMA

PATHOLOGY. This is the only benign tumour of importance in the nasopharynx. It is a tough rubbery tumour which usually arises from the lateral wall of the nasopharynx. It spreads anteriorly into the nose, orbit, ethmoids and around the maxillary antrum into the pterygoid fossa. It may also grow inferiorly into the oropharynx and superiorly into the base of the skull. It virtually never occurs in girls and its maximum age incidence is at puberty. It is said that the tumour disappears in the late teens, but many cases are described that have persisted into the thirties and forties.

Histologically the tumour consists of vascular spaces, with no contractile elements in the wall, surrounded by fibrous tissue.

CLINICAL FEATURES. The patient is nearly always a young boy with a complaint of nasal obstruction or epistaxis. If the Eustachian tube is obstructed there may be a serous otitis media. If the palate is pushed down or the nasopharynx completely filled there will be the speech defect of hyponasality.

On examination a mass which is smooth, lobulated and hard is seen on posterior rhinoscopy. Extensions of the mass may be seen in the nose or in the cheek. There may also be evidence of fluid in the middle ear. Cranial nerve palsies are rare.

INVESTIGATIONS. Radiography in the form of base of skull views and a lateral view of the skull will show a mass in the nasopharynx. Tomograms may show bone destruction, but this is rare unless the tumour is very large.

The distinguishing feature from adenoids is the tumour circulation which is shown by angiography. If an angiogram is performed in a patient with big adenoids a very vascular picture may be seen, and so the opinion of a radiologist skilled in angiography is necessary. All patients should have a CT scan and if bony destruction exists then primary surgery should not be used. If bony destruction is seen then magnetic resonance imaging is required.

Biopsy is too risky and should only be done if radiotherapy is contemplated.

TREATMENT. This depends to a large extent upon the angiographic findings. Embolization should be used if there is bone destruction with a liberal cross-circulation at the skull base, together with a vascular tumour. This may be followed by radiotherapy, but it is difficult to evaluate the success claimed by radiotherapists in this condition due to the frequent lack of pretreatment biopsy specimens.

In nearly every other circumstance, however, surgery is the treatment of choice. The approach is transpalatal and transantral. The tumour is bluntly dissected onto as small a pedicle as possible and then avulsed quickly. This latter point is important because if done properly and quickly blood loss is not too profuse and is easily controlled. If removal is slow and the pedicle torn then bleeding can reach dangerous proportions.

Cryosurgery is usually of no avail because the tumour is so vascular that an adequate ice-ball is difficult to form.

OTHER TUMOURS

The **oncocytoma** or oxyphil-cell adenoma is a tumour of minor salivary glands in the nasopharynx. It is always benign and simple removal suffices.

Plasmacytoma in the nasopharynx is usually solitary and the treatment is surgical removal via a transpalatal approach if necessary.

Craniopharyngioma and **chordoma** are extensive base of skull tumours, and reference should be made to more specialized texts.

Rhabdomyosarcoma of the nasopharynx is very rare, and is more often found in children in whom it may simulate an angiofibroma or a large adenoid mass on account of the nasal obstruction produced. Diagnosis is by biopsy. The regional nodes enlarge early, and middle-ear effusion may occur. Treatment depends on staging and good results can be expected from combination radiotherapy and chemotherapy.

Chapter 2.7

TUMOURS OF THE OROPHARYNX

PATHOLOGY. The oropharynx consists of four sites as classified by the Union Internationale Contre le Cancer (UICC):

Roof: Soft palate.
Floor: Posterior third of tongue and lingual epiglottis.
Lateral wall: Tonsil, anterior and posterior pillars.
Posterior wall: Posterior wall of pharynx from hard palate to hyoid level.

It contains squamous epithelium, lymph tissue and minor salivary glands and so tumours of these three elements can occur. Their incidence is as follows: squamous-cell carcinoma, 75 per cent; lymphoepithelioma, 5 per cent; lymphoma, 15 per cent; minor salivary gland tumours, 5 per cent. The site incidence of squamous carcinoma is: lateral wall, 45 per cent; base of tongue, 40 per cent; posterior wall, 10 per cent; soft palate, 5 per cent.

The UICC classification with respect to T staging is: T_1, a tumour less than 2 cm; T_2, a tumour between 2 and 4 cm; T_3, a tumour greater than 4 cm. The presence or absence of lymph node metastases is classified in the usual way, and the relative incidence is: N_0, 35 per cent; N_1, 30 per cent; N_2, 5 per cent; N_3, 30 per cent.

The incidence of tumours of the oropharynx in the UK is 8 per million, but it is higher in the USA, being 60 per million. The maximum age incidence is in the eighth decade and the male : female ratio is 10 : 1.

Lymphoma is limited to non-Hodgkin's types with a male : female ratio of 2 : 1 and a maximum age incidence in the eighth decade. Half of these tumours occur in the tonsil and 35 per cent have evidence of spread to other sites.

The commonest site for salivary gland tumours is the soft palate. Half of these tumours are malignant, the commonest type being adenoid cystic carcinomas.

CLINICAL FEATURES. The history is usually of sore throat, otalgia or dysphagia. Some patients have merely a feeling of a lump in the throat. About 20 per cent of tonsillar carcinomas present with a node in the neck as the only symptom.

On examination all the structures in the oropharynx should be seen perorally and with a nasopharyngeal and laryngeal mirror. The size of the tumour should be assessed not only by eye but also by palpation. A carcinoma is nearly always ulcerated, whereas lymphoma and salivary gland tumours are usually smooth enlargements. The neck should also be palpated to complete the staging.

113

INVESTIGATIONS. Radiography is not usually helpful except to see if there has been mandibular invasion. In a lymphoma, however, a pedal lymphangiograph and chest radiographs are essential. CT scanning will allow any parapharyngeal extension to be assessed.

Similarly, laboratory investigations have little to add except in the assessment of the general health of the patient. Biopsy should be performed under general anaesthesia so that the extent of the tumour can be assessed at the same time.

TREATMENT OF CARCINOMAS. Approximately 20 per cent of patients with oro-pharyngeal carcinoma are incurable for the following reasons: (1) highly anaplas-tic tumour; (2) bilateral neck nodes; (3) trismus; (4) Horner's syndrome; (5) distant metastases; (6) patient refusal of treatment; (7) advanced age; (8) poor general condition. Not all of these conditions are absolute contraindications to treatment, but the 2–3 per cent survival rate seen in patients with bilateral neck nodes, trismus and anaplastic tumours make one wonder if it is worthwhile subjecting the remaining 98 per cent to radical surgery or radiotherapy.

1. *Tonsil carcinoma.* If there are no palpable neck nodes then the primary treatment is by irradiation because the results are just as good as with surgery. If, however, there is a palpable neck node, primary irradiation cures virtually no one. These patients should be treated with a commando operation removing the fauces, part of the palate and base of tongue, part of the mandible and radical neck dissection. If the pharynx is closed primarily the oral cavity will be crippled and so reconstruction is performed with a pectoralis major myocutaneous flap. This not only gives reliable closure but the bulk makes up for the deformity that results from losing the vertical ramus of the mandible.

2. *Base of tongue carcinoma.* If the tumour is lateralized it may be dealt with as a tonsillar carcinoma, but the prognosis will be worse because the tongue will be more widely infiltrated than the tonsil.

If it is small and midline in the vallecula a supraglottic laryngectomy may be performed. This will not be successful if much tongue has to be removed because swallowing will then be too difficult. It should also be reserved for patients under the age of 60 who are unirradiated. The commonest presentation is where virtually the whole of the tongue base is involved. If surgery is to be used then a total glossectomy will be required because it will be impossible to preserve both lingual arteries. Furthermore, there will be spread into the pre-epiglottic space necessitat-ing a total laryngectomy as well. Radiotherapy is unlikely to cure a large tumour of the tongue base. On occasion the total glossectomy can be accompanied by a partial supraglottic laryngectomy instead of a total laryngectomy. The advent of myocutaneous flaps has made replacement of the tongue a straightforward procedure. The author uses a midline labiomandibulotomy approach and a large pectoralis major myocutaneous flap for reconstruction.

3. *Soft-palate carcinoma.* Because this is easily seen and assessed with spread only into the superior pole of the tonsil, radiotherapy is used as the primary treatment. If it fails the soft palate should be excised from a lateral mandible-splitting approach and replaced with a dental obturator.

4. *Posterior-wall carcinoma.* Again, for the same reasons, radiotherapy is used as the primary treatment. In the event of recurrence the posterior pharyngeal wall can be widely excised via a lateral pharyngotomy and a reconstruction performed with a medially based chest flap. A myocutaneous flap is usually too bulky for this site.

TREATMENT OF LYMPHOMAS. These should be irradiated and, if the assessment shows that they have spread outside the head and neck, chemotherapy should also be used. If a tonsil is suspected of being involved with a lymphoma it should be totally excised, since this gives the pathologist a better chance of diagnosing the type than does a punch biopsy.

TREATMENT OF SALIVARY TUMOURS. The biopsy should be incisional so that adequate treatment can be planned without the danger of previous implantation. If the tumour is a benign pleomorphic adenoma removal with a cuff of healthy tissue will suffice. If it is an adenoid cystic carcinoma or a mucoepidermoid tumour a wide excision should be planned because they are radio-resistant (p. 131).

PROGNOSIS. This depends on many factors such as type of tumour, size, neck gland metastases, age, general state of patient, etc. Lymphoma limited to the oropharynx does well, with around a 70 per cent survival rate, but it falls dramatically when it is outwith the head and neck. Adequate excision of benign salivary gland tumours should lead to a very low recurrence rate. Malignant salivary gland tumours do well in the first 5-year period (70 per cent), but poorly over 10 years (5 per cent).

With regard to squamous carcinoma, patients with tonsillar tumours survive much longer than those with base of tongue tumours. Soft-palate amd posterior-wall tumours are so rare that survival patterns cannot be accurately predicted.

Chapter 2.8

TUMOURS OF THE HYPOPHARYNX

ANATOMY. For the purposes of tumour classification the hypopharynx is divided into three areas (*Fig.* 2.8.1).

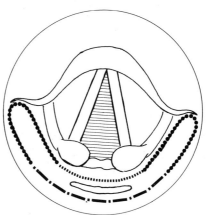

Fig. 2.8.1.   The areas of the hypopharynx.
● ● ● ● ●, Pyriform fossa.
■ ■ ■ ■ ■, Postcricoid region.
■ ▬ ■ ▬ ■, Posterior pharyngeal wall.

1. The **pyriform fossa** is paired and lies on either side of the larynx, being bounded medially by the aryepiglottic folds, laterally by the inner surface of the thyroid ala, superiorly by the pharyngoepiglottic fold and inferiorly it extends to the mouth of the oesophagus. Like the aryepiglottic fold which bounds it, the pyriform fossa has a rich lymphatic drainage and a relatively poor sensory supply resulting in tumours presenting late with lymph node metastases.

2. The **posterior pharyngeal wall** (*Fig.* 2.8.2) extends from the level of the hyoid bone above to the level of the inferior margin of the cricoid cartilage below and laterally to the posterior margins of the pyriform fossa.

3. The **postcricoid region** (*Fig.* 2.8.2) is in fact very small and is confined to the posterior surface of the larynx and extends from the posterior surface of the arytenoid cartilage and its connecting folds to the inferior surface of the cricoid

116

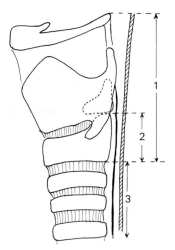

Fig. 2.8.2.   Lateral view of larynx.
1, Posterior pharyngeal wall.
2, Postcricoid region.
3, Cervical oesophagus.

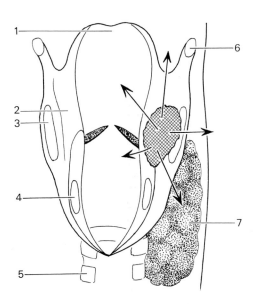

Fig. 2.8.3.   Routes of spread of tumours of the pyriform fossa.
(By courtesy of Heinemann Books.)

1, Epiglottis.   5, Trachea.
2, Pyriform fossa.   6, Hyoid bone.
3, Thyroid cartilage. 7, Thyroid gland.
4, Cricoid cartilage.

cartilage; its lateral margin is the posterior part of the pyriform fossa. Inferior to the cricoid cartilage is the cervical oesophagus but, although inaccurate, the name 'postcricoid' has been applied to the whole area around and including the mouth of the oesophagus. Postcricoid tumours *per se* are very rare and in this chapter tumours of the cervical oesophagus are included as postcricoid.

PATHOLOGY. Most of the tumours of the hypopharynx are squamous-cell carcinomas and their site incidence is as follows: pyriform fossa, 60 per cent; postcricoid/cervical oesophagus, 30 per cent; posterior wall, 10 per cent.

The pyriform fossa has the richest lymphatic drainage and so patients with tumours in this site have a 75 per cent incidence of lymph node metastases (*Fig. 2.8.3*); of these; about half will have bilateral nodes. Tumours on the lateral wall of the pyriform fossa often present as a mass in the neck—either a metastatic node or an extension of the tumour outside the laryngopharynx. If the tumour is primarily on the medial wall it will involve the larynx and cause hoarseness. Any tumour of the pyriform fossa may extend up to the tongue or downwards into the cervical oesophagus.

Most tumours diagnosed as postcricoid are either cervical oesophageal tumours 'coming up' or pyriform fossa tumours 'going down'. Because the oesophagus is involved the incidence of 'skip lesions', due to wide dissemination in the submucosal lymphatics, is high. Ten to fifteen per cent of patients have a second tumour in the oesophagus. About 20 per cent of patients with postcricoid tumours have a metastatic node when first seen. In this tumour spread also occurs to the paratracheal nodes and mediastinal nodes.

Tumours of the posterior pharyngeal wall are usually midline and exophytic. They are confined to the posterior wall until late in the disease and about 50 per cent of patients have a metastatic node when first seen.

Although squamous carcinoma is the commonest tumour, various sarcomas may occur. The carcinosarcoma or spindle-cell carcinoma is a polypoidal tumour usually arising from the posterior pharyngeal wall. It is slow-growing and relatively benign. Similarly, the leiomyosarcoma is a polypoidal non-aggressive tumour which does well with merely wide local removal.

Benign tumours such as leiomyoma, lipoma and fibrolipoma are also found.

HISTORY. The clinical picture of the large hypopharyngeal tumour is unmistakable. The patient has dysphagia at first for solids and then for fluids, with resultant aspiration and lung infections. There is weight loss of several kilograms and biochemical evidence of dehydration, protein and electrolyte deprivation and starvation. As the surrounding structures are involved, the patient will have dysphonia either due to direct invasion of the larynx or to vocal cord paralysis consequent upon recurrent laryngeal nerve involvement.

The diagnosis of the early case presents some difficulty, however. These patients will complain of a feeling of 'something' in the throat around the level of the cricoid. Unfortunately, so too will many thousands of other patients with oesophagitis or the globus syndrome. Every patient with this symptom must have a barium swallow and meal, but to pass an oesophagoscope in every one of these people would be an impossible task. Two symptoms help in sorting out patients with this symptom and a normal barium swallow; first, if they have ever had food sticking and, secondly, if they have a constant feeling of a crumb in the throat. Such cases must have an oesophagoscopy.

Although it is not premalignant, a surprisingly high proportion of these cases give a past history of the Paterson–Brown Kelly syndrome. What is more significant, however, are those patients who give a history of irradiation for thyrotoxicosis 25–30 years before.

EXAMINATION. Indirect laryngoscopy may show the presence of a frank tumour in the pyriform fossa or the posterior pharyngeal wall. It will not, however, show up a cervical oesophageal or postcricoid tumour—these will manifest themselves by oedema of the arytenoids, or by pooling of saliva in the pyriform fossae. If the recurrent laryngeal nerves have been involved one or both vocal cords will not move. In palpating the neck it is important to try to differentiate the mass which is a direct extension of a pyriform fossa tumour from a metastatic node.

Radiography. This is a mandatory investigation in all patients complaining of any dysphagia. The plain radiograph is of limited value but an enlargement of the soft-tissue shadow posterior to the trachea is suggestive of a postcricoid tumour. As a general rule if the soft-tissue shadow is wider than the body of a vertebra then it is abnormal. Tumours of the pyriform fossa may also destroy areas of the thyroid cartilage.

The key investigation is the barium swallow which should demonstrate 95 per cent of all hypopharyngeal tumours. The greatest use of this investigation is in delineating the lower end of a cervical oesophageal lesion through which an oesophagoscope may not reach. A chest radiograph will occasionally show multiple opacities which may be secondary deposits or patches of consolidation due to aspiration of food. CT scanning is useful in delineating extraoesophageal spread at the thoracic inlet.

Endoscopy. This will be done in every patient with an abnormal barium radiograph and also in those who have experienced food sticking or a feeling of a 'crumb' in the throat. The short oesophagoscope, the laryngoscope and the female small-diameter oesophagoscope are the most commonly used instruments. Not only must a biopsy be done but an accurate assessment of the extent of the tumour must be made because this will influence treatment. Bronchoscopy should also be performed to assess spread to the trachea.

TREATMENT POLICY. At the outset it should be said that the 5-year survival for any of these tumours is poor. Many of the patients present late with advanced tumours, and because of age, tumour dissemination and general condition about 1 in 3 are not treated by any modality. There is no such thing as 'palliative' radiotherapy in these tumours; they seldom have pain and radiotherapy will cause painful mucositis. Of those untreated, death will be by aspiration pneumonia in most instances. If the growth has been considered too advanced for successful treatment the general practitioner should be so informed, and he should not seek to prolong life by antibiotic therapy for intercurrent infections.

In nearly all cases it will be necessary to remove the larynx as well as the pharynx if surgery is chosen as the primary modality. On the other hand, radiotherapy does not show encouraging results, the best being about a 20 per cent 5-year survival. Another fact that must be borne in mind is the high incidence of lymphatic metastases.

Pyriform fossa. If the tumour is small and does not involve the postcricoid region radiotherapy should be the primary treatment provided there are no palpable nodes. If a node is palpable or if the tumour recurs a total laryngo-pharyngectomy should be performed. Reconstruction of this short segment may be performed with a free segment of jejunum and small-vessel anastomosis or by a pectoralis major myocutaneous flap. The main complication of this is stricture.

If the tumour involves the postcricoid region or cervical oesophagus a total laryngopharyngo-oesophagectomy will be required. Reconstruction is by either stomach transposition or colon. The patient then has postoperative irradiation.

Postcricoid. In this site the cervical oesophagus will be involved and because clearance will require to be at least a hand's breath, due to 'skip' lesions, repair with skin flaps is impractical. Because fresh tissue will be brought in for the repair and as lymph node metastases are less common, radiotherapy is the best initial treatment for small tumours. If it is successful, the patient will keep his larynx. If it fails, or if the tumour is large, a total laryngopharyngo-oesophagectomy will need to be done using either stomach or colon to replace the pharyngo-oesophagus. It is the author's custom to use stomach replacement. This operation is performed by two teams working synchronously. Intensive care facilities should be available for postoperative care. Postoperative radiotherapy is seldom used.

Posterior wall. In this site it is important to make sure of the histology of the tumour. If it is a leiomyosarcoma or a carcinosarcoma a wide local removal should be done and the patient followed closely for 5 years.

If it is a carcinoma radiotherapy should be the primary treatment unless a node is palpable, when surgery should be used. A lateral pharyngotomy is performed and the defect is replaced by a deltopectoral skin flap. In most instances these patients will be able to keep their larynx.

Chapter 2.9

TUMOURS OF THE ORAL CAVITY

The oral cavity for the purposes of UICC (Union Internationale Contre le Cancer) classification consists of: (1) the buccal mucosa, (2) the lower and upper alveoli, (3) the hard palate, (4) the floor of the mouth to the anterior tonsillar pillar, (5) the anterior two-thirds of the tongue to the circumvallate papillae.

PATHOLOGY. The vast majority of tumours within the mouth are malignant. Of these, 95 per cent are squamous carcinomas and the remaining 5 per cent consist of salivary tumours and malignant melanomas.

Oral cancer accounts for 2 per cent of all cancers registered in the UK and 1 per cent of all cancer deaths. Fifty years ago it used to be a disease almost exclusive to males with a male to female ratio of 10:1. There has been a 3 per cent annual decrease in the incidence of this disease in males over this period, and now the male to female ratio is 2:1. The maximum age incidence in both sexes is the seventh decade.

Of the squamous carcinomas 98 per cent are well-differentiated. Adenoid cystic carcinoma is the commonest salivary carcinoma found in the oral cavity, followed by mucoepidermoid tumours.

The UICC classification with respect to T staging is on the basis of size: T_1, tumours less than 2 cm; T_2, tumours between 2 and 4 cm; T_3, tumours greater than 4 cm.

Even though it would seem simple to diagnose a tumour in such an accessible site as the mouth, more than 70 per cent are in the T_2 and T_3 groups when first seen.

The nodes are staged in the usual fashion and the incidence in the oral cavity is: N_0, 70 per cent; N_1, 25 per cent; N_2, 2 per cent; N_3, 3 per cent.

The site incidence is as follows: floor of mouth, 40 per cent; tongue, 28 per cent; cheek, 12 per cent; hard palate, 10 per cent; lower alveolus, 10 per cent.

CLINICAL FEATURES. A painful ulcer or a painless lump is the patient's usual complaint. If there is pain there will be difficulty in eating and speaking. Dysphagia will also occur with any tongue fixation. Tumours on the alveoli or palate will interfere with dentures and an ulcer may cause halitosis.

Examination will show the site of the lesion and its extent. Assessment of the degree of fixation is made by asking the patient to move the tongue from side to side. Tumours may be exophytic, in which case there is not much infiltration, or ulcerative, in which case they infiltrate widely. This must be assessed by palpation.

The neck is palpated for nodal metastases. These usually occur in the submandibular areas or in the upper deep jugular chain. The tongue also has a direct line of drainage to the jugulo-omohyoid node.

The state of the teeth must be assessed because this will be important if radiotherapy is to be used. Usually, however, patients with oral cancer have very poor teeth or none at all.

INVESTIGATIONS. Laboratory investigations do not play a major part in the assessment of oral tumours. Formerly syphillis was often seen in conjunction with oral cancer but this is now very rare.

Mandibular involvement is also rare, but orthopantomograms must be performed so that not only can invasion be assessed but retained roots of any carious teeth may be seen. If the tumour is on the palate tomograms of the maxillary sinus should be taken to see if there is any penetration. CT scans are not widely used in the investigation of oral cancer but it is hoped that as magnetic resonance imaging develops assessment of tongue infiltration by tumours will be improved.

Biopsy is best performed under general anaesthesia because infiltration anaesthesia may lead to tumour extension. Also, when the patient is asleep the extent of the tumour can be assessed better. In the case of a lump on the palate incisional biopsy should be done because there is no danger of tumour spread, and accurate wide-field excision can be planned if it is malignant.

TREATMENT POLICY

General considerations. Resection of any part of the oral cavity affects chewing, swallowing, articulation and appearance. Reconstruction involves replacement of soft tissue and/or bone. Soft tissue is replaced either by a pectoralis myocutaneous flap, especially if bulk is required as in a total glossectomy, or by a free flap and small-vessel anastomosis. The best free flap is the so-called 'Chinese' flap from the forearm plus the radial artery, and often with part of the radius. This can supply missing mandible as can part of the 6th rib on a pectoralis myocutaneous flap.

Radiotherapy is fine if it is successful but if there is residual tumour or recurrence then detection is very difficult since it is so deep and biopsies tend to be negative.

Small lesions (less than 2 cm) can often be managed locally with either cryosurgery or laser excision.

Buccal carcinoma. Squamous carcinoma may be exophytic (usually at the oral commissure), ulcerative (further posterior in the mouth) or verrucous. Each is usually surrounded by an area of hyperkeratosis and if an unrepresentative biopsy is taken the tumour may be underdiagnosed and undertreated.

Exophytic and verrucous tumours should be removed surgically because good clearance can be achieved and radiotherapy often changes the histological character of verrucous tumours making a proportion anaplastic. Small tumours can be removed with primary closure but larger ones will require skin grafting.

Ulcerative tumours should be irradiated because they tend to penetrate the pterygoid area causing trismus and thereby becoming incurable. Surgery is unlikely to achieve adequate clearance in this area. In the event of recurrence, wide-field excision will be required and the defect in the cheek will require reconstruction with a myocutaneous or a temporalis flap.

This tumour is much commoner in India than in the UK and is probably related to betel nut chewing. If it occurs in an area where radiotherapy is not available, a hemimandibulectomy is to be recommended, together with the removal of the primary cheek tumour, in order to achieve adequate removal of the pterygoid muscles.

Minor salivary gland tumours occur on the buccal mucosa and often present as cysts. Local excision with an adequate margin is the first choice of treatment for these, but if it is adenoid cystic carcinoma excision over a very wide field is required together with complicated reconstruction, with either a myocutaneous flap and/or a free flap and small-vessel anastomosis.

Carcinoma of the hard palate and upper alveolus. Minor salivary gland tumours are usually benign in this site and are commoner than epithelial carcinomas. Local excision with preservation of the hard palate is usually possible, but if any doubt exists about the pathology it is better to remove some bone because it can always be filled with a dental obturator. If it is an adenoid cystic carcinoma then it will have to be widely excised with inclusion of the greater palatine nerves, since this is the usual route of spread to the cranium.

Squamous carcinoma in the hard palate is rare and may represent an extension from a maxillary carcinoma. This should be treated in the same way as maxillary tumours, that is, with a palatectomy followed by postoperative radiotherapy. The defect is filled with an obturator.

Carcinoma of the tongue. Eight out of 10 tongue tumours are on the lateral edge which means that cancer of the dorsum, tip and central surfaces is rare.

If the lesion is ulcerative and infiltrative equally good results are obtained from radon seed implantation and surgery. If the tumour is exophytic there is less infiltration and the results of surgery are better than radiotherapy.

In small tumours a partial glossectomy can be repaired with a split-thickness quilted skin graft. Up to half of the tongue may be removed with primary closure without crippling the oral cavity. If more than half of the tongue is removed it has to be replaced with a pectoralis myocutaneous flap.

Tumours of the dorsum of the tongue should be treated first with radiotherapy, total glossectomy being reserved for recurrences. Tumours of the tip can be removed locally with a 'V' excision, thus reconstituting the tip for articulation.

If a neck node is palpable a neck dissection should be performed, but if no node is palpable it is doubtful if an elective neck dissection materially alters the survival rate. If there are bilateral nodes the patient is virtually incurable and surgery should not be offered unless the tumour is in the anterior part of the floor of the mouth.

Carcinoma of the floor of the mouth and lower alveolus. Tumours in this area affect the jaw either directly or indirectly. For this reason radiotherapy should not be used as the primary treatment because later excision of bone, whether partial or total, will compromise the vascular integrity of the radiated bone and osteoradionecrosis may well occur.

If the tumour is in the anterior part of the floor of the mouth as delineated by the canine teeth, every attempt should be made to keep an arch of the mandible or else the tongue will lose all its support and the patient will have unmanageable drooling. If possible the floor of the mouth should be removed together with a partial mandibulectomy. If the whole anterior segment of the mandible is to be removed then it must be replaced by bone. Soft-tissue replacement is necessary to maintain the mobility of the anterior part of the tongue and this is probably the best site in which to use the 'Chinese' flap.

If the tumour is in the lateral floor of the mouth the mandible can be removed in a segment, if necessary, without much functional or cosmetic problem. It is preferable, however, to limit surgery to partial removal because at a later date dentures can be worn. The soft-tissue excision will involve the floor of the mouth and part of the tongue. If the tongue remnant is closed primarily to the buccal mucosa there will be some difficulty in eating and speaking. Soft-tissue replacement is therefore necessary and the choice lies between a myocutaneous flap, a free flap, or later split-thickness skin grafting.

If neck nodes are palpable on one side a radical neck dissection should be performed, but if bilateral neck nodes are palpable no surgery should be performed unless the tumour is in the anterior floor of mouth. If no nodes are palpable a suprahyoid dissection is recommended, not only for lymphatic clearance but also because it improves access to the primary site.

Prognosis. Surgery gives about a 10 per cent better cure rate than radiotherapy (a 60 per cent 5-year survival if all sites are considered), but the functional results are better if the latter treatment is successful. If there is going to be a recurrence then it is most likely to be seen in the first year. After 3 years it is unlikely that recurrence will be found.

The best functional results after surgery are likely if the patient can wear dentures because these not only help when eating but also help articulation. In order to wear dentures the patient must have a sulcus in which the flange of the denture can sit. This is why preservation of a mandibular arch is important and why thin split-thickness skin or thin free flap is a better soft-tissue replacement than bulky myocutaneous flaps.

BENIGN DISEASES OF THE ORAL CAVITY

ULCERS

Traumatic Ulcer

This is usually caused by biting or by sharp edges of broken teeth or dentures. If it does not heal when the provoking factor is removed then it should be biopsied.

Aphthous Ulcer

The aetiology of this common condition is unknown. These ulcers occur in a major and minor variety. The major form is usually one of persistent multiple ulceration continuing for many years. In the minor form a single ulcer or a small crop of ulcers appears on the mucosa several times a year, runs a short painful course and heals without scarring. Sixty-three per cent of cases of recurrent oral ulceration are of the minor variety and 12 per cent are of the major variety.

Herpetiform Ulcer

This forms 9 per cent of recurrent oral ulcers. It begins as a pin-head point which enlarges and coalesces. It goes on for several years and is commonest in women.

Non-specific Recurrent Oral Ulceration (ROU)

As well as aphthous ulcers and herpetiform ulcers, ROU can be due to some underlying disease such as vitamin B_{12}, folic acid and iron deficiency. These were found in 18 per cent of patients as compared to 8 per cent of controls. Twenty per cent of patients with ROU have a flat coeliac disease pattern on jejunal biopsy. There is no real evidence to incriminate the herpes virus. Adenovirus type 1 and *Streptococcus sargenes* have often been cultivated but their significance is not established. Food allergies are not associated with ROU. Seventy-five per cent of patients have a high level of circulating antibodies to oral mucosa. There may be a cell-mediated immunity to oral mucosal antigen in ROU and Behçets syndrome. A significant increase in HLA-DR$_5$ antigen is found in the latter syndrome. Finally it is seen sometimes in patients taking the beta-blocking drug propranolol.

Treatment is unsatisfactory. Responses to topical steroids and antibiotics are variable.

WHITE LESIONS

Fordyce's Granules

These are heterotopic sebaceous glands occurring in the oral mucosa. They present either as yellow-white pin-points, usually in the buccal mucosa, or as plaque-like configurations. They have no significance and no treatment is required.

Lichen Planus

This can occur as an intraoral disease with no accompanying skin lesions. The condition is often symmetrical, affecting the buccal mucosa, the lower lip, the alveoli and the border of the tongue. It may cause pain and on occasion this can be severe. It has no malignant potential.

Moniliasis

This presents as white multiple plaque-like lesions which can be scraped off easily. It is usually seen as a side-effect of broad-spectrum antibiotics and resolves with local fungicides.

Leucoplakia

Histologically this can be divided into three basic types: (*a*) a simple keratosis arising as a result of mild irritation; (*b*) various combinations of hyperkeratosis, parakeratosis and acanthosis; (*c*) a dysplastic type which can progress to carcinoma-in-situ. Less than 5 per cent proceed to carcinoma but in order to identify the type and the presence of any malignant change, every leucoplakic patch must be biopsied. Malignant change is commoner in females, in patients with a long history, in cases on the lateral edge of the tongue and floor of mouth, and in smokers.

RED LESIONS

Papillomas

These occur most usually on the soft palate, anterior pillar and buccal mucosa. They can also occur on the alveoli in patients with ill-fitting dentures. They have no malignant potential and simple excision suffices.

Pemphigoid

Bullous eruptions in the mouth may rarely be pemphigoid. Oral pemphigus is almost unknown.

Erythroplakia

This occurs in patches like leucoplakia and has a very high malignant potential. It should always be widely removed and a split-thickness quilted graft applied.

Granular-cell Tumour

This arises from skeletal muscle and it is not known whether it is a tumour or a degenerative or regenerative lesion. It occurs on the alveoli in the newborn in a female to male ratio of 8 : 1. It is three times more common in the upper jaw than in the lower jaw. In the adult its maximum age incidence is in the fourth decade and it can occur in any head and neck site, but 30 per cent occur in the mouth. Local excision is the treatment of choice.

Epulides

An epulis is a granuloma occurring on the gums. There are four types: (*a*) congenital: this is referred to above; (*b*) fibrous: this usually arises in the interdental papillae; (*c*) pregnancy: this is like a pyogenic granuloma and resolves when the pregnancy is over (granuloma gravidarum); (*d*) giant-cell granuloma or osteoclastoma: this usually occurs on the anterior part of the alveolus and usually on the lower jaw. The differential diagnosis includes the 'brown' tumour of hyperparathyroidism.

Haemangioma

Cavernous haemangiomas usually occur on the tongue and are best treated with cryosurgery.

CYSTIC LESIONS

Benign Lymphoepithelial Cyst

This usually occurs on the floor of the mouth. The clinical appearance is of a small grey-white nodule shining through the overlying mucosa.

Ranula

Ranulas can be either simple or cavernous. The simple variety is a true retention cyst of one of the minor salivary glands. The cavernous type is a cavernous lymphangioma and invades the fascial planes of the neck.

Dermoids

Only about 2 per cent of dermoids occur in the mouth. They may be sublingual or submental depending on their relationship to the mylohyoid muscle.

SPECIFIC TONGUE LESIONS

Median Rhomboid Glossitis

This is characterized by a reddish rhomboid-shaped area devoid of lingual papillae immediately anterior to the foramen caecum. It may represent the remnant of the tuberculum impar, but recent views suggest that it is due to infection with *Candida albicans*.

Geographic Tongue

Large or small areas of the dorsal surface of the tongue show atrophy of the filiform papillae, resulting in a smooth red mucosal surface in which the fungiform papillae become visible as little red elevations. The borders of the smooth area will usually be accentuated by a 'marginal' hypertrophy of the filiform papillae. The cause is unknown but stress has been suggested. The area becomes normal again in a few weeks or months.

Hairy Tongue

This is characterized by a hairy black-brown or yellow aspect of the dorsal surface of the tongue. Smoking seems to be a promoting factor. Aspergilli can be cultured from the surface.

Fissured Tongue

This is characterized by numerous grooves in the surface of the tongue. Along with facial paralysis and granulomatous cheilitis it can form part of the Melkerson–Rosenthal syndrome. It is also seen in syphilis, Sjögren's disease and iron-deficiency anaemia.

Lingual Thyroid

This is rare and usually occurs in women. It occurs on the posterior surface of the tongue and may cause dysphagia. When a lingual thyroid is suspected a thyroid scan should be done, since it may represent the only functioning thyroid tissue. It should not merely be diagnosed as a hypertrophic lingual tonsil and diathermied.

Chapter 2.11

SALIVARY GLAND DISEASE

SURGICAL ANATOMY

There are four main salivary glands—two submandibular and two parotids (*Fig.* 2.11.1)—and thousands of minor salivary glands. These minor glands occur throughout the entire upper respiratory tract, especially in the palate and oral cavity.

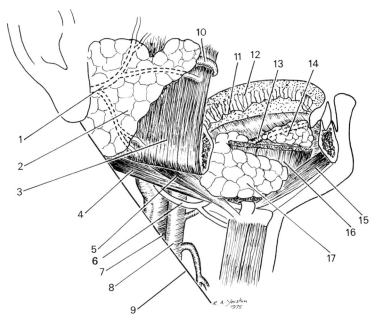

Fig. 2.11.1.   The salivary glands.

1, Outline of course of facial nerve within the parotid gland
2, Parotid gland.
3, Masseter muscle.
4, Digastric, posterior belly.
5, Stylohyoid muscle.

6, Hypoglossal nerve.
7, Internal carotid artery.
8, External carotid artery.
9, Anterior border of sternomastoid muscle.
10, Parotid duct.
11, Sublingual fold.

12, Tongue.
13, Submandibular duct.
14, Sublingual salivary gland.
15, Digastric, anterior belly.
16, Mylohyoid muscle.
17, Submandibular salivary gland.

129

The parotid gland has been likened to a lump of bread dough poured over an egg whisk—the dough representing the glandular tissue and the egg whisk the facial nerve. Most of the parotid gland lies above the nerve (the superficial lobe), the nerve lies totally surrounded by parotid tissue and the parotid tissue below the nerve is the deep lobe or retromandibular portion. Within the parotid fascia lie some lymph nodes, swelling of which may mimic parotid tumours.

The facial nerve emerges from the mastoid at the stylomastoid foramen lateral to the styloid process and immediately enters the parotid. As it enters the gland it divides into its upper and lower divisions two-thirds of the way to the mandible. The two divisions are the temporozygomatic and the cervicofacial branches, which divide into peripheral branches. The nerves to the forehead muscles and the upper and lower eyelids arise from the temporozygomatic branch and the buccal branch; and the nerves to the upper and lower lips arise from the cervicofacial branch.

The retromandibular portion of the parotid gland lies in the parapharyngeal space along with the carotid sheath, the vagus nerve, the sympathetic trunk and fat. Masses in this space, which lies lateral to the tonsil, may arise from any of these structures and may present in the pharynx, in the parotid tail, or both.

The submandibular gland lies under the mandible on the mylohyoid muscle. The posterior part bends around the posterior border of the muscle, and from this part arises the duct which runs on the floor of the mouth to open at the frenulum of the tongue.

Minor salivary glands occur throughout the upper respiratory and alimentary tracts, the commonest sites being in the buccal mucosa, the floor of the mouth and the soft palate. They also occur in the nasopharynx, the tonsil and the supraglottic larynx.

SURGICAL PATHOLOGY

There are two features of salivary gland tumours which make them unique. First, some tumours occur only in the salivary glands and nowhere else in the body, and secondly, as well as benign and malignant tumours, there are some which have very variable biological behaviour. These two facts, together with the difficulty of histopathological interpretation, have led to a profusion of classifications, none of which has been universally accepted.

The common benign tumours are the pleomorphic and the monomorphic adenomas, and the common malignant ones are the adenoid cystic carcinoma, adenocarcinoma, malignant pleomorphic adenomas and squamous carcinoma. Tumours of variable malignancy are the mucoepidermoid tumour and the acinic-cell tumour. Rarer tumours are haemangioma, lymphangioma, sarcoma, lipoma, lymphoma, metastatic tumours and the benign lymphoepithelial lesion.

The commonest non-neoplastic condition of the salivary glands is sialectasis, which provides the background in which calculi form. A number of medical conditions and allergies can cause sialomegaly and a number of conditions can mimic sialomegaly with no actual abnormality of the glands.

BENIGN TUMOURS

Pleomorphic Adenoma

This is also known as a mixed-cell tumour and comprises 60 per cent of all salivary gland tumours. In the parotid it forms 90 per cent of all benign tumours, but in the submandibular and minor salivary glands it constitutes less than 50 per cent of all tumours although it is the commonest benign tumour. The sex incidence is equal and the peak age incidence is in the fifth decade. In the parotid it is usually unilateral but bilateral tumours have been described. In the minor salivary glands the only site in which it presents with any frequency is the palate.

The tumour grows slowly with long quiescent periods and short periods of rapid growth. Some patients may have ill-defined local discomfort but it is usually symptomless apart from the lump. Pain and facial paralysis must make one consider malignancy.

The capsule of compressed normal parotid tissue varies in thickness and the tumour extends into the capsule in a lobulated fashion. This is why shelling the tumour out leads to the risk of local recurrence, which may be in several sites since some of the lobules in the capsule can be left behind. On the surface the tumour is greyish-white or blue with possible cyst formation and haemorrhage. Ten per cent of tumours are highly cellular and, although showing no malignant propensity, such a tumour is more liable to recur.

The tumours contain epithelial and mesodermal elements. The mesodermal parts arise from the myoepithelial cell which is a contractile cell surrounding the tubules draining individual acini.

Monomorphic Adenomas
Papillary Cystadenoma Lymphomatosum (Warthin's Tumour)

This is invariably benign and is found only in the parotid gland. It is much commoner in men, the male to female ratio being 7 : 1. The peak age incidence is in the seventh decade and 10 per cent of tumours are bilateral but rarely synchronously. The tumours are soft and cystic and are often fluctuant, and they probably arise from parotid tissue included in the lymph nodes which are usually present within the parotid sheath.

Oncocytoma

Oncocytoma arises from oncocytes which are derived from intralobular ducts or acini. They may undergo a diffuse multinodular hyperplasia known as onco-cytosis. It is seen most frequently in the sites of minor salivary glands, and the diagnosis must be borne in mind in the presence of lumps in the nasopharynx and larynx, especially in elderly males. It is also known as oxyphil-cell adenoma. It rarely undergoes malignant change.

MALIGNANT TUMOURS

Adenoid Cystic Carcinoma

This is the commonest malignant tumour and it may arise from any salivary tissue; it is, however, commoner in minor than in major glands. It comprises 31 per cent of minor salivary gland tumours, 2 per cent of parotid gland tumours and 15 per cent of submandibular gland tumours. The maximum age incidence is in the sixth decade and there is an equal sex incidence. The commonest presenting feature is pain and the tumour may be present for some years before diagnosis. It is some time before a mass becomes palpable or evident in many cases, and the patient may spend a few years visiting different specialists with regard to facial pain.

Lymph node metastasis is low (15 per cent) and is due to direct or contiguous invasion rather than to emboli. It tends to spread along nerve sheaths and this accounts for the large number of cases of preoperative facial paralysis (18 per cent). Distant metastases, especially to the lungs, are not uncommon.

The 5-year survival rate varies from 60 to 80 per cent but few series record more than a 30 per cent 10-year survival.

Adenocarcinoma

Adenocarcinoma forms 3 per cent of parotid tumours, and 10 per cent of submandibular and minor salivary gland tumours. The sex incidence is equal and it is one of the commoner salivary gland tumours in children.

There are three basic histological patterns—tubular, papillary and undifferentiated. The last type is usually very biologically aggressive and metastasizes instantly. There is also a 23 per cent incidence of preoperative facial paralysis.

Squamous-cell Carcinoma

This is a rare tumour in the salivary glands and almost never occurs in the minor glands. Two-thirds of the patients are men and the maximum age incidence is in the seventh decade. It is an aggressive tumour and shows no tendency to encapsulation. It grows rapidly causing pain, facial paralysis, skin fixation and ulceration. About half the patients have metastatic lymph nodes when first seen. It arises from the duct system and some pathologists deny its existence, considering them all to be high-grade mucoepidermoid carcinomas. It is also possible that some of these tumours represent metastases in parotid nodes that have spread from the lymph node into the gland.

Malignant Pleomorphic Adenoma

This has been used synonymously with carcinoma ex-pleomorphic adenoma (carcinoma arising from a mixed tumour). These designations signify two separate entities. The true malignant pleomorphic adenoma is very rare. The carcinoma arising in a mixed-cell tumour is commoner and represents 1–6 per cent of lesions of the mixed-cell category. It is commonest in the parotid, followed by the submandibular and then the minor salivary glands of the palate, lip, paranasal sinuses, nasopharynx and tonsil. The original tumour should have been there for at least 10 years. There is an accelerated recurrence rate and a high incidence of metastases (30–70 per cent). Not many series report a 5-year survival rate of more than 40 per cent.

TUMOURS OF VARIABLE MALIGNANCY

Mucoepidermoid Tumour

Since this was first described in 1945 debate about its biological classification has continued. This can be summarized as follows:

1. One view is that it is always a carcinoma whose behaviour is related to its histology. Low-grade or well-differentiated tumours act like benign mixed-cell tumours, intermediate ones are more aggressive and high-grade or undifferentiated tumours metastasize early and carry a poor prognosis.

2. The more recent view is that behaviour is not related to histological

appearance, and apparently benign tumours can eventually metastasize while initially aggressive ones can disappear with the appropriate treatment. For this reason the word 'tumour' is applied rather than 'carcinoma'.

Mucoepidermoid tumours can arise in any salivary tissue and constitute 4–9 per cent of salivary gland tumours. Nine out of 10 involve the parotid gland. In minor salivary glands, the palate is the commonest site, followed by the buccal mucosa, the tongue, the floor of the mouth, the lip and the tonsil. The age range at presentation is very wide and it is the commonest salivary gland tumour in childhood. The sex incidence is equal and the peak age incidence is in the fourth decade. If low-grade tumours are excluded there is almost a 50 per cent incidence of lymph node metastases. Five-year survivals of around 40 per cent for intermediate and high-grade tumours are reported.

Acinic-cell Tumour

This accounts for between 2 and 4 per cent of all parotid gland tumours and, like Warthin's tumours, it may be bilateral (3 per cent). It is rarely found outside the parotid gland. It is not uncommon in childhood but the peak age incidence is the fifth decade. It is of doubtful biological behaviour but 5-year survival rates of around 90 per cent make it a much more benign tumour than mucoepidermoid tumours. Attempts to predict biological behaviour from histomorphological findings have not been fruitful, but about 10 per cent do metastasize.

RARE TUMOURS

Haemangioma

Less than 20 cases of haemangioma of the parotid gland have been reported. The parotid may, however, be involved in haemangiomas occurring primarily elsewhere, like the skin overlying the gland and the infratemporal fossa. Spontaneous regression definitely occurs in some tumours so that no treatment should be offered until the age of 7 or 8, and then only if the tumour is enlarging.

Lymphangioma

There are three types of lymphangioma—simple lymphangioma, cavernous lymphangioma and cystic hygroma. The thin-walled lymph spaces invade the parotid and adjacent tissue and do not replace the glandular parenchyma. The tumours are soft and fluctuant and usually transilluminate. Total excision is virtually impossible and recurrences are common.

Sarcoma

Sarcomas may be part of the rare malignant mixed-cell tumour spectrum, but salivary glands can also be involved in osteosarcomas and chondrosarcomas of the mandible.

Lipoma

Lipomas, which are usually unilateral and lie external to the parotid, must be differentiated from fatty infiltration which is usually bilateral. Removal is uncomplicated unless it extends into the anterior compartment of the face, in which case the terminal branches of the nerve can be at risk.

Metastatic Tumours

The parotid lymph nodes may be involved by spread from carcinomas of the scalp and facial skin, especially melanomas. Adenocarcinoma from the digestive tract or urogenital system may present as parotid gland metastases.

NON-NEOPLASTIC SALIVARY DISEASE

Sjögren's Syndrome

In 1888 Mikulicz described a syndrome consisting of enlargement of the parotid, submandibular and lacrimal glands. Over the next few years the following conditions were added and Mikulicz disease became Mikulicz syndrome—tuberculosis, syphilis, sarcoidosis, recurrent parotitis of unknown aetiology and actinomycosis. Some years later, in 1933, mucous gland atrophy in the nose, larynx and vulva were added to the syndrome. Sjögren described xerostomia keratoconjunctivitis sicca and arthritis. In 1952 Godwin described benign lympho-epithelial lesion which is the same pathological process confined to the parotid gland. Sjögren's syndrome (SS) is the second most common autoimmune disease and it shows periductal lymphocytic infiltrates in multiple organs. The major salivary glands are affected in 35 per cent of cases. One in six patients will progress to full-blown lymphoma. It is classified into:

(a) Primary SS, or the Sicca syndrome, which consists only of xerostomia and xerophthalmia. These patients have a high incidence of malignant transformation and have a different genetic background to those with,

(b) Secondary SS, which consists of xerostomia, xerophthalmia and a connective tissue disorder, usually rheumatoid arthritis.

Investigation shows a raised ESR, positive rheumatoid factor, positive ANF and raised immunoglobulins. The Schirmer's test shows less than 5 mm tearing in 5 min and the salivary flow rate is less than 0.5 ml in a minute.

Definitive diagnosis is by sublabial biopsy and more sophisticated immunological tests (SS-A, SS-B antigens, etc.). Treatment is symptomatic but there should be awareness of the high risk of lymphoma. Parotidectomy is more likely to be required for diagnostic rather than therapeutic reasons. Lymphoma arising in SS has a much worse prognosis than lymphoma arising in a normal parotid.

Sialectasis

This is the salivary gland analogue of bronchiectasis—a progressive destruction of the alveoli and parenchyma of the gland accompanied by duct stenosis and cyst formation as the alveoli coalesce. Most cases are thought to be congenital and in childhood it may mimic mumps, but mumps seldom recurs. Fifty per cent have no symptoms after childhood and only a small proportion require treatment.

The typical presentation is painful enlargement of one salivary gland shortly after eating. It takes a few hours to regress and is made worse by eating again. Attacks come in runs lasting for days or weeks with long free periods of remission. These attacks are due to the main ducts being blocked by stones or epithelial debris. The parotid is a serous gland low in calcium and so the epithelial debris seldom calcifies, but in the mixed submandibular glands the epithelial debris from the necrotic ducts and alveoli calcifies and stone formation is common. Diagnosis is confirmed by sialography which shows alveolar cysts which empty poorly, duct stricture and clubbing.

Infections

The commonest infection of the parotid glands is due to the **mumps** virus. While other infections with bacteria are classically described in debilitated patients in the postoperative phase, parotitis can occur in otherwise fit patients. In young fit patients the most usual infecting organism is the **Echo** or **Coxsackie** virus. If secondary infection is not aborted in its early stages with antibiotics, parotid abscess will result. Since the infection is confined within the parotid capsule the gland becomes tense and is very painful.

INVESTIGATIONS OF SIALOMEGALY

HISTORY. The age of the patient is obviously important because mumps is much commoner in children than in adults. Although mumps can be predominantly unilateral, such a presentation should make one suspect a diagnosis of congenital sialectasis rather than mumps, especially if it happens twice. It is important to establish if the condition affects one gland or more than one. Tumours are unilateral apart from Warthin's on very rare occasions. Sialectasis also usually affects only one parotid gland although bilateral submandibular involvement is sometimes seen. Diffuse enlargement (sialomegaly) is caused not only by sialectasis but also by Sjögren's syndrome, drug allergies and a number of systemic conditions (*see below*), while tumours are always localized masses.

If the swelling is related to eating it is likely to be due to calculus disease secondary to sialectasis. No other sialomegalies are related to eating. The duration of swelling due to calculi is variable and may last from under an hour to several days. Benign tumours grow slowly, although if bleeding occurs inside a cystic tumour, such as a pleomorphic adenoma, the patient may become alarmed at a growth spurt. Malignant tumours increase in size fairly rapidly and are often associated with facial weakness.

Pain is a characteristic feature of duct obstruction by a calculus or infection (e.g. mumps). Adenoid cystic carcinoma typically presents with pain which may result in the patient seeing specialists in various disciplines associated with facial pain.

Systemic conditions such as myxoedema, diabetes, Cushing's disease, hepatic cirrhosis, gout, bulimia, AIDS and alcoholism may be associated with painless sialomegaly. Drugs such as thiouracil, phenylbutazone, isoprenaline, dextropropoxyphene and paracetamol (Distalgesic) and high-oestrogen contraceptive pills may also cause sialomegaly.

Finally, enquiry should be made into other symptoms which the patient may have, because sarcoidosis and tuberculosis may enlarge a gland as can hydatid disease.

EXAMINATION. Inspection should reveal which area is involved (*Fig.* 2.11.2), whether it is one gland or more than one, and whether it is a local mass or a diffuse swelling. Skin involvement should make one suspect a malignant tumour as should any facial weakness.

Palpation should determine whether the tumour is solid or cystic—cystic masses may be Warthin's tumours, cystic pleomorphic adenomas, branchial cysts or parasitic cysts. Solid tumours may be smooth or irregular, but this gives little help as to diagnosis because pleomorphic adenomas are often irregular and knobbly. Benign tumours are always mobile and any fixation should raise the strong suspicion of malignancy. In assessing any parotid mass one should ask the patient to clench his teeth so that the masseter is contracted; this allows one to assess if the swelling is in fact a hypertrophied masseter and it also lets one see whether or not the mass is inside the muscle (e.g. haemangioma or myxoma) or outside it. Complete examination of all the salivary glands is essential to decide whether the mass is single or multiple and whether or not other glands are affected.

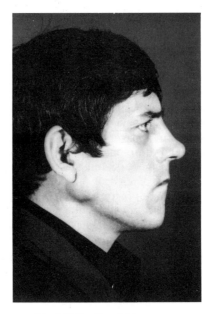

Fig. 2.11.2.   Parotid tumour.

All salivary glands should be palpated bimanually. In the submandibular area stones may be felt or moved, and in the parotid area pressure on a sialectatic gland may express pus from the duct.

No examination of this area is complete without examining the pharynx. Parapharyngeal tumours are either dumb-bell, in which case they present in the pharynx and also in the superficial lobe of the parotid, or deep lobe only, in which case they present primarily in the pharynx pushing the tonsil medially.

Clinical diagnosis of a salivary gland mass is usually not difficult but the following rarities should be kept in mind since they may mimic sialomegaly: (1) hypertrophic masseter; (2) winged mandible (in the first arch syndrome); (3) dental cysts; (4) branchial cysts; (5) myxoma of the masseter; (6) neuroma of the facial nerve; (7) facial vein thrombosis; (8) temporal artery aneurysm; (9) lipoma; (10)

lymphangioma; (11) mandibular tumours; (12) mastoiditis; (13) lymphadenitis of the preauricular node; (14) sebaceous cyst.

LABORATORY TESTS. The appropriate endocrine tests should be done to exclude diabetes, myxoedema or Cushing's disease. Rheumatoid factor, ANF and abnormal electrophoresis are often found in Sjögren's syndrome. Uric acid levels will be raised in gout. In all cases full blood and ESR investigations should be done. A Schirmer's test and salivary flow rates should be done if indicated. Electroneuronography is of help if facial nerve weakness is suspected.

RADIOGRAPHY
Plain films. Parotid stones are almost always radiotranslucent while submandibular stones are nearly always radiopaque. Intraoral films should be done in both cases. Plain films are also useful in differentiating many of the extrasalivary causes of sialomegaly.

Sialography. Sialography is the most useful investigation of salivary gland disease, but it must be performed by an experienced radiologist since artefacts can be created both by traumatic cannulization and by overfilling the gland. Its main use is in the assessment of a suspected sialectasis (*Fig.* 2.11.3). In congenital saccular sialectasis the characteristic snowstorm appearance is seen. There is extravasation of radiopaque material at the intralobular duct level and strictures and clubbing of the duct system may be demonstrated. In advanced cystic sialectasis large collections of dye are seen in the cysts and this is most marked in the post-emptying films. Both of these types of sialectasis can be mimicked by overfilling.

Pure duct stenosis is nearly always an iatrogenic artefact caused by traumatic cannulization. Some patients may stenose their parotid ducts by biting their cheeks, but submandibular duct stenosis can only be caused by operative interference in the floor of the mouth or by traumatic cannulization.

The use of sialography in tumour assessment is more restricted because clinical assessment is usually better; it can, however, give some idea of deep lobe involvement and also whether or not the mass is indeed within the parotid. It is useful when combined with a CT scan.

Scanning techniques. The early hopes that salivary glands could be scanned with technetium 99m pertechnetate have not been fulfilled. The finding that all tumours were 'cold', apart from Warthin's, has not been substantiated in the longer term and the technique is accompanied by an unacceptably large number of false-positive and false-negative results. CT scanning is of great use in the evaluation of a parapharyngeal mass and has made angiography unnecessary.

BIOPSY. On no account should a discrete salivary gland mass be subjected to incisional biopsy. Since there is a 9 in 10 chance that a single parotid mass is a pleomorphic adenoma, incising it is not only unnecessary but will almost certainly lead to a later recurrence. The only acceptable biopsy in such cases is by parotidectomy. If, however, there is skin involvement and undoubted malignancy then incisional biopsy is acceptable. Neither should a parapharyngeal mass be biopsied through the pharynx. If the mass is a chemodectoma the bleeding will be uncontrollable, and if it is a salivary gland tumour the recurrence will be unacceptable. On the other hand, diffuse enlargement of a salivary gland is probably not due to a tumour, and if a diagnosis has not been made after clinical, radiological and laboratory studies an incisional biopsy may be done. If Sjögren's syndrome is suspected then a sublabial minor salivary gland biopsy is essential.

Minor salivary gland tumours presenting in the oral cavity and upper respiratory tract have a high chance of being malignant. They are surface tumours and therefore incisional biopsy is to be preferred to excisional biopsy. This policy carries no risk of implantation but it does mean that patients with benign tumours will be subjected to a later local excision. On the other hand, if the tumour is malignant a correct treatment plan can be formulated and discussed with the patient with no danger of false security engendered by an 'excision'.

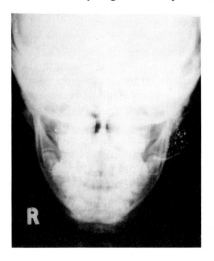

Fig. 2.11.3.   Sialograph showing saccular sialectasis.

TREATMENT POLICY

Benign Tumours

Parotid

The treatment of benign tumours of the parotid has passed through several phases during the past 30 years. Enucleation carried a high recurrence rate and so it was succeeded by enucleation and postoperative radiation. Recurrence rates were much lower in those series in which 'enucleation' meant not merely the extracapsular removal of the tumour but removal of the mass, together with a good cuff of normal parotid tissue. Since a proportion of facial weaknesses was due to these techniques, especially extracapsular enucleation, as well as the other risks, total superficial parotidectomy was next advocated. This was very successful in terms of prevention of recurrence, and the nerve was safe in the hands of skilled operators because the first step in the operation is identification of the facial nerve and its two main branches. It became evident, however, that the procedure was often too extensive; for example, removal of the upper portion of the parotid gland for a small tumour at the ear lobe seems unnecessary. Now, therefore, a hemisuperficial parotidectomy is often done (i.e. all the parotid tissue lateral to one main branch, either upper or lower, of the nerve).

Submandibular

Benign tumours in this gland are rare and are often misdiagnosed; the cause of the mass is often an enlargement of one of the overlying lymph nodes. This does not alter the fact that the operation of choice is simple removal of the submandibular gland, taking care to preserve the mandibular branch of the facial nerve, the lingual nerve and the hypoglossal nerve.

Parapharyngeal Salivary Tumours

The intraoral approach is vetoed on grounds of recurrence risk and also damage to surrounding structures. If the tumour is of the dumb-bell variety an ordinary superficial parotidectomy is performed, the nerve freed and the deep lobe removed, keeping the nerve intact. In the case of a very large tumour simple forward dislocation of the mandible doubles the retromandibular space to aid removal. If, however, even more room is required, a mandibular osteotomy at the angle may be performed.

Minor Salivary Gland Tumours

Once the diagnosis has been established by incisional biopsy, removal depends upon the site. In all sites apart from the hard palate local removal with primary closure is usually straightforward. On the hard palate there is always the possibility of extension into bone from the deep surface of the tumour. It would, however, be unnecessary to make a hole in the palate with the subsequent necessity to wear an obturator in every patient. This operation is reserved for highly cellular pleomorphic adenomas whose proven recurrence rate is more than 50 per cent. Other tumours are removed locally—the bare area on the palate can be closed with a palatal flap or left to re-epithelialize.

Malignant Tumours

Parotid

Radiation has little part to play in the primary treatment of malignant salivary gland tumours. It does, however, have an increasingly important part to play as an adjuvant to surgery, especially in adenoid cystic carcinoma which until recently has been considered radio-resistant.

Whatever else is done in the management of malignant parotid tumours there is little doubt that the whole parotid must be removed. What else is removed with it depends upon the size and position of the tumour. It will be clear once the parotid has been removed whether or not to remove the temporomandibular joint, the vertical ramus of the mandible, the mastoid, the external auditory meatus or skin. What is not so well established is what to do about the facial nerve. If the nerve is free of tumour it should be dissected out and left intact. This situation is rarely possible, however, because what one often finds is a nerve totally enmeshed in tumour with no apparent functional loss in the way of facial weakness. When the nerve is removed, immediate attempts should be made to bridge the gap with a nerve graft using the great auricular nerve which has the same diameter as the main trunk of the facial nerve. If this fails then later attempts to rehabilitate the facial paralysis can be made, provided the patient is clear of tumour, using a cross-face anastomosis technique. It is very rarely possible in parotid surgery to carry out faciohypoglossal anastomosis because the proximal piece and main branches of the facial nerve are almost always removed.

In adenoid cystic carcinoma, the nerve excision should be wide because the tumour infiltrates nerve sheaths and eventually travels intracranially. The facial nerve should be removed well into the mastoid, drilling it out of its bony canal. The great auricular and also the auriculotemporal nerves should also be removed.

In the rare cases of nodes being palpable in the neck a radical neck dissection is done, but if no nodes are palpable elective neck dissection is contraindicated.

The role of postoperative radiotherapy is not defined but consideration should be given to its use if margins of clearance are in doubt. A facial nerve graft will not be affected by radiation.

Submandibular

The operation here is wide removal of the submandibular gland, including the submental fat, the digastric muscle and the tail of the parotid. Depending on the extent of the tumour the mandible or skin may have to be removed also. Consideration may also have to be given to a full radical neck dissection. As in the parotid, if the tumour is adenoid cystic carcinoma, the lingual and hypoglossal nerves should be excised as far proximally as possible because of the infiltration of the nerve sheaths. Postoperative radiotherapy may also be considered.

Parapharyngeal Tumours

These tumours will almost certainly also affect the superficial lobe of the parotid and so the same considerations apply as are laid down in the parotid section (*see above*).

Minor Salivary Gland Tumours

These occur in any site in the head and neck and require wide-field excision.

Tumours of Variable Malignancy

Mucoepidermoid tumours and acinic-cell tumours present as apparently simple benign tumours and diagnosis is made after the excision is performed, as outlined in the section on the treatment of benign tumours. Further surgery is not indicated unless the margins are in doubt, and postoperative radiotherapy is advised. The patient should be followed at monthly intervals for the first year and 2-monthly intervals for a further 4 years in an attempt to detect recurrence. Should it recur, malignant potential is presumed and wide-field excision is undertaken followed by postoperative radiotherapy.

Sialectasis

The treatment of this depends on the severity of the attacks.

1. If the attacks of pain are mild and infrequent and if the swelling subsides in a few hours then the patient should be advised to finish each meal with a citrus drink in order to try to expel debris from the ducts. This is also helped by massage in the direction of the duct. Many patients have no further trouble after the diagnostic sialogram which flushes the ducts. Over 50 per cent will resolve with this treatment.

2. If stones are present treatment depends upon the gland in which they are situated and where in each gland they lie.

   a. In the **submandibular** gland, stones in the duct can be removed from the intraoral route by cutting down on the stone in the duct and marsupializing the duct open. If they are in the body of the gland the whole submandibular gland should be removed.

   b. In the **parotid** gland a stone in the duct is very rare and can be removed intraorally. Tympanic neurectomy, like all autonomic nerve surgery, works for a time but alternative nerve pathways are eventually formed.

3. If the stone recurs, or conservative treatment fails, a total parotidectomy should be carried out. A superficial lobectomy is insufficient and often results in a postoperative salivary fistula.

COMPLICATIONS OF PAROTIDECTOMY

Frey's Syndrome

Frey's syndrome consists of discomfort, sweating and redness of the skin overlying the parotid area occurring during and after eating. It is due to the severed ends of parasympathetic secretomotor fibres growing into the skin; when the patient eats, these fibres are stimulated (as they formerly were for the production of saliva) and they cause vasodilatation and sweating.

If asked about the symptoms 60 per cent of postparotidectomy patients will admit to some degree of this but only 20 per cent of patients actually complain of it. Spontaneous resolution within 6 months is usual, but a small number of patients require active treatment. This takes the form of a tympanic neurectomy which divides the parasympathetic pathway.

Nerve Damage

This is best avoided by using landmarks to identify and preserve the facial nerve. The two favoured by the author are:

1. The facial nerve lies 1 cm inferior and 1 cm medial to the pointed end of the tragal cartilage.

2. The angle created by the meeting of the posterior belly of the digastric muscle and the tympanic plate is bisected by the facial nerve. Identification of the nerve is aided by a facial nerve stimulator.

Salivary Fistula

This is a theoretical possibility in all superficial parotidectomies where a normal deep lobe is left *in situ* with a cut surface. Its occurrence, however, is extremely rare and it only seems to arise if a sialectatic deep lobe is left behind. It also occasionally occurs after open biopsy.

Most cases settle in a few weeks and anticholinergic drugs to cut down secretion seem to be of little value. Before removing the deep lobe it is worth trying to persuade a radiotherapist to administer the few hundred rads necessary to dry it up.

Cosmetic Deformity

After a total parotidectomy a considerable retromandibular depression occurs. This can be filled by turning up a muscle flap from the sternomastoid to fill the area.

Chapter 2.12

ANATOMY OF THE LARYNX

The larynx is an integral part of the respiratory tract and is the organ of voice production. Only the essential parts of the anatomy will be dealt with in this chapter as specialized points will be mentioned in chapters relating to the appropriate diseases.

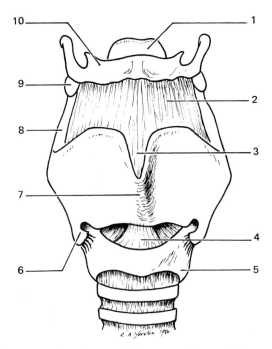

Fig. 2.12.1.   Anterior aspect of cartilages and ligaments of larynx. (Redrawn from Cunningham's *Textbook of Anatomy.*)

1, Epiglottic cartilage.   6, Inferior horn of thyroid cartilage.
2, Thyrohyoid membrane.   7, Thyroid prominence.
3, Superior thyroid notch.   8, Superior horn of thyroid cartilage.
4, Cricothyroid ligament.   9, Cartilage triticea.
5, Cricoid cartilage.   10, Hyoid bone.

SKELETON

The main part of the laryngeal skeleton is formed by the thyroid cartilage which articulates with the cricoid inferiorly. The hyoid bone lies superiorly (*Fig.* 2.12.1). The epiglottis is attached to the thyroid prominence (Adam's apple) at the level of the vocal cords and forms the anterior wall of the laryngeal compartment. Anterior to the epiglottis (between the epiglottis and the thyroid cartilage, thyrohyoid membrane and hyoid) is the pre-epiglottic fat (*Fig.* 2.12.2), an area into which cancer spreads readily. From the sides of the epiglottis two folds of mucosa pass posteriorly to be attached to the arytenoids; these are the aryepiglottic folds and they form the lateral wall of the upper laryngeal compartment (*Fig.* 2.12.3). They have a very rich lymphatic supply and so tumours of this area have a 3 in 4 chance of producing a metastatic neck node. Laterally, the space between the aryepiglottic fold and the thyroid cartilage is the pyriform fossa, which is part of the pharynx. Food passes over the back of the tongue and down the lateral food channels formed by the pyriform fossae before entering the oesophagus. Inferiorly, the aryepiglottic fold turns laterally to form the laryngeal ventricle immediately superior to the vocal cords (folds). The thick area where it turns laterally is the false vocal cord (ventricular folds) and shares the same rich lymphatic drainage.

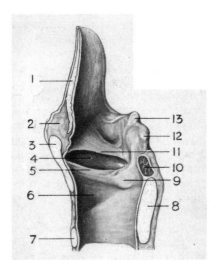

Fig. 2.12.2. Larynx, vertical median section, seen from left side.

1, Epiglottis.	9, Respiratory glottis, showing submu-
2, Adipose tissue.	cous position of arytenoid cartilage.
3, Thyroid cartilage.	10, Arytenoideus muscle.
4, Ventricle.	11, Vestibular fold or
5, Vocal cord or fold.	false vocal cord.
6, Cricothyroid membrane.	12, Corniculate cartilage.
7,8, Cricoid cartilage.	13, Cuneiform cartilage.

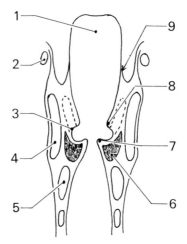

Fig. 2.12.3.   The compartments of the larynx.
1, Epiglottis.   6, Thyroarytenoid
2, Hyoid bone.   muscle.
3, Ventricle of larynx. 7, Vocal fold.
4, Thyroid cartilage.   8, Vestibular fold.
5, Cricoid cartilage   9, Aryepiglottic
                                     fold.

The laryngeal ventricle (*Fig.* 2.12.2) is the site of the primitive air sac and lies between the vocal and ventricular folds. It is the potential origin of a laryngocele.

Articulating with the upper border of the cricoid cartilage are the arytenoid cartilages to which are attached the vocal cords. The arytenoids are pyramidal in shape and have an anterior projection called the vocal process, to which the vocal cords are attached, and a lateral projection called the muscular process to which the main abducting and adducting muscles are attached (*Fig.* 2.12.4). The crico-arytenoid joint and the cricothyroid joint are synovial joints and may be affected by all synovial joint diseases. The arytenoids adduct and abduct on the cricoid, closing and opening the vocal cords. The thyroid cartilage moves in relation to the cricoid at the cricothyroid joint causing lengthening and shortening of the vocal cords (*Fig.* 2.12.2).

From the upper border of the cricoid cartilage the cricothyroid ligament arises and is attached to the thyroid prominence anteriorly and the vocal process posteriorly. The free edge is the vocal ligament. The epiglottis is composed of yellow elastic cartilage and never ossifies. The thyroid and cricoid cartilages are hyaline and begin ossifying after the age of 25 in a patchy fashion—this is well seen in radiographs of the neck in older patients.

MUSCLES

One muscle abducts (opens) the vocal cords, two adduct (close) them, one adjusts the length and two adjust the tension.

Posterior Cricoarytenoid Muscle

This paired muscle arises from the posterior surface of the cricoid and is attached to the muscular process of the arytenoid. As it contracts the arytenoid is rotated around its axis, the vocal processes move laterally and the cords abduct (*Fig.* 2.12.4).

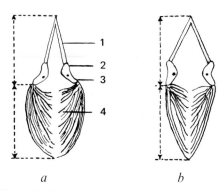

a   *b*

Fig. 2.12.4.   To show action of posterior cricoarytenoid muscle (diagrammatic).
a, The muscle 4 is at rest, the vocal process 2 is pointing medially, the muscular process 3 lies further to the side and the vocal folds 1 are only slightly separated.
b, The muscles are contracted, the conditions are reversed and the glottis is widely open.

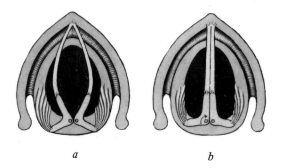

a   *b*

Fig. 2.12.5.   Showing action of the lateral cricoarytenoid muscle.
a, The muscle at rest—the glottis is open and the vocal processes are separated (note the posterior approximation of the arytenoids due to the action of the arytenoideus).
b, The muscle in action—the vocal processes are approximated and the glottis is closed.

Lateral Cricoarytenoid Muscle

This paired muscle arises from the lateral part of the cricoid arch and runs obliquely posterosuperiorly to be attached to the muscular process of the arytenoid. On contraction, the muscular process is drawn anteriorly, the vocal process medially and the cords adduct and close (*Fig.* 2.12.5). This action is aided by the **interarytenoid muscle** which is unpaired and is attached to the posterior surface of both arytenoids.

Cricothyroid Muscle

This muscle arises from the oblique line on the lateral surface of the thyroid lamina and is attached to the anterior face of the cricoid arch. As it contracts, it approximates the cricoid and thyroid anteriorly and lengthens the distance between the thyroid prominence and the arytenoids, thus lengthening the vocal cords (*Fig.* 2.12.6).

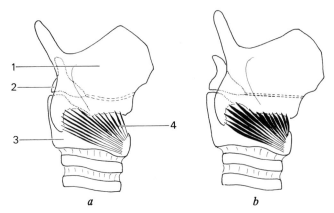

Fig. 2.12.6.   The action of the cricothyroid muscle at rest (*a*) and in action (*b*). In *b* note the approximation of the large cartilages anteriorly by the shortening of the muscle, the backward movement of the arytenoid and the lengthened vocal cord.
1, Thyroid cartilage.   3, Cricoid.
2, Arytenoid.   4, Cricothyroid muscle.

Thyroarytenoid Muscle

With its specialized free edge portion, the **vocalis muscle**, the thyroarytenoid muscle forms the bulk of the vocal cord. It is attached to the inner border of the cricoid cartilage and fans superiorly and medially to be attached to the vocal process posteriorly, the thyroid prominence anteriorly and its free edge joins the vocal ligament. On contraction they shorten the cord but their main action is to adjust the tension in the cord consequent on changes in length.

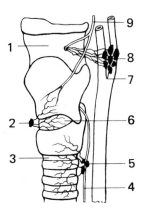

Fig. 2.12.7.   Nerves and lymphatics of larynx.
1, Hyothyroid membrane.
2, Small lymphatic gland over front of cricothyroid membrane, and lymphatics draining into it.
3, Cricotracheal membrane.
4, Recurrent laryngeal nerve.
5, Lower group of lymphatic glands.
6, Cricothyroid membrane.
7, Bifurcation of common carotid artery.
8, Group of glands at bifurcation, with lymphatics draining upper region of larynx.
9, Superior laryngeal nerve, with internal (sensory mostly) and external (motor to cricothyroid) divisions.

NERVE SUPPLY

All the above muscles, apart from the cricothyroid, are supplied by the recurrent laryngeal nerve; the cricothyroid is supplied by the external branch of the superior laryngeal nerve—a branch of the vagus (*Fig.* 2.12.7). This dual nerve supply is one of the reasons for different positions of the vocal cord after neural paralysis. The longer course of the left recurrent laryngeal nerve makes left-sided lesions commoner than right-sided ones (*Fig.* 2.12.8).

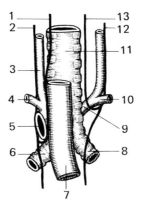

Fig. 2.12.8. To show the comparative course of the right and left recurrent laryngeal nerves (back view).

1, Left recurrent laryngeal.
2, Left vagus.
3, Left common carotid artery.
4, Left subclavian artery.
5, Aorta.
6, Left bronchus.
7, Oesophagus.

8, Right bronchus.
9, Innominate artery.
10, Right subclavian artery.
11, Trachea.
12, Right vagus.
13, Right recurrent laryngeal nerve.

BLOOD SUPPLY

The larynx above the vocal cords is supplied and drained by the superior laryngeal artery and vein which enter the larynx through the thyrohyoid membrane. The region below the cords is supplied and drained by the inferior laryngeal artery and vein—branches of the inferior thyroid artery.

LYMPHATIC DRAINAGE

The vocal cords have, to all intents and purposes, no lymph drainage; occasionally a small node on the cricothyroid membrane (*Fig.* 2.12.7) is described—the delphian node—but its involvement in tumour spread is very rare. The cords thus act as a lymphatic watershed and very effectively divide the supraglottis from the subglottis, a most important fact in partial laryngectomy.

The supraglottis drains upwards via the superior laryngeal lymphatic pedicle which pierces the thyrohyoid membrane and ends in the upper deep cervical chain (*Fig.* 2.12.7).

The subglottis drains to both the prelaryngeal and the paratracheal nodes and also directly to the lower deep cervical chain and the mediastinum (*Fig.* 2.12.7).

HISTOLOGY

The larynx is lined by two different types of epithelium—squamous over the true cord and the upper quarter of the posterior surface of the epiglottis, and low columnar ciliated over the rest of the larynx. This latter type commonly undergoes squamous metaplasia in response particularly to atmospheric pollution and smoking.

The supraglottis is rich in mucous glands and lymphatics and so metastases are commoner in supraglottic tumours than others. There are no mucous glands in the glottis and very few in the subglottis. This latter compartment has a much poorer lymph drainage than the supraglottis, accounting for the fact that only 1 in 5 patients with subglottic cancer have metastatic lymph nodes.

The mucosa of the glottis and supraglottis is firmly bound down to the underlying tissue, but not so in the subglottic region. Here, the laxity of the tissue allows a dangerous degree of oedema, especially in children, where the diameter of the area is relatively smaller than in the adult. In this situation, a degree of oedema, which would not cause too much trouble to an adult, could be fatal in childhood.

LARYNGEAL COMPARTMENTS

The larynx is divided into three different compartments, namely, the glottis, supraglottis and subglottis. This division is not only of academic anatomical interest but is of prime importance in the staging and treatment of cancer of the larynx.

The glottis is basically composed of the vocal cords from the extreme lateral edge of the cord to the inferior border of the medial surface of the cord. Anteriorly it extends from the anterior commissure (which is where the vocal cords meet) to the posterior commissure (where the arytenoids meet). Approximately half the length of the glottis is formed by the arytenoid body and vocal process (i.e. cartilage) and half by the membranous vocal cord.

The subglottis extends from the lower border of the glottis to the inferior border of the cricoid. Below this is the trachea. The subglottis is dome-shaped and is relatively small and restricted.

The supraglottis extends from the upper border of the glottis inferiorly (the ventricle of the larynx) to the hyoid bone superiorly, being bounded laterally by the aryepiglottic folds; the pyriform fossa, which is part of the pharynx, begins at the edge of the aryepiglottic folds. The suprahyoid epiglottis and vallecula are considered part of the oropharynx.

LARYNGEAL SPACES

There are three laryngeal spaces that are important in the spread of cancer and the creation of stenosis after injury:

1. *Pre-epiglottic space*: This lies between the anterior surface of the epiglottis and the hyoid body, the thyrohyoid membrane and the upper half of the thyroid cartilage. It extends from the vallecula to the anterior commissure.

2. *Interarytenoid space*: To allow the arytenoids to abduct, the mucosa between

them is lax and there is a potential space around the interarytenoid muscle which can cause problems with arytenoid movement if interfered with.

3. *Paraglottic space*: The importance of this space in the spread of laryngeal cancer has been highlighted since the advent of whole larynx sections. It is a long space that is bounded medially by the false cord, the ventricle, the vocal cords and the subglottis (i.e. the cricothyroid membrane). Laterally it is bounded by the thyroid cartilage, the cricoid cartilage and the cricothyroid muscle. Superiorly it is bounded by the aryepiglottic fold. Inferiorly it goes to the point of confluence of the subglottic mucosa and the lower border of the cricoid. Posteriorly it is bounded by the pyriform fossa and anteriorly it meets the pre-epiglottic space.

Fig. 2.12.9.   Glottis on inspiration.

Fig. 2.12.10.   Glottis on phonation.

FUNCTION

The functions of the larynx are: (1) to protect the lung, (2) to control airflow and (3) to initiate phonation. The protective function is well known to all who have choked on a crumb and have experienced the laryngeal spasm which follows. It is provided by three sphincter-like actions: (*a*) the approximation of the aryepiglottic folds assisted by the epiglottis which tilts posteriorly, (*b*) the apposition of the false cords (ventricular folds) and (*c*) the closure of the vocal cords (folds) to prevent the entry of foreign material. During this phase respiration is arrested but once the foreign particle is ejected into the hypopharynx a long inspiration occurs.

During respiration the vocal cords abduct during inspiration (*Fig.* 2.12.9), the abduction being greater during forced inspiration, and they adduct to some extent although never completely during expiration.

Adduction of the vocal cords (*Fig.* 2.12.10) is essential for clear phonation, and anything which prevents this, whether it be oedema, tumour or paralysis, results in dysphonia. The cords also adduct fully during coughing.

Voice production is fully discussed in Chapter 2.14.

Chapter 2.13

INVESTIGATION
OF LARYNGEAL DISEASE

HISTORY. As the patient gives his history it is possible to form some opinion as to the cause of the voice problem. If he is aphonic the vocal cords are not meeting, and if he is dysphonic the vocal cords are meeting but the mucosal surfaces are damaged in some way. The volume and the quality of the voice can also give some help in cases of voice strain, neuromuscular problems and hysteria.

Inquiry must be made about the onset of the problem and its progress since the onset. The onset of a vocal cord paralysis is sudden and the voice gradually improves as the mobile cord compensates. On the other hand, the onset of a carcinoma or vocal cord polyp or nodule is gradual, and the hoarseness increases as time passes. Most inflammatory conditions start fairly quickly and then gradually improve. One must inquire about precipitating and alleviating factors.

Not many laryngeal conditions, apart from cancer, arthritis and perichondritis, give rise to pain but many laryngeal conditions may cause an irritating cough. Laryngeal pain is usually referred to the ear. The larynx may also ache in voice strain.

If the arytenoids are swollen they will partially obstruct and overhang the mouth of the oesophagus causing dysphagia. Another form of difficulty in swallowing may be caused if the vocal cords fail to meet. In this event swallowing is incoordinate because the patient cannot create a positive subglottic pressure when the glottis is open, with the result that food tends to enter the trachea through the gap to give rise to bouts of coughing.

The patient's social habits must be investigated, especially with respect to smoking, exposure to occupational air pollution and vocal abuse. With regard to vocal abuse one must not forget that shouting at a deaf relative in the home is every bit as traumatic as vocal abuse at work. Ask about indigestion and reflux since mild acid burns of the interarytenoid area can cause hoarseness.

Lastly, enquiry must be made regarding the general health and past medical history of the patient.

GENERAL EXAMINATION. While examination of the larynx is of paramount importance a general examination must be performed. The neck is examined for lymph node enlargement or added masses on the larynx. The size, shape and mobility of the laryngeal framework are studied. The ears and nasopharynx are examined because tumours in these areas may paralyse the laryngeal nerves.

Myxoedema often affects the larynx and therefore the configuration of the thyroid gland and the skin, hair and nails of the patient must be examined.

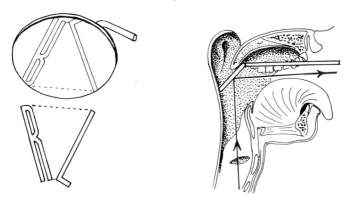

Fig. 2.13.1.   Indirect laryngoscopy.
a, The placing of the mirror against the soft palate to obtain a reflected image.
b, The right and left vocal cords are reversed in the mirror (cf. *Fig*. 2.13.2).

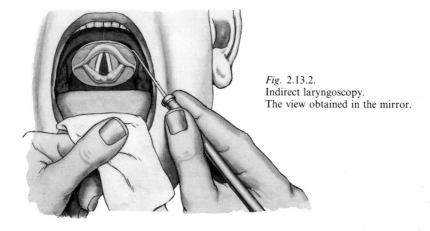

Fig. 2.13.2.
Indirect laryngoscopy.
The view obtained in the mirror.

INDIRECT LARYNGOSCOPY. It is impossible to teach indirect laryngoscopy by the written word. Nothing can take the place of practice in order to learn the skill.

The patient is asked to protrude his tongue as far as possible and the anterior part of the tongue is grasped by a swab held in the left hand. Edentulous patients should have removed their dentures. The patient is requested to breathe quietly through the mouth and the previously heated mirror is placed gently on the anterior surface of the uvula (*Fig*. 2.13.1). The light illuminates the mirror and the laryngeal image is seen as shown in *Figs*. 2.13.1 and 2.13.2. The anterior part of the larynx—the epiglottis and the anterior commissure—is seen towards the top of the mirror, and the posterior part—the arytenoids and the posterior commissure—is seen at the lower portion of the mirror. The patient's right vocal cord is on the left side of the mirror as the examiner looks at it. The patient is asked to continue to breathe gently through the mouth so that the form and colour of all parts of the larynx may be examined (*Fig.* 2.13.3). One first examines the vallecula and the tip of the epiglottis, and then the aryepiglottic folds and the pyriform fossae on each side, and from there attention is directed medially to the mouth of the oesophagus and the arytenoids. The false cords (ventricular folds) and the normally white vocal cords (vocal folds) are next inspected. It is sometimes possible to see the upper few centimetres of the trachea through the glottis. Finally, the movements of the vocal cords are studied by asking the patient to phonate 'ee' scveral times, when the glottis should normally close.

It may not be possible to do an indirect laryngoscopy on some patients due to an overactive gag reflex. In these cases the soft palate and uvula may be painted with 5 per cent cocaine hydrochloride, and the larynx may be similarly sprayed. In spite of this it may still be necessary to give some patients a general anaesthetic in order to examine the larynx, especially if there is an overhanging epiglottis.

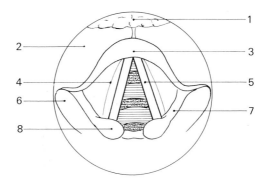

Fig. 2.13.3.   The laryngeal image on indirect laryngoscopy.
1, Dorsum of tongue.   5, Vocal fold (cord).
2, Vallecula.   6, Pyriform fossa.
3, Epiglottis.   7, Aryepiglottic fold.
4, Vestibular fold.   8, Arytenoid cartilage.

LABORATORY INVESTIGATIONS. These do not form a major part of the investigation of laryngeal disease but in appropriate cases blood may be taken for blood counts, thyroid function tests, serological tests, rheumatoid arthritis factor tests and monospot tests. In cases of suspected tuberculosis a Mantoux test may be done.

RADIOGRAPHY

1. *Plain radiographs.* Radiographs of the chest and neck may be of use in demonstrating the presence of air as, for example, in surgical emphysema or a laryngocele. The state of ossification of the cricoid and thyroid cartilage can be assessed and any displacement of the trachea will be seen. Mediastinal masses causing recurrent laryngeal nerve paralysis are usually obvious. A plain radiograph performed with and without a Valsalva manoeuvre may show an unsuspected laryngocele.

2. *Tomography.* Tomography of the larynx (*Fig.* 2.13.4) is a most useful investigation in assessing the extent of a laryngeal tumour, especially an exophytic

supraglottic tumour which obscures the vocal cords on mirror examination. It is also of importance in identifying the site and extent of a tracheal stenosis.

3. *Laryngography.* Laryngography has not lived up to its initial promise as a tool in the investigation of laryngeal disease. The larynx is first dried by giving the patient an injection of atropine, and then it is anaesthetized by a superior laryngeal nerve block. Radiopaque dye is run into the larynx by means of a catheter passed through one nostril into the pharynx. Once the dye is in the larynx the patient has a picture taken while breathing quietly, during phonation, while doing a Valsalva manoeuvre to outline the ventricles, and while doing forced inspiration.

A laryngograph has the advantage over a tomograph that it can be screened and the laryngeal movements better assessed. It is probably of most use in the assessment of subglottic stenosis.

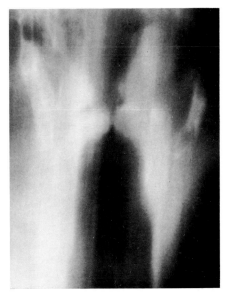

Fig. 2.13.4   Tomogram to show carcinoma of larynx involving left vocal cord and left ventricle.

4. *CT Scanning.* This technique is not used routinely in the investigation of laryngeal cancer. It is of most use in demonstrating paraglottic spread and cartilage destruction. NMR scanning may prove to be of more use in assessing tumour spread.

SPECIAL INVESTIGATIONS. These tests are applied to voice problems rather than to cases with organic disease processes.

1. *Tape recordings.* These are essential to record the progress of any case having speech therapy.

2. *Stroboscopy.* This produces an optical illusion whereby an object moving

rapidly appears to move very slowly. The illusion is obtained by viewing the larynx by indirect laryngoscopy using a stroboscope as the light source and synchronizing the illumination with the frequency of the phonated 'ee'. This arrests or slows down the rapid movement of the vibrating vocal cords and permits their inspection in any desired position by changing the phase of the light.

3. *Pitch and frequency measurements.* These measurements should be performed on all patients with voice problems. The ideal speaking pitch should be one-third of the way up the patient's range. To measure this the patient should sing his lowest note and then sing a scale so that his highest frequency can be measured. The pitch frequency of his speaking voice should then be measured and the speech therapist will then be able to adjust this to his ideal conversational pitch one-third of the way up the range.

4. *Respiratory function tests.* These tests are occasionally useful because altered breathing patterns can cause vocal abnormalities.

5. *Fibreoptic laryngoscopy.* This is a recent addition to the investigative armoury resulting from the technological advances in fibreoptic instrumentation. It is possible to pass a small fibreoptic bundle through the nose and into the larynx to examine certain areas very closely and also to avoid the need for direct laryngoscopy in some cases with an overhanging epiglottis. This technique may also be combined with stroboscopy for laryngeal examination. It is the authors' preference to use a rigid straight laryngoscope with fibreoptic illumination.

DIRECT LARYNGOSCOPY. This is the most important laryngeal investigation. It permits a close examination of the laryngeal and pharyngeal structures, it allows the extent of tumours to be assessed and biopsied, and it is a route for minor laryngeal surgery such as vocal cord stripping or removal of polyps and other benign tumours.

The Zeiss operating microscope with a 400 mm lens is used for microlaryngoscopy. With this innovation many instruments have been developed to allow for fine microscopic work to be performed on the laryngeal structures with a high degree of accuracy and thoroughness. It is unfortunate that in some otolaryngologists' minds microlaryngoscopy has become synonymous with direct laryngoscopy. While microlaryngoscopy is the procedure of choice in the assessment of benign disease, in the assessment of cancer the broader view given by direct laryngoscopy is probably of more value.

Chapter 2.14

VOICE PROBLEMS

PHYSIOLOGY OF VOICE PRODUCTION

To comprehend how a sound is produced in the larynx it is necessary to understand the Bernoulli effect. This principle states that during the steady flow of a fluid or a gas, the pressure is less where the velocity is greater. In other words, when air passes from one large space to another (i.e. from lung to pharynx), through a constriction (the glottis), the velocity will be greatest and the pressure least at the site of the constriction.

When we wish to phonate, the recurrent laryngeal nerves set the vocal cords into the adducted position, but because the vocal processes are slightly bulkier than the membranous cord a slight gap exists between the membranous cords. The lungs then expel air and the airstream passes through this chink between the vocal cords. According to the Bernoulli principle, therefore, there is a drop of pressure at this site and this causes the mucosa of the vocal cords to be drawn into the gap thus blocking it. At this time the subglottic pressure rises causing another stream of air to flow through the cords with another resultant pressure drop and closure of the gap. As this process is repeated a vibratory pattern develops at the vocal cords and the resulting sound is what we appreciate as voice. The change of this sound into speech is accomplished by the tongue, teeth, lips and palate.

At birth the vocal cords are about 7 mm long, at puberty about 14 mm long, in the adult female 15–16 mm long and in the adult male from 17 to 21 mm long. Because the anterior commissure is situated at the thyroid prominence this increased length in the male explains why men have larger 'Adam's apples' than women. The alteration in the length of the cord is produced by the cricothyroid and the thyroarytenoid muscles. Length is not the only factor in voice pitch however, both the tension or elasticity of the cord and the tracheal air pressure are important. As the cord is shortened the 'slack' must be taken up and the tension readjusted—this is done by the vocalis muscle. Increase in tension, maintaining the same length of cord, will also cause some rise in pitch. It is a well-known fact that as one speaks louder so the pitch of the voice rises. Further reference will be made to this fact in the sections on voice strain and vocal nodules.

Tension is a function of tone and tone depends on the myotatic reflex. This in turn is a function of the muscle spindles. There are a large number of muscle spindles in the laryngeal muscles, a number exceeded only in the extraocular muscles.

155

In actual phonation, pitch and pressure are associated in such a way that a slight increase of air pressure causes a considerable rise in pitch. If this were the whole story, however, the pitch of the voice would rise linearly as the loudness increased. In actual fact, increase of loudness is attained by rise of air pressure associated with decrease of elasticity of the glottis. It is a truism to state that most professional singers sing better than amateurs. The difference is defined as quality. To a large extent good singers are born rather than made. With practice, the vertical depth over which the cords meet, i.e. the medial apposing surfaces of the cords, can be increased in size; this involves hypertrophy of the vocalis and thyroarytenoid muscles. The most important factor in quality is the relationship of the size of the resonating chambers—the lungs, pharynx and upper respiratory tract—to the fundamental frequency of the note produced. It is this relationship that cannot be created by practice, and one has to be born with it.

VOICE STRAIN

This is a very common problem and will, of course, be noticed much earlier by, and cause most inconvenience to, professional voice users.

The optimum pitch of the voice is one-third of the way up the person's own range. At this pitch, optimum cordal length and tension can be maintained, as can a proper breathing pattern. If any of these factors of pitch, length, tension or breathing is altered, then some strain will be placed on the thyroarytenoid and interarytenoid muscles. The degree of voice strain will depend upon the length of time the person has practised wrong voice usage, and for how many hours each day. The type of person who is liable to get voice strain is an actor who has to project his voice abnormally loudly in poor acoustics, a preacher or a teacher who speaks too loud and at too high a pitch, a 'pop' singer with an untrained voice and poor technique or someone with an elderly deaf relative who needs constantly to be shouted at. Another very common cause of voice strain is to overuse the voice during an acute laryngitis. During an inflammatory process in the larynx some round-cell infiltration occurs in the thyroarytenoid muscle, when a myositis may be said to exist. If the voice is overused in this circumstance it will become easily tired, and permanent damage can occur to the muscle. A singer or actor therefore must cancel all performances if he has acute laryngitis. Similar pathology exists in acid burns of the larynx in reflux oesophagitis.

APPEARANCES. The larynx has a very typical appearance in this condition. Basically, it is difficult for the glottis to maintain closure, and some part of it remains open. If the thyroarytenoid muscle is most affected there will be closure of the arytenoids and posterior glottis but not of the cords—this results in an appearance of bowing (*Fig.* 2.14.1). If the interarytenoid muscle is most affected there will be closure of the cords but not of the posterior glottis, leaving a triangular gap posteriorly (*Fig.* 2.14.2) If both muscles are affected the larynx will have a keyhole appearance.

MANAGEMENT. The voice will be good in the mornings or after prolonged rest but will become 'breathy' as the muscles become fatigued with use. The best treatment therefore is voice rest for 1–2 weeks, and this must be total. The patient is instructed to use a pad and pencil to write down communications—whispering is not voice rest. After this time advice should be sought from a speech therapist to correct the causative factor, be it faulty breathing or faulty pitching of the voice.

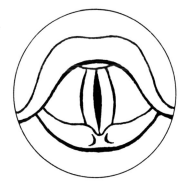

Fig. 2.14.1. Bowing of vocal cords due to thyro-arytenoid muscle weakness.

Fig. 2.14.2. Triangular gap from weakness of interarytenoid muscle.

ACID LARYNGITIS

This has been mentioned previously. It has become increasingly recognized that hypertrophy of the interarytenoid area, formerly known as pachydermia, is frequently due to acid from oesophageal reflux. This happens when the patient is supine at night and need not be accompanied by severe heartburn symptoms.

The symptom is hoarseness with anything from reddening to hypertrophy of the interarytenoid area. Gross thickening can extend on to the vocal processes where, as the result of trauma, the altered epithelium can break down causing 'contact ulcers'.

The treatment is by H_2 antagonists and antacids at night-time accompanied by the usual advice on clothing, weight and posture.

VOCAL NODULES

These are also called singer's nodes or screamer's nodes and, from this, some idea may be obtained of the aetiology. It is fashionable now for 'pop' groups to use falsetto voices on occasion. This is a trick whereby the voice is produced by vibrating the anterior part of the vocal cords, thus causing a tremendous 'shortening' effect combined with an increased cordal tension. The same is true of yodelling. This is the extreme situation, but it occurs in miniature when a natural baritone tries to sing tenor parts, and a natural contralto sings soprano. It happens, too, with anyone who pitches the voice far too high. Maximum vibration occurs in the anterior larynx and at the posterior part of this maximally vibrating portion, fibrosis and traumatic scarring occur on both cords.

Thus, typical nodules are bilateral, small and greyish-white and are situated at the junction of the anterior third and posterior two-thirds of the glottis (*Fig.* 2.14.3). This point is half-way along the membranous vocal cord because the cartilaginous vocal process forms the posterior third of the cord. The patient becomes hoarse, and the nodules need to be removed at direct laryngoscopy using microsurgical techniques. If they are very small speech therapy can sometimes improve the situation without surgery. In all cases, after surgery, the advice of a speech therapist should be obtained to correct the causative factor in voice production.

Fig. 2.14.3.   Singer's nodules.

DYSPHONIA PLICAE VENTRICULARIS

As the term implies, this is phonation with the false cords instead of the true cords. It can occur in extreme vocal cord strain, after operations on the vocal cords or for no apparent reason. The voice has a peculiar sound, almost like a duet, and is therefore called diplophonia. In some instances the patient's breathing pattern may be improved by the speech therapist with a consequent improvement in the voice. Generally, however, the results of speech therapy in this condition are not good.

SPASTIC DYSPHONIA

This is a relatively recently described condition which gives the voice a peculiar grating quality. It is usually stress-related but this is probably the only point of general agreement. The criteria for diagnosis vary so widely between speech therapists and otolaryngologists that definite diagnostic signs cannot be listed. However, the grating quality is characteristic. The usual treatment is speech therapy but decompression of the recurrent laryngeal nerve has been described.

PUBOPHONIA

Both male and female voices 'break' at puberty because of growth of the larynx. The female voice becomes more mellow but the male voice becomes deeper due to the androgenic effect on muscles. If the male voice does not 'break' abnormalities in pituitary function must be suspected. On occasion pubophonia persists with the peculiar 'breaking' quality of the voice. It should be treated by the speech therapist.

THE TRANSEXUAL VOICE

With the increasing number of sex-change operations being performed, demands are sometimes made by former males to have their voices raised in pitch. Although operations for shortening the larynx have been described they should not be done because the voice is deep due to muscle bulk rather than pure length. Again, any help for these patients comes from the speech therapist helping them adjust pitch.

Chapter 2.15

LARYNGEAL INFECTIONS

ACUTE LARYNGITIS

This is a viral or bacterial inflammation of the larynx, which very commonly presents as part of a generalized upper respiratory tract infection. On many occasions it may also occur as part of a lower respiratory tract infection. It occurs more often in smokers and other people with altered laryngeal states, such as those working in polluted atmospheres. Overuse of the voice does not cause it but merely brings it to light sooner.

DIAGNOSIS. Nowadays the diagnosis is easy because anyone who becomes dysphonic or aphonic during a cold or with an acute bronchitis has almost certainly got acute laryngitis. Formerly, however, much greater care had to be taken with the diagnosis since the febrile illness and upper or lower respiratory infection could well be diphtheria, tuberculosis or syphilis. The average laryngologist, in this country, will now see only one or two such cases in his working lifetime but in developing countries the practising laryngologist will have to keep all these conditions in mind.

The present-day diagnostic error is to miss an underlying cordal carcinoma during an upper respiratory tract infection, especially where the 'laryngitis' persists for some weeks, or to miss a vocal cord paralysis in a lower respiratory tract infection secondary to a bronchial carcinoma, or heart failure (Ortner's syndrome).

Thus in all cases of hoarseness the larynx must be seen if the problem persists for more than a week or two. In acute laryngitis the whole larynx is reddened as are the normally white vocal cords. If the condition is severe then the cords and false cords will be oedematous and pus will be seen in the interarytenoid region and perhaps even around the epiglottis.

TREATMENT. If a cold is sufficiently severe to cause laryngitis it is probably advisable for the patient to have a few days of bed rest and voice rest, since going to work and straining the voice will not only prolong the hoarseness but may permanently scar the thyroarytenoid and vocalis muscles. This is particularly important in actors and singers. During a laryngitis the muscles and spaces are infiltrated by round cells and if the normal healing processes are not allowed to take place under rest conditions, then the muscle will scar causing permanent damage. This may not be obvious in the average person, but it will certainly be noticed by a singer or actor.

Since the vast majority of these cases are due to virus infections antibiotics play no useful role, unless there is secondary infection in which case Amoxil would be the drug of choice. Steam inhalations, sweetened by the smell of menthol or tincture of benzoin, are comforting and should be used. If there is pain simple salicylic acid analgesics are usually enough but if not, one should reconsider the diagnosis and think of acute epiglottitis or perichondritis (*see* Chapter 4.3).

ACUTE ALLERGIC LARYNGITIS

This may be a manifestation of a systemic allergic problem such as a drug reaction, a local allergic reaction such as angioneurotic oedema or a contact mucositis as a result of inhaling the offending allergen in the form of dust particles.

On examination, the first two aetiological factors cause the larynx to be swollen and pale, but the contact mucositis (due to a product such as bauxite) presents as a red, swollen painful larynx not unlike that seen in acute laryngitis, but without the accompanying respiratory infection and fever. Initial treatment should be with intramuscular chlorpheniramine maleate (Piriton), 4 mg, and intravenous hydro-cortisone, 100 mg, if necessary. Because there should be a quick response to this once the precipitating allergen is removed, further respiratory obstruction should be handled by intubation rather than tracheostomy.

The less severe contact mucositis is more difficult to get rid of and occasionally persists for months in rather a painful way. Sprays such as 5 per cent glucose in glycerin may be used, together with analgesics.

Acute epiglottitis and **acute laryngotracheobronchitis** are discussed in Chapter 4.3.

CHRONIC LARYNGITIS

The aetiology of this condition is quite unknown. In a minority of instances repeated attacks of acute laryngitis will cause the chronic state to occur. In others, excessive smoking, or occupational pollution, cause metaplastic changes which alter the lining of the larynx enough to warrant a diagnosis of chronic laryngitis. It is true, however, that only a small proportion of those who smoke or are exposed to pollution suffer from chronic laryngitis. Some cases have associated chronic sinusitis with or without chronic bronchitis but, again, not all cases of sinusitis and bronchitis have laryngitis.

In summary, therefore, while a lot of associated features are recognized, the underlying cause of chronic laryngitis is unknown. Different types are recognized and described according to the laryngeal appearances. Many cases look very like cancer of the larynx, but the important diagnostic point in chronic laryngitis is that the changes are bilateral and symmetrical. It was formerly classified according to histological type (atrophic, hypertrophic) but it is not felt that this is useful.

SYMPTOMS. The common symptom to all the types is continuous hoarseness. If there is any degree of myositis there will be air wastage resulting in a breathy voice. There will also be a feeling of dryness and irritation in the throat and a frequent desire to clear the throat.

TREATMENT

Voice rest. This forms an important part of the treatment, especially in professional voice users who could do permanent damage to their voice if they did not rest it. If vocal abuse plays a part in the aetiology then voice rest must be enforced.

Speech therapy. This service must be offered to patients who do not use their voices properly.

Avoidance of pollutants. It is essential to stop smoking and to take steps to avoid or lessen exposure to environmental factors.

Local applications. Laryngeal sprays are difficult to use and have no direct therapeutic value; they are, however, comforting and medications such as glucose in glycerin or oil of pine may be used. The tongue is held forwards as for an indirect laryngoscopy and the laryngeal spray is introduced into the pharynx nozzle downwards. As the spray is used the patient inspires deeply. Sprays are especially helpful in laryngitis resulting from radiation.

Endoscopic procedures. Vocal cord stripping is of use in oedematous and hypertrophic laryngitis. It should be confined to one vocal cord at a time since the infection will inevitably involve the anterior commissure which, if bared on both sides, may lead to the formation of a laryngeal web. In most cases a biopsy will be required to confirm the diagnosis.

PERICHONDRITIS OF THE LARYNX

Because of the number of cartilages involved in the make-up of the laryngeal framework it is not unusual to find perichondritis as a response to many disease processes. Formerly it used to be seen not uncommonly as part of the symptom complex of tuberculosis, lupus and syphilis and it was also seen in typhoid, diphtheria and acute infectious fevers. Nowadays it most commonly presents as a complication of irradiation for carcinoma of the larynx. Should the larynx become swollen, painful and oedematous after radiotherapy the problem is to know whether or not there is a recurrence of the tumour concealed by the oedema. This is a very difficult situation to manage because to take deep biopsies in a search for cancer, and to expose cartilage in so doing, is a certain way to make the perichondritis worse. It is possibly better to treat the perichondritis with ampicillin and diuretics, and to delay a biopsy for as long as possible. If the larynx is still swollen and useless 6 months after radiation therapy a total laryngectomy should be performed even if the biopsies are negative. Sections of the excised larynx in such a case will almost certainly show evidence of residual cancer.

MYCOSIS OF THE LARYNX

Four main fungi are found, causing the following conditions:

Candidiasis

This occurs as a result of using steroid inhalers. The larynx looks diffusely red and the diagnosis can be confirmed by laryngeal scrapings. It usually resolves when the use of the steroid inhaler is stopped.

Blastomycosis

This is the most common fungus found and may attack the larynx primarily. It is found in grain workers in South America who are exposed to the fungus. The disease is a chronic granuloma and presents in the early stages as an intense inflammation of the larynx colouring it very dark red. There is a grey nodular surface with isolated yellow nodules and string-like secretions. Diagnosis is made by bacteriological examinations and biopsy. The latter is the more important since coexisting blastomycosis of the lungs may give a positive bacteriological finding. The finding of blastomycosis in the biopsy tissue is the only absolute diagnostic feature. It is treated by a prolonged course of a saturated solution of potassium iodide given in increasing doses from 0·3 ml daily until a maintenance dose of 2 ml is reached. The ultimate prognosis depends upon the state of the lungs.

Actinomycosis

This is due to species of *Actinomyces* and the source is usually animal hides. It is very rare in the larynx and presents as a yellow granulomatous tumour with associated glandular involvement. Treatment is by penicillin, but the prognosis depends on the response of the pulmonary lesion.

Leptothricosis

This is due to the *Leptothrix buccalis* fungus and is associated with bad dental hygiene. It usually occurs at the base of the tongue, but it may involve the larynx where it produces small, white areas in otherwise healthy mucosa. The condition has to be differentiated from keratosis of the larynx and is not dangerous. Potassium iodide may be given as for blastomycosis.

TUBERCULOSIS OF THE LARYNX

Over the past 20 years, not only has the incidence of this condition changed, but so has the clinical presentation. Formerly, laryngeal tuberculosis presented as part of a pulmonary tuberculosis affecting mainly the posterior part of the larynx. Oedema of the arytenoids and the epiglottis due to perichondritis was a feature, as were oedema and ulceration of the vocal cords. Of those cases that survived, a proportion developed scarring and stenosis of the larynx.

The chronic attenuated form of laryngeal tuberculosis is called lupus of the larynx and is contagious. It is usually secondary to well-marked lupus of the face, nose or pharynx, and the epiglottis is most frequently involved.

Since tuberculosis is so rare nowadays it is unusual for the otolaryngologist to diagnose it from mirror examination alone. The appearances are indistinguishable from those of carcinoma. There is an ulcerative vocal cord, arytenoid oedema or a verrucous overgrowth in the supraglottis. It is not invariably the case that the patient has pulmonary tuberculosis also—in fact it is now more common for the laryngeal manifestation to be the only one.

Each case must be examined at direct laryngoscopy and a biopsy taken to rule

out carcinoma. When the diagnosis has been made treatment by chemotherapy is
supervised by the tuberculosis specialist.

SYPHILIS OF THE LARYNX

This is now even rarer than tuberculosis. It may be congenital or acquired and is
more common in males than females.

Congenital syphilis of the larynx is a very severe condition which in appearance
resembles chronic hypertrophic laryngitis.

Of the acquired types, the primary and secondary stages are rarely seen in the
larynx, but if they do occur, the anterior half of the glottis and the epiglottis are
most often affected. Gumma may occur in any part of the larynx and it presents a
smooth swelling which may later ulcerate. Diagnosis is by biopsy, but this must be
confirmed by the battery of appropriate serological tests. Treatment should be
supervised by the appropriate specialist.

SCLEROMA OF THE LARYNX

This disease is prevalent in Poland, other East European countries, Egypt and
India. It starts in the nose and oral cavity and spreads downwards to involve the
pharynx and larynx. The typical lesion is in the subglottic region and takes the
form of a smooth red swelling covered by crusts. The patient complains of nasal
obstruction followed later by hoarseness, wheezing and stridor. Diagnosis is made
by biopsy, when plasma cells and hyaline bodies are seen in granulation tissue
together with the diagnostic Mikulicz cells which are large cells looking like
enormous fat deposits. If it is untreated the condition progresses to laryngotracheal stenosis. The first line of treatment is streptomycin or tetracycline, with
steroids added if there is a danger of stenosis.

LEPROSY

The larynx is involved in less than half the cases of leprosy. The epiglottis and
aryepiglottic folds become infiltrated and nodular, and later the lesions ulcerate.
Finally, scarring and contraction occur. Biopsy of the swelling will differentiate
the condition from tuberculosis and syphilis. Treatment is by a course of dapsone
which must be maintained for years.

ARTHRITIS OF THE CRICOARYTENOID JOINT

The cricoarytenoid joint and the cricothyroid joints are both synovial, and may be
affected by the same types of arthritis affecting synovial joints elsewhere in the
body. It is thus possible to get rheumatoid arthritis, infective arthritis or gout of
the larynx. Other causes of fixation of the joints are perichondritis (due to
irradiation, tuberculosis or syphilis) or trauma. In the acute phase the joint is
swollen and limited in movement, causing a large, swollen, red, immobile
arytenoid. The patient is dysphonic and has severe pain in the larynx which is
made worse by talking.

After several such attacks the joint becomes less inflamed, but more fixed. If the
joint is fixed in the adducted position the voice will be quite good, but if it is fixed

in the abducted position the characteristic feature is air wastage with a breathy voice.

The diagnosis is made by the appropriate laboratory tests for rheumatoid arthritis and the degree of fixation is established by attempting to mobilize the joint during direct laryngoscopy. This latter step is necessary to differentiate arthritis from a recurrent laryngeal nerve paralysis.

In the acute phase treatment is symptomatic and it may be necessary to add steroids to the analgesic medication. A close watch should be kept on the patient in case respiratory obstruction occurs from oedema. In the chronic phase no treatment is necessary if the position in which the joint is fixed is in adduction so that there is a good voice. If it is not, then some form of cordopexy or arytenoid operation should be performed. (p. 183).

Chapter 2.16

RARE LARYNGEAL TUMOURS

BENIGN TUMOURS

Oncocytoma

In older patients oncocytes develop. These are large cells which were originally thought to resemble tumour cells and thus the name. They have no particular significance but can undergo cystic degeneration. They are common in the minor salivary glands and thus can occur as cysts in the larynx. They are locally removed and not liable to recurrence.

Granular Cell Myoblastoma

These arise from the Schwann cell rather than muscle. They are frequent outside the larynx but 10 per cent do occur within the larynx and nearly always on the vocal cord. They can occur at any age and are subject to diagnostic error. The peculiar type of hyperplasia can be mistaken for a squamous carcinoma. When the diagnosis is established then they are removed locally and aggressive treatment is not required.

Papilloma

Single

This usually arises from the free edge of a vocal cord in adults. Histologically it is often a squamous-cell papilloma. It is liable to recurrence and may undergo malignant change. The papilloma should be removed at direct laryngoscopy, and the patient should be followed up for 5 years because of the danger of recurrence and malignant degeneration.

Multiple

These are described more fully in Chapter 4.3. They occur at any age from birth to 5 or 6 years, and although they are said to disappear at puberty this is the exception rather than the rule. They may present as scattered single papillomas all over the larynx or as a huge exuberant mass causing respiratory obstruction. They are not premalignant, but the larynx may be severely damaged from repeated removals. The papillomas can become implanted into the trachea and bronchi. Patients with this condition should be followed up at monthly intervals and the papillomas removed whenever they appear. In most instances this prevents the papillomas building up to cause respiratory obstruction which would require emergency laryngoscopy and tracheostomy.

Schwannoma

Almost 100 cases of these have been described in the larynx, ranging from the age of 3 months to 75 years with the preponderance in females. They usually occur on the aryepiglottic fold related to the superior laryngeal nerve. Only a handful of cases have been associated with multiple neurofibromatosis and almost all reported cases have been benign.

Paraganglioma

There are two pairs of paraganglia in the larynx. The first are beneath the epithelium of the anterior ends of the vocal cords and the second are between the thyroid and cricoid cartilages. Twenty-five cases have been described and most have had pain on swallowing which has disappeared on removal of the tumour. The diagnosis has been late and no malignancy has been reported. Partial laryngectomy is the recommended treatment.

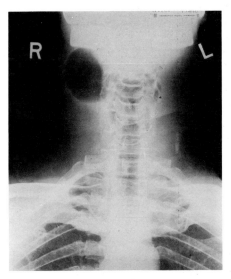

Fig. 2.16.1. Laryngocele. Radiograph showing a typical air-filled cavity.

Amyloid

Amyloid disease of the larynx occurs usually as the primary variety, not as a concomitant feature of a debilitating illness. Although uncommon, it has to be borne in mind in the differential diagnosis of the solitary laryngeal mass. It is removed locally, but it may require more radical surgery if it recurs.

Laryngocele

Lower animals have air sacs and in some humans remnants of these persist and are situated in the laryngeal ventricle. If one expands to form a laryngocele it either grows outwards through the thyrohyoid membrane and appears in the neck (external laryngocele), or it extends upwards and presents as a swelling in the vallecula (internal laryngocele). The presentation is often an intermittent neck swelling with or without hoarseness. On other occasions if the neck of the sac is blocked, the sac becomes infected and it presents as a pyocele. Laryngocele is often said to occur most commonly in trumpet players and glass-blowers but a review of the literature shows this to be false. The relationship is that if a person has a residual air sac that is liable to form a laryngocele this will occur when pressure is put upon it by blowing. The blowing *per se* does not cause the laryngocele, it only brings it to the patient's attention. It may be diagnosed by the characteristic radiographic appearance (*Fig.* 2.16.1) when the large translucent sac is seen and is made larger by the Valsalva manoeuvre. Treatment is to approach the sac from the neck, dissect it free, remove the upper half of the thyroid lamina, locate the neck of the sac, ligate it and remove the laryngocele. The repair line is reinforced by the strap muscles of the neck.

Cysts

An internal laryngocele may resemble a supraglottic cyst but it is diagnosed and differentiated by the typical radiographic appearances. A cyst occurs mainly in the supraglottis where there are a large number of mucous glands and the mouth of one of these may become blocked to cause a mucous retention cyst. Treatment is to uncap the cyst at direct laryngoscopy hoping that marsupialization will be permanent.

Vocal Cord Polypus

Although this is probably the most common laryngeal mass its aetiology is not understood. The polyp may arise from an area of unresolved infection or it may be a response to traumatic abrasion or haematoma formation. It occurs almost exclusively on a vocal cord and arises from the subepithelial connective tissue of Reinke's layer.

It may represent any of the previously listed benign tumours or it may represent an unresolved haematoma. As such, every laryngeal polyp should be removed both for biopsy and to relieve the hoarseness.

Bilateral polyps usually represent the curious disease known as Reinke's oedema. These polyps are along the whole length of the cords and are merely an oedema of the submucosal space (Reinke's space). The same appearance is seen in patients with the laryngeal manifestations of myxoedema but not every patient with Reinke's oedema has myxoedema.

Treatment is removal by microlaryngoscopy.

Prolapse of the Ventricle

This condition is of uncertain pathology. The mucosal lining of the ventricle is prolapsed so that it comes to lie on the vocal fold, where it appears as a smooth, pink, fleshy mass with a broad base. The cause of this condition is most probably the strain of coughing and the negative pressure which is exerted by the spasm. An underlying laryngocele should also be suspected and radiographs taken with and without Valsalva's manoeuvre.

Hoarseness and cough are the main complaints. Diagnosis is made at direct laryngoscopy, when replacement of the prolapsed ventricle may be effected by the blade of the laryngoscope or by forceps. A biopsy of the tissue should be taken to establish the diagnosis. Endoscopic removal of the medial portion of the projection is the most satisfactory treatment. Diathermy puncture will cause fibrosis and prevent recurrence.

Granuloma

Intubation Granuloma

Intubation granuloma occurs at two sites—the anterior commissure and on the vocal process. It is due to de-epithelializaton of cartilage resulting in low-grade perichondritis and granuloma formation. It is occasionally seen after a traumatic blind intubation, but it most commonly occurs after a long operation on a lightly anaesthetized patient where the arytenoids and posterior ends of the vocal cords vibrate against the tube. This causes abrasion and subsequent granulation tissue formation. The granuloma should be removed locally and it often recurs unless the infected cartilage is removed and the mucosa grows over the bare area.

Pyogenic Granuloma

This can occur anywhere in the head and neck region and often resembles a carcinoma. It is basically an infected granuloma and it does not recur after adequate local removal. Bleeding and ulceration also occur.

Granuloma Gravidarum

This is a pyogenic granuloma occurring during pregnancy. It is better to leave it alone until the pregnancy is over.

MALIGNANT TUMOURS

Verrucous Carcinoma

This is a tumour that is over-diagnosed by surgeons and under-diagnosed by pathologists. The patient presents with warty, white masses on the vocal cords and supraglottis that look exactly like tumour. The pathologist, however, sees a benign histological pattern with very little in the way of invasion and the surrounding inflammatory reaction. The diagnosis is, thus, difficult to establish but once established these tumours can be treated differently from squamous carcinoma. They are commoner in the male than the female and present in the sixth to seventh decade. Nodes may be present in the neck but they have a 50 per cent chance of being inflammatory rather than neoplastic.

Verrucous carcinoma has the reputation of becoming anaplastic if irradiated. This is true in 30 per cent of verrucous carcinomas outside the larynx treated by radiotherapy but no figures are available for the larynx.

The preferred treatment is surgical. This can take the form of repeated endoscopic removal or partial laryngectomy. The author has treated one such case with over 20 endoscopic removals with no recurrence now over an 8-year period.

Adenocarcinoma

Over 50 cases of adenocarcinoma have been described and most are in the glottis or supraglottis. There is 9 : 1 male to female ratio and the age-range is 23–79. Ninety per cent of patients present with nodes and 95 per cent are dead within 2 years irrespective of treatment.

Adenoid Cystic Carcinoma

Over 30 cases of adenoid cystic carcinoma have been described in the age-range 30–70 with a slight female preponderance. These tumours are usually in the sub-glottis and while nodal metastases are rare, distant metastases are common. They pursue the same slow, indolent growth that adenoid cystic carcinoma exhibits elsewhere.

Mucoepidermoid Carcinoma

Over 30 of these cases have been reported, nearly all in males. Surgery evidently leads to a 90 per cent survival.

Sarcoma

This accounts for less than 1 per cent of all laryngeal tumours and 50 per cent are fibrosarcomas. Fibrosarcoma can be well-differentiated, in which case there is a 50 per cent survival rate, or poorly differentiated, where there is a 5 per cent survival rate. It is a disease of males and is treated surgically.

Pseudosarcoma can present as a laryngeal polyp. On removal it is found to have squamous carcinoma in the stalk and sarcoma in the stroma. Of the few cases that have been reported, 70 per cent seem to have survived.

Chondrosarcoma is a difficult diagnosis to make. The difference between chondroma and chondrosarcoma only becomes evident when distant spread occurs. Most, in fact, are benign chondromas and should be treated as such. It is possible with repeated minimal surgery to keep the larynx for many years. Most tumours affect the cricoid and can present with respiratory problems or, more usually, dysphagia. Only 20 per cent affect the thyroid cartilage.

Apud System Tumours

Oat-cell carcinoma can occur in the larynx and 27 cases have been described. It is again a disease of males who smoke. Seventy-five per cent have nodal metastases and the mean survival is less than 1 year. Treatment is by radiotherapy and chemotherapy and surgery has no place in its management.

A few cases of carcinoid tumours have been described. This is more malignant outside the abdomen and it may be misdiagnosed as an anaplastic carcinoma. Diagnosis is confirmed by electron microscopy and the treatment is surgical.

Lymphoma

Over 50 cases of lymphoma of the larynx have been described and about half of them have been solitary. The common type is non-Hodgkin's lymphoma and treatment is with radiotherapy and chemotherapy.

Chapter 2.17

CANCER OF THE LARYNX

The larynx is divided, for purposes of tumour classification, into three regions—supraglottis, glottis and subglottis (*Fig.* 2.17.1). The **supraglottis** includes the laryngeal surface of the epiglottis, aryepiglottic folds, arytenoids, false cords and ventricle. The lingual surface of the epiglottis and vallecula are in the oropharynx. The **glottis** comprises the vocal cords and the anterior and posterior commissures.

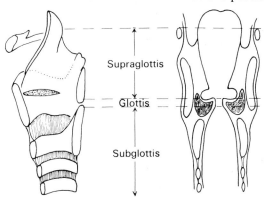

Fig. 2.17.1.   Divisions of the larynx.

The lymphatic drainage of the larynx (*Fig.* 2.17.2) is compartmentalized into the above regions. The glottis has virtually no lymphatic drainage and so acts as a watershed. The area above the vocal cords drains upwards via the superior lymphatic pedicle to end in the upper deep cervical chain. The subglottis drains both to the prelaryngeal and paratracheal glands.

Each of the three regions of the larynx—supraglottis, glottis and subglottis—is further divided into a series of sites. On the basis of the number of sites affected and also the movements of the vocal cords, the TNM system is marginally different in every region. The following is a generalization which can be applied to any region.

T_1S Carcinoma-in-situ.
T_1a Carcinoma limited to one site.
T_1b Carcinoma in two sites but within the one region.
T_2 Carcinoma affecting two regions, e.g. supraglottis and glottis, but with a mobile cord.

T$_3$ Fixation of the vocal cord.
T$_4$ Tumour outside the larynx.

Ninety-nine per cent of laryngeal cancer is squamous carcinoma and it is much more common in males and in smokers.

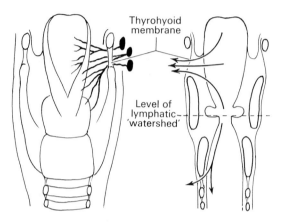

Fig. 2.17.2.   Lymph drainage of the larynx.

LEUCOPLAKIA

The word 'leucoplakia' is derived from the Greek, meaning a white patch. In the larynx these 'white patches' nearly always occur on the dorsum of the vocal cords. No assessment of their malignant potential can be made by naked-eye examination alone and so each area of leucoplakia of the larynx must be removed and submitted to histology. From this two reports are possible.

1. *Keratosis*: In this condition the white patch is due to a heaping up of keratin. This is quite benign and never becomes malignant.

2. *Dysplasia*: Although pathologists differ in their interpretation of the severity of this state, all will probably agree that this is the stage before carcinoma-in-situ. Dysplasia is premalignant and the risk of malignant changes rises as the severity of the dysplasia increases. The risk does not rise, however, above 40 per cent.

If the condition progresses to the stage of **carcinoma-in-situ** the affected vocal cords should be carefully stripped using microlaryngoscopy and the specimen sectioned. If there are any areas of invasive cancer radiotherapy should be used, but provided that it stays at the carcinoma-in-situ stage radiotherapy is contra-indicated. A policy of repeated vocal cord stripping should be adopted.

SUPRAGLOTTIC CANCER

PATHOLOGY. These tumours usually present in one of three ways: (1) as a large exophytic tumour on the laryngeal surface of the epiglottis, (2) as a relatively small discrete growth on the aryepiglottic fold and (3) as an isolated ulcerative growth on the false cord.

The supraglottic space has a rich lymphatic drainage and a high proportion of these tumours spread to lymph nodes. Roughly 1 in 3 epiglottic tumours, 3 out of 4 aryepiglottic tumours and about half the false cord tumours metastasize. Nearly all these tumours will invade the pre-epiglottic space but only a small proportion will involve the vocal cords until late in the course of the disease. This fact makes partial laryngectomy a distinct possibility in supraglottic cancer.

SYMPTOMS. While confined to the supraglottis these tumours do not affect the vocal cord and so rarely present with hoarseness. If the tumour is very large there will be some muffling of the voice. Occasionally the aryepiglottic tumours will present with painful dysphagia or on account of a lump in the neck from a metastatic node. In other words, these tumours are often diagnosed late since the supraglottis is not a region to give rise to early symptoms. Sometimes, in fact, tumours in the supraglottis are discovered accidentally by an anaesthetist during intubation for another procedure.

INVESTIGATIONS. The two key areas in assessing these tumours are the neck and the vocal cords. The neck should be carefully palpated because there is a high incidence of nodal metastases and the presence of palpable cervical nodes would necessitate a radical neck dissection. If the tumour has spread to the vocal cords no possibility exists of doing a partial laryngectomy, so they must be closely examined for evidence of spread. This is best done at direct laryngoscopy and biopsy, but if the tumour is exophytic and the laryngoscope cannot visualize the whole of the cord, a laryngograph will be of great assistance in assessing the site and mobility of the vocal cords.

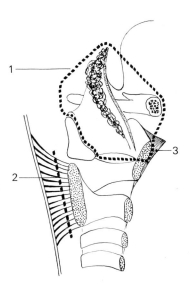

Fig. 2.17.3.   Supraglottic laryngectomy.
1, Showing the area of larynx to be removed.
2, Site of the cricopharyngeal myotomy.
3, Perichondrial flap.

TREATMENT. Before the evolution of partial laryngectomy, patients with laryngeal cancer could only be offered two alternatives—total laryngectomy or radiotherapy. For smaller tumours most surgeons rejected the idea of the rather mutilating total laryngectomy and used primary radiotherapy, reserving total laryngectomy for recurrences. With this policy, the prognosis after surgery was only about 10 per cent better than radiotherapy, but the 50 per cent who were cured by radiotherapy retained a good voice.

Supraglottic laryngectomy (*Fig.* 2.17.3) has been used for the past 25 years—more in the USA and Western Europe than the UK. It involves removing the entire supraglottis, from the vallecula to the ventricle, and joining the lower half of the larynx to the base of the tongue using a perichondrial flap (*Fig.* 2.17.4). The resultant proximity of the vocal cords to the base of the tongue makes swallowing a little difficult so the mouth of the oesophagus has to be widened by a cricopharyngeal myotomy. This operation allows the patient to retain a normal voice and gives about an 80 per cent 5-year cure (i.e. 30 per cent better than radiotherapy). If the tumour involves the tongue, the pyriform sinus or the vocal cords, the operation should not be done, nor should it be done if the patient is over 65, or if he has a bad chest. In all of these conditions the postoperative dysphagia will be of such severity that repeated aspirations may be fatal.

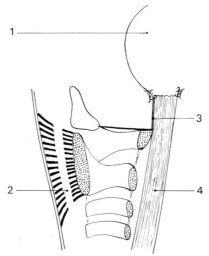

Fig. 2.17.4. Supraglottic laryngectomy. After removal of the specimen the perichondrial flap (3) is sutured to the base of the tongue (1) and supported by the strap muscle layer (4). A cricopharyngeal myotomy is done over a distance of 5 cm (2).

At one time the accepted procedure was to do a radical neck dissection in every patient on the assumption that the high incidence of metastatic glands made it likely that most patients had at least non-palpable metastases. Time showed, however, that the result of this policy gave no advantage over doing a radical neck dissection only in those cases with palpable glands, or doing a radical neck dissection as a second stage if and when glands became palpable.

In the UK present-day practice is to treat patients with metastatic nodes surgically and to treat T_1N_0 and T_2N_0 tumours with radiation. T_3N_0 and T_4N_0 tumours are also treated surgically. This means that only a proportion of patients with T_1N_1 or T_2N_1 lesions are considered for supraglottic laryngectomy.

GLOTTIC CANCER

PATHOLOGY. The glottis extends from the anterior to the posterior commissure. It consists of both cartilage and membrane—cartilage forming the posterior half and membrane the anterior half of the glottis. The length of the adult male vocal cord is about 2 cm. This should mean that if a cancer is confined to the vocal cord, it is less than 2 cm at its widest point and thus should be eminently curable.

Tumours of this region present as two distinct types: (1) a small tumour limited to the vocal cord and (2) a large tumour involving the glottis, supraglottis and subglottis—the so-called transglottic tumour. This carries a high incidence (75 per cent) of lymph node metastases because it involves the rich lymphatic fields of both the supraglottis and subglottis. These tumours also spread to the strap muscles (5 per cent) and the thyroid gland (10 per cent).

SYMPTOMS. Both tumours present with hoarseness. Why one should be seen at a very much later stage than the other is unknown, but, in theory, if every patient with hoarseness had the larynx examined within the first month then all tumours should be seen at an early stage. This is not the whole story, however, because the length of history of the transglottic variety is about the same as the glottic group. Occasionally the transglottic group will present with a gland in the neck in addition to hoarseness.

INVESTIGATION. At laryngoscopy it is essential to assess the degree of mobility of the vocal cord, and to search for any extension into the subglottis or supraglottis. It is unlikely that there will be any neck nodes palpable in the glottic tumours, but a high chance exists of such metastases in the transglottic group. Since subglottic extension is so important in the prognosis, all cases in the transglottic group should have tomographs or laryngographs.

TREATMENT. In the UK cure is achieved with radiotherapy in over 95 per cent of T_1 cases. If there is no recurrence, the patient will have a good voice, but if there is a recurrence surgery will be necessary. Either a hemilaryngectomy or a total laryngectomy may be offered. A hemilaryngectomy (*Fig.* 2.17.5) involves removing half of the thyroid cartilage with the false and true vocal cords, part of the supraglottis and the upper half of the cricoid cartilage. The resulting gap is closed by the strap muscles, fashioned so as to form a new fixed vocal cord. If a hemilaryngectomy is used as a salvage procedure after failed radiotherapy the results will be poorer than if it had been used as a primary treatment. It does, however, give the patient a chance of keeping some sort of voice instead of having to learn oesophageal speech after a total laryngectomy.

TRANSGLOTTIC TUMOURS

These seldom present until they are large and have palpable cervical nodes. The most satisfactory treatment is total laryngectomy with a radical neck dissection if

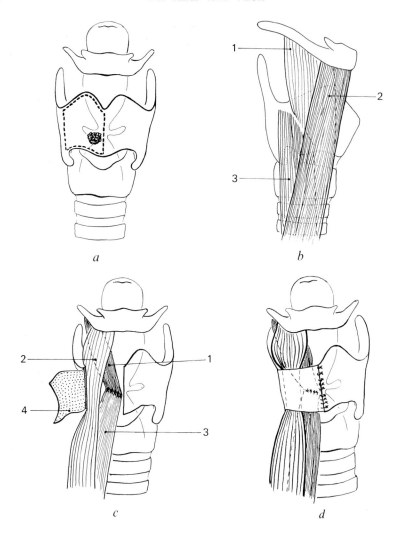

Fig. 2.17.5.   Hemilaryngectomy.
a, Showing the outline of the perichondrial flap pedicled posteriorly.
b, Lateral view showing strap muscles.
c, After the hemilarynx is removed the muscles are repositioned as shown.
d, The perichondrial flap is replaced and sutured to the remaining lamina.
1, Thyrohyoid muscle.   3, Sternothyroid muscle.
2, Sternohyoid muscle.   4, Perichondrial flap.

nodes are palpable. If there are no nodes palpable then radiotherapy is used as the primary treatment. About 40 per cent of the patients will be cured and will keep their voice. Those who recur (or who remain with a swollen larynx some months after radiotherapy) are submitted to total laryngectomy. A total laryngectomy (*Fig.* 2.17.6) involves removing the hyoid, thyroid and cricoid cartilages and several tracheal rings. When these are removed the pharynx is left open from the base of the tongue to the mouth of the oesophagus, and this is repaired in layers to form a new gullet. The upper airway is detached from the lower airway by the removal of the larynx and there is no way of joining them up again. The trachea is therefore brought out onto the surface as a permanent end tracheostome (*Fig.* 2.17.7). It will never be closed, but most patients quickly adjust to life with a permanent tracheostomy. After a few weeks they can dispense with the tracheostomy tube and conceal the hole with appropriate clothing. With effective speech therapy instruction about 60 per cent will learn to speak again in a satisfactory manner using oesophageal speech. Once the technique has been mastered the patient produces a sound from the reconstructed gullet by regurgitating air in the form of a 'belch'. Speech is produced by coordinated movements of lips, tongue, teeth and palate.

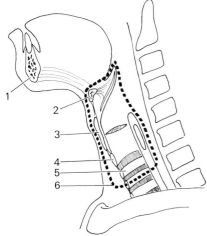

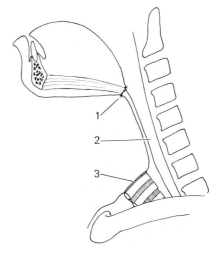

Fig. 2.17.6. Laryngectomy showing area to be removed.

1, Mandible.	4, Cricoid cartilage.
2, Hyoid bone.	5, Trachea.
3, Thyroid cartilage.	6, Line of excision.

Fig. 2.17.7. Laryngectomy showing end-result after removal.
1, Pharynx sutured to base of tongue.
2, Lumen of pharynx.
3, Permanent tracheostome.

SUBGLOTTIC CANCER

PATHOLOGY. Again, this is predominantly a squamous-cell cancer and is more common in males who smoke. The subglottis is by far the rarest region to be affected by laryngeal cancer and this is fortunate because the results are so much poorer than in cancer of the glottis and supraglottis. The subglottis is a small area extending from the lower border of the cricoid to the under surface of the vocal cords. Cancer of the thyroid gland and the trachea can spread to involve the subglottis and cancers of the subglottis spread to the thyroid gland, in 20 per cent of cases, and to the trachea. Twenty per cent also involve the strap muscles of the neck and the same percentage gives rise to cervical node metastases. There are six to eight paratracheal nodes in the mediastinum and these, too, may be involved by spread of subglottic cancer.

SYMPTOMS. If the vocal cord is involved early the presenting symptom is hoarseness, but if the tumour is lower in the subglottis the patient will present with respiratory obstruction and a normal voice. These latter cases usually present as surgical emergencies.

INVESTIGATION. Examination must be made for cervical node metastases and to ascertain the extent of spread of the tumour. Since subglottic tumours may involve the thyroid gland this should be scanned. There is a higher proportion of second primary tumours in these cases and so particular attention should be paid to the chest radiograph to see if the patient has a second chest primary tumour.

TREATMENT. Neither radiotherapy nor surgery in the form of total laryngectomy gives good results in this tumour. As things stand at the moment it is advisable to give the patient primary radiotherapy and to reserve a total laryngectomy for any recurrence. At the same time the paratracheal nodes should be removed. In the case of a large subglottic tumour presenting with respiratory obstruction a case could be made for doing an emergency laryngectomy. If a tracheostomy is done as the emergency procedure, it will have to be placed so near the tumour that there is a 60 per cent chance of the tumour implanting in the tracheal stoma unless the area is removed within 72 hours.

NEOGLOTTIS OPERATIONS

The most important thing in the development of speech after a laryngectomy is motivation. Since many of the patients who have a total laryngectomy are elderly, their motivation to attend speech therapy classes and practise oesophageal speech is not high. Only about 20 per cent of patients, therefore, develop fluent comprehensible oesophageal speech after laryngectomy. A large proportion are able to create enough sound to be understood by relatives but it is very difficult for outsiders to understand them. It is this group, therefore, that the neoglottis operations were directed at.

For many years people have attempted to create a fistula between the trachea and the oesophagus. It was in 1929 that the first such fistula was described giving speech after a laryngectomy. Since then multiple tubes have been described involving either long tunnels from the base of the tongue to the trachea or short tunnels between the trachea and the oesophagus. The aim of all these tubes is to allow air to go up but to prevent fluid coming down. For nearly every type the pattern was the same. The originator had spectacular results but they could not be repeated by other otolaryngologists. Numerous external devices were also used to produce speech, but none was superior to the ordinary electric larynx which the patient held under the chin to create a buzz in the mouth from which articulated sound could be developed.

The most promising developments in the creation of a neoglottis were the Blom–Singer valve and the Panje valve. Both involved the short-tunnel principle from the trachea to the oesophagus and both are simple to perform. It is not simple, however, to get every patient to use them correctly. There are problems with fixation with the Blom–Singer valve and problems with getting the correct length, especially if there is scarring between the trachea and the oesophagus, and with the Panje valve the problem is that the tracheal stoma has to be very large.

Although superficially attractive, these neoglottis operations have only a small part to play in the rehabilitation of the laryngectomee. Of the 75–80 per cent of patients who do not develop fluent oesophageal speech, fewer than half would want to be considered or would be suitable for consideration for a Blom–Singer valve or a Panje valve. This would be for reasons of motivation, age or difficulty in follow-up. Of the 30–40 per cent who are subjected to these procedures, only 10–20 per cent use the valves on a regular basis with good speech.

Chapter 2.18

VOCAL CORD PARALYSIS

Depending upon the cause, vocal cord paralysis may be unilateral or bilateral, complete or incomplete, giving four possible combinations, namely: (1) unilateral incomplete, (2) unilateral complete, (3) bilateral incomplete and (4) bilateral complete. Each of these presents a different clinical picture and each requires a different management.

PATHOLOGY. The recurrent laryngeal nerve is the motor nerve to all the laryngeal muscles except the cricothyroid muscle which is supplied by the external branch of the superior laryngeal nerve. This latter muscle has an adductor effect on the vocal cords, and thus a lesion which spares the superior laryngeal nerve will leave the cord lying nearer the midline than one which paralyses both the recurrent and superior laryngeal nerves. This, in effect, means that a high lesion of the vagus nerve will leave the paralysed cord further from the midline than a paralysis of the recurrent laryngeal nerve (Wagner and Grossman's theory).

Three positions of paralysed vocal cords are described: (*a*) paramedian, (*b*) intermediate and (*c*) cadaveric. There is little point in differentiating between the first two as it is of little diagnostic significance and the difference is one of only a few millimetres. Reference will only be made therefore to the paramedian and the cadaveric positions.

Another factor which controls the position of the paralysed cord is the curious fact described by Semon—'in all progressive organic lesions of the centres and trunks of the motor laryngeal nerves, the fibres supplying the abductors of the vocal cords become involved much earlier than do the adductors'. What this means, in fact, is that a partial lesion will leave the cord in the paramedian rather than the cadaveric position. Neither Semon's Law nor the site of the lesion decides the position of the cord absolutely, but both are useful guides.

It is only fair to comment that because of the considerable variability in cord position as the result of high or low lesions, neither the Wagner and Grossman nor the Semon theory is now totally accepted. On the other hand there is no satisfactory substitute theory advanced.

The most commonly affected nerve is the left recurrent laryngeal nerve, due mainly to the high incidence of bronchial carcinoma.

AETIOLOGY. Vocal cord paralysis arises as a rule from remote causes. The lesions

180

which affect **either vagus nerve** are: (1) tumours at the base of the skull, e.g. glomus jugular tumours and nasopharyngeal carcinoma; (2) bulbar paralysis; (3) peripheral neuritis due to influenza, herpes or Epstein–Barr virus; (4) high neck injuries, e.g. trauma or surgical complication of radical neck dissection; (5) metastatic node involvement; (6) basal meningitis; and (7) vagal tumours, e.g. glomus vagale or neurilemmoma.

The lesions affecting the **left recurrent laryngeal nerve** include: (1) carcinoma of the bronchus; (2) carcinoma of the cervical or thoracic oesophagus; (3) carcinoma of the thyroid gland; (4) operative trauma from thyroidectomy, radical neck dissection, pharyngeal pouch removal, cricopharyngeal myotomy, ligation of a patent ductus and other cardiac and pulmonary surgery; (5) mediastinal nodes or tumour, e.g. Hodgkin's disease; (6) any enlargement of the left atrium, e.g. mitral stenosis; (7) peripheral neuritis; and (8) aortic aneurysm.

The lesions affecting the **right recurrent laryngeal nerve** are (1) carcinoma of the thyroid gland; (2) operative trauma from thyroidectomy, pharyngeal pouch removal or myotomy procedures; (3) carcinoma of the oesophagus; (4) carcinoma of the apex of the right lung; (5) peripheral neuritis; and (6) subclavian aneurysm.

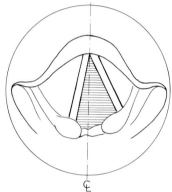

Fig. 2.18.1. Laryngeal paralysis. Mirror image to show left vocal cord in cadaveric position. (CL = centre line.)

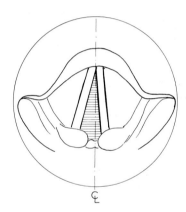

Fig. 2.18.2. Laryngeal paralysis. Mirror image to show left vocal cord in paramedian position. (CL = centre line.)

UNILATERAL ADDUCTOR PARALYSIS

As the cord will be in the cadaveric positon (*Fig.* 2.18.1) the patient will be practically aphonic at the onset of the paralysis. In a matter of a week or two the opposite cord will cross the midline on phonation and the voice will begin to return. Closure of the gap is aided by the mucosa of the normal cord becoming more lax. The paralysed cord later drops to a lower level than normal as the arytenoid falls forward. The quality of the voice at this time is harsh, warbling and breathy—a sound called diplophonia. It is almost impossible for a normal cord ever to meet a paralysed cord lying in the cadaveric position, especially posteriorly, and so a normal voice will never return unless some form of surgery is undertaken.

TREATMENT. Provided that the causative lesion is curable or is under control, this condition is worth treating because the voice is so poor and it can easily be improved. If the causative lesion is incurable it is kinder to leave the paralysis untreated unless the patient insists on surgery.

All treatment is directed to replacing the cord in the midline and this can be accomplished either endoscopically or by open operation.

Teflon injection. Using a Bruning syringe which delivers a measured amount of Teflon paste the paralysed cord is injected at direct laryngoscopy. It is better to carry out this procedure under local anaesthesia so that the patient can phonate, and Teflon paste can be injected until a satisfactory voice is produced. Once Teflon is in place it cannot be removed, so that injection must be undertaken slowly. Teflon, however, is not good if a large shift of the vocal cord is required.

Cricoarytenoid arthrodesis. Using a laryngofissure approach (in which the thyroid cartilage is split vertically near the midline) the arytenoid is exposed, the cricoarytenoid joint opened and roughened, and the arytenoid (after being rotated medially) is arthrodesed to the cricoid by means of a screw. This is sometimes known as a reversed Woodman's operation.

Implant procedures. Using a laryngofissure approach the internal perichondrium of the thyroid cartilage lamina is stripped off and the space created is filled with either the sternohyoid muscle or with a free cartilage implant, the cartilage being obtained from the upper half of the thyroid lamina.

Ishiki has described a type of laryngoplasty for this condition involving cutting a window in the thyroid cartilage and inserting a block of silastic in order to shift the soft tissues medially. This is the best procedure if a large shift is required.

BILATERAL ADDUCTOR PARALYSIS

This is the least common condition and both cords lie in the cadaveric position. There is aphonia which does not recover, and there is no possibility of developing a positive subglottic pressure. This means that the patient cannot control coordinated swallowing and food is inhaled, a situation further compounded by an inability to produce a good cough.

TREATMENT. Nearly all patients suffer from bronchopneumonia and will require a tracheostomy for removing pulmonary secretions and debris. The swallowing and inhalation problem is not helped by either Teflon injections or cricopharyngeal myotomy. If the situation is severe it may be necessary to do a total laryngectomy. In cases requiring this form of treatment the larynx and upper trachea (i.e. the trachea above the tracheostomy tube) will be oedematous and infected because they will have been acting as a sump. Usually, however, the cause is an advanced neurological disease that will in itself be fatal.

UNILATERAL ABDUCTOR PARALYSIS

This paralysis, in which one vocal cord is fixed in the paramedian position (*Fig.* 2.18.2), is most commonly due to a bronchial carcinoma at the left hilum. Every patient who is discovered to have such a paralysis in the absence of any other discoverable cause must be regarded as having a left-sided bronchial carcinoma until proved otherwise. Often it takes many months for such a carcinoma to come to light at radiography and so early bronchoscopy with cytology and carinal biopsy must always be performed. If a carcinoma causing a nerve paralysis is discovered it is generally considered to be inoperable although, if it is small, other treatment methods may have a better than usual chance of success. Many patients with lung cancer, however, present with the cord in the cadaveric position.

TREATMENT. No treatment of the paralysed cord is generally indicated because the voice problem is minimal and the other cord usually compensates.

BILATERAL ABDUCTOR PARALYSIS

The lesion is not common. Both vocal cords lie in the paramedian position, and sooner or later every patient with this condition will have stridor. The time of onset of the stridor depends generally upon the use to which the larynx is put. For example, a thin old lady who is in the house all day will not have stridor unless she gets laryngitis, but a well-built active man will have stridor on any moderate exercise, such as climbing stairs. In all cases the voice is acceptable, and in a few cases it is virtually normal.

TREATMENT. Given the two facts of stridor and a good voice, treatment must be tailored to the needs of the individual patient. Basically, a permanent tracheostomy in which a speaking tube (a valved tracheostomy tube) is worn relieves the patient both from stridor and from the danger of respiratory obstruction (and the anxiety which is engendered by this possibility). The disadvantage of this is the aesthetic fact of a hole in the neck with a tube that needs to be cleaned. One of the cordopexy operations will give the patient freedom from stridor, but will leave a slightly breathy voice which is weak. On the other hand, there is no hole in the neck, no external appliance and no social embarrassments.

If a patient has stridor he should have a tracheostomy performed and must be told that it will be there for at least 6 months. This is because recovery is possible during this time, and also because it allows him to see what life with a tracheostomy is like. If no recovery has taken place at the end of 6 months, the patient should be told of the possibility, advantages and disadvantages of cordopexy. The final decision must always be left to the patient.

A cordopexy is an operation, the objective of which is to move and fix the arytenoid, vocal process and vocal cord into an abducted position. A number of variations have been described, but only two will be outlined.

1. *External arytenoidectomy*. This is performed by entering the larynx behind the posterior lamina of the thyroid cartilage, removing the body of the arytenoid and stitching the vocal process to the thyroid cartilage. This is known as 'Woodman's operation'.

2. *Arytenoidoplasty*. This is done by a laryngofissure approach. A wire is passed from outside the thyroid lamina to enter the larynx below the vocal process; it is then passed above the vocal process to the outside of the thyroid cartilage again.

As the wire is tightened the cord is abducted. Alternatively the arytenoid can be removed via this route and the cord stitched laterally.

3. *Nerve muscle implants.* It has been claimed that cord tone and even movement can be achieved by implanting the decendens hypoglossi nerve and its endplate into the posterior cricoarytenoid. Time, however, has not borne out this operation's initial promise.

BILATERAL ADDUCTOR PARALYSIS (FUNCTIONAL APHONIA)

As the name suggests, inability to adduct the vocal cords is always bilateral and always functional, and the symptom is always aphonia. In its most severe form the voice may be barely audible because, as well as being a whisper, the severely disturbed patient will make very little effort to project the voice. One can almost imagine her deliberately making no attempt to use any throat or chest muscles in the act of voice production. The condition is most common in young females with love or work problems. On the rare occasions when it occurs in males the cause is usually to be found in promotional difficulties at work or staff incompatibilities.

One of the most helpful diagnostic features is the effort involved in creating the symptom. Mention has already been made of the associated lack of volume of the whisper. Examination shows not only that the cords are in abduction but where adduction does occur it is incoordinated—as if the patient is trying to suppress the normal reflex adduction of gagging. The single most important diagnostic feature, however, is that no matter how aphonic the patient is for speech, she will always produce a good cough when asked to, showing that normal adduction of the cords can occur.

TREATMENT. This lies outwith the field of otolaryngology. In suitable patients, quackery, such as the subcutaneous injection of sterile water accompanied by appropriate reassurances, is occasionally rewarding. In the vast majority of cases, however, the patient requires some form of psychotherapy, whether from her family doctor, a speech therapist or a psychiatrist. The otolaryngologist should limit himself to diagnosis and an explanation of the psychosomatic nature of the condition.

Chapter 2.19

LARYNGOTRACHEAL TRAUMA

After head injury, respiratory obstruction is the second most common cause of death at the roadside following an automobile accident. A high proportion of these deaths is due to such injuries blocking the airway at the upper end, either at the larynx or trachea. In a multiple injury, laryngeal fractures may well be missed because all efforts will be directed towards establishing an airway, either by tracheostomy or intubation, and dealing with the more spectacular problems in the chest, abdomen, head or limbs. At this point the laryngeal trauma is classified as 'acute' and remains in this eminently remedial state for 3 or 4 weeks. After this, the state of 'acute trauma', which is rewarding to treat, passes into a state of 'chronic stenosis' which is very unrewarding to treat. All too often this is when the problem comes to light because after 3 or 4 weeks, if the patient survives the first period, the other injuries are well controlled and attempts are made to remove the tracheostomy tube. In these unfortunate cases it is only when the patient is seen to be unable either to breathe or speak without a tracheostomy tube that the larynx is examined. To rebuild a larynx from the scarred state in order to free respiratory obstruction is relatively easy, but to make such an organ an efficient sphincter or an efficient 'voice box' is extremely difficult.

ACUTE LARYNGOTRACHEAL TRAUMA

The commonest cause of laryngeal or tracheal injury remains a road traffic accident, but with seat-belt legislation the incidence is falling. Other causes are bullet and knife wounds, damage by other sharp objects such as sticks or falling on to a sharp edge such as a kerb, and blows to the neck from such sports as karate and basketball where the neck is often extended and unprotected.

The result of a car accident depends upon the length of the front compartment of the car, and the height of the driver or passenger. At impact, if the distance is short the face will hit the steering wheel or dashboard and the result is likely to be a facial fracture. If the distance is longer, the head will extend leaving a large area of neck unprotected by the mandible and when this strikes the wheel or dash-board, the larynx is pushed back against the cervical vertebral bodies.

Under the age of 40, the thyroid cartilage is still largely cartilaginous and so, when it hits the vertebrae, the laminae are spread outwards and a fracture occurs down the prominence. When the compressing force is removed, the cartilage

185

recoils forwards, reassuming its normal shape, but with a linear fracture down the prominence. The effect of this fracture is to detach the epiglottis which will now hang free in the laryngeal lumen causing obstruction. It will also detach the anterior ends of the vocal cords which may either hang into the trachea or roll up on themselves towards the arytenoid (*Fig.* 2.19.1). As the artytenoids are pushed against the cervical vertebrae they become bruised and swollen and perhaps even disarticulated from the cricoid.

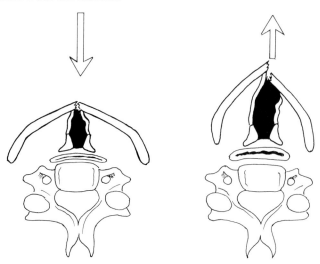

Fig. 2.19.1. Larygeal fracture. To illustrate the two phases in the younger patient. The larynx is forced backwards on to the vertebral column and the thyroid cartilage fractures down the prominence. When the larynx springs forward to regain its normal shape, the vocal cords are detached at their anterior ends.

Over the age of 40 the thyroid cartilage has lost much of its elasticity because of ossification of the cartilage. This means that as the larynx is forced back onto the cervical vertebrae the compressing force will shatter it, and when this force is removed the shattered, inelastic larynx will not recoil. The effect of this is to disorganize the cords and the base of the epiglottis, to damage the arytenoids, to narrow or close the airway and to cause a flattening of the neck (*Fig.* 2.19.2).

Minor degrees of external trauma and other injuring factors such as burns and scalds will cause only internal soft-tissue damage with no skeletal disruption. This can take the form of bruising, haemorrhage or laryngeal oedema.

The type of injury often sustained in karate or basketball is a fractured hyoid. This presents as exquisite pain over the fracture site on swallowing and also on 'springing' the hyoid by palpation.

DIAGNOSIS. As indicated in the introduction to this chapter, a laryngeal fracture is easy to miss as the associated injuries mask it. It is vital to be aware of this condition and to suspect it in any multiple injury. Bruising and other soft-tissue injury is not always dramatically obvious and indeed a major laryngeal fracture can exist in the absence of bruising.

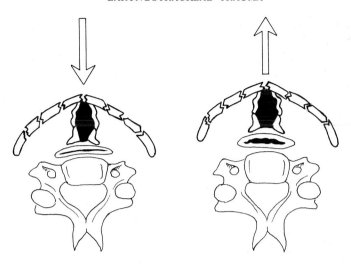

Fig. 2.19.2. Laryngeal fracture. To illustrate the extent of injury in the older patient in whom the thyroid cartilage has ossified. The initial impact shatters the cartilage which cannot recoil. The neck is flattened and the airway reduced.

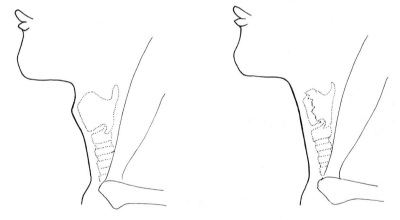

Fig. 2.19.3. Loss of normal neck outline after fracture of the larynx.

If the laryngeal lumen has been opened there will be surgical emphysema. This is diagnosed by palpating the neck and feeling the very typical crepitus. If, however, the forces applied to the larynx were sufficient to cause severe internal soft-tissue derangement without tearing the perichondrium, surgical emphysema will be absent.

In the older patient with an ossified thyroid cartilage the neck will be flattened (*Fig.* 2.19.3), and in the young patient a linear fracture may be palpated down the line of the thyroid prominence.

If there is total airway obstruction the patient will die at the roadside, but if he gets as far as hospital then the dyspnoea may not be as marked as expected.

Detached vocal cords could well increase the size of the airway initially only to decrease it again when reactive swelling occurs some hours after the injury. So it is that a patient with a fractured larynx, and say a ruptured spleen, could be admitted with shock and no respiratory obstruction. The anaesthetist could lift the detached epiglottis with his laryngoscope, intubate the patient, the spleen could be removed and on extubation the patient may well develop respiratory obstruction since by now the larynx is reactively oedematous.

Pain is a relatively minor feature; it may occur on swallowing and be transmitted to the ear.

Mirror examination may show oedematous, haemorrhagic arytenoids, mucosal tears and disorganized vocal cords. Direct laryngoscopy should be done in all suspected cases.

Plain films will show swelling within the larynx, and subcutaneous emphysema, but laryngographs do not have much importance in the acute stage because of the relative complexity of the examination and also because of the fact that the patient is seldom in a condition to cooperate with the investigation.

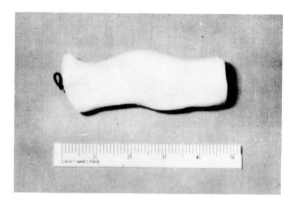

Fig. 2.19.4. Solid stent mould, made to the shape of the larynx, used to reform the shattered larynx.

TREATMENT. When the injury is slight there is no need for any treatment apart from observation in case laryngeal oedema develops. If the patient's condition deteriorates he should be put to bed and treated with humidification, oxygen and steroids, and if oedema progresses a tracheostomy should be done.

In the more severe cases there are two principles of treatment: (1) the establishment of an airway with a tracheostomy, and (2) open exploration, repair and reduction, and fixation of the fracture.

After the tracheostomy has been done, further exploration is carried out through a horizontal collar incision. It is usually possible to enter the larynx through the fracture and all torn soft tissue, such as detached cords, is stitched back into position. There should be minimal débridement.

If there is a linear fracture down the thyroid then the aim of treatment is to reduce the fracture and to prevent the anterior ends of the vocal cords from joining together to form a web. This is done by using a piece of sheeting, which is placed between the cords and is left in place for 5 weeks. The neck, but not the larynx, must be reopened to remove it.

When the thyroid cartilage is shattered the same principles are used but the larynx must be refashioned around a solid stent mould, which is made to the shape of the larynx (*Fig.* 2.19.4), wired in place and left for at least 8 weeks. This can be removed endoscopically.

Fractures of the hyoid are much easier to treat. The fracture is exposed and the piece of bone on either side of the fracture is removed leaving a gap in the hyoid which causes no functional problem.

Not all patients with tracheal avulsion or tears in the cricotracheal membrane die. If they survive long enough to get to hospital then it is possible to free the trachea into the chest and 'drop' the larynx and to suture it to the tracheal cartilage. There is no need to use a stent mould since this may result in infection and a breakdown of the anastomosis.

CHRONIC LARYNGOTRACHEAL STENOSIS

This is said to be established if the patient has not got a satisfactory airway 4 weeks after an injury. Apart from trauma other causes include:

1. *Tracheotomy.* If the tracheotomy is placed too high then the cricoid cartilage will collapse. It has been shown, however, that some stenosis is common after all tracheostomies, both at the site of the tracheotomy and at the site of the inflatable cuff on the tracheostomy tube. Post-tracheostomy stenosis, however, seldom gives rise to stridor but most commonly causes difficulty in clearing sputum.

2. *Partial laryngectomy.* If hemilaryngectomy includes more than one and one-fifth vocal cords then a McNaught keel must be used in reconstruction. Failure to do this will result in laryngotracheal stenosis.

3. *Granulomatous disease.* Stenosis may be the late result of tuberculosis, scleroma or Wegener's granuloma.

4. *Tumours.* Subglottic and tracheal tumours are dealt with in Chapter 2.17.

DIAGNOSIS. There will be difficulty in breathing, speaking and clearing secretions from the lower respiratory tract, to a greater or lesser degree, depending upon the severity of the stenosis.

On mirror examination, narrowing, web formation, granulations or oedema may be seen. The arytenoids may also be seen to be fixed. This is better assessed at direct laryngoscopy, however, because the fixation may be due to cordal scarring or fixation of the cricoarytenoid joint. These two possibilities may be assessed by moving the arytenoid at direct laryngoscopy. The extent of the stenosis, especially if it is severe, is not always possible to assess at laryngoscopy. It is in these cases that laryngography is of greatest benefit because without it no adequate preoperative planning can be done, and to operate on a tracheal stenosis without knowing its exact extent is both foolish and dangerous.

TREATMENT

Supraglottic stenosis. This may be managed by excising only the scarred area and leaving the normal functioning vocal cords. Once the scar tissue has been removed the mucosa is quilted down to avoid a dead space. The long-term results of the procedure are not as good as one would expect from this simple explanation of the procedure, but apart from wearing a permanent tracheostomy tube there is little else to offer the patient.

Glottic stenosis. If stenosis is limited to the glottis it is due either to fixation of the arytenoids or to an anterior web of the cords. In the case of arytenoid fixation the arytenoid may be removed and the cord stitched in the desired fixed position, or the vocal process may be wired laterally.

A web is best dealt with by a laryngofissure approach, excising the web and closing the larynx over a McNaught keel made of silastic.

If the whole glottis is stenosed and disorganized then it should be explored, the scar excised, the remainder refashioned as well as possible and fixed over a solid stent inlay of silicone rubber which is wired in place for 8 weeks.

Subglottic and tracheal stenosis. A very mild case may be managed by repeated dilatations but such a case is the exception rather than the rule. Most cases will require excision of the stenosed portion and re-anastomosis of the trachea. Up to 4 cm of trachea may be excised and a primary repair carried out by freeing the tracheal stump in the mediastinum down to the carina, and 'dropping' the larynx by dividing the suprahyoid muscles. It is possible to manage most problems in this way, but if more trachea has to be resected then the right main bronchus should be removed from the carina, the trachea pulled up into the neck thus straightening the left main bronchus and the right main bronchus is reattached to the left main bronchus. If the end-to-end anastomosis in the neck has been done properly it is doubtful if a tracheostomy or a stent inlay would help the procedure at all.

Cricoid stenosis. The cricoid is the only complete ring in the whole respiratory tract and if the integrity of the ring is breached a skeletal narrowing results which gives a short stricture that looks easy to sort but is in fact the most difficult to do. Many procedures listing infills, both free and pedicled, to build out the ring have been described but they are not very successful. The author has found that the best method is to excise the cricoid apart from a plate on which the arytenoids sit. The trachea is freed and the larynx dropped and the trachea joined on to the cricothyroid remnant.

These patients will have one or both recurrent laryngeal nerves divided and so will also need some form of later cordopexy.

Chapter 2.20

TRACHEOSTOMY

There has been confusion between the terms tracheotomy and tracheostomy which have in the past been used interchangeably. Etymologically, tracheotomy means making an opening into the trachea, while tracheostomy means converting this opening to a stoma on the skin surface. Thus in the operation of tracheostomy the actual opening of the trachea is tracheotomy. Tracheostomy is one of the earliest operations ever described, and there is evidence that it was performed by the Egyptians in Biblical times.

FUNCTION OF A TRACHEOSTOMY

A tracheostomy is performed to relieve an upper airway obstruction, to facilitate bronchial toilet, to decrease dead space, to assist ventilation and as an elective procedure in head and neck surgery.

Relief of Upper Airway Obstruction

An obstruction of the airway may occur with dramatic suddenness as in the case of an inhaled, impacted foreign body in the larynx. There may be a moderate urgency in acute inflammatory lesions, such as acute epiglottitis, acute laryngotracheobronchitis or the acute laryngeal oedema of the child burned by drinking from a boiling kettle. There may be the slowly progressive respiratory embarrassment, for example in laryngeal cancer which is being treated by irradiation.

Bronchial Toilet

A basic failure in respiration may require that the patient receive assistance in removing his bronchial secretions. This may occur in a central depression of the respiratory centre from coma, cerebrovascular accidents, head injury or drug overdosage; or there may be neurological problems such as poliomyelitis, cervical cord lesions, polyneuritis, myasthenia gravis or tetanus.

Dead Space

Dead space may be reduced by 30–50 per cent, thereby improving respiratory efficiency, and thus assisting the patient who has to rely on his own respiratory efforts rather than on assisted ventilation.

Assisted Ventilation

Should assisted ventilation be required this may be started with an endotracheal tube for 72 hours. While there is still no absolute proof that intubation which has been prolonged for more than 72 hours even with low-pressure cuffs causes laryngotracheal damage, it is probably safer to do a tracheostomy at this stage and to continue the intermittent positive-pressure ventilation by this means. Should the patient not have improved sufficiently in the first 3 days with an endotracheal tube, it becomes difficult to assess how much longer the tube must remain in place and each 24 hours increases the risk of serious laryngotracheal damage.

Elective Operation

In nearly all cases of major head and neck surgery it is safer to perform an elective tracheostomy, not only to maintain the airway but to protect it against haemorrhage.

TYPES OF TRACHEOSTOMY

Elective Temporary Tracheostomy

This is performed as a planned procedure, usually under general anaesthesia, as a temporary stage in the patient's management. Examples of this are in the management of recoverable coma or of inflammatory lesions such as acute epiglottitis, or as a safety measure in a head and neck malignancy operation.

Permanent Tracheostomy

In an operation involving removal of the larynx, such as a laryngectomy or laryngopharyngectomy, the tracheal remnant is brought out to the surface as a permanent mouth to the respiratory tract.

Emergency Tracheostomy

Nowadays there ought to be very few indications for this. On occasion a patient will be seen first with a large laryngeal tumour and require an emergency tracheostomy; this, however, is a situation that would only occur once every 2 or 3 years. To have to do an emergency tracheostomy in conditions such as acute epiglottitis, respiratory failure, coma, etc., is a sign of poor forward planning in the management of the patient. It is usually done under local anaesthetic if it is a true emergency and this, to the inexperienced, is a difficult, dangerous operation.

TRACHEOSTOMY TUBES

The Silver Jackson Tube

This is used for a temporary tracheostomy and consists of an outer tube and an inner tube which can be cleaned without disturbing the outer tube. It is inserted over an introducer.

Portex Tubes

These are also widely used and can be used cuffed or uncuffed. No introducers are used with them. There is no inner tube, but they are almost non-irritant. There is a wide variety from which to chose.

Radcliffe Tube

This is a right-angled tube, not used with an inner tube, which is useful in a patient with a thick, fat neck.

Durham's Tube

This is a tube with an adjustable flange and can be made to fit any size of neck.

TECHNIQUE OF TRACHEOSTOMY

This is usually done with the patient intubated and positioned with a sandbag underneath the shoulders in order to extend the neck and to pull as much trachea as possible into the operative site. A horizontal incision is marked with methylene blue two fingers' breadth above the sternum (*Fig.* 2.20.1). The incision is carried through the skin and subcutaneous tissue down to the strap muscles. These are separated in the midline, held aside with two retractors and the pretracheal fascia identifed. This is then incised in a vertical direction, avoiding the inferior thyroid veins, and the thyroid isthmus is identified (*Fig.* 2.20.2). This latter structure is freed from the trachea, clamped, divided and oversewn with 3/0 silk. The tracheal rings are then seen and at this point the cricoid should be deliberately identified, since to make an incision through the cricoid or first tracheal ring will cause laryngeal collapse and stenosis. A vertical incision is made through the third and fourth rings and a semicircle of tracheal wall is removed from either side (*Fig.* 2.20.3). The appropriately sized tracheostomy tube is inserted and the wound closed, but not tightly, with 4/0 silk sutures.

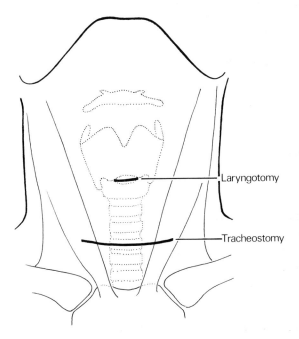

Fig. 2.20.1.   Incision for elective tracheostomy and laryngotomy.

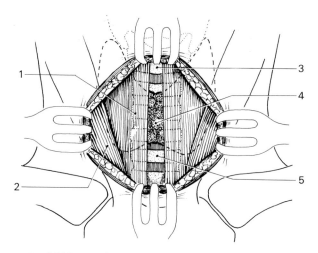

Fig. 2.20.2.   Tracheostomy—to show structures exposed.
1, Sternohyoid muscle.   4, Isthmus of thyroid gland.
2, Sternomastoid muscle.   5, Trachea.
3, Cricoid cartilage.

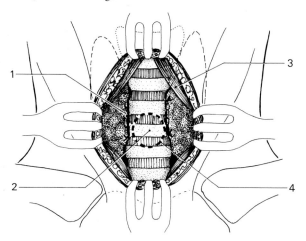

Fig. 2.20.3.   Tracheostomy—site of incision in trachea.
1, Isthmus of thyroid gland   3, Sternohyoid muscle retracted.
   divided and ligated.   4, Site of incision
2, Third ring of trachea.   in trachea.

TECHNIQUE OF LARYNGOTOMY

Our views on emergency tracheostomy have been expressed previously. If an inexperienced doctor is called to this situation he should do a laryngotomy to obtain an airway which will save life until an anaesthetist can come and intubate the patient, or a more experienced surgeon can come and do a tracheostomy. The first step in a laryngotomy is to palpate the cricoid and then the lower border of the thyroid cartilage. In the notch between the two is the cricothyroid membrane and with the head extended this lies just underneath the skin. The first thing to insert is the widest bore needle available. An alternative or later step is to incise the membrane. The space is stabbed horizontally with the blade of a knife of at least No. 10 size and the incision is lengthened. The blade is then withdrawn and the handle of the knife inserted and turned at right angles to open an airway. Special 'all in one' instruments exist to do this procedure, but it is normally such an emergency that a knife or needle is usually the most readily available instrument.

POSTOPERATIVE CARE

Nursing

A nurse who understands the care of tracheostomy patients should be in attendance for the first 48 hours and should carry out the care with sterile precautions. She should wear a mask. She should make sure that the patient has material on which to write and a bell with which to summon assistance.

Fixation of the Tracheostomy Tube

It is essential not to tie the tube too tight and not to tie the knot in a bow since this may come undone. If it is tied with tapes the head should first be flexed to relax the neck muscles. If tapes are tied with the head extended the tube may become loose on flexion when the muscles relax. The safest way is to stitch it to the skin with 2/0 silk.

Removal of Secretions

Excess secretions occur after a tracheostomy since the trachea is exposed to cold dry air and the tube acts as a foreign body and stimulates the formation of secretions. During the first 48 hours secretions should be removed half-hourly and thereafter every 1 or 2 hours. The nurse should wear sterile gloves. A sterile rubber catheter is attached to one limb of the Y-shaped plastic connector from the suction apparatus and the sterile catheter is inserted into the tracheostomy tube by means of sterile artery forceps. She then places her thumb over the open limb of the Y-shaped connection to close the air entry into the suction apparatus and withdraws the catheter. This manoeuvre should not take more than 10 seconds or else the patient will be rendered hypoxic. This is repeated until no further secretions remain.

Humidification

This is necessary to prevent crusting of the secretions and is done most simply by instilling normal saline down the tracheostomy tube at regular intervals. Humidifiers are now inexpensive and widely available and should be used constantly.

Changing the Tube

Tracheostomy tubes should not be disturbed for the first 48–72 hours, but thereafter the tube is changed daily and cleaned at regular intervals. On inserting the tube it is essential to check that it is in the trachea and not lying anterior to it in the mediastinum. If this happens respiration will not be heard through the tube and vascular erosion may occur.

Care of the Inflatable Cuff

With the advent of low-pressure cuffs one need not be as careful as formerly about letting the cuff down regularly.

Dressings

Waterproof squares are made which protect the surrounding skin from maceration from secretions and the movement of the tube edges.

Removal of the Tube

This presents no problem in the adult—the tube is removed once the patient can sleep for a night with the tube corked. The wound should then be freshened and sutured to prevent ugly scar formation. In children it is very much more difficult to remove a tracheostomy tube that has been present for more than a few days. It was thought at one time that this difficulty was psychological, but it is now thought that the subglottic region above the trachea acts as a sump and that subglottic oedema occurs. This is avoidable by using the Rees–Pracy tracheostomy tube which is fenestrated and valved so that when the patient exhales, air goes up through the larynx thus blowing out any secretions which are stagnating in the subglottis.

COMPLICATIONS

Surgical Emphysema

This is occasionally found in the immediate postoperative period and presents as a swollen area around the root of the neck and upper chest, which displays crepitus on palpation. It is due to overtight suturing of the wound and is not dangerous unless it leads to mediastinal emphysema and cardiac tamponade.

Blockage of Tracheostomy Tube

This can occur if there is lack of humidification or poor toilet. It is more likely to occur with Portex tubes than silver tubes, but presents little problem if it is recognized in time. The tube should be changed and if crusts have occurred down the trachea they must be removed by bronchoscopy.

Tracheal Erosion and Haemorrhage

The initial erosion can be caused by using a tube with the wrong curvature or by passing the tube anterior to the tracheal opening to lie on the anterior tracheal wall. A tube in this position may erode the innominate vein with almost invariably fatal results.

Dysphagia

This is fairly common in the first few days after tracheostomy. In normal swallowing a positive subglottic pressure is created by the closing of the vocal cords—which is why one cannot speak during swallowing. This is not possible with a tracheostomy tube in place, and thus swallowing is incoordinate. Another reason for dysphagia is that if an inflatable cuff is blown up it will press on and obstruct the oesophagus.

Difficult Decannulation

The problems of decannulating children have been mentioned earlier; on occasion this is due to psychological factors, but on other occasions it is due to subglottic oedema. If infection and necrosis of cartilage occur the cartilaginous tracheal rings soften, and when the tube is removed the lumen collapses causing respiratory obstruction and difficulty in decannulation. Another cause of this is tracheal stenosis due to infection because too much anterior tracheal wall has been removed at the operation, or to cricoid collapse following a high tracheotomy which involves the cricoid.

TRACHEOSTOMY VERSUS INTUBATION

If a patient requires assisted ventilation then either a tracheostomy tube or an endotracheal tube supplies an adequate route for this. Similarly, if a patient requires an airway to by-pass an obstruction then either method is equally good, given the proviso that an endotracheal tube can be inserted past or through the obstruction.

In spite of the relatively rare complication of tracheal stenosis due to an indwelling endotracheal tube, it is probably safer not to leave one *in situ* for more than 72 hours. In considering this complication of intubation it is prudent to consider the list of complications of tracheostomy listed above.

In an emergency situation, which with careful patient care should not be allowed to occur, given an equally skilled anaesthetist and surgeon, intubation will be the quicker procedure. In the hands of unskilled doctors in an emergency situation, both of the procedures are dangerous and a laryngotomy is quicker and safer. Generally, however, the procedure adopted depends upon which one the attending doctor can do better, more safely and quickly, and this will usually be intubation.

The use of hydrocortisone in inflammatory states has decreased the need for tracheostomy in an illness such as acute laryngotracheobronchitis. This is an effective and safe method and occasionally has to be complemented by intubation for a short time. Very few patients have died from an overdosage of intravenous hydrocortisone. Since this problem usually arises in children and since tracheostomy in small children is difficult owing to the anatomy, intubation is the method of choice.

In summary, therefore, one can say that while the old adage stated that 'The time to do a tracheostomy is the time you first think of it', the newer adage might be 'When you think of doing a tracheostomy, intubate, and think again'.

Chapter 2.21

NECK MASSES

In the changing pattern of the specialty it is essential that every otolaryngologist should be familiar with the diagnosis and management of masses in the neck. It is also desirable that general practitioners should have some insight into what is a fairly common complaint.

In this chapter a description will be given of the main causes of neck masses and of the management of the patient who presents with such a complaint.

BENIGN NECK MASSES

Skin and Associated Structures

The most frequent skin lump is a **sebaceous cyst** and the diagnostic feature here is the presence of a punctum. **Neurofibromas** are usually multiple flat raised areas which may be associated with *café au lait* spots and occasionally with acoustic neuromas. **Lipomas** can occur anywhere in the neck, but usually present as a supraclavicular fat pad. In the presence of enlarged glands the skin should be searched for **melanomas** or **infected scratches** (as in cat scratch fever) or boils. Some fungal infections affect the skin and subcutaneous tissue of the cervicofacial region, the commonest being **actinomycosis, tularaemia, orf** and **blastomycosis.**

Thyroid Masses

This is the commonest group of neck swellings seen in a general hospital, and the simple **goitre** with or without hyperthyroidism is most frequently found. A painful hard swollen thyroid, often accompanied by a fever, is suggestive of **thyroiditis** and in this group is included **Hashimoto's disease.** A solitary **thyroid nodule** should always be regarded with suspicion because it might be a **simple adenoma,** a **papillary carcinoma**, a **follicular carcinoma** or a **medullary carcinoma. A squamous carcinoma** or a **reticulosis** of the thyroid gland presents as a painless swelling and causes tracheal compression or recurrent laryngeal nerve paralysis.

Infected Lymph Nodes

These are the most frequent swellings encountered in general practice. Of these, the enlarged **jugulodigastric node** seen in children with tonsillitis is the commonest, and this in turn drains into the deep jugular chain to cause further lymphadenopathy. Infected skin lesions such as **cat scratch fever** and other more simple infections may also cause enlargement of cervical glands. Enlarged lymph nodes in the posterior triangle usually occur in the adult population, and the commonest causes are **infectious mononucleosis, toxoplasmosis, brucellosis** and **cytomegalovirus**. This group may also produce some lymphadenopathy in the deep jugular chain. **Parapharyngeal abscesses** may arise from either dental or tonsillar sources.

Tuberculosis

This classically affects the lymph nodes in the neck and formerly it was not uncommon for the glands to involve the skin and to form a discharging sinus. Nowadays this is rare because such enlarged neck glands are usually dealt with at a much earlier stage. Tuberculosis commonly affects glands in the deep jugular chain around the carotid bulb and occasionally all the glands in the posterior fossa are affected. As the glands enlarge they tend to become intimately associated with the walls of the major blood vessels and this makes excision difficult. While many cases have associated pulmonary tuberculosis, the neck glands may be the only manifestation of the disease. The treatment is to excise one or two glands for biopsy, and to treat thereafter with the appropriate chemotherapy.

Sarcoidosis has a similar presentation, but there is never any sign of caseation. Diagnosis is confirmed by histology or the Kveim test.

Salivary Gland Diseases

These may be included in neck swellings, as the submandibular gland lies entirely within the neck, and the tail of the parotid, in which most tumours start, is also within the neck area. These masses are commonest in middle-aged patients and are more fully discussed in Chapter 2.11.

Any diffuse swelling of these glands is probably not neoplastic but is much more likely to be due to **parotitis** (mumps), or **sialectasis** with or without calculus formation. This latter condition is to the salivary glands what bronchiectasis is to the lungs, and the contrast radiographic findings are very similar with duct stenosis and stricture, saccular and cystic spaces, and a loss of efficient functioning (*see Fig. 2.11.3*).

In the latter part of the nineteenth century Mikulicz described a syndrome consisting of swelling of all four salivary glands and of the lacrimal glands. This syndrome was later associated with keratoconjunctivitis and arthritis (Sjögren's syndrome), sarcoidosis and uveitis (Heerfordt's syndrome) and a dry mouth, dry eye complex (Sicca syndrome).

Other causes of diffuse enlargement of the salivary glands may include **diabetes, iodides, gout, thiouracil, obesity, myxoedema** and **Cushing's disease**. Parotid swelling can be mimicked by **masseteric hypertrophy, parasitic cysts** and **branchial cysts**.

The commonest benign tumour of salivary glands is a **pleomorphic adenoma** which in the parotid usually presents near the lobe of the ear. **Monomorphic adenomas** (Warthin's tumour) are usually bilateral and are cystic. The commonest malignant tumours are **adenoid cystic carcinoma** and **mucoepidermoid carcinoma**. The former invades nerves and often presents with associated nerve palsies.

Laryngocele

This is dealt with in Chapter 2.16. It is a remnant of the primitive air sac and presents at the side of the neck over the thyrohyoid membrane. It may be easily inflated and emptied of air, and it shows a characteristic radiographic appearance (*see Fig.* 2.16.1). Sometimes the mouth of the sac becomes blocked, infection supervenes and the presentation is that of a **pyocele**.

Lymphomas

This group of diseases very commonly presents primarily in the head and neck region. While the nasopharynx, tonsils or salivary tissue may be affected, the commonest sites involved are the lymph nodes in the posterior triangle or around the carotid bulb. The glands are firm, rubbery and matted together. On section they have a smooth white appearance. The various stages of **Hodgkin's disease, lymphosarcoma** and **reticulum-cell sarcoma** are seen, as are all the **leukaemias**, especially the chronic lymphatic variety.

Long-term dosage with epanutin may cause lymph node enlargement in the posterior fossa, but this is an allergic phenomenon.

Primary Tumours of Neck Structures

Tumours of the receptor cells in the carotid bulb have been given many names. On account of their histology they are called non-chromaffin paragangliomas; on account of their origin from chemoreceptors they are called chemodectomas; and on account of their site they are called **carotid body tumours**. They are very rare. They nearly always pulsate, but differentiation between their direct pulsation and the transmitted pulsation from a gland overlying the carotid bulb is very difficult. Although carotid body tumours may be moved from side to side, but not up and down, because of their attachment to the artery, the only certain way to make the diagnosis is by angiography at which the typical tumour circulation is seen. It is doubtful if they ever become malignant and metastasize, and it is very rare for them to prove fatal by local extension. Any surgery to remove them, however, carries with it a significant mortality and morbidity risk. In a young patient surgery may be carried out to remove the tumour with adequate preoperative preparations made for carotid artery by-pass. In patients over the age of 45, however, it is probably safer to leave the tumour alone.

Neurogenous tumours of the vagus nerve may be either **neurofibroma** or **neurilemmoma**, and they are all benign. The presentation is that of a mass in the lateral pharynx which pushes the tonsil medially and forwards, but at the same time there is often diffuse thickening in the neck in the upper sternomastoid region and around the tail of the parotid. These tumours are not often distinctly palpable because they lie beneath the sternomastoid muscle, the parotid gland and occasionally the great vessels. A very rare tumour of the vagus nerve which presents in the same way is the **glomus vagale** or chemodectoma of the vagus. Because of the difficulty of distinguishing neurogenic tumours from carotid body tumours all such patients should have angiography done. Neurogenic tumours should be excised, especially in the case of a malignant neurilemmoma or a glomus vagale. If the vagus nerve has to be sacrificed at operation the corresponding vocal cord will be paralysed and lie in the fully abducted position. This will require a Teflon injection to replace it in the midline and thus rehabilitate the voice.

Chondroma occurs on the cricoid or more rarely on the thyroid cartilage. It presents as a hard midline swelling and there is little clinical doubt about the attachment to laryngeal cartilage. It moves on swallowing, grows slowly and very occasionally enlarges into the laryngeal lumen. Should this happen a diagnosis of **chondrosarcoma** must be considered. A simple chondroma may be excised locally, provided that the integrity of the cricoid ring can be preserved, but a chondrosarcoma requires a total laryngectomy because it is radio-insensitive.

MALIGNANT NECK MASSES

Many carcinomas of the head and neck sooner or later metastasize to the lymph nodes of the neck which form a barrier that prevents further spread of the disease for many months. A carcinoma of the head and neck is assigned a stage which depends not only on the extent of the primary tumour (and the presence of distant metastases) but also on enlargement of the cervical lymph nodes. The current classification suggested by the UICC/AJC is shown in *Table* 2.21.1. This is a useful classification but is subject to some criticism. There is a great deal of observer error so that different observers only agree on the presence of palpable lymph nodes in about 70 per cent of patients. Furthermore, the value of the 'a' and 'b' categories is doubtful since these categories depend on a clinical opinion as to whether tumour is present in a palpable node or not and must therefore be entirely subjective. Finally, the progression from N_0 to N_3 suggests that the prognosis diminishes in that order, whereas the prognosis for bilateral nodes (N_2) is usually much worse than that for fixed nodes (N_3).

Table 2.21.1.   UICC/AJC classification of carcinoma of the head and neck

N—Regional lymph nodes
N_0—Regional lymph nodes not palpable
N_1—Movable homolateral nodes
     N_1a—Nodes not considered to contain growth
     N_1b—Nodes considered to contain growth
N_2—Movable contralateral or bilateral nodes
     N_2a—Nodes not considered to contain growth
     N_2b—Nodes considered to contain growth
N_3—Fixed nodes

The approximate distribution of patients between the four categories N_0–N_3 is shown in *Table* 2.21.2. The four categories of UICC/AJC classification will be used as convenient headings to discuss various aspects of the management of metastatic nodes in the neck.

Table 2.21.2.   Approximate incidence of lymph node metastases

N_0	70%
N_1	20%
N_2	5%
N_3	5%

Patients with no Palpable Nodes (N_0)

Some lymph nodes may be involved by tumour (occult nodes) and still be impalpable. The incidence of such occult nodes at various sites is given in *Table* 2.21.3.

Table 2.21.3. Incidence of occult nodes

Supraglottic larynx	16%
Piriform sinus	38%
Base of tongue	22%
Transglottic	11%
Glottic with a fixed cord	3%

The value of prophylactic neck dissection is doubtful. A study of the subsequent course of several hundred patients with carcinomas of the larynx, hypopharynx and mouth, who were not submitted to prophylactic neck dissection, showed that at all these sites only between 5 and 10 per cent of the patients died of uncontrolled disease in the neck, the remainder either being cured, or dying of intercurrent disease, recurrence at the primary site or distant metastases. The only patient who can theoretically be benefited by prophylactic neck dissection is the one who later dies of recurrent disease in the neck and it seems therefore that the maximum possible benefit in terms of increased survival rate is about 5–7 per cent. Against this it must be remembered that the mortality rate of radical neck dissection is between 1 and 2 per cent, so that the overall net improvement in 5-year survival figures which could theoretically be achieved by prophylactic neck dissection is reduced to around 5 per cent.

It may be that elective neck dissection has some place in the patient who is unlikely to return for follow-up and has a tumour with a known high incidence of occult nodes such as the piriform fossa, whereas there can be little or no reason for doing the operation on a patient who can readily attend for follow-up and who has a tumour such as a laryngeal carcinoma where the incidence of occult nodes is small.

Elective irradiation of the entire neck can sterilize the vast majority of occult nodes. Elective neck irradiation drastically reduced the recurrence in the same side of the neck in patients with carcinoma of the mouth, oropharynx, piriform fossa and supraglottic larynx. In a further series of patients with carcinoma of the mouth, of those patients in whom the primary had been controlled by radiotherapy almost 30 per cent later developed a metastasis in the neck, whereas no patient who had been subjected to elective neck irradiation later developed a metastasis in the neck.

Unilateral Neck Nodes (N₁)

The standard operation for dealing with metastatic glands in the neck is that of radical neck dissection described by Crile in 1906. It is generally accepted, at least by surgeons, that surgery is required to control lymph node metastases over 3 cm in the neck since these have usually been thought not to respond to radiotherapy. Small nodal metastases are more reliably sterilized by radiotherapy than larger ones. Radiotherapy has the advantage that if a node reappears after a course of radiotherapy a radical neck dissection can always be carried out, whereas radiotherapy can seldom be given with benefit for the usual diffuse recurrence which occurs after surgery.

The 'Occult Primary'

Cancer presenting with a node in the neck is mainly a disease of men (men : women, 4 : 1) with a maximum age incidence of 65 in men and 55 in women. The histology of the tumour obviously varies slightly depending on the interest of the surgeon but it appears that between one-third and one-half of all such nodes are replaced by squamous carcinoma, about a quarter by undifferentiated or anaplastic carcinoma and a similar number by adenocarcinoma if the supraclavicular nodes are involved, followed by a small number of miscellaneous tumours including melanomas, thyroid gland tumours, etc.

In about a third of patients a primary tumour can be found by investigation at the time of presentation. The primary sites in order of frequency are as follows: nasopharynx, tonsil, base of the tongue, thyroid gland, supraglottic larynx, floor of the mouth, palate and piriform fossa (head and neck sites); bronchus, oesophagus, breast and stomach (distant sites).

Careful follow-up, which will be discussed below, will later reveal a primary site in up to a third of patients. These primary sites are rather more commonly found in the head and neck than anywhere else and the sites are again those mentioned. The relative frequency of the various sites is as follows: oro- and nasopharynx, 23 per cent; thyroid, 18 per cent; laryngopharynx, 8 per cent; miscellaneous head and neck tumours, 10 per cent; lung, 21 per cent; gastrointestinal tract, 11 per cent; miscellaneous distant sites, 8 per cent. Obviously the frequency of involvement of these sites will depend to some extent on the interest of the individual surgeon.

In earlier times a malignant gland in the neck has been called a branchiogenic carcinoma, that is a carcinoma arising in a branchial remnant. Twenty-eight cases were recorded by Crile as being a branchial carcinoma, but no real search was made for a primary tumour. The nose and throat were examined in some patients; in one the branchial carcinoma was said to have extended into the piriform fossa and one had a nasopharyngeal carcinoma which was thought to be irrelevant. Chest radiographs were taken in only 11 (and in three of these definite metastases were present which may well have been lung primaries); radiographs of the skull and jaws were taken in 'several cases' only. As a result of Crile's paper many patients with a malignant node in the neck were thought to have a branchial carcinoma; since Crile had shown that treatment of this was difficult and the survival poor, it became standard practice to confine investigation to excision of the node; if squamous carcinoma was found a diagnosis of branchial carcinoma was made, no primary tumour was looked for and little further was done.

Hayes Martin was the chief opponent of this policy and urged strongly that a biopsy should be the last investigation to be done and that a search for a primary tumour must be made. He showed that these tumours were virtually always secondary to a primary tumour of the head and neck which could be treated, although he stated that a branchial carcinoma might be a real entity.

INVESTIGATION. The steps to be followed in investigating such a patient are as follows.

1. Primary sites: head and neck	Inspection, palpation, radiology, endoscopy, biopsy, cytology
2. Cervical lymph nodes	Inspection, palpation, pattern, level, aspiration, excision, morphology, histology.
3. Other primary sites	General physical examination, radiology, laboratory tests, endoscopy, biopsy, cytology.

Endoscopy is to be meticulous and should include magnification, particularly when examining the nasopharynx, the bronchi and the oesophagus. If no primary tumour is found a blind biopsy should be taken of the posterior wall of the fossa of Rosenmüller on the same side as the enlarged lymph node, of the base of the tongue and of the piriform fossa on the same side. It is also preferable to remove the tonsil on the same side and have it examined by serial section.

Bronchial cytology should always be performed by brushings, and fine needle aspiration of the node performed.

If aspiration biopsy does not give a satisfactory answer excisional biopsy must be contemplated; such a biopsy must always excise the lymph node entirely, and an incisional biopsy must never be carried out. Even then there may be serious consequences of excision including:

1. Local and possibly general spread of the disease.
2. Compromise of a subsequent neck dissection or irradiation.
3. Additional scar tissue causing difficulty in accurate palpation.
4. A false sense of security for the patient who feels that the lump has been removed.

It cannot be too strongly emphasized that excisional biopsy of a node in the neck should seldom be necessary and Martin's statement still holds true—'an enlarged lymph node should never be excised as the first or even an early step in diagnosis'; 'if, as a last resort, a cervical node must eventually be removed for diagnosis the operation must be performed by a surgeon who is able and willing to treat the primary cancer if it is later found somewhere in the head and neck.'

MANAGEMENT. In nearly all the series reported the treatment of the node with a truly occult primary has almost always been by radiotherapy. If the tumour is large and the biopsy shows a squamous carcinoma with rupture of the capsule, radiotherapy should be carried out. If one or more discrete glands in the upper part of the neck are involved a radical neck dissection should be carried out, whereas if there are one or more glands involved in the lower part of the neck radiotherapy is given; supraclavicular glands are not treated further on the presumption that they are secondary to a visceral carcinoma. This policy provided a 34 per cent survival at 3 years.

The main indications for removal of the neck nodes in the unknown primary are:

1. Where irradiation has failed, the nodes still being palpably involved, resectable and preferably on one side only.
2. A single, large, well-defined and resectable neck mass 5 cm or more in diameter.
3. Where biopsy raises suspicion of a primary tumour in the thyroid gland or a major salivary gland.
4. In the very rare case of branchiogenic carcinoma.

In those patients where the primary tumour is not found it is essential to repeat the search for a primary tumour at frequent intervals after the neck nodes have been treated. In a series of 1189 patients the primary lesion was later found in about 40 per cent, whereas a further 40 per cent died with metastatic disease and no evidence of a primary lesion. Of the survivors 16 per cent showed no further evidence of any malignant disease at any time after treatment of the neck nodes.

The follow-up may need to be continued for a very long time, since the primary tumour, particularly if it is in the tonsil, may not appear for many years.

Bilateral Neck Nodes (N₂)

Bilateral neck nodes are not common, occurring in about 5 per cent of head and neck cancers overall, more commonly from tumours of the base of the tongue, the supraglottic larynx and the hypopharynx. The accuracy of clinical diagnosis is very high. It is generally agreed that the presence of bilateral neck nodes is a very bad prognostic sign and survival rates fall to about 5 per cent in the presence of such an event. Despite this low survival rate many surgeons have advised staged or simultaneous bilateral neck dissection.

For the past 10 years or more it has been appreciated that it may not be necessary to stage operation on the two sides so that it is possible to carry out neck dissection on both sides at the same sitting with reasonable safety, although the complication rate may be as high as two in three. Formation of fistulae, sepsis, skin slough and facial oedema, which tend to persist, are the most important complications, and the postoperative death rate is about 15 per cent. Patients with supraglottic carcinoma and bilateral neck nodes have a reasonable prognosis, whereas nearly all other tumours particularly of the mouth, the oropharynx and the hypopharynx when associated with bilateral neck nodes have an extremely bad prognosis and surgery probably does not influence the natural history of the disease.

The most feared complication after bilateral neck dissection is probably increased intracranial pressure. It has been shown that tying one internal jugular vein produces a three-fold increase in the intracranial pressure, whereas tying the second side produces a five-fold increase; the intracranial pressure then tends to fall over about 8 days but not to normal. Furthermore, the pressure falls quite rapidly within the first 12 hours so that if the patient can be got over this period he is probably out of immediate danger. The methods to be used to avoid this complication include:

1. Removal of CSF (which is dangerous).
2. Keeping the patient in the sitting positon.
3. Avoiding dressings which compress the neck.
4. Infusion of mannitol.

Fixed Nodes (N₃)

The presence of fixed nodes is an uncommon event occurring in about 5 per cent of all patients with head and neck cancer. The word 'fixed' itself is one which is subject to individual interpretation and indeed very few nodes are truly fixed. A node is unlikely to be fixed until it becomes very large, i.e. 6 cm or more in diameter, but it may be fixed, even if very small, if the tumour has come out of the capsule.

Fixation to the base of the skull in the region of the mastoid process and to the brachial plexus is almost certainly a contraindication to treatment. Fixation to the skin is not necessarily a contraindication and it is possible to resect the tumour with the overlying skin which is replaced with a deltopectoral flap. On occasion, this has produced long-term survival and certainly may give very helpful pallia- tion.

When a tumour invades the arterial tree, resection of this vascular system has been described by Conley: 31 patients underwent resection of the common carotid artery for carcinoma. In 17, replacement was done by a vein graft, but the operative mortality was high (5/17). Despite this a few patients survived to live a useful life for periods up to 2 years. Six patients underwent anastomosis of the stumps of the internal and external carotid arteries. There were no postoperative deaths and two patients survived for long periods (3 and 5 years). Despite the occasional survivor reported by the highly skilled such as Conley, this technique does not appear to have become generally accepted.

MANAGEMENT OF A MASS IN THE NECK

HISTORY. The patient's age will give some guide as to the cause. Below the age of 20 the cause is likely to be inflammatory or congenital; between 20 and 40 it may be reticulotic, salivary or inflammatory; and above the age of 40 it is metastatic cancer until proved otherwise. If the cause is inflammatory the patient will usually have a pyrexia, but if it is due to infectious mononucleosis, toxoplasmosis, etc. there may only be a complaint of a vague ill-health. Tuberculosis will be associated with night sweats, and Hodgkin's disease gives the irregular Pel–Ebstein fever pattern.

Abscesses and salivary gland enlargements are painful, but most of the other conditions are painless. A history should be sought of any precipitating factors such as eating (salivary gland disease) or blowing (laryngocele). It is important to ascertain the length of the history of neck masses.

CLINICAL FEATURES. It is important to have a system of examination of the neck so that no areas are missed. The cursory running of fingers over the neck, which is commonplace, will only palpate large masses. The examiner should stand behind the patient and observe the whole neck uncovered from the hair-line to the clavicles. Palpation starts at the mastoid bone and follows the line of the trapezius muscle downwards to its junction with the clavicle. It is important to palpate beneath the trapezius muscle as this is where nodes may be felt between the flat of the fingers and the muscles from the floor of the posterior triangle to the tip of the mastoid. The line of the sternomastoid muscle is next palpated deeply under the muscle because the nodes in this region may lie about 2·5 cm from the surface of the skin. This palpation is continued down to the clavicle. At this point the examiner's fingers will be in the midline and in a position to palpate the thyroid and trachea. Futher palpation upwards in the midline allows an assessment to be made of laryngopharyngeal size and contour. In the submental region palpation laterally will include the submandibular glands and finally the parotids.

The first thing to determine about a neck mass is whether it is in the skin or deep in the neck. For example, a sebaceous cyst below the ear lobe may closely resemble a small parotid pleomorphic adenoma.

A midline mass is usually single. One may differentiate between a thyroglossal cyst and a thyroid adenoma by asking the patient to swallow and to protrude the tongue; a thyroid adenoma does not move on putting out the tongue but the thyroglossal cyst does. Chondroma of the cricoid is bony hard. Dermoids lie above the hyoid bone while thyroglossal cysts are found below it.

Posterior triangle masses are usually glandular in origin (apart from the bony hard cervical rib) and multiple. The commonest causes of small- or medium-sized unmatted soft nodes are infectious mononucleosis, toxoplasmosis, brucellosis and cytomegalovirus. Nodes from tuberculosis or a reticulosis are usually larger, matted and firm.

Supraclavicular masses are nearly always due to metastatic nodes from lung or stomach cancer depending upon the side.

Submandibular gland swellings present below the mandible but never extend below the level of the hyoid or behind the angle of the mandible. Parotid swellings are easily diagnosed as to site if they are diffuse, but small masses in the tail may be confused with jugulodigastric nodes. Generally speaking, parotid masses here are found behind the ear lobe whereas jugulodigastric node enlargement is related to the angle of the mandible.

The difficult area is around the carotid bulb, especially if the mass appears to pulsate. The differential diagnosis is between a carotid body tumour, an enlarged node due to tuberculosis, reticulosis, metastatic cancer, or a tense infected branchial cyst. Vagal tumours and nasopharyngeal metastatic glands are generally higher. A simple branchial cyst is found in this area and usually presents no difficulty in diagnosis, but if the swelling is tense it may be an infected cyst, a pyocele or a parotid abscess—all of which are painful to the touch.

Moving a painless pulsating mass does not help in diagnosis because not only carotid body tumours but also other masses lying on or adherent to the carotid artery are movable from side to side but not up and down.

Painless pulsating lumps commit the patient to having angiography done. If this investigation is not performed a surgeon may find himself in the position of operating on a neck mass which proves to be a carotid body tumour when no preparations have been made for a carotid artery by-pass.

Finally, the mobility of every mass must be assessed. If a node is fixed it does not mean that it is inoperable. It all depends upon what it is fixed to and whether the structure to which it is fixed, e.g. the mandible, can be removed along with the gland.

RADIOGRAPHY

Plain films. A plain film of the neck should always be requested because it will demonstrate such things as cervical ribs, laryngoceles, calcification in old tuberculous glands, and tracheal compression or altered direction from thyroid masses. A chest film may show pulmonary tuberculosis, mediastinal gland enlargement, bronchial carcinoma or evidence of secondary spread.

Base of skull and lateral skull films should be done if nasopharyngeal cancer is suspected.

Contrast studies. Barium studies will demonstrate oesophageal and gastric carcinomas or any oesophageal displacement. Defects in filling in the pyriform fossa will also be seen.

Laryngography is useful in primary laryngeal pathology and sialography must be done in salivary gland disease. Perhaps the most important contrast study in neck masses is carotid angiography.

Scanning techniques. Any thyroid mass demands a thyroid scan. A follicular adenocarcinoma and its metastases take up radioactive iodine, whereas no other tumour does so. A cold area may thus be the site of a carcinoma, but all nodules which are cold on scan are far from being malignant as this appearance may be due to haemorrhage or to degeneration in a cystic goitre. Hot nodules are never malignant.

CT scans of the neck are beginning to be of use in the assessment of neck masses but more for malignant than benign disease. A CT scan will show parapharyngeal extension, bone and cartilage involvement and mediastinal extension.

LABORATORY TESTS. In thyroid masses all the thyroid function tests should be done. In cases where there are multiple nodes in the posterior triangle blood should be sent for a monospot test, a toxoplasma titre, a brucella titre and a cytomegalovirus titre. If tuberculosis or sarcoid is suspected a Mantoux test and/ or a Kveim test is done.

Chapter 2.22

CANCER OF THE NOSE AND SINUSES

SURGICAL PATHOLOGY. Cancer of the nose and sinuses accounts for less than 0·1 per cent of all malignancies and about 3 per cent of all head and neck cancers. This means that there will be approximately 1 case per 300 000 population. It has a geographic propensity to affect the African, the Japanese and the Arab. It is much rarer in Western Europe and America.

The aetiology is unknown but it is not related to previous nasal disease except in the case of transitional-cell carcinoma which may be preceded by multiple polyp removals.

Definite factors in the aetiology are the dust from hard woods and nickel. Preventive measures have decreased the incidence of nose and sinus cancer in the wood and the nickel industries. Also implicated are materials used in boot making and mustard-gas production. Radiation has been implicated, as has snuff used by the Bantu tribe.

Tumours may affect the nasal skin and are usually squamous-cell cancers or basal-cell cancers. They can affect the nasal septum at the mucocutaneous junction and these are very difficult to treat because spread can occur at a very early stage into the upper lip and oral cavity. Of the tumours affecting the sinuses, 99 per cent affect the maxillary and ethmoid sinuses and only 1 per cent the frontal and sphenoid sinuses. It is often difficult to know if tumours have started in the ethmoid or in the maxillary sinus.

Ohngren describes an imaginary line going from the medial canthus through the maxillary tuberosity dividing the maxillary antrum into an anteroinferior area and a posterosuperior area. A preferred classification would be to use a line going through the middle turbinate which would split the sinuses into a suprastructure and an infrastructure.

Tumours affecting the infrastructure are quite different from those affecting the suprastructure. They may, in fact, have their origin in the teeth, the palate or the alveolar ridge and spread into the maxillary sinus rather than be originally maxillary sinus tumours that have exited from the sinus.

Suprastructure tumours will involve the upper part of the maxillary antrum and probably the ethmoid. Spread is through the multiple fissures and foramina in the orbital ethmoid area and along perineural sheaths, vascular plains and lymphatic channels. More than 80 per cent of patients present with initial bone destruction, which means that the tumours have spread into the orbit or into the infratemporal fossa.

Eighty per cent of tumours affecting the maxillary and the ethmoid sinuses are squamous-cell carcinomas. Of these a small percentage are anaplastic and the majority are well-differentiated. A report suggesting an anaplastic carcinoma should be regarded with some suspicion and the pathologist should be asked to reconsider whether or not this is a lymphoma or an olfactory neuroblastoma.

Ten per cent of tumours are of glandular origin, being adenocarcinomas or adenoid cystic carcinomas. These usually affect the nasal cavity and ethmoids.

Transitional-cell papillomas are usually benign and although it was formerly suggested that the inverting type became malignant rather than the everting type, this has not been borne out with long experience. Less than 5 per cent of these tumours turn into transitional-cell carcinomas and when they do they affect the lateral wall of the nose and ethmoids.

One per cent of nasal tumours are melanomas. These behave in one of two ways. They are either indolent and can be treated with multiple local excisions over a long period of years or they are highly aggressive, killing the patient regardless of treatment within a matter of months. They usually affect the mucosa of the nose, the septum and the ethmoid sinus.

Olfactory neuroblastoma is a neurogenic tumour arising from the olfactory bulb, thus affecting the cribriform plate and ethmoid. It has a typical histological picture but may be mistaken for a poorly differentiated carcinoma.

Sarcomas are rare but may be osteosarcoma, chondrosarcoma, fibrosarcoma or rhabdomyosarcoma.

Finally, lymphoma and plasmacytoma can mimic fast-growing maxillary tumours.

Metastases from distant tumours can implant in the nose and maxillary sinuses.

The histology dictates which of the varied treatments is appropriate for the alleviaton of the patient's problem.

CLINICAL FEATURES. Cancer of the nose and sinuses is difficult to miss. It is seldom that the diagnosis is made late due to doctor delay but it can often be held up by patient delay due to fear or dentist delay due to long continued treatment of a dental problem. The patient is unlikely to get symptoms until the tumour exits from the bony confines of the ethmoid or maxillary sinuses. The symptoms he then suffers depend on where the break in the bone occurs. If it is into the nose then he will have nasal obstruction due to a granular mass or polyps or bleeding from the nose. There may be pain in the teeth, loosening of teeth, difficulty in fitting dentures and a non-healing socket after a tooth extraction. Destruction of bone in relation to the orbit will produce proptosis, epiphora and diplopia. Invasion of nerves will cause numbness in the face or palate and invasion of the infratemporal fossa will cause trismus. Finally, skin involvement may be apparent in later presentations and less than 10 per cent will have a metastatic node in the neck. Since the sinuses themselves have no lymph drainage, the presence of an enlarged node in the neck implies soft-tissue infiltration with tumour.

ASSESSMENT OF SPREAD. The primary assessment of spread is done radiologically. Plain films and tomograms have now largely been supplanted by CT and NMR scans. CT scans, however, tend to overdiagnose the condition. Fluids in sinuses or mucosal thickening look like tumour and can lead to an overestimate of the tumour extent. However, the scans are excellent for indicating destruction of the cribriform plate, the fovea ethmoidalis or the pituitary fossa.

Sinus endoscopy should be carried out and biopsy done through an intranasal antrostomy rather than a Caldwell–Luc operation. To open tumour into the soft tissue of the cheek is against all the basic tenets of oncological surgery.

TREATMENT. Formerly radiation was used as a preoperative treatment in every case. It is now considered that many of the claims made for the preoperative use of this modality were overestimated. Most centres would now use radiation post-operatively.

The type of excision planned depends on the tumour spread and the tumour type. The least that can be done is a lateral rhinotomy and this is usually performed for the eradication of transitional-cell carcinoma. It has little place to play in the management of any other tumour except a small melanoma of a turbinate.

Tumours of the infrastructure are treated with a partial maxillectomy. This implies removal of the lower half of the maxillary antrum, the hard palate and the alveolus with preservation of the orbital floor and ethmoids. The defect is reconstructed with a dental prosthesis.

Tumours affecting the ethmoid should now be treated with a combined cranial facial approach. In this way much greater control can be secured of the cribriform plate area and also better assessment can be made of tumour extension into the orbit. Many more eyes can be saved using this approach and if they are saved their inferior support can also be preserved. There is no place for total maxillectomy with or without removal of the orbit all performed from below. The cranial facial approach thus is used for tumours that affect the ethmoids such as melanoma, olfactory neuroblastoma and adenocarcinoma.

Tumours of the septum are difficult to treat. They can invade the gingivolabial sulcus in the anterior part of the oral cavity where it is contiguous with the floor of the nose. This means that surgery will involve excision of the upper lip as well as the nose. Radiation is thus used primarily in tumours of the septum and in those that recur, a total rhinectomy and removal of the central segment of the upper lip is carried out with reconstruction by forehead flap and an Abbe lip flap.

The treatment of melanoma is primarily surgical, but it is worth giving chemothrapy because the occasional good response will be seen.

Sarcomas are treated primarily surgically with the operation being tailored to the position of the tumour. Rhabdomyosarcomas, however, do well with post-operative chemotherapy.

Lymphomas and plasmacytomas are treated with radiotherapy if they are localized, and chemotherapy and radiotherapy if they are more widespread.

The overall survival of patients with maxillary and ethmoid tumours is around 25 per cent. It is difficult to know how to improve on this, given the late presentation and lack of early symptoms.

Chapter 2.23

TUMOURS OF THE EAR

TUMOURS OF THE AURICLE

The auricle can be regarded as part of the skin of the face and thus is probably the commonest site for tumours related to the ear. The commonest types are squamous-cell carcinomas and basal-cell carcinomas, but melanoma and kerato-acanthoma can occur.

The patient is usually an elderly male with either a crusting or an ulcerating lesion on the ear. They are slow-growing and while early ones can be dealt with by minimal surgery or by radiotherapy, older people who neglect themselves may have the whole ear virtually occupied by tumour.

Squamous-cell carcinomas usually present as ulcerating granular lesions, but basal-cell tumours usually present initially either as crusts or cysts. It is only after a number of years that the surface breaks down to show the classical ulcer appearance with rolled edges. Patients usually regard these lesions as crusty dry skin and may pick at them for many years.

As long as the tumour has not entered the external meatus or has come forward into the parotid or down in between the mastoid and angle of jaw, then it can be regarded as a skin tumour. It is probably best excised surgically because cartilage will be involved and radiotherapy is less good than surgery at eradicating tumour in cartilage. If the tumour is found early then a simple wedge excision can be carried out with primary repair, but if it is larger then a total auriculectomy must be carried out and replacement of the defect can be done with a scalp flap.

More advanced cases may present with nodal metastases in the upper deep jugular chain or the parotid area. In this instance the ear must be removed together with a radical neck dissection or a parotidectomy. It implies a greater biological aggressiveness and so primary surgical treatment should be followed by radiotherapy.

CARCINOMA OF THE EXTERNAL AUDITORY MEATUS

This is a rare tumour and its incidence in the UK is one per million per year. The sex incidence is equal and this tumour is usually seen in patients over the age of 75.

Although tumours of the ear can be chemically induced in rats with azoxymethene, there seems to be no previous precipitating factor other than irradiation in carcinoma of the external auditory canal.

The external auditory canal is in two parts— a cartilaginous portion and a bony portion. Tumours arising in the cartilaginous area have little resistance and can spread anteriorly into the parotid gland or posteriorly into the postauricular sulcus. The bony portion forms a much more effective barrier to tumour spread. The lymphatic drainage can go anteriorly to the parotid lymph nodes inferiorly to the deep jugular chain and posteriorly to the mastoid lymph nodes.

The ceruminous glands of the external meatus do not produce wax and so are wrongly named. Tumours of these glands are either adenomas or adenocarcinomas and adenoidcystic carcinoma can also occur. The terms ceruminoma and hidradenoma are blanket terms for these adenomas or adenocarcinomas.

Squamous carcinoma is the commonest malignant tumour of the external meatus and as well as invading outwards it can go inwards towards the middle ear with all the subsequent complications.

Provided the tumour is lateral to the eardrum, it can be treated as a pure external meatus tumour. It is best treated by extended mastoidectomy together with excision of the temporomandibular joint and parotid. If nodes are palpable then a radical neck dissection should be performed. Postoperative radiotherapy should thereafter be considered. The prognosis is very much better than tumours invading the middle ear, but tumours confined in this way to the external auditory meatus are rare.

CARCINOMA OF THE MIDDLE EAR AND MASTOID

The age, sex and overall incidence of this tumour are the same as that of the external auditory canal. Most patients have a pre-existing chronic otitis media which has been present for 10–20 years. In addition, irradiation-induced carcinomas have been recorded and exposure to radium has been implicated also. Tumours arising in the external auditory meatus can also spread into the middle ear and it is often impossible to tell where the tumour began.

Tumours arising in the middle ear can spread into the bony Eustachian tube and thus gain access to the nasopharynx and the lateral wall of the cavernous sinus. The lymphatics of the middle ear and mastoid are less well defined, but when the tumour extends to the external meatus then the lymph nodes in the upper neck, parotid and mastoid area can be affected.

Squamous carcinoma is the commonest tumour of the middle ear. It causes extensive bone destruction involving the facial nerve, the labyrinth, the middle cranial fossa, the temporomandibular joint and the base of the skull. It also involves the IXth, Xth, XIth and XIIth cranial nerves and can extend along the Eustachian tube into the nasopharynx. As it leaves the temporal bone and involves soft tissue, it makes nodal metastases more likely and overall about 10 per cent will develop a node metastasis. The cause of death is due to a combination of intolerable pain, opiates and cranial nerve involvement, leading to aspiration pneumonia. Fatal intracranial complications can occur as can erosion of the jugular bulb and carotid artery resulting in terminal haemorrhage.

INVESTIGATIONS. Awareness of the lesion in someone with long-standing, uncontrolled chronic otitis media is a great help to early diagnosis. Substantive diagnosis is, however, made by biopsy and assessment of spread by radiology. Plain mastoid films, tomograms in the coronal and sagittal planes, and CT scans are essential to establish the extent of spread.

TREATMENT. A number of these patients will be untreatable due to cranial nerve involvement and dural involvement. There will also be the usual proportion of patients who are untreatable because of poor general condition and because of distant metastases.

Radiotherapy on its own has only about a 10 per cent 5-year survival rate, but this is tripled if surgery is added. There have been no reports of series with primary surgery and postoperative radiotherapy.

The surgery consists of excision of the temporal bone. This is begun with preliminary packing of the lateral sinus and is done with a combined temporal craniotomy and lateral approach. The temporomandibular joint, zygoma, styloid process, parotid gland and the temporal bone to the carotid artery must be removed. Soft-tissue cover is supplied by a trapezius myocutaneous flap and the facial nerve rehabilitated with a hypoglossal facial anastomosis. If lymph nodes are palpable then a radical neck dissection is performed.

After this sort of surgery the complications may be considerable, consisting of bleeding, infection, CSF leak and meningitis and hemiplegia, as well as deafness, vertigo and facial nerve paralysis. Perhaps the most lethal complication is paralysis of the IXth to XIIth cranial nerves. If these are all paralysed the patient will almost certainly die in a few months from aspiration.

GLOMUS TUMOURS

Glomus tumours arise from glomus bodies which lie on the dome of the bulb of the internal jugular vein in the hypotympanum, and may also arise from similar bodies lying on the promontory of the middle ear along the course of the tympanic branch of the IXth cranial nerve. There are thus two types of tumour. The glomus jugulare spreads widely throughout the temporal bone, while the glomus tympanicum often behaves as an indolent middle ear polyp. These tumours are very vascular and are locally invasive. The tumour grows slowly within the middle ear but will eventually perforate the tympanic membrane. The tumour may spread medially to involve the IXth, Xth and XIth nerves within the jugular foramen, and further medial spread will involve the XIIth cranial nerve. Upward and posterior spread will produce a facial paralysis. The posterior cranial fossa may be involved directly through the jugular bulb or may extend through the petrous bone. In some cases the Vth and VIth cranial nerves may also be involved. Distant metastases are exceptionally rare.

DIAGNOSIS. The earliest symptom of a glomus tumour is pulsating tinnitus. This will be followed by blood-stained otorrhoea, deafness and earache. Before the drum is perforated a red swelling is seen to arise from the floor of the middle ear and this can be seen through the tympanic membrane. If the drum is moved laterally by a Siegle's pneumatic speculum the swelling may disappear and reappear as the drum is pushed medially onto the swelling. When the tumour perforates the eardrum a polypus will be seen in the meatus and this will bleed profusely if touched. Apart from local examination, full examination of all the cranial nerves is indicated to assess the extent of the invasion. Radiographs of the temporal bones will include tomograms in both planes and a CT scan. NMR scanning will demonstrate soft-tissue extension. Jugular venography may demonstrate the extent of tumour invasion into the jugular bulb. Carotid angiography and vertebral angiography will demonstrate the blood supply of the tumour.

TREATMENT. The glomus tympanicum which is confined to the middle ear with a tympanic membrane that is still intact may be excised by tympanotomy.

The glomus jugulare tumour presents a totally different treatment problem. A proportion of patients will have unresectable tumours due to extensive skull-base involvement and these are treated with radiotherapy which may slow down the growth of the tumour. If, after appropriate assessment radiologically, it is decided that the tumour is resectable, then the possible morbidity of paralysis of the lower five cranial nerves must be balanced against the patient's age, his present morbidity and the speed of tumour growth.

Surgery involves temporal bone excision carried out by a combined temporal craniotomy and upper neck dissection to control the jugular vein.

Section 3

THE EAR

(B. A. B. Dale and A. I. G. Kerr)

Chapter 3.1

ANATOMY AND PHYSIOLOGY

ANATOMY

The ear can be divided anatomically and clinically into three parts—the external ear, the middle ear and the internal ear. The external and middle ears are concerned primarily with the transmission of sound. The internal ear functions both as the organ of hearing and as part of the balance system of the body.

The External Ear

The external ear consists of the pinna or auricle and the external acoustic meatus.

The Auricle

The auricle has two surfaces, lateral and medial; the parts of the lateral surface are shown in *Fig.* 3.1.1. The underlying skeleton of the auricle consists of a plate of yellow elastic cartilage, except for the lobule which is composed only of fat and fibroareolar tissue. The skin on the lateral surface is closely adherent to the perichondrium. The auricle is attached to the side of the head by ligaments and the largely functionless anterior, superior and posterior auricular muscles.

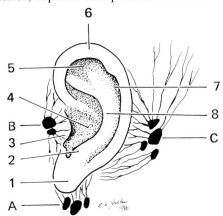

Fig. 3.1.1.   Left auricle (lateral view).

1, Lobule.
2, Antitragus.
3, Tragus.
4, Cavum conchae.
5, Fossa triangularis.
6, Helix.

7, Scapha.
8, Antihelix
   lymph nodes:
A, Superficial cervical.
B, Preauricular.
C, Postauricular.

219

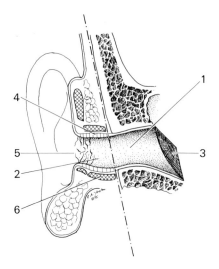

Fig. 3.1.2.   Right external auditory meatus.
1, Bony part.   4, Hair follicles and ceruminous glands.
2, Cartilaginous part.   5, Introitus.
3, Tympanic membrane.   6, Meatal cartilage.

The External Acoustic Meatus

In adults the external acoustic meatus measures about 24 mm from the introitus to the tympanic membrane, its medial limit. Since the tympanic membrane lies obliquely at the inner end of the meatus, the anterior and inferior walls are longer than the posterior and superior walls. At the junction of the inferior wall with the tympanic membrane there is a depression, the inferior meatal recess. This recess can be difficult to see and can contain an unsuspected reservoir of debris in an infected ear.

The meatus is composed of two parts: an outer or lateral third, which has a cartilaginous skeleton continuous with that of the auricle, and an inner or medial two-thirds which has a bony skeleton (*Fig.* 3.1.2.). The general direction of the cartilaginous meatus is medially upwards and backwards, while that of the bony meatus is medially, slightly downwards and forwards. There are two constrictions in the canal, one at the junction of the cartilaginous and bony part and the other in the osseous part. The meatus may be partially straightened in an adult by pulling the auricle upwards, outwards and backwards. Inconstant deficiencies of the cartilaginous meatus occur, known as the fissures of Santorini, and they may provide a pathway for infections to spread from the meatus to the parotid gland and superficial mastoid tissue or vice versa.

The skin lining the external meatus is continuous with that of the auricle. The sebaceous glands, ceruminous glands and hair follicles are present only in the cartilaginous portion. The skin is closely adherent to the underlying tissues, and for this reason furuncles in the cartilaginous portion of the canal are extremely painful due to the increased tension in the tissue.

The auricle and external meatus are supplied by branches of the Vth, IXth and Xth cranial nerves. Their distribution on the lateral surface of the auricle is shown in *Fig.* 3.1.3. The medial or posterior surface of the auricle is supplied by fibres of the great auricular nerve (C2 and C3) and the lesser occipital nerve (C2).

The **blood supply** of the auricle comes from the superficial temporal and posterior auricular arteries. The meatus is also supplied by these vessels but it receives a further supply in its inner part from the deep auricular branch of the maxillary artery. The veins accompany the arteries.

The **lymphatics** of the auricle and external meatus drain anteriorly into the preauricular (parotid) glands, inferiorly into the superficial cervical nodes along the external jugular vein, and posteriorly into the retroauricular (mastoid) glands (*Fig.* 3.1.1). The retroauricular glands also drain adjacent areas of the scalp, infection of which may produce swelling and tenderness of the mastoid area. This can lead to an erroneous diagnosis of acute mastoiditis.

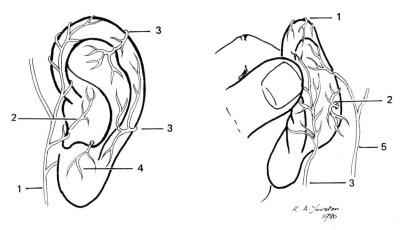

Fig. 3.1.3.   Cutaneous innervation of pinna.
1, Auriculotemporal nerve (Vth).   4, Branch of glossopharyngeal nerve (IXth).
2, Auricular branch of vagus nerve (Xth).   5, Lesser occipital nerve (C2).
3, Great auricular nerve (C2, C3).

Tympanic Membrane

The tympanic membrane, or drumhead (*Fig.* 3.1.4), separates the external meatus from the middle ear and functionally is part of the middle ear. The rim of the tympanic membrane consists of a fibrocartilage ring deficient in its superior part. This ring sits in a bony sulcus, the tympanic annulus, which lies at the medial end of the external meatus. There is a deficiency superiorly of both the cartilaginous annulus and the bony annulus known as the notch of Rivinus. This lies medial to the pars flaccida of the drum. The tympanic membrane is thin and when examined with an auriscope has a pearly grey colour with a triangular bright area, the cone of light, extending from the centre (the umbo) downwards and forwards. The membrane has an outer layer of squamous epithelium continuous with that of the meatus, a middle layer of fibrous tissue which has radiating and circular fibres, and an inner layer of mucous membrane continuous with the lining of the tympanic cavity. The fibrous tissue layer is deficient in the area of membrane bounded by the notch of Rivinus which, being less tense, is known as the pars flaccida or Shrapnell's membrane. The lower margins of this part are thickened and extend from the ends of the notch of Rivinus to the lateral process of the malleus forming the anterior and posterior folds of the membrane. The rest of the tympanic membrane is known as the pars tensa.

The **nerve supply** of the outer surface of the drum is similar to that of the adjacent external meatus. The anterior portion is therefore supplied by the auriculotemporal branch of the mandibular nerve, and the posterior portion is supplied by the auricular branch of the vagus. The inner surface is supplied from the tympanic branch of the glossopharyngeal nerve.

The outer surface of the tympanic membrane has a **blood supply** from the deep auricular branch of the maxillary artery. The inner surface receives branches from the posterior auricular artery and from the maxillary artery through its tympanic branch.

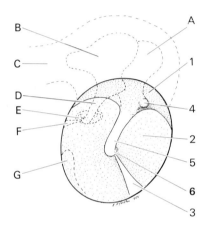

Fig. 3.1.4.   Right tympanic membrane. Broken lines indicate medial relations.

1, Pars flaccida.	A, Head of malleus.
2, Pars tensa.	B, Body of incus.
3, Cone of light.	C, Aditus.
4, Lateral process of malleus.	D, Long process of incus.
5, Handle of malleus.	E, Stapes.
6, Umbo.	F, Stapedius tendon.
	G, Round window niche.

The Middle Ear

The middle-ear cleft in the temporal bone includes the Eustachian tube, the middle ear, or tympanic cavity, and the aditus which leads posteriorly to the mastoid antrum and air cells. Anteriorly the Eustachian tube opens into the nasopharynx from which the cleft develops in early fetal life.

The middle ear, or tympanic cavity, lies between the tympanic membrane laterally and the cochlea medially. Its upper part extending above the tympanic membrane is known as the epitympanic recess or attic, and the lower part extending below the level of the floor of the external auditory meatus is referred to as the hypotympanum (*Fig.* 3.1.5).

The cavity may be described as a six-sided box, frequently likened in shape to a match-box standing on end with its vertical length greater than its breadth, but narrow in depth, particularly in its central portion where the basal turn of the cochlea forms a bulge on the medial wall. The roof of the cavity is formed by a thin plate of bone (the tegmen tympani), formed partly by the petrous part of the temporal bone and the squamous part. This plate of bone also forms the roof of the mastoid antrum and separates the tympanic cavity and antrum from the middle fossa of the skull. The floor, which is also thin, separates the cavity from the bulb of the internal jugular vein which may be exposed by bony deficiency. The tympanic branch of the glossopharyngeal nerve enters the cavity through the floor.

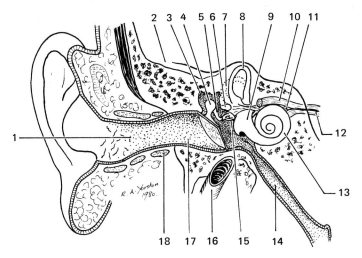

Fig. 3.1.5. Vertical coronal diagrammatic section through right ear. (After Brödel.)

1, External meatus, cartilaginous part.	10, Facial nerve.
2, Middle cranial fossa.	11, Vestibular nerve.
3, Attic.	12, Cochlear nerve.
4, Malleus.	13, Cochlea.
5, Incus.	14, Eustachian tube.
6, Position of lateral semicircular canal.	15, Stapes.
7, Position of posterior semicircular canal.	16, Internal carotid artery.
8, Superior semicircular canal.	17, Bony part of external meatus.
9, Vestibule.	18, Cartilage.

The anterior wall in its lower portion is formed by a thin plate of bone separating the cavity from the internal carotid artery. The upper portion has two openings, the lower one being the auditory (pharyngotympanic or Eustachian) tube and above it lies the canal for the tensor tympani muscle.

The posterior wall is wider than the anterior wall and in its upper part the aditus connects the epitympanic recess (attic) with the mastoid antrum. The tendon of the stapedius muscle comes out of the pyramid, a conical bony projection below the aditus. Just above the pyramid is the fossa incudis to which the short process of the incus is attached. Deep to the pyramid is a depression, the sinus tympani, which runs medial to the facial nerve and is continuous inferiorly with the hypotympanum. The facial nerve bends downwards at the level of the floor of the aditus and lies close to the posterior wall. Posterolaterally to the Fallopian canal in the aditus lies the rounded prominence of the bony wall of the lateral semicircular canal.

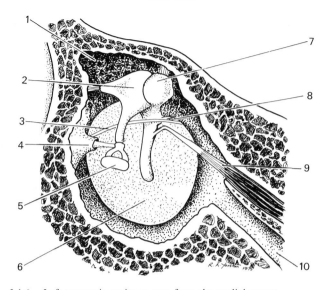

Fig. 3.1.6.   Left tympanic cavity as seen from the medial aspect.
1, Epitympanic recess.   6, Medial surface of tympanic membrane.
2, Body of incus.   7, Head of malleus and superior ligament of malleus.
3, Chorda tympani.   8, Anterior ligament of malleus.
4, Pyramid.   9, Tensor tympani in its canal.
5, Footplate of stapes.   10, Eustachian tube.

The lateral wall (*Fig.* 3.1.6) is formed mainly by the tympanic membrane and the outer bony wall of the epitympanic recess (attic). The medial wall is also the lateral wall of the internal ear. In it there are two openings (*Fig.* 3.1.7), the upper of which is the oval window (fenestra vestibuli) and below it is the niche leading to the round window (fenestra cochleae), which is closed by the secondary tympanic membrane. In front of and between these two windows lies the promontory. The surface of this bony covering of the basal coil of the cochlea is grooved for the nerve fibres of the tympanic plexus. The horizontal portion of the facial nerve is enclosed in a bony canal (the canal of Fallopius), which is sometimes deficient, and which crosses the medial wall above the oval window before turning vertically downwards at the posterior end of the window. The processus cochleariformis, containing the tendon of the tensor tympani, is situated on the anterior and superior part of the medial wall in front of the point of entry of the facial nerve from the inner ear.

The mucosal or epithelial lining of the tympanic cavity is of columnar ciliated epithelium in that part derived from the tubotympanic recess, but in a postero-superior direction there is a transition to cuboidal epithelium and finally to a flattened single-layer epithelium lining the mastoid antrum and air cells.

The Ossicles

The three ossicles, clothed in mucosa and supported by ligaments, form an articulated connection between the tympanic membrane and the oval window. The malleus consists of a head, neck, anterior and lateral processes and handle. The handle is attached to the drumhead (*Fig.* 3.1.6) and the head is situated in the attic articulating with the body of the incus, the short process of which has a ligamentous attachment to the floor of the aditus. The long process of the incus extends downwards and its lentiform process articulates with the head of the stapes. The stapes, suitably named from its stirrup-shaped appearance, has a head, a neck, two crura or limbs, and a footplate which is fixed to the margins of the oval window by an annular ligament.

The tensor tympani muscle arises from the cartilaginous part of the auditory tube, from the adjacent part of the greater wing of the sphenoid and from the bony canal in which it lies. Its tendon bends laterally around the processus cochleariformis and is inserted into the medial surface of the malleus near the neck. The nerve supply is from the motor division of the trigeminal nerve, through the otic ganglion, and its action is to tense the tympanic membrane by drawing it medially. The tendon of the stapedius muscle, after emerging from the pyramid, is inserted into the neck of the stapes. It has an action of damping the movement of the stapes by tilting outwards the anterior end of the footplate, and it is supplied by the facial nerve.

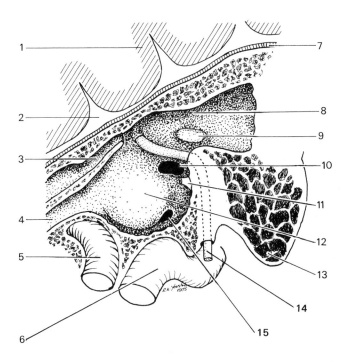

Fig. 3.1.7.   Relations of the left tympanic cavity and the facial nerve.
1, Cerebral cortex.
2, Subarachnoid space.
3, Canal for tensor tympani.
4, Eustachian tube.
5, Internal carotid artery.
6, Jugular bulb.
7, Dura mater.
8, Aditus.
9, Lateral semicircular canal.
10, Oval window.
11, Pyramid.
12, Promontory.
13, Mastoid process.
14, Facial nerve.
15, Round window.

Tympanic Ligaments and Spaces

The anterior and posterior ligaments of the malleus surround its neck and jointly form the axis ligament attached to the anterior and posterior ends of the tympanic notch. From the head of the malleus and the body of the incus a superior ligament suspends each from the roof of the attic. The posterior ligament of the incus attaches the short process of the incus to the fossa incudis in the aditus, and the annular ligament attaches the footplate of the stapes to the margins of the oval window. The folds of mucous membrane around the ossicles and ligaments form spaces or pouches in which local suppuration may occur.

Blood Vessels

The cavity is well supplied by branches arising from the maxillary, stylomastoid, middle meningeal, ascending pharyngeal and internal carotid arteries. The veins drain into the pterygoid plexus and the superior petrosal sinus. The lymphatics mainly drain into the retropharyngeal and parotid lymph glands.

Nerve Supply

This is through the tympanic plexus which lies on the promontory and is formed by the tympanic branch of the glossopharyngeal nerve and the superior and inferior tympanic branches of the sympathetic plexus of the internal carotid artery. The plexus supplies the lining mucosa of the tympanic cavity, the mastoid air cells and the Eustachian tube. Branches pass to the greater superficial petrosal nerve and the otic ganglion via the lesser superficial petrosal nerve from which secretomotor fibres are relayed by the auriculotemporal nerve to the parotid gland.

Facial Nerve

After crossing the cerebellopontine angle where it is closely related to the acoustic nerve it enters the temporal bone at the internal auditory meatus. It passes laterally, curving slightly upwards over the labyrinth until it reaches the anterior part of the medial wall of the tympanic cavity, close to the roof, just behind or medial to the processus cochleariformis. Here it bends backwards at right angles, where the geniculate ganglion is situated and passes almost horizontally, enclosed in the Fallopian canal, above the oval window and below the lateral semicircular canal. When it reaches the aditus it turns downwards behind the pyramid and continues almost vertically until it emerges at the stylomastoid foramen. The nerve then turns forward, passing lateral to the base of the styloid process, crosses the posterior belly of the digastric muscle and enters the parotid gland. It then passes between the superficial and deep lobes of the parotid gland and divides initially into two main trunks—the temporozygomatic and the cervicofacial. These then divide into peripheral branches as the nerve passes through the gland tissue until they emerge from the anterior and superior borders of the gland to supply the forehead, the upper and lower eyelid, the muscles over the cheek and nose and the muscles around the mouth. The nerve to the stapedius muscle is given off close to the pyramid. The chorda tympani nerve leaves the descending part of the facial nerve and enters the tympanic cavity which it crosses, enclosed in a fold of mucosa, to pass between the handle of the malleus and the long process of the incus. It leaves the cavity through the medial end of the petrotympanic fissure to join the lingual nerve in the infratemporal fossa.

The Eustachian Tube

The Eustachian tube (*Fig.* 3.1.5) connects the tympanic cavity with the naso-pharynx and in the adult is about 36 mm in length. From its pharyngeal end it runs upwards, laterally and backwards. In infants the tube is shorter and wider and its course is more horizontal than in adults. The tube has two parts: a pharyngeal cartilaginous part which forms two-thirds of its length, and a tympanic bony portion. The upper and medial walls of the pharyngeal portion of the tube are formed by a plate of cartilage, hook-shaped in vertical coronal sections (*Fig.* 3.1.8). The lateral wall is membranous. In the resting state the lateral and medial walls lie in apposition.

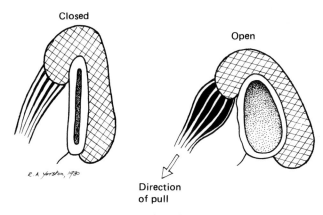

Fig. 3.1.8. Diagram to show action of tensor palati muscle in opening the Eustachian tube.

The fibres of origin of the tensor palati muscle are attached to the lateral wall of the tube so that contraction of this muscle on swallowing or yawning opens the tube, and thus equality of air pressure is maintained on both sides of the tympanic membrane. The levator palati muscle runs below the floor of the cartilaginous part of the tube and it is generally considered that contraction of this muscle opens the tube.

The bony portion of the tube lies between the internal carotid artery medially and the temporomandibular joint laterally. Above the tube is the bony canal for the tensor tympani muscle and below it lies the jugular fossa.

The Eustachian tube is lined by columnar ciliated epithelium. The submucous tissue of the cartilaginous part contains numerous mucous glands. The **blood supply** of the tube is from the ascending pharyngeal and middle meningeal arteries and from the artery of the pterygoid canal. Veins drain into the pterygoid plexus. The **nerve supply** of the cartilaginous portion of the tube is via the nervus intermedius.

The posterior aspect of the temporal bone is shown in *Fig.* 3.1.9.

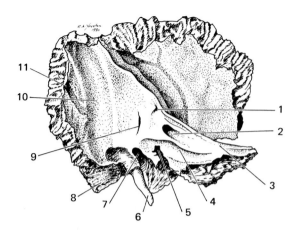

Fig. 3.1.9. Posterior aspect of left temporal bone.
1, Fossa subarcuata.   6, Styloid process.
2, Internal acoustic meatus.   7, Fossa jugularis (jugular bulb).
3, Groove for superior petrosal sinus.   8, Mastoid process.
4, Groove for inferior petrosal sinus.   9, Cranial opening of aqueduct of vestibule.
5, Canaliculus cochleae (cranial   10, Groove for transverse sinus.
  opening of perilymphatic aqueduct). 11, Mastoid foramen (for mastoid emissary vein).

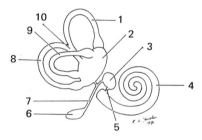

Fig. 3.1.10. Membranous labyrinth (right side lateral view).
1, Superior semicircular canal.   6, Endolymphatic sac.
2, Utricle.   7, Endolymphatic duct.
3, Saccule.   8, Posterior semicircular canal.
4, Cochlea.   9, Lateral semicircular canal.
5, Ductus reuniens.   10, Crus commune.

The Internal Ear

The internal ear within the petrous part of the temporal bone consists of a membranous labyrinth (*Fig.* 3.1.10) enclosed in a bony (osseous) labyrinth (*Figs.* 3.1.11, 3.1.12). The membranous labyrinth contains fluid known as endolymph, and the space within the bony labyrinth between its walls and the membranous labyrinth contains fluid known as perilymph. The **membranous labyrinth** contains vestibular and auditory components (*Fig.* 3.1.10). The vestibular element, which is connected to the vestibular nerve, consists of the three semicircular canals, the utricle and the

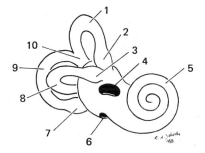

Fig. 3.1.11.   Bony labyrinth (right side lateral view).
1, Superior semicircular canal.
2, Ampulla of superior semicircular canal.
3, Ampulla of lateral semicircular canal.
4, Oval window.
5, Cochlea.

6, Round window.
7, Ampulla of posterior semicircular canal.
8, Lateral semicircular canal.
9, Posterior semicircular canal.
10, Crus commune.

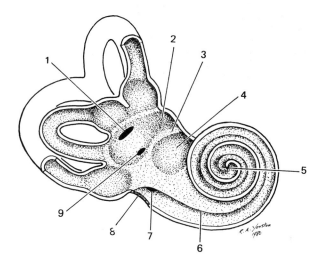

Fig. 3.1.12.   Bony labyrinth (right side lateral view partly opened).
1, Opening of crus commune into vestibule.
2, Elliptical recess (for utricle).
3, Crista vestibuli.
4, Spherical recess (for saccule).
5, Helicotrema.

6, Osseous spiral lamina.
7, Opening of perilymphatic aqueduct.
8, Round window.
9, Opening of endolymphatic aqueduct.

saccule. The auditory labyrinth consists of the cochlear duct, or membranous cochlea, and is connected to the auditory nerve. The endolymphatic sac, which lies on the posterior surface of the temporal bone, is connected to the membranous labyrinth by the endolymphatic duct which passes through the medial wall of the bony labyrinth (*Fig.* 3.1.12). The interior of the **bony labyrinth** is lined by endosteum. The central part of the bony labyrinth is the vestibule in the lateral wall of which lies the fenestra vestibuli (oval window), closed by the footplate of the stapes and the annular ligament. The medial or inner wall of the vestibule is directed towards the internal acoustic meatus and is perforated by nerve endings.

It contains two depressions—the spherical recess for the saccule and the elliptical recess for the utricle. Below the elliptical recess there is the small opening of the aqueduct of the vestibule which transmits the endolymphatic duct. The posterior, superior and inferior walls of the vestibule contain the five openings of the semicircular canals. The lateral or horizontal canal has an opening at each end but the superior and posterior vertical canals have a common opening at their non-ampullated ends, the crus commune (*Figs.* 3.1.11, 3.1.12).

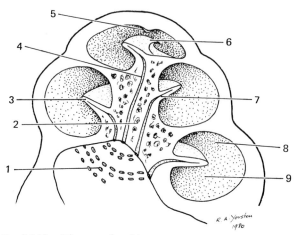

Fig. 3.1.13.   Diagram of cochlea.
1, Tractus spiralis foraminosa.   6, Hamulus.
2, Modiolus.   7, Spiral canal of modiolus.
3, Osseous spiral lamina.   8, Scala vestibuli.
4, Central canal.   9, Scala tympani.
5, Apex (contains helicotrema).

The **bony cochlea**, anterior to the vestibule, is a spiral tube wound two and a half times round its central axis or modiolus. Its base is directed towards the internal acoustic meatus and its apex towards the internal carotid artery (*Fig.* 3.1.13). From the modiolus, which contains the cochlear nerve, a hollow bony ledge (spiral lamina) projects into the lumen of the tube transmitting the branches of the nerve. This ledge commences in the vestibule just above the fenestra cochleae (round window) and ends near the apex of the cochlea at the hamulus or hook. The basilar membrane of the membranous cochlea is attached to the edge of the bony spiral lamina, and the outer surface of the membranous cochlea is attached to the inner wall of the bony cochlea thus dividing each coil of the bony cochlea into three parts: (1) the upper part, the scala vestibuli, commences from an opening in the vestibule below the spherical recess; (2) the lower part, the scala tympani, begins at the fenestra cochleae (round window); and (3) the membranous cochlea, or scala media, lies between the upper and lower parts. It is separated from the scala vestibuli by a membrane (Reissner's membrane) and contains the organ of Corti (*Fig.* 3.1.14). At the apex of the cochlea the membranous cochlea ends blindly and in this region, known as the helicotrema (*Fig.* 3.1.12), the scala vestibuli and scala tympani are continuous with one another.

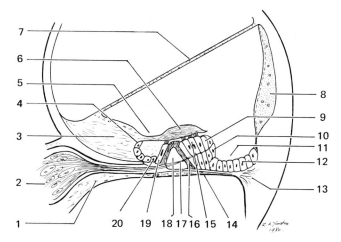

Fig. 3.1.14.   Scala media with organ of Corti.

1, Osseous spiral lamina.
2, Spiral ganglion.
3, Spiral limbus.
4, Vestibular lip of spiral limbus.
5, Inner sulcus.
6, Tectorial membrane.
7, Reissner's membrane.
8, Stria vascularis.
9, Space of Nuel.
10, Cells of Hensen.
11, Outer sulcus.
12, Cells of Claudius.
13, Spiral ligament.
14, Basilar membrane.
15, Outer hair cells.
16, Outer pillar of tunnel of Corti.
17, Nerve fibres.
18, Tunnel of Corti.
19, Inner hair cells.
20, Tympanic lip of spiral limbus.

The Membranous Labyrinth

The three membranous semicircular ducts occupying, but not filling, the lumen of the bony canals communicate with the utricle by five openings, the superior and posterior vertical ducts having a common opening (crus commune) at their non-ampullated ends (*Fig.* 3.1.10). The three ducts lie in the three planes of space, and each duct is dilated at one end to form an ampulla which contains a ridge of neuro-epithelium termed the crista ampullaris (*Fig.* 3.1.15). The hair cells of the crista have long filaments which project into a mass of gelatinous material called the cupula. Movement of endolymph in the ducts bends the cupula and hair cells which are supplied by the terminal fibres of the vestibular nerve.

The utricle, occupying the recessus ellipticus of the vestibule, contains a similar area of neuroepithelium lying in a horizontal plane. The neuroepithelium of the saccule, lying in a vertical plane, occupies the recessus sphericus. In the utricle and saccule the neuroepithelium is termed the macula, and from it hair cells are in contact with a membrane containing otoliths or ear stones (*Fig.* 3.1.15). From the utricle a small duct joins the endolymphatic duct from the saccule ending in the endolymphatic sac (*Fig.* 3.1.10) which lies between the layers of dura mater on the posterior surface of the petrous temporal bone midway between the internal acoustic meatus and the lateral sinus (*Fig.* 3.1.9).

The Membranous Cochlea

This (*Fig.* 3.1.13) is sometimes called the cohlear duct or scala media, and is a blind tube, triangular in section, coiled round a central bony pillar called the modiolus. The floor of the tube is formed by the basilar membrane, on the inner part of which lies a mound of neuroepithelium called the organ of Corti. In the lateral wall of the tube there is a layer of vascular epithelium known as the stria vascularis. The sloping roof and the third wall of the tube are formed by the vestibular (Reissner's) membrane completing the separation of the scala media from the scala vestibuli. The narrowest part of the membranous cochlea which lies within the vestibule is connected to the saccule by a fine duct (ductus reuniens) (*Fig.* 3.1.10).

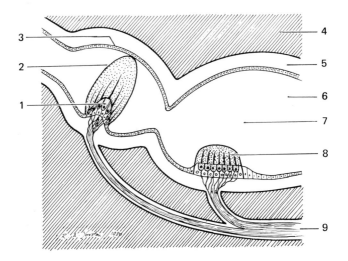

Fig. 3.1.15.   Schematic diagram of semicircular canal and utricle.
1, Hair cells.   6, Endolymph.
2, Crista.   7, Utricle.
3, Ampulla.   8, Otolith organ.
4, Temporal bone.   9, Nerve fibres.
5, Perilymph.

The **fluid system** of the labyrinth is divided into two components, endolymph and perilymph. **Endolymph**, which is contained in the membranous labyrinth, has a high potassium and a low sodium concentration. It may be produced by the stria vascularis and absorbed by the endolymphatic sac, but this is by no means proven. **Perilymph**, which occupies the perilymphatic space of the bony labyrinth, is similar to cerebrospinal fluid and contains a high sodium and low potassium concentration. While not yet proved, it is believed that perilymph is derived mainly from blood vessels, although some is derived from the cerebrospinal fluid via the cochlear aqueduct.

Organ of Corti

The organ of Corti is the sense organ of hearing and is situated on the basilar membrane of the cochlea. It consists of a complex arrangement of supporting and hair cells (*Fig.* 3.1.14). The basilar membrane and the tectorial membrane, which is in contact with the hair cells of the organ of Corti, are an integral part of the structure. In its ascent from the basal coil of the scala media to the apical coil structural changes are found in the organ, consisting of an increase in the width of the basilar membrane and in its fibrous tissue content; the tectorial membrane becomes larger; the tunnel of Corti enclosed by inner and outer rods increases in height and width; and the nerve supply to the hair cells decreases.

Blood Vessels

The main supply comes from the labyrinthine artery which arises from the basilar or anterior inferior cerebellar artery. The veins unite to form the labyrinthine vein which opens into the inferior petrosal sinus or the sigmoid sinus. Small veins pass via the aqueducts of the vestibule and cochlea to the superior and inferior petrosal sinuses respectively.

Nerve Supply

The vestibulocochlear (acoustic) nerve is formed by cochlear and vestibular parts in the internal acoustic meatus from which it emerges on the lateral side of the sensory root of the facial nerve and enters the brainstem between the pons and the medulla. The cochlear part is composed of fibres which are the central processes of bipolar cells in the spiral ganglion in the modiolus of the cochlea. The peripheral processes of the ganglion cells pierce the bony spiral lamina to reach the inner and outer hair cells of the organ of Corti. Other fibres follow a spiral course on the internal part of the basilar membrane. The vestibular part consists of the processes of the bipolar cells of the vestibular ganglion in the internal acoustic meatus. From the superior part of the ganglion, fibres pass via the superior vestibular nerve to the utricle, the ampullae of the superior and lateral semicircular ducts and the anterior part of the macula of the saccule. The inferior part of the ganglion sends fibres via the inferior vestibular nerve to the macula of the saccule and the ampulla of the posterior semicircular duct.

PHYSIOLOGY OF HEARING

External and Middle Ears

Airborne sound consists of vibrations of the atmosphere, that is, of alternate phases of condensation and rarefaction. The purpose of the auditory apparatus is to convert these vibrations in air to vibrations in the inner-ear fluids, and then to nerve impulses to be transmitted along the auditory nerve to the higher centres of hearing.

The auricle collects the sound waves to some extent, and they pass along the external acoustic meatus to the tympanic membrane which is set in motion. The vibrations of the tympanic membrane are transmitted to the malleus, incus and stapes. The malleus and incus rotate around a common fulcrum and transmit vibrations to the stapes in the oval window, causing vibrations to be set up in the endolymphatic and perilymphatic compartments of the inner ear. The conversion of sound from air into fluid is accomplished by the middle-ear structures. To some extent the lever system of the malleus and incus helps, but the main effect comes from the tympanic membrane. The ratio of the functioning area of the tympanic membrane to the area of the footplate is $14:1$, and this is combined with an ossicular lever ratio of $1\cdot3:1$. This system increases the sound pressure at the footplate to a degree which causes the fluids of the inner ear to vibrate (*Fig.*

3.1.16). The stapes moves in a rocking rather than a piston motion and, as fluids cannot be compressed, these vibrations are transmitted to the round window membrane. This reciprocal action of the oval and round windows is essential. In the normal ear the presence of the tympanic membrane and an air-containing middle ear prevents the sound-pressure waves from reaching the round window and opposing the outward movement of the round window membrane. This protection of the round window is lost where there is a large perforation of the tympanic membrane, and this is one of the factors which may produce deafness.

The tympanic membrane is at its most efficient when the air pressure in the external acoustic canal and the middle ear is equal. This is achieved by the Eustachian tube which normally opens during each act of swallowing. In this way the air pressure on both sides of the tympanic membrane can be kept equal. The stapedius and tensor tympani muscles seem to have a protective function; loud sound causes a reflex contraction of the muscles and this serves to stiffen up the conducting mechanism and possibly to protect the inner ear from damage.

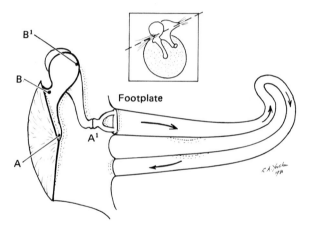

Fig. 3.1.16.   Schematic diagram of sound-conducting mechanism. Ossicular lever, AB: $A^1B^1 = 1\cdot3:1$. $BB^1 =$ axis through ligaments of malleus and incus. Inset = medial aspect of malleus and incus. Broken line = axis of rotation.

Internal Ear

The vibrations, transmitted by the stapes, produce displacement of the basilar membrane and shearing movements between the hair cells and the tectorial membrane of the organ of Corti which initiates nerve impulses in the fibres of the auditory nerve (*Fig.* 3.1.14). The greater the degree of displacement the more hair cells and hence the more nerve fibres are stimulated. It has been found that the basal portion of the cochlear duct responds to high-frequency sounds while the apex responds maximally to low-frequency stimuli. There is a gradation in response from the basal turn to the apex. The nerve fibres supplying each area of the cochlea, therefore, are stimulated by different frequencies. These fibres then transmit impulses to the auditory nuclei in the brainstem, and from there the fibres pass through the mid-brain to the auditory cortex where the impulses are perceived as sound.

The nerve impulses in response to sound are generated by the hair cells of the organ of Corti. The exact mechanism is uncertain. The electrical potentials which are set up, however, follow accurately the wave form and changes in intensity of the stimulating source. These are known as cochlear microphonics and may be picked up readily by an electrode placed on the promontory near the round window. The VIIIth nerve action potential may also be easily picked up and is now utilized in an objective test of hearing known as electrocochleography.

PHYSIOLOGY OF THE VESTIBULAR APPARATUS

The balance of the body is maintained by coordination of information from three systems: (1) proprioception, i.e. sensation from muscles, joints, tendons and ligaments; (2) the eyes; (3) the vestibular system.

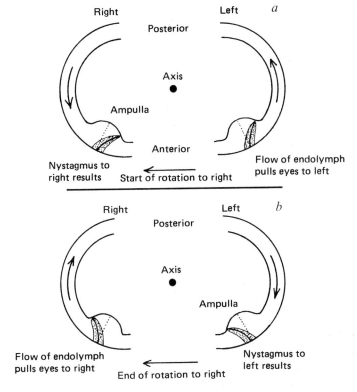

Fig. 3.1.17. Diagram of movement of endolymph in rotation tests.
a, Beginning of clockwise rotation.
b, End of clockwise rotation.

The vestibular system consists of the semicircular canals, the utricle and the saccule. The utricle and saccule respond to linear acceleration. The linear acceleration to which the body is normally subjected is gravity, and it is alterations in the position of the head in relation to the direction of gravity which stimulate selective parts of the utricle and saccule. Impulses from the utricle and saccule not only give information about the position of the head in space but initiate reflexes which tend to keep the head in the upright position and are contributory to the maintenance of muscle tonus. In modern life large horizontal linear accelerations may be added to the ever-present gravity so that the body reacts to the resultant force which is no longer vertical. The semicircular canals respond to angular (rotatory) acceleration, and stimulation of the semicircular canals gives rise to the sensation of rotation and to reflex movements of the eyes and body to counter the movement. Angular acceleration around any axis will stimulate at least one pair of semicircular canals, e.g. the horizontal canal on each side or the superior canal on one side and the posterior canal on the other side. The mechanism can most easily be explained by considering rotation in a rotating chair about a vertical axis (*Fig.* 3.1.17). Acceleration to the right will cause movement of endolymph to the left within the membranous horizontal canal and deflection of the cupula on the crista in the expanded ampulla of the canal. There is a constant impulse rate of 10–20 impulses per second in the fibres of the nerves leaving the crista. Movement of the endolymph and cupula towards the ampulla causes an increase in this impulse rate. Movement away from the ampulla causes a reduction in the impulse rate. In *Fig.* 3.1.17 it will be seen that acceleration to the right will cause an increase in the impulse rate from the crista of the right horizontal canal and a reduction of the rate on the left side. This difference in impulse rate is interpreted by the central nervous system and gives rise to the sensation of rotation to the right. The eyes will move to the left at a rate proportional to the degree of stimulation, but as the eyes can only move a limited amount laterally, a central reflex will return them to mid-position and the vestibular stimulation will again move them to the left. This constitutes nystagmus with a relatively slow vestibular component and a very much faster central component. When the acceleration stops, rotation will continue at constant velocity, the cupula on the crista will return to rest and there will be no sensation of rotation and no nystagmus. If the rotation is suddenly stopped, i.e. the equivalent of an acceleration to the left, the endolymph and cupula will continue to move to the right, the impulse rate from the left horizontal canal will reduce and the rate from the right canal will increase. There will be a sensation of rotation to the left, although the head and body are at rest; there will be nystagmus with the slow phase to the right and the quick phase to the left. It will be seen that destruction of one labyrinth with abolition of the resting impulse rate will produce imbalance of impulses arriving in the central nervous system from the two sides, resulting in the same effect as vestibular stimulation, i.e. sensation of rotation, nystagmus, righting reflexes and, if the stimulation is large enough, nausea, vomiting, pallor of the skin and sweating. Rotation carried out in this way, using controlled accelerations, may be used for testing semicircular canal function but it has the disadvantage of stimulation of the canals of both sides at the same time.

Chapter 3.2

INVESTIGATION OF EAR DISEASE

HISTORY

Deafness

Deafness is the most common symptom of ear disease, and it may vary from a degree so slight as to escape the notice of the patient to complete loss of hearing. In conductive deafness the sound appears quieter but it is not distorted. Sounds, and particularly speech, are well heard when amplified. In some cases the patient may hear better in the presence of background noise, as, for example, when travelling in a train or in a bus. This is called paracusis Willisii, and is found most typically in otosclerosis. The quality of speech is well-maintained because the patient hears his own voice clearly. In sensorineural deafness sound not only seems quieter but is distorted, the most usual distortion being the loss of high frequencies which diminishes the understanding of consonant sounds with resulting difficulties in understanding speech. The distortion also limits the benefits obtained by amplification. In severe sensorineural deafness the patient does not hear his own voice, and this leads to speech which is indistinct and expressionless.

Deafness of sudden onset may be due to occlusion of the external auditory meatus by wax or discharge, to the presence of an effusion in the middle-ear cavity, or to a blast injury perforating the drum, but this may also affect the inner ear. Sudden deafness may frequently result from inner-ear disease caused by such pathology as vascular occlusion or a virus infection. Deafness of gradual onset is typically met with in otosclerosis and presbyacusis. Hyperacusis is the sensation of discomfort or pain on exposure to loud noises. When the same tone is heard as notes of a different pitch in either ear, the condition is known as diplacusis.

Discharge

Discharge from the ear may arise from the external meatus or the middle-ear cavity. The discharge varies in type. Sometimes the patient complains of discharge when only soft wax is present. Serous or purulent discharge is seen in otitis externa because there are no mucus-secreting glands in the external meatus. Discharge from the middle ear is usually mucopurulent, but it may consist of frank pus. In chronic otitis media with a central perforation mucopurulent discharge may be profuse, while in chronic otitis media with an attic or marginal perforation the discharge may be scanty, purulent and contain epithelial debris. In the latter case it is often offensive, particularly when cholesteatoma is present. Discharge of blood from the ear commonly arises from the granulation tissue of chronic otitis media, but is sometimes due to the rupture of a blood blister in a virus infection. Occasionally bleeding is due to a malignant disease. Watery discharge may be cerebrospinal fluid after a head injury, but occasionally there is a leak after operations on the ear.

Pain

Pain in the ear may arise from the auricle, the external meatus or the middle ear and mastoid, or it may be referred from other sources. Descriptions of pain vary. It may be lancinating and paroxysmal, severe and constant, deep and boring, or intermittent. It may be aggravated by pressure on the ear, by chewing, by sneezing or by blowing the nose. The patient should be asked to point to the exact spot of the pain, because it may be felt in front of the ear, or below the auricle, over the mastoid process or deep within the meatus. Pain in front of the ear, in the region of the tragus, is probably due to a furuncle, and this pain is aggravated by chewing, by lying on the affected ear, by pressure over the tragus or by pulling the auricle. Pain felt deep in the ear or behind it may arise from the middle ear or mastoid, when it is increased by blowing the nose. Pain behind the ear may be due to an infected gland at the mastoid tip, and this may have been caused by an otitis externa, infections of the scalp or rubella. Pain located below the ear, in the cleft between the ramus of the mandible and the mastoid process, is usually due to spread of meatal infection to an infra-auricular lymph node, which may be palpable and tender.

Itching

Itching or irritation in the ear is generally associated with an otitis externa, and it may be so severe that the patient is constantly rubbing or scratching the ear, and may even abrade the skin at the meatal entrance. It may arise from the discomfort of wax, resulting in the patient attacking the wax with a hair-grip, matchstick or other such utensil, thus setting up an otitis externa.

Tinnitus

Tinnitus, or a subjective sensation of sound in the ear, is a very common, and sometimes the only, symptom of ear disease. Tinnitus may be regarded as a sign of irritation of the cochlea or upper auditory pathways, just as pain is a sign of irritation of the sensory nerves. The sounds may be continuous or intermittent, and they may be synchronous with the pulse. In otitis media pulsating noises may be met with, but they commonly occur in the absence of any aural disease. The patient is sometimes conscious of tinnitus during the whole of his waking hours, or he may hear the noises only when in a quiet room or when he is in bed at night. Tinnitus may produce extreme depression, and may render the sufferer unfit for work. The nature of the sound varies. It may be described as hissing, buzzing, rushing, hammering, as being like the escape of steam, the sound of the sea, or of bells and so on. Tinnitus may be met with in any form of ear disease, and is also a symptom of some general diseases which indirectly affect the ear through the circulation. It is a common symptom of renal affections, cardiac disease and anaemia, and it may be caused by certain drugs, such as quinine, the salicylates and ototoxic antibiotics. The possiblity of an intracranial tumour occurs to many patients, and their fears cannot be allayed without a neurological examination unless some other cause is found.

Vertigo

Vertigo may occur in certain ear diseases, and it must be regarded as a symptom of irritation of the vestibular apparatus. Rarely it may be produced by the pressure of cerumen against the tympanic membrane. It may accompany virus infections of the middle and internal ear. In cases in which the bony wall of the horizontal (lateral) semicircular canal is eroded by disease, giddiness is experienced on stooping or on suddenly turning the head. Tumours of the VIIIth nerve, cerebellar lesions such as abscess or tumour and Ménière's disease give rise to vertigo. Arteriosclerotic changes in the blood vessels of the brain are a common cause of giddiness in old people. Vertigo may be severe and of short duration, or it may be more or less constantly present in which event it is usually less severe.

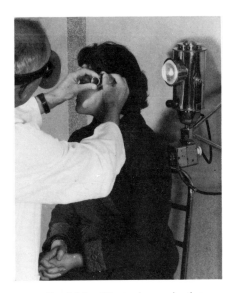

Fig. 3.2.1. Otoscopic examination.

CLINICAL EXAMINATION

In examining the ear with a forehead mirror good illumination is necessary. Any fairly powerful lamp, such as an electric bull's-eye lamp, will answer the purpose. Daylight may suffice for the examination of the external meatus, but is less satisfactory for the drumhead. The source of light is arranged on one side of the patient's head and slightly above the level of his ear (*Fig.* 3.2.1). The electric headlamp may be employed. The patient is seated sideways to the surgeon who sits opposite the ear to be examined and reflects light on to it. Before introducing a speculum the mastoid process should be examined, and any abnormality, such as a scar, redness or oedema, is noted. The auricle is next examined for inflammation, swelling or skin lesions. The external meatus is investigated for swelling of the walls, dermatitis or visible discharge, and this inspection will allow a suitably sized speculum to be selected for insertion.

In order to see the drumhead the external meatus must be straightened by pulling the auricle upwards, outwards and backwards. In infants, owing to the non-development of the bony external meatus, the auricle has to be drawn downwards and backwards. In a considerable proportion of cases these manipulations permit an inspection of the drumhead without the use of a speculum, unless vibrissae interfere with the view or the outer end of the meatus is slit-like. The speculum should have a wide mouth and an oval or circular end, and there should be three or four different sizes to suit all ages. The auricle is held up by the middle and ring fingers as the speculum, held by the thumb and index finger, is gently inserted into the meatus (*Fig.* 3.2.1). Obstructing vibrissae may be passed by a rotary movement of the speculum, but the instrument must not be inserted far enough to come in contact with the bony meatus as this part of the canal is exceedingly sensitive.

The electric auriscope, or otoscope, is more frequently employed in general practice. There are many patterns on the market. It is wise to select one which gives a good light directed through the tip of the speculum and not falling on one of the walls. There should be four or five specula of different sizes, and especially one small enough for use in infants. Some auriscopes have closed heads while others have open heads to allow the passage of wool mops or wax curettes, but the latter are generally used by specialists. Many have a fixed focus, and this may mean that the definition of the tympanic membrane is not always satisfactory. Others have an adjustable focus. Magnification is usually × 2, but it is possible to acquire one with a magnification of × 3, or even × 6, although this is too great for general use. Some patterns have an attachment for a rubber bulb, thus adapting the instrument for use as a pneumatic speculum, but frequently the rubber tube or the cement in the eye-piece becomes loose in time, and the advantage is lost.

On looking into the meatus, the skin of the posterior inferior meatal canal will probably meet the eye first. The tip of the speculum must be pointed upwards and inwards to display the membrane. In health, the drumhead presents a highly polished grey surface of which the posterior and upper part is distinctly nearer the eye than the anterior and inferior. The colour alone is not sufficient for recognition of the membrane; the handle of the malleus must also be seen. At the upper end of the handle the short process is noted as a small projection, and running backwards and downwards from this the handle of the malleus appears as a whitish-yellow streak ending at a point (the umbo) below the centre of the membrane.

For purposes of description the membrane is divided into four quadrants by imaginary lines, one drawn horizontally through the umbo while the other bisects this line at right angles (*Fig.* 3.2.2). Extending downwards and forwards from the umbo the cone-shaped light reflex is seen. This is fairly constant in position as the anterior inferior quadrant of the membrane is the only part that is approximately at right angles to the meatus, and therefore in a position to reflect the light from the mirror. The reflex may be absent owing to loss of gloss, or it may be altered in position by changes in the curvature of the drumhead. In front of and behind the short process two folds are seen on the membrane. These are called the anterior and the posterior malleolar folds. They are only very slightly marked in the normal drumhead, but become exaggerated in cases of indrawing. Above the short process the pars flaccida, or Shrapnell's membrane, fills the gap in the tympanic ring known as the notch of Rivinus. As its name implies, this part of the drumhead is less taut than the part inferior to the malleolar folds, called the pars tensa.

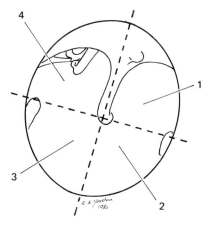

Fig. 3.2.2. Diagram of right tympanic membrane divided into quadrants.
1, Anterosuperior quadrant. 3, Posteroinferior quadrant.
2, Anteroinferior quadrant. 4, Posterosuperior quadrant.

The translucency of the drumhead varies considerably in health and, while the above description refers to one of average translucency, additional structures may be seen when the membrane is more transparent. The long process of the incus is frequently observed as a white line behind and parallel to the handle of the malleus (Fig. 3.2.2), but extending only about half its length. It is sometimes seen to end in a round spot which is the head of the stapes. At right angles to this, and extending to the posterior margin of the membrane, the tendon of the stapedius muscle presents a similar appearance. In the lower and posterior quadrant a round shadow may be seen at the circumference of the membrane which corresponds to the niche leading to the round window. The centre of the membrane may be of a pale yellow colour due to the promontory shining through, because the membrane is concave while the promontory is convex, and thus the medial wall of the middle-ear cavity is much closer to the drumhead at this part. It is occasionally possible to see the tympanic opening of the Eustachian tube through the most anterior part of the membrane.

While the normal appearance is readily recognized after a little practice, the beginner experiences considerable difficulty in distinguishing many abnormal conditions. Where difficulty exists, the short process and handle of the malleus should be looked for in the first instance, because if they are seen there is no doubt that the structure they lie in is the drumhead, however much its appearance may be altered. When they are not detected the observer must attempt to estimate the depth of the structure at which he is looking. If it is obviously nearer the eye than the membrane, the appearance may be due to a polypus, granulation tissue, wax, a foreign body or some projection from the meatal wall. If the appearances are not comparable with any condition with which the observer is familiar, the ear should be syringed or mopped out, as the presence of even a little pus or a flake of wax or desquamated epithelium may be quite misleading and give rise to an incorrect diagnosis.

A minute perforation of the membrane appears as a black spot because, as it is small, the middle ear is not lit up through it. A healed influenzal bulla gives a somewhat similar appearance. A larger perforation allows light to illuminate the middle-ear cavity. Perforations have clear-cut edges unless they are due to trauma in which case the edges may be ragged. A cicatrix is usually transparent and may appear like a dry perforation, but unless it is adherent to the medial wall of the middle ear it may be distinguished from a perforation by means of a Siegle's pneumatic speculum. This is a speculum which expands into a small chamber and is closed at its outer end by a lens. A small hollow tube, to which a valveless rubber ball is attached by rubber tubing, is let into the side. The speculum is introduced into the meatus, which it should fit closely, and an enlarged view of the drumhead is obtained. By alternately compressing and releasing the bulb, the air in the meatus is alternately condensed and rarefied. In the case of a cicatrix each movement of the rubber ball makes it flap in and out, while a perforation shows no movement, although, if the middle ear contains secretion, some discharge may be sucked out through the perforation.

An indrawn membrane presents characteristic appearances; the short process is prominent and causes the anterior and posterior malleolar folds to be much exaggerated, especially the latter which frequently present a sickle shape. The handle of the malleus is foreshortened and rotated, so that it lies in a more backward direction than usual. This change in direction brings the umbo into the upper half of the membrane and thus the light reflex is displaced, being extended or fragmented to appear as a mere spot of light at the periphery.

LABORATORY INVESTIGATIONS

In cases where there is purulent or seropurulent discharge, it is very useful to take a swab for bacteriological culture before starting treatment.

Where indicated, blood may be taken for blood counts, serological tests, thyroid-function studies, autoantibodies, renal function tests and viral studies.

HEARING TESTS

These are considered in the next chapter.

RADIOGRAPHY

1. Plain films of the temporal bone will show the degree of pneumatization of the mastoid (see Fig. 3.7.2). Clouding of the air cells can indicate infection while areas of erosion may be seen in large cholesteatomas after mastoid surgery or with malignant disease (Fig. 3.2.3).

2. Tomography of the temporal bone is useful in assessing the degree of development in congenital atresias of the ear. It can also demonstrate small areas of erosion, middle ear abnormalities and widening of the internal acoustic meatus as occurs with acoustic neuromas.

3. Computerized axial tomography (CT scan) is now widely used in investigation for acoustic neuromas or cerebellopontine angle tumours causing sensorineural hearing loss. It can be combined with an air-meatogram which can detect and outline tumours less than 1·5 cm in diameter.

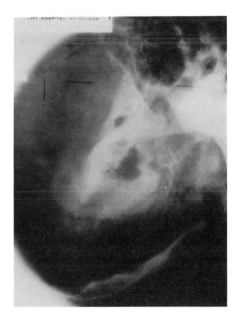

Fig. 3.2.3. Lateral view of the right temporal bone showing an irregular defect in the mastoid antrum. This was a carcinoma.

REFERRED OTALGIA

If a patient complains of earache the cause is usually determined by inspection of the external meatus and the tympanic membrane, but in a number of cases the pain is a referred one and the meatus and drumhead are normal. The ear receives sensory nerve supply from the trigeminal, glossopharyngeal and vagus nerves as well as from branches of the upper cervical roots, especially C2 and C3.

When otoscopy is normal, therefore, the cause of the pain must be sought in the scalp, neck, nose, nasopharynx, pharynx, teeth, parotid, temporomandibular joint and larynx (*Fig.* 3.2.4).

Dental pain may be referred through the trigeminal nerve and usually arises from disease of the lower molars, e.g. pulp space infections, periodontal disease, impacted unerupted teeth, especially wisdom teeth, various roots, etc. Even if the patient is edentulous, radiography in the form of an orthopantomogram may reveal a retained root or an unerupted tooth. Pain in the ear may follow dental extraction or bone infection following extraction.

The **temporomandibular** joint is a fairly common source of otalgia, and the cause is a capsular stress produced by dental malocclusion. It may be found in young people as a result of faulty mastication or in young girls when kissing is thought to be a cause. Badly fitting dentures throw a strain on the joint capsule, as does

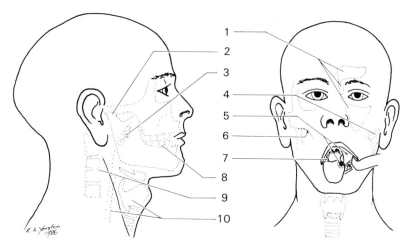

Fig. 3.2.4. Causes of referred otalgia.
1, Sinus disease.
2, Lesions of temporomandibular joint.
3, Nasopharyngeal disease (adenoids, neoplasms).
4, Parotid gland lesions.
5, Oral disease (ulcers, malignancy on tongue, etc.).
6, Infratemporal fossa carcinoma.
7, Tonsillar disease.
8, Dental causes.
9, Cervical causes (e.g. intervertebral joint disease).
10, Laryngeal and pharyngeal malignancies.

injury to the mandible. In 20 per cent of cases the pain is referred to the ear or the side of the face. Examination of the joint includes listening for a clicking sound on opening the mouth. The mandibular condyle should be palpated during jaw movements and digital pressure during movement may produce the pain. There may be limitation or asymmetry of movement and there is limitation of side-to-side movement of the opened mandible. Radiograhy of the temporomandibular joints may show no abnormality, but this does not exclude the joint as the source of the pain. The treatment lies in the hands of the experienced dental surgeon who may manipulate the joint in acute cases with immediate relief or correct the bite or change the dentures in long standing cases.

Pharyngeal causes of otalgia include acute tonsillitis, peritonsillar abscess, post-tonsillectomy pain, ulcers in the mouth and pharynx, malignant disease of the nasopharynx, pharynx and hypopharynx. The pathway of most of these is the glossopharyngeal nerve. **Glossopharyngeal neuralgia** is a primary neuralgia causing intermittent agonizing paroxysms of pain affecting the base of the tongue, the fauces and the ear. The spasms are provoked by swallowing, talking or coughing and the pain is unilateral. Treatment by carbamazepine (Tegretol) is less successful than in trigeminal neuralgia and the roots of the glossopharyngeal nerve may have to be divided by a neurosurgeon. A **tympanic plexus neuralgia** is a similar paroxysmal pain, confined to the ear, and may be initiated by touching the ear.

Nasal and sinus causes of otalgia are not common but malignant disease of the nose and sinuses may cause earache in addition to the local pain. Occasionally a malignancy in the **infratemporal fossa** or **nasopharynx** may present with otalgia and only with the later involvement of surrounding structures does the diagnosis become apparent. The onset of persistent unexplained earache in a healthy person should always be treated with suspicion and the patient should be investigated and followed up until a definite cause has been found.

The **larynx** must be examined as pain may be referred to the ear in laryngeal carcinoma or tuberculous laryngitis. There is usually, however, associated hoarseness.

Cervical causes are mainly neuralgic and may follow a whiplash injury, intervertebral joint disease or cervical spondylosis. The pain usually starts in the occiput and radiates forwards and it may involve the ear.

The parotid gland should be carefully palpated as occasionally earache is the presenting symptom of a malignant tumour, e.g. adenoid cystic carcinoma.

Chapter 3.3

AUDIOLOGY AND VESTIBULOMETRY

AUDIOLOGY

In most cases of ear disease it is essential to measure the hearing threshold and to ascertain whether deafness, if present, is conductive or sensorineural. **Conductive deafness** results from failure of the conducting mechanism to transmit the sound impulses from the external ear to the inner-ear fluids, and it may be due to blockage or diseases of the external auditory canal, the tympanic membrane, the middle-ear cavity or the ossicles. **Sensorineural deafness** can be a result of diseases of the sensor organ, the cochlea or its neural connections—the acoustic nerve and its central pathways.

In a number of cases examination of the vestibular apparatus will also be required.

Voice Tests

The distance at which the patient can hear a forced whispered voice with the opposite ear occluded in a quiet room is measured and the result recorded for each ear. A person with normal hearing should be able to hear 100 per cent of words at about 5·5 m. If the patient cannot hear a whispered voice a conversation voice is used and this distance is measured. If he cannot hear a conversation voice a raised conversation voice is used close to the ear, and it may be necessary to shout into the ear. If it is necessary to raise the voice to allow the patient to hear it is essential to prevent him from hearing with the opposite ear. This 'masking' is most conveniently done by placing a Bárány noise box, a clockwork-driven source of loud noise, over the other ear. A loud shout in the ear to be tested, with a Bárány box in the opposite ear, is still the most reliable test for total deafness. The whispered voice or conversation voice test is a simple practical method of testing a patient's ability to understand speech, which is the function of hearing most important to most people.

Tuning-fork Tests

Tuning-fork tests provide a most reliable method of determining whether deafness is of the conductive or sensorineural type. The tuning fork used should be large so that its rate of decay is not rapid and its frequency should be 512 Hz. It should have an expanded base for application to the skull. The tuning fork is struck against a resilient surface and then held so that the acoustic axis is in line with the

246

external acoustic meatus (*Fig.* 3.3.1). In this way the sound of the fork is heard by air conduction. If the vibrating tuning fork is held with its base placed firmly against the skull the sound is transmitted through the bones of the skull to the cochlea and the sound of the fork is heard by bone conduction.

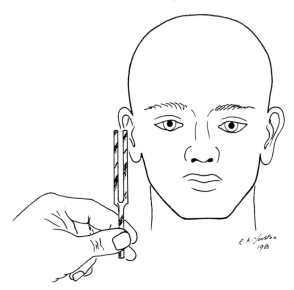

Fig. 3.3.1.   Tuning fork in the correct plane for testing air conduction.

Rinne's Test

Air conduction, in which the sound of the tuning fork is transmitted through the normal sound-conducting pathway, is much more efficient than bone conduction, in which the sound is transmitted through the bones of the skull to the cochlea. In Rinne's test air conduction is compared to bone conduction. The tuning fork still vibrating is then applied with its base to the mastoid process and the patient is asked which he hears louder. If the sound-conducting pathway is intact the tuning fork is heard much louder by air conduction than by bone conduction and Rinne's test is said to be positive. If the sound-conducting pathway is disrupted bone conduction will be better heard than air conduction and Rinne's test is said to be negative. In conductive deafness Rinne's test will be negative if the conductive hearing loss is greater than 15–20 dB.

Absolute Bone Conduction

In tuning-fork bone-conduction tests the normal sound-conducting pathway is by-passed, so that bone-conduction tests are a measure of inner-ear function. In the test of absolute bone conduction, the bone conduction of the patient is compared with that of the examiner and, assuming that the examiner has normal hearing, it is a test of the patient's inner-ear function. The turning fork is struck and its base is applied to the patient's mastoid process with the meatus occluded. The patient signals as soon as the sound of the fork is no longer heard. The tuning fork is immediately applied to the examiner's mastoid process with the meatus occluded. If the examiner, having normal hearing, can still hear the tuning fork the patient's inner-ear function is reduced and bone conduction is said to be shortened. In conductive deafness, and particularly in otosclerosis, bone conduction may be lengthened, i.e. the patient continues to hear the tuning fork when the examiner can no longer hear it.

Weber's Test

This test compares the bone conduction of the two ears and is of greatest value in cases of asymmetrical conductive deafness. The tuning fork is set in vibration and applied to the vertex of the skull in the midline and the patient is asked in which ear he hears the sound. The vibrations are transmitted equally to the cochlea on each side. In sensorineural deafness one would expect the sound to be better heard in the better ear. While this sometimes occurs it is not a regular finding, the sound being more often heard in the midline. In conductive deafness, on the other hand, the sound is heard in the more affected ear.

Provided that the patient's reply is accurate, Weber's test is very sensitive in conductive deafness. In unilateral conductive deafness, Weber's test will be heard in the affected ear where the hearing loss is only 5 dB. The student can verify this by applying Weber's test to himself and producing a mild conductive deafness by occluding the external acoustic meatus on one side. The sound of the tuning fork will be clearly heard in the occluded ear.

False-negative Rinne

This is an important observation. In unilateral total or severe sensorineural deafness Rinne's test will appear to give a negative result. Air conduction is absent, but bone conduction may be good because the sound is transmitted to the opposite cochlea. This result may lure the examiner into making a wrong diagnosis of conductive deafness. In this situation Weber's test is important. If the deafness is of conductive type, the tuning fork should be heard in the deaf ear. If Rinne's test is negative in one ear and Weber's test is not lateralized to that ear the examiner must consider that the condition may be total deafness. The final test is a loud shout in this ear with Bárány's noise box in the opposite ear.

Audiometric Tests

Pure-tone Audiometry

This is the most commonly used method of measuring hearing acuity. A pure-tone audiometer is an instrument which delivers tones of variable frequency and intensity to the ear by earphones. The frequencies usually tested are at octave steps, i.e. 125, 250, 500, 1000, 2000, 4000 and 8000 Hz. Occasionally half-octave steps, e.g. 1500, 3000, 6000 Hz, are used. The intensity can be increased or decreased for each frequency and can vary from 10 dB to 120 dB. Most audiometers used today are calibrated to the International (ISO) standard level (R.389).

Both the air conduction and bone conduction can be measured and are best done in the same manner. The best frequency to start with is 1000 Hz. A series of short signals or tone pips are put in at an intensity above the patient's suspected threshold, and the patient is instructed to signal every time he hears a sound. The intensity is reduced in 10-dB steps until no sound is heard. The signal is then increased in 5-dB steps until half of the tone pips are consistently heard. This is the patient's threshold for that frequency. The thresholds for the remaining frequencies are then measured. The bone conduction is measured in a similar fashion by putting a receiver onto the mastoid bone. The sound emitted by this is transmitted by the bones of the skull to the cochlea, thus by-passing the external and middle ears and giving a measure of inner-ear function. The results are charted as audiograms (*Fig.* 3.3.2).

In audiometry it is important to eliminate the possibility that the test sound is being heard in the opposite ear. The audiometer provides a masking noise which may be played into the opposite ear. Masking must be applied to the better ear when testing the deafer ear if the difference in threshold is found to be 40 dB or more. When testing the bone-conduction threshold the other ear should always be masked because of the ease with which bone-conduction sound is transmitted through the bones of the skull.

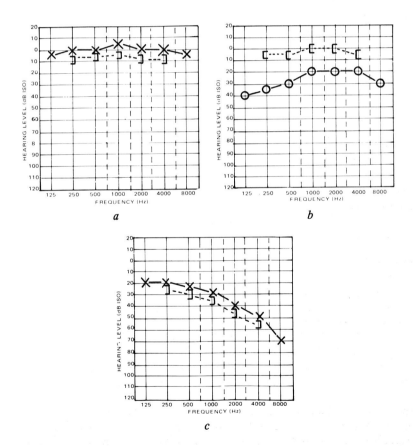

Fig. 3.3.2. Pure-tone audiograms. *a*, Normal. *b*, Conductive deafness. *c*, Sensorineural deafness. (Air conduction: right O, left X; bone conduction: right [, left].)

Speech Audiometry

This measures the patient's ability to understand speech. A series of words from a tape recorder is presented via headphones to the patient. The words are phonetically balanced to encompass the whole speech range from 500 to 2000 Hz and the intensity is varied. The results are charted by recording the total percentage of words correctly repeated by the patient at each intensity (*Fig.* 3.3.3). When hearing is normal (A) all the words will be understood if they are played loudly enough. In conductive deafness (B) all the words will be understood but they will need to be played louder than for the normal subject. In many cases of sensorineural deafness (C and D) there is a loss of ability to discriminate speech. As a result, increasing loudness may produce distortion of sounds and inability to hear 100 per cent of words. If increasing the loudness can produce an understanding of 40 per cent of the words it may be predicted that 90 per cent of sentence intelligibility will be obtained. The **speech reception threshold** can be derived from the audiogram and is usually taken as the intensity at which the patient can repeat 50 per cent of the presented words. Speech audiometry is a valuable method of assessing the actual disability produced by the deafness, and it can be used to predict the usefulness of a hearing aid or the benefit which might be obtained by an operation. It is also useful in helping to localize a lesion causing sensorineural deafness. In cochlear deafness the ability to discriminate speech is relatively well-maintained, but in retrocochlear deafness caused by disease involving the acoustic nerve or brainstem, there is often a severe loss of ability to hear speech which is far worse than the pure-tone audiogram would indicate.

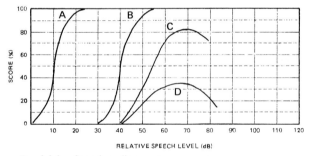

Fig. 3.3.3.   Speech audiogram.
A, Normal.
B, Conductive deafness.
C, Sensorineural deafness—good discrimination.
D, Sensorineural deafness—severe loss of discrimination.

Acoustic Impedance Audiometry

This most valuable test is now widely used and provides a quick objective measurement of the state of the middle ear. A tone played into the ear will be partly absorbed by the sound-conducting apparatus and partly reflected outwards from the surface of the tympanic membrane. The maximum absorption of sound occurs when the air pressure in the external auditory canal is the same as the air pressure in the middle ear. The amount of sound reflected by the drum is measured by a microphone and by varying the pressure in the external meatus by means of a pump attached to a manometer, a tracing of sound absorption against pressure is obtained. The sound source microphone and pump are all incorporated into a probe which is inserted into the external canal (*Fig.* 3.3.4). Because the passage of sound can be said to be impeded by the drum and ossicles, the technique is known as impedance audiometry. Some typical tracings are shown in *Fig.* 3.3.5. The middle-ear pressure can be derived from the tracing and is the pressure at which the curve peaks. Characteristic patterns are produced by fluid in the ear, by diminished middle-ear pressure due to Eustachian obstruction and by ossicular discontinuity. This technique is known as **tympanometry.**

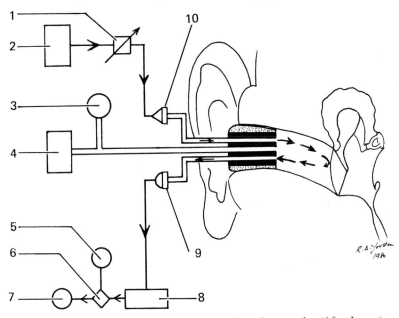

Fig. 3.3.4. Diagram showing component parts of impedance probe. (After Jerger.)

1, Potentiometer.
2, Oscillator (220 Hz).
3, Manometer.
4, Air pump.
5, Reference voltage.
6, Bridge circuit.
7, Balance meter.
8, Amplifier.
9, Microphone.
10, Loudspeaker.

The impedance audiometer can also be used to elicit the **acoustic reflexes**. The **stapedius reflex** is the more useful. When a sound of 70 dB or more above threshold is presented to the ear the stapedius muscle contracts. This immediately alters the stiffness of the ossicular chain and causes a change in the acoustic impedance of the ear which is recorded by the audiometer. The reflex threshold varies from 70 to 95 dB above the pure-tone threshold and can be used as a rough estimate of hearing ability. Because it is an objective test it can be used to detect malingerers and it can also demonstrate recruitment. The presence or absence of the stapedial reflex can also be useful in localizing lesions of the facial nerve, as the stapedius muscle is supplied by the nerve. **Contraction of the tensor tympani muscle**, the other acoustic reflex, is produced by stimulation of the sensory part of the trigeminal nerve, the usual stimulus being a puff of cold air applied to the cornea. This can also be detected by a change in the impedance.

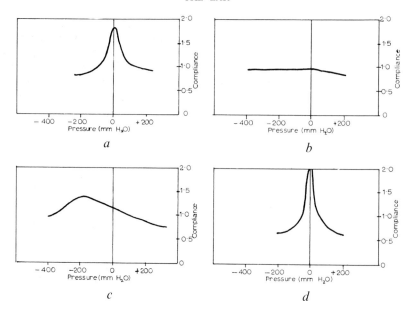

Fig. 3.3.5. Tympanograms. The horizontal axis is the pressure in the external auditory canal which can be varied by the pump. The vertical axis is compliance which is measured in millilitres and is the reciprocal of stiffness. This gives a measure of the elasticity of the drums and ossicles.
a, Normal response.
b, Fluid in the middle ear.
c, Reduced middle-ear pressure (due to Eustachian tube dysfunction).
d, Discontinuity of ossicular chain (e.g. disarticulation of incudostapedial joint).

Recruitment

Loudness recruitment is a condition which occurs in sensorineural deafness and is associated with disease of the cochlea. Quiet sounds cannot be heard by the patient but loud sounds are heard at their normal intensity or, in severe cases, at a greater intensity than normal, producing discomfort. This can result in loss of speech discrimination and intolerance of loud sounds, especially when a hearing aid is worn. Demonstration of recruitment can be used to localize the site of a lesion in sensorineural deafness as cochlear lesions are far more likely to cause recruitment than are lesions of the acoustic nerve or central connections.

Fowler's Loudness Balance Test

This is a simple and useful test for demonstrating recruitment. A tone is played alternately into the normal ear and the deaf ear and the intensity in the deaf ear is adjusted until the sounds in both ears are heard equally loudly (*Fig.* 3.3.6).

Various other hearing tests have been devised in an attempt to differentiate between cochlear lesions and retrocochlear (nerve) lesions.

Békésy Audiometry

This is a self-recording type of audiometry where the frequency of the test signal is increased automatically from low to high. The patient controls the intensity of the signal so that it fluctuates around his threshold and the level is plotted by a pen. This type of audiometry is widely used in hearing screening programmes using a continuous tone. By comparing the threshold obtained using continuous tone to that using an intermittent pulsed tone, it is possible to differentiate between some cases of cochlear and retrocochlear hearing loss. This method, however, is not very reliable and it has largely fallen into disuse.

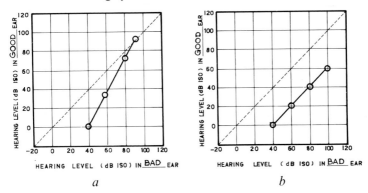

Fig. 3.3.6.   Diagram showing loudness balance charts.
a, Recruiting sensorineural deafness.
b, Non-recruiting sensorineural deafness.

Tone Decay

A tone is presented continually to the patient at an intensity of 5 dB above his threshold. In normally hearing subjects or most types of cochlear deafness the tone can be heard for 60 seconds. In patients with lesions of the acoustic nerve the sound is heard only for 5–10 seconds before it appears to die away. The intensity is then raised by 5-dB steps until the patient can hear the tone for the full minute.

Loudness Discomfort Level

Most people experience discomfort at an intensity of 90–105 dB. Patients with nerve lesions may experience no discomfort, even at the limit of the audiometer.

Acoustic Reflex Decay or Absence

Abnormally fast decay of the stapedius reflex or absence of it suggests the presence of a lesion of the acoustic nerve.

Evoked-response Audiometry

All of the foregoing tests, with the exception of impedance audiometry, are dependent on the cooperation of the patient, i.e. they are subjective. Evoked-response audiometry, also known as electric-response audiometry, is objective in that no conscious response from the patient is required. All four main types depend on either a neurogenic or myogenic response to a sound stimulus, and because the responses are small they have to be amplified and summated to give a recognizable signal.

Electrocochleography

This measures the electrical activity generated in the cochlea in response to a click stimulus. A needle electrode is passed through the tympanic membrane and held in place against the promontory near the round window. The responses obtained include the cochlear microphonics and the VIIIth nerve action potential. Its main clinical use is in threshold estimation in children who cannot be tested by other means. It is accurate to within 5–10 dB of the psychoacoustic threshold.

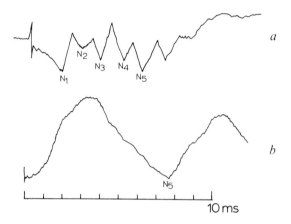

Fig. 3.3.7. Brainstem audiogram.
a, Ménière's disease with hearing loss of 50 dB. This is a normal recording.
b, Small acoustic neuroma with an average hearing loss of 40 dB.

Brainstem Electrical Responses

This technique is non-invasive. Electrical impulses occur in the area of the brainstem and mid-brain in response to sound, and these are detected by surface electrodes placed over the mastoid, forehead and vertex. It is useful in demonstrating the integrity or otherwise of some of the central connections of hearing. It can be used in the determination of the hearing threshold in children who cannot be tested by conventional means, e.g. mentally defective children, autistic children or blind children. It is accurate to within 10 or 15 dB of the psychoacoustic threshold and can be used instead of or in combination with electrocochleography.

It is now established as the most reliable audiological method of differentiating between cochlear and retrocochlear hearing losses. In a cochlear deafness, e.g. Ménière's disease, the normal pattern of waves is maintained (*Fig.* 3.3.7*a*). Where there is a retrocochlear lesion, e.g. acoustic neuroma (*Fig.* 3.3.7*b*) or other cerebellopontine angle tumours, the wave pattern is altered. The fifth wave can be delayed or absent or the whole response may be grossly abnormal. If the brainstem response is normal, the patient is very unlikely to have a retrocochlear lesion. Where the hearing loss is greater than 70 dB, however, the test becomes unreliable and other investigations must be used instead.

Myogenic Response (Crossed Acoustic Response)

There is a bilateral reflex contraction of the postauricular muscles in response to sound. These contractions can be detected and used as a hearing threshold measurement. It is non-invasive and can be done relatively easily on very young children. This test is useful as a screening procedure.

Cortical Electrical Response Audiometry

This technique detects the electrical activity occurring near the vertex by surface electrodes in response to sound. It is a very good objective measurement of hearing threshold in cooperative patients. Its main clinical use is in medicolegal work and evaluation of non-organic or psychogenic hearing loss. Pure tones are used in this test and a conventional air-conduction pure-tone audiogram can be obtained.

Tests for Non-organic Hearing Loss (NOHL)

These tests are used in cases where the patient claims to have no hearing on one or both sides, or greatly reduced hearing, and where there is no obvious cause for this. One would suspect a NOHL where pure-tone responses are inconsistent or where the patient cannot hear, in his good ear, a sound over 70 dB above his threshold put into his bad ear. Cases of bilateral hearing loss are rarer, but can be more difficult to detect as many of the tests rely on the patient having one good ear. Hospital admission and observation may be required in some cases. In tests for unilateral loss it is often useful to blindfold the patient.

Stenger's Test

When identical tuning forks are struck and held at equal distances from both ears they are heard in both ears. If one tuning fork is moved closer to one ear the patient hears only that fork although the other fork is still vibrating sufficiently for him to hear it. To do the test on a suspected 'malingerer' the examiner stands behind the patient and the tuning forks are struck and held equidistant from either ear. If the patient is claiming deafness in his left ear he will claim to hear only the fork on his right side. The fork on the left side is moved closer. If the patient is feigning deafness he will perceive only the tuning fork on the left side and will claim not to hear anything. If the patient has a genuine hearing loss on the left he will still hear the tuning fork on the right side. This test can also be done using an audiometer with two channels.

Teal Test

This can be used when the patient admits to hearing bone conduction in his 'deaf' ear. The examiner stands behind the patient and applies a tuning fork to the mastoid process of his 'deaf' ear. The patient admits to hearing it. The examiner then says that he is going to repeat the test, but puts a non-vibrating fork on the mastoid while at the same time bringing a vibrating fork close to the auricle. If the patient is malingering, he will hear the tuning fork through air conduction, but think that it is being heard through the bone. If he is really deaf he will not hear the fork.

Lombard's Test

This depends upon the fact that to the normal man the sound of his own voice is necessary for the proper regulation of its tone and loudness. The Bárány noise apparatus is adjusted to the patient's sound ear and its machinery started in order to accustom him to its grating noise. He is given a book, and told to read aloud in his normal voice and not to stop reading when the instrument is set in action. As soon as the noise begins, a man whose opposite ear is profoundly deaf will at once raise his voice and, if his deafness is absolute, may literally shout. The malingerer, on the other hand, claiming a one-sided deafness which is not real will continue to read in an even tone or in a tone only slightly elevated.

Delayed Speech Feedback

This requires a tape recorder and playback system with a capacity to delay the feedback. The patient reads aloud from a book. His voice is recorded and played back to him via earphones with a 150–300 millisecond delay. The earphones should be able to be adjusted independently so that the good ear is not stimulated. If there is a genuine deafness he will be able to read without pausing. If, however, he is feigning deafness the delayed feedback will almost certainly alter his reading pattern causing him to stammer or slow down or raise his voice as in the Lombard test. This test is very effective and will detect most, though not all, malingerers.

Stapedial Reflex

If stapedial reflexes are present and normal on both sides the patient cannot have a total loss of hearing on one side. This test can, of course, be used on cases with bilateral deafness.

Cortical Evoked Response Audiometry

This is time-consuming, but it is the most effective way of testing auditory function in suspected NOHL not detected by simpler tests. In addition, an accurate measure of threshold is obtained. 'Hearing', however, is a cortical function, and one cannot categorically say that a patient 'hears' the sound, but only that the auditory pathways are intact. This test is effective for both unilateral and bilateral cases.

VESTIBULOMETRY

Evaluation of the vestibular system must be considered only as part of the investigation of a dizzy patient. A full otoneurological history and examination must be carried out. This includes a history of the dizziness, its duration, severity, mode of onset and effect of sudden changes of position of the head. Is there associated nausea and vomiting? Is there associated deafness or tinnitus? Is the patient on any drugs likely to be causing or exacerbating the dizziness? Is there a rotatory component or a feeling of movement present? Are there any symptoms suggestive of central disease, e.g. diplopia, dysphasia or loss of consciousness?

Examination should include tests of coordination and fundoscopy as well as full cranial nerve examination, audiometry and specific vestibular tests.

Nystagmus

As the symptom of vestibular disorder is vertigo, the sign is nystagmus. It is defined as an involuntary deviation of the eyes away from the direction of gaze, followed by a return of the eyes to their original position. There are three main types of nystagmus—central, ocular and vestibular.

In **central nystagmus** the eye movements are coarse and do not fatigue. There may be vertical and oblique components as well as horizontal movements. There is often no subjective complaint of vertigo and there are usually other signs of intracranial disease present.

Ocular nystagmus tends to be pendular in type and many cases are congenital.

Vestibular nystagmus is rhythmic. It consists of a slow movement of the eyes in one direction followed by a quick return in the opposite direction. The slow component of the nystagmus is produced by impulses from the vestibule. The fast component, or recovery movement, is a central correcting reflex. The mechanism of nystagmus production is shown in *Fig.* 3.3.8. The direction of the nystagmus is named according to the direction of the quick component, e.g. nystagmus to the right means that the quick jerk is to the right. Vestibular nystagmus can be spontaneous, positional or induced.

Spontaneous Nystagmus

To examine for spontaneous nystagmus the patient's head is kept steady in the upright position and he is told to look straight forward and then to follow the finger of the examiner. The finger is held 60 cm away and is moved to the right, then the left and also up and down. Spontaneous nystagmus in any of these positions is noted. The finger should not be moved more than 40° in any direction because most people will demonstrate nystagmus at the extremes of eye movements. Nystagmus is most marked when the patient looks in the direction of the quick component and is lessened or abolished when he looks in that of the slow component. Nystagmus which is present only when the patient looks in the direction of the quick component is known as **first-degree nystagmus**. If nystagmus is also present when the patient looks straight ahead it is **second-degree nystagmus**. If it is still present when he looks in the direction of the slow component it is **third-degree nystagmus**. A patient with nystagmus to the right is requested to look at an object on his right side. The vestibular pull causes the eyes to deviate to the left. Under the influence of an anaesthetic the quick component of nystagmus is eliminated, and the slow or vestibular movement alone takes place and results in conjugate deviation. Frenzel glasses are very useful in detecting minor degrees of nystagmus.

Positional Nystagmus

Nystagmus, usually rotatory and accompanied by rotatory vertigo, may occur in certain positions of the head—commonly in the recumbent position with the head extended and turned to one side. The patient can frequently assume the position in which vertigo is experienced. Tests for positional nystagmus are done in the upright and supine positions with the head turned to either side. A nystagmus which is fatiguable and short-lasting is usually associated with a peripheral pathology. A nystagmus which does not fatigue or which is direction-changing is more likely to be associated with a central lesion. To avoid the effect of neck movements the positioning should be done slowly. (*See also* benign paroxysmal positional nystagmus, p. 332.)

Induced Nystagmus

Nystagmus can be induced by rotational stimulation, thermal stimulation and visual stimulation. Valuable information can be obtained about the state of the vestibular system by utilizing these stimuli and examining the induced nystagmus.

Rotation Tests

The principle of rotation tests has been described before, but they have limited clinical application. Both labyrinths are stimulated simultaneously. The nystagmus induced by acceleration and deceleration in a rotating chair is recorded. During acceleration a nystagmus with the fast component in the direction of rotation is set up. When a constant speed is reached a postrotation nystagmus appears with the fast component beating in the opposite direction. The chair is then decelerated quickly and a nystagmus is set up beating in the direction opposite to the rotation. After the chair stops a final postrotatory nystagmus appears which lasts for a few seconds. This is called cupulometry. The angular velocity can be adjusted so as to give a minimal stimulation, and it is possible now to obtain a measure of the vestibular threshold. Rotation can be carried out in both directions. The results obtained by rotation tests can show normal response, asymmetrical response, diminished response or no response, the latter two being associated with bilateral vestibular pathology, e.g. congenital deafness or drug-induced ototoxicity. Asymmetrical responses may be obtained in some unilateral peripheral lesions, e.g. vestibular neuronitis.

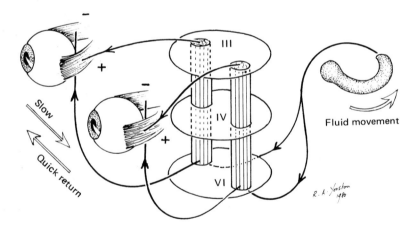

Fig. 3.3.8.   Diagram to show mechanism of cold caloric response in left ear. (Modified from Mendel, *Teach-In*, July 1974.)
Hot water would cause the fluid to move towards the ampulla of the semicircular canal (ampullopetal). This stimulates the cupula, increases the left vestibular nerve activity and causes a nystagmus in the opposite direction, i.e. with the slow component to the right.

Caloric Tests

The main advantage of the caloric test is that each labyrinth can be tested separately. Syringing the ear with hot or cold water induces convection currents

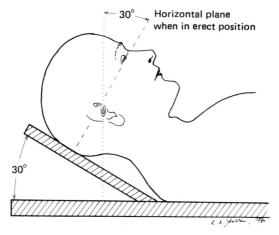

Fig. 3.3.9. Diagram showing that the lateral semicircular canals are vertical when the head is raised 30° from the supine position.

within the lateral or horizontal semicircular canals, and therefore stimulates them with resulting vertigo and nystagmus (*Fig.* 3.3.8). In the caloric test this is done under controlled conditions. The patient lies with the head at an angle of 30° above the horizontal, which brings the lateral semicircular canals into a vertical plane (*Fig.* 3.3.9). Cold syringing cools the most superficial part of the canal. This cooler fluid then tends to fall and causes a movement of the endolymph away from the ampulla. This sets up a nystagmus with the slow component going in the same direction as the fluid movement, e.g. cold stimulation of the left labyrinth produces a movement away from the ampulla of the left semicircular canal and induces a nystagmus with the slow component to the left and the fast phase to the right (*Fig.* 3.3.8). There will be a sensation of rotation to the left and, if the stimulus is great enough, nausea and vomiting. Irrigation with warm water produces exactly the opposite effect. The tests are carried out on each ear with water at 30 and 44 °C. The ear is irrigated for 40 seconds, 5 minutes being allowed between irrigations. During the test the patient is asked to keep his eyes open and fixed on an object straight above him on the ceiling. The measure of the response is the number of seconds between the commencement of the stimulation and the cessation of nystagmus. The results are recorded on a chart (*Fig.* 3.3.10). Normal variations occur in response duration, the average being 1·5–2·5 minutes, the hot reactions being slightly shorter than the cold (*Fig.* 3.3.10*a*). Where there is depression of function on one side the response to hot and cold douching on that side will be diminished; this is known as canal paresis (*Fig.* 3.3.10*b*). A canal paresis, complete or incomplete, is suggestive of a lesion in the peripheral vestibular apparatus, e.g. vestibular nerve or vestibule. In some cases nystagmus in one direction, e.g. to the left, may be more readily induced and this is known as a directional preponderance of nystagmus (*Fig.* 3.3.10*c*). It indicates dysfunction in the vestibular pathways but it is non-localizing as it can occur in peripheral or central lesions. In a number of cases there is a combination of canal paresis and directional preponderance.

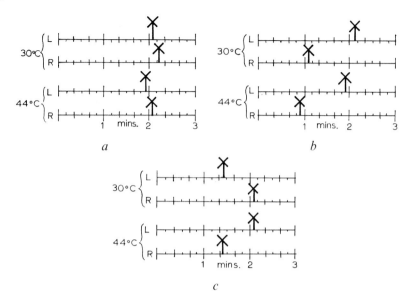

Fig. 3.3.10. Calorigrams.
a, Normal caloric responses.
b, Right canal paresis.
c, Directional preponderance to the left.

Electronystagmography (ENG)

This technique is now available in most centres and is used routinely in them. It records nystagmus on paper and enables a more thorough assessment of vestibular function to be made. There is an electric potential between the cornea and retina of some 300–1300 μV, positive at the cornea. By placing electrodes at each outer canthus and a reference in the midline, and measuring the potential difference across them, it is possible to detect eye movements. Nystagmus is shown as a saw-toothed appearance (Fig. 3.3.11). Full electronystagmography consists of a series of tests, including eye movements, head positions, with eyes open and closed, and caloric testing. In an ENG the duration of irrigation is only 30 seconds. The eyes are closed or the room darkened and the response is measured by the angle of the slow phase rather than by the duration. The steeper the angle of the slow phase the greater the nystagmus. As the nystagmus is diminishing it is useful to switch on the lights or ask the patient to open his eyes and fix them on an object on the ceiling. In nystagmus due to peripheral disease this causes a reduction in the speed and amplitude of the nystagmus of a least 50 per cent.

The ENG recording is then examined and note is taken of spontaneous nystagmus, positional nystagmus, the effect of eye closure and the caloric responses. There are three questions which can be answered by an ENG:

1. Is there spontaneous nystagmus? This will be shown by the tests with eye movements and with eyes closed.

2. Is the cause central or peripheral? Central nystagmus is irregular and abolished by eye closure. Peripheral nystagmus is regular. It is accentuated or made apparent by eye closure and is depressed by optic fixation.

3. If peripheral, which side is affected? A canal paresis localizes the disease to the side of the paresis. A directional preponderance does not.

Caloric testing with water can only safely be done with an intact tympanic membrane. If there is a perforation a caloric test can be carried out using air at 24 and 52°C. Cold caloric tests can be carried out alone using a Dundas Grant apparatus. A cold caloric test can also be done using ice-cold water. This is known as Kobrak's test and gives a quick and rough guide to vestibular function.

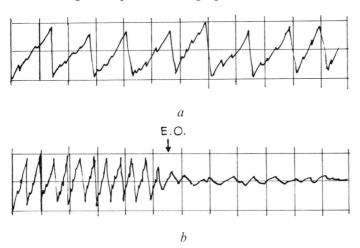

a

E.O.

b

Fig. 3.3.11. Electronystagmograms.
a, Nystagmus to the left (slow).
b, Nystagmus to the left (fast) with fixation suppression. E.O. = eyes open.

Pendulum Test (Eye Tracking)

This can be incorporated into an ENG testing routine. The patient is seated in front of a metronome which is set in motion. He is asked to follow the moving tip with his eyes. In the normal patient a sinusoidal tracing is obtained showing that both eyes are smoothly following the movement. If the trace is irregular it may indicate central disease, e.g. cerebellar dysfunction. If a metronome is not available the test can be done by using a piece of string with a weight attached at the bottom and swinging it gently.

Optokinetic Nystagmus

This test is used in many vestibular laboratories. The patient is connected to an ENG machine and a drum is rotated in front of him. The drum has vertical black stripes on a white background and the patient is instructed to look at the stripes as the drum is slowly rotated horizontally. This sets up a nystagmus which is recorded. The drum is then rotated in the reverse direction and a nystagmus again induced. Asymmetry of the responses is suggestive of a central lesion.

Fistula Test

This test is of use in detecting areas of circumscribed labyrinthitis where part of the bony wall of the inner ear has been eroded by disease with exposure of the endosteum. This condition is known as a fistula and occurs commonly in the lateral canal but can involve the other canals or the promontory. There must be a functioning labyrinth for the test to work. The test is carried out as follows: an olive-shaped earpiece attached by means of rubber tubing to a valveless Politzer bag, or the earpiece of a Siegle's speculum, or a pneumatic auriscope, is fitted tightly into the meatus. The patient is directed to look straight ahead. By squeezing the rubber bag the air pressure in the meatus is raised and the pressure is transmitted to the fluid in the labyrinth through the fistula. By releasing the bag without removing the earpiece, the pressure in the meatus is diminished and a nystagmus is induced. The direction of the nystagmus produced in this way cannot always be accurately predicted, but the effect of rarefaction is always the opposite of that due to compression. In the typical fistula, on compression, nystagmus is produced in the direction of the diseased side, the slow movement being to the opposite side. In the 'reversed' fistula sign the slow component is towards the diseased side. This reversed fistula sign may be produced in cases of undue mobility of the stapes. A positive fistula test is also obtained after a labyrinthine fenestration procedure. A minor degree of nystagmus may only be detected if the patient is wearing Frenzel glasses or is connected to an ENG machine.

Romberg's Test

This is a useful test which can be done quickly in the consulting room. The patient stands with heels and toes together and eyes closed and the direction of any swaying or falling is noted. The patient will often fall to the side of a recent peripheral lesion.

Other clinical tests may be done including walking with the eyes closed, or standing on one leg with the eyes closed, both of which may be affected in peripheral lesions. The finger–nose test is useful in detecting cerebellar disease.

Chapter 3.4

DISEASES OF THE EXTERNAL EAR

THE AURICLE

Congenital Abnormalities

Minor congenitial abnormalities such as accessory auricle or slight malformation are not uncommon and may require no treatment. More major abnormalities such as microtia and atresia of the canal are rare but are often associated with hearing difficulty. These are considered in Chapter 4.8.

Haematoma of the Auricle

This generally results from injury. An effusion of blood occurs under the perichondrium and forms a swelling on the lateral or anterior surface of the auricle, which may have a bluish tinge, and considerable pain is experienced. Suppuration may take place, resulting in destruction of cartilage, and finally in shrivelling of the auricle. If uncomplicated by inflammation, the serum becomes absorbed, but a certain amount of permanent thickening remains. Repeated trauma, as may occur in boxing or rugby football, can result in gross scarring, thickening and disfigurement of the auricle and is commonly known as 'cauliflower ear'.

TREATMENT. In the early stages, before coagulation of the blood has occurred, aspiration, with full aseptic precautions, may be employed, but may have to be repeated owing to further oozing taking place. A firm bandage is applied with pressure over the auricle. At a later stage free incision and evacuation of the haematoma may be required, but this should not be undertaken lightly because of the risk of introducing infection.

Seroma

Like a haematoma, this can result from trauma which may be minor or it can occur spontaneously. It is often painless and very fluctuant.

TREATMENT. This is essentially the same as for a haematoma.

Perichondritis of the Auricle

This may follow a haematoma, or result from the extension of infection from a furuncle on the posterior meatal wall or be a complication of a surgical procedure.

263

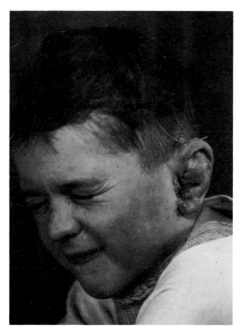

Fig. 3.4.1.   Perichondritis of the auricle.

Pseudomonas pyocyanea is the common causal organism, and the pus has a bluish tinge. There is severe pain in the ear and a rise of temperature. The auricle swells rapidly, becomes dusky in colour and its normal contour is lost, the swelling being apparent on both surfaces (*Fig.* 3.4.1). If the infection progresses, necrosis of the cartilage may take place, with the result that the auricle finally shrivels.

TREATMENT. This consists of a course of the appropriate antibiotic, preferably one active against Pseudomonas, e.g. ticarcillin. Penicillin may be given until the results of sensitivity tests have been obtained. Ichthyol, 20 per cent in water, aluminium acetate, 8 per cent in water, or magnesium sulphate paste may be used frequently as local applications to relieve the discomfort. When fluctuation is apparent, incision and drainage are required.

THE EXTERNAL AUDITORY MEATUS

Acquired Atresia

Acquired meatal stenosis or atresia can be secondary to infection, surgical procedure, accidental trauma or radiotherapy. If the stenosis is of a minor variety it may be symptomless and require no treatment. Where it is more severe or where there is total occlusion of the deep meatus causing conductive deafness, surgical correction is advisable. If there is a localized web, simple excision and packing of the canal with BIPP may suffice. In cases where the stenotic segment is longer or where there is obliteration medially by thick fibrous tissue, it is usually necessary to insert a sleeve of split-thickness skin, taken from the postauricular sulcus, to cover the underlying bone.

Injuries to the meatus are sometimes followed by a thin membrane formation which is easily destroyed by application of a silver nitrate bead.

Contracture of the introitus of the meatus may result from burns and lacerations, and a stenosed meatus may follow mastoid surgery. In these cases a meatoplasty provides the most satisfactory restoration of an adequate meatal opening. Narrowing of the external orifice of the meatus is also seen in old age and deafness may result from quite small accumulations of wax.

Hypertrophied skin lining of the meatus is encountered in association with chronic otitis externa which is often secondary to chronic otitis media. The meatal swelling may be sufficiently reduced by packing the meatus with ribbon gauze wicks soaked in 8 per cent aluminium acetate solution to permit examination of the tympanic membrane in order to exclude middle-ear disease. If this cannot be excluded the patient will require radiological examination and possibly mastoid surgery with a suitable meatoplasty.

Impacted Wax

The accumulated secretion from the ceruminous glands situated in the outer part of the meatus may form a solid, often hard, mass giving rise to deafness and discomfort in the ear. Tinnitus and disturbance of balance may occur from pressure of the wax on the drumhead, and a cough reflex due to stimulation of the auricular branch of the vagus has been described. The onset of deafness is often sudden following washing or bathing, when the entrance of water to the meatus closes a previously narrow passage for the transmission of sound by causing the wax to swell and a more profound blockage results.

DIAGNOSIS. Diagnosis is in most cases easily made by otoscopic examination, the mass or plug having a brown or yellowish colour but sometimes it is black or greyish when mixed with desquamated epithelium. The drumhead may be partially or totally obscured from view.

TREATMENT. Wax is removed either by instrumental manipulation or by syringing. The former method should be reserved for special situations and performed only by an otologist. Syringing is advised for most cases and may be carried out by trained personnel after the presence of wax has been confirmed. The most useful type of syringe for this purpose is made of brass or plated or stainless steel. It is difficult for a, patient to syringe his own ear efficiently. Any competent person may, after a little training, learn to carry out this simple procedure. Sterile saline solution, or boracic lotion (1 : 40), or a solution of sodium bicarbonate, warmed to blood heat, should be employed for syringing. After filling the syringe, bubbles of air must be expelled by pressing on the piston with the point of the syringe raised. The patient should be seated, a towel laid over his shoulder and a kidney dish held either by the patient or an assistant immediately below his ear and in close contact with the skin to catch the return flow of lotion. The patient's head is inclined slightly downwards and towards the same side to prevent the fluid from running down the neck. It is a natural reaction for the patient to tilt his head away from the stream of fluid. The auricle is pulled upwards and backwards to straighten out the meatus, and the fluid is injected along the upper wall of the meatus (*Figs.* 3.4.2,

Fig. 3.4.2.   Syringing the ear.

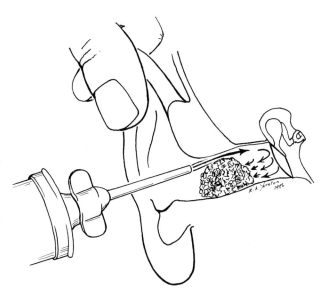

Fig. 3.4.3.   When syringing an ear the jet of water should be directed along the roof of the canal.

3.4.3). It is essential to illuminate the ear by direct or reflected light. Excessive force should not be exerted to remove wax. If the wax is hard and does not come away easily, it is better to ask the patient to instil drops of olive oil, almond oil or lukewarm sodium bicarbonate BPC, for several days to soften the wax, and then return for syringing. When the wax has been removed, the ear should be inspected to ensure that none remains. The meatus should be dried with cotton-wool mops after syringing. This is important because any abrasion of the skin during the procedure may become infected if it is left in a moist condition. Some surgeons advise that a few drops of spirit be instilled after syringing to complete this drying.

Syringing, although causing discomfort, should never produce actual pain and if such occurs syringing should cease and the ear must be inspected. Severe lancinating pain occurs if the drumhead is ruptured and this may be accompanied by intense vertigo while the returning fluid is tinged with blood. The syringing lotion should be at body temperature. If too hot or too cold a caloric response may be induced in the labyrinth and vertigo experienced by the patient. After completion of the procedure the meatus should be carefully dried and the hearing tested.

PROGNOSIS. Provided that no other cause of deafness exists in the middle or inner ear, removal of wax should restore hearing to its previous level. Prior to treatment patients should be asked about any previous ear disease, and the possible presence of a perforated eardrum, or one which has healed with a thin scar, should be kept in mind so that a warning may be given of a possible reactivation of otitis media. In such situations it may be decided that the wax should be removed by suitable instruments rather than by syringing the ear.

Keratosis Obturans

In this condition the meatus on one or both sides becomes blocked in its deep portion by a mass consisting of wax, desquamated epithelium and cholesterol. The exact cause of the formation of these hard accumulations has not been determined, but hyperaemia of the meatal skin and instability of the epidermis are possible factors. In young adults the disease has been found in association with bronchiectasis and with a chronic sinusitis. The mass is closely attached to the meatal walls and pressure effects cause absorption of bone and widening of the meatus. In severe cases the facial nerve may be exposed causing paralysis, but in most cases the initial symptoms are pain and deafness. There may also be tinnitus and discharge from the ear. Removal of the mass is often difficult and general anaesthesia is frequently required. Initially softening of the mass with sodium bicarbonate ear drops instilled daily for several days followed by syringing should be tried. Regular observation of the patient is also necessary to prevent the formation of further solid accumulations.

Foreign Bodies in the Ear

Occasionally flies or other insects become trapped in the external canal and cause great distress and discomfort by moving about trying to get back out. In such cases the ear should be filled with oil or even water, thus drowning the insect which can then be picked or syringed out. In some Eastern countries, maggots may be found in ear canals. They cause intense pain, and their presence is most likely in an ear where discharge is already present, and which has become very offensive and blood-stained. It is useless to attempt to syringe them out as they are firmly attached to the meatal walls. Chloroform water or vapour must be applied to the external meatus in order to anaesthetize or kill the maggots and so release their grip on the skin. Thereafter they may be removed by syringing.

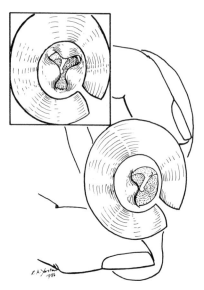

Fig. 3.4.4.   Osteomas of the ear canals.
Inset, multiple osteomas.

Benign Tumours of the External Meatus

Osteoma is the most common type of benign tumour encountered in the meatus, occurring either as multiple exostoses (*Fig.* 3.4.4) composed of ivory bone or as a single osteoma of cancellous structure. The exostoses vary in size, and arise from the walls of the osseous meatus as rounded swellings, or as a flat area of thickening of part of the meatal wall to which the term hyperostosis is applied.

AETIOLOGY. The repeated entry of cold water into the external meatus in swimming and diving is regarded as the primary cause of the condition, but other factors such as trauma, long-standing irritation, as in otitis externa, or prolonged middle-ear suppuration may be contributory.

Osteomas are slow-growing, often occurring in both ears, and are more common in men than in women.

CLINICAL FEATURES. A single cancellous osteoma or exostosis is less common than the multiple variety. It is usually attached to the posterior wall of the osseous meatus by a narrow base and appears as a smooth, rounded body which may completely fill the canal. Multiple exostoses are frequently bilateral and symmetrical, arising from the anterior and posterior osseous meatal walls. The drumhead may be almost hidden by the growths but complete blockage of the canal is unusual in this variety.

SYMPTOMS. Multiple exostoses seldom cause symptoms unless the lumen of the meatus is obstructed by accumulation of wax or epithelial debris, when the patient complains of deafness. In cases of otitis media pain may occur if there is obstruction to discharge from the middle ear or if there is a secondary otitis externa.

DIAGNOSIS. The diagnosis is generally clear on inspection, although wax and debris may first need to be removed in order to view the growth. Its bony consistence is confirmed by touching it with a probe.

TREATMENT. Multiple osteomas which are not giving rise to symptoms require no treatment, and when they are observed only as part of a routine examination their presence is best left unremarked to the patient. These growths are very hard and the visible part may resemble the tip of the iceberg. The larger submerged portion of a growth arising from the posterior meatal wall may be closely related to the facial nerve canal so that removal may cause damage to the facial nerve. When removal is necessary on account of persistent symptoms it is best effected by the use of a drill applied directly to the growths via the external meatus, which is widened if necessary by an endaural incision.

Surgery is more often necessary in the case of a single cancellous osteoma which is likely, by its continued and more rapid growth, to cause complete obstruction of the meatus. Because of its pedunculated attachment this type of oestoma may frequently be removed by applying a gouge to the pedicle of the growth and cracking it at its base. Care must be taken to protect the drumhead and middle ear by supporting the growth on its medial aspect with a curved dissector. Large osteomas may require a wider exposure by means of an endaural incision or an external retroauricular approach.

Other benign tumours of epithelial and mesenchymal origin may affect the external meatus but, apart from papillomas, these are only occasionally found.

Otitis Externa

Inflammation of the skin of the external ear canal is common. It is often due to local factors but can be secondary to an underlying acute or chronic middle-ear infection. There can be diffuse involvement of the whole ear canal or a localized area of inflammation, often described as furunculosis. The former is the more common.

The generalized form affecting the meatus, auricle and adjoining areas of skin may be primarily otological or primarily dermatological. In addition, the condition may be classifed as infective, due to bacterial, fungal or viral agents, and reactive, from contact with numerous external sensitizing agents or resulting from atopy. In many cases the disease is of mixed origin, a primary infective lesion developing an eczematous reaction and vice versa.

INCIDENCE. The incidence of otitis externa, especially fungal, is highest in tropical countries with a high humidity where the symptoms are often severe and recurrences are frequent.

AETIOLOGY. Many factors can be implicated in the onset of otitis externa. Scratching the ears with dirty fingers or with contaminated objects such as a matchstick or a hair-grip, or the use of dirty instruments may introduce pathogenic organisms to the meatus. If the skin is traumatized infection may penetrate the barrier of the stratum corneum. Syringing the ear for the removal of hard wax or badly fitting and infrequently cleaned hearing-aid earpieces may also cause minor injury and subsequent infection. In other cases allergy is the primary factor.

The development of skin allergy may be due to a large variety of antigens, many of which are contained in topical applications such as cosmetics and antibiotic preparations. Intense itching is an early symptom of sensitization and scratching often leads to secondary infection. A sensitivity reaction may result from psychological factors such as prolonged mental stress.

BACTERIOLOGY. The normal external meatus is sterile, or contains *Staphylococcus albus* alone or in combination with other non-pathogenic organisms. Less often *Staphylococcus aureus* or non-haemolytic streptococci are found. In cases of otitis externa the bacteriological flora is often mixed, and *S. aureus* and Gram-negative organisms such as *Pseudomonas pyocyanea* and *Proteus vulgaris* are present. *Escherichia coli* occurs also in mixed infections. The proportions of these organisms vary with the geographical area, *Ps. pyocyanea* being commonest in tropical and subtropical regions.

SYMPTOMS. At an early stage pain in the ear and discharge from the meatus are commonly present. Pain is usually severe in furunculosis, aural herpes and the acute primary stage of diffuse otitis externa, being preceded in the latter by a hot burning sensation and followed by a thin serous discharge which may become thicker and more profuse as the condition develops. When discharge is present a swab should be taken to determine the organisms and their sensitivity to antibiotics. If the discharge has a sticky mucoid content an underlying otitis media must be suspected. Itching is a prominent symptom in seborrhoeic dermatitis, drug sensitivity, neurodermatitis and otomycosis. Conductive deafness results from obstruction of the meatus by oedema of the walls and accumulated debris or discharge. In cases of chronic diffuse otitis externa thickening of the meatal skin causes a permanent meatal stenosis so that small amounts of wax and epithelial debris may give rise to deafness. Fissuring of the skin around the meatal introitus is associated with seborrhoeic dermatitis and eczema. Furunculosis of the posterior meatal wall may be accompanied by retroauricular oedema with protrusion of the auricle.

MANAGEMENT. It is essential in all cases to remove all debris and discharge from the ear canal. There are three reasons for doing this:

1. To allow local medication to come in contact with the diseased skin.
2. To inspect the eardrum.
3. To take a swab of the discharge if purulent and send for bacteriological examination and culture.

Cleansing of the ear canal is best done by using a head mirror and speculum to see into the canal and a fine wire probe tipped with fluffy cotton wool to clean the canal (*Fig.* 3.4.5). In some patients it is possible to use suction. The ear canal can also be cleaned using an auriscope with a removable lens but it is less satisfactory.

If there is no previous history of ear disease or if the eardrum is known to be intact, e.g. in chronic otitis externa, it is often worthwhile syringing the ear gently using normal saline or any other bland solution. The ear canal should then be gently dried using cotton wool on a wire carrier.

Further otoscopic examination should be done to visualize the drumhead and to ensure that no debris remains in the anteroinferior meatal recess (p. 220).

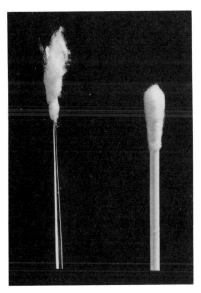

Fig. 3.4.5. Correct and incorrect applicators for cleaning ear canals.
Left. Correct: this is a wool carrier prepared so that the end of the
cotton wool is fluffed out to provide better absorption of discharge and
protect the skin of the ear canal.
Right. Incorrect: this commercially available 'cotton bud' is too large
to enter the canal. Some parents try to clean their children's ears with
them but only succeed in pushing any wax further in.

Failure to clear this pocket may result in prolonged treatment and recurrences. In
dry, scaly and crusted ears cleansing may be helped by the use of mops dipped in
sterile liquid paraffin or baby oil. Trauma to the meatal skin must be avoided and
treatment by trained staff is necessary.

Furunculosis

Boils (furuncles) are due to a staphylococcal infection of hair follicles which are
present in the skin of the outer cartilaginous part of the external meatus. They
may develop in the superficial layers of the skin or may be more deeply seated. A
boil may occur as a single lesion or as multiple lesions confined to the ear or
associated with boils elsewhere in the body. They commonly recur, particularly in
debilitated individuals and in diabetics.

CLINICAL FEATURES. Furuncles produce severe pain in the ear and tenderness in
the region of the meatus at an early stage. Swelling of the meatal walls may
occlude the meatus thus causing deafness. The superficial infection may be seen as
a small, red, circumscribed and very tender swelling on the skin of the meatus.
Deep infection is more diffuse and the skin initially shows no significant change
although the area may be tender on gentle pressure. When a boil is situated on the
anterior or inferior meatal wall chewing movements of the jaw cause increased
pain and swelling of the lower eyelid may be present. If the boil is on the posterior
wall the swelling may cause protrusion of the auricle and obliteration of the

postauricular sulcus by oedema. Infection may spread to lymph glands either anterior to the auricle or below the tip of the mastoid process. Swelling of the meatus associated with discharge from the ear may cause difficulty in deciding whether infection is limited to the outer ear or originates within the middle ear.

DIAGNOSIS. In distinguishing between furunculosis of the external meatus with oedema and acute otitis media with mastoiditis, several observations should be noted.

1. A history of recent head cold or influenza is suggestive of middle-ear infection whereas staphylococcal infection in some other area of the body may point to furunculosis.

2. Careful and gentle otoscopic examination may reveal a boil and when a normal drumhead can be seen the diagnosis is not in doubt.

3. Hearing in the affected ear is better in furunculosis than in mastoiditis. Insertion of an infant-size aural speculum into the meatus, when possible without causing undue pain, will improve the hearing if no middle-ear infection is present.

4. Pain in furunculosis is of a continuous, dull throbbing character and may last for several days until the boil bursts, or is incised, when there is a scanty yellow discharge. In acute otitis media a sharp piercing pain varying in duration and intensity occurs and is relieved by the appearance of discharge which may be copious. The presence of mucus in the discharge is pathognomonic of an otitis media.

5. Movement of the auricle and pressure on the tragus increase pain in furunculosis but not in otitis media.

6. In furunculosis maximum tenderness is present over the tragus, below and medial to the lobe of the ear and along the anterior border of the mastoid process. Tenderness in mastoiditis is more often elicited along the posterior border of the mastoid and over the mastoid antrum.

7. Obliteration of the postauricular sulcus with forward displacement of the auricle suggests a furuncle, and this is confirmed if aspiration of a fluctuant swelling yields pus on piercing skin. If it is caused by a subperiosteal abscess from mastoid infection pus is not met with until bone is reached.

8. Mastoid radiographs showing well-developed clear cells on the affected side will exclude mastoiditis but a retroauricular oedema produces some haziness of the cells compared with those of the normal side. Furunculosis and mastoiditis may occur together and if the latter cannot be excluded an exploratory operation may be justified.

TREATMENT. Local and general measures are necessary. Heat applied to the ear by a covered hot-water bottle or radiant heat relieve pain, especially if combined with the administration of sedatives. Meatal packs consisting of narrow (12 mm) ribbon-gauze wicks soaked in 10 per cent ichthammol glycerin BPC solution, gently inserted, have a soothing effect. The wicks are changed daily. Most furuncles burst spontaneously and the discharge should be removed by dry mopping, the ichthammol glycerin wicks being continued until the ear is dry. After-treatment consists in keeping the external meatus clean and applying a disinfectant such as 1 per cent solution of gentian violet in spirit. The majority of boils are due to *S. aureus* infections and, unless there is a previous history of sensitivity, a 5-day course of treatment with flucloxacillin gives a rapid relief of pain, particularly if initially given intramuscularly. Incision of a boil should be delayed until it is clearly pointing on the skin. Recurring boils are not uncommon. In persistent cases the urine should be tested to exclude diabetes mellitus. The patient is frequently a scratcher and transfers infection from the nasal vestibules which are also a source of *S. aureus* infection. In such cases the application of a chlorhexidine/neomycin cream (Naseptin) for several days will clear this carrier area. In more resistant cases the whole body requires to be washed in a bactericidal liquid soap and dried with a fresh clean towel.

Diffuse Otitis Externa

This condition occurs in acute or chronic stages in which the skin of the external meatus varies from an acute exfoliative and exudative reaction to a chronic granular or proliferative state.

The *acute stage* presents usually as a feeling of heat in the ear, soon changing to pain which is often severe and is increased by jaw movements. The appearance of a thin serous discharge is accompanied by easing of the pain. Later the discharge becomes thicker and purulent and in some infections foul-smelling. On examination the meatal skin is inflamed, swollen and very tender. Deafness of the conductive type is usually present due to accumulation of discharge and epithelial debris. Enlarged tender periauricular glands are palpable and surrounding oedema may displace the auricle. Wax is noticeably absent.

The features of the *chronic stage* are discharge and constant irritation or itching. The desire to scratch is great and severe at night-time, resulting often in reinfection and exacerbations of the acute stage. Thickening of the meatal skin with narrowing of the lumen may be present, or oedema and desquamation with superficial ulceration of the skin may occur. The drumhead is often congested, with a granular surface, and intermittent deafness results from accumulated debris.

TREATMENT. The treatment of both stages requires thorough and gentle cleansing of the external meatus, keeping the ears dry, avoiding trauma by scratching, attention to personal hygiene and the treatment of associated skin conditions.

In the acute stage local treatment may begin with gentle irrigation of the meatus with warm isotonic saline followed by dry mopping. An attempt should be made to see the drumhead and to clean the anteroinferior meatal recess. Provided that regular toilet of the meatus can be carried out treatment with ear drops may give satisfactory results. Preparations containing an anti-inflammatory corticosteroid and a broad-spectrum antiseptic are effective in many patients, e.g. drops containing gentamicin may be instilled twice daily. The possible adverse effect on the hearing by the topical use of such aminoglycosides in patients with perforated drum membranes is discussed on p. 324. Antibiotic drops and ointments should be employed circumspectly because of the risk of sensitization or secondary fungus infection, and should be related to results of bacteriological examination. In the wet stage packing of the meatus with 12 mm ribbon gauze soaked in an astringent solution such as 8 per cent aluminium acetate may produce a dry meatus. Packing should be done daily and the patient provided with a quantity of the solution so that the wick may be kept moist by applying a few drops to it three or four times a day. Occasionally the canal walls are so swollen that it is not possible to insert a pack, let alone see the eardrum. In such patients the most satisfactory treatment is

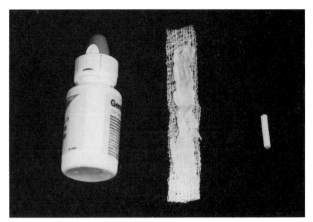

Fig. 3.4.6.   Three methods used in the treatment of otitis externa.
Left. Antibiotic/steroid ear drops.
Centre. Medication on ribbon gauze.
Right. Merocel (Xomed) wick used with drops.

the insertion of a small Merocel wick into the ear canal (*Fig.* 3.4.6). Antibiotic steroid drops are then applied and the wick expands to fill the canal. It can be left in place for 2 or 3 days, by which time the swelling has usually subsided.

Local treatment of the chronic stage requires the same meticulous toilet of the meatus. Swelling of the meatal walls may be relieved by ribbon-gauze wicks soaked in 10 per cent ichthammol glycerin. Irritation, causing reinfection by scratching, is controlled by packing the meatus with a wick impregnated with an antiseptic/cortisone cream. As the condition improves the cream may be lightly applied to the meatal walls by a wool-tipped applicator. Nocturnal itching may be relieved by sedatives, and scratching prevented by a light gauze bandage over the affected ear or by wearing a pair of clean cotton gloves.

Failure to respond to treatment may be caused by an underlying middle-ear infection, sensitivity of the skin to the local application, usually an antibiotic, or by secondary fungus infection.

Otomycosis

Mycotic infection of the external auditory meatus is prevalent in tropical and subtropical climates. The incidence in temperate climates has increased in proportion to the use of topical antibiotics which leave a medium sterilized of other organisms in which the fungus may flourish. The condition should be suspected when routine treatment fails to relieve a diffuse otitis externa, where there is continued irritation in the ear and when the mass of debris in the meatus rapidly reforms after cleansing or when the fungus can be seen on otoscopy. The fungi which are commonly found are *Aspergillus niger* and *Candida albicans*. In aspergillus infections numerous black specks may be seen in the epithelial debris. Microscopic examination of a smear from the debris will confirm the diagnosis.

TREATMENT. Treatment consists of thorough cleansing of the meatus by dry mopping and the application of nystatin, clotrimazole or econazole lotion. Amphotericin B (Fungilin) is also effective in candida infections. Alternatively, drops of 2 per cent salicylic acid in alcohol, or a ribbon-gauze wick soaked in this solution, may be applied to the external meatus. Regular attendance for treatment lasting 3 or 4 weeks is necessary for elimination of the infection.

Seborrhoeic Dermatitis of the Scalp

Seborrhoeic dermatitis, commonly referred to as scurf or dandruff, is characterized by a scaly state of the scalp with patches of erythema, visible at the hair margins and the postauricular sulcus, spreading below the lobe to adjacent areas of the face. A diffuse otitis externa frequently results, with secondary infection induced by scratching.

TREATMENT. The scalp condition should be controlled by regular shampoos, initially twice weekly, containing selenium sulphide (Selsun) or cetrimide BP. The meatus should be kept clean. An ointment containing salicylic acid, precipitated sulphur (each 600 mg) and petroleum jelly (30 g) may be applied to the meatal skin with a wool-tipped applicator to prevent further scaliness and formation of fissures at the introitus.

Dermatitis of the Auricle

Dermatitis occurs as the result of skin sensitivity and may be infective in origin or due to contact of the skin with an external substance, such as cosmetics, jewellery or hair lotions and hair lacquer, but more commonly to the topical use of antibiotics. The typical appearance is of vesication followed by a serous exudate and accompanied by severe irritation. Scratching is likely to introduce secondary infection in those cases of contact origin (*Fig.* 3.4.7).

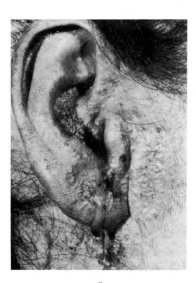 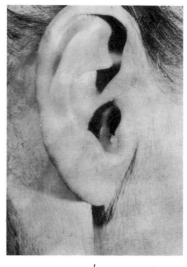

a *b*

Fig. 3.4.7. Dermatitis and otitis externa.
a, Non-infective (contact) dermatitis showing vesiculation and weeping.
b, After treatment with aluminium acetate dressings followed by betamethasone cream.

TREATMENT. In infected allergic skin conditions the use of anti-inflammatory, antiallergic steroids combined with antibacterial agents is advised. A cream containing triamcinolone acetonide (Adcortyl) or fluocinolone acetonide (Synalar) should be applied.

Neurodermatitis

In eczematous types of otitis externa resistant to treatment an underlying psychological disturbance may be present. Intense itching is the main symptom causing considerable distress to the patient with loss of sleep. Secondary infection usually produces a diffuse reaction. A disturbed mental condition may be apparent or careful enquiry may reveal a state of stress.

TREATMENT. Local measures are directed at the relief of secondary infection and the control of irritation with the topical use of antibacterial, antiallergic steroids. Prevention of further scratching is necessary and psychiatric assistance in solving the basic problem may be required.

Otitis Externa Haemorrhagica

During certain epidemics of influenza the infection shows a predilection to attack the ear, and the patient complains of severe earache and tinnitus. On inspection blood blisters of a reddish-brown or purple colour may be seen on the meatal walls (otitis externa haemorrhagica), close to the annulus and on the tympanic membrane (myringitis bullosa). The bullae are prone to spontaneous rupture, with blood-stained aural discharge which may be profuse. The infecting organism is a haemolytic streptococcus combined with a virus. These blisters may occur independently of any middle-ear lesion, and in such cases the hearing is practically normal.

TREATMENT. Incision of the bullae is not indicated unless otitis media with exudate in the middle ear is present, when there will be conductive deafness and severe pain. A course of antibiotics, either penicillin or ampicillin, may be given and sedatives may be required for the pain. The meatus may be lightly plugged with cotton wool.

Malignant Otitis Externa

The majority of reported cases of this uncommon disease have occurred in elderly diabetics. It is characterized by increasingly severe pain in the ear and purulent discharge. The organism responsible is *Ps. pyocyanea*. Granulation tissue is present in the floor of the meatus at the junction of the cartilaginous and osseous portions. Infection spreads to the deeper tissues through the normal clefts in the floor of the cartilage to involve the parotid gland and structures at the base of the skull. Despite energetic management of the local infection the disease can be progressive causing widespread osteomyelitis, intracranial complications and death.

TREATMENT. Granulation tissue should be removed and necrotic tissue excised from the meatus to which daily packs of ribbon-gauze wicks impregnated with gentamicin ointment (Cidoymcin, Genticin) are applied. It is also important to administer full doses of intravenous antibiotics which are active against Pseudomonas, e.g. ticarcillin or azlocillin. Progress of the infection necessitates wide surgical excision of all infected tissue and bone.

Chapter 3.5

ACUTE OTITIS MEDIA
IN ADULTS

Acute inflammation of the middle-ear cleft is distinctly less common in adults than in children. This is due, it is thought, to regression of the adenoids, a reduction in the number of upper respiratory tract infections and possibly, as a result of the aforementioned conditions, more effective Eustachian tube function.

EUSTACHIAN TUBE DYSFUNCTION

Normal Eustachian tube function is essential to the well-being of the middle-ear cleft. If there is either an anatomical or a functional blockage of the Eustachian tube problems soon arise. The Eustachian tube normally opens during swallowing or yawning, and when it does air passes from the nasopharynx into the middle ear. If the tube does not open part of the air in the middle ear becomes absorbed and the patient will notice this as a mild hearing loss and feeling of pressure in the ear. If the process continues and the tube does not reopen then a serous exudate occurs which is associated with a more severe hearing loss, discomfort in the ear, occasionally tinnitus and, in some patients, dizziness.

TREATMENT. This is directed at eliminating infection in the nose, sinuses or postnasal space, combined with the patient attempting to autoinflate the middle ear. Local decongestants or systemic decongestants can also be tried as well as treatment of any underlying allergic element. Occasionally the posterior end of the inferior turbinate can impinge on the Eustachian tube orifice, causing intermittent or even chronic obstruction. Surgical removal of this 'mulberry' enlargement is indicated and will often relieve the patient's symptoms.

ABNORMAL PATENCY OF THE EUSTACHIAN TUBE

An unduly open or patulous Eustachian tube is sometimes associated with atrophic changes in the mucous membrane of the nose and pharynx. The mucosa of the whole tube may be affected or changes may be limited to the pharyngeal opening. It may occur in elderly patients, particularly those with debilitating disease and marked weight loss. Congenital anomaly may account for a small number of cases.

Patients suffering from this condition complain of the loudness of their own voice (autophony) while their hearing is reduced for other voices and sounds. They may be aware of their own breath sounds and the patient's breathing can be heard through an auscultation tube inserted into the external meatus. On examination the characteristic sign is the inward and outward movements of the drumhead accompanying respiration.

TREATMENT. In patients suffering from atrophic rhinitis or pharyngitis, measures appropriate to those diseases should be employed. The insertion of a grommet in the drumhead will sometimes give symptomatic relief. If the symptoms are distressing to the patient it is worth injecting a little Teflon paste into the anterior part of the Eustachian cushion.

ACUTE CATARRHAL OTITIS MEDIA

This usually occurs after an upper respiratory tract infection, particularly sinusitis or influenza. It is thought that simple oedema of the Eustachian tube mucosa prevents proper opening and closing of the tube. Clinically it presents with deafness and 'popping' in the affected ear and a feeling of pressure. There is no pain. The nasal and pharyngeal symptoms are those of an upper respiratory tract infection.

On examination, there is usually nasal obstruction with a mucopurulent nasal discharge. The pharynx may or may not be congested. The affected tympanic membrane is retracted, sometimes acutely, but its colour is normal or slightly pink with a few dilated surface vessels. There is no pyrexia or malaise.

Audiometry, if done, will show the deafness to be conductive in type and of a slight to moderate severity.

TREATMENT. The treatment is expectant because the condition normally resolves as the upper respiratory tract symptoms disappear. Nasal decongestants such as oxymetazoline combined with an oral decongestant syrup, e.g. brompheniramine, may prove helpful. The Eustachian tube may be inflated once the acute nasal symptoms have subsided. This may be done by autoinflation by Valsalva's method, politzerization or Eustachian tube catheterization, in that order, until the tube opens and the hearing returns. In Valsalva's autoinflation the nostrils are pinched to close them and the patient is asked to make a forced expiration with his mouth shut. If this succeeds, air enters the middle ear cavity with a cracking noise. Politzerization is carried out with a Politzer bag about the size of a large orange, connected to an olivary nozzle. The nozzle is inserted into the nostril of the affected side to close it and the other side of the nose is pinched shut. The patient is given a sip of water and is told to swallow it. At the moment he does, just as the larynx is seen to rise, the Politzer bag is sharply compressed expelling air through the closed nasal cavity. Once again a successful inflation is accompanied by a cracking noise. Should both these measures fail, a Eustachian catheter is passed, tip down, along the floor of the nose until it reaches the posterior nasopharyngeal wall. With the catheter steadied at the anterior nares, the tip is rotated through a right angle medially and the catheter gently withdrawn until the tip is held up against the posterior end of the nasal septum. Once again, the catheter is steadied and rotated through 180° with the beak passing downwards and laterally to lie in the nasopharyngeal end of the Eustachian tube. A Politzer bag is attached and air is blown through the catheter, while the surgeon listens through a stethoscope, the other end of which is placed in the patient's external meatus. Air may be heard to bubble or crackle through the Eustachian tube or, if it is patent, a blowing sound will be heard.

ACUTE MIDDLE-EAR EFFUSION

This may be considered as a more severe variety of catarrhal otitis media where the tube is either completely blocked or blocked for a longer time. The cause is commonly an upper respiratory tract infection, but to this may be added an allergic component such as severe hay fever and barotrauma (see p. 349).

The symptoms again are more marked. The hearing loss tends to be more severe and there may be discomfort sufficient to require the use of mild analgesics. In addition, tinnitus and a feeling of blockage and imbalance are not uncommon.

Examination will show the eardrum to be congested and often there is a dark orange hue to it. It may be retracted, and when pneumatic otoscopy is carried out there is little or no movement of the drum. It is important that the batteries in the auriscope are in good condition because if they are running down the normal eardrum often appears dull and dark red. As the eardrum tends to be retracted the light reflex, if present, will be at the periphery anteriorly instead of the umbo. It is in this condition that fluid levels may be seen. If they are present it means that there is some air left in the middle ear and the outlook for a rapid recovery is usually better.

TREATMENT. This is along similar lines to catarrhal otitis media. If the fluid and deafness persist, it is usually worthwhile proceeding to a myringotomy with examination of the postnasal space in case there is a nasopharyngeal tumour present.

ACUTE SUPPURATIVE OTITIS MEDIA

This is much commoner in children but it does occur in adults. It can follow an upper respiratory tract infection which is often viral initially or it can be secondary to the introduction of water through a perforation.

The organisms responsible are similar to those in children, i.e. adenovirus, rhinovirus or bacteria. The commonest bacteria isolated are, in order of prevalence: *Pneumococcus, Haemophilus influenzae, Streptococcus pyogenes* and *Staphylococcus aureus*. Recent work suggests that *Branhamella catarrhalis*, a beta-lactamase producing organism, may be increasing in importance.

CLINICAL FEATURES. The onset can be fairly sudden in adults. The first symptom is of a dull ache inside the ear and this can then become more severe, sometimes radiating to behind the ear. The ear feels dull and there is quite marked hearing loss. There may be slight unsteadiness as well as headache in the parietal area and tinnitus. Fever in an adult is unusual.

Examination will show the eardrum to be very red and in severe cases there will be marked bulging outwards of the membrane with loss of the surface anatomy. If the eardrum has perforated or if there was a pre-existing perforation, there will be a copious mucopurulent, and occasionally blood-stained, discharge, coming from the ear. A bacteriology swab should be sent if pus is present.

Once the eardrum ruptures the pain will decrease to a dull ache and analgesics will probably not be necessary.

TREATMENT. Any existing upper respiratory tract infection should be treated in the usual manner. In the absence of pus, empirical treatment should be started.

A 5-day course of antibiotics should be instituted. Usually in adults oral treatment is adequate and the antibiotics of choice are: (a) ampicillin or amoxillin, (b) co-trimoxazole, (c) cefaclor, (d) erythromycin, (e) penicillin. Simple analgesics such as aspirin, paracetamol or occasionally codeine phosphate are usually sufficient. Where the pain is severe, it is very occasionally necessary to carry out a myringotomy under general anaesthesia but in adults this is rarely required.

If there is a long-standing perforation and the patient is suffering recurrent attacks of otitis media, it is worthwhile considering a myringoplasty to seal the drum.

Where the response to treatment is unsatisfactory in that discharge or pain continues, it may be that the wrong antibiotic has been given and when bacterial sensitivities are available the appropriate antibiotic should be given. If discharge and pain persist, despite the patient having been given adequate doses of the correct antibiotic, a mastoid reservoir of infection may exist and appropriate investigation should be undertaken. There is no proven place for local antibiotics or decongestants in acute suppurative otitis media.

Chapter 3.6

CHRONIC OTITIS MEDIA

Chronic otitis media is less common than in preantibiotic days and it is usually less severe. It still does, however, take up a considerable amount of clinic time and operating time dealing with either active chronic otitis media or the sequelae of previous otitis media. The main complaint of the patient is deafness and, if there is active infection, intermittent foul-smelling discharge. Pain is rarely complained of unless there is a coexisting otitis externa. If pain is a feature as well as deafness and discharge, there may be an underlying malignancy in the ear or an impending mastoiditis or extradural abscess.

CHRONIC MIDDLE-EAR EFFUSION

This condition, known in children also as serous or secretory otitis media, can occur in adults. The basic cause is chronic Eustachian tube dysfunction or obstruction due to blockage of the tube in the middle ear or nasopharynx. Occasionally there may be adhesions in the middle ear or thickened mucosa blocking off the Eustachian tube opening, these will usually be seen as an abnormality on otoscopy. Much commoner is obstruction or oedema at the nasopharyngeal end, often associated with upper respiratory tract infection, e.g. chronic sinusitis, nasopharyngitis or allergic rhinitis. Not uncommonly no abnormality is found, despite thorough examination and investigation. The presence of an unexplained chronic middle-ear effusion, especially in an older person, should immediately raise the suspicion of nasopharyngeal carcinoma.

CLINICAL FEATURES. The principal complaint is of a blocked feeling in the ear with a variable amount of discomfort and occasionally tinnitus or mild vertigo. The patient is unable to clear the ear by autoinflation.

On examination, the characteristic feature is retraction of the drumhead in whole or part. Retraction of the pars tensa is seen and the handle of the malleus appears shortened and to lie in a more horizontal position. The lateral process of the malleus may thus appear more prominent. Partial or localized retraction may involve any segment of the drumhead but often produces an appearance in which the membrane is draped over the incudostapedial joint or appears to adhere to the promontory. The drum often has a dark or orange hue to it and occasionally a fluid level may be seen.

Examination of the nose may reveal signs of sinusitis or allergic rhinitis. Occasionally a tumour, e.g. nasopharyngeal angiofibroma or carcinoma, may be seen in the nose but they are more commonly detected on examination of the nasopharynx.

INVESTIGATION. Audiometry will reveal a conductive hearing loss and there will be diminished or absent mobility of the tympanic membrane. On pneumatic otoscopy a tympanogram will show a flat curve. Sinus radiography and views of the postnasal space should be taken to detect sinusitis or a space-occupying lesion in the nasopharynx and treatment should be directed to any appropriate coexisting disease.

TREATMENT. If the condition persists despite treatment of any underlying sinusitis or if no cause can be found, the patient should undergo an examination of the postnasal space with biopsies of any suspicious areas. Myringotomies should be carried out. If there is thick or serous fluid present, grommets should be inserted even if there is a postnasal tumour present. Where the drum is collapsed or atrophic grommets may be inserted anteriorly, but if the atelectasis is long-standing they are unlikely to be beneficial, and the patient would be better served by having a hearing aid. If the condition persists after the grommets have come out, long-term ventilation tubes such as a T-tube or titanium tubes should be used.

CHRONIC SUPPURATIVE OTITIS MEDIA

This can be conveniently divided into two main clinical types. The first variety, which tends to follow a more benign clinical course, is virtually always a complication of acute otitis media where there is a persisting perforation in the tympanic membrane. It, therefore, usually starts in childhood and is relatively much commoner then. It can be considered as the **tubotympanic type** because in many cases the persisting or recurring infection spreads via the Eustachian tube to the tympanic cavity. It rarely gives rise to any serious complications. The other main type is more aggressive and if untreated usually follows a relentless course of destruction of the middle ear, mastoid antrum and occasionally the inner ear. It can be considered as the **tympanomastoid** variety and always carries a significant risk of serious complications. Although the symptoms may be very similar, the two conditions will be described separately because of the difference in their management.

Tubotympanic Otitis Media

The main pathological condition in this type of disease is a perforation of the eardrum resulting from acute otitis media. The perforation does not heal after the initial acute attack because there has been persistence of the infection and, if this continues for long enough, the edges of the perforation are covered by squamous epithelium from the outer surface joining the mucosa of the middle ear so that the perforation is lined by epithelium. A patient with such a perforation is liable to persisting or recurring discharge secondary to upper respiratory tract infections, but middle-ear infection may also result from bacteria entering the middle ear through the perforation from the external meatus. The perforation is always a central perforation, that is, it is surrounded by part of the pars tensa throughout

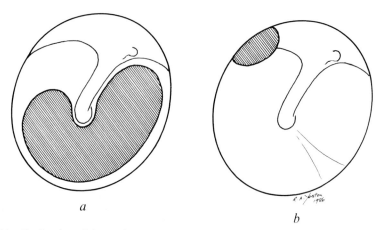

Fig. 3.6.1.   Perforation of the eardrum.
a, Central or anterior perforations are usually associated with tubotympanic disease.
b, Attic and posterior perforations or retraction pockets are associated with atticoantral disease.

its circumference. The perforation may be anterior, posterior, kidney-shaped or subtotal, but it is always surrounded by drum remnant (*Fig.* 3.6.1*a*).

CLINICAL FEATURES. The main symptom of tubotympanic disease is mucopuru-lent discharge which may be intermittent or persistent. There is also deafness which may vary from trivial to moderately severe, that is, averaging about 40 dB. More severe deafness is unusual and is due to involvement of the ossicular chain either by adhesions or by necrosis causing a break in the link.

Examination of the ear will confirm the presence of a central perforation. It is essential that all discharge be removed from the ear so that the tympanic membrane may be completely examined. The discharge is removed by mopping or by suction. There may also be some otitis externa due to prolonged discharge. In all cases the nasal cavities, nasopharynx and pharynx must be examined because it is in the upper respiratory tract that the source of infection will be found. The common causes of ascending infection are infected tonsils and adenoids and sinusitis. Hearing tests, including tuning-fork tests and pure-tone audiometry, will confirm the presence of conductive deafness. Radiography of the nasal sinuses will frequently be required to exclude sinusitis. Radiography of the mastoids will usually show that the mastoids are cellular, but if there has been prolonged infection they may be of the sclerotic type but there will be no evidence of bone destruction. A swab of the ear discharge will be submitted for bacteriological investigation.

Complications are rare and are not serious. With prolonged discharge a polypus, which is a swelling of the middle-ear mucosa, may project through the perforation into the external auditory meatus. This may require removal before the tympanic membrane can be seen adequately and the true nature of the disease assessed. Chronic discharge from the ear leads to otitis externa and this may require treatment before the tympanic membrane can be adequately inspected. A much more unusual complication is fixation of the ossicles by fibrosis. The ossicular chain may be broken by absorption of bone, particularly the long process of the incus. These lesions of the ossicular chain may cause more severe deafness.

TREATMENT. Treatment of the infection consists of eliminating upper respiratory tract infection first. This may require the removal of tonsils or adenoids or the treatment of sinusitis, etc. Provided this is done it is not usually difficult to control the ear infection by local treatment. The local treatment consists of thorough cleaning of the ear, and this is best done by mopping under direct vision which will require the use of a forehead mirror or headlamp. Alternatively, the ear may be cleaned using suction under the vision of an operating microscope. After cleaning, antibiotics are inserted, preferably on a pack. The choice of the antibiotic will depend on the bacteriology. There will be a high incidence of Gram-negative infections such as *B. proteus* or *Pseudomonas pyocyanea* so that antibiotics such as gentamicin, neomycin or framycetin will be required. It is usual to combine the antibiotic with hydrocortisone to reduce the likelihood of skin-sensitivity reactions. There is a theoretical risk that these antibiotics, which are ototoxic, may penetrate the oval or round window to cause sensorineural deafness, but there is no evidence yet that this can occur. If it is not possible for the patient to attend for treatment he should be instructed to mop out the ears twice daily, using cotton wool on a wooden carrier with a long fluffy end firmly attached to the carrier, rather than the commercially available ear mops. With the mop made up as described the ear can be cleaned right down to the tympanic membrane with no pain and no risk to the middle-ear structures. After mopping, the antibiotic ear drops are instilled with the head on the side so that the affected ear is uppermost. After the drops are inserted the tragus is pressed inwards to encourage the drops to pass into the middle ear. In the vast majority of cases the infection can be controlled by these measures.

However, once the ear is dry, there is always the risk of ascending infection from the upper respiratory tract or infection from the outside via the external meatus. These patients should be warned not to get water into their ears when washing or swimming and, if the patient gets a cold, he should not blow his nose as this may cause massive movement of nasal discharge up the Eustachian tube to the middle ear. If there is recurring discharge or if there is deafness sufficient to cause disability, closure of the perforation by myringoplasty should be considered.

Tympanomastoid Otitis Media

In this type of infection the bone of the attic, antrum or mastoid process is involved as well as the mucosa of the middle-ear cleft. It is therefore also referred to as atticoantral disease (*Fig. 3.6.1.b*). As erosion of bone may extend to adjacent vital structures there is always a danger of serious complications. The bony involvement may give rise to granulations or polypi. These may be true granulation tissue but are more often the result of inflammatory swelling of the mucosa of the ear. Their presence, however is usually evidence of bony involvement.

PATHOLOGY. There are three basic pathological findings in the tympanomastoid type of disease:

1. Cholesteatoma.
2. Granulation tissue with osteitis.
3. Cholesterol granuloma.

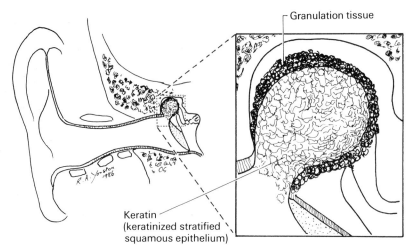

Fig. 3.6.2. Attic cholesteatoma starts as an ingrowth of squamous epithelium which gradually expands superiorly, medially and posteriorly into the mastoid bone.

1. *Cholesteatoma.* The term is a misnomer. When first described in the nineteenth century this condition was thought to be a tumour containing cholesterol. Despite the fact that neither of these is true, the name has stuck and is widely used. The term keratoma has recently been introduced but has yet to be universally accepted.

Cholesteatoma consists of a sac of keratinizing squamous epithelium surrounded by granulation tissue. The surface layers of the epithelium keep producing keratin and this results in the naked-eye appearance of a thin-walled sac containing white cheesy material (*Fig.* 3.6.2). Most cholesteatomas, if untreated, will continue to expand and destroy surrounding structures, although this may take many years.

The granulation tissue on the outside of the sac produces lysozymes and this gradually erodes the ossicles, eardrum and mastoid bone. In children, cholesteatoma tends to be more aggressive and destructive.

Pathogenesis. There are several theories as to how cholesteatoma arises:

a. Congenital cholesteatoma. This is unrelated to chronic suppurative otitis media. It arises from cell rests and occurs in the posterior cranial fossa, where it is known as an epidermoid cyst, the temporal bone and occasionally in the middle ear.

b. Metaplasia. It is well known that metaplasia can occur in respiratory mucous membrane, e.g. in the larynx or where a nasal polyp protrudes from the nose. It is, therefore, likely that metaplasia can occur in the middle-ear mucosa and may account for a small number of cholesteatomas.

c. Ingrowth of squamous epithelium. In all perforations of the tympanic membrane the squamous epithelium extends around the edge of the hole to the medial surface of the drum remnant. Some cholesteatomas seem to arise from extension of this squamous epithelium further into the middle ear.

d. Retraction pocket. The most widely accepted explanation of the origin of cholesteatoma is that it starts as a retraction pocket of the tympanic membrane.

Where the Eustachian tube is blocked, the tympanic membrane tends to be retracted in the posterosuperior segment and in the attic region where the membrana flaccida is thin. This is frequently seen in the later stages of secretory otitis media (*see* Chapter 4.10) when the drum becomes atrophic. A simple retraction pocket causes little trouble as the dead epithelium readily passes into the meatus and is carried to the exterior by the normal migration. If the retraction pocket becomes more marked as the process continues, a sac may be formed with a narrow neck. At this stage the dead squames may not be able to escape through the narrow neck and the condition is now a cholesteatoma. Once formed a cholesteatomatous sac will continue to grow at the expense of any structure in its path (*Fig.* 3.6.2). Structures immediately at risk are the long process of the incus, the Fallopian canal containing the facial nerve, and the dense bone of the horizontal semicircular canal. Slightly more remotely, the tegmen may be eroded to expose the middle fossa dura, the sigmoid sinus may be eroded with risk of sinus thrombosis or the dura of the posterior fossa may be exposed to allow direct access into the posterior fossa towards the cerebellum.

Problems of function of the Eustachian tube leading to secretory otitis media are extremely common and it seems likely that, in most cases, cholesteatoma arises from this cause during childhood.

2. *Granulation tissue.* This is basically a low-grade osteitis of the mastoid bone. It may be localized to one area, e.g. posterosuperior meatal wall and middle ear, or extend throughout the middle ear and mastoid. It can also cause destruction of surrounding structures.

3. *Cholesterol granuloma.* This can be seen on its own or in combination with either cholesteatoma or granulations. The naked-eye appearance is of dark brown gelatinous material, often with a lot of bone destruction, and if present in the middle ear gives the eardrum a dark blue or black appearance. Histological examination shows it to consist of cholesterol crystals surrounded by foreign-body giant cells and granulation tissue.

CLINICAL FEATURES. The symptoms and bacteriology are very similar to those of tubotympanic otitis media. The main symptom is again of discharge from the ear which may be persistent or recurrent. The discharge, however, is purulent rather than mucopurulent and it is frequently foul-smelling. Deafness is again usually present and may vary from trivial to severe because of frequent involvement of the ossicular chain. If granulations or polypi are present, bleeding from the ear may be noted. The onset of symptoms is insidious so that the patient may be unaware of the starting point of the disease, but in many cases the condition commences in childhood.

On examination, purulent discharge which is frequently offensive has to be mopped out before the tympanic membrane can be adequately seen. Polypi or granulations may have to be removed by surgery before the nature of the condition can be fully assessed. In contrast to tubotympanic otitis media the perforation in the dangerous type is usually attic or in the posterosuperior segment of the tympanic membrane. The perforation is marginal, that is, it extends to the bony annulus of the drum (*Fig.* 3.6.1b). Polypi or granulations may be seen to occupy such perforations or may protrude through them into the ear canal. Cholesteatoma may be seen as a greyish substance projecting from or filling an attic or a marginal perforation.

INVESTIGATIONS. Hearing tests, including tuning-fork tests and pure-tone audiometry, will be required. Radiography will usually show a sclerotic mastoid. The mastoid is small and poorly developed with a low middle fossa and a far-forward lateral sinus. If the mastoid was previously cellular there may be secondary sclerosis tending to obliterate the cells. A larger cholesteatoma sac may be seen as an area of radiotranslucency with a clearly outlined bony margin.

TREATMENT. Before treatment can commence, an accurate assessment of the nature and degree of the disease process must be made. Examination of the ear using an operating microscope will frequently be required with or without a general anaesthetic. Aural polypi or granulations may require removal before the underlying drum can be adequately visualized. If there is no evidence of cholesteatoma the treatment described for tubotympanic otitis media may be used, and this may also be applicable after the removal of granulations or polypi if no cholesteatoma is seen. If the infection is not controlled by this conservative treatment, surgical treatment will be required.

In most cases of cholesteatoma surgical treatment will be required. If cholesteatoma is seen in an attic perforation or in a posterosuperior perforation it is not usually possible to assess the extent of the cholesteatomatous sac unless there is also radiographic evidence of a bony defect. Such evidence is usually only seen in the larger cholesteatomas. If the hearing is good it is tempting to wait until it deteriorates before advising treatment, lest the hearing be further damaged by the surgery. However, if expectant treatment is applied, there may be a sudden loss of hearing from trivial to severe if the long process of the incus is eroded. It will then be very difficult to restore the hearing to its previous level. It is more likely that a good level of hearing will be maintained by early surgical treatment which will prevent further extension of the cholesteatoma to the ossicles. Such surgery may require removal of parts of the ossicular chain to make the ear safe, although this may require sacrifice of the hearing. In addition to the risk to hearing there is the distinct possibility of facial paralysis, labyrinthitis or an intracranial complication if cholesteatoma is not controlled. It is for this reason that surgical treatment will be required in the majority of cases to control the cholesteatoma.

THE SURGICAL TREATMENT OF CHRONIC OTITIS MEDIA

In all cases the aim of the treatment is to produce a safe, dry ear and, if possible, to restore or improve the hearing. Whether this can be achieved will depend upon the nature and extent of the disease.

Myringoplasty

This operation consists of closing a central perforation in the tympanic membrane, in the tubotympanic type of chronic suppurative otitis media. The indications for the operation are recurring discharge from the ear and/or deafness causing disability. At routine medical examination it is not unusual for candidates to be found with central perforations of the eardrums, of which they are entirely ignorant. These people may be unaware of any deafness and may be able to swim

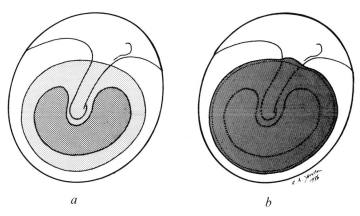

a   *b*

Fig. 3.6.3.   Onlay myringoplasty.
a, The surface epithelium is raised or removed around the perforation.
b, The temporalis fascia graft is trimmed to size and laid over the raw surface. It is held in place by covering it with gelatin sponge.

or get upper respiratory tract infections without developing symptoms. In these cases it is meddlesome to interfere.

Before myringoplasty is considered the ear should be dry and free from infection, preferably for several months. The fascia covering the superficial surface of the temporalis muscle is the material most used for grafting because it is strong and very thin. It can be obtained by the incision used to gain access to the ear or through a separate incision in the temporal region. The eardrum is prepared for receiving the graft by removing the squamous epithelium on its outer surface, or this epithelium may be turned forwards as a flap. The temporalis fascia is then applied and the flap replaced (*Fig.* 3.6.3). Alternatively, mucosa can be separated from the inner surface of the drum and the graft applied on its inner aspect. A combination of onlay and underlay techniques may be used.

How well the graft will take will depend upon the size of the perforation, because the graft will rely for its blood supply on vessels growing in from the periphery. Therefore, it will depend on whether the drum remnant is vascular, or scarred and avascular. This operation will be successful in the majority of cases, both improving the hearing and reducing the likelihood of infection ascending to the middle ear. In a few cases the hearing deteriorates as a result of the drum becoming too thick and immobile. In a very few cases severe sensorineural deafness occurs. Myringoplasty can be combined with operations to reconstruct the ossicular chain.

Radical Mastoidectomy

For many years this was the standard operation for treating chronic suppurative otitis media, whether associated with granulations or cholesteatoma. In this operation the mastoid air cells were exenterated and the posterior meatal wall and outer attic wall were removed so that the external meatus and the site of the mastoid air cells were opened into one large cavity. In addition, the tympanic membrane and ossicles were removed, and the remains of the tympanic annulus and the Eustachian tube were curetted (*Fig.* 3.6.4). This operation had two

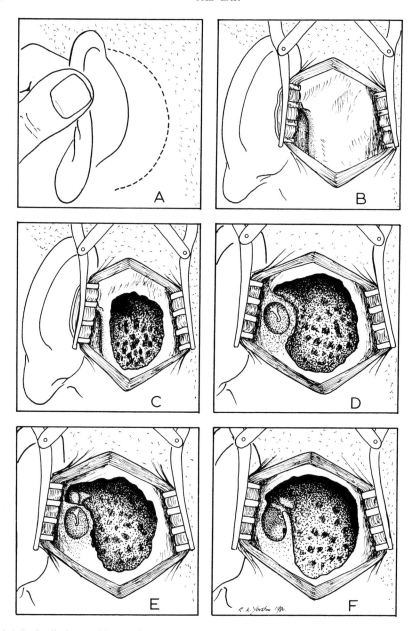

Fig. 3.6.4.   Radical mastoid operation.
A, Skin incision.
B, Area of operation exposed.
C, Mastoid antrum opened.
D, Outer or lateral part of posterior bony meatal wall removed, but inner end, or bridge, remains.
    Drumhead is visible.
E, Most of the bridge has now been removed, body of the incus and head of the malleus are revealed.
F, Radical operation completed. Malleus and incus, with the drumhead, have been removed, and facial
    spur lowered. Prominence of lateral canal, facial nerve, stapes, promontory and niche leading to the
    round window can all be seen on medial wall of operation cavity.

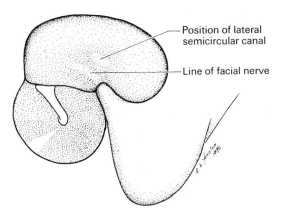

Position of lateral semicircular canal

Line of facial nerve

Fig. 3.6.5. The healthy mastoid cavity should be lined with thin skin. The malleus and drum membrane are left if feasible, and any perforation is repaired. Ossicular reconstruction, if required, can be performed at the initial or a later operation.

disadvantages: (1) the patient was left severely deaf and (2) there was recurrent ascending infection from the Eustachian tube.

Modified Radical Mastoidectomy

At the present time this is still the most frequent operation carried out for chronic suppurative otitis media of the dangerous type. The mastoid cells are again exenterated and the outer wall of the attic and the posterior meatal wall are removed so that the meatus, attic and mastoid cells are opened into one large cavity. However, the remains of the eardrum and ossicles are not disturbed unless they are diseased. If cholesteatoma involves the ossicles, parts of these may have to be removed to open up the diseased processes. In most cases this operation will retain the hearing at the preoperative level, provided that no damage is done to the drum remnant and the ossicles. An important part of this operation is a meatoplasty to enlarge the external auditory meatus. This will give good access to the cavity for dressings. Later it will allow entry of air so that the cavity is more likely to be lined by squamous epithelium and a dry ear achieved (*Fig.* 3.6.5).

Combined-approach Tympanoplasty

The main disadvantage of a modified radical mastoidectomy is that the patient is left with a large cavity which may preclude him from swimming, because water getting into the ear may cause infection. Cold air and water may also cause vertigo. It is, therefore, attractive to try to remove the diseased processes without leaving behind a cavity exposed to the exterior. In combined-approach tympanoplasty the mastoid cells are opened by a postaural approach. This exposure can be continued forwards towards the attic. By extending the exposure downwards through the posterior wall of the middle ear just lateral to the facial nerve, a large part of the middle-ear cavity can also be exposed. In most cases the disease may be eradicated by this approach but it is not suitable for an extensive cholesteatoma. Even when the cholesteatoma is small there is a risk of leaving squamous epithelium undisturbed and, therefore, of a recurrence of the cholesteatoma. For this reason the patients who have had combined-approach tympanoplasty carried out require careful, skilled follow-up, and the operation should only be done where this follow-up can be undertaken. The other advantage of this approach is that where reconstructive procedures are carried out, the site of the reconstruction can be kept under vision when the eardrum is grafted and when the meatal pack is inserted. Thus the surgeon can be sure that the ossicular reconstruction has not been disturbed by these procedures.

Tympanoplasty

Repair of the eardrum or myringoplasty has already been described. It is well-recognized that sound transmission directly from the drum to the head of the stapes will give excellent hearing. Nature often achieves this with a scarred drum or by adherence of a cholesteatoma membrane to the stapes. However, surgically it is very much more difficult to achieve these excellent results. Where there is loss of the ossicular chain it is now more usual practice to try to reconstruct a functioning chain, using mainly the patient's own incus or, if it is diseased, a homograft incus, to reconstitute the ossicular chain. Where the malleus and stapes are intact and mobile, the gap between the two can be bridged by reshaping the incus so that a sound connection is obtained between them. If the malleus and the stapes are mobile but the superstructure of the stapes has been lost, the incus again may be used to bridge the gap between the handle of the malleus and the footplate of the stapes. If the stapes footplate is immobile as a result of adhesions or tympanosclerosis, stapedectomy will usually be required using a piston which is attached either to the handle of the malleus or the long process of the incus if that is present. Not infrequently the handle of the malleus or the incus is fixed in the attic by adhesions. In these cases the head of the malleus and the incus are removed and, if this mobilizes the malleolar handle, the drum reconstruction can be carried out in a manner similar to that already described for the intact malleus.

Where the patient's own incus is diseased or is absent, a homograft incus or malleus can be used and is just as effective. If there is total loss of bones and ossicles, it is possible to insert a complete homograft eardrum and ossicles and in expert hands worthwhile hearing results can be achieved.

These reconstructive procedures are surgically difficult and the results can be poor if the replaced ossicles are absorbed or where adhesions form and refix the ossicles. Occasionally adhesions can be prevented by inserting silastic sheeting at the initial drum repair and establishing a more healthy middle-ear space.

When the time comes for the ossicular reconstruction the silastic can be removed and the ossiculoplasty performed in conditions which should give more reliable results. In some cases the primary cause of the problem, Eustachian tube dysfunction, persists and the reconstructed drum and ossicles become adherent to the promontory. These unfortunate patients will then have to accept the hearing loss or use a hearing aid.

Although the results of tympanoplasty are improving, they are still unsatisfactory in a significant number of cases, e.g. 30 per cent or more where the incus is missing, and the surgeon must be honest with himself and the patient when considering surgical intervention.

TUBERCULOUS OTITIS MEDIA

Tuberculous otitis media is now a rare condition in Great Britain. Cases of tuberculous otitis media may be divided into two groups: (1) in infants and very young children who are fed, in whole or in part, on unsterilized cow's milk which contains the bovine type of tubercle bacillus. Suppurative otitis media in an infant, which is not responding to treatment, should make one think of tuberculous middle-ear disease. (2) In the advanced stages of pulmonary tuberculosis disease of the middle-ear cleft sometimes occurs.

PATHOLOGY

Infection by way of the Eustachian tube. Tuberculous infiltration of the mucous membrane spreads up the tube to the tympanic cavity, or infectious particles may be insufflated up the Eustachian tube during the acts of coughing and sneezing. Invasion of the labyrinth occurs first of all through the oval and round windows. In advanced cases there is caries and necrosis of the bony labyrinth capsule. In rare cases there is a tendency to spontaneous cure of the tuberculous labyrinthitis.

Infection by the bloodstream. If the Eustachian tube and tympanum appear to be healthy, while the mastoid process alone is diseased, the probability is that infection has occurred by way of the bloodstream.

SYMPTOMS. The onset appears to be painless, in marked contrast to the early stages of pyogenic otitis media. The lymph glands surrounding the ear are often enlarged. In the early stage the discharge is watery, and later it may be flocculent; in the advanced stages, where mixed infection is present, it is offensive and purulent. Pale granulations may be seen and these recur rapidly after removal. Paralysis of the facial nerve may occur and multiple perforations in the tympanic membrane may sometimes be seen in adults. Involvement of the labyrinth is of frequent occurrence, and takes place at a comparatively early stage of the disease. Tuberculous labyrinthitis, like tuberculous otitis media, appears to have a quiet onset, in marked contrast to the violent symptoms produced by an attack of acute purulent labyrinthitis.

COMPLICATIONS. Tuberculous otitis media and interna do not, as a rule, give rise to intracranial complications, although tuberculous granulation tissue on the dura mater is frequently met with at operation. A number of cases, however, have been reported where a tuberculoma of the brain has occurred, the cerebellum being the most likely site.

DIAGNOSIS. This is made by attention to the following points: (1) The clinical characteristics of the case already described. (2) Examination of the aural discharge for tubercle bacilli. (3) Microscopic examination of granulations removed from the middle ear or mastoid. (4) Culture. (5) The findings at operation—enlarged caseous glands, presence of necrosed bone, pale flabby granulations, putty-like pus in the tympanic antrum, extensive caries of the bone and necrosis of the labyrinthine wall.

TREATMENT. This consists of intensive chemotherapy with antituberculous drugs, but surgical treatment may also be required.

Chapter 3.7

EXTRACRANIAL COMPLICATIONS
OF OTITIS MEDIA

Complications of otitis media, either acute or chronic, occur when the infective process spreads beyond the confines of the middle ear. This happens less often now than in the past, due to better and more widely available antibiotics, a healthier population and more effective surgical treatment. The same antibiotics, however, have altered the classical presentation of many of the complications and this can lead to difficulty in diagnosing potentially fatal conditions. The importance of early recognition of complications of middle-ear suppuration can hardly be stressed enough.

Infection in the middle ear commonly involves the mastoid by direct extension, but other surrounding structures may be involved. This can occur by direct spread through an area eroded by disease, or through a congenital dehiscence or a fracture line. The other mode of spread is by thrombophlebitis of emissary veins.

ROUTES OF INFECTION. From the middle ear and mastoid antrum infection may spread in the following directions (*Fig.* 3.7.1):

1. **Medially** to the labyrinth, through the oval window, round window or by erosion of the lateral semicircular canal. Occasionally there may be erosion of the promontory or the other semicircular canals. Meningitis commonly occurs in this way.

2. **Superiorly** towards the middle cranial fossa resulting in an extradural abscess or in an abscess of the temporal lobe; meningitis occasionally results from spread of infection by this route.

3. **Posteriorly** towards the posterior cranial fossa producing (*a*) an extradural abscess between the sigmoid sinus and its bony wall (perisinus abscess) or an abscess medial to the sinus, (*b*) septic thrombosis of the sigmoid sinus, (*c*) meningitis beginning in the posterior cranial fossa, (*d*) cerebellar abscess.

4. **Inferiorly** through the floor of the tympanum producing a septic thrombosis of the bulb of the internal jugular vein.

Complications are more likely to arise from chronic otitis media than from acute otitis media and are conveniently divided into two groups—extracranial and intracranial. They are not mutually exclusive, however, as one complication may precede or lead to another, e.g. labyrinthitis may lead to meningitis or mastoiditis may lead to an extradural abscess.

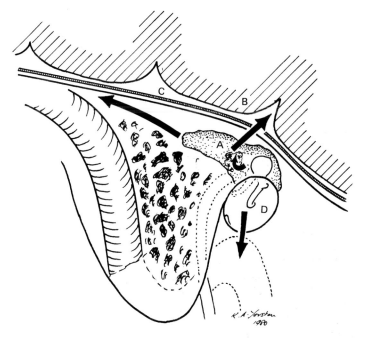

Fig. 3.7.1.   Routes of spread of infection from middle-ear cavity and mastoid.
A, Medially (acutely curved arrow) to labyrinth.
B, Superiorly to middle cranial fossa.
C, Posteriorly to posterior fossa and sigmoid sinus.
D, Inferiorly to jugular bulb.

EXTRACRANIAL COMPLICATIONS OF OTITIS MEDIA

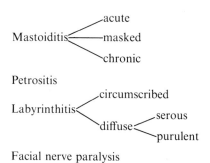

Mastoiditis — acute / masked / chronic

Petrositis

Labyrinthitis — circumscribed / diffuse — serous / purulent

Facial nerve paralysis

ACUTE MASTOIDITIS

In infancy, with the exception of the tympanic antrum and a layer of small cells in its lateral wall, the mastoid process contains no cells, the bone being diploic. This acellular or infantile type of mastoid process persists throughout life in about 20 per cent of people. It may be converted to a compact acellular mastoid by the

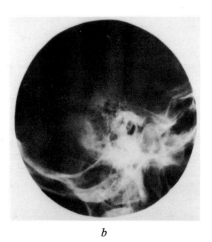

a

Fig. 3.7.2.   Radiographs of the mastoid.
a, Acellular mastoid (left).
b, Well-pneumatized mastoid (right).
c, Chronic mastoidits (left). Same patient as *b*, showing clouding and loss of definition of cells. At operation the cells were full of granulation tissue.

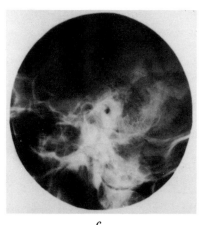

b   *c*

laying down of cancellous bone in the marrow spaces (*Fig.* 3.7.2*a*). In normal circumstances the infantile mastoid process becomes pneumatized (*Fig.* 3.7.2*b*), but between the acellular and pneumatic types there are intermediate stages. Controversy still exists as to which comes first, failure of pneumatization or infection, some otologists believing that failed pneumatization is the result of infection and not the precursor. Studies of the histopathology of acute mastoiditis have shown that, in some cases, during the process of healing the lumen of the air cell is filled with granulation tissue in which new bone is formed. There is then the possibility that an originally pneumatic process may become sclerotic, although such an occurrence is held by some to be rare.

Mastoiditis is a complication of otitis media in which infection spreads from the tympanic antrum to involve the bony walls of the cells of the mastoid process. The infection may be acute or chronic.

AETIOLOGY. Acute mastoiditis arises from an acute otitis media by extension of infection from the mastoid antrum to the air cells, and occurs therefore in a cellular temporal bone. In many cases of acute otitis media infection, although present in the cellular system, produces no bone destruction, but in severe acute infections there is a greater inflammatory reaction resulting in pus formation, increased tension, resorption of bone with loss of trabeculation and the formation of an empyema. Eventually the inflammatory process may erupt through the lateral surface to produce a subperiosteal abscess. An untreated abscess may spread in several directions: (1) through the periosteum and skin covering the mastoid process; (2) into the external meatus to simulate a discharging furnucle; (3) through the medial aspect of the mastoid tip into the digastric fossa (Bezold's mastoiditis); (4) through the posterior root of the zygoma beneath the temporal fascia (zygomatic mastoiditis) causing slight oedema of the upper eyelid as an early sign; (5) through the canal for the mastoid emissary vein or through the temporo-occipital suture to form an abscess posterior to the mastoid process; (6) beyond the confines of the middle-ear cleft giving rise to intracranial complications.

SYMPTOMS. The symptomatology of the majority of cases of acute mastoiditis seen in hospital practice has been modified or obscured by previous unsuitable or inadequate antibiotic therapy. In acute otitis media, pain behind the ear and tenderness over the area of the mastoid antrum are commonly present but are relieved by successful antibiotic treatment. Increasing pain, or the return of pain, and increasing mastoid tenderness are therefore significant. Tenderness occurs not only over the mastoid antrum (MacEwen's triangle) but may be elicited on pressure over the mastoid tip and posterior border. In an untreated case of mastoiditis discharge from the ear will usually have increased with extension of the disease, but in a 'masked' case discharge may be absent and the perforation may have healed. Fever is not marked in adults but may be high in children, in whom a rising pulse rate is a potential danger signal. Deafness is present in most cases but varies in severity. Local signs vary with the stage and extent of the infection.

In the case of periostitis gentle palpation over the mastoid area may reveal thickening of the periosteum on the affected side. Later there is oedema of the soft tissues with displacement of the auricle downwards and outwards which is often seen more easily from behind the patient (*Fig.* 3.7.3). If a subperiosteal abscess forms there is a fluctuant swelling behind the ear. Narrowing of the external meatus due to sagging of the posterosuperior meatal wall is a significant finding on otoscopy, which may reveal a perforated drumhead with pulsating discharge or an intact one which has a thickened or full appearance. Patients generally look ill and feel off colour and disinterested. Those with pain and systemic disturbances are more anxious and aware of their illness.

DIAGNOSIS. In some cases difficulty may arise in distinguishing between mastoiditis and furunculosis of the posterior meatal wall with cellulitis (*see* p. 271). Considerable help in arriving at a diagnosis of mastoiditis may be obtained from radiography of the mastoids by comparing films of the affected and unaffected sides in different views of the temporal bone. Anatomical asymmetry of the mastoid process is found in 12 per cent of patients. The radiograph shows the type of mastoid process and the extent of cellular development. In early cases of mastoid infection, slight blurring of the cellular outlines is present on the affected

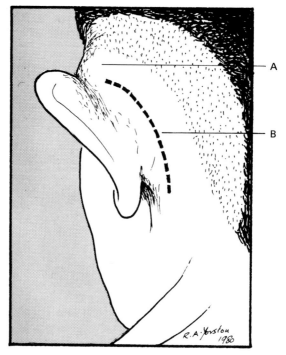

Fig. 3.7.3.   Posterior view of left ear in acute mastoiditis showing (A)
ear pushed inferiorly and laterally. B = line of incision.

side and the outline of the bony plate of the lateral sinus becomes more
prominent. Increasing opacity with pus formation is followed by loss of cellular
outlines or trabeculation, by destruction of bone proceeding eventually to formation of an abscess cavity. The radiological appearances should at all stages be
correlated with the clinical manifestations and follow-up radiography is often
necessary.

Blood examination generally shows a polymorphonuclear leucocytosis and the
ESR is increased, except possibly in those patients who have had antibiotic
treatment.

TREATMENT. The incidence of acute mastoiditis has been greatly reduced since
the advent of antibiotic treatment, particularly with penicillin. The majority of
cases of acute suppurative otitis media now resolve by early and adequate
treatment with parenteral penicillin combined, if necessary, with paracentesis. The
presence of pus in the middle ear may be associated with increased tension
requiring relief by surgical drainage, otherwise some permanent loss in hearing
may result.

When the clinical features of mastoiditis develop the patient should be confined
to bed and antibiotic administration commenced. Until pus from the ear is
available for bacteriological examination, penicillin should be given by intramuscular injection starting with 1 million units (benzyl penicillin) followed by 500 000

units 6-hourly. Lack of improvement in the patient's condition in 48 hours is an indication for a change of antibiotic or a cortical mastoidectomy.

The indications for the cortical mastoid operation, also known as Schwartze's operation, are: (1) continued pain and mastoid tenderness for more than 2 or 3 days despite antibiotic therapy in full dosage and adequate drainage by paracentesis; (2) increasing constitutional signs, e.g. fever and rising pulse rate; (3) copious pulsating discharge, rapidly refilling the meatus after mopping out; (4) sagging of the meatal wall, increasing oedema over the mastoid process or zygoma; (5) symptoms or signs of labyrinthine or intracranial complication; (6) onset of facial paralysis; (7) persistent suppurative otitis media for more than 2 weeks despite efficient treatment; (8) progressive deafness.

MASKED MASTOIDITIS

This serious and treacherous condition, associated with an unresolved or latent otitis media, is the result of inadequate treatment with antibiotics. Failure to recognize the state of the infection and to apply vigorous treatment may result in the development of an intracranial complication such as meningitis or lateral sinus thrombosis. At the present time it occurs mostly after the administration of oral penicillin given for too short a period of time and, in some cases, in inadequate dosage, particularly at night-time.

DIAGNOSIS. Many cases are referred to hospital because of the persistence of pain, deafness, fever and discharge or because of the appearance of an intact unresolved reddish drumhead. Others are seen on account of recurrence of these symptoms after an apparent recovery. The persistence of deafness is an important symptom. There may be mastoid tenderness and headache with a slight rise in temperature. The drumhead is usually congested and full or thickened in appearance. Mastoid radiographs show opacity or haziness with, in some cases, loss of cellular outlines on the affected side (*Fig.* 3.7.2*c*).

TREATMENT. Admission to hospital for observation and adequate treatment is necessary. Resumption of full antibiotic therapy is justifiable in the absence of acute signs of mastoiditis, a watch being kept on the patient's general condition, temperature chart, tympanic membrane, mastoid process and hearing. In the absence of early signs of improvement, and whenever some doubt exists, a cortical mastoidectomy should be done to provide effective drainage of the middle ear and reduce the possibility of permanent conductive deafness.

The Cortical Mastoid Operation (Schwartze's Operation)

The aim of this operation is to remove all infected mastoid cells. A postaural incision is made (*Fig.* 3.7.3), the mastoid bone is exposed and MacEwen's triangle identified. The cortex is removed using a drill, although where an abscess is present the cortex will be soft and necrotic. Each group of cells is systematically explored and cleared so as to leave an appearance such as in *Fig.* 3.7.4. Particular attention is paid to removing infection in the tip cells and the cells in the sinodural angle. If necessary the zygomatic cells are removed. If the plates of bone overlying the dura mater and the lateral sinus appear healthy they are not opened to expose these structures, but unhealthy bone in these situations must be removed and the

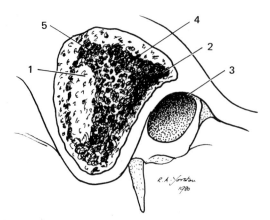

Fig. 3.7.4. Completed cortical mastoidectomy.
1, Lateral sinus plate.   4, Dural plate.
2, Aditus ad antrum.   5, Sinodural angle.
3, External auditory meatus.

dura and sinus wall examined for extension of disease. A swab of pus will be taken routinely for culture and sensitivity, and any granulation tissue should be sent for histological examination. The wound is sutured and a rubber drain is left in the lower part of the incision. The drain is removed after 24 to 48 hours and the stitches are removed in 1 week.

Lack of healing or continued meatal discharge suggests that some infected cells may have been missed or that spicules of infected bone have been left in the cavity, and in either case the wound may have to be reopened.

CHRONIC MASTOIDITIS

This is considered under Chronic Otitis Media (p. 282).

PETROSITIS

This is seen less frequently now and may occur in acute or chronic form in a pneumatized petrous bone. It is due to direct extension of infection from the middle ear or mastoid. It may present as part of a mastoiditis, or may follow a cortical mastoidectomy for mastoiditis, usually 2–3 weeks after, but occasionally several months later.

PATHOLOGY. The pathology is essentially that of the mastoid infection which precedes it. Infection may be confined to the petrous bone, or it may extend intracranially and result in a localized meningitis or an extradural abscess in the middle or posterior fossa. Spread may also occur downwards and cause abscess formation in the pharynx. Occasionally spontaneous drainage through the middle ear may result in recovery.

CLINICAL FEATURES. There is severe unilateral headache, spasmodic in type, and usually retro-orbital, supraorbital or temporal in distribution, due to irritation of the related nerves. In the presence of otitis media, such headache with diplopia due to paralysis of the abducens nerve (Gradenigo's syndrome) is almost diagnostic of the condition. A slight rise of temperature may accompany the onset of the headache. Following mastoidectomy a sudden recurrence or increase of discharge, often with pulsation, may suggest a petrositis. Other transient features may occur, such as facial palsy and vertigo with vestibular nystagmus due to labyrinthine irritation. Lumbar puncture should be performed. The cerebrospinal fluid may be under slightly increased pressure, but is otherwise normal. Any departure from normal findings, such as a slight increase in cells, is an indication for early surgical exploration. Disappearance of symptoms may indicate resolution, but if this is of sudden onset it may signify intracranial rupture and the development of meningitis or extradural abscess.

DIAGNOSIS. Diagnosis is made from: (1) persistent otorrhoea following cortical mastoidectomy, (2) clouding and rarefaction of petrous apical cells on radiography (Towne's or Stenver's view) and (3) the discovery of a fistulous track leading to the petrous apex on revision of the operation.

TREATMENT. In the early acute stages treatment is that of the associated otitis media and mastoiditis, and includes vigorous antibiotic therapy with the appopriate drug after sensitivity tests have been carried out. The pain may be sufficiently severe to require morphine. As a rule mastoidectomy is indicated and a search must be made for the presence of a fistula leading to the petrosal apex, and, when found, it must be curetted to facilitate drainage. When the condition is chronic, or when it becomes manifest after the failure to obtain a cure with a simple cortical mastoid operation, a radical mastoidectomy may be required.

LABYRINTHITIS

This is a common complication of otitis media and, if suspected, must be treated vigorously and promptly. Failure to do so may lead to total sensorineural deafness or meningitis. The least severe form is circumscribed labyrinthitis, also known as paralabyrinthitis, and this is easily the most common type. Serous labyrinthitis is less common, but more serious. The least common but most dangerous variety is purulent labyrinthitis which inevitably leads to a total and permanent loss of vestibular and auditory function.

PATHOLOGY. **Circumscribed labyrinthitis** is almost invariably due to a fistula, i.e. cholesteatomatous erosion of the bony capsule of the labyrinth, usually the lateral semicircular canal but occasionally the promontory or other canals. **Diffuse labyrinthitis** may be an extension of the circumscribed type but it more frequently follows invasion through the oval or round windows, especially the former. It involves the peri- and endolymphatic spaces. Diffuse labyrinthitis may be serous or purulent. In **serous labyrinthitis** there is a general non-purulent inflammation of the labyrinth with occasionally a fibrinous or serous exudate. In **purulent labyrinthitis** there is infiltration of the spaces by polymorphs, pus cells and destruction of the vestibular and cochlear structure. Occasionally the bony capsule becomes involved.

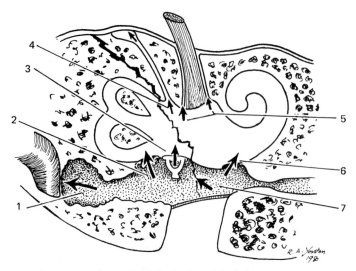

Fig. 3.7.5.   Routes of spread of infection into labyrinth.
1, Blood spread.   5, Subarachnoid sleeve of VIIIth nerve.
2, Fistula of lateral semicircular canal.   6, Round window.
3, Oval window.   7, Fracture line.
4, Cochlear aqueduct.

Labyrinthitis may follow an acute otitis media, tuberculous otitis media or chronic otitis media. Other causes of labyrinthitis include trauma, blood-borne infection, bacterial or viral, and meningitis (*Fig.* 3.7.5).

CLINICAL FEATURES

Circumscribed labyrinthitis. There may be an initial bout of vertigo and deafness in the formative stage of the fistula. Once the fistula is established the main complaint may be of intermittent vertigo brought on by sudden movements, cold water or air in the ear or, in more advanced cases, by moving the auricle. There is usually evidence of chronic otitis media on otoscopy and the diagnosis is confirmed by demonstrating a fistula sign, but a negative fistula sign does not rule out a fistula (p. 261). There may be a slight sensorineural hearing loss in addition to the conductive hearing loss due to otitis media.

Serous labyrinthitis. This may follow circumscribed labyrinthitis or any of the other causes mentioned. There is hearing loss, occasionally pain and tinnitus, but the main feature is vertigo, associated with nausea and vomiting. There may be a sensation of objects moving from the diseased to the healthy side, i.e. nystagmus towards the diseased side. The patient invariably is bed-ridden, at least initially, and lies on the unaffected ear and looks towards the diseased side because this reduces the vertigo. As a rule there is no pyrexia. Caloric reactions, if tested after the acute phase, are diminished on the affected side.

Purulent labyrinthitis. The symptoms are similar to those of serous labyrinthitis but the vertigo and vomiting may be more frequent and severe. Nystagmus, although initially directed towards the diseased ear, soon changes direction towards the good ear. Total deafness develops. Caloric testing should not be done during the acute phase because it can exacerbate the vertigo, but if done later a canal paresis is commonly found on the affected side. There is no pyrexia unless there is an intracranial complication.

TREATMENT

Circumscribed labyrinthitis. Suspicion of labyrinthine erosion by cholesteatoma or granulations is an indication for surgery. Tomography may show labyrinthine erosion. The mastoid is cleared of disease by a modified radical mastoidectomy. The fistula may be exteriorized if caused by cholesteatoma. In some cases the cholesteatoma can be removed and the fistula is covered by temporalis fascia.

Serous labyrinthitis and purulent labyrinthitis. Bed-rest is essential in the initial stages. Sedation with labyrinthine sedatives is required, dimenhydrinate BP (Dramamine), promethazine theoclate BP (Avomine) or prochlorperazine (Stemetil) being useful. Parenteral antibiotics in adequate dosage are required. A combination of penicillin and sulphonamide can be used empirically until swab results are known. Most patients settle on this regime. If the precipitating cause were an acute exacerbation of chronic otitis media this can be dealt with subsequently. Occasionally a myringotomy will be required in acute otitis media, and occasionally it is necessary to deal surgically with a mastoiditis. In a few cases persistence of symptoms with evidence of intracranial irritation may call for exploration and a labyrinthectomy.

Chapter 3.8

INTRACRANIAL COMPLICATIONS OF OTITIS MEDIA

There has been a marked reduction in incidence of these complications over the past three decades, the reasons for this being the same as for extracranial complications. When they do occur, however, their morbidity and mortality are still high. Even today a person who has a brain abscess has a 40 per cent chance of dying from it. It is vital, in any suspected case of intracranial extension of disease, to liaise closely with the neurosurgeons and neuroradiologists. The only exception to this rule being a small extradural abscess where the diagnosis is made during the course of exploratory mastoid surgery.

INTRACRANIAL COMPLICATIONS OF OTITIS MEDIA

Extradural abscess

Lateral sinus thrombosis

Otitic hydrocephalus

Meningitis

Brain abscess ⟨ temporal lobe / cerebellum

Subdural abscess

Cortical thrombophlebitis

EXTRADURAL ABSCESS

An extradural abscess consists of a collection of pus between the bone and the dura mater. Unless it is opened and drained it is frequently followed by other intracranial complications. It is more common in the posterior than in the middle cranial fossa, in some cases forming between the lateral sinus and the bone of the posterior cranial fossa (perisinus abscess) (*Fig.* 3.8.1.). Extradural abscess occurs more commonly in acute than in chronic middle-ear suppuration. In chronic purulent otitis media it is met with chiefly in cases of cholesteatoma and in acute exacerbations of chronic suppuration. The extent of the abscess varies greatly; it may be quite small or, in chronic cases, it may attain a considerable size.

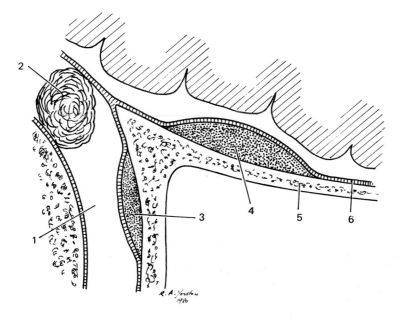

Fig. 3.8.1.   Diagram showing extradural abscess formation and lateral sinus thrombosis.
1, Lateral sinus.   4, Extradural abscess.
2, Thrombus in lateral sinus.   5, Tegmen tympani.
3, Perisinus abscess.   6, Dura mater.

CLINICAL FEATURES. The symptoms are rarely characteristic and the majority of extradural abscesses are only discovered at the time of operation. The condition is associated with deep-seated boring pain, tenderness on tapping over the temporal bone or posterior fossa, and rise of temperature. If the abscess is large, there may be evidence of compression of the brain. There are rarely any localizing symptoms although occasionally paresis of the VIth nerve may be encountered.

DIAGNOSIS. This is not easy as a rule. The relief of pain by the spontaneous evacuation of a large quantity of pus, or the aspiration of much pus by mopping or aspiration through the external meatus, may suggest the diagnosis. The continuation of pain, pyrexia and a raised pulse rate after operation for a mastoid complication should suggest the probability of the presence of a deeper-seated collection of pus.

TREATMENT. This consists of opening the abscess and evacuating its contents by free removal of the bony wall. When the abscess is opened the pus flows out in a pulsating manner. The affected dura mater may be covered with red 'healthy' granulations, or it may be greyish-green and slough-like. Removal of the under-lying bony wall should be continued until the whole abscess cavity has been freely exposed. The cortical or the radical operation—according to circumstances—is performed at the same time. The patient should be carefully watched in order to detect the first signs of further intracranial complications, e.g. sinus thrombosis, brain abscess or meningitis.

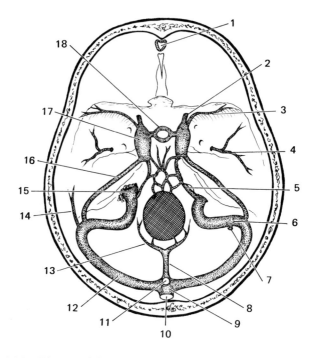

Fig. 3.8.2.   Diagram of the venous sinuses of the skull. (After Hollinshead.)

1, Superior sagittal sinus (anterior part).	10, Superior sagittal (posterior part).
2, Ophthalmic vein.	11, Straight.
3, Sphenoparietal.	12, Transverse.
4, Middle meningeal.	13, Marginal.
5, Inferior petrosal.	14, Petrosquamous.
6, Sigmoid.	15, Jugular bulb.
7, Emissary vein.	16, Superior petrosal.
8, Occipital.	17, Cavernous.
9, Torcular (confluence of sinuses).	18, Intercavernous.

LATERAL SINUS THROMBOSIS

This condition used to account for about 30 per cent of all cases of intracranial complications in the preantibiotic era, but now it occurs much less frequently and today makes up less than 10 per cent of the total. About half of these are associated with other intracranial complications, usually cerebellar abscess or meningitis. It is still a dangerous condition which must be recognized as early as possible and treated vigorously.

PATHOLOGY. The initial lesion is inflammation of the wall of the sinus secondary to local infection. This can be due to local venous thrombophlebitis but it is usually a result of an extradural perisinus abscess, which has sometimes been present for a considerable time. It occurs in both acute and chronic mastoid infections, although more frequently in the former. The local inflammation in the wall of the sinus results in thrombus formation which can spread to involve the whole lumen. In untreated or rapidly developing cases the thrombus may extend

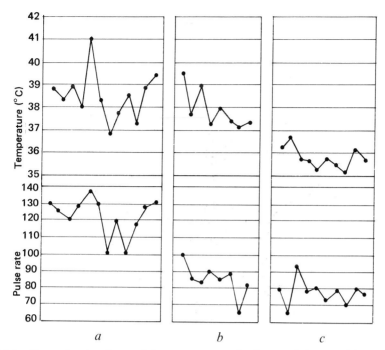

Fig. 3.8.3.   Charts showing characteristic temperatures and pulse rates in intracranial complications. *a*, Lateral sinus thrombosis. *b*, Otogenic meningitis. *c*, Brain abscess.

in either direction to involve the superior petrosal sinus (rare), cavernous sinus (rare), torcular (rare), jugular bulb (common) or the internal jugular vein (rare) (*Fig.* 3.8.2). The thrombus tends to stop where two vessels meet. If the thrombus becomes infected an abscess can develop and this may result in pieces of infected clot breaking away and being carried to other parts of the body. A pyaemia therefore occurs and abscesses are set up in the lungs and other organs. If the infection breaches the medial wall of the sinus, meningitis, subdural abscess or brain abscess can develop.

CLINICAL FEATURES. Sinus thrombosis may run its course without symptoms, particularly where antibiotics have been used, and be found later at a definitive operation for the underlying chronic otitis media. The classical presentation, now rarely seen, consists of the occurrence of chilly sensations or rigors in which the temperature rises suddenly to 39·5 or 40 °C and falls again as rapidly (*Fig.* 3.8.3*a*), the fall being accompanied by profuse sweating. There may be only one rigor daily, usually in the afternoon or evening, or several. There is a concomitant rise in the pulse rate. A high evening temperature for several days after a mastoid operation calls for exploration of the sinus. In the intervals between the rigors the patient is free from symptoms, although in advanced cases there is persistent pyrexia. Headache and vomiting occasionally occur, the tongue is dry, there may be herpes on the lips, an enlarged spleen and a congested optic disc. Lumbar puncture, which should only be done if a brain abscess has been excluded, may demonstrate raised cerebrospinal fluid pressure, particularly when complete occlusion is present. In such cases the Tobey–Ayer test is positive. This consists of compressing the jugular vein of the normal side which causes a rise in cerebro-spinal fluid pressure in the manometer connected to the lumbar puncture needle, while compression of the vein on the affected side produces little or no rise in pressure. Occasionally oedema is present in the neighbourhood of the mastoid emissary vein (Griesinger's sign).

If the thrombosis extends into the neck torticollis may develop, and there may be tenderness over the line of the jugular vein. Occasionally a cavernous sinus thrombosis can occur. As a result of escape of portions of the clot into the general circulation pneumonia or lung abscess may arise. If the particles are small, metastatic abscesses may appear in other parts of the body, especially in the subcutaneous tissues or in the bones and joints.

DIAGNOSIS. The conditions with which sinus thrombosis is most likely to be confused are malaria, typhoid fever, bronchopneumonia and erysipelas. The diagnosis of sinus thrombosis is suggested by the occurrence of rigors in the course of middle-ear suppuration; it is more difficult if the condition is complicated by the presence of meningitis or brain abscess, both of which must be treated first. Examination of the peripheral blood will show a polymorphonuclear leucocytosis. In severe infections a falling haemoglobin can occur. Blood cultures are rarely of value.

TREATMENT. Early energetic antibiotic therapy often makes operative treatment unnecessary. A combination of antibiotics to which upper respiratory tract organisms, including anaerobes, are sensitive, and which cross the blood–brain barrier, is recommended. A combination of flucloxacillin, co-trimoxazole and metronidazole should be started pending the results of bacterial culture and sensitivities. When active surgical intervention is required this consists of remov-ing the primary focus of disease by performing a cortical mastoidectomy in cases due to acute middle-ear suppuration, and a radical operation in cases of chronic suppuration. If sinus thrombosis is present the bone cells near the lateral sinus will be soft, and obviously infected. The sinus plate will have granulations on it, and there may be a perisinus abscess. If these signs are found the lateral sinus should be carefully exposed as far superiorly as the middle fossa dura and inferiorly towards the jugular bulb. A healthy lateral sinus has a glistening blue wall. If it appears greyish-yellow or brownish-green, a needle attached to a syringe should be inserted to ascertain if it is patent. If it is thrombosed or contains pus the infected thrombus should be removed, after incising the wall of the sinus, and evacuation should proceed until free bleeding occurs from both superiorly and inferiorly. Thereafter the sinus is obliterated by packing a bismuth iodoform pack between it and the sinus plate. The sinus and cavity are packed with BIPP and the wound left open to be closed at a second stage some 7 days later. The persistence of infected emboli after this procedure is dealt with by tying off the internal jugular vein, although this is now rarely necessary.

Septic thrombosis can follow injury to the sinus during mastoid operations. Injury to the wall should be treated by application of a piece of temporalis fascia or muscle to arrest the bleeding. Should rigors occur postoperatively the case is treated as a sinus thrombosis.

PROGNOSIS. The prognosis of sinus thrombosis is more favourable since the introduction of antibiotics. It is more favourable than that of brain abscess if an operation is performed before systemic infection has occurred, and if there is no other intracranial complication. With antibiotics and timely surgery a cure is to be expected.

OTITIC HYDROCEPHALUS

This is rare. It is unfortunately a misnomer as there is no hydrocephalus (i.e. enlargement of the ventricular system). In fact the ventricles in this condition are often smaller than usual. It occurs most frequently in children, adolescents and young adults. It is thought to arise because of thrombosis of the lateral sinus which may extend to the torcular. The associated ear infection is the probable underlying cause and there may be abnormalities of the venous sinuses of the skull (*Fig.* 3.8.2) so that the affected sinus drains most of the cerebral blood flow. This causes a rise in intracranial pressure, due to inadequate absorption of cerebrospinal fluid by the arachnoid villi, which is the source of the symptoms. Similar clinical features are found in benign intracranial hypertension from other causes.

CLINICAL FEATURES. The patient complains of intermittent severe headaches occurring several times a day. When the headaches are severe there may be slight clouding of the conscious level and vomiting. Intermittent dizziness is present and unilateral or bilateral VIth nerve palsies and papilloedema develop. An intracranial space-occupying lesion must be excluded by a CT scan and following this a lumbar puncture will show markedly raised intracranial pressure.

TREATMENT. The mastoiditis is treated medically or surgically as appropriate. Also steps are taken to reduce intracranial pressure which is achieved medically by a combination of steroids and diuretics. Daily lumbar puncture is helpful. If the papilloedema persists for more than 3 weeks there is a risk to long-term visual acuity, and permanent drainage by a ventriculoperitoneal shunt or reduction of pressure by a subtemporal decompression may be required.

MENINGITIS

This accounts for about one-third of all intracranial complications, only brain abscess being more common. Even with the armamentarium of antibiotics available today it can still be fatal and must be suspected in all cases of otitis media where there are symptoms and signs suggestive of intracranial spread of disease. Like the other complications of otitis media it is decreasing in incidence.

PATHOLOGY. Meningitis is an infection of the pia mater which invests the brain, the arachnoid mater which is closely adherent to the under surface of the dura mater, and the cerebrospinal fluid which lies between these two layers. It can occur during an acute infection but is more commonly associated with chronic otitis media. There are several ways in which infection can reach the meninges: (1) direct extension through the dura mater due to thrombophlebitis of communicating veins, erosion by disease or surgery, or congenital or traumatic dehiscences; (2)

extension of disease from an extradural abscess or lateral sinus thrombophlebitis; (3) extension of a suppurative labyrinthitis via the cochlear aqueduct or the subarachnoid sleeve of the VIIIth nerve.

As in other infections there is often an initial inflammatory response with production of serous fluid. This stage can be identified readily, for instance with extradural abscesses. Granulations develop in the dura mater around the abscess and this causes irritation of the pia-arachnoid layers which respond by producing a serous effusion. If the abscess drains spontaneously or is drained surgically the effusion gradually subsides and this **serous meningitis** settles. If, however, the local infection is not controlled infection may then spread into the pia-arachnoid layers. There is initially a cellular reaction to this and polymorphonuclear leucocytes increase in number, and this is followed by the appearance of bacteria in the cerebrospinal fluid and a **purulent meningitis**. The disease may remain localized initially but with the purulent stage developing it rapidly becomes diffuse. In some cases, in which the bacteria are virulent, there is only a very brief serous phase before the onset of the purulent phase. In an untreated or a rapidly progressive infection the surface of the brain becomes affected causing a meningoencephalitis and a widespread and usually fatal cerebral dysfunction occurs.

The bacteria commonly associated with meningitis are *Haemophilus influenzae*, streptococci and pneumococci. Occasionally *Bacillus proteus* or *Pseudomonas pyocyanea* may spread from a chronic mastoid infection.

CLINICAL FEATURES. Headache and neck stiffness are the two cardinal features of **serous meningitis**. The headache is severe and may be initially localized to the side of the disease but later becomes generalized. There will be neck stiffness and tenderness, most easily tested by lifting the patient's head off the pillow. Photophobia may be present, occasionally associated with vomiting due to raised intracranial pressure. The patient's initial conscious level may be normal but usually there is slight confusion and irritability with occasional episodes of drowsiness. There may be an initial rigor but often the temperature is slightly elevated from 38 to 38·5 °C.

As the disease progresses and **purulent meningitis** supervenes so the headaches become extremely severe. The neck becomes rigid, there is a positive Kernig's sign (an inability to extend the knee with the hip flexed to 90°). There may be severe neck pain. Photophobia is marked and there is frequent vomiting. The level of consciousness varies but there is marked confusion, irritability with occasional periods of excitement during which the patient may cry out or talk incoherently. The reflexes are increased initially but later, as the condition advances, may be reduced. There is a persistently high temperature (39·5–40 °C) (*Fig.* 3.8.3*b*) with a fast and weak pulse.

In the final stages paralysis may develop and can affect various parts of the body and the cranial nerves, especially the IIIrd and the VIth, with the production of squinting. Optic neuritis is frequently seen while the pupils are contracted and equal and react sluggishly. Coma supervenes before death.

DIAGNOSIS. Meningitis has been aptly described as the great imitator and must be diagnosed and treated at an early stage for the best chance of survival. If the clinical features suggest the possibility of either a brain abscess or a subdural abscess, a CT scan must be carried out first. If this is negative the definitive test is lumbar puncture. The features suggestive of an intracranial abscess are variable morning headache as opposed to the continuous headache of meningitis, a slightly elevated (*Fig.* 3.8.3*c*) or even reduced temperature, drowsiness, focal signs and epileptic fits. If CT scanning is not available, a radioisotope scan or arteriography may be required.

Lumbar puncture can reveal a great deal of information. The normal pressure of the cerebrospinal fluid is 80–120 mmH$_2$O and in meningitis it is raised. It is important that there should be no blood in the fluid sent for examination, and therefore the first few drops should be allowed to escape. Four cells per cubic centimetre may be regarded as normal. If the fluid is under tension, but clear and sterile, and the cellular content is not increased, the meningitis is still at the serous stage. On the other hand, if the fluid is under pressure and is turbid from the presence of leucocytes, purulent meningitis may usually be diagnosed. If organisms are present in addition, there can be no doubt. Biochemical examination of the cerebrospinal fluid in meningitis will show diminished or absent glucose, raised protein and globulin, and lowered chloride.

TREATMENT. Without waiting to identify the organisms responsible parenteral antiobiotic therapy should be instituted. Two to 4 megaunits of penicillin are given 6-hourly, combined with 2 g of sulphonamide 6-hourly. Swabs from the ear and fluid obtained at lumbar puncture are cultured to discover the organisms and determine their sensitivities, and antibiotic therapy is continued with the appropriate drug until the cerebrospinal fluid and clinical examination are normal. Other antibiotics routinely used include ampicillin and cloxacillin, cephaloridine and occasionally chloramphenicol or gentamicin. Intrathecal penicillin, 10 000 units in 5 ml, may be introduced at the initial lumbar puncture if the fluid is turbid. Surgery of the underlying ear disease should be carried out when the patient's general state permits. Labyrinthectomy may be required in the presence of concomitant suppurative labyrinthitis.

PROGNOSIS. An uncomplicated meningitis has a more favourable outlook than one associated with a sinus thrombosis, brain abscess or labyrinthitis.

CIRCUMSCRIBED SEROUS MENINGITIS

This is a very rare complication of chronic otitis media. In response to nearby infection a localized serous meningitis develops and forms a cyst in the subarachnoid space. It usually occurs in the posterior cranial fossa and produces symptoms by pressure on surrounding structures. Clinical features include headache, giddiness, ataxia, deafness, tinnitus, nystagmus, dysdiadokokinesia and past-pointing. Occasionally the cysts burst spontaneously, but if they enlarge exploration of the posterior cranial fossa is usually required with drainage of the cyst. Differentiation between this condition and a cerebellar abscess can be extremely difficult.

BRAIN ABSCESS

Brain abscess is the commonest intracranial complication of ear disease making up over one-third of the total numbers. Ear disease, on the other hand, is the commonest cause of brain abscess and accounts in some series for about half the total. Cerebellar abscesses nearly always arise from ear disease. Today the overall mortality from brain abscesses is quoted at around 40 per cent. The earlier the diagnosis is made and treatment instituted, the more likely are the chances of recovery, but there is a significant morbidity rate in the survivors in terms of epilepsy. Suspicion and early diagnosis, therefore, are vital if the prognosis is to improve.

PATHOLOGY. An abscess develops close to the site of the original infection, so otogenic brain abscesses arise in the temporal lobes and the cerebellum. The majority are associated with chronic otitis media although acute infections account for a significant number. Cerebellar abscess is due to: (1) extension of infection from the mastoid posteriorly and medially through the triangular area bounded by the superior petrosal sinus above, the labyrinth and facial nerve anteriorly, and the lateral sinus laterally—there is usually a preceding extradural abscess; (2) septic thrombosis of the sigmoid sinus which is usually associated with a perisinus abscess; (3) labyrinthitis.

Temporal lobe abscess, the more common abscess, is caused by spread of infection through the roof of the middle ear or mastoid antrum, again frequently preceded by an extradural abscess. The dura mater, pia arachnoid and brain become adherent to the inflamed tissue, and after an initial local surface encephalitis the infection spreads to the subcortical white matter. More rarely the abscess is due to septic thrombosis of one of the pial veins of the temporal lobe or cerebellum. Infection by this route, which is common in cases of acute middle-ear suppuration, may result in multiple abscesses.

Once infection is established in the brain, if unchecked, it involves more tissue which becomes necrotic and an abscess is formed. The presence of infection stimulates oedema of the surrounding tissue and results in increased intracranial pressure, distortion of surrounding structures and functional disturbance of them. Continuing infection causes tissue destruction, a further displacement of brain tissue across the midline and eventually death, usually from mid-brain damage.

CLINICAL FEATURES. The symptoms and signs produced are due to three factors; (1) increased intracranial pressure, (2) focal disturbance of function, (3) systemic disturbance.

1. *Increased intracranial pressure*. Headache is the dominant symptom and is usually generalized and worse in the morning. Vomiting often occurs, especially in cerebellar lesions. Drowsiness, confusion and lethargy develop as pressure increases and finally coma supervenes. Papilloedema may be present but its absence does not rule out raised intracranial pressure. The temperature is often subnormal in the early stages unless there is coexisting meningitis and the pulse is often slow (*Fig. 3.8.3c*).

2. *Focal signs*. These are variable. Homonymous hemianopia is a valuable sign in temporal lobe abscess, as is nominal dysphasia. Cerebellar abscesses give rise to ataxia and nystagmus. In very ill patients these signs may be difficult to elicit.

3. *Systemic disturbance*. Although there may be little initial systemic upset, as

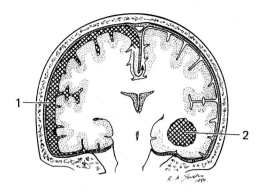

Fig. 3.8.4.   Diagram showing a subdural abscess and a temporal lobe abscess.
1, Subdural abscess. This may remain localized or can spread to involve the whole of the cerebral hemisphere and track under the falx cerebi to involve the other hemisphere.
2, Temporal lobe abscess. This tends to remain localized but can, in severe cases, rupture into the ventricular system.

the infection progresses the patient becomes very ill and emaciated. There is pyrexia, loss of appetite, exhaustion and a furred tongue. There is raised ESR and a polymorphonuclear leucocytosis. A severe rise in temperature often occurs if an abscess ruptures into the ventricular system.

Temporal Lobe Abscess
This is more common than cerebellar abscess and gives rise to a typical clinical picture (*Fig.* 3.8.4).

CLINICAL FEATURES. Headache is common and is usually generalized. If there has been a preceding extradural abscess the headache may be more severe on the affected side and be associated with tenderness over the temporal lobe. The headache classically is worse in the morning and it is exacerbated by coughing, sneezing or straining. Vomiting is occasionally seen. Mental changes may be minimal initially and consist of subtle changes in personality and mild confusion. As the intracranial pressure increases, however, the patient will become lethargic and listless, and then drowsy. Drowsiness is a danger signal as it indicates early tentorial herniation and mid-brain compression. Papilloedema may be present at this stage.

Nominal dysphasia is a feature of temporal lobe abscesses and it suggests involvement of the speech area of the dominant cerebral hemisphere. The speech area is located in the frontotemporal region and is usually on the left side of the brain in a right-handed person and on the right side in a left-handed person. The earliest focal sign is usually a homonymous hemianopia. If this sign is present the patient has visual field defects affecting the same sides of both retinas, and he will be unable to see objects on one side, i.e. to the right if there is a lesion of the left temporal lobe. The defect is due to interruption of the fibres of the optic radiation as they pass near the temporal lobe and, if the lesion is small, it may present early as a superior quadrantic visual defect. This test is elicited by standing in front of the patient and comparing his visual fields with the examiner's. In an unconscious or drowsy patient the sign may be elicited by flashing a light or a handkerchief

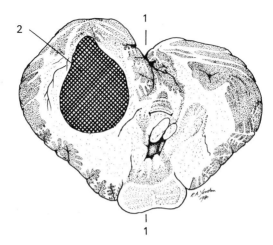

Fig. 3.8.5.   Cerebellar abscess. 1–1 indicates what would be the normal midline of the cerebellum and demonstrates the midline shift due to swelling of the abscess-containing cerebellar hemisphere (2).

near the eye and trying to elicit the blink reflex and comparing the sides. An expanding lesion may cause contralateral paralysis of limbs and even a hemiplegia if the internal capsule is affected. Pupillary abnormalities and oculomotor palsies are suggestive of transtentorial herniation and are danger signs. Epileptic fits are not uncommon but, unless they are focal, are of little localizing value. Sudden onset of coma associated with a high fever indicates that the abscess has ruptured into the lateral ventricle and is of a grave prognostic significance.

Cerebellar Abscess

This abscess (*Fig.* 3.8.5) is less common than temporal lobe abscess by a ratio of 1 to 4 or 5.

CLINICAL FEATURES. Headache is again a feature and tends to be sub-occipital and may be associated with nuchal rigidity. Vomiting is common and papilloedema is seen more often than in temporal lobe lesions. Confusion and drowsiness occur if the intracranial pressure increases and will progress to coma and death if untreated.

Truncal and limb ataxia gives rise to unsteadiness, and Romberg's test is positive. Other signs of cerebellar disease are past-pointing and dysdiadokokinesia. In the latter test the patient is asked to pronate and supinate his forearms alternately. If there is unilateral cerebellar disease present he will be unable to do the test efficiently on that side. Nystagmus is usually present and is coarser and of greater amplitude than that due to labyrinthitis. As a rule it is directed towards the affected side. Later signs consist of a VIth nerve palsy and dysarthria.

DIAGNOSIS. Once suspected it is essential to obtain neurosurgical advice as the investigation and treatment are neurosurgical. Lumbar puncture is contraindicated, even if a concomitant meningitis is suspected, because of the risk of coning. The investigations carried out depend on local facilities but they must be done with utmost urgency.

1. *Plain skull radiography*. This is useful as it may show a midline shift if the pineal gland is calcified.

2. *Computerized axial tomography scan*. A CAT or CT scan is the best investigation, if available. It is quick, non-invasive and extremely accurate in localizing abscesses, especially when it is combined with contrast enhancement. As well as delineating the abscess, intracranial shift, cerebral oedema and hydrocephalus can all be demonstrated.

3. *Electroencephalography*. This can be of use but in posterior fossa lesions it is of less help.

4. *Brain scan*. Radioactive technetium is injected intravenously and the brain scanned by a gamma camera. It is very valuable in supratentorial lesions and is non-invasive.

5. *Arteriography*. This is still recommended as an important investigation because it shows intracerebral shifts, avascular areas and areas of increased vascularity. It is not without risk, needs a general anaesthetic, unless the patient is comatose, and its accuracy can be doubtful.

TREATMENT. This is primarily neurosurgical. High doses of antibiotics which cross the blood–brain barrier are given parenterally. Some help may be obtained from swabs from the offending ear. Once the abscess is localized it is drained via a burrhole. This may be followed by repeated aspiration and instillation of antibiotic. In some cases a craniotomy is performed and the abscess with its capsule, if well-defined, is removed.

In an emergency, if there is no immediate neurosurgical help available and the patient is deteriorating rapidly, a temporary improvement may be obtained by giving 500 ml of 20 per cent mannitol intravenously combined with 4 g of dexamethasone. This may reduce the cerebral oedema sufficiently to prevent coning and allow the patient to be transported to a neurosurgical unit.

The causative ear infection should be dealt with as soon as the patient's general condition permits. A radical mastoidectomy is recommended for chronic disease and a cortical mastoidectomy for acute infections.

COURSE AND TERMINATION. If untreated a brain abscess ends fatally with increasing drowsiness, stupor and eventually coma which continues until death.

PROGNOSIS. Even today the mortality for brain abscesses may be as high as 40 per cent. A further 40 per cent are left suffering from some degree of permanent disability, usually epilepsy. If there is meningitis associated with the brain abscess the prognosis is worsened.

SUBDURAL ABSCESS

This is an extremely rare complication of otogenic infection and it is serious, with a poor prognosis. The mode of spread is similar to other intracranial infections but pus collects in the subdural space (*Fig.* 3.8.4). This causes increased intracranial pressure, midline shift and transtentorial herniation. The patient is extremely ill, has severe headache and, as infection spreads to involve the cerebral cortex, develops focal signs of hemiplegia or hemianaesthesia. Drowsiness progresses rapidly to coma. Epileptic fits may start. Neurosurgical referral is a matter of urgency and investigations are similar to those for brain abscess.

The treatment consists of draining the subdural space and in some acute cases this may have to be done on a presumptive diagnosis in order to save the patient's life.

CORTICAL THROMBOPHLEBITIS

This again is rare and diagnosis is usually made after the patient has been fully investigated and found not to have any of the other complications. It is a localized thrombophlebitis affecting the cortical veins. It gives rise to a clinical picture of focal signs which can include focal epilepsy, hemiparesis or hemianaesthesia, and variable drowsiness and headache. Diagnosis is by exclusion of an intracranial abscess or meningitis. Treatment is by antibiotics.

OTOSCLEROSIS

In normal conditions the membranous labyrinth is surrounded by two distinct layers of bone. The inner of these two, the labyrinth capsule proper, is composed of dense bone directly derived from the cartilaginous capsule of the otic vesicle in the embryo. For good hearing it is necessary that the nerve structures of the inner ear should be immediately surrounded by this layer of dense non-vascular bone. Enclosing this cartilaginous bone, but distinct from it, there is the ordinary lamellar bone derived from the mucoperiosteum of the middle ear and from the osteogenic layer of the dura mater. These two layers are partially separated from one another in the embryo, and also in infants, by a well-marked lymph space. In young subjects, remains of fetal cartilage are sometimes to be found in the promontory near the anterior margin of the oval window.

Otosclerosis is a common disease. Probably 1 person in every 200 suffers from the affection. In many cases otosclerosis is present, unsuspected, in the labyrinth capsule and only becomes manifest when it involves the hearing mechanism.

AETIOLOGY. The disease is much more common in females than males. There is a marked hereditary tendency to otosclerosis in certain families, and in nearly 50 per cent of cases a history of deafness in the family can be obtained. The disease usually becomes manifest between the ages of 18 and 30, but it may begin earlier. There appears to be a close relationship between the onset of deafness and the onset of puberty or the occurrence of pregnancy.

PATHOLOGY. The bony changes vary according to the duration of the disease. At first the normal bone is absorbed and replaced by vascular spongy osteoid tissue. The process advances along the blood vessels. Later the new bone becomes thicker and less vascular. The most common site of disease is the promontory in the region of the anterior margin of the oval window, and in advanced cases the stapes becomes ankylosed in position by a mass of spongy new bone. Various reasons have been given to explain this 'site of election' for bone disease in otosclerosis. It may be worthy of note that in this region there is an anastomosis between the vessels of the middle ear and those of the labyrinth capsule. Of greater possible significance is the fact that in this area is located the **fissula ante fenestram**, a vestigial structure which frequently contains cartilaginous remnants and which is particularly prone to otosclerotic change.

SYMPTOMS. The chief symptoms are gradually increasing deafness and tinnitus. The noises are often referred to the head rather than the ear and occasionally cause the patient more discomfort than the deafness. If tinnitus is marked, the case is likely to progress rapidly. Paracusis Willisii is frequently present, i.e. the patient states that he can hear better in a noisy place such as a railway carriage or motor car. Various explanations have been put forward to account for paracusis, the most probable being that patients suffering from otosclerosis, and consequently unable to hear lower tones, obtain more advantages than normal people from the raising of their friends' voices in a noisy place, as they (otosclerotics) are not distracted by the low-pitched hum of machinery to the same extent as people with perfect hearing. Otosclerotics speak in a low, well-modulated voice, very different from the loud, harsh speech of an advanced case of nerve deafness. Giddiness is a rare symptom, but may be present in varying degree even to the extent of true paroxysmal vertigo.

EXAMINATION. In otosclerosis the tympanic membrane is usually normal. In about 10 per cent of cases a flamingo-pink blush may be seen through the membrane, usually behind the handle of the malleus. This is due to hyperaemia of the promontory and affords good evidence that the otosclerotic process is in an active phase. The Eustachian tube is usually patent. On the other hand, the presence of scars in, or opacity or retraction of, the drumhead in association with Eustachian obstruction by no means precludes the diagnosis of otosclerosis. Otosclerosis may coexist with middle-ear suppuration.

Tuning-fork tests show a negative Rinne's test and Weber's test is lateralized to the more affected ear. Audiometry confirms the presence of a conductive deafness with, usually, normal inner-ear function. Sometimes there may be a diminution of inner-ear function, earlier than can be accounted for by presbyacusis.

There are rare cases of otosclerosis in which the focus of spongy change does not affect the region of the oval window but involves the capsule of the cochlea at a separate spot. In such cases there is no paracusis, and tuning-fork tests give the results normally obtained in a case of sensorineural deafness. It has been suggested that if a young or middle-aged patient suffers from nerve deafness for which no other cause can be found, and if in her or his family there are individuals suffering from typical otosclerosis, the case should be regarded as one of cochlear otosclerosis.

TREATMENT. Patients with otosclerosis hear well with a hearing aid, but as treatment is usually sought in early adult life or in middle age, surgical treatment is usually preferred.

The surgical treatment of otosclerosis was revolutionized by the introduction of direct mobilization of the stapes by Rosen in 1953. This gave excellent results initially, but it soon became apparent that the stapes refixed in practically all cases. In 1958 the operation of stapedectomy was introduced when the stapes was removed and replaced by a prosthesis. The operation is best carried out under general anaesthesia using controlled hypotension, although it can also be done under local anaesthesia. It is essential to use a good operating microscope. The exposure is achieved using an aural speculum. The skin of the posterior bony meatal wall is incised to form a U-shaped flap (*Fig.* 3.9.1), which is raised towards the annulus tympanicus which is then elevated from the underlying bone

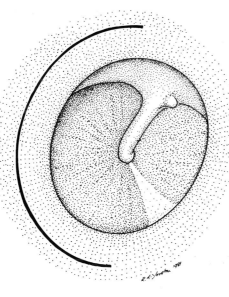

Fig. 3.9.1.   The stapedectomy incision. The incision is made in the
skin of the posterior meatal wall parallel to the tympanic ring from 12
o'clock to 6 o'clock.

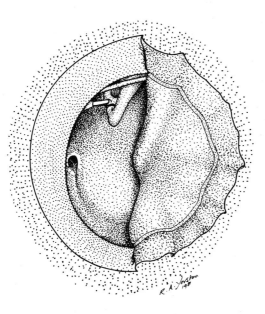

Fig. 3.9.2.   The middle ear exposed. The skin has been elevated from the bone, the fibrous ring has
been lifted from the annular sulcus and, together with the tympanic membrane, has formed a flap
which has been reflected anteriorly with the handle of the malleus as a hinge, exposing the posterior
half of the tympanic cavity.

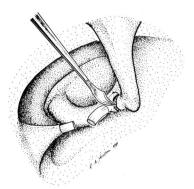

Fig. 3.9.3.   The incudostapedial joint is disarticulated after division of the stapedius tendon.

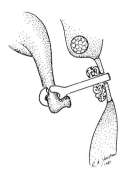

Fig. 3.9.4.   The footplate of the stapes has been drilled to take a Teflon piston of 0·6 mm diameter. The piston is crimped round the long process of the incus and projects 0·5 mm into the vestibule. Gelfoam is packed round the piston.

so that the posterior half of the tympanic membrane can be folded forwards, hinged on the handle of the malleus, to expose the posterior half of the tympanic cavity (*Fig.* 3.9.2). Extra exposure is obtained by removing bone around the posterosuperior margin of the bony rim. The superstructure of the stapes is removed (*Fig.* 3.9.3); a limited opening is made through the footplate of the stapes and a Teflon piston is inserted with its looped end around the long process of the incus and its free end inserted into the opening through the stapes footplate. The opening in the footplate may be sealed by a vein graft or by surrounding the piston by gelfoam or fat (*Fig.* 3.9.4).

There are many modifications of technique in stapedectomy but satisfactory improvement in hearing is obtained in more than 80 per cent of cases with closure of the air–bone gap in the great majority. The extent of the improvement will, of course, be limited by any sensorineural loss. This high success rate has to be balanced against a possible postoperative deterioration of hearing, amounting to total loss in under 5 per cent of cases. Because of this risk to the hearing the operation should only be carried out on the ear with the poorer hearing.

COMPLICATIONS. The most important complication is loss of hearing and this may occur at the time of the operation but it may not occur until many months later. For this reason operation on the second ear should only be considered after at least 6 months, and many surgeons believe that operation on the second ear should never be performed. Sudden hearing loss is particularly liable to occur after sudden changes in pressure and patients should avoid diving and only fly in pressurized aircraft. In a small number of cases a fistula may develop between the fluids of the inner ear and the middle ear via the new opening in the footplate of the stapes. This will give rise to fluctuating hearing and to intermittent vertigo. When such symptoms occur the ear should be explored and the operation revised with closure of the opening into the labyrinth.

PROGNOSIS. Patients should be assured that the progress of the disease is usually very slow, that no brain disease is present, that the condition is not dangerous to life and does not result in absolute deafness. Pregnancy, illness and accident may cause a rapid increase of the deafness and tinnitus. If the affection comes on early in life, the prognosis is poorer from the hearing point of view.

Chapter 3.10

SENSORINEURAL DEAFNESS

The term 'sensorineural deafness' is used when the cause of the deafness is in the cochlea or in the auditory nerve. The term 'sensory deafness' is sometimes used when the lesion is in the cochlea, and 'neural' or 'retrocochlear deafness' may be used when the lesion is in the auditory nerve. Sensorineural deafness may be so slight that the patient is quite unaware that he has a hearing loss, or it may be so severe that there is no useful hearing at all. The majority of cases, of course, fall in between these two extremes. When a patient presents complaining of deafness it should be possible, without any real difficulty, to make a diagnosis of conductive or sensorineural deafness if the methods of investigation described in Chapter 3.2 are followed.

The disability of sensorineural deafness is relatively greater than that of conductive deafness. This is because the patient's hearing is distorted due to the loss at different frequencies being affected to a varying degree; in the majority of cases the higher frequencies are more affected than the lower, leading to difficulty in hearing the consonant sounds which are so important for speech discrimination. In addition, many patients have tinnitus, and those with a cochlear lesion have loudness recruitment. A patient with a sensorineural deafness therefore hears with less difficulty in a personal one-to-one situation than in a crowd, or in the presence of background noise.

Whether the lesion is in the cochlea or the auditory nerve can usually be determined by a series of audiometric tests. In general, the presence of recruitment (p. 252) means that the lesion is in the cochlea, and if recruitment is absent the lesion is likely to be in the auditory nerve. Lesions in either site will reduce the discrimination for speech but the loss of discrimination will be relatively more marked in neural lesions. In most cases a final pathological diagnosis can be made by careful history taking and clinical examination, paying particular attention to associated symptoms and signs.

DEAFNESS DUE TO INFECTION

Viral Deafness

Mumps can cause sudden sensorineural deafness which is usually unilateral. The deafness is generally severe or total and comes on about the fourth or fifth day of the disease. The deafness is occasionally accompanied by vertigo. The hearing loss is permanent.

Deafness due to measles is less common than mumps and causes a permanent severe bilateral high frequency loss. The resulting disability is marked, especially in young children who have not acquired speech. The virus is thought to reach the inner ear from the subarachnoid space through the cochlear aqueduct. Myringitis bullosa haemorrhagica occurs in the presence of viral infections, usually influenzal. Several blood-stained bullae are seen on the surface of the drum. They cause severe pain and, as they are also present on the medial surface of the eardrum and there is an associated serous otitis media, there is a conductive deafness. In a small proportion of patients viral labyrinthitis also occurs with a sensorineural deafness and vertigo.

Herpes zoster oticus (Ramsay Hunt syndrome), as well as giving herpetic vesicles on the external ear and the inside of the cheek, with a lower motor neurone facial palsy, can be associated with a severe sensorineural deafness and vertigo (*see* Chapter 3.15).

Bacterial Sensorineural Deafness

Suppurative Labyrinthitis

Progressive infection of the inner ear is now relatively rare and is more likely to complicate chronic than acute otitis media. In serous labyrinthitis there is non-purulent inflammation of the labyrinth with a fibrinous or serous exudate. The associated subtotal sensorineural hearing loss and vertigo can be reversed by prompt administration of the appropriate antibiotic systemically and by limited mastoid surgery to control the chronic ear infection. In purulent labyrinthitis where there is suppuration within the labyrinth, the hearing loss is total and irreversible, and treatment should be aimed at limiting the spread of infection to the internal auditory meatus with meningitis. Adequate systemic antibiotics followed by mastoid surgery and labyrinthectomy may be required. Labyrinthitis may be secondary to meningitis and is one of the few causes of total loss of hearing in both ears.

Syphilis

With the adequate treatment of syphilis by penicillin, it seemed likely at one time that syphilitic ear disease would be eradicated. However, in recent years it has become apparent that syphilis must not be ignored as a cause of sensorineural deafness. It is more likely to be a complication of congenital syphilis than of late-acquired syphilis, although the incidence of the former is decreasing. The disease causes osteitis of the otic capsule as well as changes in the membranous labyrinth. In congenital syphilis the deafness is likely to commence in the third, fourth or fifth decades, whereas in acquired disease the age of onset is always over 35 years of age. The deafness is bilateral and progressive and the associated tinnitus can be very loud. Diagnosis is made by specific serological testing with the VDRL, TPHA and FTA abs tests. Diagnosis is important as treatment can be effective in improving the hearing and lessening the tinnitus. Optimum treatment is with 500 000 iu of penicillin four times a day intramuscularly for 12 days, with prednisolone, 30 mg per day. Thereafter the antibiotics are stopped and the prednisolone dosage reduced. Follow-up is important to detect relapse, when further treatment is beneficial. Long-term steroids in low dosage may be required.

PRESBYACUSIS

The term 'presbyacusis' is used to describe hearing loss resulting from degenerative changes of ageing. In sensory presbyacusis there is high-tone hearing loss associated with atrophy of the organ of Corti commencing at the basal end of the cochlea. In neural presbyacusis there is a loss of neural elements. This produces no consistent audiometric pattern of loss, but there is marked loss of speech discrimination out of proportion to the pure-tone loss. Degeneration of the stria vascularis produces a flat type of audiometric loss but with good speech discrimination. The hearing may also be affected by alteration in the conduction along a defective basilar membrane. These types of presbyacusis may occur as distinct entities or may occur in combination. The hearing loss is symmetrical in the two ears and progression is usually slow. The deafness may become evident at any time beyond the third decade, but patients do not usually become concerned about their deafness until the speech range is affected. Characteristically old people complain of difficulty in understanding speech, even though the speech appears to be loud enough. They also have difficulty in hearing in the presence of background noise so that they find group conversations difficult to follow. The difficulty in understanding speech is due to the inability to hear higher frequencies which means that consonant sounds, which carry most of the meaning of speech, cannot be heard properly. Recruitment of hearing also adds to the distortion. Loss of the neural elements may result in very poor discrimination of speech. These difficulties are made worse by lack of concentration associated with the slowing down of mental processes.

Understanding the disability of presbyacusis helps in its management. In speaking to such patients it is essential to speak slowly and distinctly, and not to shout. For patients with a neurosensory loss of greater than 30 dB over the speech frequency range, a hearing aid is helpful. In those with neural presbyacusis poor speech discrimination may limit the beneficial results.

OTOTOXICITY

It has long been recognized that quinine and the salicylates may cause deafness. Fortunately this deafness is usually reversible when the drugs are stopped. During the past 40 years therapeutically valuable drugs have been introduced which may cause a relative toxic action on the cochlea or vestibule. The most frequent effects are seen with the antibiotics (particularly the aminoglycosides), diuretics (particularly ethacrinic acid and frusemide), antiepileptics, beta blockers and cytotoxic drugs. If two potentially ototoxic drugs are given, such as an aminoglycoside and diuretic, their toxic effect may be synergistic. Many drugs which are ototoxic are also nephrotoxic, and as most of them are excreted through the kidney, their effects are more pronounced if renal failure is present.

TOPICAL OTOTOXICITY

Ear drops containing ototoxic drugs such as neomycin, gentamicin, polymyxin and framycetin are widely used for the treatment of otitis externa and chronic otitis media. There is considerable evidence that drugs can be absorbed through the round window membrane into the fluids of the inner ear and, in theory, these drugs could be absorbed in the same way. Although such ear drops are very widely used there is no convincing evidence that sensorineural deafness has resulted. The risk of spread of the infection from the middle ear to the inner ear is much greater. In patients with perforations of the eardrum there is a much greater risk of sensorineural deafness being caused by antiseptics used to clean the ear prior to operations. Topical chlorhexidine in alcohol has been blamed for such deafness.

OTHER CAUSES OF SENSORINEURAL DEAFNESS

Otosclerosis generally causes conductive deafness but it is often accompanied by sensorineural deafness, particularly when the otosclerotic process becomes evident in early life. A mixed hearing loss, the greater proportion of which is sensorineural in type, may be seen in some patients in whom there is a strong family history of otosclerosis, and cochlear otosclerosis is then diagnosed. If it occurs in younger patients systemic long-term fluoride therapy will halt its progress. In Ménière's disease the most distressing symptom is vertigo, but the hearing loss can be a marked problem in those patients with bilateral disease. Due to recruitment, distortion may be a marked feature. Other patients, particularly in the sixth decade, may have a fluctuant low-frequency hearing loss of the type associated with Ménière's disease, but without the vertigo. They are thought to have cochlear endolymphatic hydrops and often respond to long-term vasodilator therapy. Paget's disease can affect the temporal bone, and produce a mixed hearing loss. The conductive element is due to ankylosis of the stapes in the oval window, but stapedectomy is to be avoided as there is an appreciable risk of a dead ear, and the speech discrimination is often very poor. There is no evidence that calcitonin improves the hearing acuity or reduces the tinnitus.

Neurosensory deafness due to trauma, and perilymph leaks are discussed in Chapter 3.14.

SUDDEN IDIOPATHIC DEAFNESS

This term is used for deafness that comes on extremely suddenly so that the patient is actually aware of the moment of the onset of the deafness. It can also be applied when a patient wakes up in the morning and finds that he has become deaf. The deafness may be accompanied by tinnitus and there is often distortion of hearing and also a resonance effect so that sound of one frequency produces a feeling of resonance in the ear. No other signs of ear disease are discovered on clinical examination. On pure-tone audiometric testing virtually any pattern of hearing loss can be found. Patients with greater loss at higher frequencies have a poorer prognosis than those with a low-frequency loss. In most cases there is quick recovery from the deafness within hours, days or weeks. If there is no recovery within 3 weeks it is unlikely to occur spontaneously. This tendency to spontaneous recovery makes assessment of treatment difficult. Important diagnoses such as bleeding into an acoustic neuroma and perilymphatic leak must be excluded. In the remainder if there is no sign of spontaneous improvement the patient is assumed to have anoxia or a viral infection. These patients are admitted to hospital and given an intravenous infusion of low-molecular-weight dextran to lessen sludging of the blood, they breathe a mixture of 5 per cent carbon dioxide in air as a vasodilator and, provided there is no contraindication, are given steroids. Unfortunately a high proportion of these patients are initially treated as though they have Eustachian tube obstruction and time is lost in initiating treatment. To have any reasonable chance of success this should begin within 1 week of the original episode of sudden hearing loss.

HEARING AIDS

A modern hearing aid consists of a microphone to pick up sound, a transistorized amplifier and a receiver which is connected to the patient's ear. In a body-worn hearing aid the microphone and amplifier are in the portion of aid worn on the body. The receiver is worn in the ear connected to the amplifier by a lead. In an ear-level aid the microphone, amplifier and receiver are all contained within the aid which is worn behind the ear. From the receiver a small plastic pipe carries the sound into the external auditory meatus. Hearing aids are designed to give the best reception for the speech frequencies and are, therefore, not of great benefit outside this range. The range of amplification is usually from about 250 to 4000 Hz. Amplification should be uniform from 750 Hz upwards but the lower frequencies can be decreased at a rate of 12 dB per octave. This reduced amplification in the lower frequencies helps to prevent masking of the higher frequencies by the amplified low tones. The frequency response of the aids can be adjusted to the patient's requirements so that a patient with severe high-tone loss may require more amplification in the higher frequencies and less amplification in the lower tones. Similarly, the acoustic gain may vary so that the severely deaf can be helped by powerful aids. In many hearing aids there is a tone control which can be used to increase slightly the gain in the higher frequencies which can help in understanding of speech. One of the problems of patients who wear hearing aids is that powerful amplification is required to hear sounds of moderate intensity. If to this is added a very loud sound, the amplification may produce an intolerable sound level. In some hearing aids these very loud sounds can be controlled by automatic volume control. This is particularly useful in patients who have recruitment of hearing.

Where the deafness is of the conductive type there is little difficulty in obtaining good results with a hearing aid. The choice in such patients is whether they should have the slight inconvenience of wearing a hearing aid or whether surgical treatment is indicated to overcome the deafness. In sensorineural deafness the benefit from a hearing aid is never so good as in conductive deafness. In sensorineural deafness there is always distortion and this may be increased by amplification. The commonest type of hearing loss in sensorineural deafness is one where the high tones are affected more than the low tones. This means that the consonant sounds which carry most of the meaning of speech are less well heard than the vowel sounds which act as carriers for the consonants. To understand speech, as well as being able to hear that someone is speaking, requires that the consonants be clearly heard and amplification may achieve just this. However, if the drop of acuity for the higher frequencies is very steep it may be virtually impossible to increase the understanding of the consonants without producing intolerable loudness of the lower-tone vowel sounds. Recruitment is also a problem for the patient with cochlear deafness because quiet sounds may be amplified to a comfortable level but loud sounds may be amplified to the level of discomfort. Recruitment also distorts and compresses the loudness scale and this produces further distortion in hearing speech.

Fitting a hearing aid not only consists of choosing the most suitable instrument for the deaf person but it also includes accurate fitting of the aid so that it is comfortable, and in particular so that the earpiece fits closely to the ear without causing pain or discomfort. If the earpiece is loosely fitting, sound will escape from the external auditory meatus and reach the microphone in the body of the aid. This produces the squealing noise known as 'feedback'. Obviously feedback is more likely to occur where the microphone is close to the ear, as in an ear-level aid, and is less marked in body-worn aids where the microphone is worn on the chest. The greater the amplification the more likely is feedback to occur.

Once the aid has been fitted the patient must be given full instructions in its use. He/she will have to be warned that it takes time and perseverance to get the best use of a hearing aid. The biggest problem initially is that of background noise. In addition to speech which they mainly wish to hear, they will hear surrounding noise which they may not have heard for a considerable time. This background noise not only distracts them from hearing speech they wish to hear but may actually mask it and make it difficult to hear. With perseverance this problem can, to some extent, be overcome, and as those with normal hearing learn to ignore the sounds they do not wish to hear, a deaf person can do the same when wearing a hearing aid. It is a problem, however, that may not be overcome in all patients. Similarly, tolerance to loud sounds increases as the patient gets accustomed to wearing the aid. After the aid has been fitted and full instructions about its use are given, follow-up visits to the hearing clinic should be arranged so that a check can be made on the manner in which the patient is using his aid. Patients who are confined to home or to residential establishments, such as hospitals or homes for the elderly, should if possible be visited, not only to instruct the patient, but to instruct the staff in the problems of those who wear hearing aids.

Where the hearing loss is severe and where only limited benefit is obtained from the hearing aid, instruction in lip-reading may be of great benefit. The combined help from an aid and lip-reading may produce better results than either alone. The use of the hearing aid may be augmented by fittings which allow the patient to hear directly from television sets or from telephones, and they may be able to pick up from loop systems in halls, lecture theatres, etc. which are fitted to help the deaf. At home, for the severely deaf, the doorbell may be connected to the house lighting system so that the house lights flash when the doorbell is rung and extra loud extension bells may be used for the telephone. These measures may help to prevent a deaf person from being, and feeling, isolated. The very severely deaf may require speech therapy to delay the deterioration of speech which occurs when a patient is unable to hear his own voice. This should be instituted as soon as the speech starts to deteriorate because it is extremely difficult to improve speech once it has become poor.

Cochlear Implants

Cochlear implants are still at an early stage of development. They are a means of electrical stimulation of the cochlea by sound waves. The electrodes can be placed on the promontory within the scala tympani or on the cochlear nerve. They are useful in the totally deaf to give an auditory rhythm signal which can greatly aid lip reading, and are to be thought of as an adjunct to a rehabilitation programme. At present even multichannel stimulation gives no ability to comprehend speech.

PSYCHOGENIC DEAFNESS AND MALINGERING

Non-organic hearing loss is of two types. In psychogenic deafness the patient is unaware that he is simulating deafness and that his symptoms are not due to organic disease. The other type of non-organic hearing loss is malingering where the subject is quite aware that his hearing is normal and that he is feigning deafness to avoid some situation of responsibility. The incidence of psychogenic deafness is difficult to assess. In the past authors have disagreed greatly, some feeling that it is very common whereas others have suggested that it is very rare. It can usually be suspected where clinical examination of the ears shows no abnormality but hearing tests and audiometry show a greater degree of deafness than the clinical impression of the patient's ability to communicate would suggest. Repeated audiograms usually give different results on each occasion which is unusual in organic lesions with a cooperative patient. At the present time it should be fairly easy to diagnose psychogenic deafness as there are now, in addition to tests requiring subjective cooperation, objective tests which can give a fairly clear idea of the threshold of hearing. If there is still doubt about the organic nature of deafness after pure-tone audiometry, Békésy audiometry and acoustic reflexes have been done, cortical evoked-response audiometry or electrocochleography should give an accurate estimate of hearing.

In malingering, where the patient complains of total deafness in one or both ears, it is usually possible by simple tests to demonstrate that his responses are not honest. If he complains that his deafness is only partial the problem is rather more difficult, but the approach to testing will be the same as in psychogenic deafness when a battery of tests will usually reveal the true nature of his deafness. More difficult still are patients who have been partially deafened by noise or blast or by accident, and who wish to exaggerate their symptoms for compensation reasons. This is at present a common event. Repeated audiometry with different results on each occasion should lead the examiner to suspect exaggeration of the deafness, but final assessment may again require much more detailed analysis. Details of these tests are given on page 255.

Chapter 3.11

TINNITUS

Tinnitus is the sensation of sound not brought about by simultaneously externally applied mechanoacoustic or electrical signals. This definition excludes vascular sounds and bruits. Almost every ear disease and cause of deafness can be associated with tinnitus, and the great majority of tinnitus sufferers have some measurable hearing loss. Many patients mention their tinnitus as an aside while describing their ear symptoms, but in some patients it is the tinnitus which is the major annoyance and presenting symptom. It is estimated that 1 per cent of the adult population has tinnitus of a degree which causes severe annoyance, and in some patients it becomes the dominant factor in their life, leading to depression and occasionally to suicide.

The first essential in treating a patient complaining of tinnitus is to come to an accurate diagnosis of the cause of their hearing loss. Often this is obvious and easily treated, such as Eustachian obstruction, an exacerbation of chronic otitis media or wax occluding the external auditory meatus. When these are dealt with, the hearing improves and the tinnitus disappears. If no obvious cause is found, tests can be carried out to find the pitch, the loudness and the maskability of the tinnitus. These tests are particularly important if the patient is claiming compensation for a noise-induced or traumatic tinnitus. Normally the pitch of the tinnitus is found to be at or around the frequency of the maximal hearing loss. The loudness is usually within 15 dB of the patient's pure-tone threshold at the frequency of pitch matching, and the tinnitus is usually masked by narrow band masking at that frequency and at an intensity within 20 dB of that threshold. These are, however, purely audiological measurements and in no way indicate to the observer the intensity of the tinnitus which is apparent to the patient, as recruitment may well be present.

When the tinnitus is associated with neurosensory deafness the choice of treatment is between a hearing aid, a tinnitus masker and a hearing aid/masker combination. Hearing aids are only helpful to those who have a hearing loss sufficient to warrant the issuing of an aid to increase hearing acuity (35 dB loss over the speech frequency range). As well as aiding the patient's hearing, if an appropriate aid with maximal gain at around the frequency of the tinnitus is fitted, the increased awareness of background sound will make the tinnitus less apparent, and many patients find the use of an aid very helpful. If the neurosensory hearing loss is less than that for which an aid is required a masker can be tried. This is basically a small instrument the shape of a behind-the-ear hearing aid which produces a masking sound which obliterates the sensation of the patient's own tinnitus. It is psychologically much more acceptable than the tinnitus, as it is more tonal in quality and is controllable. As there is adaptation to a prolonged sound stimulus, the masker should be used for short periods of less than 2 hours at a time. A proportion of patients have residual inhibition following a period of masking, that is their own tinnitus disappears for a while, completely in the lucky few, but usually the tinnitus is still present at a reduced intensity. In a small proportion of patients the tinnitus is sound-sensitive, that is it increases in intensity in the presence of noise, and in these a tinnitus masker is unhelpful. In many patients with central or bilateral tinnitus, bilateral maskers may be required. The hearing aid/tinnitus masker combination is used for the severely deaf when output of a simple masker is probably insufficient for adequate masking. Masking devices are recommended to be used before periods of quietness, as when sitting reading in the evening or before going to bed at night.

Despite claims to the contrary, there is virtually no place for drug treatment of tinnitus. Intravenous lignocaine, which is not without risk, can alleviate tinnitus in a proportion of patients for a short period of time, but is totally impractical for long-term use. Oral analogues of type I cardiac dysrythmics are ineffective at less than toxic levels, there is little evidence that fluoride reduces the tinnitus associated with otosclerosis, although it may stop it from getting worse, and calcitonin is equally ineffective in dealing with the tinnitus of Paget's disease of the temporal bone, although it may reduce the pulsating sensation due to the increased vascularity of the bone. Many tranquillizers and antidepressants can cause tinnitus as a side-effect and the otologist should try and reduce the number and dosage of drugs the patient is concurrently ingesting.

Tinnitus patients, especially those who have been sufferers for many years, often become depressed and dependent. A special tinnitus clinic where a longer consultation period is available to give psychological support is helpful. Clinical psychologists can make a contribution by teaching methods of relaxation.

VERTIGO

Vertigo is a hallucination of movement. The term should be regarded as the symptom of a vestibular system lesion, whether peripheral or central, and should not be restricted to a sensation of rotation, but should also include linear motion as in tending to stagger to one side. It is often difficult for the patient fully to describe his sensations, and in taking a full and accurate history the feeling of vertigo should be differentiated from other types of dizziness such as fainting, light-headedness, drop attacks, postural hypotension and claustrophobia.

It is most important to obtain a full and accurate history from the patient as often the signs are minimal or non-existent. A full description of the sensation should be obtained with special reference to precipitating factors (e.g. neck movements), associated symptoms (e.g. deafness, tinnitus), and frequency and duration of attacks. Inquiries into the past history should include a report of any trauma to the head or neck as well as a full medical history. It is important to ask about drug and alcohol ingestion as these are very common causes of 'dizziness'.

Clinical examination should include an otological, neurological and cardiovascular evaluation. The ears should be examined for wax, indrawing of the drum, the presence of fluid or infection with or without a perforation, or signs of previous surgery. Neurological examination commences with a search for spontaneous nystagmus, evaluation of the cranial nerves, especially the IIIrd to Xth, and tests of cerebellar function, coordination and balance. If a history of a positional vertigo is obtained, positional tests should be carried out.

Cardiovascular examination consists of palpation of the carotid arteries and auscultation for bruits, measurement of blood pressure and assessment of the pulse. Neck movements should be tested.

The investigations required depend on the history and examination but audiological tests are usually required. Vestibular tests are often helpful as are routine skull and mastoid radiographs as well as radiography of the internal auditory meati. Blood tests which may be indicated include a full blood count, fasting blood sugar and tests for syphilis.

Not every audiometric, vestibular or blood test need be done on every patient. The investigation should be appropriate to the individual problem, e.g. it is not appropriate to carry out full caloric tests on an infected ear.

The causes of vertigo are many and varied, and some fall into the provinces of cardiology, neurology or psychiatry. All may present to the otologist and it is important for him to keep an open mind until a diagnosis is made and to initiate treatment or refer the patient as necessary.

Acute vestibular failure. Acute vestibular failure occurs when there is a sudden input of discordant information to the vestibular nuclei, as for example following labyrinthectomy. The patient feels a sensation of acute rotatory vertigo, is most comfortable lying still, and often has a feeling of nausea or is vomiting. Over the following days a process of central compensation takes place. First the patient is able to sit up in a chair in reasonable comfort, and after a few more days can walk in a straight line. However, any sudden head movement will at this stage still induce staggering. If the lesion causing acute vestibular failure is unilateral, peripheral and static, normal balancing function should return in 6 weeks.

Positional vertigo. A positional vertigo is one in which a specific head movement such as turning over onto one side in bed, or reaching for an object above head level with the neck rotated causes vertigo of short duration. Other head positions are not accompanied by this sensation, and if the vertigo is restimulated by the specific head position it can be controlled by returning the head to a neutral position.

Compensation from a vestibular lesion. The rate at which a patient compensates from a vestibular lesion depends on four factors:

1. The younger the patient the faster the compensation.
2. A patient compensates quicker from a peripheral lesion, e.g. labyrinthitis, than from a central one, e.g. brainstem vascular thrombosis.
3. A patient compensates quicker from a unilateral lesion than from a bilateral one, e.g. vestibulotoxic drug.
4. A patient compensates from a static lesion, e.g. labyrinthectomy, but not from a variable one, e.g. Ménière's disease.

It is useful to subdivide vertiginous patients into four main groups:

1. The positional vertigos.
2. Vertigo as an isolated symptom.
3. Vertigo plus deafness plus tinnitus.
4. Vertigo plus other signs of neurological disease.

THE POSITIONAL VERTIGOS

Benign Paroxysmal Positional Nystagmus

This, the benign form of positional nystagmus, is characterized by brief, sudden attacks of vertigo precipitated by head movements. There are no other aural symptoms although the vertigo may be accompanied by a slight feeling of nausea. The disease is thought to be due to inorganic deposits on the cupula of the posterior semicircular canals and there is often a preceding virus-type illness. Similar symptoms can arise after a head injury.

CLINICAL FEATURES. There is usually no abnormality on otoscopy or audiometry. The diagnosis is made on the history and by demonstrating nystagmus during neck movements. The usual procedure adopted is to have the patient sit on a couch looking straight ahead. The examiner then tells the patient what he is going to do and asks him to keep his eyes open and look straight ahead. He then turns the patient's head to one side, at the same time leaning him back so that his head ends up hanging over the end of the couch. If the test is positive there will be a few seconds' latent period followed by a rotatory nystagmus lasting up to 30 seconds, the fast component of which is directed towards the undermost ear. The patient is brought back to the original position when again there may be a short bout of vertigo and nystagmus. The test is repeated to the other side and again to the affected side. It will be found that the nystagmus fatigues and after three or four attempts it may not be present. If, however, the nystagmus does not fatigue and is irregular the condition may be central or **malignant positional nystagmus**. Vestibular tests may show no abnormality since the nystagmus is rotatory unless there are electrodes placed above and below the eyes to pick up vertical components.

TREATMENT. Avoidance of the provoking position is often all that is required, but some patients, especially post-traumatic cases and elderly patients, may require labyrinthine sedatives. Most cases settle within a few months but some may persist for years.

Disequilibrium of Ageing

As the body ages, degenerative changes occur in most organs, the vestibular apparatus being no exception. Pathological studies have demonstrated degenerative changes in the maculae and the cristae, and it seems reasonable to assume that neuronal degeneration occurs in other parts of the vestibular pathways. The symptoms are varied but usually consist of vague imbalance or staggering, often associated with movement. In some patients there may be associated cervical spondylosis and this can exacerbate the symptoms. There is often little of note on examination and audiometry is normal for their age. Vestibular tests are indicated only if there is doubt about the diagnosis.

TREATMENT. This is supportive. Vasodilators such as cyclandelate (Cyclospasmol) may be tried, as may labyrinthine sedatives if the dizziness is severe enough. In those who have cervical spondylosis a cervical collar can be useful for a short time.

Central (Malignant) Positional Nystagmus

When the patient's head is put in the critical position a coarse, variable nystagmus is set up. There is no latent period and the nystagmus is non-fatiguable. It is seen with tumours of the posterior cranial fossa or the mid-brain, with disseminated sclerosis and with vascular lesions. Vertigo is often less than expected.

VERTIGO AS AN ISOLATED SYMPTOM

Vestibular Neuronitis

This condition is frequently preceded by a virus infection or a febrile illness. It is characterized by severe vertigo of sudden onset without deafness or tinnitus and with no signs of neurological involvement. Caloric tests show a canal paresis on the affected side. Treatment is symptomatic. Young people recover quickly but an older person may be unsteady for months following an attack. Other names sometimes used for this affliction are epidemic vertigo and epidemic labyrinthitis, the latter, however, being literally incorrect as there is no cochlear involvement.

Disseminated Sclerosis

Acute severe vertigo, identical to that in vestibular neuronitis, may occur in disseminated sclerosis. It can present without signs of the disease elsewhere but more usually occurs in an established case.

Drugs

Many drugs can give rise to dizziness as a side-effect and a careful drug history is essential. The aminoglycosides (streptomycin, kanamycin, gentamicin, etc.) are well-known as ototoxic drugs and may cause both cochlear and vestibular damage. Most drugs, however, give rise to less well-defined symptoms. Commonly used drugs which can give rise to symptoms of unsteadiness include all the labyrinthine sedatives, oestrogens such as ethinyloestradiol BP and norethisterone (Primolut N), diuretics such as bendrofluazide BP and frusemide BP and antibiotics such as nalidixic acid (Negram), co-trimoxazole (Septrin) and metronidazole (Flagyl).

Miscellaneous

Other conditions which can cause symptoms of unsteadiness include anaemia, hypotension often during antihypertensive therapy, diabetes mellitus and migraine. Psychogenic dizziness sometimes occurs and it may need several visits and tests before this conclusion is reached. Epilepsy can sometimes be preceded by a vertiginous aura.

VERTIGO PLUS DEAFNESS PLUS TINNITUS

Ménière's Disease

Ménière's disease is characterized by deafness and tinnitus as well as by vertigo, loss of balance, nausea and vomiting, and thus involves both the cochlear and vestibular components of the inner ear.

PATHOLOGY. The most consistent histological finding in Ménière's disease is a dilatation of the endolymphatic compartment of the inner ear (*Fig.* 3.12.1). The aetiology of this endolymphatic hydrops is unclear, but its presence infers an abnormality of endolymph formation or absorption. Local ischaemia has been put forward by many as a cause, thus prompting the widespread use of vasodilators and stellate ganglionectomy. Another proposed aetiology is that there is faulty absorption of endolymph by the endolymphatic sac, and this has been given some support by the results of surgery on this structure. Other causes which have been put forward at one time or another include allergy, focal infection, biochemical disturbance, vitamin deficiency, endocrine disturbances and viral infections.

CLINICAL FEATURES. The outstanding features are vertigo, vomiting, tinnitus and deafness. The onset of the vertigo is often sudden, usually without warning, and

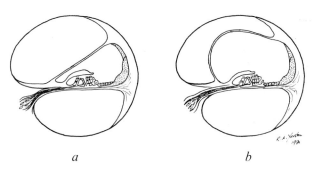

Fig. 3.12.1. Diagram showing dilatation of the endolymphatic compartment of the cochlea in Ménière's syndrome.
a, Normal.
b, Ménière's syndrome.

may render the patient completely helpless within seconds of the onset. If support is not at hand the patient may fall and injure himself. Vomiting may accompany the dizziness or may follow it. There is frequently a feeling of tension in the head or tinnitus during the attack and this passes off afterwards. Similarly deafness may occur during an attack, the patient often noticing it only when the incapacitating vertigo is settling. In the early stages of the disease the hearing may return to normal after attacks, but if the condition progresses and attacks recur deafness becomes established and more severe. Between attacks clinical and cochlear examination may be completely negative and the diagnosis may have to be assumed after a careful consideration of the history. The typical attack may be modified in that instead of vertiginous episodes there may be a constant sense of imbalance with occasional exacerbations and periodic increases in the hearing loss with slight nausea only. Fullness or pressure in the ear and suboccipital headaches are common features. During a severe attack sweating, bradycardia and diarrhoea may occur, probably as a result of vagal stimulation.

If the patient is seen during an attack he is completely disorientated, and unable to stand or do anything for himself. He will usually lie down as still as possible as any movement exacerbates the vertigo. Nystagmus is present but its direction is not indicative of the side of origin of the symptoms. If the patient is seen just after an acute attack has settled there will be sensorineural deafness, often associated with distortion of sounds.

DIAGNOSIS. Ménière's disease must be differentiated from other causes of sensorineural deafness and tinnitus. The diseases most likely to give rise to problems in differentiation are acoustic neuroma, labyrinthitis and, occasionally, intracranial disease and syphilis.

Examination in Ménière's disease usually reveals normal intact tympanic membranes with a negative fistula test. The patient is neurologically normal apart from a sensorineural hearing loss, usually detectable by tuning-fork tests. Audiometry will show a sensorineural hearing loss, except in early cases. The hearing loss is frequently of a low-tone or flat type but any pattern may occur. Speech audiometry usually is in keeping with the pure-tone audiogram. Recruitment is frequently present, impedance audiometry is normal and there is no tone decay. In early cases the hearing loss is fluctuant, improving between attacks and this is a useful finding at follow-up audiometry. In more advanced cases there may be a persistent moderate or severe sensorineural loss.

Vestibular tests may be normal in the early case between attacks, but later a canal paresis or hypofunction is found on the affected side. Radiography of the mastoids will be normal as should be views of the internal auditory meati.

In advanced Ménière's disease the acute symptoms frequently disappear, leaving an imbalance which may be constant or may recur at intervals without nausea. An anxiety state is quite commonly observed in those patients who have had several disabling acute attacks. The occurrence of associated migraine is not unknown. Lermoyez's syndrome may be a variant of the disease. It consists of a progressive loss of balance over days or weeks with increasing deafness and headache which terminates with a paroxysm of vertigo, to be followed by immediate improvement in the hearing and other symptoms.

TREATMENT. This is initially medical but a number of patients may benefit from a surgical procedure.

Medical treatment. Many cases can be controlled by antihistamine labyrinthine sedatives such as prochlorperazine maleate (Stemetil), cinnarizine (Stugeron) or promethazine theoclate (Avomine). Because many of these patients are anxious they may be helped by anxiolytics or tranquillizers. Betahistine hydrochloride (Serc) appears to be the most useful recent addition to the medical armamentarium and is routinely prescribed for most patients by a number of doctors. It is a histamine analogue and is thought to work by causing local vasodilatation and thus reducing the vertigo with occasional hearing improvement and relief of tinnitus. Other vasodilators employed include nicotinic acid and thymoxamine (Opilon). Attempts to reduce the labyrinthine hydrops by fluid and salt restriction and diuretics is widely practised and is probably worthwhile in cases uncontrolled by other methods. Medical treatment controls the condition in over two-thirds of patients.

During the acute attack sedation is essential and vomiting may necessitate intramuscular administration of a labyrinthine sedative. Other drugs useful in the acute attacks are chlorpromazine hydrochloride (Largactil) and promethazine hydrochloride (Phenergan), while phenobarbitone and hyoscine are effective alternatives.

Surgical treatment. Decompression of the endolymphatic sac is gaining in popularity as a method of reducing the vertigo, with some hope of reduction of tinnitus and preservation and occasionally improvement in hearing. It is now being done earlier in cases uncontrolled by medical treatment where there is still useful hearing in the affected ear. Vestibular neurectomy has been advocated. It relieves the vertigo but the hearing continues to diminish and it is an intracranial procedure. Stellate ganglionectomy is still practised with some success. In the persistently vertiginous patient where there is no useful hearing in the affected ear surgical destruction of the labyrinth may have to be considered. This, however, is a last resort and should be used as such because a number of patients develop bilateral disease. Selective destruction of the vestibular labyrinth with preservation of hearing may be achieved by applying ultrasound to the affected lateral semicircular canal.

PROGNOSIS. This depends upon the response to the various forms of treatment. If treatment does not control the attacks the outlook is bad for the affected ear. At the same time, remission occurs so frequently that it is difficult to be precise in prognosis after one attack. The disease may be bilateral in up to 40 per cent of cases and therefore conservatism is essential.

Labyrinthitis

Inflammation of the labyrinth due to any cause gives rise to symptoms of vertigo, deafness and tinnitus.

Viral Labyrinthitis

This may occur during the course of an exanthematous disease such as mumps or measles or as part of an influenza-type illness. The vertigo is usually transient and the association of the symptoms and signs of the disease makes the diagnosis clear. Deafness may be complete.

Vertigo may occur as part of herpes zoster oticus (p. 360). Treatment is symptomatic.

Bacterial Labyrinthitis

This may be circumscribed, serous or suppurative (p. 301). There is usually a history of otorrhoea and hearing loss and there is evidence of otitis media on otoscopy. Treatment is that of the cause.

Labyrinthitis secondary to meningitis can occur in both viral and bacterial infections. Infection passes along the subarachnoid space from the base of the brain into the internal acoustic meatus and then along the nerves and vessels to the labyrinth. Usually both the cochlear and vestibular compartments are affected, although the symptoms may not be immediately noticed because of the accompanying meningitis. Occasionally the disease is bilateral. The resulting deafness is complete. The vestibular symptoms pass off rapidly in adults but in children they may last as long as 1 year. Treatment is directed towards the meningitis with symptomatic treatment for the vertigo.

Acoustic Neuroma

This must always be considered in the differential diagnosis of unilateral sensorineural hearing loss (see Chapter 3.13). Vestibular symptoms are extremely variable and may consist only of intermittent slight unsteadiness. Tinnitus is a common occurrence.

Syphilis

Syphilis (p. 58) can mimic Ménière's disease and histologically can give endolymphatic hydrops. It should always be suspected and serological tests should be carried out routinely in all vertiginous patients.

Labyrinthine Trauma

Non-operative

Vertigo can follow labyrinthine concussion or fractures of the temporal bones. In some cases, especially after a fracture, this can be severe and require bed-rest and labyrinthine sedatives. In others there is a vague unsteadiness, worsened by quick head movements, which may take months to settle.

Postoperative

A **perilymph fistula** may occur after a stapedectomy or it can follow a sudden pressure change, e.g. diving or sneezing. There is intermittent vertigo associated with a deteriorating or fluctuating sensorineural hearing loss. Treatment is by surgical repair of the fistula, usually by covering it with fat or fascia. In tympanoplasty or mastoid surgery excessive manipulation of ossicles or accidental exposure of the vestibule may result in sensorineural deafness, tinnitus and variable vertigo.

Miscellaneous

Other conditions which can give rise to symptoms of deafness, vertigo and tinnitus include wax occluding the external auditory meatus, Eustachian tube obstruction, serous otitis media and labyrinthine haemorrhage due to a blood dyscrasia.

VERTIGO WITH SIGNS OF INTRACRANIAL DISEASE

Vertigo is a common feature of intracranial pathology, but it often tends to be of a minor degree and is masked by the other features of the disease.

CNS Neoplasms

Vertigo may occur in tumours, primary or secondary, involving the brainstem, cerebellum or mid-brain. Other signs of intracranial disease are usually evident. If electronystagmography is done it will be found that the nystagmus is irregular and enhanced by eye opening.

Posterior-inferior Cerebellar Artery Thrombosis

This is known as the lateral medullary syndrome. The onset of the condition is associated with severe vertigo. The development of ipsilateral cerebellar signs and a Horner's syndrome, together with a contralateral hemianalgesia, indicates the true nature of the condition. Deafness may or may not be found.

Vertebrobasilar Ischaemia

This presents as transient episodes of vertigo associated with other signs of brainstem dysfunction, e.g. diplopia, dysarthria, loss of consciousness. It is due to microemboli originating from plaques of atherosclerosis in the major arteries. These attacks affect elderly people with generalized atherosclerosis and often precede a stroke. Treatment is by referral to a cardiovascular physician. The term is also commonly used to denote vertigo associated with neck movements and cervical disc disease (*see* Disequilibrium of ageing, p. 333).

Chapter 3.13

CEREBELLOPONTINE ANGLE TUMOURS

Lesions of the cerebellopontine angle are of interest to otologists as they present in the Ear, Nose and Throat Department. In addition, they are important as if left undiagnosed or untreated can endanger the patient's life due to pressure effects on the brainstem. Acoustic neuroma represents 8 per cent of all intracranial tumours and 80 per cent of cerebellopontine angle tumours. They arise from the Schwann or neurilemmal cells. As the medial portion of the cranial nerves are covered by glial stroma they are situated laterally, and virtually always originate within the internal auditory meatus. The commonest nerve of origin is the superior vestibular, followed by the inferior vestibular and rarely the cochlear. They are commoner in females than males in the ratio of 3 : 2 and usually present in the fourth decade or above, although they are also rarely encountered in children and young adults. Ninety per cent are unilateral, although they can be bilateral in von Recklinghausen's disease.

PATHOLOGY. The tumour cells arise from the neurilemmal sheath. Histologically two different patterns can be differentiated. In the first or fasciculated type the cells are arranged in an orderly fashion of parallel cells, and intercellular fibres form interwoven bundles with alternating nuclei and fibrous zones. In the second or reticular type there is a disorderly loose network of cells of variable shapes with intercellular vacuoles and cysts. In the latter type haemorrhage can occur, giving rise to sudden increase in size and therefore marked symptoms such as acute vertigo or sudden deafness. Sometimes the tumours are surrounded by arachnoid cysts due to a secondary arachnoiditis; these can occur both in the cerebellopontine angle, and laterally causing local expansion of the internal auditory meatus (*Figs.* 3.13.1, 3.13.2).

NATURAL HISTORY. The tumour originates laterally and expands and presses on the other contents of the internal meatus, that is the cochlear and facial nerves and the internal auditory artery. Thereafter, it expands medially into the cerebellopontine angle. No nerves are within the tumour but are stretched over it and gradually become thin and attenuated. By the time it attains 2·5 cm in diameter it will indent the brainstem and the anterosuperior portion will come in contact with the Vth and VIth cranial nerves. Meanwhile the inferior extension will press on the IXth and Xth cranial nerves. The anterior inferior cerebellar artery is on its medial

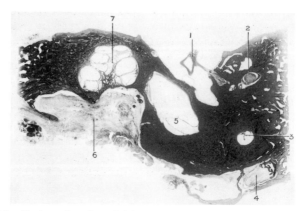

Fig. 3.13.1.   Horizontal section of right ear in a case of acoustic neurinoma. (× 3.)
1, Head of stapes with stapedius.   4, Tumour.
2, Facial nerve.   5, Lower part of utricle.
3, Posterior canal with haemorrhage in   6, Dilated internal meatus with tumour.
   perilymph space.   7, Cochlea.

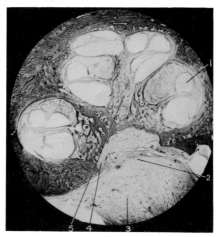

Fig. 3.13.2.   Acoustic neurinoma. Axial section through right cochlea. (Note the infiltration of the scala vestibuli and scala tympani by delicate connective tissue.)
1, Dilated cochlear canal, basal coil.   4, Cochlear nerve, which is
2, Capsule of tumour.   compressed by tumour tissue.
3, Tumour tissue.   5, Central canal of modiolus.

aspect and further pressure on the brainstem will cause shift of the fourth ventricle with compression of the aqueduct and hydrocephalus.

SYMPTOMS. The commonest presenting symptoms are unilateral deafness or tinnitus, or a combination of both. The duration of the deafness is related to the size of the tumour. If hearing loss is the only symptom, and it is of more than 10 years' duration, an acoustic neuroma is most unlikely as a tumour which has been growing for longer than this period will give other cranial nerve or brainstem symptoms. As bleeding can occur into a reticular type of neurilemmoma the deafness can be sudden. Balance disturbance is rarely severe, as the tumour expands slowly and the loss of vestibular function is compensated for as it occurs. Discomfort around the ear and mastoid area, which is referred pain from pressure on the posterior fossa dura, is common. Trigeminal symptoms occur before facial nerve symptoms as sensory nerves are less resistant to loss of function from stretching than motor ones. Numbness of the face, paraesthesia and facial pain can all occur. Facial nerve involvement includes absence of blinking or mild weakness of the eyelids. Visceral efferent effects include reduction of taste threshold and reduced lacrimation. Diplopia due to pressure on the VIth cranial nerve, and hoarseness due to involvement of the IXth and Xth nerves are rare and late symptoms.

SIGNS. All patients have some unilateral neural hearing loss. Seventy per cent have some evidence of ataxia on balance testing, 55 per cent have trigeminal nerve impairment, the earliest sign of which is loss of corneal reflex, and 48 per cent have nystagmus, either of a vestibular or cerebellar type. Facial nerve impairment can be elicited in 30 per cent, usually of the sensory element as lack of taste on electrogustometry or loss of lacrimation on Schirmer's test, but occasionally also involving loss of motor power. In large tumours diplopia is found.

CRITERIA OF SUSPICION. The further investigation of a patient with a suspected acoustic neuroma is audiological and radiological. The following should be regarded as criteria of suspicion for such further testing:

Unilateral deafness of less than 10 years' duration.
Sudden deafness with retrocochlear elements which do not respond to steroids.
Poor speech discrimination in relation to pure-tone threshold.
Spontaneous nystagmus with eyes closed on electronystagmography without a history of disequilibrium.
Absence of caloric response with near normal hearing.
Hearing loss with reduced corneal reflex.
Local pain.

FURTHER AUDIOLOGICAL INVESTIGATION. There is a large number of audiological tests which can help in differentiating between a cochlear and a retrocochlear hearing loss. Many of them give an unacceptable proportion of false-positive and false-negative results, and carrying out a large battery of tests, as was common a few years ago, does not increase the accuracy of the conclusion. There are two tests which are now recognized to be far superior to the others. Brainstem-evoked response audiometry has only a 3 per cent false-negative rate and, where it is available, this is undoubtedly the test of choice in demonstrating a retrocochlear lesion by an increased latency between the N1 and N5 waves. The second most valuable test is that of stapedial reflex decay, which has an accuracy in excess of 65 per cent. These two tests only demonstrate whether a hearing loss is cochlear or retrocochlear. There are of course many other causes of a retrocochlear deafness. It should be realized that, at presentation, about 25 per cent of patients with an acoustic neuroma have a pure-tone threshold hearing loss of greater than 70 dB.

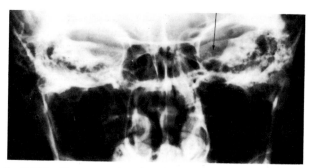

Fig. 3.13.3.   Posteroanterior view showing enlargement of the right internal acoustic meatus due to acoustic neurinoma.

In this group further audiological investigation is very limited, and the accuracy of any results obtained is poor.

RADIOLOGICAL INVESTIGATION. Radiological investigation can be divided into three phases:

Examining the configuration of the internal auditory meatus.
Examining the contents of the meatus and the cerebellopontine angle.
Examining the relationship of the tumour to the brainstem.

EXAMINING THE CONFIGURATION OF THE INTERNAL AUDITORY MEATUS. This can be done in one of three ways—plain films in the transorbital projection, multidirectional tomography, and high-resolution computerized tomography with magnification by reconstruction zoom. In transorbital plain films, the height of the two meati is measured and compared (*Fig.* 3.13.3). A difference in height of 2 mm or more is undoubtedly pathological, and a difference of 1·5 mm is suspicious. Plain films will demonstrate expansion due to an acoustic neuroma in 75 per cent of patients, but the finding of a normal meatus does not exclude a tumour and the finding of a wide meatus does not prove the existence of one.

Multidirectional tomography is only marginally superior to plain films but has the additional disadvantage of giving off appreciable radiation close to the lens of the eye.

High-resolution CT scanning with magnification by reconstruction zoom is the most accurate of these three investigations, but this facility is only available on third- and fourth-generation scanners with special expensive software.

INVESTIGATION OF THE CONTENTS OF THE MEATUS AND CEREBELLOPONTINE ANGLE. Before considering the choice of radiology in this section, it should be remembered that acoustic neuromas can be divided into three types:

Type A are purely intrameatal.
Type B expand to 25 mm within the cerebellopontine angle.
Type C have a diameter of greater than 25 mm within the angle.

Type A and B tumours give purely otological symptoms, whereas type C tumours give 'neurological' symptoms, i.e. symptoms due to compression of other cranial nerves or the brainstem or the cerebellum.

CT scanning with intravenous contrast enhancement pick up all type C tumours, and third- and fourth-generation scanners will also pick up type B tumours of greater than 10 mm within the cerebellopontine angle. However, small type B and all type A tumours are missed by this investigation.

To demonstrate this smaller group some form of cisternography is required. There are two methods of doing this, by gas cisternography with a third- or fourth-generation CT scanner, or by pantopaque cisternography with conventional films. They are equally accurate; the former can be carried out at the same time as the CT scan with intravenous contrast enhancement. The latter can leave small oil droplets within the cerebellopontine angle which would cause artefacts on any subsequent scanning. Cisternography should not be carried out in patients with type C tumours, as it will not delineate them fully, and it can be highly dangerous as these patients may have hydrocephalus due to displacement of the fourth ventricle.

EXAMINING THE RELATIONSHIP OF THE TUMOUR TO THE BRAINSTEM. This third stage in radiological investigation is only undertaken in type C tumours after they have been demonstrated. It is not therefore part of the diagnostic work up to prove the presence of such a lesion, but is sometimes necessary as a preoperative precaution when there is doubt about the nature of the mass, as to whether it is primarily within the cerebellopontine angle, or is an exophytic tumour of the brainstem or cerebellum or is a basilar artery aneurysm. Amipaque CT cisternography is the method of choice after hydrocephalus has been ruled out. If the latter is present it is contraindicated due to the risk of coning, and vertebral angiography is then the alternative investigation.

DIFFERENTIAL DIAGNOSIS. Acoustic neuromas comprise 80 per cent of cerebellopontine angle tumours. Second in frequency are meningioma followed by neuroma of the VIIth nerve or cranial nerves within the jugular foramen. Congenital cholesteatoma can occur within the apex of the petrous bone or within the cerebellopontine angle itself. Somewhat rarer are dilatations or aneurysms of the basilar or vertebral arteries.

TREATMENT OF ACOUSTIC NEUROMA. Once an acoustic neuroma has been diagnosed, it should be removed provided the risks of operation are acceptable in relation to the patient's life-expectancy. Certainly tumours in patients under the age of 60 should be removed. Small 'otological' tumours in the more elderly should be watched by carrying out CT scanning with enhancement at yearly intervals to gauge the rate of expansion. There are basically three surgical approaches to the cerebellopontine angle—via the middle fossa, translabyrinthine, and via the posterior fossa.

The middle fossa approach is relatively difficult with limited access, and should only be considered for small intracanallicular tumours. Hearing can be preserved, and the facial nerve is easily identified and protected. Bleeding from branches of the anterior inferior cerebellar artery at the end of the operation can be troublesome.

The translabyrinthine route is safer with wider access and the facial nerve can be identified relatively early in the operation so that the risk of inadvertent damage is kept to a minimum. All hearing is of course lost.

A lateral posterior fossa approach gives good access for large tumours, the posterior wall of the internal auditory meatus is drilled away early in the procedure and the facial nerve can be identified laterally and thereafter protected. Hearing can be maintained.

Recent advances in surgery of acoustic neuromas have reduced the mortality to a very low figure and morbidity is within acceptable limits. The use of the operating microscope has been more important than the development of new surgical approaches in attaining this improvement.

Chapter 3.14

OTOLOGICAL TRAUMA

Despite the fact that the ear lies in a protected position—the inner ear is within the hardest bone in the body, and the middle ear is protected by the curving external auditory meatus—it is liable to trauma in a variety of ways. Foreign bodies can occlude the external auditory meatus or be pushed through the tympanic membrane; the middle-ear mucosa, tympanic membrane and the inner ear can all be damaged by sudden pressure change; the middle ear, ossicles, and inner ear can be involved in fractures of the temporal bone; and the cochlea can be damaged by prolonged noise exposure.

FOREIGN BODIES IN THE EAR

Foreign bodies, both animate and inanimate, may be found in the external ear. The latter are more frequent, especially in children, and are often introduced by the patients themselves. Children tend to insert foreign bodies when they are bored, and the commonest objects found are pieces of paper, rubber, pencil, beads, buttons, shells, peas and beans. Foreign bodies rarely cause trouble, unless the tympanic membrane has been ruptured, and they may remain undetected for years. Indeed, some complications result from ill-directed attempts at their removal. Gentle inspection will reveal the object in most cases. If it is not seen, the ear may be gently syringed, as a very small foreign body may lie out of sight in the anterior recess of the meatus.

In removing foreign bodies three facts should be remembered. First, the narrowest part of the external auditory meatus, the isthmus, is situated near its mid-point in the bony part. Secondly, foreign bodies of vegetable origin, such as nuts, peas and beans, are hygroscopic and should not be syringed, as if the first attempt fails, they will swell up and impact against the meatal walls. Thirdly, no attempts should be made to remove smooth spherical objects such as beads by forceps: as the forceps close the object will inevitably be pushed deeper down the meatus.

As a general rule, most foreign material can be removed by gentle syringing. This is particularly so if it consists of several particles. Larger objects lying superficial to the isthmus should not be syringed, as there is a risk of wedging them in that area. They, and all material of vegetable origin, should be removed with a fine hook. Beads which have a diameter less than that of the isthmus can be syringed; larger ones are better removed with a hook. Attempts at removal of foreign bodies in children should not be prolonged because of the pain produced and the fright engendered. In such cases it is wiser to remove it under general anaesthetic with the help of the operating microscope. In rare instances repeated attempts at removal may drive the object into the middle ear, and an external operation may be required for its extraction.

Animal foreign bodies in the external meatus are rarely met with in the UK, but are found in Eastern countries. Maggots cause intense pain, and their presence is most likely in an ear where discharge is already present and which has become offensive and blood-stained. It is useless to attempt to syringe them out as they are firmly attached to the meatal walls. Chloroform water or vapour must be applied to the external meatus in order to anaesthetize or kill the maggots and so release their grip on the skin. Thereafter they may be removed by syringing.

HEAD INJURY WITH FRACTURE OF THE TEMPORAL BONE

Gross fractures of the temporal bone are divided into longitudinal and transverse in relation to the axis of the petrous temporal bone (*Fig.* 3.14.1).

Longitudinal fractures are commoner (80 per cent) and almost a quarter of them are bilateral. They result from blows to the temporal and parietal area. The fracture line starts at the squamous temporal bone, runs across the posterosuperior part of the external auditory meatus, over the roof of the middle ear, along the carotid canal to the region of the foramen spinosum. The fracture line can sometimes be seen in the external auditory meatus, the tympanic membrane is

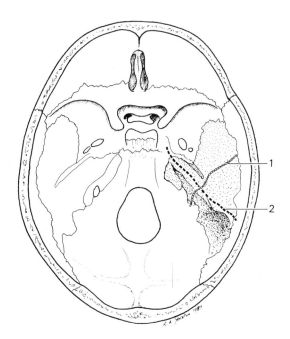

Fig. 3.14.1.   Fractures of the petrous temporal bone.
1, Transverse fracture.   2, Longitudinal fracture.

frequently torn, the inner ear is usually spared as it lies within dense bone, and the resulting deafness is therefore conductive in type. There can be some accompanying neurosensory deafness due to labyrinthine concussion which is typically maximal at 4 kHz. The fracture line is relatively easily visualized on appropriate radiographs.

The conductive deafness of a longitudinal fracture can have several causes. There is frequently blood, sometimes accompanied by cerebrospinal fluid in the external and middle ears. It is important that the blood clot is left alone, as untimely interference can lead to the introduction of infection into the middle ear giving rise to otitis media, which if prolonged may lead to a permanent perforation. Similarly, ear drops should not be used. If cerebrospinal fluid otorrhoea occurs, systemic antibiotics to which upper respiratory tract bacteria are sensitive and which cross the blood–brain barrier (i.e. co-trimoxazole) should be used. Cerebrospinal fluid otorrhoea most commonly ceases spontaneously and it is only very rarely that surgical intervention is required to close a tear in the middle fossa dura. Within a few weeks the blood will disappear from the external and middle ear, and in uncomplicated cases the perforation will heal and hearing will return to normal.

More severe and permanent conductive deafness can be due to damage to the ossicles. In order of frequency these are, disruption of the incudostapedial joint, massive dislocation of the incus, fracture of the stapedial arch, fracture of the malleus, and fixation of the head of the malleus and incus due to displacement of the outer attic wall. If inner-ear function is satisfactory these ossicular problems can be corrected by tympanoplastic techniques or stapedectomy (*see* Chapter 3.9). Rarely a fracture can involve the Eustachian tube, leading to refractory seromucinous otitis media requiring long-term grommet insertion. Late conductive deafness due to aseptic necrosis of the long process of the incus can occur some years after the head injury.

Transverse fractures of the temporal bone are less common (20 per cent) and result from blows on the occipital region. The fracture arises from the foramen magnum, passes around or through the jugular and hypoglossal foramina, through the internal auditory meatus and ends in the middle cranial fossa in the region of the foramen lacerum and foramen spinosum. As the fracture runs across the axis of the petrous temporal bone, the inner ear and the facial nerve are frequently involved and the patient complains of neurosensory deafness which is frequently total, vertigo and a lower motor neurone facial palsy. These fractures are less readily demonstrable on radiography and a patient with a post-traumatic dead ear, both as regards hearing and balance, is assumed to have had a transverse fracture. No treatment is available for the neurosensory deafness. As the vestibular lesion is peripheral and total, central compensation occurs. As temporal bone fractures are frequently associated with multiple trauma requiring prolonged bed rest, the patient may have largely compensated for his vestibular damage by the time he is able to move about. The facial palsy is frequently temporary, but if it is complete and prognostic indicators are bad, decompression of the Fallopian canal is indicated (*see* Chapter 3.15).

HEAD AND NECK INJURY WITHOUT FRACTURE

Head and neck injury without fracture can give rise to both peripheral and central lesions.

In the peripheral ones, which tend to be due to blows to a fixed head, a large pressure wave passes through the bones of the base of the skull, and there is excessive movement of the stapes. As regards hearing this leads to a cochlear hearing loss of a 'traumatic' type, that is, it is maximal at around 4 kHz. This hearing loss is very variable in degree, it can be near maximal or only minor. A proportion of it is 'concussional' in type and it therefore recovers in time, although the hearing of patients with a marked immediate post-traumatic deafness is unlikely to return to near normal levels. The peripheral vestibular damage affects either the semicircular canals or the otolith organs. In the former, an electronystagmograph will show a latent spontaneous nystagmus, fixed in direction, with the eyes closed, and bithermal caloric stimulation will demonstrate a canal paresis. If the otolith organs are damaged benign paroxysmal positional nystagmus occurs. This is thought to be due to loose otolithic particles stimulating the cupola of the posterior semicircular canal. The prognosis in post-traumatic benign paroxysmal positional nystagmus is different from that of the idiopathic type, in that the symptoms and signs last longer. However, when they do disappear, they rarely return (see Chapter 3.12).

The central lesions from head and neck injury without fracture are thought to be due to rapid acceleration or deceleration of a mobile head. The brain is damaged due to its movement relative to the skull, and the brainstem is particularly liable to bruising due to its pivotal position. Tearing and damage to the VIIIth nerve can also occur. Electronystagmography shows spontaneous nystagmus in some or all head positions with the eyes open, and central compensation for this kind of central vestibular lesion is slow and incomplete. Whiplash injuries to the neck are due to rapid acceleration and extension, and are thought to cause vestibular symptoms because of injury to the sympathetic nervous system which can lead to ischaemia of the labyrinth. Patients can develop classical symptoms of Ménière's disease following head and neck injury. This could be due either to imbalance of the autonomic nervous system causing ischaemia and thereafter endolymphatic hydrops, or alternatively the latter could be secondary to damage to the endolymphatic duct by a fracture line.

LABYRINTHINE WINDOW RUPTURE

The perilymph is connected to the cerebrospinal fluid by the cochlear aqueduct. The pressure in the perilymphatic system can be altered by explosive and implosive forces. In the explosive ones the increased cerebrospinal fluid pressure transmitted through the cochlear duct is secondary to coughing, sneezing or an unsuccessful Valsalva manoeuvre. In the implosive type, there is raised middle-ear pressure due to such things as blast, severe acoustic trauma, closed head injury or barotrauma. The symptoms are of fluctuating hearing loss, fluctuating tinnitus and intermittent vertigo. This diagnosis should always be suspected when these symptoms follow some abrupt change of middle-ear or intracranial pressure. The symptoms can postdate the episode of barotrauma by several days. The fistula sign is positive and vertigo and nystagmus can be stimulated by moving the tympanic membrane with a Siegle's speculum. About half the patients also have benign paroxysmal positional nystagmus. A useful diagnostic point in differentiating between a labyrinthine window rupture and true Ménière's disease is that in the former ataxia persists between acute attacks of vertigo, whereas in the latter, once the attack of vertigo has settled, the patient has no persisting imbalance. The stapediovestibular ligament ruptures more frequently than the round window membrane. The ultimate diagnosis is operative when the middle ear is exposed by a tympanotomy approach, and both windows should be carefully observed for evidence of perilymph building up. This can be quite difficult, especially if an adequate hypotensive anaesthetic is being used which reduces intracranial pressure. The leak is repaired by elevating the surrounding mucous membrane, and applying a fat graft. The results are good as regards the cessation of vertigo but disappointing as regards improvement of hearing. This is probably due to the fact that the original wave of raised perilymph pressure has also damaged the intracochlear membranes. This is markedly different from the perilymph leak following stapedectomy, when the outlook for improvement of hearing is good.

DIVING AND BLAST INJURIES

Diving and blast injuries can affect both the middle and inner ears.

Barotraumatic Otitis Media

Barotraumatic otitis media, or otitic barotrauma, occurs when the air pressure within the middle ear is markedly less than that of the surrounding atmosphere. It occurs due to rapid descent, whether in an aircraft or while diving. The passage of air down the Eustachian tube on ascending is passive, but the passage of air up the tube on descent is always active, being aided by the opening of the mouth of the tube by the tensor and levator palati muscles. If there is a pressure differential between the nasopharynx and middle ear of 90 mmHg or above, the mouth of the tube 'locks' and the muscular contraction is insufficiently strong to overcome this. If the Eustachian tube lining is oedematous due to an upper respiratory tract infection, the locking will take place at a lower pressure differential. The tympanic membrane becomes pushed inwards around the middle-ear contents and there is vascular engorgement of the mucosal lining with ecchymosis and transudation of fluid which contains blood. The patient complains of discomfort or pain in the ear affected, there is conductive deafness sometimes accompanied by tinnitus and occasionally vertigo. On inspection the drum is indrawn and pink and there may be a fluid level. If a haemotympanum has occurred this will be dusky blue in colour.

Treatment consists of teaching the patient to carry out the Valsalva manoeuvre. If this fails politzerization or Eustachian catheterization is carried out. If fluid is present a myringotomy may be necessary and occasionally, in resistant cases, grommet insertion may be required until the middle-ear mucosa has returned to normal.

For those who have previously suffered from the condition, a decongestant nasal spray is a useful prophylactic measure on further flights.

Blast Injury

Blast injuries can occur due to explosions or a slap on the pinna. This causes a very rapid positive wave which is followed by a much longer negative wave. It is the former which has the greater energy and causes the damage. This takes the form of a reniform punched-out perforation in the anterior segment of the pars tensa, with an accompanying conductive deafness. There is frequently also inner-ear damage and the presence of a tympanic membrane perforation in no way protects the inner ear. There is a severe neurosensory deafness and tinnitus, more marked at higher frequencies, most of which is recoverable, although after severe explosions a proportion of the cochlear hearing loss is permanent. Some patients also complain of vestibular symptoms, most commonly benign paroxysmal positional nystagmus. Labyrinthine window rupture is also a recognized complication of blast injuries.

NOISE-INDUCED DEAFNESS

It has long been recognized that exposure to loud noise will cause sensorineural deafness and it is well-known that boiler makers, coopers and workers in noisy factories will become deaf after prolonged exposure.

Traumatic exposure to noise may also occur in sports such as shooting and in other recreations, particularly with the introduction of very high amplification of music etc. in the entertainment world.

The first effect of exposure to excessive noise is a temporary loss of hearing, maximal at 4–6 kHz, which is often accompanied by tinnitus. The effect is only temporary and is known as temporary threshold shift. The rate of recovery occurs in an exponential fashion and for practical purposes hearing has returned to near normal levels after 12 hours. Ears which have not been exposed to much previous noise show more temporary threshold shift than ears which have been so exposed for a long time. The degree of temporary threshold shift and its rate of recovery bears no relationship to the susceptibility of a particular individual to inner-ear noise damage. If the exposure to noise is repeated and prolonged, a permanent threshold shift may occur. Again the frequencies initially affected are around 4–6 kHz. As exposure continues what starts as a localized audiometric dip at these frequencies becomes broader and lower frequencies become increasingly affected (*Fig.* 3.14.2). In severe cases all frequencies above 500 Hz may be involved and a smooth mid- and high-frequency hearing loss develops. The rate at which permanent threshold shift proceeds depends on the intensity of the noise, the duration of exposure, the individual susceptibility of the patient and, to a lesser degree, the frequency analysis of the offending sound, high-frequency noises and pure tones being more injurious than low-frequency ones. Permanent threshold shift is irreversible and is due to damage to the outer hair cells of the organ of Corti. Histologically the signs of degeneration are most marked in the area of the basal turn of the cochlea which subserves the 4 kHz frequency. In severe cases, virtually all components of the cochlea, the outer hair cells, the supporting cells, the pillar cells, Reissner's membrane and the nerve fibres in the osseous spiral lamina, show signs of damage. The degree of noise-induced deafness is roughly equal in both ears, as they are subject to the same sound pressure levels. It should, however, be remembered that in some situations such as shooting, using hand tools, and driving heavy goods vehicles and tractors, one ear receives considerably more noise exposure than the other and an asymmetric hearing loss will be found. Where there is doubt as to whether a noisy environment is traumatic, the degree of noise should be measured using a sound-level meter. If there is continuous exposure to noise for 8 hours in any one day, the sound level should not exceed 90 dB(A). A doubling of intensity in sound-pressure levels should be accompanied by a halving of exposure time, for example 93 dB(A) is a safe level for only 4

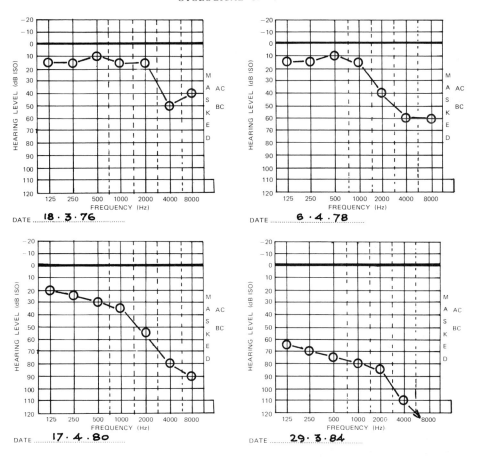

Fig. 3.14.2. Noise-induced sensorineural deafness. The record for the left ear was practically identical and has been omitted for the sake of clarity. The patient was a weaver in a jute mill.

hours. In many industries, as well as a fairly constant background noise, there are superimposed fluctuating or impulsive sounds, and complicated calculations are required to estimate the damage risk criteria to the workers.

Occupational deafness is a recognized industrial disease and employers have a duty to protect their workers from noise damage. Ideally the noise level should be reduced at source, but this may often prove impractical for economic reasons. If noise levels remain unsafe, some form of ear protection will have to be provided. This can take the form of foam inserts, plastic plugs or earmuffs. Of these the last are most effective, but even well-fitting earmuffs only provide attenuation of 30 dB at the lower and 50 dB at the higher frequencies. Training and constant supervision of the workers will be required, and routine audiometry to monitor the efficiency of the hearing protection programme is advisable.

Medicolegally the degree of hearing impairment is measured by pure-tone audiometry. Both air and bone conduction measurements are required. In circumstances where doubt exists about the accuracy of these measurements further tests such as speech reception threshold and cortical evoked response audiometry may be required. The hearing disability is any lack or restriction of ability to perceive everyday sounds in the manner or within the range considered normal for human hearing. The relationship between hearing impairment and hearing disability is not linear. The disability expressed as a percentage, as a function of average hearing threshold loss, is considered to build up slowly at first, then to increase quite rapidly and finally to increase more slowly to 100 per cent.

SURGICAL TRAUMA

Damage to the inner ear resulting in sensorineural deafness is a risk in every operation on the ear. It is most likely to occur when the inner ear has actually been opened, as in stapedectomy. However, it may also occur from excessive movement of the drum or ossicles being transmitted to the inner-ear fluids. Excessive drilling, chiselling or needling of the footplate may cause sensorineural deafness, and bony fragments dropping into the vestibule are another important cause. It follows that the structures of the ear must be manipulated with extreme gentleness, with good exposure using an operating microscope. A bloodless field is essential and this is best obtained using general anaesthesia with controlled hypotension. In some cases sensorineural deafness follows ear surgery after a period of good hearing. A perilymph fistula through the oval window after stapedectomy is relatively common and causes fluctuating deafness and vertigo. A revision operation is required. After stapedectomy hearing may be lost after sudden atmospheric pressure changes, but sometimes sensorineural deafness occurs without any apparent cause.

Chapter 3.15

THE FACIAL NERVE

The facial nerve is the most emotive nerve in the human body. Our expression reflects our innermost feelings and damage to this nerve is obvious to the onlooker and may produce quite inappropriate feelings of depression in the sufferer. Paralysis of the nerve is surprisingly common. Hard data on incidence is lacking because often the paralysis is fleeting and does not require medical attention, but about 20 per 100 000 population per year is the usual figure quoted for Bell's palsy. Less common causes are trauma, infection or tumour.

The prognosis of facial paralysis depends not only on the cause but also on the degree of damage to the nerve. The three classic degrees of pathology are termed:

1. *Neuropraxia.* This is a physiological block with no anatomical disruption which is temporary, it lasts only a few days and a full return of function is expected.

2. *Axonotmesis.* The axon sheath is intact but the axon is divided, i.e. a more severe lesion. Distal degeneration of the nerve fibres occurs, the sheath remains intact and most of the fibres tend to regenerate. Unfortunately a degree of mismatching may occur, with subsequent loss of axons and wrongly placed axons. In the face this phenomenon may be demonstrated as synkinesis (mass movement).

3. *Neuronotmesis.* In this severe lesion the whole nerve is severed. Degeneration of the distal segments occurs and there is even greater propensity to mismatch regenerating axons. A neuroma may form at the lesion from excessive fibrosis and scarring and terminal nerve filaments. Unless this lesion is accurately repaired, the end-results of this condition are poor.

There have been many attempts to further clarify this rather clumsy classification. The most notable being on anatomical description.

Class I: Only the axon itself is affected in a physiological block. This is the same condition as neuropraxia.

Class II: This is a more severe injury which results from a division in the individual axon but not in the surrounding perineurium.

353

Class III: The axon and perineurium are divided but not the endoneurium.
Class IV: The axon, perineurium and endoneurium are all divided but not the nerve sheath itself.

Class V is synonymous with neuronotmesis. Classes II, III and IV are synonymous with axonotmesis.

It is somewhat naive to suppose that all the 7000 motor axons and 3000 secretomotor axons carried by the VIIIth nerve will all undergo exactly the same degree of damage and thus a variety of possibilities is likely in a traumatized intact nerve.

ANATOMY

The facial nerve is essentially a motor nerve. The voluntary fibres arise in the precentral gyrus and course down through the internal capsule to the brainstem. They are joined by involuntary emotional fibres which originate in the more central areas of the brain, e.g. thalamas and hippocampus, as well as the secretomotor fibres from the salivatory nuclei. There is bilateral innervation of the forehead from the central nervous system but not the peripheral nervous system. Therefore, clinically in an upper motor neurone lesion the forehead has normal movement but in a lower motor neurone lesion the whole side of the face is affected. The fibres impinge on the VIIth nerve nucleus which is sited in the brainstem. The fibres then course back to pass around the VIth nerve nucleus, thereby creating an elevation in the floor of the fourth ventricle. The fibres leave the cerebellopontine angle in association with the VIIIth cranial nerve and nervus intermedius. They travel across the arachnoid space to the internal auditory meatus where the VIIth nerve lies anterosuperiorly. This is the site of the narrowest bony portion of the canal and has been implicated as the site of swelling in Bell's palsy. A mild constriction leads to vascular engorgement with more swelling and eventually a paralysis. The nerve courses laterally in the labyrinthine segment between the cochlea and the superior semicircular canal to the geniculate ganglion. Here the main trunk of the nerve turns posteriorly but the greater superficial petrosal nerve is given off anteriorly. This is joined by sympathetic fibres from the internal carotid plexus which form the deep petrosal nerve. Together as the Vidian nerve they course forward to enter the pterygopalatine fossa to synapse in the ganglion and be distributed in the fibres of the maxillary division of the Vth nerve. (*Fig.* 3.15.1).

Clinical testing of this part of the VIIth nerve is achieved by Schirmer's test. A dry piece of blotting paper, 0·1 mm thick, 5 mm wide and 30 mm long, is inserted under the lower eyelid and the distance the filter paper is wet after 5 minutes can be compared with the good side. A difference of greater than 90 per cent is significant.

From the genu the VIIth nerve enters the middle ear at the processus cochleariformis adjacent to the tensor tympani. It courses posteriorly in this tympanic portion, then turns inferiorly in a second genu to enter the mastoid portion. In this area it runs close to the footplate of the stapes and surrounds it by about 180° in the posterosuperior portion. This is also the commonest place for the nerve to be dehiscent from its covering bony Fallopian canal and attention should be paid in surgery to avoid damage. A branch comes off the nerve as it enters the mastoid

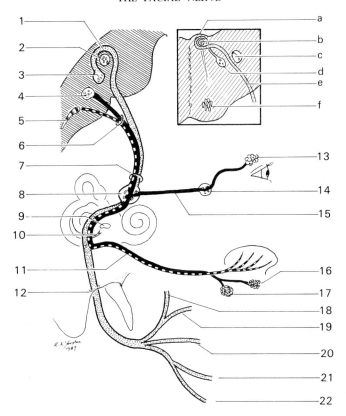

Fig. 3.15.1. Scheme of facial nerve.

1, Motor root of VIIth nerve.	9, Oval window.	16, Sublingual gland.
2, VIth nerve nucleus.	10, Nerve to stapedius.	17, Submandibular gland.
3, Motor nucleus of VIIth nerve.	11, Chorda tympani.	18, Temporal motor branch.
4, Superior salivary nucleus.	12, Stylomastoid foramen.	19, Zygomatic motor branch.
5, Tractus solitarius.	13, Lacrimal gland.	20, Buccal motor branch.
6, Nervus intermedius.	14, Sphenopalatine ganglion	21, Mandibular motor branch.
7, Internal auditory meatus.	15, Greater superficial petrosal	22, Cervical motor branch.
8, Geniculate ganglion.	nerve.	

Inset: Intrapontine course of
    VIIth nerve.

a, Colliculus facialis.	c, Spinal trigeminal nucleus.
b, VIth nerve nucleus.	d, Motor nucleus of VIIth nerve.

e, Motor root of VIIth nerve.
f, Pyramid.

portion, the nerve to stapedius. This may be tested by the stapedius reflex. A loud noise is put in either the ipsilateral or contralateral ear and the reflex causes the stapedius tendon to contract suddenly. This may be seen on tympanometry as a flick and is evidence of a functioning VIIth nerve down to this branch. Absence of the reflex may be the result of many other disorders (e.g. hearing), as well as a VIIth nerve lesion.

Slightly more distal to this branch is the chorda tympani. This branch courses anteriorly across the middle-ear space between the incus and the malleus to join the lingual nerve and supplies taste to the lateral aspect of the anterior two-thirds of the tongue. This branch may be tested by simple taste testing with salt, sour, bitter and sweet substances. However, it can be tested accurately by passing a small electric current across the tongue, the patient recording the presence of a metallic taste. Many variations on this theme are described but none has gained widespread acceptance. Again the good and affected sides are compared.

The chorda tympani also supplies the submandibular glands. Submandibular salivary flow, consistency, pH and secretion rates have all been suggested as prognostic indicators in facial palsy, but have not gained widespread clinical acceptance.

The nerve courses inferiorly to exit at the stylomastoid foramen when it is sheathed in multiple layers of connective tissue. It swings forward to enter the substance of the parotid gland, and here may be identified by several anatomical landmarks.

1. Tragal pointer—the nerve lies 1 cm medial and deep.
2. Bisection of the angle between the digastric muscle and the mastoid bone.
3. Bisection of the angle between the mastoid process and the vaginal process of the tympanic bone.

In neonates the mastoid portion is poorly formed and the VIIth nerve is extremely superficial and hence at risk from trauma.

The superficial and deep lobes of the parotid are not really divided by the facial nerve, the nerve merely passes through the substance of the gland and the term superficial and deep relate to surgical principles rather than anatomical ones. Here the nerve divides, rejoins and divides and, having formed the pes anserinus (goose's foot), sends off branches to the face. Initially the zygomaticotemporal and the buccolabial branches separate and thereafter the peripheral branches are formed.

The hallmark of the temporal bone is variation. The course of the VIIth nerve is no exception. The majority of abnormalities are dehiscence of the bony covering of the nerve, but commonly posterior displacement of the nerve placing it intimately with the lateral semicircular canal leads to surgical disaster. Duplication or triplication of the mastoid portions are also well-recognized. The extratemporal facial nerve is also very variable. The trunk may occasionally divide within the temporal bone prior to exiting the stylomastoid foramen, the course through the parotid gland is also unpredictable.

BELL'S PALSY

The commonest cause of facial palsy is idiopathic or Bell's palsy. This is a lower motor lesion of unknown cause. Possible aetiological theories include viral, vascular or autoimmune causes, but none has been proven. It is likely that a wide variety of insults produce the end-result, i.e. facial paralysis. The site of the lesion in Bell's palsy is similarly confusing. Initially the chorda tympani was implicated, but with the passage of time the mastoid, tympanic portions, labyrinthine portions and now the brainstem are thought to be the sites of swelling and inflammation of the nerve. Sporadic reports of postmortem studies identifying pathology in the different anatomical sites are not common enough to be statistically useful and operative findings of swelling of the nerve at various sites are similarly not confirmed by the body of world opinion. Decompression of the nerve in the mastoid regions was commonly practised at one stage, with or without splitting of the nerve sheath. Spilling out of the nerve from the sheath was taken as confirmatory evidence of pathology. It has since been shown that simple splitting of the sheath of a normal nerve does not spill out the nerve contents, but division of the perineurium does cause spilling. The proven facts of Bell's palsy are, therefore, lacking.

INVESTIGATION. Clinically Bell's palsy begins with a rapidly progressing stiffness or numbness of the face and there may be associated pain. The palsy may remain incomplete over several days, in which case the prognosis is good, and well over 90 per cent have a full recovery. Total paralysis associated with severe pain and advancing age indicates that the lesion is severe and the prognosis may be less good. Only 20 per cent of patients in a recent series with these parameters had a good recovery. Clinical examination should exclude any demonstrable cause for the palsy. It is essential to look at the tympanic membranes, palpate the parotid glands and do a full neurological examination to exclude causes of other facial nerve palsy.

The extent of the palsy must be assessed by testing all muscle groups, i.e. the forehead, orbicularis oculi, orbicularis oris and platysma. An overall impression is noted but unfortunately no clear reproducible method of charting facial movements has been established.

An audiogram should be done to exclude any inner or middle-ear hearing abnormality and a chest radiograph taken to exclude any general systemic conditions, such as sarcoidosis. Once the diagnosis has been established the patient wishes to be reassured about the prognosis. Apart from the functional clinical aspects, the most accurate diagnostic test lies in the field of electrophysiology. This test is known as electroneuronography.

Other tests, e.g. the retention of the stapedius reflex and the blink reflex, are associated with a good prognosis, but loss of these reflexes does not necessarily mean a poor prognosis. A normal Schirmer's test, normal electrogustometry and normal submandibular salivary flow are all good prognostic indicators.

The electrophysiological tests depend on stimulation of the VIIth nerve at the stylomastoid foramen and some form of assessment of consequent facial muscular function.

The maximal excitability test is conducted by placing a stimulating electrode over the area of the VIIth nerve as it leaves the stylomastoid foramen and increasing the voltage or amplitude of the stimulus until all the muscle groups are functioning. The voltage and amplitude are noted and compared with the good side. A percentage comparison is said to indicate the percentage of fibres in the nerve which have degenerated.

A more accurate adaptation of this is evoked electromyography (electroneuronography) whereby a supramaximal voltage is used (*Fig.* 3.15.2). This uses a maximal excitability twitch voltage plus 20 per cent to ensure that all fibres are stimulated. A recording of electrical activity in the facial muscles, called the action potential, is noted. The height of this action potential is compared with the good side and a percentage comparison made. This reflects the number of functioning fibres and if less than 5 per cent are functioning severe degeneration has occurred. If there is degeneration to this extent from any cause the prognosis for recovery is poor.

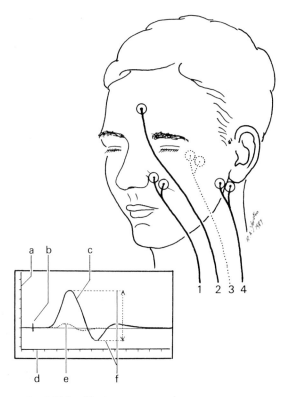

Fig. 3.15.2.   Electroneuronography.
1, Recording electrode.   3. Alternative position for
2, Reference electrode.   recording electrode.
                           4, Stimulating electrode.

Inset: Recording.
a, Amplitude scale.   d, Time-scale.
b, Stimulus point.   e, Affected nerve response.
c, Normal nerve response. f, Amplitude measured.

Many other electrical tests described in the past have now become obsolete. The electroneuronography test is not without problems, however. It can only measure conductivity between the stylomastoid foramen and the facial musculature. This means that any intratemporal bone lesion cannot be assessed until distal degeneration reaches the stylomastoid foramen, i.e. at least 48 hours. The stimulus must be applied about 20 times before accurate recording can take place because the electrical resistance of the skin changes in this time. At least five stimuli are used and are averaged through a computer. Each stimulus is mildly painful, which discourages a good follow-up. The placement of the stimulating electrode may be critical and considerable experience on the part of the operator is neccessary to achieve reproducible results.

Occasionally there is a nil result despite good facial movement. This is a recognized phenomenon which defies scientific explanation but is uncommon.

TREATMENT. The treatment of the condition is similarly confused. The standard treatment is steroids in various forms (ACTH, prednisolone, cortisone), although no valid trials have confirmed the usefulness of this method. They make the patient feel better but have not been shown to have any effect on the prognosis of the palsy.

Surgical decompression of the nerve is contentious. The decision to do this to avoid a poor end-result relies on the results of the prognostic electrophysiological tests.

Total decompression from the internal auditory meatus to the stylomastoid foramen is becoming more popular and has many advocates. However, such a major procedure as this requires some form of neurosurgical expertise and should not be undertaken lightly.

There are many other causes of facial palsy.

1. Trauma

Fractures of the petrous temporal bone occasionally damage the facial nerve. The longitudinal fracture produces a paralysis in 10 per cent of cases and the transverse fracture paralysis in 40 per cent. The site of the lesion is commonly at the geniculate ganglion. The decision to operate is dependent on the electroneuronographic findings. More than 90 per cent degeneration of the fibres within 2 weeks of the injury indicates a poor prognosis unless the site of damage is inspected and repaired. The nerve may be contused, in which case regenerating fibres may be misdirected along the greater superficial petrosal nerve rather than the nerve trunk. The greater superficial petrosal nerve should be clipped to prevent this occurrence. A sharp piece of bone may impinge into the nerve which should be removed, as the nerve may be transected. The ends should be held in apposition by light sutures. Extratemporal trauma is not common. Occasionally peripheral branches are damaged by direct trauma.

Iatrogenic trauma is more common. All ear operations run the risk of facial nerve damage, particularly if the nerve is exposed. In particular a mastoidectomy has a high risk because a sharp cutting rotating burr is used in close proximity to the nerve. A nerve overhanging the stapes footplate may be damaged during a stapedectomy. Acoustic neuroma removal invariably involves manipulation of the facial nerve with varying consequences. The facial nerve in a baby is very superficial due to poor pneumatization of the mastoid. It is at risk if forceps are applied to the head during delivery. Removal of a parotid tumour can damage the facial nerve or some of its divisions. To avoid this care is taken to localize the nerve trunk as it exits from the stylomastoid foramen. Intraoperative facial nerve stimulation prevents the surgeon damaging the nerve.

2. Tumours

Despite the size and proximity of an acoustic neuroma, the facial nerve is relatively rarely paralysed, but often at operation is found splayed out over the tumour. All types of temporal bone tumour can cause facial paralysis, which is usually a sign of spread of the disease, and include squamous-cell carcinoma, glomus tumours, adenocarcinoma, metastatic tumours and mesodermal neoplasia. The less aggressive benign tumours such as cholesteatoma cause paralysis by pressure effects rather than infiltration. A facial palsy complicating a parotid tumour suggests malignancy. Facial neuromas are uncommon. They can occur anywhere on the nerve and surprisingly often do not present with facial paralysis but with aural symptoms. The principles of treatment of these conditions are removal of the underlying tumour, excision of the affected portion of the nerve and the placing of an interposition graft.

3. Infection

Although a viral cause has been implied as the causative factor in Bell's palsy, the evidence is inconclusive. Herpes zoster definitely causes a facial palsy in the Ramsay Hunt syndrome; painful vesicles are seen on and around the tympanic membrane near the time of paralysis. The prognosis is generally poorer than for a Bell's palsy. Infectious mononucleosis may also present with this mononeuropathy. If the Fallopian canal is dehiscent any middle-ear infection may produce a paralysis. Acute otitis media complicated by a facial paralysis demands operative intervention and drainage through a myringotomy incision. Paralysis complicating a cholesteatoma indicates erosion of the Fallopian canal which requires exploration of the mastoid.

4. Central Causes

Any brainstem or higher central lesion may affect facial movement. Clinically this may be obvious by the sparing of the forehead movement due to bilateral innervation. Occasionally a peripheral lesion may present in this manner, as the fibres which supply the forehead are carried centrally in the nerve in its temporal portion and may be protected from external pressure.

5. Other Causes

These include sarcoidosis and other granulomatous lesions which can affect the intra- and extratemporal portions of the nerve. Vascular lesions, particularly those associated with diabetes, may also produce a paralysis. There are many other uncommon causes of facial palsy, including the ingestion of heavy metals, spirochaetal and fungal infections. Occasionally it is congenital.

Hemifacial spasm

This is an uncommon condition mainly of elderly people in whom the face twitches involuntarily. It is analogous to trigeminal neuralgia. The cause is probably an abnormal vascular loop which lies on the root of the facial nerve as it exits the pons. The treatment is to elevate this loop off the nerve via a posterior fossa craniotomy.

SECTION 4

PAEDIATRICS

(D. L. Cowan)

Chapter 4.1

TONSILS AND ADENOIDS

Infections of the pharynx and tonsils are discussed in Chapter 2.3.

TONSILS

The Function of the Tonsil

The full details of the immunological functions of the tonsil are as yet not totally understood. The tonsils are grouped as secondary lymphatic organs. The palatine tonsils contain 10 per cent lymphatic cells and constitute approximately 0·2 per cent of all lymphocytes in the adult. Cytologically these are subdivided into small lymphocytes (45 per cent), centrocytes (35 per cent), centroblasts (15 per cent) and plasma cells (2·5 per cent). The centrocytes and centroblasts are germinal centre cells. Plasma cells develop from lymphocytes and produce immunoglobulins.

Proliferation of lymphocytes is induced by contact with antigens or polyclonal activators (polysaccharides and lipopolysaccharides from the membranes of bacterial yeasts and viruses).

From the clinical point of view, it has been suggested that tonsillar hypertrophy is a physiological process, indicating B-lymphocyte proliferation, while sunken atrophic tonsils indicate a collapse of the B-cell activity and a 'collapse' of the defence process. It may be, therefore, that small atrophic tonsils are more often the seat of infection of a chronic sort and as such have become redundant and worth removing.

Tonsillectomy

The operation of tonsillectomy, with or without the removal of adenoids (p. 370), is the surgical procedure most frequently performed in the hospitals of the U.K.

INDICATIONS. The indications for removal of tonsils in adult life are: (1) repeated attacks of acute tonsillitis, affecting the general health and causing frequent absences from work, and (2) one attack of peritonsillar abscess (quinsy) because further acute inflammation of the tonsils is apt to produce a further quinsy.

The indications for removal of tonsils in children are the subject of some controversy, mainly between paediatricians, who favour conservatism, and otolaryngologists who are more surgically inclined, given certain criteria in the history and certain clinical appearances. When this has been said, it must be admitted that the clinical criteria of what constitutes a septic tonsil are not measurable, and each surgeon, from his experience, decides his own base-lines. The appearances which suggest tonsillar sepsis are: (1) the presence of enlarged palpable lymph nodes in the deep cervical chain when there is no acute inflammatory lesion to account for them; (2) the presence of a band of congestion along the free edge of the palatoglossal fold (anterior faucial pillar) in the absence of acute inflammation of the pharynx; and (3) the presence, either on inspection or after squeezing the tonsil with a spatula, of purulent material in the crypts of the tonsils. Given these three criteria, the tonsils may be considered to be unhealthy; given two of the three criteria the tonsils may be suspected of being unhealthy; given only one it may be thought unnecessary to recommend surgical removal on clinical grounds alone.

It will be noted that the size of the tonsils is not one of the criteria of their sepsis. It often happens in children that tonsils which are judged to be unhealthy are also large, but in adults the small buried tonsil may prove to be more septic than the larger one. Nor would a tonsil whose surface shows open crypts be deemed more unhealthy than one with a smooth surface unless pus can be seen in the crypts.

History plays a vital part in the assessment for surgery, and history depends on the case records of the general practitioner and upon the parents. Thus the letter from the family doctor, especially if it is documented, may play a vital role in the surgical opinion. Only he can assess the effect of repeated infections on the general health of the child. Parents vary in the way that they describe the illnesses of the child. Those who are anxious for surgery will exaggerate the frequency and severity of the sore throats, while parents opposed to surgery may minimize them. By the same token results are difficult to assess because the parents who have successfully pressed for surgery may well paint a different picture from those who have had reservations about the operation and who may ascribe many subsequent illnesses as dating from the operation. Between these two extremes is the vast majority of cases in which the practitioner's letter and the parents' story are in agreement.

Appetite is investigated, and in particular any change in appetite associated with the onset of a sequence of tonsillitis. Loss of appetite may be an indication of tonsillar sepsis, and many children eat much better following tonsillectomy. It has been shown that on average they make a sudden gain in weight after the operation, and that this levels out later. On the other hand, a poor appetite is no indication for tonsillectomy if the tonsils are healthy. It has been said in other chapters, and it must be repeated, that tonsillectomy has no effect on allergy. However, removal of septic tonsils may help allergic patients by improving their general health.

It is true that hearing loss may improve following the removal of tonsils and especially adenoids (p. 439). This will occur if the hearing loss is conductive and is due to catarrh or infection in the auditory (Eustachian) tube or middle ear. The operation has no effect on other forms of deafness, so that if a history of deafness is obtained the tympanic membranes must be examined and audiometry carried out.

The classic history of tonsillar sepsis in children is of frequent sore throats which affect the general health of the child. There may be abdominal pains from mesenteric adenitis, a poor appetite which persists between attacks, a loss of energy and a disinclination for games, and a change of temperament leading to tantrums or crying for little reason in a child who was formerly free from these. There may be frequent colds or sore ears.

There is a popular belief that tonsils should never be removed before a certain age on the basis that the child will grow out of the succession of sore throats. It is true that the frequency of tonsillitis diminishes the older the child becomes, but each case must be judged on its merits. There can be little justification for delaying surgery until a certain birthday if the child is having repeated severe tonsillitis which affects the general health. On the other hand, there is equally no ground for recommending surgery unless the criteria in the history or on clinical examinaton are fulfilled. In the latter case, when sore throats are few or slight, it is wiser that the child should be kept under observation at regular intervals until either the attacks stop or they become more severe and more frequent. Some paediatricians advise long-term antibiotics in such cases.

There is the case in which, without any previous history of tonsillitis, a child develops several attacks in rapid succession and usually in spite of one or more antibiotics having been given on each occasion. This history suggests a virus infection which persists unaffected by therapy. If the child recovers completely from this 'series' of attacks then there is no indication to remove the tonsils as it is assumed that the virus infection has 'burned itself out'. It is only when these attacks occur on a repetitive basis that tonsillectomy need be considered.

It is generally accepted that the role of focal sepsis in tonsils was exaggerated in the past and tonsillectomy for rheumatic or renal disorders is now less commonly recommended unless the tonsils require removal on their own account. Some children who are due for cardiac surgery may be recommended for tonsillectomy if the criteria of sepsis are found, because of the danger of subacute bacterial endocarditis.

In a few cases tonsils are removed because of size alone. Such children have tonsils which, although not inflamed, meet in the midline and cause gross difficulty with speech, swallowing and breathing. There is loud snoring and often choking attacks at night, and there have been reports of cor pulmonale on this account. During the day the child is constantly blocked and mouth breathes loudly. These children are most commonly under the age of 2 and tonsillar hypertrophy of this degree is one of the causes of the **sleep apnoea syndrome**. This is a syndrome in which the sleep pattern is disturbed in an episodic pattern with marked fluctuations in the Po_2 and Pco_2 levels when measured during sleep. Other causes of this are varieties of skeletal facial abnormalities, e.g. the Pierre–Robin syndrome.

CONTRAINDICATIONS. There are no absolute contraindications to tonsillectomy as such, but as in any surgical procedure it is vital that the patient is medically assessed and concomitant or unassociated conditions are recognized and treated appropriately. Because haemorrhage is the most dangerous complication of tonsillectomy, it is vital that any possible bleeding disorder or clotting problem is identified by appropriate screening measures before surgery. Intelligent history-taking with this in mind will often raise the index of suspicion.

Tonsillectomy is not performed during epidemics of poliomyelitis, although these are now uncommon in Western countries as a result of inoculation. There was evidence to suggest that the virus may gain access to the exposed nerve sheaths and so give rise to the more fatal bulbar form of the disease.

Tonsillectomy is an elective operation and should not be undertaken in the presence of respiratory tract infections, or during the period of incubation after contact with one of the infectious diseases, or if there is tonsillar inflammation. It is much safer to wait some 3 weeks after an acute inflammatory illness before operating because of the greatly increased risk of postoperative haemorrhage. Tonsillectomy can be performed at any age if there are sufficient indications for their removal.

CHOICE OF OPERATION. There were two methods of removing tonsils—by the guillotine or by the dissection method. The guillotine method is shorter, but is no longer taught. Dissection is the method of choice.

POSTOPERATIVE CARE. In the immediate postoperative period, careful monitoring of vital signs is essential so that any reactionary haemorrhage (*see below*) can be recognized early. It is important that all patients are encouraged to move the muscles of the throat during the first postoperative week. This means chewing, talking, drinking, etc. The nature of the food is unimportant, but if the pharyngeal muscles are kept moving then the slough will be shed more quickly from the tonsil fossa allowing healing to take place. Patients should be warned that otalgia may be the predominant complaint. This is a referred pain that rarely indicates any otological problem.

Sensible use of analgesics postoperatively is important. Aspirin and associated products should be avoided due to their effect on the coagulation process and to their recently suggested possible association with the development of Reye's syndrome in the under twelves. Paracetamol in tablet or liquid form is an adequate alternative.

COMPLICATIONS. **Reactionary haemorrhage** occurs within a few hours of the operation and may be severe. It may occur after either form of operation, and is treated by a return to the theatre when the vessel is ligated under anaesthesia. If there has been much loss of blood a transfusion may be given, but this is less liable to be required if the nursing staff is alert and prompt action is taken.

Secondary haemorrhage occurs some 5–8 days after the operation, and is due to infection often associated with a refusal on the part of the patient to eat. Chewing food keeps the muscles of the throat active and appears to keep the tonsil beds free from infection. If food is refused the slough becomes septic and bleeding occurs at the time of its separation. A similar haemorrhage may occur if a patient is incubating an upper respiratory tract infection at the time of surgery. The patient should be readmitted to hospital; an appropriate dose of morphia for adults or heroin for children is injected, and a course of systemic antibiotics ordered. This is usually enough to control the bleeding, and only rarely is a transfusion necessary. It is not common to have to anaesthetize the patient and search for the bleeding point. The haemoglobin level of the blood should be ascertained and, if necessary, a course of ferrous fumarate (Fersamal) or some other iron preparation is prescribed. The patient can usually be discharged in 48 hours provided that he is eating well.

Infection may occur after operation. A pyrexia is not uncommon on the morning after tonsillectomy, but this usually settles after the bowels are opened, helped by an aperient if necessary. Prolongation of the pyrexia should be treated by systemic antibiotics for 5 days.

Pain on swallowing is common for the first week after tonsillectomy until the slough has separated.

Speech is affected until the slough separates, but if care has been taken to modify removal of adenoids in children with insufficient soft palates there should be no long-term deterioration in speech.

RESULTS. The only result that should be claimed for the operation is freedom from attacks of acute tonsillitis. It will not stop the transient pharyngitis before upper respiratory tract infections, and during this pharyngitis there will be congestion of small islands of lymphoid tissue on the posterior and lateral walls of the pharynx and in the lingual tonsil. Head colds will not disappear following surgery, although they may decrease in frequency and severity. Appetite may improve initially. Attacks of otitis media should diminish, especially if the adenoids have also been removed, and a conductive deafness should improve, again especially when adenoids have been removed at the same time. Snoring and mouth breathing should disappear, but occasionally a confirmed mouth breather will be helped by breathing exercises.

In the adult relief from acute tonsillitis ensures the success of the operation.

ADENOIDS

Adenoid tissue arises from the junction of the roof and posterior wall of the nasopharynx, and is composed of vertical ridges of lymphoid tissue separated by deep clefts. It differs from tonsillar tissue in that it contains no crypts, is bounded by no capsule and is covered by ciliated epithelium. Adenoids are present at birth, continue throughout childhood and atrophy at puberty, although persistence into adult life is not uncommon.

Adenoids are liable to inflammatory changes. **Acute adenoiditis** may occur alone or in association with rhinitis or tonsillitis. It produces pain behind the nose and postnasal catarrh, lack of resonance of the voice, nasal obstruction and feeding difficulties in babies and it is often accompanied by cervical adenitis. Treatment is that of acute rhinitis. **Chronic adenoiditis** may result from repeated acute attacks or from infection in small adenoid remnants. The main symptom is postnasal catarrh which is got rid of by hawking or by snorting in young children, and the secretion is seen to hang down behind the soft palate as tenacious mucopus. Treatment consists of removal of the infected adenoids or adenoid remnants.

Adenoid Hypertrophy

The enlargement may be simple or inflammatory, and the symptoms may be referable to hypertrophy, to infection or to both.

SYMPTOMS. Symptoms due to hypertrophy are produced, not from the actual size of the lymphoid mass, but from the relative disproportion in size between the adenoids and the cavity of the nasopharynx. This leads to nasal obstruction, which manifests itself in the following ways:

1. In infants enlarged adenoids may interfere with feeding because the baby has to stop sucking intermittently in order to take a breath. This makes feeding a

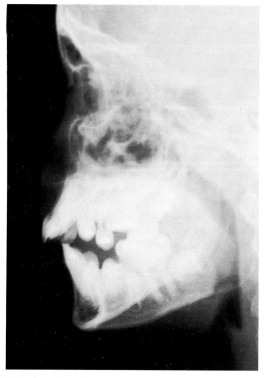

Fig. 4.1.1.   Lateral radiograph of child with protruding upper incisors suggesting mouth breathing. The dental gap may be seen, while
the nasal airway is completely free and is being used.

wearisome process for both mother and child. The infant tires easily, takes
insufficient food and fails to thrive. It may also have noisy respirations and a wet
bubbly nose. Removal of even a small mass of adenoid tissue in such a case is
often sufficient to result in an immediate improvement.

2. In older children nasal obstruction leads to mouth breathing, a habit which
is very difficult to break. Mouth breathing is abnormal, and no normal baby will
breathe through the mouth. Once the habit of mouth breathing due to obstruction
is established, however, the child has little desire to use the nose for respiration.
Therefore, the sooner the condition is corrected the better chance there is for the
re-establishment of the nasal mechanism.

3. The voice loses tone, and becomes nasal and lifeless. It must be shown that
the fault is entirely due to adenoids. Movement of the palate may be demonstrated
by a palatogram, and if it is impaired, speech therapy should be given before and
after a modified removal of adenoids to give good results.

4. There is nasal discharge, partly due to mechanical obstruction at the
posterior nares, and partly to a secondary chonic rhinitis.

The term 'adenoid facies', which used to be applied to the child with an open
mouth, a vacant expression and an underslung lower jaw, is in many instances a

misnomer. It has been shown that many of these children, whose mouths remain open, are breathing normally through the nose and the defect is one of dental malocclusion, with consequent inadequate musculature of the mouth. This should be treated by remedial exercises and orthodontic measures. Children who have enlarged adenoids do not develop these skeletal and muscular changes and, after removal of adenoids, no re-education is necessary. The differential diagnosis may be made by lateral radiography of the nasopharynx (*Fig.* 4.1.1), which will demonstrate a normal nasal airway in the resting phase, and by the cold spatula test. This consists in holding a cold metal spatula against the upper lip below the nose and estimating the nasal airway during normal respiration by the amount of steaming produced on the spatula.

The other symptom arising from adenoid hypertrophy is deafness due to the adenoid mass obstructing the openings of the auditory tubes. This diminishes air entry to the middle ears.

Symptoms due to infection are also referred to the nose and middle ears. Infection of the adenoids will cause an infection of the mucous membrane of the nose, and vice versa. This, in turn, may lead to an obstruction to the drainage of secretion from the paranasal sinuses and thus to infection of the sinuses. Removal of adenoids is usually sufficient to clear up most cases of sinus involvement in children. More serious is the effect of spread of infection from the adenoids along the auditory tubes to give recurring attacks of acute otitis media, or to perpetuate a chronic otitis media. Enlarged infected adenoids are also a contributory factor in secretory otitis media.

CLINICAL FEATURES. On posterior rhinoscopy a lobulated mass of the same colour as the mucous membrane is seen in the nasopharynx (*Fig.* 4.1.2). It may be

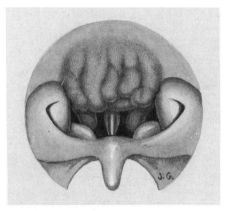

Fig. 4.1.2. Adenoids as seen by posterior rhinoscopy.

so slight as to form only a moderate projection which does not encroach on the posterior nares, or it may hang down and obscure either part or the whole of the septum and choanae. The growths occasionally extend laterally to lie in close relation to the openings of the auditory tubes (the tubal tonsils). In rare instances

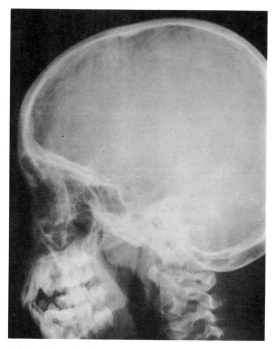

Fig. 4.1.3.   Lateral radiograph showing a large mass of adenoids.

the adenoids extend into the pharynx and project below the soft palate. Examination with a postnasal mirror can sometimes be carried out in young children. If not, it is never necessary to palpate the nasopharynx unless under general anaesthesia. Lateral radiographs of the nasopharynx will demonstrate the presence and size of adenoids (*Fig.* 4.1.3).

DIAGNOSIS. The diagnosis is usually easy, but in the case of young infants it may not be possible to come to a definite conclusion prior to operation. In such cases it is wiser to give an anaesthetic and to palpate the postnasal space, and if adenoids are present they may then be removed. In all cases anterior rhinoscopy should be carried out to eliminate any other cause of nasal obstruction. The possibility of coexistent infection of the paranasal sinuses must not be forgotten.

TREATMENT. If adenoid hypertrophy is not well-marked and the symptoms are slight, surgical treatment should not be advised. Simple breathing exercises may suffice in such cases. The patient should be reassessed after an interval of a few months. When, however, one or more of the cardinal symptoms are present, no time should be lost in removing the adenoids. It is not a sufficient contraindication to operation that the adenoids tend to atrophy at puberty.

COMPLICATIONS OF ADENOIDECTOMY. Among these, incomplete removal must be mentioned. This occurs in part because the removal of adenoids is a blind operation and in part because the adenoids are a diffuse mass which are not encapsulated. The adenoids may be partly detached and hang down below the soft palate as a tag. This can usually be removed later, although removal of adenoid remnants at a later date is made more difficult by fibrous scarring. Adenoid remnants produce symptoms by virtue of the sepsis they may contain, and persisting deafness or middle-ear infection may be experienced.

Hypernasality may occur after removal of adenoids from children whose soft palate is insufficient to close the nasopharynx during speech. Their speech is often affected, even before operation, and surgery may have been sought because of this. The inadequate palate may depend upon a large pad of adenoids for any contact during phonation. If this large adenoid mass is completely removed to relieve aural or nasal symptoms, the insufficient palate may then be unable to close off the nasopharynx. Nasal escape occurs and hyponasality has been converted into the more serious hypernasality. This may be sufficiently severe to require correction by pharyngoplasty. If the condition is diagnosed preoperatively, and nasal or aural complications demand relief, it is possible to remove the upper part of the adenoid mass, thus leaving a lower ridge of adenoid tissue against which the defective palate may continue to make contact.

Reactionary haemorrhage shows itself shortly after the operation by persistent bleeding from the nose. This does not, as a rule, respond to sedation by diamorphine injection. Very frequently there is a copious vomit containing much fresh blood. The pulse rate increases and the blood pressure drops. Experience shows that the best treatment is to return the child to the theatre where a postnasal pack is inserted under anaesthesia, and is removed on the following morning, again under anaesthesia. If blood loss is severe or prolonged before being controlled a blood transfusion will be required.

Secondary haemorrhage from the adenoid bed may occur, although uncommonly, 4–10 days after the operation. It is usually not sufficiently severe to justify a postnasal pack, and it generally responds to sedation and antibiotic therapy.

Chapter 4.2

THE CATARRHAL CHILD

Nasal catarrh and a history of frequent colds in children are commonly encountered in general practice and in the outpatient clinics of both paediatricians and otolaryngologists. The history varies a great deal, depending upon the insight of the parents, and it may not be a simple matter to reduce a rambling story to clinical facts. It all too often happens that the parents form preconceived and perhaps inaccurate ideas and will stress some parts of the history and minimize or omit others. Yet an accurate history is essential, and is best obtained by the family doctor from his knowledge of the family, the house and the illnesses of the child and the siblings.

PREDISPOSING FACTORS. Certain factors may predispose to the problems met with in the catarrhal child.

Environment. This includes the occupation, financial status and intelligence of the parents; the size, hygiene, surroundings and structure of the house; the nourishment, overcrowding and cleanliness of the children; the previous illnesses of the parents and the children, etc. Chronic catarrh in the child is more often, but by no means exclusively, found in the poor, who live in overcrowded conditions, often in areas polluted by smoke, and whose diet is unsatisfactory from the point of view of balance and vitamin content.

Virus infections. These are brought into the home from buses, trains, factories, offices, schools, supermarkets, etc. by parents or older children, and such infections may be increased in virulence by passage through several hosts. Overcrowding and lack of fresh air in the home increase the chance of infection spreading, and this is especially true during epidemics of upper respiratory tract infections of virus origin. Indeed, at the other end of the social scale, the families living in an atmosphere of overhot central heating are just as exposed to the spread of virus infection. Young children attend nursery schools in greater numbers, and from an earlier age, and are thus doubly exposed to infection. There are two main types of respiratory viruses. The first type enter the cells of the respiratory tract where they multiply to cause respiratory infections, and among these are the influenzal and para-influenzal viruses, the adenovirus, the respiratory syncytial virus and the rhinovirus. The second type enter the respiratory cells where they cause no local trouble but spread by the bloodstream to give rise to the exanthemata such as measles, rubella, varicella, etc.

Allergy. Allergy is frequently hereditary in origin, and the child of two atopic parents stands a 75 per cent chance of producing symptoms of nasal allergy. In many cases this is a food allergy, where the allergen is often milk, or an infantile eczema which may lead to nasal catarrh, and often ultimately to hay fever or bronchospasm.

Nasal polypi. Rather surprisingly, as nasal allergy is so common in children, allergic nasal polypi are rarely, if ever, seen. The unilateral antrochoanal polypus often presents as a visible swelling behind the soft palate and requires surgical removal. Multiple ethmoidal nasal polypi are only seen in childhood in association with mucoviscidosis, and hence this condition must be searched for if a child with nasal polypi is seen. Surgical removal is the only available treatment, and recurrence is the rule rather than the exception.

Vasomotor rhinitis. This is as common in older children as it is in adults. The turbinates appear engorged and hypertrophied and do not have the pallor of the allergic turbinate. The major complaint is that of nasal obstruction, but persistent rhinorrhoea with or without sniffing is not common.

Snuffly baby. There is no doubt that some babies produce more nasal secretions than others and especially when feeding they will have difficulty breathing through their nose. Some mothers worry more about this than others, but in general terms the baby is not ill and gradually the secretions will become less troublesome. Decongestant nose drops should be avoided except in acute exacerbations and choanal atresia must be excluded (*see* p. 377).

Immotile cilia syndrome. Children with recurrent unexplained chest infections or chronic obstinate nasal catarrh may have this problem. The condition is not totally understood at present and it may affect any part of the respiratory epithelium and be associated with localized immunoglobulin deficiencies. Diagnosis is difficult but usually requires biopsy of the affected mucosal area.

CLINICAL FEATURES. The complaints include nasal catarrh, frequent upper respiratory tract infections which may proceed to lower respiratory tract infections, sore throats, sore ears, lack of apetite, pallor, insomnia often with spasms of non-productive coughing, and lack of normal growth and development.

From a clinical aspect one must consider other factors which may uncommonly predispose to nasal catarrh. Hypothyroidism may occasionally play a part. Hypogammaglobulinaemia may rarely predispose to a susceptibility to upper respiratory tract infections, giving rise to a condition known as the antibody deficiency syndrome in which the child cannot produce a sufficient natural resistance to infection. Mucoviscidosis may underlie a frequency of upper and lower respiratory tract infections and should always be suspected in intractable cases.

The catarrhal child should be thoroughly investigated by the family doctor and the paediatrician to exclude these factors before treatment is undertaken, or before he is examined by the otolaryngologist. If referral is made in the first instance to an ear, nose and throat clinic, the specialist should endeavour to establish, in taking the history, that there is no general medical problem requiring attention before recommending treatment, and especially before he recommends surgery. The best results are achieved by a collaboration between the two specialists.

The natural history of the catarrhal child who presents no factors, such as recurrent tonsillitis, otitis media or bronchial trouble, requiring a specific form of treatment is one of slow improvement. The symptoms are at their height when the child goes to school, either when the town child goes to nursery school or when the country child, reared perhaps in isolation on a farm, goes to primary school, at which he first comes into close contact with numbers of other children. Absences are frequent in the first year at school and, again provided that infected tonsils or middle ears do not develop, the natural sequence of events is for the child to develop his own immunity, if he is allowed to do so, and he may well outgrow these infections by the time he reaches the age of 8 or 9 years.

There are many children who do not pursue this course, which is relatively benign, in spite of frequent absences from school. Such children develop recurring infections of lymphoid tissue of the pharynx and nasopharynx, when their illnesses become more serious. They have frequent attacks of follicular tonsillitis, or of acute or chronic otitis media. Some develop bronchitis at an early age and a proportion of these may degenerate into bronchiectasis. In this group treatment must be positive rather than expectant because such children may be sowing the seeds of ill-health later in life.

Lastly there is the allergic group who may progress from infantile eczema to allergic rhinitis, perhaps with exacerbations of hay fever at the pollinating season, and so to asthma. Many of these children appear to grow out of their allergy when the eczema finally heals, but an appreciable percentage persist with nasal catarrh and stuffiness, so that their allergens should be sought for and, where possible, avoided or treated.

TREATMENT. In the early stages this should be medical and hygienic in the widest sense. Training may have to begin with the parents by teaching them how to house, feed and look after their children. Early training in nasal hygiene and nose blowing prevents infected mucopus lying in the child's nose. No hard-and-fast rules can be laid down for the timing of this, but when a child goes to school he should be capable of blowing his own nose, and should be aware of when this is required. Yet it is not uncommon to give a child a swab and ask him to blow his nose in the outpatient department only to find that a 9-year-old has no idea of what this means. Mucopus lying in the child's nose obstructs air entry into and drainage from the nasal sinuses. Simple nose breathing exercises allow the nasal mucosa a chance to recover its normal function. Nasal mucus, containing the bactericidal lysozyme, and the ciliated epithelium are the best natural defences a child has against infection. If they are aided by good home conditions and a well-balanced diet with plenty of vitamins the child's natural resistance to disease will be greatly strengthened.

Antibiotics should be reserved for serious infections, and not prescribed for the common cold. Certain children, however, may require antibiotic therapy for any acute infection, and among these are sufferers from mucoviscidosis or children with congenital cardiac lesions. Some susceptible children may be given a long-term course of antibiotic therapy under the supervision of the paediatrician.

Children with nasal allergy may be treated with antihistamines and by nasal drops for acute exacerbations only. Oxymetazoline hydrochloride (Iliadin) drops, 0·05 per cent or 0·025 per cent for infants, are probably those used most commonly. Many children combine a basic atopy with a mild chronic rhinitis, and they present the greatest problem in therapy. A metered nasal spray delivering 50 μg doses of beclomethasone dipropionate (Beconase) (up to 400 μg daily) has proved to be very successful in treating these children. Adrenal function is not suppressed and there appear to be no complicatons from long-term therapy. The treatment is safe and effective.

Surgery is reserved for those children in whom clinical features warrant it. Many children improve following the removal of adenoids when the discharge from the nose is mucopurulent or when there have been attacks of otitis media. Tonsillectomy is justified in those children who have recurrent attacks of acute tonsillitis with clinical evidence of sepsis in the tonsils. Proof punctures of the maxillary sinuses may be required if radiography suggests infection, and in those cases in which pus is aspirated it should be cultured and the appropriate antibiotic given, either by mouth or by direct injection into the sinus through an indwelling polythene tube for 5–7 days.

Surgery to reduce the bulk of the turbinates is becoming increasingly popular for the most chronic sufferers of perennial rhinitis. In the under-tens this is best done by submucosal diathermy which produces fibrosis and hence shrinkage. In older children simple surgical reduction is of help, although care must be taken to prevent adhesions developing postoperatively.

SINUSITIS IN CHILDREN

The paranasal sinuses develop during childhood. At birth the maxillary, ethmoidal and sphenoidal sinuses are present and the frontal sinuses begin to grow shortly after birth as the nasofrontal ducts. The **maxillary** sinuses grow into the body of the maxilla, occupying the space left as the primary and secondary teeth move towards the alveolar margin. The floor of the antrum is level with the floor of the nasal cavity about the age of 7 years, and thereafter growth proceeds rapidly until the sinus attains its full size with the eruption of the wisdom teeth. The **ethmoidal** and **sphenoidal** sinuses enlarge to form recognizable sinuses between the ages of 4 and 6 years. The **frontal** sinus develops more slowly, and is not recognized as a sinus until its cupola appears above the level of the roof of the orbit radiographically, about the age of 8 years.

Acute Sinusitis

This may occur in children as a direct extension of an acute rhinitis, but, as the openings of the sinuses into the nasal cavity are relatively larger in children, they rarely close to set up the conditions for acute sinusitis. Acute maxillary sinusitis is uncommon. Acute ethmoidal sinusitis may only show itself when the infection has spread through the lamina papyracea to cause an orbital cellulitis (*Fig.* 4.2.1). Acute frontal sinusitis may occur in the older child and produce symptoms identical to those in the adult, except that there is more often a visible swelling in the forehead over the affected sinus due to an osteomyelitis of the frontal bone.

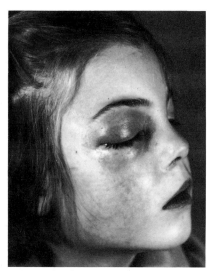

Fig. 4.2.1.   Acute ethmoiditis with orbital cellulitis in a child aged 6.

Treatment is by antibiotics, giving a broad-spectrum antibiotic in full doses.
Inhalation should not be prescribed for a young child, in whom it may produce
laryngeal oedema, or for any child being treated at home because of the danger of
the inhalation fluid beng spilled down the child's front. Local decongestant drops
of oxymetazoline hydrochloride (0·05 per cent or 0·025 per cent for infants) should
be used in conjunction with the antibiotic therapy.

Chronic Sinusitis

Chronic sinusitis in children is usually confined to the maxillary sinus. Chronic
maxillary sinusitis may develop in children who suffer from repeated head colds
and in whom drainage of the infected mucopus is hampered by enlarged adenoids,
by a deflected septum or by enlargement of the turbinates from nasal allergy. The
symptoms are persistent nasal catarrh of a mucopurulent character, frequent,
protracted head colds and nasal stuffiness. The repeated upper respiratory tract
infections may cause recurrent bronchitis, bronchiectasis or pneumonia, and
children with mucoviscidosis are generally considered to be prone to sinus
infection. Examination of the nose shows mucopus either in the floor of the nasal
cavity or in the middle meatus. The mucosa of the inferior turbinate may be
congested and swollen. In children with an underlying allergy there is often a small
swollen area in the floor of the nose opposite the anterior end of the inferior
turbinate.

   Radiography should be carried out in all children suspected of sinus infection,
and a lateral view to show the nasopharynx should always be requested. The films
may be misleading. Many children are incapable of clearing their noses by
blowing, and the nasal secretions which remain in the nasal cavities, combined
with the swelling of the nasal mucous membrane, result in a lack of air entry into
the sinuses. This may give a false impression of sinus opacity on the radiograph,
and it requires a paediatric radiologist to read the films accurately. The opacity

from infection is much more dense, while a fluid level in a sinus is diagnostic of infection. Thickening of the mucous lining of the maxillary sinuses may be due to allergic oedema or to a chronic infection of the sinuses. A solitary polypoid swelling in the floor of the maxillary sinus may be due either to nasal allergy or to a cyst within the sinus.

Diagnostic proof puncture is performed on those children who show radiographic evidence of sinus disease. This should be an aspiration proof puncture and not an antral wash-out, the latter will expel not only the antral contents but also those of the nasal cavities into the receiver, and this may give a false impression of sinus infection. If mucopus is obtained on aspiration of the maxillary sinus, it can only have come from the sinus, and should be sent for bacteriological culture and sensitivity tests. A Higginson's syringe may then be attached to the cannula and the sinus washed clear of infected contents. This is often curative, but if infection recurs a polythene tube may be threaded through the cannula and the sinus washed out through it, or the appropriate antibiotic instilled directly into the antrum.

Whether or not mucopus is obtained from the sinus the adenoids are removed if they are present, and some authorities believe that removal of adenoids alone without proof puncture will clear up any sinus infection by improving the nasal airway and thus aerating the sinus.

Nose drops of oxymetazoline hydrochloride (0·05 per cent) should be prescribed. They are best administered to a child by laying him flat on his back on a bed with his head hanging over the side. If he sniffs in as the two drops are instilled into each side the medication is thus dispersed throughout the nasal cavities.

It is uncommon for children to require further sinus surgery. Some surgeons perform intranasal antrostomy on children for chronic sinusitis, and some even advocate such an operation routinely when the tonsils and adenoids are removed if there is radiographic opacity of the sinuses. There seems to be little to commend this, and there are few criteria for intranasal antrostomy in children. It should be borne in mind that childhood is a period of upper respiratory tract infectons; that most children improve with simple conservative therapy including proper nose blowing and nose breathing; that radiography may show sinus opacity which is due simply to a lack of air entry into the sinuses; and that nasal allergic oedema is frequently combined with a mild chronic rhinitis to cause persistent catarrh.

By the same token it is even more uncommon for radical sinus surgery to be undertaken in childhood, except in the case of complications of sinusitis which do not resolve with antibiotics, or in the case of malignant diseases when biopsy of the intrasinus tumour is necessary.

Conservatism should be the standard practice in the catarrhal child in whom the aims of treatment should be the establishment of free drainage, the training in proper nose blowing to evacuate the catarrh so drained into the nasal cavities, and nasal breathing to allow the nasal mucus and the cilia to fulfil their physiological functions.

CONGENITAL CHOANAL ATRESIA

Embryology

A detailed discussion of the embryology of the nose is not necessary in a book of this size, but it is important to have some visual image of the development of the

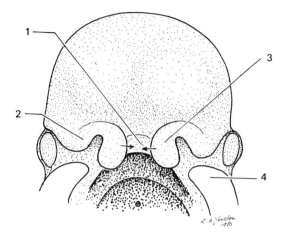

Fig. 4.2.2.   Schematic drawing of a 12-mm embryo showing the nasal placodes with their medial and lateral processes and the frontonasal process which ultimately forms the nasal septum and the anterior part of the palate.
i, Frontonasal process.   3, Medial nasal fold.
2, Lateral nasal fold.   4, Maxillary process.

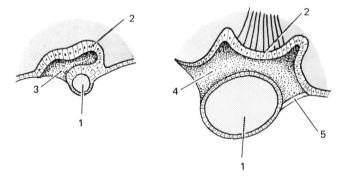

Fig. 4.2.3.   Schematic drawings to show the development of the nasal cavity and to demonstrate how failure of absorption of the bucconasal membrane can lead to choanal atresia.
1, Primitive palate.   4, Anterior naris.
2, Olfactory epithelium.   5, Bucconasal membrane.
3, Nasal sac.

nose so that congenital abnormalities of the palate, with or without cleft lip, and of the choana may be understood (*Figs.* 4.2.2, 4.2.3).

The nose, mouth, palate, sinuses and pharynx all develop from the cranial portion of the primitive foregut. The nose starts as two epithelial thickenings known as the nasal placodes, which appear above the stomatodeum about the end of the first month of fetal life. These placodes deepen to form olfactory pits which lie between the medial and lateral nasal processes. The medial processes fuse to form a central elevated part known as the frontonasal process. The lateral nasal processes approach each other so that the frontonasal process is compressed to form the nasal septum. This will in due course grow posteriorly and totally divide

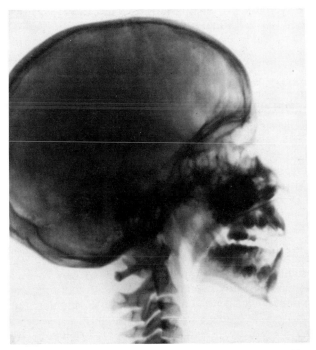

Fig. 4.2.4.   Complete choanal atresia. Lipiodol has been injected into the nasal cavity, but none has passed beyond the posterior border of the hard palate.

the two nasal cavities. The remaining free lower surface of the frontonasal process forms the primitive palate, and ultimately the anterior palate. At the same time as this is happening maxillary processes below grow medially to meet ultimately in the midline as the posterior part of the palate, thus dividing the stomatodeum into nasal and oral cavities.

Any breakdown in this developmental procedure will give rise to abnormalities ranging from a submucous cleft of the palate to the more severe forms of bilateral cleft lip and palate.

Posteriorly each nasal cavity is still closed by the thinned-out posterior wall of the original nasal sac, called the bucconasal membrane, and if this process is arrested choanal atresia will result.

CLINICAL FEATURES. Choanal atresia is usually unilateral but bilateral cases occur and these are observed at birth because the infant has the greatest difficulty in breathing, and the condition constitutes a neonatal emergency. Because nasal breathing is normal, the neonate strives for breath while keeping the lips tightly closed. The accessory muscles of respiration are used, the alae nasi dilate, and eventually the lips are sucked inwards and part as cyanosis appears. A few gulping respirations are taken through the mouth, the lips close tightly again and the sequence continues. Emergency treatment consists of the insertion of an oral airway which is fixed in place to ensure respiration until curative surgery can be undertaken. The symptoms of unilateral atresia are those of nasal obstruction, including snoring, but are slight in infancy or childhood, and are often not complained of until later in life. Examination of the nose will show thick gelatinous secretion in the affected side, and no airway can be demonstrated by holding a cold plated spatula below the nares—only the clear side steaming the plating. Posterior rhinoscopy may be undertaken in the older child and will show the occlusion. A probe or a soft rubber catheter cannot be passed through the affected side into the nasopharynx. If doubt still exists, radiopaque oil may be instilled into the suspected side of the nose, and lateral radiography will show that it is arrested at the choana (*Fig.* 4.2.4).

TREATMENT. Treatment of the infant with a bilateral atresia consists of perforation of the occlusion. If this is membranous in origin perforation is easy, and the membrane may be opened widely. If it is osseous, it must be opened by a proof puncture trocar and cannula, or by a special instrument devised for the purpose. The opening is widened by nibbling forceps.

Although some surgeons feel that the newly fashioned openings should be kept patent by the insertion of indwelling tubes, many problems have been encountered using this technique. Assuming continued follow-up can be guaranteed, the openings will be maintained by regular bouginage with urethral bougies. Initially this needs to be done under general anaesthetic every 2 months, but as the child grows the intervals between bouginage may be extended.

A unilateral atresia may be similarly dealt with if it is diagnosed in infancy. If it is not recognized until later in life the operative approach is through an incision at the junction of the hard and soft palates. The soft palate is retracted, and the occlusion is removed together with part of the posterior edge of the septum and the border of the hard palate.

Chapter 4.3

LARYNGEAL STRIDOR

ANATOMY. In order to understand how laryngological problems in children differ from those in adults, it is necessary to appreciate the anatomical differences. During fetal life the larynx descends from the level of the basiocciput at the sixth week to lie opposite the 2nd, 3rd and 4th cervical vertebrae at birth. At the age of 6 years it is opposite the 5th cervical vertebra, and at puberty the larynx lies opposite C6, a position which it occupies throughout adult life (*Fig.* 4.3.1). The lumen of the larynx and trachea in the child is small, especially in proportion to the rest of the body. The anteroposterior length of the glottis at birth is 7–9 mm and its lateral width in full abduction is 6 mm. Thus the area of the glottis in the newborn is some 24 mm². From this it is apparent that 1 mm of oedema in the neonate will reduce the area of the glottic space by 50 per cent to 12 mm². The

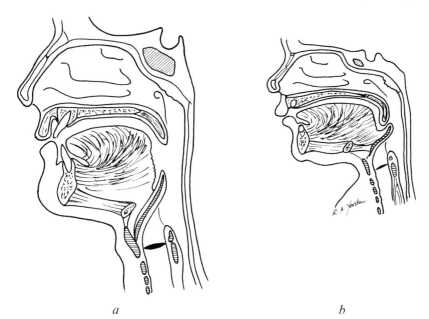

a   *b*

Fig. 4.3.1. Diagram to compare the position of the larynx in the adult (*a*) and the child (*b*).

381

diameter of the immediate subglottis at birth is 5–7 mm and that of the trachea is 6–8 mm. The area of this region is thus about 9π and this is reduced by 1 mm of oedema to 4π, or to 44 per cent of normal. By the same token 1 mm of oedema in a 3-mm bronchus reduces its area to 11 per cent of normal. The trachea is 4 cm long at birth, 5·5 cm at about the age of 7 years and 9–15 cm in length in the adult.

The neonate's larynx is tilted downward so that the epiglottis lies in close relationship to the glottis, and the angle between the glottis and the tongue is more acute in infancy than in childhood. The infant's epiglottis is less rigid than later in life and it is folded longitudinally at its free lateral edges although its base is quite broad. The infantile cartilage is relatively longer and more tubular than that of the child. In certain cases this longitudinal fold is very marked, and this has been called an exaggerated infantile epiglottis, and it may account for infantile stridor. As growth proceeds, and chondrification stiffens the epiglottis, the longitudinal fold opens so that the cartilage becomes omega-shaped, and this persits throughout childhood until the enlargement at puberty occurs and the epiglottis assumes the normal adult shape. In a percentage of cases the longitudinal fold either does not open, or opening becomes arrested at the omega-shaped stage, so that an infantile or childish epiglottis may be found throughout life.

The other laryngeal cartilages which are also soft at birth tend to become more firm as growth proceeds. The subepithelial tissue of the subglottis area becomes less lax during development. At puberty the larynx grows more rapidly, the rate being much more apparent in boys when the voice breaks.

The most common feature of laryngeal disorder in infants or children is **stridor**, with or without hoarseness. Stridor is the noise produced by an obstruction to the passage of air in and out of the lower respiratory tract. It may be inspiratory, expiratory and mixed inspiratory and expiratory. Laryngeal stridor is usually inspiratory, bronchial stridor is usually expiratory and the rare inspiratory and expiratory variety must bring to mind the possibility of an abnormal vessel arising from the aortic arch.

The following account will deal almost exclusively with the common laryngeal inspiratory stridor. Allergic or infective bronchospasm is the commonest cause of expiratory stridor but the otolaryngologist should always bear in mind the possibility of an inhaled foreign body, such as a peanut or a bead, in these cases.

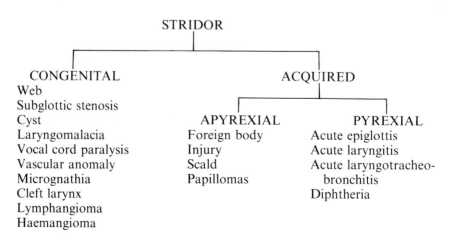

STRIDOR

CONGENITAL
Web
Subglottic stenosis
Cyst
Laryngomalacia
Vocal cord paralysis
Vascular anomaly
Micrognathia
Cleft larynx
Lymphangioma
Haemangioma

ACQUIRED

APYREXIAL
Foreign body
Injury
Scald
Papillomas

PYREXIAL
Acute epiglottis
Acute laryngitis
Acute laryngotracheo-
  bronchitis
Diphtheria

CONGENITAL ANOMALIES

Laryngeal Atresia

This represents the ultimate in stenosis and is inconsistent with life unless it is recognized at birth and a tracheostomy performed. It is, in fact, a web filling the whole larynx and it is commonest in the subglottic region (*Fig.* 4.3.2).

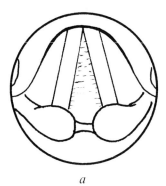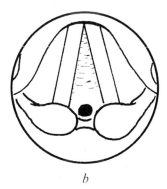

a   *b*

Fig. 4.3.2.   Laryngeal atresia.
a, Complete web.   *b*, Partial web.

Congenital Laryngeal Web

This consists of a membrane lying between the vocal cords, always at the anterior part of the glottis. The membrane is quite tough and the degree of stridor and aphonia is proportional to the size of the web. A small web will cause little respiratory difficulty and may safely be left until the larynx has stopped growing since it only causes slight dysphonia and no dyspnoea. A large web, however, should be dealt with immediately because the only alternative will be a permanent tracheostomy (*Fig.* 4.3.3). The thyroid cartilage is divided in the midline and the web is excised. If the larynx were to be closed at this point, the raw anterior ends of the vocal cords would adhere causing further glottic stenosis and so it is

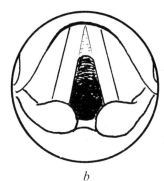

a   *b*

Fig. 4.3.3.   Laryngeal web.
a, Large.   *b*, Small.

Fig. 4.3.4.   McNaught keel.

necessary to close the larynx over a McNaught keel (*Fig.* 4.3.4). This is made of 0·18-mm thick tantalum sheeting and it is left in place for at least 5 weeks. During this time the patient breathes with a temporary tracheostomy. After 5 weeks the keel is removed.

Medium-size webs may be removed at microlaryngoscopy, the anterior ends of the vocal cords being injected with steroid to try to prevent adhesions forming. The use of the laser beam has greatly reduced the problems of postoperative scarring and adhesions.

Subglottic Stenosis

This may be caused by a congenital narrowing of the cricoid cartilage. It is said to be established if the internal diameter of the cricoid ring is less than 3·5 mm. It can also be caused by an improperly performed high tracheostomy (*see* Chapter 2.19).

Cleft Larynx

Cleft larynx is really a high tracheo-oesophageal fistula. In its complete form, where the cleft goes through the whole lamina of the cricoid cartilage and the posterior wall of the trachea, death from aspiration of food and saliva is inevitable. If the cleft does not go completely through the cricoid lamina, however, it can be repaired in layers and the cleft closed.

In very minor cases the U-shaped indentation of the cricoid lamina fills with granulations and these interarytenoid granulations seen on laryngoscopy may be misdiagnosed as pachydermia.

Congenital Cysts

Congenital cysts of the larynx occur as developmental anomalies in the ventricle and saccule, as true retention cysts of the supraglottis and as laryngoceles. They project into the laryngeal lumen and produce dysphonia and stridor in proportion to their size. Small cysts can be uncapped and drained at direct laryngoscopy but larger cysts will require to be dealt with using suspension laryngoscopy and the techniques of microlaryngeal surgery.

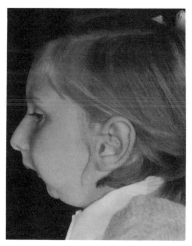

Fig. 4.3.5. Hypoplasia of the mandible (micrognathia).

Micrognathia

Micrognathia (hypoplasia of the mandible, *Fig.* 4.3.5) can cause stridor or an inadequate airway because the tongue is displaced posteriorly. In the Pierre–Robin syndrome a cleft palate is associated with micrognathia and the stridor is marked. The treatment of this is the Beverly–Douglas procedure in which the tongue is fixed anteriorly. Micrognathia may also be seen in the Treacher Collins syndrome.

Vascular Anomalies

These may cause a chronic stridor in infants often accompanied by a persistent brassy cough. If disorders of swallowing accompany the condition it is called 'dysphagia lusoria'. The common causes are: (1) a right aortic arch, (2) a double aortic arch, (3) a vascular constricting ring formed by a patent ductus arteriosus or a ligamentum arteriosum and the pulmonary artery or aortic arch, (4) an abnormal right subclavian artery and (5) an abnormal innominate artery. Diagnosis is made by a lipiodol swallow (*Fig.* 4.3.6) or by arteriography. At bronchoscopy a pulsatile swelling may be seen on the right anterolateral tracheal wall some 2 cm above the carina, and is best seen if the head of the baby is not overextended. If this swelling is occluded by the tip of the bronchoscope (*a*) the right radial and right temporal pulses will stop if there is an abnormal innominate artery, (*b*) the right radial pulse stops but the right temporal pulse is unaffected if there is an abnormal subclavian artery and (*c*) neither pulse is obliterated if there is a double aortic arch. The treatment is carried out by a thoracic surgeon.

Laryngomalacia

This is the name now used for what used to be called 'congenital laryngeal stridor'. It is the most common condition causing an inspiratory stridor at or shortly after birth. It may persist throughout infancy. There is abnormal flaccidity of the

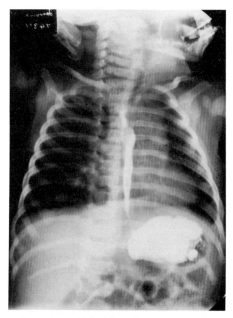

Fig. 4.3.6.   Lipiodol swallow in dysphagia
lusoria due to congenital vascular ring.

laryngeal cartilages allowing the laryngeal structures to vibrate like a small
elongated reed. On inspiration the airflow draws the laryngeal tissues into the
lumen, thus causing an inspiratory stridor which is worse during exertion such as
crying.

Diagnosis is made at laryngoscopy at which the larynx is often difficult to
expose, being placed high under the base of the tongue. During induction of
anaesthesia the stridor increases with struggling but disappears when the depth of
anaesthesia required for laryngoscopy is reached. The sharply infolded soft
epiglottis is seen, and if the tip of the laryngoscope cannot be inserted under the
epiglottis a bronchoscope should be used to examine the vocal cords, which are
normal. After the laryngoscope is withdrawn into the vallecula and respiration
becomes more forceful the soft epiglottis will be seen to be tugged downwards into
the glottis with each inspiration to cause stridor. This stridor can be stopped by
inserting the laryngoscope or bronchoscope into the epiglottic chink.

The usual course of the condition is that the stridor is noticed shortly after
birth, increases during the first few months of life and thereafter remains static.
Most cases usually develop enough firmness in the laryngeal structures for the
condition to disappear by the age of 2. The condition is distinguishable from
lesions affecting the vocal cords by the fact that the cry is normal. The treatment is
symptomatic with reassurance to the parents and early antibiotic therapy for
upper respiratory tract infections.

Congenital Laryngeal Paralysis

This is a rare condition in children and if present is usually associated with other anomalies. A complete account of the causes and management is given in Chapter 2.17.

Congenital Laryngeal Tumours

Congenital Haemangioma and Lymphangioma

These are usually found in the subglottic area or on a vocal cord and are only distinguishable histologically. A purplish subglottic swelling may either be a haemangioma of the subglottis or an indentation and erosion of the subglottis by an abnormal vessel or aneurysm. Fifty per cent of children with subglottic haemangiomas will have haemangiomas elsewhere in the body, and these are usually easily seen. Because of this no biopsy or treatment should be attempted until the situation has been more fully assessed by angiography. If the airway is threatened a tracheostomy should be performed and this is required in some 30 per cent of cases. No other treatment may be necessary because the growth of the larynx may resolve the airway problems. Systemic use of steroids has been advocated but most reports are unconvincing. External radiation has been abandoned due to the risks of malignant change in the thyroid gland, but Benjamin from Sydney, Australia, recommends the insertion of a radioactive gold grain with a half-life of 4·7 days. This is inserted into the haemangioma through a small incision using microsurgical techniques.

APYREXIAL ACQUIRED STRIDOR

Laryngeal Trauma

Foreign bodies in the larynx are uncommon because they are either coughed out or cause fatal obstruction within a few minutes if help is not to hand. In the desperate acute situation the child should be turned upside down and its back slapped. If the child arrives at hospital with a foreign body lodged in the larynx it usually means that there is sufficient airway to allow careful induction of general anaesthesia and removal at laryngoscopy.

Scalds and burns of the larynx occur when a child inhales superheated steam, drinks a boiling liquid or is rescued from a fire. The supraglottic oedema may settle with conservative measures such as inhalations, sprays and steroids, but intubation for 2–3 days may occasionally be required.

Injury to the larynx is less common in children than in adults since there is more 'give' in the pliable laryngeal cartilages. The shortness of the neck makes laryngeal injury from an automobile accident rare in children. The commonest cause is from beatings, attempted strangulations and running into a 'neck-high' wire or clothes rope during play.

Multiple Laryngeal Papillomas

Multiple papillomas are the most common laryngeal tumours in children but in the whole spectrum of laryngeal disease they are rare. They may be present at or soon after birth but more commonly they arise about the age of 2 years. Their cause is unknown but it is probable that they are due to a virus, not unlike that which causes warts elsewhere on the body. Strength is given to this theory by the fact that they are implantable, especially down the trachea, after numerous

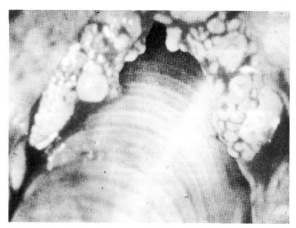

Fig. 4.3.7.   Multiple papillomas of the larynx seen at microlaryn-goscopy.

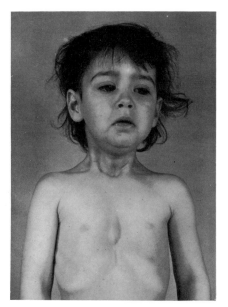

Fig. 4.3.8.   The appearances in severe dyspnoea in a child with multiple papillomas of the larynx.

intubations, and they are also transmissible since mothers have grown warts on their fingers after managing a child who has had a tracheostomy for the condition.

At laryngoscopy the papillomas look like bunches of wart-like excrescences, pinkish-white in colour; they may be sessile or pedunculated and are always multiple (*Fig.* 4.3.7).

Symptoms depend upon the size and position of the growths. If the vocal cord is affected at all there will be dysphonia, and if the papillomas are big enough to compromise the airway there will be stridor (*Fig.* 4.3.8).

The principle of treatment is to remove the papillomas as they appear, without damaging the larynx in the process, and to wait for the normal resolution of the condition. It is also important to do everything possible to prevent spread down the tracheobronchial tree, and to this end avoidance of a tracheostomy is important when one considers how the tumour is implantable.

Many treatments have been advocated over the years—administration of oestrogens, cautery with podophyllin, trichloracetic acid or chromic acid, ultrasonic therapy, irradiation, vaccine therapy and local idoxuridine. None of these is as successful as careful and repeated local removal, aided by the microscope, and regular 2-monthly follow-up of the patient until the condition resolves. The advent of the laser beam microlaryngeal techniques has proved highly successful in destroying the papillomas and reducing the frequency of their recurrence. More recently the use of antiviral interferon therapy has aroused considerable interest and there is, at present, a multicentre trial taking place in the UK into the use of interferon therapy.

Prognosis is always hopeful although treatment may be prolonged. Spontaneous disappearance of the growths may occur at any age.

INFLAMMATORY CONDITIONS

Simple Acute Laryngitis

This is a condition to be taken seriously because of the danger of oedema. Supraglottic oedema begins in the arytenoids and spreads to the aryepiglottic folds and the false cords. Subglottic oedema occurs only below the vocal cords in the lax subglottic submucosal spaces. In neither case do the vocal cords become oedematous.

Laryngeal Diphtheria

This is now seldom found in the developed countries as a result of immunization, but in the developing world it may still affect young childrem. There is hoarseness, progressive stridor, dysponea and distress. The membrane may or may not affect the fauces, but it spreads from the larynx down the trachea. The smell is characteristic, and the clinical features include retraction of the suprasternal, intercostal and epigastric areas. Cyanosis precedes a livid pallor. Penicillin, if given promptly, will abort the condition, failing which a tracheostomy will be necessary. Antitoxic serum should be administered in this event, and combined with penicillin or erythromycin.

Acute Epiglottitis

This is seen in children more commonly than in adults and while it may present as part of a generalized upper respiratory tract infection, it may also occur on its own. It is an infection of winter caused as a rule by *Haemophilus influenzae* type B, in which there is inflammation and oedema of the supraglottic structures.

DIAGNOSIS. The usual presentation is with fever and severe pain deep in the throat, especially on swallowing. If allowed to progress unchecked the inflammatory oedema will track through the vast lymphatic spaces of the supraglottis—especially the aryepiglottic folds—and will cause muffling of the voice and respiratory obstruction. Since these spaces are larger in children than in adults, it is a more dangerous disease in childhood.

Examination with a mirror shows a bright red epiglottis, which will become very swollen as the disease progresses. The oedema will later be seen in the aryepiglottic folds and arytenoids, and examination will also become progressively more difficult since it becomes painful and difficult to protrude the tongue.

TREATMENT. Treatment is to put the child in an atmosphere of moist oxygen. Sedation must be given cautiously, if at all, in case the respiratory centre is depressed. Chloramphenicol is the antibiotic of choice and it should be given intramuscularly or preferably intravenously. Amoxycillin or ampicillin is no longer advised as the haemophilus organisms are now sufficiently often resistant to make its use inappropriate. Fluids should be given by mouth or, if dysphagia is severe, by infusion. It is an error to assume that the airway will remain patent, because it may block suddenly at any moment. If the child is becoming tired or the vital signs are deteriorating then it is better to perform nasotracheal intubation early in the illness. Intubation is now considered preferable to tracheostomy as it is non-invasive and avoids the possible fatal complications of tracheostomy. Having said that, however, intubation does require the ready availability of a skilled paediatric laryngologist or anaesthetist, and if these are not available then tracheostomy should be carried out.

By carrying out early nasotracheal intubation the mortality from this condition has dropped from about 6 per cent to 0·9 per cent.

Acute Laryngotracheobronchitis

This condition is sometimes referred to as acute laryngotracheitis, acute obstructive subglottic laryngitis or 'croup', although the condition which the general public call croup bears little relation to this serious virus infection. It is a disease of the winter months which is found more often in temperate climates, and in large conurbations as opposed to the countryside. This may be due as much to overcrowding and the ease with which the virus spreads as to the presence of 'smog'. The parainfluenzal 1 virus is probably the main organism, while the usual pathogens, streptococcus, staphylococcus, pneumococcus and *H. influenzae,* may appear secondarily. The disease most commonly attacks those between the ages of 6 months and 3 years.

CLINICAL FEATURES. This is a disease of the subglottis and later of the trachea and bronchi, and it follows rapidly upon an apparently simple upper respiratory tract infection which suddenly worsens with hoarseness, a croupy cough rather like a seal's bark and progressive stridor. The temperature rises to about 38·5 °C with a corresponding rise in pulse rate. Respirations are rapid and laboured and there is inspiratory stridor and expiratory wheeze. Intercostal and suprasternal retraction is marked. The child is toxic and restless from hypoxia and hypercapnia, his face is pale with a cyanotic tinge which may not improve after he is placed in an incubator in an atmosphere of moist oxygen. As toxicity and respiratory obstruction increases his restless tossing wears off and the child lies exhausted and semiconscious.

INVESTIGATION. On examination the pharynx may be congested and the larynx, when examined directly, shows congestion with subglottic inflammatory oedema which may narrow the conus elasticus to a slit 1 mm wide. The mucosa of the trachea and bronchi is congested and covered with viscous secretion which may dry to leave crusting in the lumen. Bronchoscopy is not advised because of the subglottic oedema. Force would be required, and this would further damage the tissues with the possibility of permanent fibrotic narrowing. The condition is diagnosed from acute epiglottitis by the absence of supraglottic oedema, the presence of sticky secretions and a normal lateral radiograph of the neck.

TREATMENT. This consists of placing the child in the moist air of a croupette, the humidity being kept high to prevent crust formation in the tracheobronchial tree. Sedation is better avoided, but fright at hospital admission may aggravate the respiratory problems and rectal Seconal may be helpful provided that the dose does not depress the cough reflex which is essential for survival. Toxicity is very marked, and may prevent a child from coughing or even expelling secretion that has been coughed into the mouth. Suction must be available to assist the child when necessary. Antibiotics may be given intravenously, cephaloridine, or ampicillin with cloxacillin being the drugs of choice, but the essentially virus nature of the disease means that too great reliance must not be placed on them. Fluids are essential, and to prevent repeated disturbance of the child an intravenous infusion may be set up and the antibiotics injected into it.

Special nursing is essential, and frequent pulse and respiratory rates are recorded. A rising pulse rate and increased respiratory difficulty with restlessness, the use of the accessory muscles, and the lack of improvement of the colour of the face are indications for nasotracheal intubation. Once again, if skilled help is not available then consideration to perform tracheostomy should not be delayed. Intubation should not be delayed in the presence of lack of improvement with medical treatment, and repeated aspiration of secretions is necessary through the tube. The instillation of 1–2 ml of sterile normal saline solution and immediate aspiration may prevent crusting, especially if a further 1 ml is slowly injected thereafter to lie in the bronchial tree. If this fails and respiratory difficulty increases, the crusts may have to be picked out with forceps at bronchoscopy.

Death is due to asphyxia and poor gas exchange in the terminal bronchi leading to progressive hypoxia of the heart and brain.

Using these methods the mortality rate from laryngotracheobronchitis has been drastically reduced. Problems of a serious nature will only occur if admission to hospital is delayed.

Chapter 4.4

ENDOSCOPY

In the adult indirect laryngoscopy is commonly performed, and the larynx is illuminated by light reflected from a laryngeal mirror held against the soft palate while the tongue is pulled forwards. Most children, even older children, will not tolerate indirect laryngoscopy on account of fear or the sensation of choking, and when laryngoscopy is required it is performed directly and usually under general anaesthesia. In many centres no general anaesthetic is given, but most surgeons prefer that the child should be unconscious so that examination may be conducted methodically and without haste.

LARYNGOSCOPY

Laryngoscopy should be performed in all cases of stridor or hoarseness. It is unscientific and potentially dangerous to diagnose the cause of stridor in an infant or of hoarseness in a child on the basis of probability from the published lists of relative frequency. The anaesthetic is required for a short duration only, but the depth of anaesthesia must be such that an inspection may be carried through without the vocal cords going into spasm. The larynx is first inspected with the tip of the laryngoscope inserted into the funnel of the infantile epiglottis or below the upper edge of the child's epiglottis. This is the point of maximal stimulation for laryngeal spasm and it should be performed first while the anaesthetic is deep. At this stage the ventricular folds (false cords), the vocal cords (true cords), the ventricle, the anterior commissure, the posterior commissure and the subglottis are examined. The tip of the laryngoscope is then withdrawn and inserted into the vallecula, and the movements of the vocal cords may be studied without fear of spasm while consciousness returns and respiration resumes. If the laryngoscope is left within the laryngeal vestibule during this phase spasmodic adduction of the cords is likely to occur as anaesthesia lightens. Not only may the movement of the cords be studied, but in infants the movement of the epiglottis should be examined for any tugging during inspiration.

BRONCHOSCOPY

Bronchoscopy is required in many cases of stridor and in all cases of suspected foreign body inhalation. It should always be preceded by laryngoscopy during

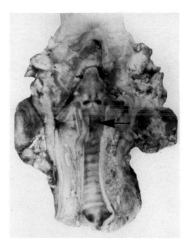

Fig. 4.4.1. Subglottic ectopic thyroid tissue (arrowed).

which the subglottis has been examined. To insert a bronchoscope without preliminary laryngoscopy is to risk missing a lesion in the subglottis. *Figure* 4.4.1 shows the postmortem appearance of a baby who died from asphyxia. The cause of the stridor, which was ectopic thyroid tissue in the subglottis, had never been found in spite of several bronchoscopies in a hospital where preliminary laryngoscopy was not routinely practised.

Bronchoscopy is a difficult and potentially hazardous procedure in the infant and young child. In the first place the lumen of the bronchoscope is so small that the occasional bronchoscopist without a telescope may be unable to determine the various bifurcations of the bronchi. In a premature infant or neonate it may be only possible to pass a 2·5 mm bronchoscope as the outside diameter is 4 mm (*Table* 4.4.1). If the bronchoscope selected is a little tight the next smaller size should be used. The narrowest part of the airway is the subglottis and even a little oedema can greatly narrow the airway of a neonate.

The bronchoscopes now used (*Fig.* 4.4.2) have two main side-arms. One of these has a connection which fits on to the anaesthetic gas supply and the other is connected to a fibreoptic cable and light source. This system allows the anaesthetist a controlled airway and enables the operator to make a full, unhurried

Table 4.4.1. Bronchoscopes used for children, relating the size of the instrument to the age of the child

Size marked on bronchoscope (mm)	External diameter (mm)	Age range
2·5	4·0	Premature/neonate
3·0	5·0	Neonate–3 months
3·5	5·7	4–12 months
4·0	7·0	12–36 months
5·0	7·8	3–9 years
6·0	8·2	Over 9 years

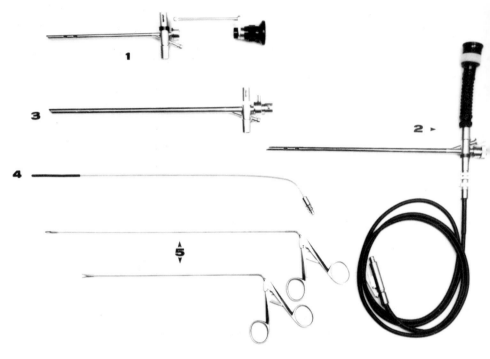

Fig. 4.4.2.   Bronchoscopic instruments for use in children.
1, 2.5-mm Storz bronchoscope.   3, 4.5-mm Storz bronchoscope.
2, 3.5-mm Storz bronchoscope with fibre   4, Suction tube.
   light cable and anaesthetic attachment.   5, Grasping forceps.

examination of the trachea and bronchi. It is of the utmost importance that there
is full cooperation between the surgeon and anaesthetist so that each knows what
the other is doing. A fully experienced paediatric anaesthetist is necessary. There
are several anaesthetic techniques used. If there is any question of upper airway
obstruction, the child must not be paralysed. A local spray of 1 or 2 per cent
lignocaine applied to the epiglottis, larynx and trachea will reduce laryngeal spasm
so that the bronchoscope may be passed. If the upper airway is normal and the
examination is for a bronchial foreign body or diagnosis of lower respiratory tract
pathology, then a muscle relaxant such as suxamethonium may be used. This
makes passing of the bronchoscope much easier as the cords remain abducted.

   After viewing the larynx, a bronchoscope of suitable size is selected and it is
gently passed through the cords with the bevel in contact with one cord (*Fig.* 4.4.3)
until it enters the trachea. If it is even a little tight a smaller bronchoscope should
be used.

   During the procedure the child should be connected to an electrocardiographic
monitor. If the pulse rate starts to slow it suggests the patient is becoming hypoxic
and the surgeon should then withdraw the bronchoscope till it lies in the trachea
and wait until the anaesthetist is happy the situation has stabilized.

   Orientation can be difficult in a neonate or infant to the occasional bronchosco-

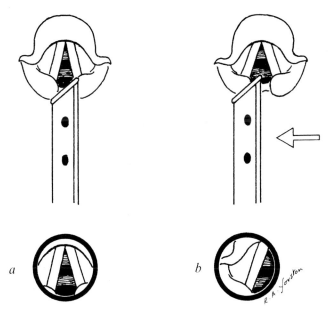

Fig. 4.4.3. Introduction of bronchoscope.
a, View on approach to glottis, with handle of bronchoscope on right.
b, Tip of bronchoscope moved to the left, and slipped between cords
    during inspiration.

pist, and often this is because the bronchoscope has been passed straight into the right main bronchus.

The structures are extremely small in an infant and many surgeons use telescopes which can be passed along the bronchoscope to examine both straight ahead and at various angles. There is also a wide selection of cup, serrated and peanut forceps available.

Other ventilating bronchoscopic systems are available, some incorporating Venturi jet systems. Great care must be taken in using high-pressure insufflation systems in young children because of the danger of creating a pneumothorax. Fibreoptic flexible bronchoscopes suitable for infants and young children are now available but have not yet been widely used.

MICROLARYNGOSCOPY

Microlaryngoscopy in children differs little from that in adults apart from the size aspect. The laryngoscope holder is placed not on the chest wall but on a table positioned above the child. The endotracheal tube should be as small as the anaesthetist can manage.

Microlaryngoscopy is used routinely in many paediatric units. It has the advantage that, by clamping the laryngoscope in place either by a suspension apparatus or by a snake-arm which can be locked, both hands are left free for intralaryngeal manipulations and the image is enlarged. Photography and ciné-photography are more easily undertaken.

Chapter 4.5

INTUBATION AND TRACHEOSTOMY

Intubation and tracheostomy are performed for relief of airway obstruction, to facilitate bronchial toilet and to assist ventilation. It is worth remembering that in neonates and infants a modest oedema may imperil the airway. In a neonate the anteroposterior diameter of the glottis averages 8 mm and the width in full abduction is some 6 mm, giving an area of 24 mm^2. With 1 mm oedema this is halved to 12 mm^2. Similarly, the lumen of the subglottis may be reduced to about 30–40 per cent of normal by an oedema of 1 mm.

Respiratory distress may follow acute obstruction of the airway in the region of the larynx (acute epiglottitis or laryngeal oedema); acute lower respiratory infections (acute laryngotracheobronchitis, bronchiolitis, staphylococcal pneumonia); or failure of respiration in meningitis, head injury or poisoning. Respiratory distress may lead to circulatory failure which may not be recognized until hypoxia and acidaemia reach a critical level. If the oxygen content of arterial blood falls below 85 per cent cyanosis occurs, and this is a more precise sign of hypoxia than restlessness or impaired consciousness. Peripheral cyanosis and coldness develop with a fall in the systemic blood pressure. Arterial blood gas analysis is frequently carried out in the management of respiratory distress in children, and if the pH falls below 7·2 units while the $P\text{CO}_2$ rises to over 65 mmHg, the prognosis becomes more grave. Following relief of the airway obstruction, there is an immediate improvement in these levels. Many surgeons of experience, however, still prefer to make a clinical assessment of the appropriate time to intubate or to perform a tracheostomy.

Oedema arises from inflammatory causes as a rule, but an oedema may be produced by the passage of a bronchoscope or an anaesthetic tube which is too wide. Any tube introduced into the trachea must slip easily through the subglottis. If force is required the tube is too wide. Such induced oedema may be slight and transitory, but the presence of an indwelling tube over any length of time may have more lasting and serious results. Therefore, if intubation is to be the method of choice for treatment the tube must be the correct size to lie easily within the subglottis, and the length of intubation must be controlled. Such pressure necrosis is not confined to the subglottis but may appear in the posterior end of the glottis.

INTUBATION

Intubation is to be preferred if the natural course of the disease is expected to be short. It is the method of choice for the relief of airway problems if the cause lies in the neighbourhood of the larynx.

Rees pioneered intubation in Britain and used a polyvinyl tube. This has now been superseded by silastic tubes which are basically inert and cause very little local tissue damage. These tubes become malleable at body temperature and hence conform to the various contours they traverse.

Infants and young children tolerate nasotracheal intubation without distress and only very rarely do they require any form of sedation. There are no set limits to the time that an infant can be safely intubated but, depending on the degree of movement of the child etc., tubes can be tolerated for periods of up to 4–6 weeks without complications.

TRACHEOSTOMY

Tracheostomy is the method of choice for relief of airway problems if intubation is impossible or if relief of upper airway obstruction or assisted ventilation is required for periods longer than 4–6 weeks. If there are severe burns and damage to the laryngeal mucosa, then it is probably advisable to proceed straight to tracheostomy rather than risk continued mucosal irritation by leaving an endotracheal tube in the larynx. Whenever possible it is performed under general anaesthetic given by a skilled paediatric anaesthetist who can frequently pass an endotracheal tube, however small, to maintain oxygenation. The incision is a short transverse one, midway between the lower border of the thyroid cartilage and the suprasternal notch. The neck must be well extended. Dissection is carried between the veins and below the thyroid isthmus if possible. If this is impossible the isthmus is clamped and divided in the midline. An incision is made through two tracheal rings, preferably the third and fourth. It is unwise in the infant or child to remove any tracheal cartilage because this weakens the anterior tracheal wall and may interfere with functional healing. The endotracheal tube is removed as the appropriate size of tracheostomy tube is inserted. A small skin incision may need no suturing. The tracheostomy tube is tied around the neck with the head flexed. If it is tied with the head extended the strap muscles are taut, and when the head is later flexed the tapes become loose and the tube may come out of the trachea.

The same argument regarding oxygenation obtains as with intubation, although the tubal lumen is greater because the lumen of the trachea exceeds that of the subglottis. There is a difference of opinion as to whether silver or plastic tracheostomy tubes should be used. It is argued that the lower end of the silver tube excoriates the tracheal mucosa during movements of the head and neck. On the other hand, the safety factor of the double tube is very considerable and many lives have been saved by the prompt removal of the inner tube. The plastic tube may excoriate less, but the tube walls are thicker so that the lumen is less. Most surgeons have a personal preference for a particular type of tube and they should always use the tube that they and their staff are accustomed to rather than experiment with a variety of different types.

Whichever tube is used in the infant one must bear in mind the high level of the infant larynx and the thickness of subcutaneous tissue in the infant's neck. If an infant is nursed propped up after tracheostomy there is a considerable danger of the head rolling forward and occluding the lumen of the tracheostomy tube. The patient should be nursed in an atmosphere of moist air because the warming and moistening functions of the nasal mucosa have been by-passed and cold dry air inhaled through the tracheostomy tube or, for that matter, the intubation tube, is irritating to the bronchial mucosa and much secretion is produced. The tube must be cleaned at frequent intervals, and this is more easily done if a silver tube has been inserted because the inner tube may be taken out for cleaning and the airway is then perfectly clear. In order to clean the plastic tube it must be removed and another one reinserted. Aspiration of pulmonary secretions is effected by passing a catheter through the lumen of the tracheostomy tube.

COMPLICATIONS. Complications are subcutaneous emphysema from a leak around the tube due either to the tube being too small or because it has slipped out of the trachea. When the fault is corrected recovery ensues. Pneumothorax and mediastinal emphysema are usually due to the tube having come out of the trachea, or to an extensive dissection of the tissues in the lower neck. Deaths occur following tracheostomy, but these are more often due to the disease for which the operation was performed. Deaths from complications of the operation, blockage of the tube, crusts in the bronchi, displaced tube or improperly inserted tube, account for less than 25 per cent. The mortality rate is relatively higher in infants under 1 year of age.

DECANNULATION. Decannulation is frequently a problem if the tracheostomy tube has been worn for a length of time.

Irrespective of age a tracheostomy which has been performed for an acute problem, scalds, acute epiglottitis, acute laryngotracheobronchitis, etc. may be extubated within a week. It is necessary to assess at laryngoscopy that the acute obstruction has been relieved, and, if this is so, the tube may be removed while the child is still under the anaesthetic. The neck wound is closed by the finger and thumb and the surgeon and anaesthetist watch the recovery from the anaesthetic. If there is no stridor and no dyspnoea an occlusive dressing is applied and the incision heals, usually without the need for a suture. If stridor is found during recovery from anaesthesia the tracheostomy tube is reinserted and a further trial made a few days later.

In the case of the tracheostomy which has been in place for some time assessment must be made at laryngoscopy that the cause has been relieved, that the airway through the glottis and subglottis is satisfactory and that there is no stenosis above the tracheostomy tube. Assessment can be made by soft-tissue lateral radiography to ensure that the alignment of the airway has not been distorted by the tube.

In the absence of stenosis, and if a bronchoscope of the correct size passes easily to the carina, there should be no physical reason why the tube should not be occluded for increasing periods until it is blocked both day and night. Some surgeons advocate a progressive procedure by replacing the tracheostomy tube with succeeding tubes of diminishing size, so that closure is effected slowly, and the final suturing may be made easily. The Rees–Pracy tube is fenestrated and has a valve attachment so that the child may use the larynx for speech, and it has an occluding tube for use before decannulation. It is reasonable to suppose that if a child can have the tube occluded day and night for some time without respiratory embarrassment he will accept its removal with equanimity. This seldom happens because he has been so dependent on the tube for so long that a crisis develops at the suggestion that he could do without it. On the other hand if he wakens from an anaesthetic without the tube, he will accept the position. Thus, if it can be demonstrated that there is no stenosis, it is usually possible to close the opening in layers or by swinging skin flaps, and when the child recovers consciousness and breathes easily he is happy.

If a stenosis is found above the tube on tracheoscopy there are physical problems to be overcome. They take the form of compression of the anterior tracheal wall either because the upper lip of the tracheostome is tilted backwards, or the lower lip is pressed downwards and outwards, or the posterior tracheal wall has been displaced backwards by the tube. These effects may be produced or exaggerated by too small an incision in the tracheal wall or over-extension of the neck during tracheostomy. Some surgeons anticipate these difficulties at the time of operation by stitching the tracheal opening forward to hold it in place, while others try to correct the defect when the incision is eventually closed.

SUBGLOTTIC STENOSIS

Subglottic stenosis has now become one of the most common causes of chronic upper airway obstruction in infants and children. It may be congenital or acquired.

Congenital subglottic stenosis is less common and less severe than the acquired form and as such can usually be managed conservatively. Airway obstruction can result from a cricoid cartilage that is small in diameter or eccentrically shaped with luminal compression. The majority of children will outgrow the condition and if the airway is threatened then a tracheostomy may be required to allow this growth to occur. Most children will be decannulated by the age of 2.

Acquired subglottic stenosis may be a result of direct trauma or high tracheostomy, but is most commonly found after a period of prolonged intubation either during the neonatal period or following cardiac surgery. Premature neonates with a variety of metabolic and respiratory problems may often require prolonged endotracheal intubation with or without assisted ventilation and if the intubation has to be repeated frequently, often in emergency situations, the risk of subglottic mucosal damage and resulting subglottic stenosis is undoubtedly increased. The incidence of this complication seems to vary considerably in different centres. In Edinburgh, a meticulous method of fixing the tube, supported by avoidance of infection and regular physiotherapy, has revealed a zero incidence of subglottic stenosis in 458 consecutive carefully documented neonates with endotracheal intubation. It would seem, therefore, that attention to the detail of fixing the tube to avoid dislodgement should lead to a considerable reduction in the incidence of acquired subglottic stenosis. Figures from elsewhere quote the incidence between 2 and 8 per cent.

Children with significant acquired subglottic stenosis will require tracheostomy and this should be done between the fifth and sixth tracheal rings to avoid interference if surgical repair is required. Most authorities agree that surgical repair should not be attempted until the age of 2 at a minimum.

Many methods of surgical repair have been advocated over the years and, as is so often the case in surgery, this usually indicates that none of these has been universally successful. Endoscopic methods, including dilatation and the injection of steroids have generally been abandoned, as allowing further growth will usually be sufficient to permit decannulation.

Excision of the stenosed area always presents a surgical challenge. A variety of methods from total excision of the affected area with end-to-end anastomosis to simple scar excision and stenting (with or without skin graft) have been documented. Results are difficult to analyse, but generally speaking these have been unsuccessful due to recurrence of the stenosis.

Success has been obtained by procedures that allow for expansion of the trachea in conjunction with scar excision. The castellated tracheal incision in the laryngotracheoplasty procedure can be successful in the older child and if the stenosed area is not too close to the vocal cords. Complete midline division of the posterior plate of the cricoid in conjunction with a costal cartilage graft to the upper anterior tracheal rings allows good expansion of the upper trachea, and if this is maintained by an Aboulkir Teflon stent left in place for 3 months, decannulation may be possible. This Teflon stent greatly reduces the formation of granulation tissue (as compared to previously used silastic stents) and reduces the chance of the stenosis.

Subglottic stenosis tends to attract a surgical approach, but nowadays with home suction apparatus a child of any age can quite easily be managed at home with a tracheostomy tube. Fenestrated tubes or valved tubes can be used, but even if they are not used the child can very often learn to pass enough air through his larynx for perfectly adequate speech. As the child grows the stenosed area will become increasingly less significant and decannulation will become possible without surgical interference.

These children indeed present a problem, but surgery should not be rushed into by the inexperienced until all the possibilities have been carefully considered.

Chapter 4.7

TUMOURS OF THE HEAD
AND NECK

By far the commonest swellings in the neck are cervical lymph nodes and in children the commonest cause is inflammation. The jugulodigastric gland that lies at the upper end of the deep cervical lymph chain drains the tonsils and surrounding area of the pharynx. Swelling of this node is, therefore, extremely common and is discussed in more detail in the chapter on tonsils and adenoids.

INFLAMMATORY CONDITIONS AFFECTING NECK NODES

Infectious Mononucleosis (Glandular Fever)

This is more commonly an affliction of older children and there is now an accepted relationship between the Epstein–Barr virus (EBV) and infectious mononucleosis. Its infectivity seems to be low and spread requires close direct contact (hence, the 'kissing' disease). The diagnosis can be confirmed by a suggestive clinical picture, typical changes, the peripheral blood (large atypical mononuclear cells), a positive heterophil antibody test (Paul–Bunnell or monospot tests), IgM antibody to the EBV and, finally, non-specific liver function tests. Complications can be severe and can include serious airway obstruction due to cervical oedema, neurological problems and even cardiac involvement. There is no specific treatment and in particular antibiotics should be avoided. Ampicillin is specifically contraindicated in view of the definite association between its use in infectious mononucleosis and the development of toxic skin eruptions.

Cytomegalovirus Infections

This may in the first instance be congenital, having been passed to the fetus from the mother. Mild infections may result in significant deafness.

In the older child the disease may mimic infectious mononucleosis, often with hepatic complaints as well as cervical adenitis. Diagnosis is by excluding glandular fever and by demonstrating a significant use of antibody titre during the illness.

Cat Scratch Disease

Seventy-five per cent of reported cases of this problem occur in children and are usually associated with the careless handling of animals. Adenitis will develop in the area related to the original lesion, although this may be virtually unidentifiable. The disease is a benign one which can be confirmed by a positive skin test to cat scratch antigen. The treatment is purely symptomatic and antibiotics do not influence the course of the disease.

Toxoplasmosis

This can present either as a congenital infection of the newborn, in which case it produces an acute and often severe illness, or else a less severe acute febrile illness in childhood. The congenital infection may produce major damage to the central nervous system including the eye.

The causative organism, *Toxoplasma gondii*, is a crescentic protozoan which is strictly intracellular, multiplying only within the cytoplasm of the host. The acquired infection in childhood usually presents with lymph node involvement and only very occasionally are there other organisms involved. Enlarged cervical glands may persist for months so that biopsy may be required to exclude tuberculosis, lymphadenitis or lymphomas. Treatment is rarely required in the acquired form.

Salivary Gland Swellings

Apart from mumps (epidemic parotitis), diseases of the salivary gland in children are congenital. Congenital absence has been described. Enlargement, particularly of the sublingual glands, has been reported in children with cystic fibrosis. Symmetrical painless swelling of the parotid and lacrimal glands, often accompanied by reduced secretion of saliva and tears (Mikulicz's syndrome), is a rare complication of leukaemia and tuberculosis. Salivary calculi have only very rarely been reported in children and almost always these have involved the submandibular gland. Swelling of the affected gland on eating food is characteristic of the disorder. Sjögren's syndrome of salivary and lacrimal gland swelling, dry mouth, painful dry eyes and arthritis has been recorded in children on rare occasions. Tumours such as haemangiomas, lymphangiomas, mixed salivary tumours and lymphomas can occur but again are extremely rare.

Suppurative Parotitis

Suppurative infection of the parotid gland, usually with *Staphylococcus aureus*, may occur in the newborn and in debilitated children. The affected gland is swollen, painful and tender. Pus can sometimes be expressed from Stensen's duct. The condition is always unilateral. Treatment should be vigorous with antibiotics in large doses. Should an abscess form this may have to be drained.

Recurrent Parotitis

In this condition there is recurrent painful swelling of sudden onset of one or both parotid glands, lasting about 1 or 2 weeks. During attacks the orifice of Stensen's duct may appear red and oedematous. It may sometimes be possible to express some pus from the duct and a commonly found organism is *Streptococcus viridans*. These attacks, which may occur at intervals of weeks or months, usually commence between the ages of 3 and 6. They cause considerable discomfort at the time but are rarely associated with any systemic upset.

Treatment should be by gentle massaging of the affected gland, the use of sialogogues (e.g. acid sweets) once the really acute symptoms have settled and antibiotics during the acute attacks. Penicillin is sometimes prescribed on a long-term prophylactic basis if the condition is particularly recurrent. The condition resolves by puberty and hence surgery should be avoided.

BENIGN TUMOURS IN THE NECK

Cystic Hygroma (Lymphangioma)

Although some authors have attempted to classify cystic hygromas, it would seem that they are a single entity. Lymphatic vessels develop as spaces in embryonic tissue and if these fail to communicate with the thoracic duct or the internal jugular vein, cystic swelling will develop. About half of the cysts have been present since birth and the remainder develop during childhood. The swelling, which may attain a very considerable size, is predominantly found in the posterior triangle of the neck, but there may be extensions to the hypopharynx and larynx. The cyst is smooth, firm, fluctuant, not bound down, and it transilluminates. Histologically it consists of a multilocular cyst enclosing clear lymph within thin walls. Removal of the cyst for cosmetic reasons is not difficult if it is small, but poses problems of access and of complete removal when it involves the hypopharynx and larynx in which regions there is an appreciable recurrence rate.

Dermoid Cyst

This may involve the floor of the mouth in the midline or it may appear in the submental region below the mylohyoid muscle. The cyst is spherical and because of its thick walls it feels soft yet solid. Enlargement within the mouth may cause feeding problems, and should it enlarge into the hypopharynx it may hamper respiration. Microscopically it resembles a dermoid elsewhere in the body, having a thick fibrous capsule and containing hairs and epithelial debris which may discharge through the sinus. It is removed either through the floor of the mouth or via a submental incision, depending upon the situation of the sinus.

Thyroglossal Cyst

The thyroid gland forms from the foramen caecum near the base of the tongue and descends into the neck behind the hyoid bone. If its attachment to the tongue does not atrophy it leaves the thyroglossal duct inside which a cyst may form. About half of all the thyroglossal cysts are first noticed in childhood, presenting as a symptomless lump in the midline of the neck below the level of the hyoid bone. It moves on swallowing because of its attachment to the thyroid gland, and on protruding the tongue because it originally derives from the base of that organ. It may also present as a midline infected cyst. Treatment is removal through a neck incision and dissection upwards to the tongue, the hyoid bone being divided and the central part removed with the tract.

Anomalies of the Second Branchial Groove

Persistence of the second branchial groove may present as a cyst, a sinus or a fistula. Because second groove anomalies are by far the commonest, these lesions are known as branchial cysts, sinuses or fistulae.

Branchial Cyst

A branchial cyst may occasionally open on to the lateral wall of the pharynx on the palatopharyngeal fold, or in the floor of the external auditory meatus at the junction of its cartilaginous and bony parts, but it usually appears at the anterior border of the sternomastoid muscle at the junction of its middle and upper thirds. The cyst represents the remnants of the first branchial cleft and is removed through an incision along the anterior border of the sternomastoid muscle.

Branchial Sinus

This sinus from the second branchial groove usually presents as a small opening along the anterior border of the sternomastoid muscle. These may discharge mucoid material. Treatment is by surgical removal of the sinus and tract after filling the tract with a dye such as methylene blue. The tract often runs close to the bifurcation of the common carotid artery.

Branchial Fistula

The inferior opening of the fistula is again commonly along the anterior border of the sternomastoid and it runs superiorly and medially between the external and internal carotid arteries, lateral to the hypoglossal nerve to open into the pharynx in the area of the tonsillar fossa. These can be demonstrated radiographically by the injection of radiopaque dye and treatment is by surgical excision.

MALIGNANT TUMOURS OF THE HEAD AND NECK

Lymphomas

Eight per cent of all childhood malignant tumours are lymphomas, with 4 per cent being Hodgkin's and 4 per cent being non-Hodgkin's lymphomas. Less than one-quarter of these will present with cervical neck gland enlargement. The diagnosis depends on suspicion backed up by histological confirmation. Treatment depends very much on the staging of the tumour and as this involves extensive investigations, the management should be undertaken by a team, including radiologists, haematologists, oncologists and radiation oncologists. At least 80 per cent of those with localized neck lymphoma can now expect to be cured by combined therapeutic approaches.

Burkitt's Lymphoma

Although this is a rare tumour in the UK, it is quite a common tumour in endemic malarial areas. It commonly presents in the lower jaw but it can occur in the nasopharynx and in the other extranodal areas. There have been several findings of the Epstein–Barr virus (EBV) in the aetiology of Burkitt's lymphoma. Treatment results with chemotherapy for localized Burkitt's lymphoma are excellent.

Rhabdomyosarcoma

Rhabdomyosarcoma represents the most common soft-tissue neoplasm of the head and neck found in children. The tumour is most commonly seen in Caucasian children under the age of 12, usually presenting as a painless mass. Distant metastases are frequently present, especially in regional lymph nodes, lung and bone marrow. All children suspected of having this disorder should have a thorough examination of the head and neck as well as a complete radiological investigation of the primary site to try and define the true size of the tumour. Histological diagnosis should be obtained as soon as possible by simple biopsy. Once the diagnosis has been made a thorough search for metastatic disease must be undertaken. Treatment must be individualized according to the findings and the management should once again be undertaken by a team, including the surgeon, radiation oncologist and paediatric oncologist. The most frequent sites for the tumour are the orbit, the oral cavity and pharynx, and the face and neck region. Results of treatment have improved considerably since systemic chemotherapy in conjunction with full-dose radiation have been started, and survival figures of between 50 and 75 per cent disease-free after 5 years can now be confidently expected.

TUMOURS OF THE NOSE AND SINUSES

Congenital Tumours

Congenital tumours are occasionally met with, either externally or within the nasal cavity (*Fig.* 4.7.1).

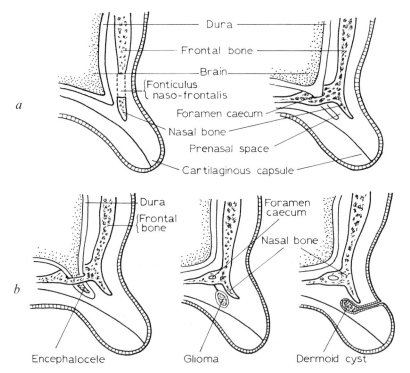

Fig. 4.7.1. Congenital tumours of the nasal cavity.
a, Dorsum of nose at birth.
b, Congenital neoplasms of nose at birth.
(Redrawn from Wang and Macomber in *Reconstructive Plastic Surgery* by Converse; Saunders, 1964.)

Glioma

This is a solid tumour which may present externally at the root of the nose which becomes broadened, or it may appear intranasally from the roof or the lateral wall of the nasal cavity. It arises from a failure of the dural process to become sealed off in the foramen caecum during embryonic development. The external tumour is subcutaneous, firm and elastic to the touch, and it must be distinguished from a dermoid cyst. The intranasal type resembles a small nasal polypus on inspection and it may appear in the nasal vestibule. It is firm to the touch with a probe and does not enlarge when the baby cries, a fact which distinguishes it from an encephalocele. The glioma is composed of neuroglial tissue and astrocytes, and is not malignant. It should be removed completely.

Encephalocele

This is a herniation of dura mater which enters the nose through the foramen caecum or through a dehiscence in the cribriform plate of the ethmoid bone. The

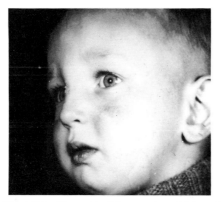

Fig. 4.7.2. Dermoid of the nose in a child aged 18 months. The sinus opening on the external nose has become infected.

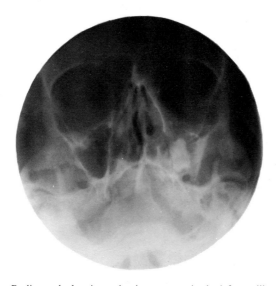

Fig. 4.7.3. Radiograph showing a dentigerous cyst in the left maxillary sinus.

cyst contains cerebrospinal fluid and occasionally, cerebral tissue. It is smooth, freely movable on its stalk, readily compressible and enlarges with crying. In view of its composition it is dangerous to puncture the cyst to determine the nature of its contents in case an intracranial infection results. The removal involves neurosurgery, and the deficiency in the floor of the skull is closed at the same time.

Dermoid Cyst

This is an external midline cyst on the dorsum of the nose which contains hair and amorphous material. It may open on to the surface by a small sinus (*Fig.* 4.7.2) through which hair may protrude. This serves to distinguish it from an external glioma. The cyst tends to extend widely beneath or between the nasal bones towards the base of the skull, so that surgical removal may be an extensive procedure which may necessitate plastic reconstruction.

Chapter 4.8

DEAFNESS IN CHILDREN

EMBRYOLOGY OF THE EAR

A working knowledge of the embryology of the ear is important, because with increasing frequency otologists are operating upon children with congenital conductive deafness either to restore the hearing or to provide a meatus into which a hearing aid may be inserted. As the inner ear develops separately from the outer and middle ears, abnormalities may be identified in an independent way. The outer and middle ears develop from the first and second branchial arches and the first branchial cleft, while the inner ear develops from the otocyst which is an outgrowth of the hindbrain.

The External Ear

The **pinna** develops from six distinct hillocks or tubercles, and is fully formed by the twelfth week of fetal life. A hillock from the first branchial arch forms the tragus, while the remainder of the pinna develops by fusion of the other tubercles from both the first and second arches. The **external meatus** is not fully developed until much later in fetal life, and in fact does not become completely canalized until the seventh month. The meatus develops by canalization of a solid core of epithelial tissue from the medial end laterally. This tissue forms the superficial layer of the tympanic membrane and the deep meatus.

The Middle Ear

The **Eustachian (pharyngotympanic) tube** and the **middle-ear cavity** develop as the tubotympanic recess, opening from the foregut through a slit-like orifice, and it becomes tubular as its distal end expands to form the tympanic cavity (*Fig.* 4.8.1). As this distal end expands it envelops the developing ossicles, the tendons of the intratympanic muscles and the chorda tympani nerve. The myxomatous tissue, of which this layer is originally composed, becomes changed after birth into the middle-ear mucoperiosteum. The **ossicles** develop early in fetal life and are of full adult size at birth. They are of complex origin, those above the level of the facial nerve being from the first arch while those below the level of the facial nerve derive from the second arch. Hence the first-arch tissues make up the body of the malleus and the body and short process of the incus, while the second-arch tissues form the manubrium of the malleus, the long process of the incus and the main structure of

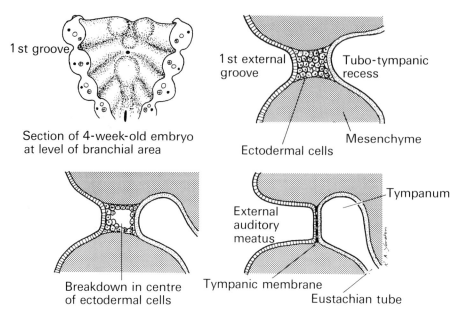

1st groove

Section of 4-week-old embryo
at level of branchial area

1st external
groove

Tubo-tympanic
recess

Ectodermal cells

Mesenchyme

Breakdown in centre
of ectodermal cells

External
auditory
meatus

Tympanum

Tympanic membrane

Eustachian tube

Fig. 4.8.1.   Development of tympanic membrane, tympanum and Eustachian tube.

the stapes, in addition to forming the hyoid bone and the styloid process of the
mastoid.

The Tympanic Membrane

This develops at the same time as the solid deep meatus becomes canalized in the
seventh fetal month. The fibrous middle layer of the membrane arises from part of
the first-arch tissues, and it may sometimes present as a thick bony plate in
children with meatal atresia.

The Inner Ear

The inner ear develops early in fetal life from the otocyst which, during the first
month of fetal life, divides into a utriculosaccular part and a part containing the
endolymphatic duct and sac. The cochlea develops as an invagination of the
saccular part and is fully formed by the eleventh week. The semicircular canals
develop from the utricle at about the same time, and the whole system is complete
by the twentieth week.

CONGENITAL CONDUCTIVE DEAFNESS

The complicated embryology allows for a great variety of congenital malforma-
tions (*Fig.* 4.8.2) involving the pinna, the external meatus, the tympanic membrane, the middle-ear cavity and the ossicles. There are many classifications of
these abnormalities but, from the standpoint of congenital conductive deafness,
the most important are defects in the external meatus which prevent sound waves
reaching the tympanic membrane, and abnormalities of the ossicular chain which
interfere with the transmission of sound to the inner ear. Parents are quite often

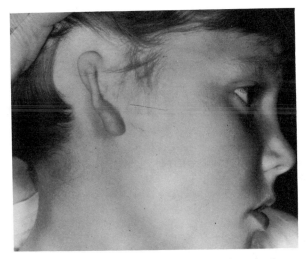

Fig. 4.8.2.   Congenital malformation of auricle and atresia of meatus.

more worried about the appearance of the baby from abnormalities of the pinna, and demand correction, but are less concerned about the consequence of such defects on hearing. In previous years surgical attempts to help the hearing have been hampered by lack of knowledge of the full nature of any congenital defect beyond what may be discovered on examination. The recent advances made in polytomography of the middle-ear cleft and the inner ear have made for greater accuracy in assessment. Unless there is a normal cochlea and a middle-ear cleft with a demonstrable ossicular mass, surgical approaches will have nothing to offer.

Meatal Atresia

This may be unilateral or bilateral. There may be complete atresia or the meatus may end in a blind depression. A variety of abnormalities of the pinna may or may not be associated with this. If the abnormality is unilateral and the other ear is normal, surgery should not be considered until later in life.

With a bilateral meatal atresia surgery should be considered, and the normally accepted age for this is between 18 months and 2 years. Should there be deformity of the pinna in addition to the meatal defect the plastic surgeon should be consulted because he may wish to refashion the auricle at a later age.

Provided that the cochlea has been shown to be normal and that a middle-ear space with an ossicular chain has been demonstrated on polytomography, surgical intervention should be advised. The main problems associated with this microsurgery, which should only be undertaken by those experienced in the field, are avoiding the facial nerve (which may run an abnormal course), establishing a sufficiently wide meatus and creating some form of conduction pathway for sound.

Maintaining a patent meatus without restenosis is a major challenge and all authorities are in agreement that some kind of epithelial lining must be established if the newly fashioned meatus is to remain patent. The most successful method of doing this is to wrap a split-thickness skin graft around a suitable length of scleral silastic sponge with the skin surface against the sponge. This prosthesis should then be inserted into the new meatus and the skin resutured over the surface. After 2 months the incision should be reopened and the scleral sponge removed. This will leave a good skin-lined external meatus. Even successful operations may only allow the child to wear an air-conduction, rather than a bone-conduction, hearing aid, and it is important that parents of the child are made fully aware of the difficulties of this problem.

Ossicular Abnormalities

Congenital conductive deafness may occur unilaterally or bilaterally in children with either normal external auditory meati or in association with other abnormalities of the craniofacial skeleton, e.g. Treacher Collins syndrome. In these children careful and full otoscopic and audiometric evaluation is vital. By far the most common cause of bilateral conductive deafness is secretory otitis media (*see* Chapter 4.10), and this must be excluded.

Assuming a 60–70 dB conductive loss has been identified and secretions are not present, an exploratory tympanotomy should be undertaken. If access is poor an endaural tympanoplasty approach is recommended. Ossiculoplasty techniques must then be undertaken to reconstitute some sort of ossicular continuity. The problem of whether or not to proceed to stapedectomy in children is not wholly established, but in general terms this should be avoided if at all possible. The danger of sensorineural loss in the operated ear must never be forgotten.

SENSORINEURAL DEAFNESS

Figures for the occurrence rates of children born with significant bilateral sensorineural (perceptive) deafness vary from country to country, and from series to series, but in general in the UK it is accepted that significant bilateral sensorineural loss occurs in approximately 1 in 1000 live births. Babies and young children are not born with the ability to speak and hence to acquire speech they require the input of sound. For acquisition of speech the important years of life are the first 2 years, and thus it is vitally important that children born with a significant loss should be identified before reaching the age of 1 year, and preferably before the age of 9 months.

With modern evoked response brainstem results the diagnosis of significant deafness may be made shortly after birth. It is not yet known at exactly what age hearing aids should be fitted but if the diagnosis is definite, aids can certainly be fitted from the age of 3 months.

AETIOLOGY. In the first instance it must be realized that, despite all our knowledge of the causes of sensorineural deafness in children, in approximately 50 per cent of children so diagnosed no known cause can be proved. Obviously, therefore, much further work and study must be undertaken into this subject because, until the cause can be established in almost every child, there is little that can be accomplished in the way of prevention. The more common causes of severe sensorineural loss are discussed.

Prenatal causes. **Hereditary prenatal causes** include a number of well-recognized syndromes associated with bilateral or unilateral sensorineural hearing loss.

Waardenburg's syndrome is of dominant transmission and the child exhibits some or all of the following characteristics—shortening of the eye fissures, hypertrichosis of the eyebrows which may meet in the midline, heterochromia of the iris, and a white forelock. The hearing defect is of a sacculocochlear (Scheibe) type resulting in bilateral or unilateral perceptive loss.

Alport's syndrome is an autosomal dominant condition affecting boys more than girls, and consists of progressive glomerulonephritis and a progressive sensorineural loss which is usually bilateral.

Klippel–Feil syndrome displays congenital abnormalities of the cervical vertebrae giving a short neck with a low hairline at the back. There may be a perceptive loss which is usually severe.

Usher's syndrome results in retinitis pigmentosa with progressive visual loss and a progressive sensorineural hearing loss in a small proportion of these children.

Cretinism is a congenital hypothyroidism which may be associated with a moderate bilateral sensorineural hearing loss.

Treacher Collins syndrome is transmitted by an irregular dominant gene affecting the embryo during the second month. The facial appearances are typical and consist of an absent frontonasal angle, antimongoloid slant of the eyes with notching of the lower lids and some medial loss of eyelashes, hypoplasia of the mandible with a large mouth and abnormal hair on the cheeks. The pinnas lie lower than usual and may be normal or underdeveloped, while the external meati may be normal or stenosed. The ossicles are often fused and deformed and there may be cochlear abnormality, so that the hearing loss may be conductive, sensorineural or both.

Other syndromes resulting in deafness are less commonly found and include **Refsum's**, **Jervil–Lange Neilson's**, and the so-called **Leopard** syndrome. Reference should be made to paediatric textbooks for their clinical features.

Non-hereditary prenatal causes arise from maternal infections of viral origin occurring in the first trimester of pregnancy. The most frequent are **influenza, rubella, glandular fever** and **cytomegalovirus (CMV) infection**. Maternal **syphilis** is now a less frequent cause of congenital sensorineural deafness, and as such tends to be overlooked, but the increase of the disease in younger girls means that it should be borne in mind. **Drugs** taken by the pregnant mother may affect the hearing of her baby. Thalidomide was a supreme example, but streptomycin, quinine, salicylates and alcohol may give rise to sensorineural deafness of varying severity.

Perinatal causes. **Haemolytic disease of the newborn** (hyperbilirubinaemia) has fortunately become increasingly uncommon, but the problems of **prematurity** and **anoxia** are assuming greater significance. The cochlea is a particularly sensitive organ, and any period of anoxia will result in damage to the cochlear nuclei producing a dramatic loss in hearing frequencies above 1000 c/s (1 kHz).

Postnatal causes. **Head injury**, especially if it involves the petrous bone, may cause either conductive or sensorineural deafness. **Ototoxic drugs** such as streptomycin, dihydrostreptomycin, kanamycin, bacitracin, neomycin, gentamicin and quinine affect the cochlea. **Loud noise**, such as gunfire or prolonged exposure to the noisy music of discotheques, may give rise to hearing loss. The modern habit of wearing 'walkman' radio sets presents a potential hazard. Of the infections, **measles** is usually associated with conductive deafness from middle-ear involvement, but it has been known to cause a sensorineural deafness. Meningitis, either meningococcal or pneumococcal, may result in severe perceptive deafness, while tuberculous meningitis produces considerable deafness from a direct invasion of the cochlea or the VIIIth nerve.

INVESTIGATION. Most health authorities maintain an 'at risk' register of families in whom possible prenatal and perinatal causes exist, such as deaf parents, consanguinity, previous miscarriages, previous deaf children, maternal virus illnesses, premature births, neonatal anoxia, jaundice, etc. In this way such babies are earmarked for special screening, usually by a health visitor in the first instance, with regard to deafness during the first 6 months of life. These are simple tests— the quiet sounding of a rattle, the rustling of paper, the chink of a spoon in a cup, and the quiet human voice—all of them being carried out in the home but beyond the baby's vision so that he is not alerted. A high degree of training in such tests is required of the health visitor, and on her report, usually after a second test in case the first has been a false reading due to an upper respiratory tract infection, the baby is further tested at a clinic. The normal responses of a hearing baby to such tests are: 2–3 months, the 'startle' reflex of 'freezing', blinking or frowning; 5 months, the eyes turn towards the sound; 6–7 months, the head turns to locate the sound.

As has already been stated, 'at risk' registers will only identify about 50 per cent of the deaf children. General practitioners in the UK now run well-baby clinics and health visitors are trained in the skills of distraction audiometry. It is hoped, therefore, that if distraction audiometry is routinely carried out at these clinics at the age of 6–7 months, the deaf children who may have been missed will be successfully identified.

From a practical point of view it is therefore not really possible to glean accurate information on routine screening and testing of infants much before the age of 6 months. However, it is thought that the inner language develops from approximately the third to the sixth month, and that receptive speech begins from the eighth month. Therefore if a baby has a significant sensorineural hearing loss requiring a hearing aid the diagnosis should be made before the eighth month if at all possible. Full testing of an infant's hearing is not an easy task, and it should be carried out by a team experienced in this field.

Prior to any actual testing taking place a detailed family history must be obtained, the details of the mother's pregnancy must be carefully noted, and a full history taken of the perinatal and postnatal occurrences. A general paediatric examination, including a neurological investigation, is undertaken, and the otologist must examine the ears, nose and throat. Once these have been completed hearing tests should be carried out in a sound-proofed room by a technician with an assistant who is good with children. The child must be mentally able and willing to cooperate, and if conditioned techniques are to be used the child must be able to be conditioned. Other children and distractions should be avoided. The techniques available are:

Distraction techniques. As has already been stated, from the age of about 6–7 months a normal baby will search for the source of a sound by turning his head towards the noise, and hence meaningful sounds are used. A fairly accurate assessment can thus be made of the child's hearing thresholds at a variety of frequencies. As the child grows beyond the age of 1 year various voice distraction tests may be used, and again a fairly accurate assessment of hearing thresholds may be established by a competent technician.

Conditioning techniques. After about 2·5 years the child can be taught to make some simple movement, e.g. building up bricks or some other progressive toy, in response to sounds to which it is known that he responds. First, he is allowed to see the sound source, which could be a xylophone being struck or a free-field audiometer. Once he appears to understand the game the sounds are made out of his sight, and his responses to a variety of sounds at different thresholds can be noted. When the child has been thus conditioned an accurate assessment of hearing loss becomes possible, and actual audiograms can be prepared.

Pure-tone audiometry. The age at which a child can be subjected to pure-tone audiometry varies according to the nature of the child and the skill and patience of those testing him. Most children between the ages of 4 and 5 years can be persuaded to cooperate so that a pure-tone audiogram may be obtained.

Impedance audiometry. This can be used in most children, but it is not a particularly helpful technique in the diagnosis of sensorineural hearing loss. It is, however, extremely useful for identifying any superimposed middle-ear condition, and thus it should be included routinely in the assessment of any child suspected of having significant sensorineural deafness.

Electric response audiometry. This is now being increasingly used in threshold measurements in infants and young children. It is indicated if there is difficulty or uncertainty using conventional distraction techniques; if there is a likelihood of hearing disability, e.g. child of deaf parents or maternal rubella; if the child is too young for conventional testing and there are doubts as to its hearing ability.

The technique involves presenting the child with sound stimuli. Surface electrodes then detect the electrical activity in the cochlea or brain in response to the sound and after passing this through an averaging computer, the response is displayed on a screen (*Fig.* 4.8.3).

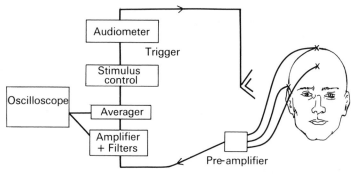

Fig. 4.8.3.   Basic ERA set-up. The sound stimuli generated by the audiometer in response to a trigger stimulus from the control are relayed to a loudspeaker or headphones. Surface electrodes, or transtympanic electrodes in electrocochleography, then detect changes in potential and these are amplified and pass to the averager where the summated potentials are displayed on the oscilloscope.

Cortical evoked response audiometry. This test, also known as the slow vertex response, was first developed in the 1960s and detects the response at the vertex. It has proven to be unreliable in young children because of the length of time it takes and the fact that it is affected by sleep, anaesthetics and sedatives. It has been supplanted by the other techniques.

Brainstem evoked response audiometry. This is now widely used to estimate hearing thresholds in infants. In a neonate it can be performed while the child is sleeping, or after a feed. Once the infant is 2 or 3 months old it may need sedating and trimeprazine syrup, or chlorpromazine may be used. Some centres prefer to give general anaesthesia but in many cases this can be avoided. Surface electrodes are applied to the mastoid, vertex and forehead and the auditory stimulation is by 2000 or 4000 broad-band click or tone bursts. The response is recorded and the intensity reduced until the N5 wave disappears (*Fig.* 4.8.4).

Electrocochleography. In electrocochleography an insulated needle electrode is inserted through the tympanic membrane to lie on the promontory. Again a series of clicks or tone bursts are used. The number varies with the size of the response

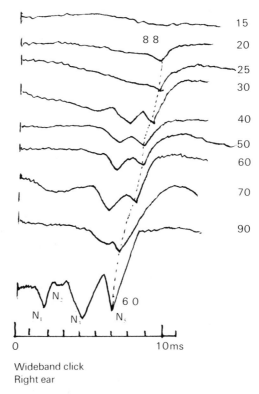

Fig. 4.8.4.   Brainstem responses in a child. A series of clicks at 90 dB intensity give a normal series of negative peaks (N_1–N_5). The intensity of the sound stimulus is then gradually reduced and all the peaks, except N_5, disappear. Eventually, at 15 dB, the N_5 peak is no longer visible and this would suggest the hearing threshold in that ear to be 20 dB or better.

from 64 to 512 or more. The threshold is estimated by identifying the action potential (AP) and reducing the intensity of the auditory stimuli until the AP is no longer seen.

Electrocochleography is a very accurate method of estimating hearing threshold and can get to within 5 or 10 dB of the psychoacoustic threshold, but in children requires a general anaesthetic. Brainstem audiometry is slightly less accurate but will estimate to within 15 dB of threshold and should be considered first. Bellman et al. (1984), reviewing their experience of both techniques, suggest that both, if possible, should be available and found both reliable.

Auditory response cradles. These are now being evaluated as a method for screening the hearing of neonates. The infant is placed in the cradle and subjected to sound stimuli of 80 dB. The response of the child to the sound is monitored by sensors which detect cardiovascular changes, respiratory changes and movements and are fed to an inbuilt computer which will 'pass' or 'fail' the child. If two fails occur under good conditions brainstem audiometry is then carried out. Initial experience by Bennet et al. (1980) suggests this to be an effective way of screening neonates.

Speech development. Although significant hearing loss should ideally be diagnosed before the age of 1 year, in reality the diagnosis is often missed, and suspicions may not be raised until it becomes obvious that speech development is delayed. It is impossible to generalize, but the following landmarks of normal speech development are worth noting:

1 year	—	2–3 words with meaning
18 months	—	20 words with meaning
21–24 months	—	beginning to string words together
2·5 years	—	250 words.

There are many causes of delayed speech development, but if a child has no words with meaning by 18 months, and no sentences by 30 months, it is vital that deafness be excluded before further opinions are sought.

MANAGEMENT. When a child is diagnosed as having a significant sensorineural hearing loss in both ears, the child, the parents and all associated with the education of the child will require continued guidance and help from people throughout the child's life. As yet there is no surgical management of this condition, and so all efforts must be channelled towards amplification of sound so that it may be heard by the child (*Fig.* 4.8.5) and towards giving continued support to the parents and teachers. Such support comes from a panel which should include an otologist, a paediatrician, a visiting teacher of the deaf, an educational psychologist and a speech therapist. This team should maintain close contact with the child's general practitioner and the community health service, under whose control educational provisions are made.

Once the child is old enough for a reliable assessment of hearing to be made, and with expert help this may be as early as 8 months, hearing aids will have to be fitted to match the hearing loss. The age at which this may be accomplished varies with the infant, the skill of the examiners and the cooperation of the parents. The examiners may be audiometricians or teachers of the deaf, many of whom have

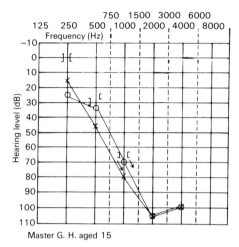

Master G. H. aged 15

Fig. 4.8.5. Audiogram of an early diagnosed rubella deafness who is managing well at a normal school with two postaural high frequency-type commercial hearing aids. He has good speech.

undergone audiological training and are competent to give such information in quite young children. Parental cooperation is often difficult to achieve, because confirmation of deafness in a baby proves to be a highly emotional shock to the parents, many of whom refuse to accept the diagnosis.

The design of hearing aids has advanced at a considerable rate in the past few years and the greatest advances have been, first, the development of radio aids and, secondly, the miniaturization of aids so that in-the-ear aids are now replacing postaural aids. The radio aids, in which the mother or teacher wears a microphone transmitter and the child wears the receiver/hearing aid, have revolutionized the quality and clarity and amplitude of sound supplied to the child. These can be used as ordinary aids or switched to direct contact between microphone and receiver so that much more significant auditory input can be received. The major advantage of this system is in the child's education, as it now means that he or she can attend the local school (or university) and merely hand the microphone to the teacher at the commencement of a class. Some children are quite content to drift along in their original school placement while others, with the help of a radio aid, have the potential and urge to learn more (*Fig.* 4.8.6). These children are, of course, the ones who pick up lip reading and quickly learn to communicate.

The in-the-ear or module-type aids are of particular benefit to the less severely deaf. They are adjusted individually to amplify only those frequencies that are defective. They fit into the ear, and hence are neat, and make use of the sound-collecting functions of the pinna.

From this it will be apparent that merely to issue a child with hearing aids and dismiss him from the clinic can never succeed. Continued care and advice on a regular basis from the visiting teacher of the deaf and the educational psychologist are vital to the education of both the child and the parents.

Although it has not always been the case, it is now felt that binaural hearing

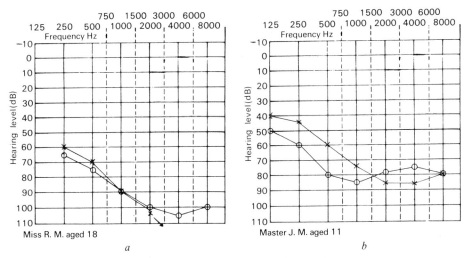

Fig. 4.8.6.   Audiograms to show the benefit of an early diagnosis and management.

a, This girl had a profound congenital deafness which was diagnosed early. There was no recordable bone conduction. She was educated at a normal school initially wearing a body-worn aid, then a radio aid with the occasional use of two powerful postaural commercial aids. She has good speech and has obtained university entrance qualifications.

b, This boy, with a similar deafness, was not diagnosed until late and attended initially a school for the profoundly deaf. He is now at a school for the partially deaf and wears a radio aid. His speech is poor and his progress is slow.

offers the maximum advantage to any deaf child, and it is now the practice to issue all bilaterally deaf children with a hearing aid for each ear at as early an age as possible. As the child grows up the ear moulds will require to be changed constantly to fit the enlarging external meati. Further, as speech and response to speech develop, increasingly detailed assessments of the child's hearing capabilities can be made, and the most appropriate hearing aid for the hearing loss can be supplied. As technology develops, increasingly sophisticated ear-level hearing aids are being produced and so most deaf children will soon be able to be issued with ear-level aids before they attend any form of primary education.

Some children with a mixed type of deafness of some 35–45 dB loss over the range of hearing may manage well enough in a primary school with favourable positioning in class, an understanding primary teacher and constant help from a visiting teacher of the deaf. The problem arises with these children when they are transferred to a secondary school with different teachers for each subject, and when foreign languages are taught. Unless the child has a real desire and ability to learn, is helped by the visiting teacher of the deaf, and possibly encouraged to wear hearing aids for the first time, he may be in considerable difficulty (*Fig.* 4.8.7). Not the least of his problems is what he may consider to be the stigma of being fitted with an aid for the first time at the age of 12 years.

It must be the aim of all those associated with the education of the deaf child constantly to encourage him to utilize whatever level of hearing he has towards the development of speech. Further, it is their duty, when the child is nearing school-leaving age, to guide the child in the choice of a job most suited to the individual handicap. Only in this way can the deaf child be helped to integrate with the

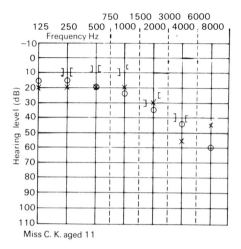

Fig. 4.8.7. Audiogram of a girl who was struggling at school, but whose school work improved dramatically after she was fitted with two vented intra-aural hearing aids with low-frequency cut.

hearing community, and although at present this appears to be less than satisfactory it is hoped that in time the problems of the severely deaf may be greatly ameliorated.

The problems of the multiple-handicapped child are much more serious. The combination of severe hearing loss with defective vision, physical impairment or mental retardation presents enormous problems of schooling, and the environment chosen must be that which is best suited to the principal handicap, whatever the hearing level.

UNILATERAL DEAFNESS

Unilateral severe deafness may occur in a number of the syndromes discussed, and **mumps** tends to give a unilateral deafness rather than a bilateral one. Provided that the hearing in the other ear is normal there is no impairment of speech or of hearing during normal conversation with the child. The totally deaf ear may pass unrecognized until the healthy one becomes damaged by otitis media or middle-ear secretion, when the observant mother may become aware that the child is more deaf than would appear likely from an acute otitis media in one ear. Further, the free-field sweep testing of children commonly used early in school life will not show up a unilateral deafness because both ears are tested together. Such children may not be recognized for years until they complain, possibly casually, that they cannot hear in one ear. On other occasions the child may be seen in practice with an acute otitis media, and is routinely tested for hearing loss. It is a simple matter on these occasions to test each ear with a Bárány noise box in the other, and children seem to enjoy this. With such a test a total deafness may be discovered unilaterally, and in these cases a search should be made for the cause, e.g. mumps, head injury, etc. A young child may show no emotion on learning that one ear is deaf, but an older child may become quite upset. The management of such a child in school is to inform the class teacher that the child must always be placed with the good ear towards the teacher. In the same way, the parents should ensure that a unilaterally deaf child sits with the deaf ear next to the wall and the good ear towards the room.

Chapter 4.9

ACUTE OTITIS MEDIA
AND MASTOIDITIS

IN INFANCY

Acute otitis media may affect infants of any age, the highest incidence being 16–24 months. It is frequently not discovered until discharge occurs, and it is safe to assume that many cases are never suspected, but recover from the antibiotics prescribed for some undiagnosed pyrexial illness. There are many factors in the aetiology. The wide, horizontally placed Eustachian tube, which opens at a lower level in the infant's nasopharynx and middle-ear cavity than in those of the child or adult, may allow easy access of infection into the infantile tympanum, and it affords easy drainage of mucopus from the middle ear (*Fig.* 4.9.1). The infant has a poorly developed immunity to upper respiratory infections of virus origin or bacterial sequelae. The infant's lymphoid tissue in the pharynx and especially the nasopharynx is in a state of active growth and prone to infection. The middle-ear content of mesenchyme forms a medium for pathogens to multiply. Teething with its congestion of the gums and general upset may be associated with earache, not only a referred otalgia but also a middle-ear congestion from an infection spread via the Eustachian tube lymphatics. Otitis media is liable to recur in these children with further teething. The predominantly horizontal positon of the young baby allows stagnation of regurgitated milk or of vomit in the pharynx or nasopharynx which may infect the Eustachian tube. This was very noticeable about 30 years ago when epidemic gastroenteritis of a lethal type was associated with an infantile otomastoiditis. Home hygiene and parental ignorance play their part in the frequency of infantile otitis media.

The *symptoms* are those of a pyrexial upper respiratory tract infection associated with crying, disturbed nights, upset feeding habits and head rolling. In older infants the hand may be put to the affected ear or the head may be banged against the side of the cot. The first indication that the middle ear has become infected may be the appearance of a mucopurulent discharge. This is a late feature because of the thickness of the infant's tympanic membrane and when it occurs it may signify the acute necrotizing otitis media with a large perforation or an upper marginal involvement denoting destruction of bone. Such a perforation is more common in the debilitated infant, and frequently followed measles or scarlet fever before these were treated routinely by antibiotics.

422

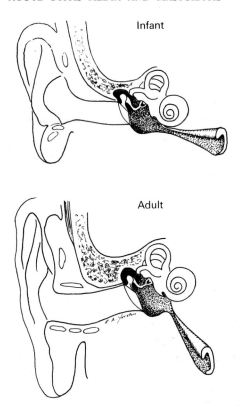

Fig. 4.9.1.   Showing that the infant Eustachian tube is shorter, relatively wider, and more horizontal than the adult.

BACTERIOLOGY. The common organisms, streptococcus, staphylococcus, *Haemophilus influenzae* and pneumococcus, are all responsible, and when discharge occurs it is important to a full resolution that sensitivity tests are carried out on a swab of the mucopus. A number of cases of otitis media are of virus origin.

CLINICAL FEATURES. These are not easily seen but must be sought in all infants presenting with pyrexia and screaming. If no sufficient cause is found in the chest or abdomen for such symptoms the ears should always be suspected. The younger the infant the more difficult it is to discover evidence of middle-ear disease. The tympanic membranes are not easy to inspect. The meatal walls are in apposition but may be separated by downward traction of the auricle. The meatus may contain epithelial debris which must be gently cleaned out with a fine wool-tipped wire probe. It often helps to moisten the wool so that the epithelium adheres to it and this facilitates removal. The baby's tympanic membrane appears to be a continuation of the upper meatal wall, and is placed obliquely, almost horizontally. It is a dull grey colour, opaque and showing no light reflex. Congestion is slow to appear although there may be peripheral flushing. The drumhead rarely appears angrily inflamed, a greyish-red or a dirty red colour being more usual.

Before perforation the drum may look yellow and there may appear a slight downward sagging instead of the usual bulging in the older child.

Radiography of the mastoids is unhelpful in infancy because pneumatization is limited and the middle-ear infection will reduce air entry into the mastoid antrum and small developing cells to give a hazy appearance which may be reported as an opacity.

TREATMENT. Antibiotics are used. If there is a discharge, little may be lost by waiting for sensitivity tests, and it is better to treat on the results of these than to prescribe haphazardly. When discharge occurs in the first known attack of otitis media in an infant it is a late feature, and accuracy in selecting the correct antibiotic is essential for a complete cure. Many of the chronic middle-ear infections stem from a random choice of antibiotics in the first attack.

In the majority of cases there is no discharge, so that the selection of an antibiotic is made on probability as far as the infecting organism is concerned. The choice lies between penicillin and ampicillin or amoxycillin. Many people prefer to give ampicillin or amoxycillin because of the sensitivity of *Haemophilus influenzae* to these antibiotics. In severe cases drugs should be given intramuscularly for 48 hours and then the drugs can be given orally for another 5 days, making 1 week in all. If there is no marked improvement after 48 hours and the child is still fretful, the eardrum is still flushed, feeding has not been restored and the nights are still disturbed, it must be assumed that the organisms are resistant to the antibiotic and another regimen must be started. Erythromycin, co-trimoxazole or a cephalosporin are all suitable alternatives. Whatever the antibiotic used, it is essential that a full course be given to obtain a complete resolution and it may be wise to admit the baby to hospital so that this can be achieved. Any discharge is treated by dry mopping with wisps of cotton-wool, preferably by a trained nurse. Persistence of pain, in spite of changed antibiotic therapy, or increasing pain, justifies myringotomy and it enables a swab of the pus to be obtained for sensitivity tests.

PROGNOSIS. Most cases recover completely. Some appear to recover but relapse quickly and continue to recur as soon as the antibiotic is discontinued. This is due either to incorrect antibiotic choice, insufficient dosage being given by the parents, or because the initial infection was due to a virus. These infants often carry a collection of sterile secretions in their middle ears between acute attacks and may be noted to be constantly rubbing their ears. Diagnosis can be confirmed by impedance audiometry and treatment is to carry out myringotomy and insertion of grommet tubes on a prophylactic basis.

IN CHILDHOOD

Acute otitis media has been shown in many surveys to be very common in childhood. The adequate control of the infection by antibiotics means that it is largely treated by the family doctor and that cases are referred to hospital only when such treatment has failed.

Acute Catarrhal Otitis Media

This is more often diagnosed in adults than in children, and it occurs following an upper respiratory tract infection when the Eustachian tube becomes blocked either from catarrh in its lumen or by oedema of its walls or both. The relatively wider lumen of the child's tube may block less easily but the main symptom, that of some hearing loss, is less often complained of by the child, and is not apparent to the mother unless she is watching for it, or unless the catarrh is bilateral. When it is found, there is a history of preceding head cold followed rapidly after the acute symptoms recede by some loss of hearing. There is, as a rule, no pain and no constitutional upset. The obstruction is due in many cases to hypertrophied adenoids which have enlarged with the nasopharyngeal congestion, but it may follow an antrochoanal polypus, descent in an aeroplane, diving or underwater swimming by a child with a congested nose.

CLINICAL FEATURES. The tympanic membrane is indrawn so that the short process of the malleus is thrust into prominence while the handle appears foreshortened. The light reflex is altered. In slight cases it appears to be split in two, one part at the tip of the handle of the malleus (the umbo) and the other at the periphery. Later it becomes narrow and elongated as drum retraction proceeds. As a rule the membrane is normal in colour but there may be a few dilated vessels running along the malleolar handle. If a faint pink colour appears in the membrane it suggests congestion of the mucosa of the middle-ear cavity, while a yellow colour of the drum denotes serous fluid in the tympanum. Hearing loss is conductive in type, and Rinne's test, to which children reply accurately as a rule, is negative.

TREATMENT. This aims to restore the patency of the Eustachian tube by politzerization but this should not be performed if there is mucopus in the nose or congestion of the nasal mucous membrane. In such an event simple decongestants are prescribed, and these may result in a spontaneous reopening of the Eustachian tube. As this takes place there is often a complaint of cracking or popping noises in the ears due to the sticky tubal walls separating and this often distresses the child. Should spontaneous cure not have occurred when the child is re-examined in a week, politzerization should be performed. The mechanism is explained to the child who is shown what is expected of him so that the manoeuvre should be successful at the first attempt. In particular he is warned that his ears will 'pop' and that immediately after this voices will sound very loud, but that this will quickly settle to normal. If politzerization is properly conducted it should not have to be repeated. Eustachian catheterization is frightening to a child and painful. It may be done under anaesthetic but it is often more appropriate in persistent cases to carry out a myringotomy.

Recurring attacks of catarrhal otitis media with succeeding head colds, or a persisting slight hearing loss with indrawn eardrums, will call for removal of adenoids or treatment of an allergic rhinitis if the lateral radiograph of the nasopharynx shows no enlargement of the adenoids.

Acute Suppurative Otitis Media

Provided that the tympanic membrane is intact the middle-ear cavity can only be infected by the bloodstream, which is exceedingly rare, or via the Eustachian tube. The Eustachian tube is infected principally from the adenoids, especially the lymphoid tissue adjacent to the cushion of its pharyngeal opening, but any inflammation of the nasopharynx may infect the tube. Adenoids may be infected alone, but more commonly in association with or immediately following infection of the tonsils, the nasal cavity or the nasal sinuses. It thus follows that acute otitis media is a sequel to acute tonsillitis, acute coryza, some of the infectious fevers, especially measles and scarlet fever, and acute sinusitis. Infection may be forced into the Eustachian tubes of a child with an upper respiratory tract infection or with mucopus in the nose if he dives or swims under water. The development of an aerotitis is likely during descent if the child has nasal catarrh which has not been blown clear. If the tympanic membrane is perforated an acute otitis media may follow any of the conditions mentioned, but in addition infected material may be carried direct into the tympanum through the perforation, and swimming or washing the hair may produce an attack.

From the *bacteriological* standpoint the most common pathogens are the haemolytic streptoccus, *Staphylococcus pyogenes, H. influenzae* and the pneumococcus, while adenovirus or rhinovirus infections of the middle ear are not uncommon, and may be an initial stage to be followed by the pathogens. It is only possible to determine the organism with certainty if aural discharge has occurred, and in this event it should be routine practice to take a swab for sensitivity tests.

The principal symptom is pain, sudden and severe, which may waken the child screaming and crying at night. There will usually be a history of a preceding upper respiratory tract infection, but this is not invariable. Unless the condition is bilateral or unless there is defective hearing in the other ear deafness may not be noted by the parents. The child is ill, flushed and pyrexial and his pulse is rapid. If the drumhead has ruptured, or if there has been a previous attack resulting in an unhealed drum there will be a discharge of mucopus which may be profuse. The sudden appearance of discharge is associated with relief from pain.

CLINICAL EXAMINATION. The difficulties experienced in assessing an infant's drumhead have been mentioned. There are fewer problems with children because the development of the osseous meatus results in the tympanic membrane assuming a position close to that found in adult life. It is extremely uncommon to find wax obscuring the acutely inflamed drum, but there may be desquamated epithelium in the meatus or adhering in a patchy fashion to the membrane. The phases of acute otitis media give typical drum changes. In the earliest stage there may be slight indrawing of the membrane which is normal in colour except for dilated blood vessels along the handle of the malleus. Dilated vessels appear peripherally and run across the drumhead to the malleolar handle so that there are radiating engorged vessels. The surface of the membrane, which has been grey or pink, becomes red and shortly this redness covers the whole surface of the drum so that individual vessels are not recognizable to the naked eye. The light reflex disappears at this stage because the drum begins to bulge outwards into the meatus. This is due to the middle-ear cavity being filled with mucopus which cannot escape either into the Eustachian tube or the mastoid antrum, and as the other walls are osseous, tension causes the tympanic membrane to bulge. It is this tension which gives rise to the pain.

There may be mastoid tenderness in an acute otitis media because, with the continuity of mucosa from the tympanum through the aditus to the mastoid antrum and mastoid cells, spread of inflammation occurs. A child with severe earache will not welcome the palpating finger or thumb, especially if it is thrust on to the mastoid process with the question, 'Is that sore?'. Palpation should be carried out very gently with the examiner standing behind the child and the forefinger of each hand palpating the tip of the mastoid, the surface and finally the region of the mastoid antrum where tenderness may be expected.

Radiography of the mastoids may show haziness of the cells due partly to lack of air entry and partly to mucosal congestion, and these findings do not imply mastoiditis unless there is intercellular breakdown.

Hearing tests will show a conductive hearing loss of moderate severity. Rinne's test will be negative, and although children usually respond well to this test they may resent the application of the tuning fork to the affected mastoid process.

DIFFERENTIAL DIAGNOSIS. This is to be made from other causes of earache (*Fig.* 4.9.2). Furuncle of the external meatus gives pain located to the front of the

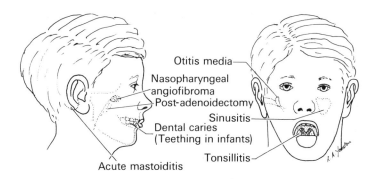

Otitis media
Nasopharyngeal angiofibroma
Post-adenoidectomy
Sinusitis
Dental caries (Teething in infants)
Tonsillitis
Acute mastoiditis

Fig. 4.9.2. Causes of otalgia in childhood.

ear and aggravated by chewing or by lying on that side. There is tenderness on pulling the auricle and on pressure over the tragus, while spread to the glands will cause them to be tender on pressure. The posterior auricular gland lies close to the mastoid tip but careful palpation over the mastoid process will locate the area of maximum tenderness. In a furuncle there is no mucus in the discharge from the ear, and hearing is normal or only slightly reduced by the swelling of the boil which is usually easily seen at the meatal entrance. Referred pain from a carious tooth is common in children, and less often a referred pain may arise in the temporomandibular joint and is associated with some loss of side-to-side mobility of the mandible when the jaw is open. Earache is sometimes complained of in older girls, in the 11–12-year bracket, when no cause can be found clinically or radiologically. In all these referred otalgia cases the tympanic membranes are normal, thus excluding a local cause. Should dental inspection and radiography of the teeth, sinuses, nasopharynx and mastoid be negative there is usually some psychosomatic cause.

TREATMENT. This varies with the severity of the pain, and in mild cases no treatment may be required apart from analgesics at night. Many cases need no more than this, and the universal prescription of antibiotics may create more problems than it solves because recovery from pain in a mild attack is so rapid that the mother tends to stop treatment before completion of the course. This leads to recurrences and to antibiotic resistance. In more severe attacks antibiotics are necessary, but the correct selection of the drug is not easy if the drumhead is intact. As a general rule, amoxycillin or ampicillin should be given intramuscularly if necessary and the situation reassessed at 48 hours. If normal resolution is taking place, the drug should be continued orally for another 5 days. If not, a switch should be made to erythromycin, co-trimoxazole or penicillin and the drug used for 5 to 7 days.

Treatment of an acute otitis media with discharge is much more accurate because a swab should be taken routinely and sent for culture and sensitivity. Until the results are available, ampicillin is given orally and is continued for 7–10 days if the organisms are sensitive. If the pathogens are resistant to ampicillin, the appropriate antibiotics should be given for at least 7 days.

Nasal decongestant drops of 0·5–1 per cent ephedrine hydrochloride may be given if the nose is stuffy or catarrhal. The diet should be appetizing, and attention should be given to a plentiful fluid intake.

PROGNOSIS. A complete recovery is to be expected with proper treatment. Pain disappears, temperature settles, the tympanic membrane reverts to a normal colour, any perforation heals and hearing returns to normal.

Recurrences are common and, just as babies may have an otitis media with the eruption of each tooth, so children may have an acute middle-ear infection with each sore throat or cold. If there is a definite co-relationship between the ear infections and adenoiditis or adenotonsillitis, then surgical removal of these may be indicated. If, however, as often happens in young children there is no obvious precedent cause, then the frequency of ear infections may be reduced by myringotomies and insertion of grommets. An alternative approach, which should be considered especially if the otitis media appears seasonal (i.e. worse in the winter), is to administer a prophylactic antibiotic at half the standard dose over the period where the child is at risk. Antibiotics which have been used include sulphonamide.

ACUTE MASTOIDITIS

Acute mastoiditis, once an extremely common condition in infancy and childhood, is now infrequently seen because of the better treatment of acute otitis media. Such cases as occur have either been untreated or have been given incorrect or inadequate antibiotic therapy. The difficulty of diagnosing acute otitis media in infancy accounts for the fact that most cases of acute mastoiditis seen over the past 20 years have occurred in infants under the age of 2 years. Acute infection of the mastoid antrum and cells is probably present with each attack of acute otitis media by virtue of the mucosal continuity between the tympanum and the mastoid process, but as long as the aditus remains patent an acute mastoiditis does not develop. The factors which lead to an acute otitis media, therefore, are those which predispose to acute mastoiditis.

CLINICAL FEATURES. The classic symptoms of acute mastoiditis, earache followed by aural discharge with relief from pain, succeeded by cessation of discharge with recurrence of pain, do not necessarily obtain, especially in babies. In infancy and in young children mastoid infection may present, even with a subperiosteal abscess, without any aural discharge on account of the thickness of the drumhead which does not readily perforate. It follows that mastoiditis must be suspected in every case of acute otitis media in this age-group. Should the discharge lessen or cease with returning pain the diagnosis is certain. The retroauricular swelling (*Fig.* 4.9.3) is often the first indication that the parents or the practitioner can see to associate a fretful pyrexial baby with ear infection.

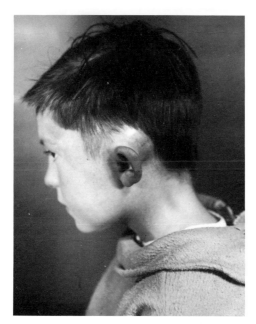

Fig. 4.9.3.   Acute mastoiditis with subperiosteal abscess.

The most satisfactory method of examining clinically for evidence of mastoid infection is to palpate from behind the child (*Fig.* 4.9.4). The fingers are fixed on the neck and both mastoid processes are gently palpated with the tips of the forefingers. In this way a comparison may be made between the two sides. Normally one can palpate the surface of the mastoid bone through the skin and recognize the supramastoid ridge and the depression over the mastoid antrum. It must be borne in mind that the mastoid antrum is much higher in infants, and relatively higher in children, than it is in adults. In the early stages of acute mastoiditis thickening of the periosteum dulls the surface palpatory sensation as if a sheet of rubber dam were interposed between the finger and the mastoid surface. When pus breaks through the surface to form a subperiosteal abscess the superficial skin becomes red and the abscess pushes the auricle downwards and forwards, because pus usually erupts from cells close to the antrum. Fluctuation develops and may be palpated.

Hearing tests show a conductive deafness if the child is old enough to cooperate. Radiography of the mastoids should not be required if clinical examination has been properly conducted, but if it is done opacity of the mastoid cells and possibly some breakdown will be seen.

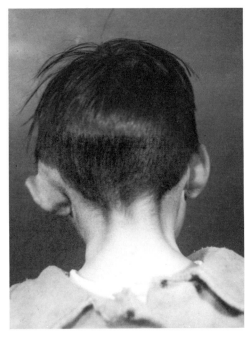

Fig. 4.9.4.   Acute mastoid abscess seen from behind.

DIFFERENTIAL DIAGNOSIS. This is to be made from a furuncle with extension to the posterior gland over the mastoid tip, and from an infected cyst in the same area. In both of these the inflammatory swelling is much lower than a subperiosteal abscess. A furuncle may be visible at the meatal entrance, the tragus is tender and there is pain on moving the auricle. An infected cyst has no origin in the middle ear and the tympanic membrane is normal.

TREATMENT. In acute mastoiditis in infants or children treatment should be by admission to hospital where, if there is aural discharge, a swab is taken and the appropriate antibiotic is given in full dose. Should there be no aural discharge penicillin is given intramuscularly in doses of 500 000 u twice daily for 48 hours whether there is an abscess or merely periosteal thickening. If the organisms are penicillin-sensitive the abscess will have decreased in size markedly or the periosteal thickening will have largely disappeared within 48 hours and tenderness will be less. In this event penicillin should be continued orally for a further week.

In those cases where the skin remains red over a fluctuating abscess, or where pyrexia and tenderness continue, the mastoid should be opened. Pus will appear either on the incision being made or on the mastoid cortex being opened, and this should be cultured. In infants much of the clearing out of cells may be accomplished with sharp spoons and the cavity is laid bare and the mastoid antrum opened before the incision is closed. In children a more formal cortical (Schwartze) operation is required, the cell galleries, including, very often, the zygomatic cells, being opened up. A drain may be inserted before closure. When sensitivity test results are available from the pus, a course of the appropriate antibiotic is given for a week.

The results in the uncomplicated case are usually excellent, hearing is restored and the tympanic membrane returns to normal.

Chapter 4.10

SECRETORY OTITIS MEDIA

This complex condition, which has been recognized for a century but which only began to assume its enormous frequency since about 1940, is also called non-suppurative otitis media, seromucinous otitis media, exudative otitis media or simply 'glue ear', which describes the consistency of the fluid in most cases but avoids any suggestion about its origin. There are those who would differentiate the condition depending upon the viscosity of the middle-ear fluid, reserving the name of serous otitis media for the more acute development of thin middle-ear fluid, often in association with barotrauma. On the other hand, a low-viscosity middle-ear fluid is frequently found in children unassociated with any pressure changes and, until there is universal agreement regarding the aetiology of middle-ear fluids, it is more convenient not to subdivide the condition.

Embryologically the middle-ear mucosa and that of the mastoid antrum and cells derive from the upper respiratory tract. Ciliated columnar epithelium is confined to the Eustachian tube, the part of the tympanum in the neighbourhood of the tubal orifice and the hypotympanum. Elsewhere in the tympanum ciliated cuboidal epithelium is found, while in the mastoid the lining is of flattened epithelium. Mucus-secreting goblet cells are to be found in the tympanum, and biopsy of the middle-ear mucosa of children with secretory otitis media shows hyperplasia of the mucus-secreting elements and infiltration into the mucosa of monocytes and lymphocytes. Electron microscopy shows an increase of the serum-secreting cells if the fluid is serous, but a decrease or absence of the elements and a degeneration of the ciliated epithelium when the fluid is mucous.

Cytologically the fluid contains polymorphonuclear leucocytes, macrophages and cell debris, but no ciliated columnar cells and no eosinophils are present.

Biochemically the viscid fluid contains glycoproteins and nucleoproteins, the former by virtue of its molecular weight accounting for the mechanical properties of mucus, but the protein-bound carbohydrate, showing as oligosaccharide side-chains, and the mucous strands which are present combine to produce the glue-like fluid. Protein is found in the greatest concentration in serous fluids, while deoxyribonucleic acid, present in high concentration in cell nuclei, is found especially in purulent fluid.

Recent work shows the presence of immunoglobulin-producing plasma cells (IgA, IgG and IgM) and macrophages in the Eustachian tube and middle-ear cavity in this condition, suggesting that the middle ear may be protected by an immunological defence system.

AETIOLOGY. In spite of considerable investigation over the past 15 years, the cause of secretory otitis media has not yet been determined. Sade was of the opinion that the viscous middle-ear effusion is of the same nature as true mucus and is largely composed of glycoprotein; and that the mucus-secreting cells produce this in excessive amount because of deficient ventilation of the tympanic cavity, probably due to an altered function of the muscles of the Eustachian tube. Palva and Raunio agreed that there was evidence that the middle-ear mucosa actively secretes many proteinic substances into the tympanum. There seems to be general agreement that the fluid is not a transudate which would result from a hydrostatic imbalance between vascular and extravascular compartments with normal permeability, and it may occur when the aero- and hydrodynamics of the middle ear are interfered with. A transudate is the probable explanation of the fluid in barotrauma.

Secretory otitis media reached its considerable proportions at a time when antibiotics were widely prescribed for all pyrexial illnesses, and this has prompted the theory that inadequate or incorrect antibiotic therapy might result in an incomplete resolution of an otitis media, or that the casual organisms were of low virulence. However attractive this theory may be it does not account for the frequency with which the fluid is found bilaterally in children, while bilateral acute otitis media is uncommon.

The repeated association of the disease with an upper respiratory tract infection, especially in the epidemics of parainfluenzal and respiratory syncytial viruses, has led to the vital theory of aetiology, but the persistently negative findings during searches for viruses in the middle-ear fluid has cast doubt on this. Similarly, the absence of eosinophils in the fluid has negated an allergic aetiology, however much the embryologically respiratory type of epithelium in the tympanum might suggest this possibility.

The similarity between secretory otitis media and the catarrhal deafness due to Eustachian obstruction inevitably leads to the Eustachian tube coming under suspicion from the aetiological viewpoint, and this is reinforced by the appearance of fluid in the tympanum of patients with a nasopharyngeal tumour. The fact that the great majority of cases of secretory otitis media are bilateral suggests a central cause rather than a unilateral one.

The condition is most commonly met within the 4–6-year age bracket, and almost exclusively in children under the age of 9 years, and this leads to enlarged adenoids being suspected. The difficulty of removing all the nasopharyngeal lymphoid tissue has been stressed, that part around the Eustachian tubal opening being the most difficult. But the main bulk is generally well removed so that hypertrophy of adenoids *per se* cannot be the principal cause. Maw (from Bristol), in what is probably the first reported, properly controlled, randomized clinical trial into adenoidectomy in secretory otitis media, shows with statistically significant figures that adenoidectomy has a significant therapeutic effect in approximately 40 per cent of children with secretory otitis media. Hibbert (from Liverpool) suggests in two separate papers that, although the actual volumetric size of the adenoids bears no relation to the presence or absence of secretions, the actual postnasal-space airway is smaller in children with secretory otitis media compared to age-matched controls.

To tie all these ideas together one must propound a theory that would agree with the frequency of a bilateral hearing loss, the cytological evidence suggesting an underlying infection, the sterility of the fluid, and, very frequently, the absence of pain. It is postulated that, owing to a dysfunction of the Eustachian tube, the fluid in the middle-ear cavity is not cleared by ciliary activity as it would be in a case of acute suppurative otitis media which one might expect to paralyse ciliary action.

Middle-ear fluid and conductive hearing loss are frequent in children with a cleft palate, and it has been quoted in percentages of up to 90 per cent of cases. It may well be that the exposure of the nasopharynx and the tubal openings due to the cleft leads to a chronic nasopharyngitis or to a chronic infection of the Eustachian tubes. With a cleft palate the insertions of the levator palati and tensor palati muscles are poorly anchored and thus the action of these muscles is less effective than in a normal child. Function improves after surgical repair of the palate, but Holborow suggested that the fracture of the hamulus during this repair, to release the tendon of the medial part of the tensor palati, or damage to the nerve supply during dissection, or postoperative scarring might interfere with muscular function controlling patency of the Eustachian tube. While these factors may obtain in children with cleft palate, the mechanism whereby tubal opening and function fails in the healthy child is less apparent.

Another group of children in whom middle-ear fluid is reported by many to be common is those suffering from mucoviscidosis, but other workers disagree with this view.

Each theory, therefore, can be refuted as failing to support the established clinical features of the condition, and at present the aetiology must remain unknown.

SYMPTOMS. The principal and often the only complaint is of hearing loss, and it may be discovered at any age from the infant who is slow to show evidence of hearing or talking, through the toddler stage in which speech defects point to a hearing loss, to the schoolchild whose oral work is poorer than his written work. The loss may be discovered accidentally at a routine school sweep hearing test. It may never be noted at home, especially such homes where there is a large family and a televison, radio or taperecorders blare all day so that the ambient noise level is such that everybody shouts. It may be missed by the school teacher who normally talks loudly in the classroom, but it is the exception that the teacher, especially in a primary class, does not suspect some hearing loss in a child. It is often suspected or recognized by the mother, who may continue to have suspicions for months or even years before taking any action. It may be taken for disobedience by the father or for inattention at school.

There is frequently no history of a precipitating cause of the deafness, so insidious is the onset, but there is usually a story of an upper respiratory tract infection before any recurrence of deafness in a child who has been successfully treated and whose parents are alert for any signs of hearing loss.

Pain is not a common symptom, but it does occur in a percentage of cases, often following a head cold. One may expect that any increase of middle-ear fluid due to outpouring of mucus or mucopus with upper respiratory tract infection will increase tension within the tympanum and so cause pain.

The history of frequent head colds, nasal stuffiness or catarrh, sore throats or nasal allergy is little different from that obtained in any group of children, and there are no specific features to suggest an aetiology.

CLINICAL FEATURES. Examination of the nose and pharynx of the child and radiology of the sinuses and nasopharynx may reveal nothing diagnostic, but may show the presence of adenoids and of catarrh in the nose. Inspection of the tympanic membranes and hearing tests, including audiometry, must be undertaken with care and accuracy for a diagnosis to be made.

The tympanic membrane may be occluded by wax, and if this cannot be removed in a conscious child with a hearing loss it should be removed under anaesthesia. In a proportion of cases evidence of middle-ear fluid will be obtained. Once the tympanic membrane is visible it should be examined with some form of magnification because the naked-eye examination will miss many of the drum changes. Many children are frightened by examination through a microscope, even if held in the hand and not wall-mounted, but will permit examination through an auriscope, and lenses giving $\times 3$ or $\times 6$ magnification are to be preferred to the standard $\times 2$ lens.

The colour of the tympanic membrane varies from normal grey to a red, but not the angry red of inflammation, rather a dull red colour. There may be dilated blood vessels on the surface of the membrane running along and parallel to the handle of the malleus or peripherally as a palisade especially from the meatal floor. The membrane may be amber-coloured or straw-coloured, suggesting a serous fluid in the middle-ear cavity, or slate or inky blue indicating that the fluid in the tympanum contains blood pigment. Against these colour changes the handle of the malleus stands out starkly white. The drumhead is rarely transparent if the fluid is highly viscid but air bubbles or a fluid level may occasionally be seen through the membrane if the fluid is serous. The contours of the tympanic membrane are altered. Indrawing of the drum is shown by a prominence of the short process of the malleus and a shortening of its handle. In many cases the drum is full rather than bulging, and this is often seen posteriorly, while if fullness occurs with retracted membrane it appears to be sagging on the lower part like a 'pot belly'. Many drums show retraction pockets, particularly in the attic region or in the posterior quadrant.

Occasionally small spots are seen on the drumhead, and have been likened to sago grains. In our experience it is more frequent to discover small pinkish or roseate spots, either single or arranged discretely in a coral necklace formation below the umbo. The nature of these is obscure and incision through such a spot at myringotomy is unrewarding except that they are contained within the membrane and appear vascular. They may be akin to the spot left after an influenzal myringitis heals, and we tend to regard them as evidence of a healed or healing virus infection of the tympanum.

The tympanic membrane should be examined with a pneumatic speculum when characteristically it will be found to lack normal mobility. The lining of the retraction may be withdrawn outwards on applying negative pressure unless it has become adherent to the underlying ossicles.

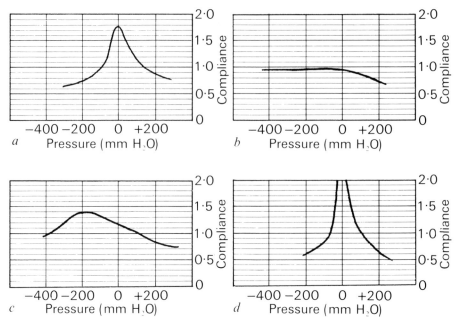

Fig. 4.10.1. Tympanograms.
a, Normal response.
b, Fluid in the middle ear.
c, Reduced middle ear pressure, due to Eustachian tube dysfunction.
d, Discontinuity of the ossicular chain, e.g. incudostapedial disarticulation.

Hearing tests should be carried out not only to determine the degree of hearing loss but also the type of deafness. Children respond confidently and on the whole accurately to Rinne's test, and in younger children the loudness of the response often matches the loudness of the sound which the child hears. In other words, the child will reply more loudly when the tuning fork is placed on the mastoid than when held at the meatal entrance. Pure-tone audiometry in the age-group in which this is feasible will show a conductive loss of at least 40 dB throughout the hearing range. Impedance tympanometry will show a flat 'tympanogram' which is typical of secretory otitis media (*Fig.* 4.10.1) and will differentiate this condition from Eustachian obstruction and otosclerosis.

Radiography of the mastoids may show no abnormality but it usually shows haziness of the mastoid cells on account of a lack of air entry. Once the condition has been established for some years, or in cases of recurring middle-ear fluid, there may be breakdown of the intercellular walls. If the mastoid process is acellular no erosion is seen.

TREATMENT. In the early case medical treatment has a part to play. In any series of cases a percentage of children diagnosed clinically as having secretory otitis media is found at operation to have dry middle ears. Therefore either the initial diagnosis was incorrect or the fluid has drained during the period of waiting for admission to hospital. It follows that medical treatment may help those whose deafness has lasted for a short time, say, 2 months, although this is an arbitrary figure. The only way in which this fluid can escape is along the Eustachian tube into the nasopharynx. If the fluid drains along the Eustachian tube the cilia of the middle-ear cavity and the tube must have recovered their function. It has been shown that antibiotics have no part to play in the treatment of secretory otitis media, indeed it has been shown that they cannot be recovered from the middle-ear fluid in secretory otitis media whereas they are recovered from the mucopus of a suppurative otitis media. There is as yet no specific drug available on the market which will cure the disease. Numerous trials have been carried out using both decongestant drugs or mucolytic agents and no statistical evidence exists to prove satisfactorily the efficacy of any oral medication in the treatment of this condition. It is probably a fact that in any given 2-month period, about 20 per cent of children with proved secretory otitis media will recover normal function and hearing spontaneously. The difficulty lies in identifying this group.

The treatment of the established case is myringotomy and aspiration of the fluid, performed under general anaesthesia and with the help of the operating microscope. Wax is first removed and the tympanic membrane inspected. Any debris or crusting lodged in a retraction pocket should be removed with care because the underlying drum is atrophic and may tear.

The incision for myringotomy may be made posteriorly or anteriorly or both. The double incision is recommended by some surgeons when the tenacious nature of the glue makes aspiration difficult, and a second incision allows air to enter the tympanic cavity and so prevents negative pressure from increasing the difficulty of aspiration.

Aspiration is continued until no more fluid can be obtained. If the fluid is serous this is rapidly evacuated, but if it is glue-like it is frequently observed that after the middle-ear fluid has been aspirated a further source of glue appears from the attic region posterior to the malleus. This must come from the mastoid antrum and adjacent mastoid cells, and it has been held up above the fold separating the attic from the tympanum until the suction applied in the middle ear withdraws it. There is considerable negative pressure behind this because there is no means of air getting distal to the glue, and if contact is broken between the suction tube and the glue it disappears rapidly into the attic.

The problems created by retraction pockets remain to be dealt with, the danger being that it is from these that cholesteatoma may develop. First, the exact site of the pocket is determined and with the aid of the suction tube it is discovered whether the epithelium of the pocket is adherent to the ossicles. This epithelium is thin because of the loss of the lamina propria, and when it is not adherent it may be sucked out into the meatus as a dry, crinkled inelastic protrusion. When it adheres to the ossicles underlying it, aspiration produces no withdrawal. The exact mechanism accounting for retraction is as yet imperfectly understood, but it follows continuing or recurring secretory otitis media and has been ascribed to prolonged intratympanic vacuum. This is hard to understand if the Eustachian tube remains patent, although, as has been stated, negative pressure is undoubtedly present distal to the glue-like secretion in the attic and mastoid antrum. The atrophic epithelium of the posterosuperior quadrant is invariably retracted upwards and posteriorly towards the aditus and, while this may point to negative pressure distal to the aditus exerting an influence on the pocket, it does not explain the primary lesion of the loss in this area of the drum of its lamina propria.

Treatment of the retraction pocket depends upon whether the lining is fixed or mobile. If mobile, a reventilation may occur either naturally or following the insertion of a grommet, but others suggest that the appropriate treatment is to excise the pocket, insert a grommet and remove the adenoids. Even if the posterosuperior quadrant does not heal after excision of the pouch a perforation in this area is much safer than the reformation of a pocket.

The question of whether or not to insert a grommet tube to ventilate the middle-ear cavity after routine myringotomy and aspiration is debated in the literature between those who do and the smaller number who do not. Some state that the mucosal secretion of many proteinic substances into the middle-ear cavity explains why myringotomy alone does not effect a cure. They add that this secretory capacity can only be stopped by the drying effect of air through a grommet starting a degeneration of the secretory epithelial cells and glands. There have been a number of comparative studies of hearing improvement with and without grommet insertion. Shah examined a series in whom a grommet had been inserted anteriorly in one ear and he found in the period between 6 weeks and 6 months postoperatively that 80 per cent of the ears with the grommet had normal hearing compared with 20 per cent of cases with no grommet. Richards in a similar test reported better hearing as long as the grommet remained in position, but after extrusion there was little difference to be made. They reported that all the grommets had been rejected 2 years after insertion, that there was no significant difference in hearing thresholds between ears, that fluid was still present in 30 per cent of the cases irrespective of whether a grommet had been inserted or not, and that the thin scars on the tympanic membranes were more frequent in the ears that had had grommets which suggested to them that grommets may inhibit healing.

If a grommet is inserted it may be placed posteriorly or anteriorly depending upon the preference of the surgeon. Those who place it anteriorly regard this as being more physiological because air normally enters the tympanum through an anterior orifice and it is in the anterior part of the tympanum that the secretory cells abound and have to be dried off. While the tube remains in place (from 2 months to 2 years and the period is longer with the anteriorly placed tube), care must be taken to avoid water entering the middle ear through the grommet. There have been some recent studies that suggest that, while swimming, water does not in fact reach the tympanic membrane due to eddy currents in the external meatus. It is my practice not to forbid swimming but to recommend the use of a commercial ear plug or a cotton-wool ear plug impregnated with petroleum jelly, kept in place by a cap. Care must also be taken at times of hair washing and having a bath. The grommet is either rejected spontaneously or may be removed, preferably under an anaesthetic because this is momentarily painful. Healing occurs more quickly after extrusion than after removal.

Opinion is divided as to whether a routine removal of adenoids should be performed. Bennett believed that removal of adenoids would cure 75 per cent of retraction pockets. Many surgeons routinely remove adenoids after myringotomy while others restrict removal to those children with a history of earache or with blocked noses and catarrh due entirely to adenoidal hypertrophy. Some postulate that there is a degree of adenoidal hypertrophy which is insufficient to cause obstruction but sufficient to maintain negative pressure around the orifice of the Eustachian tube with each inspiration. As has been stated already, Maw has produced convincing evidence that adenoidectomy plays a definite part in the treatment and that this is probably related as much to the size of the nasopharynx as to the size of the actual adenoids. It is by no means the case that adenoids are palpably enlarged in all cases of secretory otitis media. There is no doubt that adenoids are not solely to blame for the condition as some children who get recurrent secretory otitis media have no demonstrable adenoids.

RESULTS. The immediate result of treatment is a hearing improvement in every case. This lasts for a variable length of time depending upon how completely the fluid has been aspirated, because if there is still viscid fluid being produced or entering the tympanum from the mastoid antrum and cells, hearing loss will slowly recur. The insertion of a grommet will not avert this because if glue gets into the lumen of the grommet, it will solidify there, thus defeating the ventilating object of its insertion. In most cases there is a favourable report from the parents 4 weeks after surgery, and in these cases the eardrum has healed and looks normal while tuning-fork tests and audiometry show that hearing has been restored. If there has been a mobile retraction pocket reventilation may have occurred. Continued follow-up may show that this recovery is not maintained, and recurrences are found in 15–35 per cent. Even if allowance is made for the difficulty of aspirating all the viscid secretion, this is a disappointingly high figure. If these are true recurrences, and not merely the reappearance of fluid which has not been completely aspirated, doubt must be cast on the aetiological importance of adenoids, because most surgeons remove them routinely.

Recurrences are once again treated by myringotomy and at the second, or certainly at the third, myringotomy most surgeons will insert a grommet. Mawson reports that 35 per cent of cases require a second grommet and 11 per cent need a third. It is important, especially if retraction pockets are present, that recurrences are seen as soon as a hearing loss is suspected, and that they are treated energetically. Complete recovery can occur after recurrences and this is why each subsequent deterioration in hearing should be investigated and treated. The disease does appear to burn itself out by the age of puberty when, although the ravages of the drumhead may be seen, there is no middle-ear fluid.

The long-term results, as far as hearing is concerned, are reasonably good. Mawson and Fagan, who routinely inserted a grommet, reported 65 per cent with a hearing loss of less than 20 dB and 26 per cent with a 20–30 dB loss. Cowan and Brown, reporting on 456 cases in whom routine insertion of grommets was not performed, quote 73 per cent with a hearing loss under 10 dB and a further 11 per cent with a loss of 10–30 dB. They also reported on the appearance of the tympanic membrane 6–12 years following myringotomy, when their results were assessed, and found 62·5 per cent normal, 7 per cent with retraction pockets, 7 per cent with tympanosclerosis, 1·5 per cent with a perforation and 22 per cent showing atelectasis, atrophy or scarring. Mawson and Fagan reported 60 per cent abnormal membranes on follow-up, 30 per cent of which were due to tympanosclerosis.

Tympanosclerosis is seen much more frequently in children since secretory otitis media became prevalent, and it appears to occur more often if grommets are inserted. The figures of Cowan and Brown and Mawson and Fagan have been given. MacKinnon reported that tympanosclerosis occurred after myringotomy in 33 per cent of cases with grommets and in 8 per cent of those without grommets.

A percentage of cases defy treatment by repeated myringotomy and aspiration with or without grommet insertion, and they continue to show evidence of fluid in

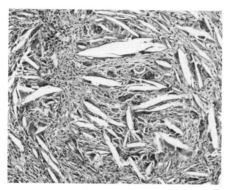

Fig. 4.10.2.   Cholesterol granuloma. (× 130.)
(By courtesy of the *Journal of Laryngology and Otology*.)

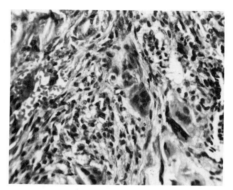

Fig. 4.10.3.   Cholesterol   granuloma   showing haemosiderin. (× 400.)
(By courtesy of the *Journal of Laryngology and Otology*.)

the middle ear, often rapidly after treatment. There may or may not be recurring earache. Radiography of the mastoids may show an acellular sclerotic process, but more frequently there is a cellular process with breakdown of the bony cell walls between the hazy cells. The proper treatment is to open the mastoid, when the cells will be found to contain a sticky greenish-brown or black secretion, and a reservoir of such necrotic material is found typically in the periantral cells and in those in the tip, although the whole process may be involved. Histology shows this to be cholesterol granuloma consisting of cholesterin spaces, foreign body giant cells (*Fig*. 4.10.2) and occasionally haemosiderin (*Fig*. 4.10.3). It has been found that in these cases dissection should be carried forward above the meatal roof to expose the short process of the incus because cholesteatoma may be present in the attic.

The other major complication of secretory otitis media is the development of cholesteatoma from the retraction pocket, and this is discussed on p. 286.

Haemotympanum

It has been stated that the tympanic membrane in a case of secretory otitis media may show a slate-blue or inky-blue colour denoting the presence of blood pigment in the middle-ear fluid. In the absence of any history of head injury which might cause bleeding into the tympanum, such a chance finding was formerly regarded as idiopathic. Haemotympanum was first described in 1927 and what was at one time thought to be an unusual condition became a much more common one when secretory otitis media was widespread. These blue drums are seen fairly often and if followed up the blue colour may, occasionally, be noted to move anteriorly through the tympanum as the secretion makes its way slowly to the Eustachian tube. More often it remains and myringotomy produces on aspiration a greenish-brown glue-like secretion. This may not be curative in spite of repeated myr-ingotomies and, on opening the mastoid, cells filled with greenish-black choles-terol granuloma will be found and should be exenterated before a cure can be obtained.

Adhesive Otitis Media

The persistence in the middle-ear cavity of glue-like fluid in an untreated case may result in the formation of adhesions which bind the tympanic membrane to the medial wall of the middle ear. They may also adhere to the ossicles, thus diminishing their function and causing conductive deafness. This may be the precursor of tympanosclerosis or it may coexist with this condition.

Tympanosclerosis

Tympanosclerosis may occur as a result of the middle-ear process which leads to secretory otitis media or as a consequence of treatment of that condition, or it may appear later in life without any previous history. It represents an imperfect healing process in response to inflammation. At its simplest, tympanosclerosis is represen-ted by what used to be called a 'chalk patch' on the drumhead or white plaques appearing on the surface of the tympanic membrane. They are due to hyaline degeneration of a collagenous type in which calcium is deposited to give a white colour. In children in whom the hyalinosis is confined largely to the tympanic membrane there will be a conductive deafness commensurate with the size of the plaque, but averaging some 30 dB loss. Small discrete plaques may leave hearing at the lower limit of normality and the membrane may remain mobile as tested with a pneumatic speculum. Larger thick plaques seriously hamper mobility of the drum, and may be so large and so thick as to appear solid on palpation with a probe. In cases with middle-ear fluid it may be impossible to incise through such a plaque.

The more serious type of tympanosclerosis occurs when the hyalinosis involves the tympanum, with the formation of dense adhesions between the drumhead and the ossicles or the medial tympanic wall—the chronic adhesive catarrh as de-scribed above. In addition, hyaline plaques may form and calcify in the tympanum to affect mobility and articulation of the ossicles. It does seem to be generally thought that tympanosclerosis is much more frequent in children since secretory otitis media became so widespread than it was when chronic otitis media was the commonest chronic aural condition in childhood. Mawson is of this opinion, and points out that any fluid lying undisturbed in a middle ear will undergo fibroblastic organization; this is true not only of glue but also of suppurative otitis media inadequately treated by antibiotics.

The association of grommet insertion and tympanosclerosis has been discussed and it seems likely that tympanosclerosis of the drumhead may be increased by grommets, but not necessarily middle-ear tympanosclerosis.

Treatment of tympanosclerosis depends upon the extent of the condition. Gibb describes an operation for the removal of a large plaque in the membrane with satisfactory healing and improvement in hearing to near-normal. Small plaques which do not diminish hearing require no treatment. Surgery to remove middle-ear extensions should only be undertaken if the patency of the Eustachian tube can be demonstrated. Ideally the ossicles should be remobilized and adhesions divided, but arthrodesis, especially of the incudomalleolar joint, may be such as to defy all manipulations. Some surgeons advocate extensive reconstruction to create an air-filled cavity. Siirala suggested that if the drumhead adheres to the ossicles and promontory, the membrane should be separated and a wide air space, including the tympanum, the mastoid antrum and mastoid air cells, be fashioned. In order to prevent recurrence of adhesions, he recommended α-chymotrypsin and corticosteroids postoperatively.

The chance of adhesions and arthrodeses reforming after surgery is considerable, and a hearing aid may have to be issued in this event, and in all cases with a blocked Eustachian tube.

Index

abscess(es)
  brain, 37, (*Figs.* 3.8.4–5) 311–15
  dental, maxillary sinusitis and, 42
  extradural, (*Fig.* 3.8.1) 304–5
  nasal, 24
  neck space, 104–8
  orbital, secondary to recurrent acute sinusitis, 36
  parapharyngeal, 199
  retropharyngeal, (*Fig.* 2.5.1) 104–5
  subdural, 37, 315–16
  subperiosteal, 297, (*Figs.* 4.9.3–4) 428–31
  of tonsils, (*Fig.* 2.3.1) 85–6
achalasia, (*Fig.* 2.4.6) 100
acid laryngitis, 157
acinic-cell tumour, 133
  treatment of, 140
acoustic nerve, anatomy of, 233
acoustic neuroma, 337, (*Figs.* 3.13.1–3) 339–44
  facial pain due to, 65
acquired immune deficiency syndrome (AIDS), 91
acquired meatal atresia, 264–5
acquired subglottic stenosis, 400–1
acquired syphilis, 59
acromegaly, 71, 72
actinomycosis
  of larynx, 163
  of neck, 198
acute miliary tuberculosis, pharyngeal, 92–3
acute otitis media
  in adults, 278–81
  in children, 422–8
acute pharyngitis, 89
acute sinusitis, in children, 375–6
acute tonsillitis, 84–5
adenocarcinoma
  of larynx, 169–70
  of salivary gland, 132
adenoid cystic carcinoma
  of larynx, 170
  oral, 121, 123

adenoid cystic carcinoma (*cont.*)
  of salivary gland, 131–2
  treatment of, 140
adenoids, (*Fig.* 4.1.2) 367–71
  when to remove, in secretory otitis media, 438–9
adenoma
  of parotid gland, 199
  of salivary gland, 130–1
ageing
  cosmetic facial surgery and, 69–70
  deafness due to, 324
  disequilibrium of, 333
agger nasi, 4
agranulocytosis, pharyngitis in, 91
AIDS, pharyngitis and, 91
alcohol, chronic pharyngitis and, 89
allergic reactions
  allergic laryngitis, acute, 161
  allergic rhinitis, 51–3
  nasal allergy in children, 373, 374, 375
allergy testing, 17–18
Alport's syndrome, 413
amitriptyline, in vasomotor rhinitis, 40
amyloid disease, of larynx, 167
anaemia, fissured tongue in, 128
anatomy
  of ear, (*Figs.* 3.1.1–15) 219–33
  of facial nerve, (*Fig.* 3.15.1) 354–6
  of hypopharynx, (*Figs.* 2.8.1–3) 116–18
  of larynx, (*Figs.* 2.12.1–8) 142–9
    developmental, (*Fig.* 4.3.1) 381–2
  of nose, (*Figs.* 1.1.1–7) 3–10
  of parapharyngeal space, (*Figs.* 2.5.2–3) 105
  of pharynx, (*Fig.* 2.1.1) 77–9
  of retropharyngeal space, (*Fig.* 2.5.1) 104
  of salivary glands, (*Fig.* 2.11.1) 129–30
  of submandibular space, 107
angiofibroma, of nasopharynx, 111–12
angiography
  carotid, 207
  in nasopharyngeal angiofibroma, 111

443

angioma, nasal, 57
angioneurotic oedema, 161
animal foreign bodies, in ear, 267, 346
animals, allergy to, 51
anosmia, in maxillary sinusitis, 43
antibiotic therapy
    in acute mastoiditis, 298–9, 430
    in acute otitis media, 281, 424
    in acute sinusitis, 35
    in chronic otitis media, 285
    in lateral sinus thrombosis, 308
    in meningitis, 311
    in vestibulitis, 40
antifungal agents, 61
    for pharyngeal infections, 91
antihistamines, oral, 52–3
antroscopy, (Figs. 1.2.4–5) 16
    in maxillary sinusitis, 43
antrostomy
    in children, 377
    intranasal, 35
    in maxillary sinusitis, (Figs. 1.7.1–2) 44–5
aphonia, 180–4
    functional, 184
aphthous ulcer, 125
apud tumour, of larynx, 170
arthritis, of cricoarytenoid joint, 164–5
arytenoidoplasty, 183–4
Asche's forceps, 23
aspergillosis, 61
atrophic rhinitis, 40–1
    following turbinectomy, 39
audiology, 246–56
    audiometric tests see audiometry
    in children, 414–17
    non-organic hearing loss, tests of, 255–6,
        328
    tuning-fork tests, (Fig. 3.3.1) 246–8, 255
    voice tests, 246
audiometry, 248–56
    Békésy, 252–3
    in children, 414–17
    disability assessment, in occupational deaf-
        ness, 351–2
    evoked response, (Fig. 3.3.7) 253–5, (Figs.
        4.8.3–4) 415–17
        in acoustic neuroma diagnosis, 341
        in children, 416
        in malingerer, 256
    impedance, (Figs. 3.3.4–5) 250–1, 415
    pure-tone, (Fig. 3.3.2) 248–9, 415
    speech, (Fig. 3.3.3) 250, 256
auricle
    anatomy of, (Fig. 3.1.1) 219–20
    carcinoma of, 212
    cutaneous innervation of, (Fig. 3.1.3) 221
    diseases of, 263–4
    embryology of, 409
autophony, 278–9

bacteriology
    of external meatus, 270
    of nose, 12
balance, physiology of, 235–6
balloon nasal packs, 32
barium contrast studies
    barium swallow
        in achalasia, (Fig. 2.4.6) 100
        in dysphagia, 103
        for hypopharyngeal tumour, 118, 119
        in pharyngeal disease, 82
        in pharyngeal pouch, (Fig. 2.4.4.) 96
    of neck masses, 207
barotraumatic otitis media, 349
bat ears, 68–9
Becker otoplasty operation, 69
Behçet's syndrome, 125
Békésy audiometry, 252–3
Bell's palsy, 356–9
betel nut chewing, buccal carcinoma due to, 123
Beverly–Douglas procedure, 385
Bezold's mastoiditis, 297
biopsy
    in pharyngeal disease, 83
    of salivary gland tumours, 137–8
birth trauma, septal deviation due to, 21, 22
blast injuries, to ear, 349–50
blastomycosis, 91
    of larynx, 163
    of neck, 198
blepharochalasis, 69
blepharoplasty, 69
Blom–Singer valve, 178, 179
blood disorders, pharyngitis in, 90–1
blood supply
    of eustachian tube, 227
    of external ear, 221
    of external nose, 4
    of internal ear, 233
    of larynx, 147
    of middle ear, 226
    of nasal septum, (Fig. 1.1.4) 6
    of tympanic membrane, 222
blow-out fracture of eye, (Fig. 1.3.6) 27
bouginage, oesophageal, 99, 100
brain abscess, 311–15
    cerebellar, (Fig. 3.8.5) 314–15
    temporal lobe, (Fig. 3.8.4) 313–14
brain tumours, vertigo due to, 338
brainstem audiogram, (Fig. 3.3.7) 254
brainstem evoked response audiometry, 254
    in acoustic neuroma diagnosis, 341
    in infants, 416
branchial anomalies, 404–5
branchiogenic carcinoma, 203
Branhamella catarrhalis, 280
breast carcinoma, trans-sphenoidal hypophy-
    sectomy and, 72
bronchoscopy, in children, (Figs. 4.4.2–3; Table
    4.4.1) 392–5

'brown' tumour, *versus* epulis, 127
brucellosis, 199
buccal carcinoma, 122–3
Burkitt's lymphoma, 405
burn(s)
    laryngeal, in children, 387
    oesophageal, corrosive, 98–9

cacosmia, in maxillary sinusitis, 43
café au lait spots, 198
calculus, of tonsil, 87
Caldwell–Luc operation, (*Fig.* 1.7.2) 45
caloric tests, (*Figs.* 3.3.8–10) 258–9
    Kobrak's test, 261
    using air, 261
cancer *see* carcinoma; tumours
Candida albicans, 61, 91
    median rhomboid glossitis and, 127
candidiasis, of larynx, 163
carcinoma,
    of auricle, 212
    of external auditory meatus, 212–13
    of hypopharynx, 116–20
    of larynx, 162, 169–70, 171–9
    of middle ear and mastoid, 213–14
    of nasal sinuses, 210–11
    of nasopharynx, 109–11
    of neck, 201–8
    of oral cavity, 121–4
    of oropharynx, 113–15
    of parotid glands, 199
    of thyroid, 198
'cardiospasm', 100
carotid body tumours, 200
CAT scans *see* CT scans
cat scratch disease, 198
    in children, 402–3
catarrh, 13
    catarrhal child, 372–80
'cauliflower ear', 263
cautery
    in epistaxis control, 30–1
    of turbinates, in chronic rhinitis, 38–9
cavernous sinus thrombosis, 24, 37
cerebellar abscess, (*Fig.* 3.8.5) 314–15
cerebellar artery thrombosis, vertigo in, 338
cerebellopontine angle tumours, (*Figs.* 3.13.1–3)
    339–44
cerebrospinal fluid rhinorrhoea, 28–9
cervical myalgia, 66
cervical neuralgia, 66
Chevallet, fracture of, (*Fig.* 1.3.1) 21
children
    audiometric tests in, 254–5
    endoscopy in, 392–5
    intubation and tracheostomy in, 396–9
    nasal examination in, 15–16
    removal of foreign body from ear, 346

children (*cont.*)
    removal of tracheostomy tube, 196, 197, 398–9
chin, cosmetic surgery on, 69
'Chinese' flap 122, 124
choanal atresia, congenital, (*Figs.* 4.2.3–4) 377–80
choanal polyp, 55
cholesteatoma, of middle ear, (*Fig.* 3.6.2) 286–8
chondroma, of cricoid, 200–1, 206
chondrosarcoma, of larynx, 170
chordoma, 112
chordopexy, 183–4
chromoglycate, sodium, 53
chronic rhinitis, 38–41
chronic sinusitis, 42–50
    in children, 376
cicatrix, on tympanic membrane, 242
cilia (nasal)
    immotile, 11
    mucociliary clearance test, 18
    structure of, (*Figs.* 1.1.8–9) 10–11
circumscribed serous meningitis, 311
cisternography, of acoustic neuroma, 343
cleft larynx, 384
cleft palate, 434
clinical examination
    of ear, (*Fig.* 3.2.1) 239–42
    of neck, 206–7
    of nose, 13–16
    in secretory otitis media, in children, 435
cocaine
    in cautery procedures, 30, 31
    in nasal examination, 14
cochlea, embryology of, 410
cochlear implants, 327–8
common cold, 34
    in children, 372
computerized axial tomography *see* CT scans
conductive deafness, 237
    congenital, 410–12
    otosclerotic, 317–21
    stapedectomy for, (*Figs.* 3.9.1–4) 318–21
congenital abnormalities
    of auricle, 263, (*Fig.* 4.8.2) 410–11
    causing conductive deafness, 410–12
    causing laryngeal stridor, 383–7
    of oesophagus, 102
congenital choanal atresia, (*Figs.* 4.2.3–4) 377–80
congenital cholesteatoma, 286
congenital epulis, 127
congenital haemangioma, of larynx, 387
congenital laryngeal paralysis, 386–7
congenital sialectasis, 134
congenital subglottic stenosis, 400
congenital syphilis, 58
congenital tumours, of nose and sinuses, 406–8
contact mucositis, of larynx, 161
Converse otoplasty operation, 69
cordopexy, 183–4

Corynebacterium diphtheriae, 88
corrosive burns, of oesophagus, 98–9
cortical evoked response audiometry, 255
  in malingerer, 256
cortical thrombophlebitis, 316
cortical venous thrombosis, 37
cosmetic facial surgery, 67–70
Cottle septoplasty, 25
Cottle's area, (*Fig.* 1.1.3) 6
cradles, auditory response, 417
craniopharyngioma, 112
cretinism, 413
cricoarytenoid muscles, anatomy of, (*Figs.* 2.12.4–5) 144–5
cricoid stenosis, 190
cricothyroid muscle, anatomy of, (*Fig.* 2.12.6) 146
'croup', 390
croupette, 391
CSF otorrhoea, following head injury, 347
CSF rhinorrhoea, 28–9
CT scans
  of acoustic neuroma, 342–3
  of brain abscess, 315
  in ear disease, 243
  in laryngeal disease, 153
  in nasal disease, 20
  in nasopharyngeal carcinoma, 110
  of neck masses, 208
  of nose and sinus tumours, 210–11
  in pharyngeal disease, 82
  of salivary gland tumours, 136
cupped ears, 69
Cushing's disease, 199
  pituitary, 71, 72
cystic hygroma, in children, 404
cyst(s)
  dental, 49
  of larynx, 168, 384
  of maxillary sinus, 48–9
  of neck, 198, 404–5
  oral, 127
  of tonsil, 87
cytomegalovirus infection, 199
  in children, 402

dandruff, 275
deafness
  in children, 409–21
  history of, 237
  in Ménière's disease, 334–7
  noise-induced, (*Fig.* 3.14.2) 350–2, 413
  sudden idiopathic, 325–6
  tests for suspected malingerer, 255–6, 328
  see also conductive deafness; sensorineural deafness
decongestants (nasal)
  in allergic rhinitis, 52

decongestants (nasal) (*cont.*)
  overuse of, 39
  in rhinosinusitis, 35, 36
  in vasomotor rhinitis, 40
dental abscesses, maxillary sinusitis and, 42
dental cysts, 49
dermabrasion, 70
dermatitis
  of auricle, (*Fig.* 3.4.7) 275–6
  of scalp, 275
dermoid cyst
  of neck, 404
  of nose, (*Fig.* 4.7.2) 408
dermoids, oral, 127
desensitization treatment, 53
deviated septum, (*Fig.* 1.3.2) 21–2
diabetes, 199
diagnostic proof puncture, 16
  in children, 377
diathermy, in chronic rhinitis, 39
diphtheria, 88
  laryngeal, in children, 389
diplacusis, 237
diplophonia, 158, 181
direct roof puncture, in maxillary sinusitis, 43
disseminated sclerosis, vertigo due to, 334
driving injuries, to ear, 349
Dohlman's operation, 97
drug-induced
  ototoxicity, 324–5, 413
  sensorineural deafness, prenatal, 413
  vertigo, 334
dry nose (rhinitis sicca), 41
Durham's tracheostomy tube, 193
dysphagia, 101–3
  due to pharyngeal disease, 80
  'dysphagia lusoria', (*Fig.* 4.3.6) 385
  following tracheostomy, 196–7
  management of, 101–3
  in oesophageal stricture, 99
  in Paterson–Brown Kelly syndrome 94, 95
  in pharyngeal pouch, 96
dysphonia plicae ventricularis, 158

ear
  anatomy of, (*Figs.* 3.1.1–15) 219–33
  cosmetic surgery on, 68–9
  disease, clinical investigation of, 237–45
  embryology of, (*Fig.* 4.8.1) 409–10
  external, diseases of, 263–77
  physiology of, 233–6
  trauma to, 345–52
  tumours of, 212–15
  see also conductive deafness; sensorineural deafness
ear drops, ototoxic, 325
earache *see* otalgia
eardrum *see* tympanic membrane

earmuffs, 351
electric larynx, 178
electric response audiometry *see* evoked response audiometry
electrocautery, 31
electrocochleography, 254
    in children, 416–17
electroneuronography, in Bell's palsy, (*Fig.* 3.15.2) 357–8
embryological cysts, of maxillary sinus, 48–9
embryology, of ear, (*Fig.* 4.8.1) 409–10
encephalocele, 407–8
endolymph, 232
    in balance physiology, 235–6
endoscopy
    bronchoscopy, in children, (*Figs.* 4.4.2–3; *Table* 4.4.1) 392–5
    laryngoscopy
        in children, 392, 395
        direct, 154
        fibreoptic, 154
        indirect, (*Figs.* 2.13.1–3) 151–2
        microlaryngoscopy, 154, 395
    in nasal examination, 15–16
epanutin, allergy to, 200
epiglottitis, in children, 389–90
epistaxis, 30–3
    due to angioma of the sinus, 57
Epstein–Barr virus
    in glandular fever, 90
    nasopharyngeal carcinoma and, 109
    in tonsils, 84
epulis 127
erythroplakia, oral, 126
ethmoid sinus
    anatomy of, 9–10
    carcinoma of, 210–11
    drainage of, 35
    radiography of, 18–20
    surgery to, 48
eustachian tube
    anatomy of, (*Fig.* 3.1.5) 227
        in infants, (*Fig.* 4.9.1) 422
    dysfunction, 278–80
        chronic, 282
    embryology of, 409
evoked response audiometry, (*Fig.* 3.3.7) 253–5, (*Figs.* 4.8.3–4) 415–17
    in acoustic neuroma diagnosis, 341
    in children, 416
    in malingerer, 256
examination *see* clinical examination
explosions, otological trauma due to, 349–50
external auditory meatus
    anatomy of, (*Fig.* 3.1.2) 220–1
    atresia of, 411–12
    diseases of, 264–77
    tumours of, (*Fig.* 3.4.4) 268–9
external ear
    anatomy of, (*Figs.* 3.1.1–3) 219–21

external ear (*cont.*)
    diseases of, 263–77
    embryology of, 409
    physiology of, 233–4
extradural abscess, (*Fig.* 3.8.1) 304–5
    secondary to frontal sinusitis, 37
eye involvement *see* ocular involvement

face-lift operation, 69–70
facial fibrous dysplasia, 58
facial nerve, 353–60
    anatomy of, 130, (*Fig.* 3.15.1) 354–6
        in middle ear, 226
    Bell's palsy, 356–9
facial neuroma, 359–60
facial pain, 64–6
    in adenoid cystic carcinoma, 135
facial paralysis, following parotidectomy, 139–40, 141
facial surgery, cosmetic, 67–70
facial trauma, 21–9
    blow-out fracture, (*Fig.* 1.3.6) 27
    frontal sinus fracture, 26
    frontoethmoid fracture, 26
    Le Fort fractures, (*Fig.* 1.3.8) 28
    zygomatic fracture, (*Fig.* 1.3.7) 27
fibreoptic laryngoscopy, 154
fibroangioma, of nasal septum, 57
fibrolipoma, hypopharyngeal, 118
fibroma, nasal, 57
fibrosarcoma, laryngeal, 170
fibrous dysplasia, facial, 58
fissured tongue, 128
fistula
    oroantral, 49–50
    perilymph, 338
    test, 261–2
food, allergy to, 52
Fordyce's granules (oral), 126
foreign bodies
    in ear, 267, 345–6
    in larynx, of children, 387
    nasal, 62–3
Fowler's loudness balance test, 252
fracture(s)
    facial, (*Figs.* 1.3.6–8) 26–8
    nasal, (*Fig.* 1.3.1,3) 21–5
    septal, (*Fig.* 1.3.1) 21–2
    temporal bone, 346–7
Frey's syndrome, 141
fontal sinus
    anatomy of, 9
    chronic sinusitis of, (*Figs.* 1.7.3–4) 45–8
    drainage of, 35
    fracture of, 26
frontoethmoid fracture, 26
fungal infection
    of external auditory meatus, 274–5

fungal infection (*cont.*)
 of larynx, 162–3
 nasal, 61
 of neck, 198
 pharyngeal, 91
fungi, allergy to, 51
furunculosis, of external meatus, 271–3

geographic tongue, 127
gigantism, 71, 72
gingivitis, ulcerative, 87–8
glandular fever (infectious mononucleosis), 90–1, 199
 in children, 402
 versus acute tonsillitis, 85
glioma, nasal, 406–7
globus syndrome, 97–8
 versus hypopharyngeal tumour, 118
glomus tumours, 214–15
glomus vagale, 200
glossectomy, 123
glossitis, median rhomboid, 127
glossopharyngeal neuralgia, 64, 244
glottis
 anatomy and physiology of, 148–9
 cancer of, 175
 stenosis of, 190
'glue ear' *see* secretory otitis media
goitre, 198
gout, 199
Gradenigo's syndrome, 301
granular-cell tumour, oral, 126–7
granuloma
 of larynx, 169
 nasal, 58–61
granuloma gravidarum
 of larynx, 169
 of oral cavity, 127
Griesinger's sign, 308
grommets, in children, 438, 439
Guérin fracture, 28

haemangioma
 of larynx, congenital, 387
 of parotid gland, 133
 of tongue, 127
haematoma
 of auricle, 263
 of nasal septum, 23–4
haemolytic disease of the newborn, 413
Haemophilus influenzae, on nasal swab, 12
haemorrhage
 following adenoidectomy, 371
 following tonsillectomy, 366
haemorrhagic telangiectasia, hereditary, 32–3

haemotympanum, 441
hair transplants, 70
hairy tongue, 127–8
Hansen's disease, 93
Hashimoto's disease, 198
hay fever, 51
head injury, otological trauma following, 346–8
headache, 65
 in acute sinusitis, 35
 in maxillary sinusitis, 43
 in vasomotor rhinitis, 40
Heaf test, 59
hearing aids, 326–8
 in children, 417–119
 in infants, 412
 with tinnitus masker, 330
hearing tests *see* audiology; audiometry
Heerfordt's syndrome, 199
Heller's operation, 100
hemifacial spasm, 360
hemilaryngectomy, (*Fig. 2.17.5*) 175
hereditary haemorrhagic telangiectasia, 32–3
herpes zoster, 65
herpes zoster oticus (Ramsay Hunt syndrome), 323
herpetiform ulcer, oral, 125
Horner's syndrome
 nasopharyngeal carcinoma and, 110
 in pharyngeal disease, 82
house dust mite, allergy to, 51
Hutchison's teeth, 58
hyperacusis, 237
hyperbilirubinaemia, 413
hyperprolactinaemia hypogonadism, 74
hypertelorism, 26
hypopharynx
 anatomy of, 77–8
 biopsy of, 83
 clinical examination of, 81
 tumours of, 116–20
hyposensitization treatment, 53

imaging techniques
 for brain abscess, 315
 in nasopharyngeal carcinoma, 110
 for salivary gland tumours, 136
immotile cilia syndrome, 373
immunoglobulin E, 51
impedance audiometry, (*Figs. 3.3.4–5*) 250–1, 415
indirect laryngoscopy, (*Figs. 2.13.1–3*) 151–2
infections
 facial palsy due to, 360
 of larynx, 160–5
 of neck space, 104–8
 of pharynx, 84–93
see also under specific infections

infectious mononucleosis (glandular fever), 90–
        1, 199
    in children, 402
    versus acute tonsillitis, 85
influenza 34
    otitis external haemorrhagica and, 276
innervation *see* nerve supply
insects, in ear, 267, 346
internal ear
    anatomy of (*Figs.* 3.1.10–15) 228–33
    physiology of, 234–5
intubation
    in children, 396–7
    versus tracheostomy, 197
iodides, 199
itching
    in neurodermatitis, 276
    in otitis externa, 238

Jarjavay, fracture of, (*Fig.* 1.3.1) 21
Jervil–Lange Neilson's syndrome, 413

Kartagener's syndrome, 11, 18
keratoma, 286
keratosis obturans, 267
ketoconazole, 61
Kiesselbach's plexus, (*Fig.* 1.1.4) 6
Klebsiella rhinoscleromatis, 61
Klippel–Feil syndrome, 413
koilonychia, (*Fig.* 2.4.1) 94, 95
Koplik's spots, 89
Kveim test, 60

labyrinth, trauma to, 337
labyrinthine window rupture, 348–9
labyrinthitis
    bacterial, (*Fig.* 3.7.5) 301–3, 337
    deafness due to, 323
    vertigo due to, 337
    viral, 323, 337
laryngeal atresia, at birth, (*Fig.* 4.3.2) 383
laryngeal nerve, lesions of, 180–4
laryngeal sprays, 162
    laryngeal stridor, in children 381–91
laryngectomy
    hemilaryngectomy, (*Fig.* 2.17.5) 175
    supraglottic, (*Figs.* 2.17.3–4) 174
    total, (*Figs.* 2.17.6–7) 175–7
laryngitis, 160–2
    in children, 389
laryngocele, (*Fig.* 2.16.1) 167–8, 199–200
laryngography, 153
laryngomalacia, 385–6
laryngoscopy
    in children, 392, 395
    direct, 154
    fibreoptic, 154

laryngoscopy (*cont.*)
    indirect, (*Figs.* 2.13.1–3) 151–2
    microlaryngoscopy, 154
laryngotomy, technique, (*Fig.* 2.20.1) 194–5
laryngotracheitis, acute, 390–1
laryngotracheobronchitis, acute, 390–1
larynx
    anatomy of, (*Figs.* 2.12.1–8) 142–9
        developmental, (*Fig.* 4.3.1) 381–2
    diseases of, 150–4
        in children, 381–91
    electric, 178
    infections of, 160–5
    trauma to, 185–90
    tumours of, 166–70
        benign, 166–9
        congenital, 387
        malignant, 169–70, 171–9
lateral medullary syndrome, 338
lateral sinus thrombosis, (*Fig.* 3.8.2) 306–9
Le Fort fractures, (*Fig.* 1.3.8) 28
leiomyoma, hypopharyngeal, 118
leiomyosarcoma, hypopharyngeal, 118, 120
Leishmaniasis, 62
Leopard syndrome, 413
leprosy, 62
    of larynx, 164
    of pharynx, 93
leptothricosis, of larynx, 163
Lermoyez's syndrome, 336
leucoplakia
    of larynx, 172
    of oral cavity, 126
leukaemia, acute, pharyngitis in, 91
lichen planus, oral, 126
lingual thyroid, 128
lingual tonsil, hypertrophy of, 87
lipoma
    of hypopharynx, 118
    of neck, 198
    of salivary glands, 133
Little's area, (*Fig.* 1.1.4) 6
Lombard's test, 255–6
Ludwig's angina, 107–8
lupus, of pharynx, 93
lupus vulgaris, 59
lymph nodes, of neck
    infection of, 198–9
    metastases to, 201–6
lymphangioma
    of larynx, congenital, 387
    of neck, 404
    of parotid gland, 133
lymphatic drainage
    of external ear, (*Fig.* 3.1.1) 221
    of external nose, 4
    of larynx, 147, (*Fig.* 2.17.1) 171–2
    of nasal cavity, 6
lymphoma
    of head and neck, 200

lymphoma (cont.)
  in children, 405
  of larynx, 170
  of nose and sinuses, 211
  of pharynx, 91, 113, 115
lysol burn, pharyngeal, (Fig. 2.4.5) 98

McNaught keel, (Fig. 4.3.4) 384
maggots, in ear, 267, 346
magnetic resonance imaging
  in nasopharyngeal carcinoma, 110
  in oral tumours, 122
malingerer (deafness), 255–6, 328
Mallory–Weiss syndrome, oesophageal perforation in, 100
maskers, for tinnitus, 329–30
mastoidectomy, radical, (Figs. 3.6.4–5) 289–91
mastoiditis
  acute, 295–99
    in children, (Figs. 4.9.3–4) 428–31
  masked, 299–300
  versus furunculosis of external meatus, 272
maxillary sinus
  anatomy of, 8–9
  carcinoma of, 210–11
  clinical examination of, 16
  cysts of, 48–9
  infection of, 42–5
  radiology of, 18
measles, deafness due to, 323, 413–14
meatus see external auditory meatus
mediastinitis, following oesophageal perforation, 100
melanoma
  of neck, 198
  of nose, 210
  of oral cavity, 121
Melkerson–Rosenthal syndrome, fissured tongue in, 128
Ménière's disease, 325, (Fig. 3.12.1) 334–7
  versus labyrinthine window rupture, 348–9
meningitis, 309–11
  circumscribed serous, 311
  deafness due to, 414
  following acute rhinosinusitis, 37
  following CSF leak, 29
mentoplasty, 69
metastatic tumours
  of parotid gland, 134
  to neck lymph nodes, 201–6
micrognathia, (Fig. 4.3.5) 385
microlaryngoscopy, 154, 395
middle ear
  anatomy of, (Figs. 3.1.5–9) 222–8
  embryology of, 409–10
  physiology of, 233–4
migraine, periodic migrainous neuralgia, 66
Mikulicz cells, 164

Mikulicz's syndrome, 134, 199, 403
moniliasis (thrush)
  nasal, 61
  oral, 126
  pharyngeal, 91
monospot test, 82
moulds, allergy to, 51
mouth see oral cavity
mucociliary clearance test, 18
mucocoeles, of frontal sinus, 45–6
mucoepidermoid tumour
  of larynx, 170
  of salivary glands, 132–3
  treatment of, 140
mucormycosis, 61
mucus (nasal), 6–7, 10
mumps, 135, 420
  deafness due to, 322–3
  versus sialectasis, 134, 135
Mustardé otoplasty operation, 69
Mycobacterium leprae, 62
Mycobacterium tuberculosis, 59
mycosis, of larynx, 162–3
myoblastoma, of larynx, 166
myofacial pain dysfuncton syndrome, 66
myringitis bullosa haemorrhagica, 323
myringoplasty, (Fig. 3.6.3) 288–9
myringotomy, in children, 437–9
myxoedema, 199

nasal cavity, anatomy of, 4–7
nasal cilium, structure of, (Figs. 1.1.8–9) 10–11
nasal decongestants see decongestants
nasal deformities, rhinoplasty for, 67–8
nasal granulomas, 58–61
nasla packing, (Fig. 1.4.1) 31–2
  following turbinectomy, 39
nasal polyps, 54–5
  in children, 373
  ethmoidal sinus surgery for, 48
nasal provocation test, 18, 52
nasal septum
  anatomy of, 4–6
  fibroangioma of, 57
  tumours of, 211
nasal sinuses
  anatomy of, 7–10
  development during childhood, 375
  fibreoptic examination of, 16
  radiography of, (Fig. 1.2.6) 18–20
nasal smears, in allergic rhinitis diagnosis, 52
nasal sprays, steroid, 53
nasal swabs, caution in interpretation of, 16
nasal trauma, 21–9
nasal vestibule, anatomy of, 4
nasopalatine artery, anatomy of, 6
nasopharyngeal angiofibroma, 111–12
nasopharyngeal carcinoma, 109–11

nasopharyngoscope, (*Fig.* 1.2.2) 15
nasopharynx
    anatomy of, 77
    biopsy of, 83
    clinical examination of, 14–16, 80–1
neck
    clinical examination of, 81–2
    injury, otological trauma following, 347–8
    tumours, 198–208
        in children, 402–6
neck space infections, 104–8
Nelson's syndrome, 71, 72
neoglottis operations, 178–9
neonates
    bronchoscopy in, 393–5
    hearing screening of, 417
    septal abnormalities in, 21–2
nerve supply
    to eustachian tube, 227
    to external ear, (*Fig.* 3.1.3) 220–1
    to internal ear, 233
    to larynx, (*Figs.* 2.12.7–8) 147
    to middle ear, 226
    to nose, (*Figs.* 1.1.5–6) 7
    to tympanic membrane, 222
neuralgia (facial), 64–5
    atypical, 66
    glossopharyngeal, 64, 244
    postherpetic, 65
    Sluder's, 66
    trigeminal, 64
neurilemmoma, of vagus nerve, 200
neuroblastoma, olfactory, 210
neurofibroma
    of neck, 198
    of vagus nerve, 200
neuroma, facial, 359–60
neurosensory deafness *see* sensorineural deafness
noise-induced deafness, (*Fig.* 3.14.2) 350–2, 413
non-organic hearing loss, 328
    tests for, 255–6
non-suppurative otitis media *see* secretory otitis media
nose, cancer of, 209–11
nose picking, vestibulitis due to, 40
nosebleeds *see* epistaxis
nostrils, closure of, in atrophic rhinitis, 41
nuclear magnetic resonance (NMR) imaging
    in laryngeal disease, 153
    in nasal disease, 20
nystagmus
    benign paroxysmal positional, 332–3
    electronystagmography, (*Fig.* 3.3.11) 260–1
    optokinetic, 261

oat-cell carcinoma, of larynx, 170
obesity, 199

occupational deafness, 350–2
ocular involvement
    blow-out fracture, (*Fig.* 1.3.6) 27
    of ethmoidal tumours, 211
    in frontal sinusitis, 46
    in nasopharyngeal carcinoma, 110
    in sarcoidosis, 60
    see also nystagmus
odontophagia, 80
oesophageal reflux, acid laryngitis and, 157
oesophageal speech, 177
    neoglottis operation and, 178–9
oesophageal tumours, cervical, 118, 120
oesophagitis, *versus* hypopharyngeal tumour, 118
oesophagus
    achalasia of, (*Fig.* 2.4.6) 100–1
    corrosive burns of, 98–9
    management of dysphagic patient, 101–3
    perforation of, 99–100
    stricture of, 99
oncocytoma, 131
    of larynx, 166
    of nasopharynx, 112
optokinetic nystagmus, 261
oral cavity
    benign diseases of, 125–8
    carcinoma of, 202
    tumours of, 131–4
orbital cellulitis, following recurrent acute sinusitis, 36
orf, of neck, 198
organ of Corti, anatomy of, (*Fig.* 3.1.14) 232–3
oroantral fistula, 49–50
oropharynx
    anatomy of, 77
    biopsy of, 83
    clinical examination of, 81
    infections of, 84–93
orthopantomogram, 20
Ortner's syndrome, 160
ossicles
    anatomy of, (*Figs.* 3.1.5–6) 224–5
    congenital abnormalities of, 412
    embryology of, 409
    trauma to, 347, 348
osteoma
    of external meatus, 268–9
    nasal, 57–8
osteomyelitis, in diploic bone, 36
otalgia, 238
    causes of, in childhood, (*Fig.* 4.9.2) 427
    referred, 238, (*Fig.* 3.2.4) 243–5
otitic barotrauma, 349
otitic hydrocephalus, 309
otitis externa, 269–71
    diffuse, 273–4
    haemorrhagica, 276
    itching in, 238
    malignant, 276–7

otitis media (in adults)
    acute, 278–81
    barotraumatic, 349
    chronic, 283–93
        middle ear carcinoma and, 213–14
        surgical treatment of, (*Figs.* 3.6.3–5) 288–92
    extracranial complications, 294–303
    intracranial complications, 304–16
    nature of discharge in, 237–8
    tuberculous, 292–3
otitis media (in children), 422–42
    acute, 422–8
    acute mastoiditis and, 428–31
    secretory, 432–42
otomycosis, 274–5
otoplasty, 68–9
otorrhoea, CSF, following head injury, 347
otosclerosis, 317–21
    mixed hearing loss due to, 325
otoscopic examination, (*Fig.* 3.2.1) 239–42
ototoxicity, 324, 413
    topical, 324–5
oxyphil-cell adenoma, 131
ozaena, 41

packs, nasal, (*Fig.* 1.4.1) 31–2
Paget's disease, 325
pain
    facial, 64–6
    pharyngeal, 80
    see also otalgia
palatine tonsils *see* tonsils
Panje valve, 178, 179
papillary cystadenoma lymphomatosum, 131
papilloma
    laryngeal, 166–7
        in children, (*Figs.* 4.3.7–8) 387–9
    nasal, 56
    oral, 126
paracusis Willisii, 237
    in otosclerosis, 318
paraganglioma, of larynx, 167
paranasal sinuses, anatomy of, 7
parapharyngeal abscesses, 199
parapharyngeal space, infection of, (*Figs.* 2.5.2–3) 105–6
parotid glands
    anatomy of, 130
    tumours of, 130–4, (*Fig.* 2.11.2) 136, 199
        clinical examination, 207
        otalgia in, 245
        treatment of, 138–41
parotidectomy, complications of, 141
parotitis
    in children, 403–4
    epidemic (mumps), 199, 403
patch tests, 52

Paterson–Brown Kelly syndrome, 82, (*Fig.* 2.4.1) 94–5
    atrophic pharyngitis in, 90
    hypopharyngeal tumour and, 119
pemphigus, oral, 126
pendulum (eye tracking) test, 261
perforation
    of nasal spetum, 24, 29, 59
    of oesophagus, 99–100
    of tympanic membrane, (*Fig.* 3.6.1) 284
        chronic otitis media and, 283–5, 287–8
perichondritis
    of auricle, (*Fig.* 3.4.1) 263–4
    of larynx 162
perilymph, 232
    fistula, 338
periodic migrainous neuralgia, 66
peritonsillar abscess (quinsy), (*Fig.* 2.3.1) 85–6
petrositis, 300–1
pharyngeal pouch, (*Figs.* 2.4.3–4) 96–7
pharyngitis, 89–91
    acute, 89
    atrophic, 90
    in blood disorders, 90–1
    chronic, 89–90
pharynx
    anatomy of, (*Fig.* 2.1.1) 77–9
    benign disease of, 94–103
    clinical examination of, 80–3
    infections of, 84–93
        otalgia due to, 244
physiology
    of hearing, 233–5
    of nose, 10–12
    of vestibular apparatus, 235–6
Pierre–Robin syndrome, 385
pinna *see* auricle
pituitary gland, trans-sphenoidal hypophysectomy, 71–4
plasma-reactive immunosorbent test (PRIST), 52
plasmacytoma
    of nasopharynx, 112
    of nose and sinuses, 211
pleomorphic adenoma, of salivary glands, 132
Plummer–Vinson syndrome *see* Paterson–Brown Kelly syndrome
politzerization, 425
pollens, allergy to, 51
polyps
    choanal, 55
    nasal, 20,54–5
        in children, 373
postherpetic neuralgia, 65
Pott's puffy tumour, 36
pregnancy
    epulis in, 127
    granuloma gravidarum of larynx, 169
    prenatal causes of deafness, 413
prematurity, sensorineural deafness and, 413

presbyacusis, 237, 324
prick test, 52
PRIST, 17, 52
provocation tests (nasal), 18
pseudohypertelorism, 26
pseudosarcoma, of larynx, 170
psychogenic dizziness, 334
psychogenic hearing loss, 255–6, 328
pubophonia, 159
pyoceoele, of frontal sinus, 46
pyriform sinus tumours, 80

quinine, deafness due to, 324
quinsy (peritonsillar abscess), (*Fig.* 2.3.1) 85–6

Radcliffe tracheostomy tube, 193
radical mastoidectomy, (*Figs.* 3.6.4–5) 289–91
radio aids, 417
radioactive sorbent test (RAST), 52
radiography
    of acoustic neuroma, (*Fig.* 3.13.3) 342
    in ear disease, 242–3
    of hypopharyngeal tumour, 119
    in laryngeal disease, 152
    in mastoiditis, (*Fig.* 3.7.2) 297–8
    in maxillary sinusitis diagnosis, 43
    of nasal bones, 18
    of nasal sinuses, (*Fig.* 1.2.6) 18–20
    of nasopharyngeal carcinoma, 110
    of neck masses, 207
    of oesophageal disease, 103
    in Paterson–Brown Kelly syndrome, (*Fig.* 2.4.2) 95
    in pharyngeal disease, 82
    in sialomegaly, 137
radon seed implantation, for carcinoma of tongue, 123
Ramsay Hunt syndrome, 323
ranula, 127
RAST, 17, 52
Recklinghausen's disease, 339
recruitment
    problems of, in hearing aid design, 326–7
    in sensorineural deafness, 252, 322
recurrent oral ulceration (ROU), 125
Rees–Pracy tracheostomy tube, 196, 398–9
Refsum's disease, 413
Reinke's oedema, 168
Rendu–Osler–Weber disease, 32–3
retropharyngeal abscess, (*Fig.* 2.5.1) 104–5
Reye's syndrome, 366
rhabdomyosarcoma
    in children, 405–6
    of nasopharynx, 112
    of nose, 211

rheumatoid arthritis, of cricoarytenoid joint, 164–5
rhinitis
    allergic, 51–3
    atrophic, *versus* scleroma, 61
    chronic, 38–41
    vasomotor, in children, 373
rhinitis caseosa, 41, 43
rhinitis medicamentosa, 39
rhinitis sicca, 41
rhinolalia, 13
rhinoliths, nasal, 63
rhinomanometry, 18
rhinoplasty, 67–8
rhinorrhoea, cerebrospinal fluid, 28–9
rhinosinusitis, acute, 34–7
rhinosporidiosis, 61
rigors, in sinus thrombosis, 307, 308
Rinne's test, 247
    in children, 427, 436
    false-negative, 248
Romberg's test, 262
Rosen otoplasty operation, 69
rotation tests, 258

saccharine-clearance test, 18
saddle nose, 67, 68
salicylates, deafness due to, 324
salicylic acid hypersensitivity, 51, 54
salivary glands
    anatomy of, (*Fig.* 2.11.1) 129–30
    diseases of, 129–41, 199
        in children, 403–4
    infections of, 135–8
    tumours of, 113, 121, 123, 130–4
        investigations of, 135–8
        oncocytoma, 112
        prognosis of, 115
        treatment of, 115, 138–41
    see also parotid glands; Sjögren's disease
sarcoidosis, 199
    nasal lesions in, 60
sarcoma
    of hypopharynx, 118, 120
    of larynx, 170
    of nose, 210, 211
    of salivary glands, 133
scanning techniques *see* CT scans; imaging techniques; NMR scanning
scarlet fever, *versus* acute tonsillitis, 85
Schneiderian papilloma, 56
schwannoma, of larynx, 166–7
Schwartze's operation, (*Figs.* 3.7.3–4) 299–300
    in children, 430–1
    indications for, 299
scleroma 61
    of larynx, 164
    of pharynx, 93

scratches, to neck, 198
screamer's nodes, 157
scurf, 275
sebaceous cyst, of neck, 198
seborrhoeic dermatitis, of scalp, 275
secretory otitis media, 282–3
 in children, 432–42
semicircular canals, embryology of, 410
Semon's law, 180
sensorineural deafness, 237, 246, 322–8
 audiometric tests of, 248–56
 in children, 412–14
 due to perilymph leaks, 348
 loudness recruitment in, 252, 322
 noise induced, (*Fig.* 3.14.2) 350–2
septic cavernous thrombosis, 4
septoplasty procedure, 24–5
septum (nasal)
 deviation of, 21–2
 fractures of, (*Fig.* 1.3.1) 21–2
 perforation of, 24, 29, 59
 surgery to, (*Figs.* 1.3.4–5) 24–5
 trauma to, 21–3
seroma, of auricle, 263
serous otitis media *see* secretory otitis media
shingles, 65
sialectasis, 134–5, 199
 treatment of, 140–1
sialography, 136
sialomegaly, 130
 investigations of, 135–8
sicca syndrome, 41, 134, 199
Siegle's pneumatic speculum, 252
Silver Jackson tracheostomy tube, 192
Simpson's gun, 39
singer's nodules (*Fig.* 2.14.3) 157–8
sinus headache, 65
 in acute sinusitis, 35
 in maxillary sinusitis, 43
 in vasomotor rhinitis, 40
sinus thrombosis, (*Fig.* 3.8.2) 306–9
sinuses (nasal)
 angioma of, 57
 surgical drainage of, 35, (*Figs.* 1.7.1–4) 44–50
 tumours of, 56–8, 209–11
sinusitis
 acute, 34–6
  recurrent, 36
 in children, 375–7
 chronic, 42–50
  surgical procedures for, (*Figs.* 1.7.1–4) 44–50
Sjögren's disease, 134, 199, 403
 atrophic pharyngitis in, 90
 biopsy in, 138
 fissured tongue in, 128
skin tests, 52
 for allergies, 17
sleep apnoea syndrome, 103
 tonsillar hypertrophy in, 365

Sluder's neuralgia, 66
smears (nasal), 17
smell, altered, in maxillary sinusitis, 43
smoking
 chronic laryngitis and, 161, 162
 chronic pharyngitis and, 89
snoring, 103
snuffly baby, 373
sodium chromoglycate, 53
spastic dysphonia, 158
speech audiometry, (*Fig.* 3.3.3) 250
 delayed speech feedback test, 256
speech development, normal stages of, 417
speech, oesophageal, 177
 neoglottis operation and, 178–9
speech problems, in pharyngeal disease, 80
speech therapy, 327
sphenoid sinuses
 anatomy of, 10
 radiography of, 18–20
 surgery to, 48
sphenoiditis, 35
sprays
 laryngeal, 162
 nasal, 53
'squashed' noses, 21
stapedectomy (*Figs.* 3.9.1–4) 318–21
Staphylococcus albus, on nasal swab, 12
Staphylococcus aureus
 carriers, 12
 in vestibulitis, 40
steam inhalations, 161
Stenger's test, 255
steroid inhalers, laryngeal candidiasis due to, 163
steroid therapy
 nasal sprays for allergic rhinitis, 53
 slow-release depot solution, 53
Stewart's granuloma, 60–1
stricture, oesophageal, 99
stridor
 in children, 381–91
 in vocal cord paralysis, 183
stroboscopy, 153–4
subdural abscess, 315–16
 secondary to frontal sinusitis, 37
subglottic cancer, 177–8
subglottic stenosis, 190
 in children, 384, 400–1
submandibular gland
 anatomy of, 130
 tumours of, 130–2
  treatment of, 139, 140
submandibular space, infection of (Ludwig's angina), 107–8
subperiosteal abscess, 297
sudden idiopathic deafness, 325–6
supraglottic cancer, 172–5
supraglottic laryngectomy, (*Fig.* 2.17.3) 174
supraglottic stenosis, 189–90

surgical procedures
  blepharoplasty, 69
  Caldwell–Luc operation, (*Fig.* 1.7.1) 45
  cordopexy, 183–4
  cortical mastoid (Schwartze's) operation,
      (*Figs.* 3.7.3–4) 299–300
  cosmetic facial surgery, 67–70
  laryngectomy, (*Figs.* 2.17.6–7) 175–7
      hemilaryngectomy, (*Fig.* 2.17.5) 175
      supraglottic, (*Figs.* 2.17.3–4) 174
  laryngotomy, (*Fig.* 2.20.1) 194–5
  mastoidectomy, (*Figs.* 3.6.4–5) 289–91
  mentoplasty, 69
  myringoplasty, (*Fig.* 3.6.3) 288–9
  otoplasty, 69
  polypectomy, 54
  rhinoplasty, 68
  sinus drainage, 35, (*Figs.* 1.7.1–4) 44–50
  stapedectomy, (*Figs.* 3.9.1–4) 318–21
  tracheostomy, (*Figs.* 2.20.1–3) 193
  tympanoplasty, 291–2
surgical trauma, to ear, 352
swabs (nasal), caution in interpretation of, 16
syphilis, 58–9
  fissured tongue in, 128
  of larynx, 164
  oral tumours and, 122
  of pharynx, 91–2
  sensorineural deafness due to, 323–4, 413
  vertigo due to, 337

tape recordings, of voice problems, 153
Teal test, 255
teeth
  abscesses of, 108
  cysts of, 49
  facial pain due to, 65
  Hutchison's, 58
  infection of, maxillary sinusitis and, 42
  otalgia due to, 243–4
Teflon injection, of vocal cord, 182
temporal arteritis, 66
temporal bone fractures, 346–7
temporal lobe abscess, (*Fig.* 3.8.4) 313–14
temporomandibular joint
  facial pain due to, 66
  as source of otalgia, 243–4
thiouracil, 199
thrombophlebitis, cortical, 316
thrush (moniliasis)
  nasal, 61
  oral, 126
  pharyngeal, 91
thyroarytenoid muscle, anatomy of, 146
thyroglossal cyst, 404
thyroid masses, 198
  clinical examination of, 206
  scanning techniques for, 207–8

thyrotoxicosis, hypopharyngeal tumour and,
      119
Tine test, 59
tinnitus, 238–9, 329–30
  in Ménière's disease, 334–6
Tobey–Ayer test, 308
tomography
  in laryngeal disease, (*Fig.* 2.13.4) 152–3
  of nasal sinuses, 20
tongue
  carcinoma of, 114,123
  haemangioma of, 127
  specific lesions of, 127–8
tonsillectomy, 363–7
tonsillitis
  acute, 84–5
  chronic, 86
tonsillolith, 87
tonsils, 363–7
  anatomy of, 78–9
  carcinoma of, 113, 114, 115
  function of, 363
  infections of, 84–8
  pain in, 80
toxoplasmosis, 199
  in children, 403
trachea, trauma to, 185–90
tracheostomy, 191–7
  in children, 397–9
  definition, 191
  technique, (*Figs.* 2.20.1–3) 193
tracheotomy
  definition, 191
  laryngotracheal stenosis following, 189
trans-sphenoidal hypophysectomy, 71–4
transexual voice, 159
transplants, hair, 70
trauma
  facial, 21–9, 359
  laryngotracheal, 185–90
  nasal, 21–9, 67–8
      epistaxis due to, 30–3
  to ear, 263, 345–52
  to larynx, in children, 387
  see also fracture(s)
traumatic ulcer, oral, 125
Treacher Collins syndrome, 385, 413
trench mouth, 87
trigeminal neuralgia, 64
tuberculosis, 199
  of larynx, 163–4
  nasal, 59
  of pharynx, 92–3
  of tonsil, 87
tuberculous otitis media, 292–3
tularaemia, of neck, 198
tumours
  acoustic neuroma, (*Figs.* 3.13.1–3) 339–44
  cerebellopontine angle, (*Figs.* 3.13.1–3) 339–
      44

tumours (*cont.*)
  of ear, 212–15
  of external meatus, 268–9
  facial, 349–60
  of hypopharynx, 116–20
  of larynx, 166–70
  nasal, 56–8
  of nasopharynx, 14, 109–12
  of neck structures, 200–1
    in children, 402–6
  of nose and sinuses, 209–11
    in children, 406–8
  of oral cavity, 121–4
  of oropharynx, 113–15
  of parotid glands, 130–4, (*Fig.* 2.11.2) 136,
      199
    clinical examination, 207
    otalgia in, 245
  pyriform sinus, 80
  of salivary glands, 113, 121, 123, 130–4
    investigation of, 135–8
    treatment of, 138–41
  see also carcinoma
tuning-fork tests, (*Fig.* 3.3.1) 246–8
  of non-organic hearing loss, 255
turbinates (nasal), anatomy of, 4
turbinectomy, total inferior, 39
turbinoplasty, 39
tympanic membrane
  anatomy of, (*Fig.* 3.1.4) 221–2
  embryology of, 410
  myringoplasty, (*Fig.* 3.6.3) 288–9
  myringotomy, in children, 437–9
  otoscopic examination of, (*Fig.* 3.2.2) 240–2
  perforation of, (*Fig.* 3.6.1) 284
    chronic otitis media and, 283–5, 287–8
tympanometry, (*Fig.* 3.3.5) 251
tympanoplasty, 292
  combined approach, 291–2
tympanosclerosis, 439, 441–2

U3P operation, 103
ulcerative gingivitis, 87–8
ulcers, oral, 125
Usher's syndrome, 413
uvulopalatopharyngoplasty (U3P) operation,
    103

vacuum sinus headache, 65
vagus nerve, tumours of, 200
vascular headache, 66
vasomotor rhinitis, 38, 40
  in children, 373
verrucous carcinoma, of larynx, 169
vertebrobasilar ischaemia, 338
vertigo, 239, 331–8
  tests of, 256–62
vestibular apparatus, physiology of, 235–6
vestibular neuronitis, 333–4
vestibulitis, 40
vestibulometry, 256–62
Vidian nerve, 7, 53
Vincent's angina, 87
viral infections
  in common cold and influenza, 34
  deafness due to, 322–3
vocal abuse, 150, 156, 162
vocal cord, paralysis of, 180–4
vocal cord polypus, 168
vocal nodules, (*Fig.* 2.14.3) 157–8
voice problems, 155–9
  dysphonia plicae ventricularis, 158
  laryngitis, 157, 160–2, 389
  pitch and frequency measurements, 154
  pubophonia, 159
  spastic dysphonia, 158
  transexual voice, 159
  vocal abuse, 150, 156, 162
  vocal nodules, (*Fig.* 2.14.3) 157–8
voice tests, 246
  speech audiometry, (*Fig.* 3.3.3) 250, 256
von Recklinghausen's disease, 339

Waardenburg's syndrome, 412–13
Walsham's forceps, 23
Warthin's tumour, 131, 199
wax (impacted), 265–7
  syringing technique, (*Figs.* 3.4.2–3) 265–7
Weber's test, 248
Wegener's granuloma, nasal involvement, 60
whiplash injury, 66, 348
Woodman's operation, 183
  reversed, 182

Ziehl–Neelsen stain, 59, 62
zygomatic fracture, (*Fig.* 1.3.7) 27